ACTS

THE NIV APPLICATION COMMENTARY

From biblical text . . . to contemporary life

THE NIV APPLICATION COMMENTARY SERIES

THE NIV APPLICATION COMMENTARY

From biblical text . . . to contemporary life

AJITH FERNANDO

ZONDERVAN.com/
AUTHORTRACKER
follow your favorite authors

We want to hear from you. Please send your comments about this book to us in care of zreview@zondervan.com. Thank you.

ZONDERVAN

The NIV Application Commentary: Acts
Copyright © 1998 by Ajith Fernando

This title is also available as a Zondervan ebook.
Visit www.zondervan.com/ebooks.

Requests for information should be addressed to:

Zondervan, *Grand Rapids, Michigan 49530*

Library of Congress Cataloging-in-Publication Data

Fernando, Ajith.
  Acts / Ajith Fernando.
    p. cm.—(The NIV application commentary)
  Includes bibliographical references.
  ISBN 978-0-310-49410-2
  1. Bible. N.T. Acts (book)—Commentaries. I. Title. II. Series.
  BS 2625.3.F47 1998
  226.6'077—dc21   98–21272

Royalties from the sale of this book will be used for the promotion of Christian Literature and Education in Sri Lanka.

Printed in the United States of America

10 11 12 13 14 15 16 /DCI/ 25 24 23 22 21 20 19 18 17

To

My dear wife,

Nelun,

Friend

and

Partner in life and ministry,

And to

Our children,

Nirmali and Asiri,

Sources of great joy and satisfaction,

With gratitude to God

For his beautiful gift

Of family.

Contents

The NIV Application Commentary Series

When complete, the NIV Application Commentary
will include the following volumes:

Old Testament Volumes

Genesis, John H. Walton
Exodus, Peter Enns
Leviticus/Numbers, Roy Gane
Deuteronomy, Daniel I. Block
Joshua, Robert L. Hubbard Jr.
Judges/Ruth, K. Lawson Younger
1-2 Samuel, Bill T. Arnold
1-2 Kings, Gus Konkel
1-2 Chronicles, Andrew E. Hill
Ezra/Nehemiah, Douglas J. Green
Esther, Karen H. Jobes
Job, Dennis R. Magary
Psalms Volume 1, Gerald H. Wilson
Psalms Volume 2, Jamie A. Grant
Proverbs, Paul Koptak
Ecclesiastes/Song of Songs, Iain Provan
Isaiah, John N. Oswalt
Jeremiah/Lamentations, J. Andrew Dearman
Ezekiel, Iain M. Duguid
Daniel, Tremper Longman III
Hosea/Amos/Micah, Gary V. Smith
Jonah/Nahum/Habakkuk/Zephaniah,
    James Bruckner
Joel/Obadiah/Malachi, David W. Baker
Haggai/Zechariah, Mark J. Boda

New Testament Volumes

Matthew, Michael J. Wilkins
Mark, David E. Garland
Luke, Darrell L. Bock
John, Gary M. Burge
Acts, Ajith Fernando
Romans, Douglas J. Moo
1 Corinthians, Craig Blomberg
2 Corinthians, Scott Hafemann
Galatians, Scot McKnight
Ephesians, Klyne Snodgrass
Philippians, Frank Thielman
Colossians/Philemon, David E. Garland
1-2 Thessalonians, Michael W. Holmes
1-2 Timothy/Titus, Walter L. Liefeld
Hebrews, George H. Guthrie
James, David P. Nystrom
1 Peter, Scot McKnight
2 Peter/Jude, Douglas J. Moo
Letters of John, Gary M. Burge
Revelation, Craig S. Keener

To see which titles are available,
visit our web site at www.zondervan.com

NIV Application Commentary
Series Introduction

THE NIV APPLICATION COMMENTARY SERIES is unique. Most commentaries help us make the journey from the twentieth century back to the first century. They enable us to cross the barriers of time, culture, language, and geography that separate us from the biblical world. Yet they only offer a one-way ticket to the past and assume that we can somehow make the return journey on our own. Once they have explained the *original meaning* of a book or passage, these commentaries give us little or no help in exploring its *contemporary significance*. The information they offer is valuable, but the job is only half done.

Recently, a few commentaries have included some contemporary application as *one* of their goals. Yet that application is often sketchy or moralistic, and some volumes sound more like printed sermons than commentaries.

The primary goal of The NIV Application Commentary Series is to help you with the difficult but vital task of bringing an ancient message into a modern context. The series not only focuses on application as a finished product but also helps you think through the *process* of moving from the original meaning of a passage to its contemporary significance. These are commentaries, not popular expositions. They are works of reference, not devotional literature.

The format of the series is de⸱⸱⸱ned to achieve the goals of the series. Each passage is treated in three sections: *Original Meaning, Bridging Contexts,* and *Contemporary Significance.*

THIS SECTION HELPS you understand the meaning of the biblical text in its first-century context. All of the elements of traditional exegesis—in concise form—are discussed here. These include the historical, literary, and cultural context of the passage. The authors discuss matters related to grammar and syntax, and the meaning of biblical words. They also seek to explore the main ideas of the passage and how the biblical author develops those ideas.[1]

---

1. Please note that when the authors discuss words in the original biblical languages, the series uses the general rather than the scholarly method of transliteration.

After reading this section, you will understand the problems, questions, and concerns of the *original audience* and how the biblical author addressed those issues. This understanding is foundational to any legitimate application of the text today.

Bridging Contexts

THIS SECTION BUILDS a bridge between the world of the Bible and the world of today, between the original context and the contemporary context, by focusing on both the timely and timeless aspects of the text.

God's Word is *timely*. The authors of Scripture spoke to specific situations, problems, and questions. Paul warned the Galatians about the consequences of circumcision and the dangers of trying to be justified by law (Gal. 5:2–5). The author of Hebrews tried to convince his readers that Christ is superior to Moses, the Aaronic priests, and the Old Testament sacrifices. John urged his readers to "test the spirits" of those who taught a form of incipient Gnosticism (1 John 4:1–6). In each of these cases, the timely nature of Scripture enables us to hear God's Word in situations that were *concrete* rather than abstract.

Yet the timely nature of Scripture also creates problems. Our situations, difficulties, and questions are not always directly related to those faced by the people in the Bible. Therefore, God's word to them does not always seem relevant to us. For example, when was the last time someone urged you to be circumcised, claiming that it was a necessary part of justification? How many people today care whether Christ is superior to the Aaronic priests? And how can a "test" designed to expose incipient Gnosticism be of any value in a modern culture?

Fortunately, Scripture is not only timely but *timeless*. Just as God spoke to the original audience, so he still speaks to us through the pages of Scripture. Because we share a common humanity with the people of the Bible, we discover a *universal dimension* in the problems they faced and the solutions God gave them. The timeless nature of Scripture enables it to speak with power in every time and in every culture.

Those who fail to recognize that Scripture is both timely and timeless run into a host of problems. For example, those who are intimidated by timely books such as Hebrews or Galatians might avoid reading them because they seem meaningless today. At the other extreme, those who are convinced of the timeless nature of Scripture, but who fail to discern its timely element, may "wax eloquent" about the Melchizedekian priesthood to a sleeping congregation.

The purpose of this section, therefore, is to help you discern what is time-less in the timely pages of the New Testament—and what is not. For example, if Paul's primary concern is not circumcision (as he tells us in Gal. 5:6), what *is* he concerned about? If discussions about the Aaronic priesthood or Melchizedek seem irrelevant today, what is of abiding value in these passages? If people try to "test the spirits" today with a test designed for a specific first-century heresy, what other biblical test might be more appropriate?

Yet this section does not merely uncover that which is timeless in a passage but also helps you to see *how* it is uncovered. The author of the commentary seeks to take what is implicit in the text and make it explicit, to take a process that normally is intuitive and explain it in a logical, orderly fashion. How do we know that circumcision is not Paul's primary concern? What clues in the text or its context help us realize that Paul's real concern is at a deeper level?

Of course, those passages in which the historical distance between us and the original readers is greatest require a longer treatment. Conversely, those passages in which the historical distance is smaller or seemingly nonexistent require less attention.

One final clarification. Because this section prepares the way for discussing the contemporary significance of the passage, there is not always a sharp distinction or a clear break between this section and the one that follows. Yet when both sections are read together, you should have a strong sense of moving from the world of the Bible to the world of today.

THIS SECTION ALLOWS the biblical message to speak with as much power today as it did when it was first written. How can you apply what you learned about Jerusalem, Ephesus, or Corinth to our present-day needs in Chicago, Los Angeles, or London? How can you take a message originally spoken in Greek and Aramaic and communicate it clearly in our own language? How can you take the eternal truths originally spoken in a different time and culture and apply them to the similar-yet-different needs of our culture?

In order to achieve these goals, this section gives you help in several key areas.

First, it helps you identify contemporary situations, problems, or questions that are truly comparable to those faced by the original audience. Because contemporary situations are seldom identical to those faced in the first century, you must seek situations that are analogous if your applications are to be relevant.

Second, this section explores a variety of contexts in which the passage might be applied today. You will look at personal applications, but you will also be encouraged to think beyond private concerns to the society and culture at large.

Third, this section will alert you to any problems or difficulties you might encounter in seeking to apply the passage. And if there are several legitimate ways to apply a passage (areas in which Christians disagree), the author will bring these to your attention and help you think through the issues involved.

In seeking to achieve these goals, the contributors to this series attempt to avoid two extremes. They avoid making such specific applications that the commentary might quickly become dated. They also avoid discussing the significance of the passage in such a general way that it fails to engage contemporary life and culture.

Above all, contributors to this series have made a diligent effort not to sound moralistic or preachy. The NIV Application Commentary Series does not seek to provide ready-made sermon materials but rather tools, ideas, and insights that will help you communicate God's Word with power. If we help you to achieve that goal, then we have fulfilled the purpose for this series.

The Editors

General Editor's Preface

ONE OF THE ATTRACTIONS of the book of Acts is that it gives a picture of the church in action. It tells the story of early church leaders actually doing the work of ministry. It is an exciting story, a story that, if read carefully, allows us no chance of thinking that being a Christian is an armchair exercise. It is a book well named: Acts.

One of the attractions of this particular commentary on Acts is that it gives us repeated pictures of the church in action around the world by one who is intimately involved in the work of the church in the beautiful country of Sri Lanka. Ajith Fernando is a scholar of the Word. But he is also a frontline doer of the Word. As president of Youth for Christ in Sri Lanka, he has lived his life in a way that mirrors many of the stories told of the early church in Acts. As Zondervan editor Jack Kuhatschek noted after reading Fernando's work on Acts, "It gives the practical perspective of one who has lived through many of the items discussed in Acts."

Knowing why we believe is extremely important. Feeling good about the faith that energizes us signals the powerful working of God's Spirit within our lives. But unless our lives take on the Acts-like quality that this biblical book tells in narrative form—living out what it means to be a Christian—we have missed the essence of the faith.

What are the signs that we are responding in faith to God's gracious actions toward us? The book of Acts seems to talk about three important things.

The first and perhaps the most important is personal evangelism. One occasionally hears that personal evangelism is the calling of a special few, while the rest of us have other callings, important but different. But even a cursory reading of the book of Acts belies that notion. The church leaders and church members who star in this story *all* do the work of evangelism. One comes away from reading Acts with a distinct notion that personal evangelism is a way of living out all the other vocations of life to which God calls us. It permeates our total being. The unevangelizing life is not worth living, at least from the perspective of Acts.

The second sign is Bible study. Personal evangelism is not a content-less sharing of feelings. In order to do it well, one must have something to talk about, a story to tell, a creed to espouse, a joy with which we can inspire a cynical world. The figures in Acts—Peter, Paul, and many others—articulate the gospel story in a way that betrays concentrated study and thinking.

Bible study means more than sitting down and reading a good book. It means reading with the goal of doing something with the knowledge gained by that reading. It means studying not only with the mind of a scholar but with the heart of an activist. It means studying in order to teach what we learn to others who have not heard the story that surpasses all others.

The third sign is recognizing the people to whom we tell the story: not just people who have not heard, but people who have chosen to follow an alternate path—the way of magic and the occult. In his commentary, Fernando calls this the ability to do "effective contextualization." Some aspects of evangelism are universal, "necessary for every place whatever the background." But others have cultural features that must be discerned in order to show that the particular strength of the gospel story meet the needs of particular peoples. The listeners in Acts were lured by the false promises of major philosophies and occultism. Not surprisingly, people today are tempted by similar worldviews. We must learn how to tell the story to these people who need to hear it.

In short, we must act. We must let our actions be part of the long history of the acts of the Christian church. Make no mistake: Our acts are part of the larger story of the Christian church. When you read, study, and act on this biblical book, you make yourself a part of the story.

Terry C. Muck

Author's Preface

I WAS A UNIVERSITY STUDENT when I took the commentary on Acts in the New International Commentary series by F. F. Bruce from my lay-preacher father's library and read through it page by page, footnotes and all, over a period of about six months. I was hooked on the study of Acts! Around 1976, as I was completing my studies at Fuller Theological Seminary and preparing to return home, I again launched on a personal study, this time of the first fifteen chapters of Acts. I spent several months trying to learn what an evangelistic community should be like, all in preparation to my taking over the direction of the evangelistic community of Youth for Christ. Naturally the book of Acts has had a big part to play in our ministry, both in teaching and in application. A few years later, when my wife and I moved to a church where the attendance had dropped to zero and worked for its renewal, the book of Acts naturally became like a textbook. This church is now quite healthy, consisting primarily of converts from Buddhism and Hinduism and led by a wonderful pastor under whom we serve.

After having spent so much time studying, teaching, and applying Acts, I had a growing conviction that I should write down some of the things we had learned. But I felt that we should try to apply Acts for at least fifteen years before going into print. When that time came (1991), I began to despair about the possibility of a market for books of expositions by a relatively unknown author like myself, and I delayed the project for a more opportune time. But I kept preparing new expositions on Acts. I was delighted when I received the invitation from Zondervan Publishing House to write the volume on Acts in The NIV Application Commentary Series and when the Board of YFC granted me a sabbatical to work on this. I am grateful for this opportunity to combine my dual passions—the theology and practice of evangelism and New Testament studies—into one book.

My wife and I decided that, because of the ages of our children, this sabbatical should be spent in Sri Lanka. It was loaded with setbacks, especially as I had to suddenly take over as principal of Colombo Theological Seminary in addition to my much reduced load of personal ministry. I am grateful to my many friends, too many to name individually, who helped me get the books I needed for my studies. We do not have the type of libraries in Sri Lanka that contain the resources needed for a book like this one. Particularly I had no recourse to journals.

The one thing I, as an Asian, found difficult to adjust to is the format of the series that divides the discussions on the passages into three sections. My preferred style would have been to integrate the three areas into one discussion, which, I believe, is how theory and practice appear in the Bible and is also how we think. I am grateful for the patience of the Zondervan editors as I struggled to work within this pattern. I apologize for my failure to enter fully into the philosophy that permits the separation of original meaning, bridging contexts, and contemporary significance.

During this sabbatical, I traveled on many weekends (often with a younger Christian) for ministry in new churches reaching out to people of other faiths. I often traveled by bus, and observing and chatting with people during these long trips gave me a sense of Matthew 9:36: "When he saw the crowds, he had compassion on them, because they were harassed and helpless, like sheep without a shepherd." Ministering among workers who had answered the call to reap this plentiful harvest, as well as among people who had come to Christ from other faiths (who represented this harvest), gave me a real sense of what happened in the book of Acts. I also spoke at a few YFC evangelistic camps, where I had the opportunity to commend Christ to non-Christians and to answer their questions about and objections to the Christian gospel. I believe these experiences helped me greatly in applying Acts to today.

My basic approach to each passage studied was to spend several hours studying the text inductively before consulting commentaries and other resources. I am grateful to my teachers Drs. Robert A. Traina and Daniel P. Fuller for introducing me to the challenge and thrill of inductive Bible study. I am also grateful to my teacher Dr. Robert Coleman, who showed me the great blessings that could be reaped through applying the book of Acts. Drs. Arthur Glasser and Donald Demaray helped me develop skills in using the Scriptures to derive guidelines for theology and practice. Drs. John Oswalt and Joseph Wong helped me grow in my conviction of the historical reliability of the Bible, which has influenced this study much. The footnotes indicate how helpful to me many wonderful commentaries on Acts were.

There are many other people I need to thank for their help on this book. I must thank the people connected with Zondervan and this series, who read my manuscript and helped in numerous ways—Jack Kuhatschek, Terry Muck, Scot McKnight, and Verlyn Verbrugge. This is the second time I have had the privilege of working with Jack, who has become both a friend and partner in the gospel and has helped me greatly as a writer.

My YFC colleagues did much to release me and reduce my pressure during this sabbatical. I am particularly grateful to Timothy Godwin, who worked hard at doing things that I should I have done myself. My secretary, Helen

Fernando, managed to protect me from appointments so that I could be released to write. Mayukha Perera and volunteers S. Sugunaraj and Dilly Fernando helped me with my computer problems. Suri Williams directed the YFC work ably during my absence and tolerated two postponements of my return to YFC. My colleague at the Colombo Theological Seminary, Ivor Poobalan, read portions of the manuscript and offered valuable suggestions. The members of my small group—Mylvaganam Balakrishnan, Brian Blacker, and Suri Williams—were a great encouragement to me throughout my writing. Many friends and relatives in Sri Lanka and abroad faithfully prayed for this project.

My biggest debt is to my dear wife, Nelun, and to my children, Nirmali and Asiri, who enthusiastically supported me through this sabbatical even though I was exhausted most of the time and thus did not make a very good family member. It is a joy to dedicate this, my largest ever literary project, to them.

Ajith Fernando
Christmas, 1997

Abbreviations

Apostolic Fathers	*The Apostolic Fathers* (trans. J. B. Lightfoot and J. R. Harmer, ed. and Rev. Michael W. Holmes, 2d ed. [Grand Rapids: Baker, 1992])
BAFCS	*The Book of Acts in Its First Century Setting* (ed. Bruce Winter, et al., 5 vols. [Grand Rapids: Eerdmans, 1993–1996])
BAGD	*A Greek-English Lexicon of the New Testament and Other Early Christian Literature*
BEB	*Baker Encyclopedia of the Bible*
Boring, Hellenistic Commentary	*Hellenistic Commentary to the New Testament* (ed. M. Eugene Boring, Klaus Berger, and Carsten Colpe [Nashville: Abingdon, 1995])
Bruce, *Circle*	*The Pauline Circle* (F. F. Bruce [Grand Rapids: Eerdmans, 1985])
Bruce, *Paul*	*Paul: Apostle of the Heart Set Free* (F. F. Bruce [Grand Rapids: Eerdmans, 1977])
Bruce, *Steps*	*In the Steps of the Apostle Paul* (F. F. Bruce [London: Candle Books, 1995])
BST	The Bible Speaks Today
DJG	*Dictionary of Jesus and the Gospels* (ed. Joel B. Green, Scot McKnight, and I. Howard Marshall [Downers Grove, Ill.: InterVarsity, 1992])
DPL	*Dictionary of Paul and His Letters* (ed. Gerald F. Hawthorne, Ralph P. Martin, and Daniel Reid [Downers Grove, Ill.: InterVarsity, 1993])
EBC	*Expositor's Bible Commentary*
EDBT	*Evangelical Dictionary of Biblical Theology*
ExpTim	*Expository Times*
Ferguson, Backgrounds	*Backgrounds of Early Christianity* (Everett Ferguson, 2d ed. [Grand Rapids: Eerdmans, 1993])
Gk.	Greek
ICC	The International Critical Commentary
IDB	*The Interpreter's Dictionary of the Bible*
ISBE	*The International Standard Bible Encyclopedia* (rev. ed., 1979–1988)

Josephus, *Complete Works*	*Complete Works of Josephus* (trans. William Whiston [Grand Rapids: Kregel, 1960 rprt])
Keener, *BBC*	*The IVP Bible Background Commentary: New Testament* (Craig S. Keener [Downer's Grove, Ill.: InterVarsity, 1993])
KJV	King James (or Authorized) Version
Ladd, *Theology*	*A Theology of the New Testament* (George E. Ladd, rev. Donald A. Hagner [Grand Rapids: Eerdmans, 1993])
lit.	literal or literally
Louw and Nida	*Greek-English Lexicon of the New Testament: Based on Semantic Domains*
LXX	Septuagint (Greek translation of Hebrew Bible)
Metzger, *Textual*	*A Textual Commentary on the Greek New Testament* (Bruce M. Metzger, 3d ed. [London and New York: United Bible Societies, 1971])
n.	note
NAC	The New American Commentary
NASB	New American Standard Bible
NBCTCE	*New Bible Commentary: 21st Century Edition* (eds. D. A. Carson et al. [Downers Grove, Ill.: InterVarsity, 1994])
NDCEPT	*The New Dictionary of Christian Ethics and Pastoral Theology*
NIBC	New International Bible Commentary.
NICNT	The New International Commentary on the New Testament
NIDNTT	*The New International Dictionary of New Testament Theology*
NIGTC	New International Greek New Testament Commentary
NIV	New International Version
NIVAC	NIV Application Commentary
NRSV	New Revised Standard Version
Ramsay, *BRD*	Ramsay, William M. *The Bearing of Recent Discovery on the Trustworthiness of the New Testament* (William M. Ramsay [Grand Rapids: Baker, rprt 1979])
REB	Revised English Bible
Reclaiming Friendship	*Reclaiming Friendship: Relating to Each Other in a Frenzied World* (Ajith Fernando [Scottdale, Pa., and Waterloo, Ont.: Herald Press, 1993])

Abbreviations

RV	American Standard (or Revised) Version
SJT	*Scottish Journal of Theology*
Supremacy	*The Supremacy of Christ* (Ajith Fernando [Wheaton: Crossway, 1995])
TDNT	*Theological Dictionary of the New Testament*
TNTC	Tyndale New Testament Commentaries
TOTC	Tyndale Old Testament Commentaries
trans.	translation
TynBul	*Tyndale Bulletin*
UBS4	*Greek New Testament* (4th ed. [United Bible Societies, 1993])
YFC	Youth for Christ
Zerwick and Grosvenor, *Analysis*	*A Grammatical Analysis of the Greek New Testament* (Max Zerwick and Mary Grosvenor [Rome: Biblical Institute, 1981])
Zerwick, *Greek*	*Biblical Greek: Illustrated by Examples* (Max Zerwick [Rome: Editrice Pontificio Instituto Biblico, 1963])
ZPEB	*The Zondervan Pictorial Encyclopedia of the Bible*

Introduction

SOME SCHOLARS HAVE REGARDED ACTS as the most important book in the New Testament,[1] or at least as its pivotal book, coming as it does between the Gospels and the letters.[2] It records the origin and growth of the Christian movement, telling us how the first believers lived out Christianity. It describes its message and ministry, and its life—including its triumphs and trials, the passions that drove it, and the source of the power that energized it. Any Christian wanting to know how to be a disciple of Christ in this world should turn to Acts to know how the first Christians lived. A recent topical study of Acts was therefore appropriately entitled *The Master Plan of Discipleship*.[3] Furthermore, Acts is a deeply inspiring book. Martyn Lloyd-Jones, who calls it "that most lyrical of books," writes: "Live in that book, I exhort you: it is a tonic, the greatest tonic I know in the realm of the Spirit."[4]

This introduction to Acts will concentrate on issues I have deemed as important to a commentary on Acts that focuses on application. For more detailed discussions on topics that usually appear in introductions, the reader is directed to the many excellent commentaries available (cf. the bibliography).

Authorship and Date of Writing

THE EXTERNAL EVIDENCE available for the authorship of Acts, gleaned from the writings of the church in the first few centuries, is unanimous that the author was Luke. When we look for internal evidence (found in Scripture itself), we note that Acts is linked closely with the third Gospel, which indicates common authorship. Both are addressed to the same person, Theophilus (Luke 1:3; Acts 1:1). Acts begins by summarizing the contents of a "first book," whose contents correspond with the Gospel of Luke. Longenecker says, "Stylistically and structurally the Gospel of Luke and the Acts of the Apostles are so closely related that they have to be assigned to the same author."[5]

---

1. Barclay, *Acts*, 1.
2. A. Harnack; cited in E. F. Harrison, *Introduction to the New Testament* (Grand Rapids: Eerdmans, 1971), 235.
3. Robert E. Coleman, *The Master Plan of Discipleship* (Old Tappan, N.J.: Revell, 1987).
4. Martyn Lloyd-Jones, *The Christian Warfare* (Edinburgh: Banner of Truth, 1976), 274; cited in Stott, *Acts*, BST, 9.
5. Longenecker, "Acts," 238.

However, both Acts and the third Gospel have been written anonymously. But Acts is unique in that it contains ninety-seven verses during Paul's journeys where the third person is replaced by the first person plural—the so-called "we passages," which claim to be the observations of an eyewitness. Claims that this was a literary device used for effect—especially that the first person plural was commonly used for accounts of sea travel—have been adequately countered elsewhere.[6] Note, for example, how several other sea voyages are narrated in Acts in the third person.[7] We know from Paul's letters that Luke was his companion in Rome (Col. 4:14; 2 Tim. 4:11; Philem. 24). When we realize that the tradition that Luke wrote the third Gospel and Acts goes at least as far back as the early second century and that the church in the early centuries was unanimous about the fact Luke wrote the two books, we are inclined to accept the traditional interpretation. As Ward Gasque says, "If Luke did not write the Third Gospel and Acts, it is difficult to explain how the tradition connecting his name with these documents ever arose, since he is otherwise an insignificant figure in the early Church."[8]

Luke writes in good literary Greek, which has led to the conclusion that he must have been well educated. He was probably a Gentile, though this claim has been challenged. While there is no unanimity about where he came from, a strong early tradition connects him with Antioch of Pisidia.[9] Paul refers to him as "our dear friend Luke, the doctor" (Col. 4:14) and shows Luke as faithfully sticking with him at a time when most other Christians had shunned him, that is, during his second imprisonment in Rome (2 Tim. 4:11).

Scholars have placed the date of writing of Acts from early to mid-60s of the first century to much later in the century (some estimates go as far as the late second century).[10] The most evident point used in support of an earlier date is the fact that the book ends so abruptly with events that should be dated around the early 60s.

Acts As Historical Document

WE HAVE COMPARATIVELY longer discussions on historical issues than would be expected in a commentary of this type. This is because the pluralistic mood that is prevalent today, with its radically new understanding of the

---

6. See especially Hemer, *Acts*, 312–34.

7. See 9:30; possibly 11:25–26; 13:4, 13; 14:26; 17:14; 18:18, 21 (from D. J. Williams, *Acts*, 3–4).

8. W. W. Gasque, "Luke," *ISBE*, 3:179.

9. Ibid.

10. For a listing of the various positions on the date of Acts and the defense of an early date, see Hemer, *Acts*, ch. 9.

gospel as being on equal footing with other ideologies, can be sustained by "Christians" only if they deny the historical reliability of the New Testament records.[11] As this seems to be common in some circles today, I felt that it was relevant on occasion to occupy myself with historical matters. I wish for my readers to sense that the book of Acts is rooted in concrete history, as I believe that influences the way we approach the study and application of the truths contained in Scripture.

The prologue of the Gospel of Luke, which applies to Acts as well, indicates that Luke intended to write an account that was historically accurate (Luke 1:1–4). Yet from the end of the nineteenth century, the "Tübingen school" associated with F. C. Bauer, which was skeptical of the historical value of the biblical documents and dominated biblical scholarship, viewed Acts as a late second-century document that contained an idealized fictional account of the early church. This was the heyday of the liberal movement, which was antisupernatural and discounted the historicity of records of miraculous events in the New Testament. Today, while there is no consensus on the dating of Acts, it is generally placed much earlier than the late second century. There are three basic ways of looking at the historicity of Acts among scholars today.

Theology, Not History

THERE HAS BEEN a welcome emphasis on the theology of Luke in recent times, especially because many commentaries of an earlier era focused so much on the history that they paid little attention to the theology of Acts. It is clear that Luke had a theological aim along with a historical one in his choice of material. For example, though the ministry in Derbe yielded "a large number of disciples" (14:21), there is only a single sentence about Paul's ministry there. The ministry in Athens yields a correspondingly less number of converts—only "a few" (17:34)—but it occupies nineteen verses (17:16–34). This contrast suggests that Luke chose the material he stressed in his account depending on the subject matter rather than merely using earthly indicators of success. He selected certain events because of the value they had in communicating the truths he wanted to emphasize.

Unfortunately, some of those who have focused on the theology of Acts, such as Ernst Haenchen and Hans Conzelmann, deny the historical value of Acts.[12] They have pointed to the supposed contradictions among the Gospels and between Paul's letters and Acts, as well as to alleged historical inaccuracies, in stating their case for rejecting the trustworthiness of Acts.

---

11. For a fuller discussion of the issues involved see my *Supremacy*, ch. 6.
12. Haenchen, *Acts*; Hans Conzelmann, *Acts*, Hermenia (Philadelphia: Fortress, 1987).

Introduction

History and Theology

WE CAN BE thankful that many recent studies have focused on the theological message of Acts without denying its historical value. Works with this emphasis include the commentaries emphasizing structure by David Gooding and Robert Tannehill,[13] and the studies of the theology of Luke-Acts by Howard Marshall, Roger Stronstad, and Harold Dollar.[14] This approach to Acts can be called "theological history"—a narrative of interrelated events from a given place and time, chosen to communicate theological truths. This commentary likewise does not place false dichotomies between theology and history. It views God as acting in the arena of history and through that revealing his ways and his will to his people.

The Scottish scholar Sir William Ramsay (1851–1939) did much to shift scholarly thinking in the direction of a positive view of the historical trustworthiness of Acts. Ramsay was a lecturer in classical art and archaeology at Oxford University when he went to Asia Minor for archaeological work. While there, he went through a remarkable change of convictions, which he chronicles in his book *The Bearing of Recent Discovery on the Trustworthiness of the New Testament.*

Ramsay found no trustworthy maps of the New Testament era, so he had to make his own. This forced him to read the original sources, such as Christian inscriptions and "the Acts of the Apostles [which] had to be read anew." He reported that he "began to do so without expecting any information of value regarding the condition of Asia Minor at the time when Paul was living." This was because he had accepted the current view that Acts "was written during the second half of the second century by an author who wished to influence the minds of the people in his own time by a highly wrought and imaginative description of the early church."[15]

When Ramsay came to Acts 14:6,[16] he thought he had found a predictable error by the author. It read, "They . . . fled [from Iconium] to the Lycaonian cities of Lystra and Derbe and to the surrounding country." The common view among scholars at the time, based on material by Cicero and Pliny the Elder from about a century before the New Testament era, was that Iconium was a city in Lycaonia. Ramsay thought that the author of Acts had used

---

13. David Gooding, *True to the Faith: A Fresh Approach to the Acts of the Apostles* (London: Hodder and Stoughton, 1990); Robert C. Tannehill, *The Narrative Unity of Luke-Acts: A Literary Interpretation;* vol. 2, *The Acts of the Apostles* (Minneapolis: Fortress, 1994).

14. I. Howard Marshall, *Luke: Historian and Theologian* (Grand Rapids: Zondervan, 1970); Roger Stronstad, *The Charismatic Theology of St. Luke;* Harold Dollar, *St. Luke's Missiology: A Cross-Cultural Challenge.*

15. William M. Ramsay, *BRD,* 37–38.

16. Ramsay denotes this as 14:5 in ibid., 39.

Xenophon to obtain the idea that Iconium was in Phrygia (from his popular *Anabasis*, written four hundred years before the events recorded in Acts). Ramsay assumed that Luke, not knowing about the region, took this information and transposed it to the first century, by which time the boundaries had shifted so that it was no longer true. It was, says Ramsay, like "speaking of going from Richmond to Virginia or from London to England. The expression does not ring true."[17]

But as Ramsay investigated the matter further, he found out that Acts was entirely correct. In the first century Iconium was indeed a city in Phrygia, not Lycaonia. He notes too that the author of Acts mentioned that the people of Lystra spoke "in the Lycaonian language" (14:11), which would have meant a change from the language spoken in Iconium. Inscriptions demonstrated that Phrygian was spoken in Iconium until the end of the second century. Ramsay realized that this historical comment had been inserted into Acts because the contrast had struck Paul, who had undoubtedly mentioned it to Luke.[18] Ramsay goes on to note the description of the gods of the people of Lystra as Zeus and Hermes (14:12), and through his research realized that "Zeus and Hermes were commonly regarded in that region as associated gods."[19]

Ramsay was impressed! He began to realize that Acts might be a valuable source of historical information. He titles the chapter describing what happened to him through this study of Acts 14, "The First Change of Judgment."[20] In a subsequent chapter entitled "General Impression of Trustworthiness in the Acts," Ramsay writes:

> The more I have studied the narrative of Acts and the more I have learned year after year about Graeco-Roman society and thoughts and fashions, and organization in those provinces, the more I admire and the better I understand. I set out to look for truth in the borderland where Greece and Asia meet, and found it here. You may press the words of Luke in a degree beyond any other historian's, and they stand the keenest scrutiny and the hardest treatment, provided always that the critic knows the subject and does not go beyond the limits of science and justice.[21]

Between 1893 and 1915 Ramsay wrote ten books on Paul and Luke. The most famous of these was his *magnum opus*, entitled *St. Paul: Traveller and Roman*

---

17. Ibid., 40.
18. Ibid., 42.
19. Ibid., 48.
20. Ibid., ch. 3.
21. Ibid., 89.

Citizen (published first in 1895), which charted the entire life of the apostle.[22] Scot McKnight says of this book, "Here the real Paul seems to grab the reader and takes the reader with him throughout his journeys."[23] One should note that the historicity of Acts has been defended throughout the twentieth century in books written by classicists or historians who have achieved fame in the field of New Testament studies. The following names come to mind: classics lecturer turned New Testament scholar, F. F. Bruce; classics professor from New Zealand, E. M. Blaiklock;[24] Oxford historian A. N. Sherwin-White;[25] and classics schoolteacher turned New Testament researcher from England, Colin Hemer.[26] The latest to join this distinguished list is a brilliant historian from Russia, Irina Levinskaya.[27]

Drama and Adventure

THE THIRD SIGNIFICANT approach to Acts, represented by R. I. Prevo, claims that Acts is like a popular novel or a historical romance. It is said to aim at edification in an entertaining form; many features are there simply to enhance the readers enjoyment and delight.[28] The resemblances of Acts to ancient novels has long been noted,[29] and there is no doubt that Luke wrote in a lively and entertaining way. A recent study has observed that "the story of Paul's sea journey and shipwreck in Acts 27 is rich in nautical detail and high adventure that seems to serve no other purpose than to heighten the drama and the suspense."[30] However, that should not cause us to discount the historical trustworthiness of Acts.

Howard Marshall has given four pointed criticisms of this approach. (1) Acts is part of a twofold work, and the Gospel of Luke and Acts follow

---

22. William M. Ramsay, *St. Paul: Traveller and Roman Citizen* (Grand Rapids: Baker, 1949 reprint). This book was unfortunately not available to me.

23. Scot McKnight, "Sir William Ramsay: Archaeologist: Re-Tracing Acts," *More Than Conquerors*, ed. John Woodbridge (Chicago: Moody, 1992), 306.

24. E. M. Blaiklock, *The Acts of the Apostles*, TNTC (Grand Rapids: Eerdmans, 1959). This commentary was different from the others in the Tyndale series, being what was called a historical commentary.

25. A. N. Sherwin-White, *Roman Society and Roman Law in the New Testament* (Grand Rapids: Baker, 1978, reprint of 1963 ed.).

26. Hemer, *Acts*.

27. Irina Levinskaya, BAFCS, vol. 5, *Diaspora Setting* (1996). See especially the preface (vii–x) for a description of her scholarly pilgrimage.

28. R. I. Prevo, *Profit with Delight: The Literary Genre of the Acts of the Apostles* (Philadelphia: Fortress, 1987).

29. C. K. Barrett, *Luke the Historian in Recent Study* (London: Epworth Press, 1961), 15, 55; cited in Howard Marshall, *A Fresh Look at the Acts*, 18.

30. William W. Klein, Craig Blomberg, and Robert L. Hubbard, *Introduction to Biblical Interpretation* (Dallas: Word, 1993), 345.

a similar method and style. But the Gospel is clearly *not* a historical novel. (2) Could Luke have got away with writing a novel of the early church so soon after the events? Such inventions usually belong to a later generation. (3) Large sections of Acts cannot be considered in the category of historical novel writing; they have different concerns. (4) The features of novels found in Acts also appear in good history too.[31] Having said that, we add that we should not lose sight of the features of delight, drama, and adventure that characterize this book. Even now, whenever I think of Paul's voyage and shipwreck, I get an eerie feeling because of the impact that vivid chapter has had on me.

Paul in Acts and the Epistles

A MAJOR OBJECTION to the view that the author of Acts was a close companion of Paul is the claim that the apostle as portrayed in Acts is very different to the one who emerges from his letters. The letters show him in constant conflict with those who resisted the free admission of the Gentiles to the church, whereas in Acts the problem is largely settled in chapter 15 and not mentioned again. Furthermore, Paul's acceptance of the rules laid down by the Jerusalem Council, his circumcision of Timothy, and his undertaking of a rite of purification in Jerusalem are considered incompatible with themes found in Galatians. Finally, the strong emphasis on the atoning death of Christ and justification by faith that is found in the Paul of the letters is said to be missing in the Paul of Acts.

Let me respond to this briefly by saying that the purposes and occasions of Acts and the letters are different. We usually look at the Paul in the letters as a theologian responding to needs in the churches. In Acts, however, we see him as a missionary, a charismatic founder of Christian communities. Such differences help explain the different emphases. The apostle did not object to circumcision as a Jewish rite, so he had the half-Jew Timothy circumcised in order to enhance his credibility in ministry.[32] But when circumcision was presented as a means of salvation, he strongly opposed it. His decision to participate in a purificatory rite in the Jerusalem temple is in keeping with his teaching in the letters about becoming a Jew in order to win the Jews (1 Cor. 9:20).[33]

Paul was indeed uncompromising when it came to the fundamental principles of the faith, such as salvation by faith alone. But where these principles were not affected, he was willing to adapt himself to his audience. While

---

31. Marshall, *Fresh Look*, 19–21.
32. See our comments on 16:1–3.
33. See our comments on 21:20–26.

justification by faith in Christ and the message of the cross are not given as much emphasis in the summaries of his speeches that Luke records as they receive in the letters, these teachings are always implied and sometimes explicitly stated.[34]

While we should recognize that the purposes for writing and the theological emphases of Luke and Paul differ, we do not need to imply that they contradict each other. For a complete picture of who Paul was, we must look at both his letters and the historical description of his life in Acts, just as we must do if we want a reliable biography about any famous author. Looking at only one specific type of literature will not serve as comprehensive guide to the life and thinking of an individual.

The Speeches of Acts

SPEECHES PLAYED AN important role in the history books of the period before and during the first century, "often constituting 20 to 35 percent of the narrative."[35] Rhetoric, or the art of persuasion, was considered primary to education in the first-century Greco-Roman world. As Conrad Gempf explains, "Rhetoric was, to the ancients, *power*, whether for good or for ill. In the Graeco-Roman world, *speaking* was central to success." Thus in ancient history books, "speeches are not mere commentary on events nor accompaniment to events: speeches must be seen *as* events in their own right." In other words, "ancient historians tended to focus on battles *and* speeches as the events that shaped history."[36] So it is not surprising to find that Acts has thirty-two speeches (excluding short statements), which make up 25 percent of the narrative.[37]

The speeches in Acts have been the subject of much study and discussion since the 1920s, when scholars like Henry Cadbury and Martin Dibelius treated them as creations of Luke intended to buttress the "history" that he was presenting.[38] The writings of some early historians, such as Thucydides and Josephus, who clearly invented materials for the speeches they recorded, were taken as typical of Hellenistic historiography—a style that was then projected to Luke. It was in response to this challenge that a young Scottish

---

34. See 13:38–39; 20:17–38 and our comments on these verses.

35. David E. Aune, *The New Testament in Its Literary Environment* (Philadelphia: Westminster, 1987), 124.

36. Conrad Gempf, "Public Speaking and Published Accounts," *BAFCS*, vol. 1, *Ancient Literary Setting*, 260, 261 (italics his).

37. Aune, *Literary Environment*, 124–25.

38. For a summary of these developments, see Conrad Gempf, "Public Speaking," 291–98. For a more detailed study, see W. Ward Gasque, *A History of the Interpretation of the Acts of the Apostles* (Peabody, Mass.: Hendrickson, 1989).

classics scholar, F. F. Bruce, gave a now-famous lecture, "The Speeches in the Acts of the Apostles," in 1942.[39] It gave him a name as a New Testament scholar, a field he later made his vocation with great distinction.

Responses to the scholarly discounting of the historical value of Acts continued, climaxing in a major work by another classicist turned New Testament scholar, Colin J. Hemer, who died in 1987 (before the last three chapters of his monumental work, *The Book of Acts in the Setting of Hellenistic History*, was completed). His treatment on the speeches of Acts was pieced together by the editor of this posthumous publication, Conrad Gempf, and included as an appendix. It defends the basic historicity of the speeches while conceding that what we get are not verbatim reports. Hemer said, "The brief summary paragraphs we possess do not purport to reproduce more than perhaps a *précis* of the distinctive highlights."[40]

The editor of Hemer's work, Conrad Gempf, has, in a separate publication, elaborated on the nature of reporting speeches in ancient historiography. He has shown that simply because a speech fits in with the historian's purposes and convictions does not necessarily mean it has been invented by the historian. Historians may report speeches colorfully and rhetorically according to their own style, but that does make them unfaithful records of what took place. Gempf's conclusion is that just as good ancient historians recorded speeches in ways that, according to their standards, were historically appropriate and faithful representations of the events, it is probable that the author of Luke-Acts did the same.[41]

In this commentary we will approach the speeches as recording essentially what was said by those alleged to have given them. They are most certainly summaries and paraphrases of much longer talks, and they faithfully report what was said. Through them we receive an understanding of how the leaders of the church faced their evangelistic, apologetic, pastoral, and theological challenges, and of how the opponents of Christianity and the Jewish and Gentile leaders of the day responded to Christianity.

Major Themes of Acts

JESUS' STATEMENT OF the Great Commission in Acts 1:8 is the key text in this book, highlighting the two main themes of Acts: the Holy Spirit and witness.

---

39. Published as F. F. Bruce, *The Speeches in the Acts of the Apostles*, Tyndale New Testament Lecture, 1942 (London: Tyndale, 1943).

40. Hemer, *Acts*, 418.

41. Gempf, "Public Speaking," 259–303. For a summary of Gempf's view see his, "Acts," *NBCTCE*, 1071–72. We have discussed the alleged contradictions between Paul's letters and his speeches in Acts above.

Jesus' disciples will become witnesses only after the Holy Spirit comes on them. Jesus then gives the geographical sequence in which the task of witness will be carried out—they will begin with Jerusalem, then move to Judea and Samaria, and culminate with witness to the ends of the earth. This sequence provides an outline for the book of Acts (see below).

In this section I will only lightly describe the various themes that gain prominence in the book of Acts. The reader is directed to the Subject Index at the back for a summary of the points highlighted in this commentary.

The priority of evangelism. From chapter 1, where the Great Commission is recorded (1:8), right up to the end of the book, the great activity that dominates this book is evangelism. An interesting realization dawned on me as I was coming to the end of this commentary: The two major methods used in evangelism in Acts were the winning of attention through miracles and apologetics. All the messages recorded in Acts had a strong apologetic content. The evangelists sought to show that Christianity withstood the questions that the people were asking, and the records of the speeches indicate that their evangelism was strongly content-oriented. The chart on "Evangelistic Preaching in Acts" gives a summary of the methods and message of the first evangelists.

The power of the Holy Spirit. Many have felt that Acts should be called "The Acts of the Holy Spirit." The first chapter records the promise of the Holy Spirit (1:4–5, 8), the second his descent, and the rest of the book his work in and through the church.

Community life. Acts presents a vibrant community that was passionate about mission, with the members caring for each other, pursuing holiness, and dealing with matters that affected its unity. In the description of community we also see Luke's characteristic concern for the poor (which is more pronounced in his Gospel).

Teaching. Not only is teaching presented as something done with Christians, in Acts it is also part of the evangelistic process.

Prayer. Fourteen of the first fifteen chapters of Acts (ch. 5 excepted) and many of the later chapters mention prayer; in Acts, as in Luke's Gospel, prayer is a key theme.[42]

Breaking human barriers in Christ. In keeping with the geographical order presented in the Great Commission (1:8), Luke shows how the gospel spread from Jerusalem to Judea and Samaria and to the ends of the earth. In this process Gentiles are saved; he describes the way the church handled

---

42. On prayer in Luke-Acts, see M. M. B. Turner, "Prayer in the Gospels and Acts," *Teach Us To Pray*, ed. D. A. Carson (Grand Rapids: Baker, 1990), 59–75; P. T. O'Brien, "Prayer in Luke-Acts: A Study in the Theology of Luke," *TynBul* 24 (1973): 113–16.

that witness as well as other social differences among Christians, leaving us with the strong impression that human barriers were broken in the early church and giving us reasons why that is so.

The place of suffering. Like much of the rest of the New Testament, there is much reflection on suffering in Acts. Here the suffering faced by the church is mostly on account of opposition to the gospel.

The sovereignty of God. Allied to the emphasis on suffering is the underlying theme that God is working out his sovereign purposes even through suffering. This is the dominant theme of the passage that describes the church's reaction to the first experience of suffering (4:23–31).

The Jewish reaction to the gospel. A surprising amount of space is given to attempts of the church to evangelize the Jews and to Paul's perseverance with this task in spite of many disappointments. Acts begins with the apostles' asking Jesus when he will restore the kingdom to Israel (1:6) and ends with an affirmation that because of the hardness of the hearts of the Jews, the gospel is being taken to the Gentiles (28:25–28).

The legal status of Christianity. Luke is eager to give the impression that the Roman authorities did not consider Christianity to be a dangerous or illegal movement. Acts also contains examples of the eloquent defense of the Christians faith before the state.

Applying the Book of Acts Today

WE SAID THAT Luke had both a theological aim and a historical one in writing Acts, and that the events he chose to stress were chosen because of the value they had in presenting truths he wanted to communicate. Our task is to find those truths and to see what abiding principles we can glean from them that we can apply to our thoughts, lives, and ministries today. How do we go about gleaning abiding principles from these stories?

One method that is popular today is allegorizing—seeing consistent spiritual parallels to the incidents presented and looking for what is sometimes called the "deeper meaning" of the text. This was a common method of interpretation in the early church and is often associated with the church father Origen. For example, the three stages of Lazarus following his death have been taken to be teaching three stages of a Christian's spiritual life (see John 11). (1) His stage in the tomb as a corpse represents the unregenerate stage. (2) His stage after being raised from the dead but before he is freed from the bondage of his grave clothes represents the carnal stage. (3) The stage after being loosed from the grave clothes represents the spiritual stage.

Though such allegorizing is an effective means of communicating truth, it may not be the intention of the author of the passage. True, sometimes the

Evangelistic Preaching in Acts

	2:1–47	3:1–26	8:26–39	10:1–48	13:14–52	14:6–20	17:16–34
	On the day of Pentecost	After temple gate healing	Philip, the Ethiopian	At Cornelius's home	At the Pisidian synagogue	At Lystra	At Athens
Audience	Palestinian and dispersion Jews	Jerusalem Jews	God-fearer	God-fearers	Jews of dispersion and God-fearers	Gentiles	Intellectual Gentiles
A. BEFORE THE PREACHING EVENT							
1. How the hearers were prepared before the preaching event	Speech in their own languages (5–12); The events surrounding Jesus (22–24)	A crippled man leaps and praises God (6–10)	Reading a messianic scripture passage (28–33)	A godly man has a vision with instruction to call a preacher (1–6)	They had come for worship (14)	Lame person healed during preaching (8–10); Called gods, sacrifices offered (11–13)	Days of dialogue in the synagogue and marketplace (17); They discuss among themselves (18)
2. How the preacher is prepared	Infilling with the Holy Spirit (1–4)		Command: Angel to travel (26); Spirit to go near (29)	Peter has a vision, is given specific instruction (9–20)			Deep distress over the idols (16)
3. How attention is won	Tongues attract the crowd, Peter uses that to lead into the gospel (4–21)	Healing aroused interest (1–10); Peter says it was done by faith in Jesus' name (11–16)	Do you understand what you are reading? An invitation (30–31)	God working directly through a vision (1–6)	As visitors they are invited to speak (15)	Through a healing (8–11)	Socrates' method (dialogue in marketplace) in Athens (17); Religiosity as stepping stone (22–23); Quoting their poets (28)

B. THE PREACHING EVENT

	2:1–47	3:1–26	8:26–39	10:1–48	13:14–52	14:6–20	17:16–34
1. What triggers the preaching event	The people's questions and ridicule (13–14)	The people's astonishment (12)	Philip's question about what he was reading (34)	Dialogue about what they had experienced (25–33)	An invitation to speak (15)	Attempts to offer sacrifices to them (11–14)	An invitation to explain what he is teaching at the Areopagus (19–21)
2. Introduction	Explanation of tongues phenomenon (14–21)	Answers questions about miracle (12–16)	A passage answering his questions (34–35)	A conclusion from the dialogue (34–35)	Israel's history is recounted (16–22)	Don't do this. We are just humans (15)	Contact through their religiosity and need for unknown God (22–23)
3. This is good news			About Jesus (35)	Of peace through Jesus (36)	That resurrection fulfills promises to the fathers (32)	Their preaching (7) from idols to living God (15)	About Jesus and the resurrection (18)
4. God the Creator						Made heaven, earth, sea, and everything in them (15)	Made world, everything in it (24); Creator of all humans (26)
5. God who is supreme						Re: the destiny of nations (16)	Lord of heaven, earth (24); Determines destiny of nations (26)
6. God's action in Israel's history		God of our fathers (13); Predicting blessing of Messiahs (22, 24); Covenant to Abraham (25)			Summary of history (16–22)		

B. THE PREACHING EVENT (cont.)

	2:1–47	3:1–26	8:26–39	10:1–48	13:14–52	14:6–20	17:16–34
7. The living God						The living God (15)	Not confined to temples (24); Not in need of our help (25); Not made by humans from silver etc. (29)
8. God speaking in nature and history						Left a testimony via rain, crops, food, joy (17)	God's superintending nations makes humans search him (27)
9. Authenticated by the Scriptures	Re: descent of Spirit (16); Resurrection (25–31); Exaltation(34–35)	His death, reign, ministry were prophesied (18, 21–26)	Message answers questions about Isa. 53	All the prophets testify about him (43)	The resurrection fulfills Scripture (32–37)		
10. Gospel fulfills human aspiration					Jews' aspirations fulfilled in Jesus (16–23)		The God they did not know but wanted to (23)
11. God's accessibility							He is not far from us (27)
12. Human religiosity							Evidence of religiousness (22–23); Made to search for God (27)

	2:1–47	3:1–26	8:26–39	10:1–48	13:14–52	14:6–20	17:16–34
13. God and human nature							All humanity created from one stock (26); God's offspring, depending on him for existence (28)
14. John the Baptist as forerunner				Christ's ministry began after John's baptism (37)	John points to Jesus as climax of his work (24–25)		
15. Jesus' life and ministry	Miracles are God's accreditation of Christ (22)			Did good, healed all under the devil's power (37–38)			
16. Death announced		You killed author of life (15, also 13–14)	The theme of the talk (32–35)	Killed by hanging on a tree (39)	Executed unjustly (28)		
17. Christ's death and God's sovereignty	According to God's set purpose and foreknowledge (23)	Death—a fulfillment of prophecy (18)	Death—a fulfillment of prophecy (32–35)		Death fulfilled prophecy fully (27, 29)		
18. The resurrection as proof	God raised him up (24); Foretold in OT (24–31)	Whom God raised up (15)		God raised him, caused him to be seen (40)	God raised him (30)		God raised him as proof of all this (31)
19. We are witnesses	All witnesses of the resurrection (32)	Of resurrection (15)		Of his life and ministry (39); Chosen to see risen Christ (41)	Those who saw are witnesses of resurrection (31)		

B. THE PREACHING EVENT (cont.)

	2:1–47	3:1–26	8:26–39	10:1–48	13:14–52	14:6–20	17:16–34
20. Christ's kingship, sovereignty, and victory	Exaltation (33); experiencing Spirit (33); OT predictions are evidences (34–35); He will rule till enemies defeated (34–35)	He will remain in heaven until all is fulfilled (21); Culminating in his return (20–21)					Will judge the world with justice through Christ (31)
21. Christ the only Savior and Judge and warnings	Warning, plea to be saved from corrupt generation (40)	If you don't listen to him, you will be cut off (23)		Judge of the living and the dead (42)	Note the warning to scoffers by prophets (40–41)		
22. Jesus is Lord, Christ, Son of God, Savior, etc.	Events from miracles to sending of Spirit show that he is Lord, Christ (22–36)	God glorified his servant (13); Holy and Righteous One, author of life (14–15)					
23. Conviction	You killed him (23, 36) Convicted, they seek guidance (37)	You handed over Jesus to be killed (13–15)					
24. Repentance and conversion	Repent and be baptized (38)	Repent (19); Blessing, when people turn from wickedness (26)	Must have talked about baptism (see 36)			Turn from useless things to the living God (15)	Commands all men everywhere to repent (30)
25. Recognition of ignorance		You acted in ignorance (17)				In past he let nations go their own way (16)	In past God overlooked ignorance (30)

	2:1–47	3:1–26	8:26–39	10:1–48	13:14–52	14:6–20	17:16–34
26. Forgiveness of sins	To those who repent and are baptized through his name (38)	Sins wiped out (19)		Through his name (43)	Through Jesus (38) and justification (39)		
27. Belief in Christ		Listen to everything he tells you (22)	[If you believe (37)]	Results in forgiveness (43)	Results in justification (39)		
28. God's election to salvation	The promise is for all whom the Lord will call (34)	Jesus appointed for and sent first to the Jews (20, 26); Heirs of promise (25); Can lose it through rebellion (22–23)			Those appointed to eternal life believe (48)		All people everywhere commanded to repent (30)
29. Joining the body of Christ	Be baptized (38)	Refusal results in cutting off (23)	Baptism (see 36)				
30. The invitation	Repent, be baptized for forgiveness (38); The promise is for you (39); Warning and pleading (40)	Repent, turn to God (19); Listen to Jesus (22); Consequence of rejection (23); God's good plan for them (24–26)	Given by the hearer: "Why shouldn't I be baptized?" (36)	Response before an invitation is given (44)	In the form of a warning (40–41); Those who follow urged to continue in God's grace (43)		General call to repentance (30)
31. Other blessings of salvation	Repent etc. to receive Spirit's gift (38)	Times of refreshing (19); Christ's second coming (20–21); Promises given to heirs (25); Turned from wickedness (26)					

B. THE PREACHING EVENT (cont.)

	2:1–47	3:1–26	8:26–39	10:1–48	13:14–52	14:6–20	17:16–34
32. Actively resisting personal glory		Don't stare at us, as if it was by our power (12); It was through Christ (16)		Refuses veneration: "I am only a man" (26)		Tear clothes, rush, shout, "We ... are ... human" (14–15)	
C. AFTER THE EVENT							
1. Response to the message	3000 added (41)	Leaders are disturbed and arrest Peter and John and try them (4:1–3, 5–22); Many believe, and the number grows to 5000 (4:4)	A request to be baptized (36); He goes on his way rejoicing (39)	Holy Spirit comes on all who heard; speaking in tongues (44–46); Jewish believers astonished (45)	Invited to speak again (42); Some follow and talk (43); A big crowd next time but Jews oppose (44–45); Gentile converts (48); Persecution, expulsion (50)	Jews from nearby towns win over the crowd. Paul stoned, presumed dead and dragged out of city (19)	Some sneer at resurrection (32); Some want to hear more (32); Few believe (34)
2. Follow-up procedures	Those who accept are baptized (41)		Philip taken away! (39)	Baptized, Peter stays on a few days (48)			Become followers of Paul (34)
3. Body life	Vibrant Christian community (42–47)	Radical sharing (4:32–37)	Probably none	Words of acceptance to Gentiles (47)	Word spreads (49); Filled with joy and Holy Spirit (52)	Disciples look after the injured Paul (20)	Followers of Paul (34)

author intended the allegorical method of interpreting truth, as in the allegory of the vine and the branches (John 15:1–8). But usually that intention is clear from the words of the passage itself. If the author does not intend his passage to be used in this way, then, if we use allegorical method, we are simply using it to illustrate some truths. These truths may be valid, but only because they come from somewhere else in Scripture. This method is not the way to get at the teaching intended by the author of Acts.

Others suggest that unless a narrative passage explicitly teaches a principle to follow, we should not use it in a normative way.[43] Gordon Fee helpfully distinguishes between concluding from a passage that "we must do this," when we should be saying that "we may do this."[44] However, out of the belief that "*all* Scripture is God-breathed and is useful for teaching, rebuking, correcting and training in righteousness" (2 Tim. 3:16), I believe we can go beyond this general approach to glean normative truth from the narratives of Acts even if a specific proposition is missing.[45] Note, for example, Paul's comments regarding God's judgment on Israel during Old Testament times: "Now these things occurred as examples to keep us from setting our hearts on evil things as they did.... These things happened to them as examples and were written down as warnings for us" (1 Cor. 10:6, 11). To Paul, Old Testament history was a collection of revelatory happenings, that is, events used by God to reveal his nature and purpose to humanity. In keeping with this principle, in Romans 4 and Galatians 3 Paul used God's dealings with Abraham to construct his theology of justification by faith and not works.

Sometimes what we have in narrative passages are examples to inspire us. Hebrews 11 uses Old Testament figures as inspiring examples of persevering faith for us to follow. Paul specifically asked the readers of his letters to follow his example (1 Cor. 4:6; 11:1; Phil. 3:17). For example, "Take note of those who live according to the pattern we gave you" (Phil. 3:17). Acts is the place from which to receive that pattern. We believe that through the lives and ministries of the apostles, God acted in ways that reveal his will and his ways to humanity.

We must, of course, be cautious about how we use this principle. We must carefully distinguish principles that are normative and those that are specific to certain situations and therefore not applicable to all situations. Take, for example, Gamaliel's advice to leave the Christians alone because

---

43. This seems to be the approach advocated in Gordon Fee and Douglas Stuart, *How to Read the Bible for All Its Worth* (Grand Rapids: Zondervan, 1982), 97.

44. Ibid.

45. On this see the discussion in Klein, Blomberg, Hubbard, *Introduction to Biblical Interpretation*, 350–51.

if Christianity is not of God, it will fail; and if it is of God, the Jewish leaders cannot stop it (Acts 5:38–39). God certainly used this advice to the advantage of the church, but it is not a principle always to be followed. If we did so, we could end up accepting as from God the growth of Islam, Sai Bäba's cult, and the Jehovah's Witnesses!

Or again: Klein, Blomberg and Hubbard point to the different models of church government and organization found in Acts. They show how "Congregationalists, Presbyterians, and Episcopalians all legitimately point to passages in Acts to support their views of church structure and leadership."[46] This should tell us that different styles of leadership and structure are acceptable within the body of Christ and that we should look for the most appropriate one that does not break biblical principles. In doing this, we will look for models as practiced in the early church and recorded in Acts that suit our particular situation.

In other words, we must be careful about how we apply the narratives of Acts. One important key is to look for Luke's purpose for including an event in Acts. If we find a theme given special attention in Acts, then we may be able to find a pattern emerging that can give us normative principles. For this reason we will sometimes go into greater depth in the "Bridging Contexts" sections in order to establish the normativeness of a principle. We will refer to other incidents and statements in Acts, and perhaps elsewhere in Scripture, to substantiate that normativeness.

Acts as a Radical Challenge to Today's Church

CONTEMPORARY CHRISTIANS WHO read Acts with an open mind will find themselves challenged with pointed applications by what happened in the early church. I will mention only a few here (see the Subject Index for elaboration of these points).

- To a society where individualism reigns and where the church also seems to have adopted a style of community life that "guards the privacy of the individual," the early church presents a radical community where the members held all things in common.
- To a society where selfishness is sometimes admired and each one is left to fend for himself or herself, Acts presents a group of Christians who were so committed to Christ and the cause of the gospel that they were willing to sacrifice their desires for the good of others.
- To a society where pluralism defines truth as something subjective and personal, Acts presents a church that based its life on certain

---

46. Ibid., 350.

objective facts about God and Christ—facts that were not only personally true but also universally valid and therefore had to be presented to the entire world.

- To a society that denies absolute truth and therefore shuns apologetics and persuasion in evangelism in favor of dialogue, Acts presents a church that persuaded people until they were convinced of the truth of the gospel. Instead of aiming at mutual enrichment as the main aim of interreligious encounter, as many do today, the early church proclaimed Christ as supreme Lord with conversion in view.
- In an age where specialization has hit evangelism so much that we rarely find churches that emphasize healing also emphasizing apologetics, Acts presents a church where the same individuals performed healings and preached highly reasoned, apologetic messages.
- In an age when many churches spend so much time, money, and energy on self-preservation and improvement, Acts presents churches that released their most capable people for reaching the lost.
- In an age where many churches look to excellence in techniques to bring success, Acts presents a church that depended on the Holy Spirit and gave top priority to prayer and moral purity.
- In an age when many avenues are available to avoid suffering and therefore many Christians have left out suffering from their understanding of the Christian life, Acts presents a church that took on suffering for the cause of Christ and considered it a basic ingredient of discipleship.

Outline of Acts

Prologue (1:1-2)
A. **Preparation for Pentecost (1:3-26)**
   1. Instructions Before the Ascension (1:3-8)
   2. The Ascension (1:9-11)
   3. After the Ascension (1:12-26)
B. **Witness in Jerusalem (2:1-7:60)**
   1. The Day of Pentecost (2:1-47)
      a. The Coming of the Spirit (2:1-13)
      b. Peter's Pentecostal Speech and the People's Response (2:14-42)
      c. The New Community (2:43-47)
   2. Healing at the Temple and Its Consequences (3:1-4:31)
      a. A Cripple Cured (3:1-10)
      b. Peter's Speech (3:11-26)
      c. Evangelism Proscribed by the Sanhedrin (4:1-22)
      d. The Believers Respond with Prayer (4:24-31)
   3. Radical Community (4:32-5:11)
      a. Radical Sharing (4:32-35)
      b. Radical Generosity (4:36-37)
      c. Radical Discipline (5:1-11)
   4. The Apostles Before the Sanhedrin (5:12-42)
      a. Continuing Power (5:12-16)
      b. Arrest, Trial, and Beating (5:17-40)
      c. After the Beating (5:41-42)
   5. The Appointing of the Seven (6:1-7)
   6. The Ministry and Martyrdom of Stephen (6:8-7:60)
      a. Stephen's Ministry (6:8-10)
      b. Accusations Against Stephen (6:11-15)
      c. Stephen's Speech (7:1-53)
      d. Stephen's Death (7:54-60)
C. **Witness in Judea and Samaria and the Beginnings of Gentile Evangelism (8:1-11:18)**
   1. The Church Is Scattered (8:1-4)
   2. Philip's Ministry (8:5-40)
      a. Public Ministry in Samaria (8:5-25)
      b. Personal Ministry with the Ethiopian (8:26-40)

Bibliography

Commentaries and Expositions

Alexander, J. A. *A Commentary on the Acts of the Apostles.* Edinburgh: Banner of Truth Trust, 1984, reprint of 1857 ed. Loaded with exegetical and devotional gems, though dated.

Arrington, French L. *The Acts of the Apostles: An Introduction and Commentary.* Peabody, Mass.: Hendrickson, 1988. Brief, incisive comments from a charismatic perspective.

Barclay, William. *The Acts of the Apostles.* The Daily Study Bible. Rev. ed. Edinburgh: Saint Andrew, 1976. Devotional insights arising from a great background knowledge.

Barrett, C. K. *A Critical and Exegetical Commentary on the Acts of the Apostles.* Vol. I. on chapters 1–14. ICC. Edinburgh: T. & T. Clark, 1994. A replacement volume in the ICC series. Takes a moderately critical approach to the issue of historical accuracy. Possibly the most comprehensive treatment of the Greek text available in English.

Bruce, F. F. *The Book of the Acts.* NICNT. Rev. ed. Grand Rapids: Eerdmans, 1988. Unparalleled for how it makes the historical background accessible to the general reader.

_____. *The Acts of the Apostles: Greek Text with Introduction and Commentary.* NICGT. Grand Rapids: Eerdmans, 1990. Notes on the Greek text.

Calvin, John. *Calvin's Commentaries: The Acts of the Apostles 1–13.* Trans. John W. Fraser and W. J. G. McDonald. *The Acts of the Apostles 14–28.* Trans. John W. Fraser. Grand Rapids: Eerdmans, 1965, 1966. Sage comments from one of the greatest expositors ever.

Carter, Charles W., and Ralph Earle. *The Acts of the Apostles.* Grand Rapids: Zondervan, 1973. Helpful application.

Chrysostom, Saint. "Homilies on the Acts of the Apostles." *A Select Library of the Nicene and Post-Nicene Fathers of the Christian Church.* Vol. 11. Ed. Philip Schaff. Grand Rapids: Eerdmans, 1989 reprint. Classic expositions by the great fourth-century expositor.

Clements, Roy. *The Church That Turned the World Upside Down.* Cambridge: Crossway, 1992. Brilliant exposition on the first half of Acts by one of this generation's outstanding expositors.

Faw, Chalmer E. *Believers Church Bible Commentary: Acts*. Scottdale, Pa.: Herald, 1993. A shorter work with good application.

Gempf, Conrad. "Acts." *NBCTCE*. Ed. D. A. Carson et al. Downers Grove, Ill.: InterVarsity, 1994. Exceptionally insightful comments despite its brevity.

Gooding, David. *True to the Faith: A Fresh Approach to the Acts of the Apostles*. London: Hodder and Stoughton, 1990. Emphasis on structure. Filled with deep devotional and theological insight.

Haenchen, Ernst. *The Acts of the Apostles: A Commentary*. Trans. R. McL. Wilson. Philadelphia: Westminster, 1971. Focus on theology, discounts historical reliability.

Harrison, Everett F. *Interpreting Acts: The Expanding Church*. Grand Rapids: Zondervan, 1986. Godly scholarship with reverent application.

Keener, Craig S. *The IVP Bible Background Commentary: New Testament*. Downer's Grove, Ill.: InterVarsity, 1993. Helpful insights on the cultural and historical background of the text.

Kistemaker, Simon J. *New Testament Commentary: Exposition of the Acts of the Apostles*. Grand Rapids: Baker, 1990. Good all-round larger commentary.

Knowling, R. J. "The Acts of the Apostles." *The Expositor's Greek Testament*. Vol. 2. Ed. W. Robertson Nicoll. Grand Rapids: Eerdmans, 1974 reprint. On the Greek text.

Larkin, William J., Jr. *Acts*. IVP New Testament Commentary Series. Downers Grove, Ill.: InterVarsity, 1995. Brief, reliable notes with relevant application.

Lenski, R. C. H. *The Interpretation of the Acts of the Apostles*. Minneapolis: Augsburg, reprint of 1934 ed. Good on application.

Longenecker, Richard. "The Acts of the Apostles." *EBC*. Vol. 9. Grand Rapids: Zondervan, 1981. Possibly the best all-round medium-sized commentary for a general reader.

Marshall, I. Howard. *The Acts of the Apostles*. TNTC. Grand Rapids: Eerdmans, 1980. Short but insightful comments from a master of the Lukan writings.

Morgan, G. Campbell. *The Acts of the Apostles*. Old Tappan, N.J.: Revell, 1924. Expositions with keen devotional insight.

Munk, Johannes. *The Acts of the Apostles*. Anchor Bible. Garden City, N.Y.: Doubleday, 1967. Briefer than the other books in this series.

Ogilvie, Lloyd J. *The Communicator's Commentary: Acts*. Dallas: Word, 1983. Brief expositions.

Polhill, John B. *Acts*. The New American Commentary. Vol. 26. Nashville: Broadman, 1992. A helpful all-round medium-sized work.

Robertson, Archibald Thomas. *Word Pictures in the New Testament*. Vol. 3. *The Acts of the Apostles*. Grand Rapids: Baker, reprint of 1930 ed. Helpful and inspiring comments on Greek meanings, though dated—not having the benefit of recent semantic studies.

Stott, John R. W. *The Message of Acts*. BST. Downers Grove, Ill.: InterVarsity, 1990. Sheer exposition with flashes of brilliant application from one of the great expositors of the twentieth century.

Tannehill, Robert C. *The Narrative Unity of Luke-Acts: A Literary Interpretation*. Vol. 2. *The Acts of the Apostles*. Minneapolis: Fortress, 1994. Refreshing focus on the structure and message of Acts.

Thomson, J. G. S. S. "Studies in the Acts of the Apostles." *Bright Words*. I received photocopies of this helpful series of twenty-nine expositions on Acts, which appeared in the magazine *Bright Words* in the late 1950s and early 1960s, from my friend Rev. John Kyle, but I do not have the dates of the individual articles.

Wagner, C. Peter. *The Acts of the Holy Spirit*. Vol. 1: *Spreading the Fire;* vol. 2: *Lighting the World;* vol. 3: *Blazing the Way*. Ventura, Calif.: Regal, 1994–1995. Strong on contemporary missiological application.

Wesley, John. *Explanatory Notes Upon the New Testament*. London: Epworth, 1966 reprint. Brief but pithy comments.

Williams, David John. *Acts*. NIBC. Peabody, Mass.: Hendrickson, 1990. An outstanding all-round shorter commentary, especially helpful for preachers.

Willimon, William H. *Acts*. Interpretation: A Bible Commentary for Teaching and Preaching. Atlanta: John Knox, 1988. Lively, relevant expositions.

Other Significant Works on Acts[47]

Coleman, Robert E. *The Master Plan of Discipleship*. Old Tappan, N.J.: Revell, 1987. Topical study of Acts; rich in devotional and practical insight.

Dollar, Harold. *St. Luke's Missiology: A Cross-Cultural Challenge*. Pasadena, Calif.: William Carey Library, 1996. Refreshing! Missiology based on serious Bible study.

Harrison, Everett F. *The Apostolic Church*. Grand Rapids: Eerdmans, 1985. Helpful topical study of Acts.

Hemer, Colin J. *The Book of Acts in the Setting of Hellenistic History*. Ed. Conrad Gempf. Winona Lake: Eisenbrauns, 1990. A brilliant defense of the historical reliability of Acts.

Marshall, I. H. *A Fresh Look at the Acts of the Apostles*. Sheffield: Sheffield Academic Press, 1992. Basic contemporary introduction to Acts.

---

47. See also the abbreviations for other books consulted in this commentary.

Bibliography

Shenk, David W., and Ervin R. Stutzman. *Creating Communities of the Kingdom: New Testament Models of Church Planting.* Scottdale, Pa.: Herald, 1988. Relevant application of Acts.

Stronstad, Roger. *The Charismatic Theology of St. Luke.* Peabody, Mass.: Hendrickson, 1984. Theology from a charismatic perspective.

Winter, Bruce, et al., eds. *The Book of Acts in Its First Century Setting.* Grand Rapids: Eerdmans, 1993–1996. Five volumes out of six available. An extremely helpful series for advanced study. Vol. 1: *Ancient Literary Setting*, ed. Bruce Winter and Andrew D. Clarke (1993); vol. 2: *Graeco-Roman Setting*, ed. David W. Gill and Conrad Gempf (1994); vol. 3: *Paul in Roman Custody*, Brian Rapske (1994); vol. 4: *Palestinian Setting*, ed. Richard Bauckham (1995); vol. 5: *Diaspora Setting*, Irina Levinskaya (1996).

Acts 1:1–8

IN MY FORMER book, Theophilus, I wrote about all that Jesus began to do and to teach ²until the day he was taken up to heaven, after giving instructions through the Holy Spirit to the apostles he had chosen. ³After his suffering, he showed himself to these men and gave many convincing proofs that he was alive. He appeared to them over a period of forty days and spoke about the kingdom of God. ⁴On one occasion, while he was eating with them, he gave them this command: "Do not leave Jerusalem, but wait for the gift my Father promised, which you have heard me speak about. ⁵For John baptized with water, but in a few days you will be baptized with the Holy Spirit."

⁶So when they met together, they asked him, "Lord, are you at this time going to restore the kingdom to Israel?"

⁷He said to them: "It is not for you to know the times or dates the Father has set by his own authority. ⁸But you will receive power when the Holy Spirit comes on you; and you will be my witnesses in Jerusalem, and in all Judea and Samaria, and to the ends of the earth."

Original Meaning

ACTS 1 INTRODUCES many themes that are important to the whole book: Jesus' life and ministry, his sufferings as a fact predicted in the Old Testament, the importance of and evidence for the resurrection, the importance and power of the Holy Spirit, the priority of witness, the Great Commission with its scope extending to the ends of the earth, the missionary attitude as opposed to parochialism, the kingdom of God, the importance of truth and of Scripture in the Christian life, the role of the apostles, the ascension and second coming of Christ, and the importance of prayer and fellowship. As such it is a key to understanding the book of Acts. Because of this we will devote comparatively more space to it even though it is one of the shorter chapters.

The Former Book (1:1–2a)

THE OPENING SECTION of Acts contains a prologue along with a historical introduction. The author begins by referring to his "former book," gives the name of the recipient (Theophilus), and summarizes the contents of the earlier book (the Gospel of Luke). Theophilus means "friend of God" or "loved by God," but it is unlikely, as some (e.g., Origen) have suggested, that this name is a symbol for an anonymous person or group of people. This particular name was in use at that time, and the description of Theophilus as "most excellent" (see Luke 1:3) suggests that a real person is meant. "Most excellent" could suggest that a high government official is being addressed, but that is not a necessary inference as it was also used as a "form of polite address."[1] In those days, it was common for books to be dedicated to distinguished persons.[2]

If Luke's first volume describes "all that Jesus *began* to do and to teach *until* the day he was taken up to heaven," we can assume that this second volume describes what he *continued* to do and to teach (through his Spirit) *after* he was taken up.[3] Luke uses the word "all" in both the Gospel and Acts in a general way that the context must define. Thus, "we cannot assume he meant his Gospel to be any more exhaustive than Acts."[4]

Teaching and Instructions Before the Ascension (1:2b–8)

IN THE FORTY days before Jesus' ascension, his primary ministry related to the truth of the gospel (vv. 2b–3). (1) He gave "instructions ... to the apostles" (v. 2). The verb for instructing (*entellomai*) has the idea of commanding or giving orders. This must refer to the commands given in verses 4 and 8 not to leave Jerusalem until the Spirit comes and to preach the gospel to the ends of the earth (cf. Luke 24:46–48). These instructions were given "through the Holy Spirit" (v. 2), which introduces a key theme of Acts: All Christian ministry depends on the activity of the Spirit in the minister and in the ones ministered to.

(2) Luke then reports that Jesus' appearances were proof of his resurrection (v. 3a). The objective reality of the resurrection was the ultimate proof of the amazing claims that the apostles were to make about Jesus (17:31). The fact that the apostles were witnesses to this resurrection was a key to their preaching.[5] So right at the start of his book, Luke presents the resurrection as an event attested by "many convincing proofs."

(3) Jesus "spoke about the kingdom of God" (v. 3b), which refers to the reign or rule of God and was a key to his teaching. There are fewer references

---

1. Longenecker, "Acts," 253.
2. See Bruce, *Acts*, NICNT, 30, for examples of such dedications.
3. Ibid.
4. Longenecker, "Acts," 253.
5. See 1:22; 2:32; 3:15; 5:32; 10:39–41; 13:30–31.

to the kingdom in Acts (8:12; 19:8; 20:25; 28:23, 31), but they are important, considering that "the book begins (1:3) and ends on that theme (28:31)."[6] In the New Testament letters, while the kingdom is mentioned, what receives emphasis is the church, the body of Christ. But there is a close connection between the church and the kingdom (Matt. 16:18–19). According to the Gospels, the kingdom of God came with the events of the life, death, and resurrection of Jesus, and it finds its consummation in the return of Christ as Judge and King. In our discussion of 2:14–41 we will show why the biblical teaching on the reign of Christ should be an important ingredient of our evangelistic message.

Verses 4–5 present the crucial promise of the gift of baptism with the Holy Spirit.[7] The word *baptizō* basically means dip or immerse.[8] But it can take different meanings that must be determined by considering the context in which the word appears. It can mean "to wash ... with a view to making objects ritually acceptable," and can thus be translated "wash" or "purify." It can also mean "to employ water in a religious ceremony designed to symbolize purification and initiation on the basis of repentance—'to baptize.'" And in a figurative extension of the idea of immersion, it can mean "to cause someone to have a highly significant religious experience."[9] Related to this last definition is Jesus' question to James and John in Mark 10:38, "Are you able ... to be baptized with the baptism with which I am baptized" (NASB). This extends the meaning of immersion to a deluge or an overwhelming flood of suffering.[10]

Some of the other places where the baptism with the Holy Spirit is mentioned suggest an experience akin to the third use of *baptizō*. When Luke records this promise in his Gospel, Jesus says, "Stay in the city until you have been clothed with power from on high" (Luke 24:49). Acts 1:8 also says that when the Holy Spirit comes, the disciples will receive power. Describing what happened when this promise was fulfilled, Luke writes that the disciples "were filled with the Holy Spirit" (Acts 2:4). The words "power" and "filled" in these verses suggest that the baptism with the Holy Spirit involves an experience of God's fullness.

It must have saddened the heart of Jesus to hear his disciples ask about the time of restoring the kingdom to Israel (v. 6). He had taught them about the kingdom of God, but they talk about the kingdom of Israel. John Stott points out that

---

6. John B. Polhill, *Acts*, 82.

7. Many scholars today prefer to use the expression "baptism *in* the Holy Spirit." But we will stick to the NIV rendering of this expression: "baptism *with* the Holy Spirit."

8. BAGD, 131.

9. The definitions are from Louw and Nida, 536, 537, and 539 respectively.

10. Larry W. Hurtado, *Mark*, NIBC (1989), 176.

the verb, the noun and the adverb of their sentence all betray doctrinal confusion about the kingdom. The verb *restore* shows that they were expecting a political and territorial kingdom; the noun *Israel* that they were expecting a national kingdom; and the adverbial clause *at this time* that they were expecting its immediate establishment.[11]

Jesus' answer about not knowing times and dates set by the Father (v. 7) is consistent with what he said elsewhere on the topic of the timing of the last things (cf. Matt. 24:36, 42, 44; 25:13; Luke 12:40).

Verse 8 begins with "but" (*alla*), suggesting that Jesus is presenting an alternative aspiration for the disciples. Their primary concern should not be the political power that will come with the restoration of Israel's kingdom. It should be the spiritual power that will come through the baptism with the Holy Spirit, which will enable them to be witnesses "to the ends of the earth." This verse presents an outline and summary of Acts. The Holy Spirit's power and witness is the theme of the book. "The geographical terms provide a sort of 'Index of Contents'. . . 'in Jerusalem' covers the first seven chapters, 'in all Judea and Samaria' covers 8:1 to 11:18, and the remainder of the book traces the progress of the gospel outside the frontiers of the Holy Land until it at last reaches Rome."[12]

In a sense the disciples were already witnesses for they had seen the risen Lord; that was the key to their witness (1:22). But they also needed "power" to be effective witnesses, power that would come from the Holy Spirit. The way the Holy Spirit makes witnesses and empowers witness must cover the entire witnessing process, and this is well illustrated in Acts.[13]

Bridging Contexts

THE BOOK OF ACTS has been aptly called the "Acts of the Holy Spirit," for all that the church achieves is through the Spirit. In this first chapter Luke shows how the church prepared for the reception of the Spirit. For us today it gives essential ingredients for Spirit-anointed ministry.

Objective facts and subjective experience. The first few verses of Acts show an important factor in all of Acts—that the combination of the objective and the subjective are important aspects of the Christian religion. The mention of "many convincing proofs that he was alive" (1:3a) shows that Christianity is based on objective facts. The teaching "about the kingdom of

11. Stott, *Acts*, 41 (italics his).
12. Bruce, *Acts*, NICNT, 36–37.
13. See below on "The Holy Spirit and mission."

God" (1:3b) must also have included much that came under this category. The evangelistic preaching in Acts certainly contained many objective facts about the nature of God and the life and work of Jesus (see the chart on "Evangelistic Preaching in Acts" in the Introduction). Becoming a Christian involves assenting to those facts, and growing in the Christian life involves growing in the knowledge of those facts.

But Acts 1 also stresses the subjective experience of Christians. Thus, verses 4–5 refer to the baptism with the Holy Spirit, which, as noted above, includes a subjective experience of the power of the Spirit. To prepare to be witnesses of these great objective truths, one must have power coming from the indwelling Holy Spirit (v. 8). Peter's sermon at Pentecost climaxed with a statement of the objective truth: "God has made this Jesus, whom you crucified, both Lord and Christ" (2:36). But in response to the people's query about what they are to do, he says that if they repent and are baptized in the name of Jesus for the forgiveness of their sins, they "will receive the gift of the Holy Spirit" (2:38). The context indicates that the gift of the Holy Spirit includes, among other things, a subjective experience of him.

Acts, then, shows a church that was able to integrate the subjective and the objective aspects of Christianity.

Teaching and revival. From what we read in verses 2–5, we can infer that one of the key ways Jesus prepared his apostles for the revival that followed at Pentecost was to give them sound teaching. The place of biblical teaching in revival has been debated, and sometimes great outpourings of revival have been criticized for being low on preaching and teaching the Word. This was not the case with Peter's speech at Pentecost, and several spiritual awakenings have been recorded where the Word was uncompromisingly taught.[14] Whatever may have happened *during* a revival, it is well established that, as in Acts, Bible teaching has always been done *before* a revival. The great historian of revival, J. Edwin Orr, has said that a theological awakening must precede a revival of religion. Dr. John Mackay writes, "First the enlightened mind, then the burning heart. First a revival of theological insights, and then the revival we need."[15]

This is what happened under King Josiah when a newly discovered Book of the Law was read and a mighty revival was sparked (2 Kings 22–23). The principle we glean, then, is that if we wish to prepare for revival today, we must be faithful in teaching the Word to our people.

---

14. See J. Edwin Orr, *The Fervent Prayer: The Worldwide Impact of the Great Awakening of 1858* (Chicago: Moody, 1974), 111–20; idem, *Campus Aflame: Dynamic of Student Religious Revolution* (Glendale, Calif.: Regal Books, 1971), 217–19.

15. Both quotations are from David McKee, *The Wonder of Worship* (Ahmedabad, India: Jiwan Sahitya Sanstha, 1967), 16.

Baptism with the Holy Spirit. As already noted, the references to the baptism with the Holy Spirit suggest an experience of fullness with the Spirit. When does this take place? And what type of experience is it? Over these two questions there has been much debate in the church. Part of the problem is that the experience promised to the disciples and its fulfillment were in many ways unique, unrepeatable events. The same can be said of some of the other experiences of the coming of the Spirit to new believers in Acts. As a result, we have in the church an array of interpretations of what this means today.

A traditional evangelical explanation is that, while in Acts there were unique experiences of this baptism with the Holy Spirit, for us today such a baptism takes place at conversion, and the term *baptism* is used for initiation into the body of Christ and the resultant experience of the Spirit.[16]

But there are also many evangelicals who see this baptism as a second definite work of grace, distinct from conversion, one that usually takes place some time after conversion. It raises Christians to a higher plane in their experience and enables them to enjoy the fullness of the Spirit. Different emphases are found within this particular interpretation. The Wesleyan holiness movement has emphasized holiness of heart and life, or entire sanctification, as resulting from this baptism.[17] The Charismatics and Pentecostals have emphasized the power for witness and the sign gifts, such as tongues.[18] Evangelicals like D. L. Moody and R. A. Torrey emphasized power for service, especially for witness, as the result of this baptism.

Somewhat similar to the view of Moody and Torrey is that of Martyn Lloyd-Jones, who wrote that while the baptism with the Holy Spirit may take place at conversion, it usually takes place later and lifts a person to a higher level of spiritual experience.[19] But Lloyd-Jones seems to have left room for subsequent baptisms with the Holy Spirit. In fact, he seems to use this expression also to refer to what we usually call revival, when the power of God

---

16. See James D. G. Dunn, *Baptism in the Holy Spirit* (London: SCM, 1970); Wayne Grudem, *Systematic Theology* (Grand Rapids: Zondervan, 1994), 763–87; Frederick Dale Bruner, *A Theology of the Holy Spirit*, (Grand Rapids: Eerdmans, 1970); John R. W. Stott, *Baptism and Fullness* (Downers Grove, Ill.: InterVarsity, 1976).

17. See Laurence W. Wood, *Pentecostal Grace* (Wilmore, Ky.: Francis Asbury, 1980); Wilber T. Dayton, "Entire Sanctification," *A Contemporary Wesleyan Theology*, vol. 1, ed. Charles Carter (Grand Rapids: Zondervan, 1983).

18. See Howard M. Ervin, *Conversion-Initiation and the Baptism in the Holy Spirit* (Peabody, Mass.: Hendrickson, 1984); Stronstad, *The Charismatic Theology of St. Luke.*

19. Martyn Lloyd-Jones, *Joy Unspeakable: Power and Renewal in the Holy Spirit* (Wheaton: Harold Shaw, 1984). See also Michael A. Eaton, *Baptism with the Spirit: The Teaching of Martyn Lloyd-Jones* (Leicester: Inter-Varsity, 1989), and Tony Sargent, *The Sacred Anointing* (Wheaton: Crossway, 1994).

comes on groups of people through the outpouring of the Holy Spirit.[20] This seems to have been the view of some Puritans as well. "Apparently detecting in the phrase no consistent, technical meaning, they took it to mean 'effusion in Spirit' or 'inundation in Spirit' and felt free to pray for revival in the terms, 'Oh, baptize us afresh with the Holy Spirit!'"[21]

One of the strongest arguments for the conversion-initiation position is the apparent use of this expression for everyone in the church in 1 Corinthians 12:13: "For we were all baptized by one Spirit into one body—whether Jews or Greeks, slave or free—and we were all given the one Spirit to drink."[22] Others, however, have countered this claim. Howard Erwin argues that the first part of this verse refers to the Spirit's work of incorporating believers into the body as expressed by water baptism, while the second part refers to a subsequent experience, a Pentecostal-type baptism in the Spirit. According to this interpretation, "the parallelism [between the first and second parts of this verse] is not *synonymous*; it is *synthetic* in which the second metaphor supplements the first."[23] The question of how Paul could say that "all" have had this experience is answered by stating that "in the apostolic age, the baptism in the Spirit, in a Pentecostal sense, was the norm." But what of the fact that many of these supposedly Spirit-baptized people were carnal and babes in Christ (cf. 1 Cor. 3:1–2)? Erwin answers that "the Pentecostal baptism in the Spirit is for power-in-mission. . . . The manifestations of the Spirit's charisms are neither evidence of, nor contingent upon, spiritual maturity."[24]

What do we do with such differences of interpretation? Note first that there is little explicit teaching about how one enters into this baptism in the more didactic segment of the New Testament, the letters. But there are certain things we can be sure of. The baptism with the Holy Spirit implies a full experience of the Spirit, which among other things empowers us for witness. Paul makes fullness of the Spirit mandatory for Christians with the imperative: "Be filled with the Spirit" (Eph. 5:18).[25] Here, however, the result of the fullness is true, heartfelt worship (5:19–20).

---

20. Martyn Lloyd-Jones, *Revival: Can We Make It Happen?* (London: Marshall Pickering, 1986), 49–54.

21. D. A. Carson, *Exegetical Fallacies* (Grand Rapids: Baker, 1984), 47. Carson directs our attention to Iain Murray, "Baptism with the Spirit: What Is the Scriptural Meaning?" *Banner of Truth Magazine* 127 (April 1974): 5–22.

22. Grudem, *Systematic Theology*, 767–68; Dunn, *Baptism in the Holy Spirit*, 127–31.

23. Erwin, *Conversion-Initiation*, 100.

24. Ibid., 102.

25. Some have understood this statement as meaning "Be filled in your spirit." But, as Leon Morris points out, even if this were the meaning, it could be achieved only through the work of the Holy Spirit (*Expository Reflections on the Letter to the Ephesians* [Grand Rapids: Baker, 1994], 176–77).

The early church showed that being filled with the Spirit was mandatory for Christians by making it a basic qualification for those who were to administer the distribution of food (Acts 6:3). Therefore, even if this baptism refers to conversion-initiation, Christians who are not experiencing God's fullness in their lives are a scandal, an anomaly. The baptism with the Holy Spirit should open the door to their moving on to experience all that it implies: God's fullness. And they must seek this fullness with all their heart. The entrance into that experience may be through a crisis or a process. We know that, given the human make-up, we often take leaps forward in our spiritual lives through crisis experiences. Therefore, whether a crisis is mandatory or not, it is a genuine experience of growth to many Christians.

Whatever one may call it and however one may enter it, what is important is for all Christians to experience what the baptism with the Spirit implies: the fullness of God's Spirit and power in witness. The supreme place the Holy Spirit has in ministry in Acts is evidenced right from chapter 1. The ministry that the apostles will have can be fulfilled only with the Spirit's power (1:8). So important was this that they were not to launch out on the urgent mission for which they had been so consistently prepared by Christ (1:4–5) until they received this power. More urgent than the mission at this time was having the right equipment to carry out the mission. This, then, is the abiding principle we glean from the emphasis on baptism with the Spirit in Acts 1: The fullness of the Spirit is essential for Christian life and ministry.

Two implicit rebukes. The question that the disciples asked about the time of restoring the kingdom to Israel elicits two implicit rebukes from Christ (vv. 6–8): about eschatological inquisitiveness and about parochialism.[26] Despite his earlier statements that no one knows the time of the end events, they still ask him about it. And when Jesus is thinking about "the kingdom of God" (v. 3) and "the ends of the earth" (v. 8), they are thinking about their own nation. Twenty centuries later these two errors are still seen in the church.

The Great Commission. We have said that the Great Commission (1:8) gives something of an outline and summary of Acts. This is an indication how important this commission is. Acts 10:42 contains another form of this commission. "He commanded us to preach to the people and to testify that he is the one whom God appointed as judge of the living and the dead." Each of the four Gospels has a different form of the Great Commission (Matt. 28:18–20; Mark 16:15; Luke 24:46–49; John 20:21), and each one presents unique facets of the commission. We do not know when Acts 10:42 was uttered, but all the others were uttered between the resurrection and the ascension. We must, then, conclude that this commission was uppermost in Christ's thinking during the days before his ascension.

---

26. Clements, *The Church That Turned the World*, 16.

This realization clearly implies that "his last command" should be "our first concern." As the pioneer missionary to Muslims in India and Persia, Henry Martyn (1781–1812), said, "The Spirit of Christ is the spirit of missions, and the nearer we get to him, the more intensely missionary we must become."

The concept of witness. None of us can be witnesses in the same sense as the apostles were, for we have not seen the risen Lord as they did. Yet even their preparation to be witnesses would not be complete until they received the Holy Spirit (1:8). On our part, when we believe their witness regarding what they had seen and heard and entrust ourselves to Christ based on that belief, we too can experience the risen Lord through the indwelling Holy Spirit. As the book of Acts unfolds, we see that not only the apostles but also the other Christians were active in witness (8:1, 4). In the same way we too must witness for him. Yet for our witness to be effective, it must be witness; that is, it must come out of a firsthand knowledge of the risen Christ. Like the apostles, we too must say, "We cannot help speaking about what we have seen and heard" (Acts 4:20).

The Holy Spirit and mission. This passage shows us how important the Holy Spirit is to our understanding of mission and how important mission is to our understanding of the Holy Spirit (vv. 2, 5, 8). The rest of the book of Acts expounds this theme. The Spirit is the one who regenerates and sanctifies us so that we experience the risen Christ to whom we witness (vv. 4–5; cf. John 3:5–8). He fills individuals with special anointings to face special challenges in witness (Acts 4:8, 31; 6:10; 7:55; 13:9). He gives boldness in witness (4:9–13, 31; 13:9–11) and encourages his people in a way that helps them to grow in numbers (9:31). Just as the Spirit enabled the first Christians to speak in other tongues (2:4), he is the one who gives the words to speak in witness, in keeping with the promise of Christ (Mark 13:11). He directs people to special witnessing situations (10:19) and forbids them to go to some places they want to go (16:6–7). He calls people to their special mission (13:2) and sends them on their way (13:4). Finally, he directs the church to important doctrines relating to the mission of the church (15:28).[27] The Christian mission and ministry, then, can only be done in the power of the Spirit.

Contemporary Significance

INTEGRATING THE OBJECTIVE **and the subjective.** How difficult we find integrating the subjective and the objective aspects of Christianity today. The early church, therefore, challenges us here.

---

27. See Roland Allen, *The Ministry of the Spirit: Selected Writings of Roland Allen,* ed. David M. Paton (Grand Rapids: Eerdmans, 1962), 3–12.

We have churches that are "strong on the Bible" but which show little vitality because they suffer from a dead orthodoxy. Segments of the evangelical movement were for many years weak on the experiential aspects of the faith, especially when it came to evangelism—until the charismatic movement burst into the scene.

This may well explain why, until recently, the gospel made such little inroads in Asia, despite years of missionary activity. Asia has a rich heritage of spirituality, and it found the rational and activist evangelical message unappealing and unfulfilling. Throughout the history of the church there were movements—like the charismatic, the Wesleyan holiness, and the Moravian movements—that brought back the subjective aspects of the basic Christian gospel. But often these churches lacked solid biblical teaching. I believe we are presently seeing, in far too many evangelical churches, a reaction to the dry orthodoxy of the earlier generations that is dangerously influenced by the postmodern mood of our day (see next section), which emphasizes the subjective at the expense of the objective.

Yet the history of the church is studded with beautiful examples of Christian leaders and movements that integrated the warm heart and the sound mind. From earlier centuries I think of the apostle Paul, Origen, John Chrysostom, St. Augustine, the Puritans, Blasé Pascal, John Wesley, Jonathan Edwards, and Charles Finney. In our century I can think of Dietrich Bonhoeffer, E. Stanley Jones, Martyn Lloyd-Jones, J. I. Packer, Jack Hayford, Henri Nouwen, and John Piper. It would be good for us to linger with these giants so that something of their ability to integrate the warm heart and the sound mind might rub off on us.

However, we find it difficult to linger with such people because the demands of our rushed and specialized age make this difficult. The integration we are talking about comes from grappling with many areas of life at the same time, and that is difficult in our specialized world. We prefer to have our specialist scholars and specialist spiritual writers. As long as we permit such fragmentation of truth, we are going to have an anemic church that does not know the depth of what it means to know God out of a foundation of objective reality and an experience of deep spirituality. From Acts 1, then, we can infer that the ideal Christian teaching is done by Spirit-empowered individuals whose teaching is grounded on the objective facts of the gospel and should result in evangelism.

Truth and the postmodern mood. Verses 2–3 show us what an important place truth has in Christianity. But each of the three statements there runs counter to the thinking of what may be called the postmodern mood of the day. The onset of the postmodern era has been placed by different scholars at dates ranging from the early 1970s to the early 1990s. Some of its characteristics will emerge in the discussion below.[28]

(1) We said that the "instructions through the Holy Spirit" given by Jesus (v. 2) were primarily about the Great Commission—to make disciples of all the nations, baptizing them and teaching them (Matt. 28:19–20). Christ promised that such a ministry would result in people leaving their other religions in order to follow him. But this command runs directly counter to religious pluralism, which is a key postmodern emphasis. According to pluralism, no ideology can claim to possess absolute truth; all the religions are more or less equals in the universe of faiths. Veith points out that while modernists argued in various ways that Christianity is not true, postmodernists do not argue this way. Their main objection is to the Christian claim to have the only ultimate truth.[29]

Postmodernists are eager to share their beliefs with others so that people can learn from them. But as they see it, no group should attempt to convert others to their side out of a belief that they possess absolute truth. Yet this is precisely what Christians aim to do. Therefore two questions have become important for contemporary Christians: "Why do we still hold to the uniqueness of the Christian gospel?"[30] and, "Why do we still proclaim Christ in this pluralistic age?"[31]

(2) Luke's next statement about the truth of the gospel (v. 3a) gives the heart of our answer to these two questions: We can be so bold as to proclaim this message as unique, just as Paul was bold when speaking to the pluralists in Athens, because the resurrection is the ultimate proof of its uniqueness (17:31). Belief in the resurrection, which is the cornerstone of the gospel, has been well attested: "After his suffering, he showed himself to these men and gave many convincing proofs that he was alive" (1:3a). But the postmodern mind revolts against the idea that religious reality can be founded on objective facts. Into this environment we must go with the message that Christianity is absolutely true and that this assurance comes from Jesus' resurrection,

---

28. For introductions to postmodernism from a Christian perspective, see Stanley J. Grenz, *A Primer on Postmodernism* (Grand Rapids: Eerdmans, 1996); J. Richard Middleton and Brian J. Walsh, *Truth Is Stranger Than It Used to Be* (Downer's Grove, Ill.: InterVarsity, 1995); Gene Edward Veith Jr., *Postmodern Times* (Wheaton: Crossway, 1994).

29. Veith, *Postmodern Times*, 19.

30. See Sir Norman Anderson, *Jesus Christ: The Witness of History* (Downers Grove, Ill.: InterVarsity, 1985); Stephen Neill, *The Supremacy of Jesus* (London: Hodder and Stoughton, 1984); A. Fernando, *Supremacy*.

31. See Lesslie Newbigin, *Truth to Tell* (Grand Rapids: Eerdmans, 1991), and Vinoth Ramachandra, *The Recovery of Mission* (Carlisle: Paternoster, 1996). For a comprehensive response to pluralism and its influence within and without the church, see D. A. Carson, *The Gagging of God: Christianity Confronts Pluralism* (Grand Rapids: Zondervan, 1996).

which attests all that he claimed for himself and his gospel. The resurrection, in turn, is attested by many infallible proofs.

The loss of trust in objective truth is one of the keys to understanding postmodernism. In the scientific realm, the idea of an ordered universe following the fixed laws of Newtonian physics with its absolutes of space and time has come under fire. Einstein's theory of relativity showed that what was earlier regarded as absolute (space and time) was sometimes relative to the observer's frame of reference. The theory caught on and triggered what came to be called a revolution in science. Einstein brought in a new absolute, the velocity of light. But many extended this idea of relativity to other spheres, such as to religion and morals—something that Einstein never intended. Relativity became relativism—there are no absolutes.

In other areas of science as well the idea of objective reality came under fire. In the Newtonian model the world was considered mathematically ordered, and mathematics, with its logical axioms, was considered an effective tool for gaining knowledge of the physical world. Euclidean geometry, which was considered an appropriate way to describe physical reality, was built on ten principles, such as the principle that the shortest distance between two points is a straight line. These principles have also been questioned since the eighteenth century, and people have realized that there may be a chasm between what is mathematically true and what is physically true. Perhaps the most radical challenge has come from Quantum physics, which seems to violate the basic canons of logic or common sense.[32] The result of all this is the devaluing of the importance of objective truth.

Philosophically there has also been a shift in focus. The Enlightenment, the mother of the modern era, focused on rationalism, championing cause and effect. But postmodernism is a child of existentialism, which focuses attention not on objective facts "out there" but the contents of our own minds, the ideas we have "in here." Thus, truth is considered subjective, arising from you—the subject—rather than from something or someone outside you. In this environment personal truth is important: You have your truth coming from your particular experience, and I have mine. No one can claim to have truths that are absolute and should be universally applied.

The devaluing of the rational shows in the means used today to persuade people. My study of postmodernism was sparked off when I realized that it was influencing what people are watching on TV in Sri Lanka (mostly Western programs). As a youth worker and father of two teenage children, I felt

---

32. For a helpful analysis of these changes in science, see Nancy R. Pearcey and Charles B. Thaxton, *The Soul of Science* (Wheaton: Crossway, 1994). I am indebted to this book for much of what I have written on science.

I needed to look into this more closely. I was amazed to find out how many advertisements sought to persuade the viewers not by rational arguments about the value of the product but by emotional impressions that made people feel good about the product.

The postmodern existentialist mood has significantly influenced today's church.[33] I would go so far as to say that, in many segments of evangelicalism, experience is replacing the Bible as the supreme source of authority. If we examine books and teaching on practical topics, we often find that statistics, research, and testimonies of what people have experienced are given as authoritative guidelines. In much of Christian management teaching, the authorities are the management gurus. The Bible is used only as a quote book or a book out of which illustrations are found, only to buttress truths that have been found elsewhere. It should be the reverse: We should get our truths from the Bible and go to the world in order to find ways to illustrate those truths. David Wells says of those who theorize about Christian behavior primarily within North American evangelicalism: "While they tip their hats in the direction of the Bible, [they] quickly look the other way when they get down to the serious business of devising technique for the Church's life. In a historic sense, theology is thus disappearing."[34]

Many evangelical preachers, writers, and worship leaders today often prefer to focus almost entirely on the more soothing subjective and experiential aspects of the Christian religion. The devotional time of many evangelicals is confined to receiving some inspiring thoughts from a devotional book. Once again, the primary source of feeding is not the Bible but the inspiring story: "It feels good, so it must be from God."

Unfortunately, much of evangelical preaching today caters to this feel-good mentality. The time devoted to preaching is getting less and less as elements like testimonies get more prominence. Entertainment has replaced passion for the truth as a major means of attracting people to the gospel. But a problem develops when we get used to associating feeling good with divine activity: We begin to think that something wrong is God's will simply because it makes us feel good. Tragic statistics emerging from the West indicate, in terms of sexual morality, little difference between the behavior of Christians and of non-Christians; sad to say, in other words, the Bible is no longer the primary factor in determining Christian behavior.[35]

---

33. See Charles Colson with Ellen Santilli Vaughan, *The Body: Being Light in Darkness* (Dallas: Word, 1992).

34. David F. Wells, *No Place for Truth: Or Whatever Happened to Evangelical Theology* (Grand Rapids: Eerdmans, 1993), 109.

35. See Veith, *Postmodern Times*, 16–18.

All the above are evidences that the evangelical movement has been markedly influenced by the postmodern emphases on feelings and on the subjective at the expense of absolute, objective truth. Such emphases may well lead to evangelicals opening the door to pluralism. When the experience grows stale or when "the dark night of the soul" comes (as it surely will), there is no solid ground to keep on affirming the uniqueness and absoluteness of Christianity. The experiences and testimonies we have relied on will not be sufficient to see us through these dark times. I fear that many within the evangelical movement, by their neglect of the truths of Christianity, have already slipped unawares to what may be called a proto-pluralist position. The challenge for us today is to find the means of proclaiming the objective truths of Christianity in ways that are relevant and attractive to postmodern society. What gives us hope is the knowledge that this postmodern quest for an authentic subjective experience can be only ultimately satisfied by God through Christ.

(3) The third aspect of the truth of the gospel presented in Acts 1 is the teaching "about the kingdom of God," which includes the importance of submitting to the rule of the transcendent God. This is the last thing that postmodern people want to do. Rather than looking for a God out there, they are discovering the god within them. New Age analyst Theodore Roszak says that our goal is "to awaken the god who sleeps at the root of the human being."[36] This is one reason why the New Age movement has grown so rapidly in this era. There we have enough of the divine to satisfy the incurable religiosity of the human being (this is something that secular humanism of the modern era could not do). But the divine here is not a transcendent, supreme God, for such a god would be an affront to the quest for self-actualization that many are involved in. What we have instead is a pantheistic approach to reality, where everything, including ourselves, is part of the divine. Swami Mukthananda, who had a great influence on Werner Erhard (founder of EST and FORUM), captures this mood well: "Kneel to your own self. Honor and worship your own being. God dwells within you as you."[37] In other words, the message of the kingdom, of the rule of a supreme God, offends those influenced by New Age pantheism.

In summary, the gospel clashes with the pluralism, the subjectivism, and the pantheism of our day. Finding relevant and effective ways of presenting the gospel of Jesus Christ is a great challenge, to which we must devote our-

---

36. Theodore Roszak, *Unfinished Animal* (New York: Harper and Row, 1977), 225, quoted in Douglas R. Groothuis, *Unmasking the New Age* (Downer's Grove, Ill.: InterVarsity, 1986), 21.

37. Quoted in ibid.

selves with much vigor and commitment.[38] On the one hand, we have an evangelistic responsibility to adapt our methods so that the unchanging gospel is communicated in a way that will make our people want to listen to it.[39] On the other hand, we have the pastoral responsibility of helping develop Christians who know how to study and apply the Scriptures to their daily lives—that is, people who practice their belief in the supreme authority of Scripture in a postmodern world.

Bible teaching in preparation for revival. In a study of Josiah's revival, Lewis Drummond writes, "A spiritual awakening always soars on the wings of the Word. No matter how long people neglect the truth of God, one day it will surface and accomplish its wonder work."[40] This should be an encouragement to ministers of the Word who yearn for revival. They toil in what seems like barren ground, see little visible fruit, and may be greatly tempted to shift the emphasis of their ministries from uncompromisingly proclaiming the Word of God to entertaining Christians with "feel-good" preaching.

Let us remember that Jesus also had the crowds leave him because of what he taught after his initial success. "This is a hard teaching," they said. "Who can accept it?" (John 6:60). But he persevered with the few who remained. Acts 1 shows that even with the disciples, after more than three years of concentrated teaching, they had not really understood one of the central aspects of Jesus' teaching—the kingdom of God. But what he had taught them finally blossomed in their lives. With the empowering of the Spirit they went out, proclaimed the good news, and sparked off the most powerful revolution the world has ever seen. The words of Paul, given in a different context, apply to the ministry of teaching too: "Let us not become weary in doing good, for at the proper time we will reap a harvest if we do not give up" (Gal. 6:9).

Unbalanced emphases. Each of the emphases within the church regarding the Holy Spirit can lead to unbalanced Christianity. The danger with the conversion-initiation interpretation is that it can take away a yearning for God's fullness and create a class of half-baked Christians who are not experiencing everything that God wishes them to enjoy.

On the other hand, those who emphasize the idea that the baptism with the Spirit empowers one for mission can neglect the vitally important aspect of living holy lives and having the fruit of the Spirit. This is happening so often now

---

38. See Lesslie Newbigin, *The Gospel in a Pluralistic Society* (Grand Rapids: Eerdmans, 1989); Timothy R. Phillips and Dennis L. Okholm, editors, *Christian Apologetics in the Postmodern World* (Downer's Grove, Ill.: InterVarsity, 1995).

39. See Leighton Ford, *The Power of Story* (Colorado Springs: NavPress, 1994), and Charles Stromer, *The Gospel and the New Spirituality* (Nashville: Thomas Nelson, 1996).

40. Lewis Drummond, *Eight Keys to Biblical Revival* (Minneapolis: Bethany House, 1994), 35.

that it should be a major concern that the charismatic movement must address. This is corrected by the Wesleyan emphasis on entire sanctification, on the fullness of the Spirit empowering us to live holy lives (1 Thess. 5:19–24).

The Wesleyan emphasis, however, can give rise to an unhealthy perfectionism, with unbiblical measures brought in to evaluate whether one is entirely sanctified or not. This I also see as a danger of those meetings where people tarry for the Holy Spirit. It is mandatory that we tarry until we know that we have all of God. But we should not identify with this fullness anything not given in the Bible as an essential accompaniment of the fullness. On our part, the question we should always be asking is: "Do I have all that the Scriptures say I should have?"

The priority of the Spirit for Christian ministry. The relationship between the Holy Spirit and mission was a factor that was neglected in the history of the church, as the South African missiologist David J. Bosch points out:

> By the second century A.D. the emphasis had shifted almost exclusively to the Spirit as the agent of sanctification or as the guarantor of apostolicity. The Protestant Reformation of the sixteenth century tended to put the major emphasis on the work of the Spirit as bearing witness to and interpreting the Word of God. . . . Only in the twentieth century has there been a gradual rediscovery of the intrinsic missionary character of the Holy Spirit. This came about, *inter alia*, because of a renewed study of the writings of Luke.[41]

One of the pioneers here was an English Anglican clergyman, Roland Allen (1868–1947), who, after short tenures as a missionary in China and priest in England, came to some radical convictions that he wrote in several books and articles published between 1912 and 1930. Of particular interest is his book, *Pentecost and the World: The Revelation of the Holy Spirit in the "Acts of the Apostles."*[42] He stood up for indigenous churches that did not have to depend on foreign missions but which should depend on the Holy Spirit. When these writings were first published, his "ideas about 'handing over' responsibility to new Christians and trusting the Holy Spirit seemed not only radical but irresponsible."[43]

Allen knew that his ideas were far ahead of their time and even predicted to his son that his work would not be taken seriously until about 1960. This

---

41. David J. Bosch, *Transforming Mission: Paradigm Shifts in Theology of Mission* (Maryknoll, N.Y.: Orbis, 1991), 115.

42. Reprinted in Allen, *The Ministry of the Spirit*, 1–61.

43. Charles Henry Long and Anne Rowthorn, "Roland Allen, 1868–1947: 'Missionary Methods: St. Paul's or Ours?'" in Gerald T. Anderson et al., *Mission Legacies: Biographical Studies of Leaders of the Modern Missionary Movement* (Maryknoll, N.Y.: Orbis, 1994), 385.

prophecy was more than fulfilled, and today he is considered one of the most influential missiologists of the twentieth century. One of the earliest to pursue his emphasis on the link between the Holy Spirit and mission was an American Christian Reformed missionary to Nigeria, Harry Boer, whose influential book, *Pentecost and Mission*,[44] was published in 1961. Today, thankfully, there is much thinking and writing on this topic, but it is one that we can never take for granted.

Acts 1 implies that ministry should not be done without the minister's experiencing the Spirit. Often Christian workers with serious spiritual problems refuse advice to stop their work and spend some time alone with God, trying to get their spiritual life back together. Usually the reason given is that their work will crumble if they take such a break. But even more serious than that is to have people doing God's work in the flesh, for then the most noble work is being done in an ignoble way and God's name is being dishonored.

It is easy for us to get distracted and find security in other things that serve as substitutes to the power of the Spirit. Excellent programming using the best of modern technology, management techniques, and building facilities can produce impressive results. Someone once said that 95 percent of what happens in many evangelical churches could be done without the Holy Spirit. Many people will come to these churches attracted by the comprehensive program the church offers. People want a weekly religious dose, and, in our entertainment-oriented culture, a church that provides an entertaining program will attract people, just like a good concert or sporting event will attract people. But Christian ministry is ministry in the Spirit. Without the Spirit's power, our excellent programs are ultimately futile.

So whoever we are and whatever we do for God, our great desire should be to be filled with God's Spirit so that our work will spring from his resulting power. As Jacob did when he faced the challenge of meeting his brother Esau, we must cry out, "I will not let you go unless you bless me" (Gen. 32:26). This attitude is well expressed in a story that Dr. Martyn Lloyd-Jones told about an old Welsh preacher who was preaching at a convention in a small town. The people were already assembled, but the preacher had not come. So the leaders sent a maid back to the house to fetch him. She came back and reported that he was talking to somebody and she did not want to disturb him. They said, "That is strange because everybody is here. Go back and tell him that it is after time and he *must* come." She went again and returned with the same report: "He *is* talking to somebody." The leaders asked, "How do you know that?" She answered, "I heard him say to this other person who is with him, 'I will not go and preach to these people, if you will

---

44. Harry R. Boer, *Pentecost and Mission* (Grand Rapids: Eerdmans, 1961).

not come with me.'" The wise leaders replied, "Oh, it is all right. We had better wait."[45]

Eschatological inquisitiveness. How curious it is that despite all the warnings about the inappropriateness of date-setting regarding the end times, Christians continue to make specific predictions and authoritatively pronounce that some event in world history is a sign that the end is near or that the end will come in a certain number of days, months, or years. How can Christians continue to do this when church history testifies to many specific predictions that were not fulfilled, leaving sincere believers bewildered in their wake? And how can Christians be so gullible as to be taken in by yet another such prediction?

There are many reasons for this. (1) Many of those who make these predictions are godly people, so we do not easily dismiss what they say. Some claim to have a gift of prophecy, which makes rejecting what they say appear like rejecting God's special message. Yet Paul says that even if he himself or an angel preaches something different from the original revelation of the message that the Galatians received, the new message is to be rejected (Gal. 1:8). Our final authority is the Word of God. While what a godly person or someone with the gift of prophecy says should be regarded with utmost seriousness, if it contradicts Scripture, it must be rejected.

(2) The Bible predicts that certain things will happen in the end times, and we are seeing many of these things happening today. This heightens our sense of excitement over the possibility that we are living in the end times. The appearance of signs that seem to be definite fulfillments of such prophecies suggest that it can happen any day. The biblical attitude under such circumstances is for us to be ready and to be active in the work of the kingdom. This surely is the teaching of Christ in his eschatological discourses (e.g., Matt. 24–25). Matthew 24:44–46 summarizes this attitude well:

> So you also must be ready, because the Son of Man will come at an hour when you do not expect him.
>
> Who then is the faithful and wise servant, whom the master has put in charge of the servants in his household to give them their food at the proper time? It will be good for that servant whose master finds him doing so when he returns.

Acts 1 also shows us that while eschatological inquisitiveness is not acceptable, eschatological expectation is—note that the angels say that Christ will come back in the same way as he went into heaven (1:11). This attitude to end-time events is well expressed in the answer John Wesley gave when

---

45. D. Martyn Lloyd-Jones, *Authority* (London: Inter-Varsity Fellowship, 1958), 88.

asked what he would do if he knew this day was his last: "I would spend it just as I intend to spend it now." He then read off his schedule for the day. We should always be ready for his coming, but we should never fall into the trap of date-setting.

Jesus' answer to the disciples (1:8) suggests that our primary work should be evangelism. That is what prepares the world for the coming of Christ. Jesus himself said, "This gospel of the kingdom will be preached in the whole world as a testimony to all nations, and then the end will come" (Matt. 24:14). The great New Testament theologian George Ladd calls this "perhaps the most important single verse in the Word of God for God's people today"; it "is the clearest statement in God's Word about the time of our Lord's coming."[46] In actuality, the signs and the teaching of the end time can be an effective tool in evangelism. There is a natural curiosity about what will happen in the future, which interests people in what the Bible has to say. But let us never fall into the trap of going beyond what the Bible allows us to teach.

Parochialism. The second implied rebuke in Jesus' answer to the disciples' question about restoring the kingdom to Israel is about their parochialism. His reply is in terms of "the ends of the earth." According to the New Testament, there is no room in the Christian life for parochialism, racism, and prejudice. We will look at the issues of prejudice when we discuss Peter's visit to the home of Cornelius (Acts 10). What we see in Acts 1 is a parochialism of such heightened interest in one's own affairs that there was relatively no interest in the affairs of others. Jesus' answer was to develop a mission orientation—a reminder to us that our responsibility does not stop until the gospel has reached "to the ends of the earth."

At various times in its history, the church has lost its vision for the world. But God always called key servants and opened their minds to understand the Scriptures and what they have to say about the church's mission to the world (Luke 24:45–48). When the Protestant movement was missing this emphasis, for example, God sent people like the Moravians and John Wesley (1703–1791)—who said, "The world is my parish"—to bring it back.

It is not always educated scholars like Wesley whom God uses to revive missionary interest in the church. He sometimes uses "provincials," like the apostles. As a young man William Carey (1761–1834) tried to make the Baptists aware of this vision. He told a minister's meeting to consider "whether the command given to the apostles to teach all nations [Matt. 28:19–20] was not obligatory on all succeeding ministers to the end of the world, seeing that the accompanying promise was of equal extent." They rejected what he said, but

---

46. George Eldon Ladd, *The Gospel of the Kingdom* (Grand Rapids: Eerdmans, 1959), 123–24.

he persisted. He wrote a tract entitled, *An Inquiry into the Obligation of Christians to Use Means for the Conversion of the Heathen*. He himself responded to the call, and the Baptist Missionary Society was born.[47] This type of story has been repeated countless times in the history of the church, including the ministry I have worked with these past twenty-one years, Youth for Christ/Sri Lanka.

The continuing need for revival of missionary interest arises because of our natural tendency to parochialism. The challenges at home can appear to be so great that we can lose sight of our responsibility to the world. The missionary vision is usually inconvenient, for it places on us many demands to which we must respond—and that not for our benefit but for others. We may have to make structural changes we are uncomfortable with. But under Spirit-empowered, visionary leadership, we can keep this vision of missions burning. William Booth was too old and sick to attend one of the important anniversaries of the Salvation Army. So he sent a telegram, which was not to be opened until the anniversary meeting. It contained only one word: "Others." William Temple is credited with the statement: "The Christian church is the one organization in the world that exists purely for the benefit of non-members." Mission!

Great Commission Christians. Like a good motivator, Jesus constantly kept before his disciples a vision of the work they had been entrusted with. This is a good model for all leaders. Often people in the rank and file can get so engrossed in their particular work that they lose sight of the grand vision. Some may become so involved in maintenance or fighting fires that they lose sight of the vision. Consequently, demotivation and stagnation set in, which result in slow death. As someone has said, "The church that lives for itself will die by itself." Swiss theologian Emil Brunner once wrote, "A church exists by mission as fire exists by burning."

Leaders have the responsibility to place this grand vision before the people. Jesus is our model here. He talked of the significance of this mission (Matt. 24:14); he presented the need and the challenge to the people (9:36–38); he responded to objections to it (John 4:35–38); he gave himself as the model to follow (20:21); he showed them where it should be done (Matt. 28:19; Mark 16:15; Acts 1:8) and how it should be done (Matt. 10:5–42; 28:19–20; Luke 24:46–48; Acts 1:8). Note how there was creativity, variety, motivation, and instruction in the way he presented this commission. Following this example is one of the greatest responsibilities of a leader. I have felt that, next to the call to pray for and enable my colleagues, my next most important responsibility is to place before the movement I lead (Youth for Christ) the vision, in all its glory, of our particular call to go to unreached youth with the gospel of Christ.

---

47. Taken from Kellsye M. Finnie, *William Carey: By Trade a Cobbler* (Eastbourne: Kingsway, 1986), 28–36.

When we realize the important place that the Great Commission had in the early church, I think we can endorse the use of phrases like "Great Commission Christian" and "Great Commission Lifestyle." Some object to these phrases, thinking that they will detract people from other aspects of Christian mission, such as fulfilling the social mandate. This can happen and has, alas, happened with Christians who have overemphasized the Great Commission. But it *should not* happen. The social mandate is clear in the Bible, especially in the Old Testament.[48] We must never be afraid to be fully biblical. True, combining these two elements of mission is not easy, as we have found in our own ministry with the poor. But when was biblical ministry easy? Thank God that there is a noble history of evangelicals who put into practice this dual commitment to the social and evangelistic aspects of our mission.[49]

In view of the urgency of Jesus' commission, we should all seek to be Great Commission Christians[50] and endeavor to have all Christian organizations and churches to be Great Commission movements.[51] We should constantly live under the influence of our mission, so that we are willing to pay whatever price is required in order to reach the lost. Mission, of course, includes involvement across the street and around the globe. It is the responsibility of Christian leaders first to burn with passion themselves for mission and to pay the price of such commitment (see 1 Cor. 9); then, out of the credibility won from such passionate commitment, they must constantly keep the vision of mission before the people they lead.

Witnessing Christians. On the strictly personal level, a Great Commission Christian is first and foremost a witness. E. Stanley Jones (1884–1973), an

---

48. For an explanation of these matters see, John R. W. Stott, *Christian Mission in the Modern World* (Downer's Grove, Ill.: InterVarsity, 1975); Bruce J. Nicholls, ed., *In Word and Deed: Evangelism and Social Responsibility*, (Grand Rapids: Eerdmans, 1986); Lausanne Committee for World Evangelization and World Evangelical Fellowship, *Evangelism and Social Responsibility: An Evangelical Commitment* (Exeter: Paternoster, 1982).

49. See Donald Dayton, *Discovering an Evangelical Heritage* (New York: Harper and Row, 1976).

50. On this see Robert E. Coleman, *The Great Commission Lifestyle* (Grand Rapids: Revell, 1992).

51. Among the many available introductions to the Great Commission and its implications for the church are Paul Borthwick, *How to be a World Class Christian* (Wheaton: Victor, 1991); idem, *A Mind for Missions* (Colorado Springs: NavPress, 1987); Michael Griffiths, *Shaking the Sleeping Beauty* (Leicester: Inter-Varsity, 1980); Robertson McQuilkin, *The Great Omission* (Grand Rapids: Baker, 1984); John Piper, *Let the Nations Be Glad: The Supremacy of God in Missions* (Grand Rapids: Baker, 1993); John T. Seamands, *Harvest of Humanity* (Wheaton: Victor, 1988); Max Warren, *I Believe in the Great Commission* (London: Hodder and Stoughton, 1976). The U.S. Center for World Mission (Pasadena, Calif.) has produced a helpful mission education and involvement package, *Vision for the Nations*, which includes a "Participants Reader" and thirteen video lectures.

American missionary in India, had an effective evangelistic ministry with the intellectuals of India and through his writings became a mentor to many Christian ministers in Asia. In his youth he struggled with whether he was called to be a lawyer or a preacher. He finally decided that he would become a preacher and be "God's lawyer"—"to present his brief for him, to plead his case." Many relatives and friends came to hear the first sermon he preached in his home church. After six sentences he made a mistake, using a nonexistent word, "indifferentism." He saw that it brought a smile to a young lady in the audience—and his mind went blank! After a long silence, he managed to blurt out, "Well, friends, I'm sorry to tell you, but I've forgotten my sermon!"

He began to walk back to his seat in the first row in shame when he heard God telling him, "Haven't I done anything for you?" He replied, "Why, yes, of course you have." "Then couldn't you tell that?" came the question. "Perhaps I could," he said. So, instead of taking his seat, he turned around in front and said, "Friends, as you see, I can't preach, but you know my life before and after conversion; and while I can't preach, I do love the Lord, and I will witness for him the balance of my days." Jones says that he "said some more things like that to fill in the awful blank." After the service, a young man came up to him and said, "I want to find out what you have found."[52]

Jones did ultimately become God's lawyer. He immersed himself in the Scriptures and also in India's culture, and he effectively presented the claims of Christ to the intellectuals in that culture until he was almost ninety years old. But he always viewed preaching as witness: "As 'all great literature is autobiography,' so all real preaching is testimony."[53]

If something that the Bible testifies about is not true in our lives, we must stop all our activity and grapple with God until we know that it is true for us, just as the disciples waited in Jerusalem, devoting themselves to prayer (1:14). To believe in the Bible is to believe that what it says works, does in fact work. Jones tells the story of a young preacher who said, "I've been perjuring myself. I've been preaching things not operative within me. I'm through with this unreality. I'll give God till Sunday to do something for me. And if he doesn't do something for me before Sunday, someone else can preach. I won't." He took Saturday off as a day of retreat. God met him, and he went into the pulpit a new man. That Sunday the congregation got the shock of their lives—they had a new minister! The congregation found themselves seeking what their young minister had found.[54]

---

52. Related in E. Stanley Jones, *A Song of Ascents: A Spiritual Autobiography* (Nashville: Abingdon, 1968), 65–66.

53. Ibid., 66.

54. E. Stanley Jones, *The Word Became Flesh* (Nashville: Abingdon, 1963), 149.

Acts 1:9-26

❦

AFTER HE SAID this, he was taken up before their very eyes, and a cloud hid him from their sight. ¹⁰They were looking intently up into the sky as he was going, when suddenly two men dressed in white stood beside them. ¹¹"Men of Galilee," they said, "why do you stand here looking into the sky? This same Jesus, who has been taken from you into heaven, will come back in the same way you have seen him go into heaven."

¹²Then they returned to Jerusalem from the hill called the Mount of Olives, a Sabbath day's walk from the city. ¹³When they arrived, they went upstairs to the room where they were staying. Those present were Peter, John, James and Andrew; Philip and Thomas, Bartholomew and Matthew; James son of Alphaeus and Simon the Zealot, and Judas son of James. ¹⁴They all joined together constantly in prayer, along with the women and Mary the mother of Jesus, and with his brothers.

¹⁵In those days Peter stood up among the believers (a group numbering about a hundred and twenty) ¹⁶and said, "Brothers, the Scripture had to be fulfilled which the Holy Spirit spoke long ago through the mouth of David concerning Judas, who served as guide for those who arrested Jesus—¹⁷he was one of our number and shared in this ministry."

¹⁸(With the reward he got for his wickedness, Judas bought a field; there he fell headlong, his body burst open and all his intestines spilled out. ¹⁹Everyone in Jerusalem heard about this, so they called that field in their language Akeldama, that is, Field of Blood.)

²⁰"For," said Peter, "it is written in the book of Psalms,

"'May his place be deserted;
let there be no one to dwell in it,'

and,

"'May another take his place of leadership.'

²¹Therefore it is necessary to choose one of the men who have been with us the whole time the Lord Jesus went in and out among us, ²²beginning from John's baptism to the time when

Jesus was taken up from us. For one of these must become a witness with us of his resurrection."

²³So they proposed two men: Joseph called Barsabbas (also known as Justus) and Matthias. ²⁴Then they prayed, "Lord, you know everyone's heart. Show us which of these two you have chosen ²⁵to take over this apostolic ministry, which Judas left to go where he belongs." ²⁶Then they cast lots, and the lot fell to Matthias; so he was added to the eleven apostles.

THIS SECTION OF ACTS describes Jesus' ascension into heaven, the obedience of the disciples to his command that they wait in Jerusalem for the promised Holy Spirit, and one of the main activities that they performed during this waiting period, namely, to choose a successor to Judas Iscariot.

The Ascension (1:9–11)

JESUS' ASCENSION TAKES place after his giving the Great Commission for the last time (v. 9). In the early church the ascension was associated with Christ's exaltation to God's right hand (see Eph. 1:20–21; Phil. 2:9; Heb. 1:3; 2:9). The expression "he was taken up" carries this idea, for "the Jews thought of heaven as 'above' and earth as 'below.'"[1] The cloud also expresses this thought, "for in biblical language the cloud often served as a symbol of divine glory (cf., e.g., Ex. 16:10; Psa. 104:3)."[2] The words "before their very eyes" show that Luke wants us to know that "something objective took place."[3]

The upward gaze of the disciples is interrupted by the appearance of two men (v. 10), whose white clothes suggest that they are angels (see Matt. 28:2–3; John 20:12). There is a mild rebuke implied in their question about standing and "looking . . . into the sky" (v. 11a). It reminds us of the angelic rebuke that the women received as they were looking for the living among the dead (Luke 24:5). The disciples always seem to be one step behind the surprising moves of God!

The expression "men of Galilee," which in 2:7 is in essence a "disparaging label," may suggest a divine reminder "that the apostles were provincials who had a worldwide task ahead of them."[4] The angels specifically give

---

1. Williams, *Acts*, 24.
2. Ibid., 25.
3. Ibid.
4. Faw, *Acts*, 31.

Jesus' post-ascension abode as "heaven" (1:11b). The promise that he "will come back in the same [exalted] way" (v. 11c) would have helped make some sense out of Jesus' repeated statements to the disciples about his second coming. This prospect encourages Christians to "live self-controlled, upright and godly lives in this present age while we wait for the blessed hope—the glorious appearing of our great God and Savior Jesus Christ" (Titus 2:12–13).

Waiting Prayerfully (1:12–14)

THE APOSTLES' RETURN from the Mount of Olives to Jerusalem was a Sabbath day's walk (v. 12), which, according to the Mishnah,[5] was a little less than three-fourths of a mile. Since this happened forty days after Easter, it was a Thursday, not a Sabbath day. The disciples "went up to the upper room, where they were staying" (v. 13a, NASB). While the definite article suggests that this room was a well-known place, we cannot tell which room it was.[6] It must have been a good place for prayer as it was "above the tumult of the crowded streets and beyond the prying eyes of passersby."[7]

Luke's list of who had gathered in this upper room (v. 13b) includes the eleven apostles—the same list as given in Luke 6:14–16, but without Judas. The order, however, has been changed; this list begins with the three prominent apostles who alone appear later in Acts—Peter, John, and James. Women are also mentioned, in keeping with Luke's practice of giving a prominent place to women in his writings. Faithful women were with Jesus during his ministry to minister to his needs (Luke 8:2–3); they were also prominently featured on the days of his death (23:27–31, 49, 55–56) and resurrection (24:1–10). Thus, it is not surprising to find them here as well (Acts 1:14). "Given the culture's usual downplaying of women's public roles, the equal participation of women is noteworthy, especially their apparent mixing with the men."[8] The early disciples were carrying on what Christ demonstrated about breaking human barriers. They will soon realize more revolutionary implications of this truth (Acts 10; 15; Gal. 3:28).

Mary, Jesus' mother, is also mentioned here—her only appearance in Acts (v. 14). Luke had presented her as a model of trust and obedience in his Gospel (Luke 1:38). Now we see that she "not only gave birth to her Son;

---

5. A compilation of Jewish oral tradition of interpretations of the law, completed around A.D. 200.

6. Among the suggestions are: where the Last Supper was held (Luke 22:11–12), where Jesus met the disciples after the resurrection (John 20:19), where they were on the day of Pentecost (2:1), and where Mary the mother of Mark lived (cf. 12:12).

7. Longenecker, "Acts," 260.

8. Keener, *BBC*, 325.

she also assisted in the birth of the church."[9] The undue veneration of her by some should not hinder us from appreciating the important role she played in the history of salvation.

Various theories have been given to explain who the brothers of Jesus mentioned here (and elsewhere in the New Testament) are, especially by those who believe in the perpetual virginity of Mary. C. K. Barrett says, "The present verse contributes nothing to the arguments for or against any of these theories, though it is fair to add that the most natural meaning of *adelphos* [the word used here] is blood-brother, that foster-brother is not impossible, and that cousin is very improbable."[10] We know that Jesus appeared to James after his resurrection (1 Cor. 15:7). The unbelief of the brothers, which was still there as late as six months before this death (John 7:5), is now gone.

Luke-Acts abounds with references to prayer (mentioned thirty-one times in Acts and appears in twenty of its chapters).[11] Thus, it is not surprising to find that, as the followers of Jesus wait for the promised baptism of the Spirit, they "all joined together constantly in prayer" (v. 14). The word translated "together" (*homothymadon*) literally means "with one mind or passion" and is a favorite word of Luke.[12] Older translations translated it "with one mind," following its etymological meaning. There is some question as to whether this word takes its etymological sense here, and the newer translations render it as "together" (the meaning it generally takes in the Septuagint).[13] But the thought of unanimity in community life is a key theme in Acts, one that we will discuss in connection with other passages that unmistakably indicate this idea (4:32; 6:5; 15:25). The word translated "constantly" "is often connected with prayer (Acts 1:14; 2:42, 46; Rom. 12:12; Col. 4:2).... It means resolute, sometimes obstinate, persistence."[14] The idea of "prevailing prayer" comes from this word.

Choosing Judas's Successor (1:15–26)

TO FIND A replacement for Judas, Peter addresses a group of "believers [lit., brothers] . . . numbering about a hundred and twenty" (v. 15). "The term 'brothers,' used here for the first time in Acts, may have been the earliest

---

9. Kistemaker, *Acts*, 60.

10. Barrett, *Acts*, 90.

11. For the variety of occasions for, and of locations and times of, prayer in Acts, see Coleman, *Master Plan of Discipleship*, 107–9.

12. Ten of the eleven times it appears in the New Testament are in Acts.

13. See Barrett, *Acts*, 88–89.

14. Barrett, *Acts*, 88. Romans 12:12 is mistakenly recorded as Acts 12:12 in Barrett's book.

Christian designation for church members."[15] With his concern for accuracy in reporting, Luke likes to qualify his numerical data with a cautious "about," especially if a round number follows (2:41; 4:4; 10:3; 19:7). As this may not be the exact number present, the number one hundred and twenty is probably not significant, and Luke may simply be saying that the room was full. But the figure did have some significance for Jews, and this may be in Luke's mind here.[16] Whatever the case, it reminds us of how few disciples there were in those first days and of how much they were able to accomplish with the empowering of the Spirit.

Peter views Judas's act of betrayal as a fulfillment of Scripture (v. 16). That, however, does not take away from the pain of what happened, for, as Peter says, "he was one of our number and shared in this ministry" (v. 17). Peter's view of the divine authorship of the Old Testament Scriptures is evidenced in his words, "Brothers, the Scripture had to be fulfilled which the Holy Spirit spoke long ago through the mouth of David" (v. 16).

Luke's digression about how Judas died (vv. 18–19) uses the word "wickedness," which shows that, while the betrayal was predicted in Scripture, it was a serious act of treachery. This eliminates the views of those who try to "rehabilitate" Judas by showing that his motives for betraying Christ were honorable. Jesus said, "The Son of Man will go as it has been decreed, but woe to that man who betrays him" (Luke 22:22).

There are significant differences between Luke's account of Judas's death here and that of Matthew (Matt. 27:1–10). According to Craig Keener, "these similarities and differences can be explained on the basis of two authors reporting different details and ancient historians' freedom on such details."[17] Richard Longenecker has presented plausible explanations for these differences.[18]

Peter's predictions in verse 20 are from Psalm 69 and 109. The early Christians saw David, the righteous sufferer, and his enemies as types of Christ and his enemies (the antitypes).[19] Differences between David and Jesus and between David's enemies and Judas in these psalms can be explained by the fact that the antitype is always greater than the type.

The theme of God's sovereign will at work in the suffering and death of Christ is one that occurs several times in the apostles' preaching, espe-

---

15. Williams, *Acts*, 31.

16. "According to a Jewish tradition of uncertain date, 120 elders first passed on the law in the time of Ezra. Then again, the Dead Sea Scrolls required one priest for every ten men, so 120 may be the number of people a team of twelve leaders could best accommodate...." (Keener, *BBC*, 326).

17. Ibid.

18. Longenecker, "Acts," 263–64.

19. Derek Kidner, *Psalms 1–72*, TOTC (Downer's Grove, Ill.: InterVarsity, 1973), 245.

cially to Jews.[20] When the disciples faced the first outlawing of evangelism, they again reflected on the sovereignty of God as it was manifested in the most terrible event in history: the death of Christ (4:25–28). This perspective helps us believe that God will turn the evil done to us into good (cf. Gen. 50:20). It would have helped take away the bitterness that the disciples must have had over the betrayal of Jesus by one who had been so close to them.

Peter felt that it was "necessary" to find a replacement for Judas (v. 21). The same verb "it is necessary" (*dei*) is used here as in verse 16, which presented the necessity of Judas's betrayal (though in v. 16, the verb is in the imperfect tense, "it was necessary"). Thus, the early church followed Jesus' practice of having exactly twelve apostles. When the community that gave rise to the Dead Sea Scrolls "chose a group of leaders which included twelve special officials, it was meant to symbolize that this community was the true remnant of Israel, faithful to God even though the rest of the nation was apostate."[21] The same can be said here.

Note that the first period of the church's growth was in Israel and that in the Gospels the apostles had a special role in relation to Israel (Luke 9:1–6; 22:28–30). "The filling up of the number was probably meant to indicate that the task of witness to Jesus as the Messiah of the Jews was to be continued after the resurrection."[22] The qualifications required for the replacement had to do with the role of the apostles as witnesses (Acts 1:21–22). Later, Peter would say that those who saw the risen Lord were "witnesses whom God had already chosen" (10:41). Witnessing to the resurrection was a crucial, never to be repeated, role of a select group of men in the early Christian church.

The church cast lots since they felt a need for direct divine guidance on the final choice between the two equally qualified people. But the use of lots comes only after prayer for God's guidance. That prayer shows what we should be looking for most in a leader: "Lord, you know everyone's heart. Show us which of these two you have chosen" (v. 24). The believers had found two people with suitable external qualifications, but those would be useless if the person's heart was not right. Only God knows the hearts of people unerringly, so they ask his help. Like most of the other apostles, the new apostle Matthias does not appear again in Acts. Later tradition presents him as a missionary to the Ethiopians.

---

20. See Acts 2:23; 3:18; 8:32–35; 13:27, 29.
21. Keener, *BBC*, 325–26.
22. Marshall, *Acts*, 63.

Bridging Contexts

LIKE THE PREVIOUS PASSAGE, this one continues the preparation of the church for Pentecost and for launching out on its mission. Again we will see principles that help the church today in preparing for mission.

The importance of the ascension. Though Jesus' ascension (vv. 9–11) is not often mentioned today among Christians, "in the primitive preaching the resurrection and ascension of Jesus represent one continuous movement and together constitute his exaltation."[23] As this is of great importance to our evangelistic message, we will discuss it in our treatment of Peter's message at Pentecost (2:17–36).

Prayer and revival. Luke clearly wants to communicate the fact that a key way in which the disciples prepared for the coming of the Spirit was through prayer (vv. 13–14). The connection between these two factors is well established in the Bible, especially in the Lukan writings.[24] Arthur Matthews goes so far as to say that "the spiritual history of a mission or church is written in its prayer life."[25] This passage, therefore, has much to teach us about prayer.

The idea of "prevailing prayer" (cf. above) presents one key to powerful praying: praying without giving up until the answer comes. Jesus said that we "should always pray and not give up," and gave the parable of the persistent widow to illustrate that point (Luke 18:1–8). But why do we need to keep on praying? Is God so reluctant to answer our prayers that we have to keep on asking him? No, he is not reluctant to give, but often we may not be ready to receive his gift. Prayer makes us ready, for in communion with God our hearts are attuned to his will.

Furthermore, prayer is a way of engaging in spiritual warfare against Satan and his forces. Battle language is often used for prayer (cf. Rom. 15:13; Col. 4:12). Immediately after Paul's famous exposition on spiritual warfare in Ephesians, he says, "And pray in the Spirit on all occasions with all kinds of prayers and requests" (Eph. 6:18). F. F. Bruce observes that there is a strong connection between Ephesians 6:18 and the section on spiritual warfare that precedes it.[26] In other words, prayer is a form of spiritual warfare. Note too that God has chosen to send most of his blessings to earth through human

---

23. Bruce, *Acts: Greek Text*, 103.

24. Luke 3:21–22; 11:13; Acts 4:31; 8:15. For discussions on prayer in Luke-Acts, see M. M. B. Turner, "Prayer in the Gospels and Acts," *Teach Us To Pray*, ed. D. A. Carson (Grand Rapids: Baker, 1990), 59–75; P. T. O'Brien, "Prayer in Luke-Acts: A Study in the Theology of Luke," *TynBul* 24 (1973): 113–16.

25. R. Arthur Matthews, *Born for Battle* (Waynesboro, Ga.: STL Books, 1978), 72.

26. F. F. Bruce, *The Epistles to Colossians, to Philemon, and to the Ephesians*, NICNT (Grand Rapids: Eerdmans, 1984), 411.

instruments, and praying is one of those instruments he uses. Finally, God in his sovereign wisdom has chosen the best time for sending an answer to prayer; until then, we "should always pray and not give up."

If "together" in verse 14 does mean unanimous, then this accords with a principle that Jesus presented: "If two of you on earth agree about anything you ask for, it will be done for you by my Father in heaven" (Matt. 18:19). Regardless of the meaning of this word, we know that the prayer talked about here is group prayer, in which "all joined together constantly" (Acts 1:14). Often great prayer movements start with one or more individuals with a burden to pray, who share this burden with others, and then keep on praying with them until the blessing comes.[27]

The pain of defection. The pain of defection by people who have been close to us (vv. 15–20) is something we often face in ministry. Paul expressed this pain when he said, "Demas, because he loved this world, has deserted me and has gone to Thessalonica" (2 Tim. 4:10). Such pain can leave us embittered and hinder our spiritual freedom and fruitfulness in ministry. Peter's discussion of Judas's action does not overlook the seriousness of his act of betrayal, but it does see it from the perspective of God's sovereignty, for he saw it predicted in Scripture (Acts 1:16–20). This approach to personal hurt from colleagues has much to say to us today.

Choosing leaders and making decisions in the church. We noted above that it was significant for the early church's ministering among the Jews to have exactly twelve apostles (vv. 21–22). But as the narrative of Acts proceeds, especially as it enters the phase of Gentile evangelism, the apostles receive less prominence. Only Peter, James, and John have individual roles in Acts, and none of these apostles is mentioned after chapter 15, by which time a non-apostle, James the brother of Jesus, had become leader of the church in Jerusalem. Thus, the number twelve is not intended to be a precedent to follow in church organization. This points us to the transitory nature of some of the events recorded in Acts. There is, however, "no exegetical support in any New Testament text"[28] for the idea that the choice of Matthias to replace Judas was a mistake, and that "Paul ... was God's man for the filling of the gap."[29] Matthias's not being mentioned again in Acts is shared with eight other apostles!

We also cannot say that the use of lots by these disciples was wrong. If it was a blind use of lots, then it would certainly have been wrong. But these believers had been careful to use all other available means of choosing the

---

27. For more on community prayer in Acts see below and the discussions on 4:23–41; 12:1–19; 13:1–4.

28. William W. Klein, Craig L. Blomberg, and Robert L. Hubbard, *Introduction to Biblical Interpretation* (Dallas: Word, 1993), 348.

29. Campbell Morgan, *Acts*, 21.

leaders, such as prayer and the requirements of adequate experience of and a relationship with Christ. Lots were used only after they had two candidates for one position who seemed to have the same qualifications. Lots were used in decision making in a variety of circumstances in the Old Testament.[30] Proverbs 16:33 observes about this process: "The lot is cast into the lap, but its every decision is from the Lord." "According to the biblical usage, lots seem to have been used only when the decision was important and where wisdom or biblical injunctions did not give sufficient guidance. One of the advantages of the casting of lots was the impartiality of the choice."[31]

It is probable that the disappearance of the practice of casting of lots in Scripture is related to the coming of the Holy Spirit, who is now the great Guide of the believers (Rom. 8:14; Gal. 5:18). The fact that it is mentioned just before the record of Pentecost may suggest that Luke wants to highlight the truth that this is a symbol of the end—the signing off, as it were—of the old era.

Acts does not give us a fixed method of community decision making. But there are common features here and in other decision-making episodes that can be helpful to us.[32] (1) Throughout the decision-making process was theological reflection, which most often involved the use of Scripture. This same feature is present in the other key community decisions (4:23–31; 6:1–6; 10:1–11:18; 14:26–15:35).

(2) The language used here suggests that the two names were proposed by the whole community. Thus, the community had a part in arriving at the decision, but so did Peter as leader. This interplay between congregational participation and direction by a leader appears in other important decisions taken by the church in Acts (6:1–6; 10:1–11:18; 14:26–15:35).

(3) Peter's role in directing the church through theological reflection accords with the biblical understanding of leadership. As God is the real leader of the church, the human leader's task is to direct people to God's will, which is most clearly recorded in the Scriptures. In other words, the leader's primary task is to direct people to God's Word. Note that in the list of qualifications for elders in 1 Timothy 3, the only ministry-related qualification cited is that an elder should be "able to teach" (1 Tim. 3:2; the rest of the qualifications relate to character, reputation, and family life). In our study of 6:1–6 we will note how a leader performs this "ministry of the Word."[33]

---

30. Lev. 16:8–10; Num. 26:55–56; Josh. 14:2; Judg. 1:3; 20:9; 1 Chron. 24:5–19; Neh. 11:1; Prov. 18:18.

31. "Casting of Lots," *BEB*, 1356. The only other time it appears in the New Testament is the soldiers' casting lots for Jesus' garments (Matt. 27:35).

32. See Luke T. Johnson, *Decision Making in the Church: A Biblical Model* (Philadelphia: Fortress, 1983).

33. For an exposition of this understanding of leadership, see my *Leadership Lifestyle: A Study of 1 Timothy* (Wheaton: Tyndale, 1985).

---

(4) The choosing of Matthias also shows us that prayer should play a critical part in our strategy of appointing leaders. Note how Jesus spent the night in prayer before choosing his twelve apostles (Luke 6:12–13). In Luke-Acts, as Robert Stein points out, "prayer preceded every major decision or crisis in the life of Jesus and the early church."[34] Prayer is important before making any decision because it gets us in tune with God, so that we are receptive to his voice. In Antioch, for example, it was as the church was praying (and fasting) that the Holy Spirit spoke to them about separating Saul and Barnabas to the task of missions (13:2).

Here in 1:24 is a clear petition for guidance ("Show us . . ."). Prayer had an equally important part in the process of selecting and appointing elders in the first churches that Paul and Barnabas founded (Acts 14:23). From Jesus' instructions to "ask the Lord of the harvest, therefore, to send out workers into his harvest field" (Matt. 9:38), we can conclude that prayer has an important role to play in the recruitment of mission workers.

(5) As already noted, the prayer in verse 24 implies that the disciples needed to have confirmed for them the inner nature of the person's heart, which only God's knows. Christian ministry is essentially spiritual in nature, and external qualifications are useless if a person's heart is not right with God.

PRAYER AND REVIVAL. Just as Pentecost came after constant prayer by the disciples, the history of the church demonstrates that revival also comes only after persistent prayer. Revival is something that God sends sovereignly, and therefore we cannot predict when it will come. But, as revival historian J. Edwin Orr observes, "no great spiritual awakening has begun anywhere in the world apart from united prayer—Christians persistently praying for revival."[35] I have heard a statement, attributed to Matthew Henry, that when God wants to do something special in the world, he first gets his people to start praying.

In the 1850s, for example, the United States was in a weak spiritual state, as people were preoccupied with concern for material things. In 1857 a quiet forty-six-year-old businessman, Jeremiah Lanphier, felt led to start a noontime weekly prayer meeting in New York City, in which business people could meet for prayer. Anyone could attend, for a few minutes or for the entire hour. On the first day Lanphier prayed alone for half an hour. But by

34. Robert H. Stein, *Luke*, NAC (Nashville: Broadman, 1992), 192. See also ibid., 51–52.

35. Quoted in Wesley L. Duewel, *Mighty Prevailing Prayer* (Grand Rapids: Zondervan, 1990), 135.

the end of the hour six men from at least four denominational backgrounds had joined him. Twenty came the next week and forty the week after. Soon they decided to meet daily, and the group swelled to over one hundred. Pastors who came started morning prayer meetings in their own churches. Soon similar meetings were being held all over America. Within six months there were more than ten thousand meeting daily in New York City alone. This was the start of what is now termed "The Great Awakening" in North America. It is estimated that in a two-year period (1857–1859), two million people were led to Christ (out of a population of thirty million).[36]

The prayer that took place in Jerusalem was persistent or prevailing prayer. This can happen today as well. The Lord sometimes gives a burden to someone, which he or she shares with others. They pray about this over an extended period of time, and with time they find that the Lord has wonderfully answered their prayers. It is a simple principle, but one that we must be regularly reminded of, given our natural tendency to drift toward prayerlessness.

In 1949, in the village of Barvas in the Hebrides Islands (off Scotland), the parish minister along with his church leaders began to pray for revival. In the same village two sisters in their eighties, whose poor health did not allow them to attend worship, prayed in their cottage for revival in Barvas. God gave them a promise: "I will pour water on the thirsty land, and streams on the dry ground" (Isa. 44:3). On the other side of Barvas, knowing nothing about the others, seven young men met three nights a week in a barn to pray for revival. They committed themselves to prayer in keeping with Isaiah 62:6–7:

> I have posted watchmen on your walls, O Jerusalem;
> > they will never be silent day or night.
> You who call on the LORD,
> > give yourselves no rest,
> and give him no rest till he establishes Jerusalem
> > and makes her the praise of the earth.

The result of all this prayer was wave upon wave of revival over the entire island, through which thousands were converted and/or filled with the Spirit.[37] Note how specific portions of Scripture spurred these people to persevere in prayer, just like Christ's promise to his disciples of baptism with the Spirit. The Scripture causes us to look beyond our present experience and to yearn for the fullness God wants us to experience. This, in turn, stimulates prevailing prayer.

---

36. Taken from Wesley L. Duewel, *Revival Fire* (Grand Rapids: Zondervan, 1995), 128–31.
37. For the full story, see ibid., 306–18.

Often an individual has a burden that may not be shared by others but which triggers individual prevailing prayer. In November 1844 George Mueller began to pray for the conversion of five individuals. He says, "I prayed every day without one single intermission, whether sick or in health, on the land or on the sea, and whatever the pressure of my engagements might be." After eighteen months of such praying, the first of the five was converted. Five years later the second came, and the third after another six years. In his sermon Mueller said that he had been praying for thirty-six years for the other two, but they still remained unconverted. His biographer says that one of those two "became a Christian before Mueller's death and the other a few years later."[38]

Often, as in the case of an adult but rebellious child or an unconverted spouse, we can do little directly to change the person. Advice and rebuke may only worsen the situation. But we can persevere in prayer for them. History is replete with examples of answers to such prayers.[39]

Healing the hurts inflicted by colleagues. The pain that comes from hurt caused by colleagues who leave a group can be deep in the life of a Christian. The fellowship in Christ that we have with other believers is one of the greatest blessings of being a Christian. But this means that we expect more from our brothers and sisters in Christ than from others. As a result, the pain of disappointment is also greater in our relationships with Christians. I have encountered so many people who are bitter about being betrayed by other Christians that it appears to me as if we are having an epidemic of such bitterness today.

This bitterness can greatly hinder one's own spiritual life. It will battle with the love of God poured into our hearts by the Holy Spirit (Rom. 5:5)—a battle that can be draining and lead to our being spiritually exhausted and losing the glow of the Spirit. Our lives and ministries suffer as a result. The pain of betrayal can also lead us to become hesitant to trust others enough to enter into relationships of spiritual accountability with them. We settle for superficial relationships, and, if this is in a working environment, we allow the job description to rule the relationship, so that we share only what is necessary to do the job properly. Such living is unscriptural.

The description of Judas's defection in Acts 1 should teach us something about how to handle the pain of defection. The community that these first believers helped forge was not afraid of deep spiritual accountability, for they "were one in heart and mind" (4:32). In other words, they seemed to have

---

38. Roger Steer, *George Mueller: Delighted in God* (Wheaton: Harold Shaw, 1975), 267.

39. See Ruth Bell Graham, *Prodigals and Those Who Love Them* (Colorado Springs: Focus on the Family, 1991).

overcome the blow of disappointment and developed principles of account-ability. Paul too was deeply hurt by defection, apostasy, and unfaithfulness, but he kept opening his life to others and making himself vulnerable to more hurt. He felt hurt right up to the end of his ministry (2 Tim. 4), but he also helped develop many church leaders and left a huge legacy of fruitfulness when he died. Thus, learning how to overcome the hurt of betrayal is an important discipline to cultivate in the Christian life.

I can see two words of encouragement in this passage for Christians wounded by their fellow Christians. (1) Even Jesus' own disciples experi-enced the pain that we are experiencing. The language used here for Judas's defection is restrained, but it does not hide the tragedy and the pain. In this case there must have been great humiliation, for verse 19 says, "Everyone in Jerusalem heard about this." It would be a scar on Jesus' reputation. David Gooding presents what may have been heard in Jerusalem like this:

> You say Jesus is the Son of God, Israel's Messiah, Savior and Restorer, come to right our wrongs and to expose the priests' corrupt abuse of their sacred office for money? How then did he not know any better than to choose a man like Judas to be one of his chief companions, rep-resentatives and executives—and, if you please, treasurer of his group?[40]

Sometimes our biggest anger about betrayal by friends has to do with the humiliation it causes us.

All this should give us hope. Several years ago I suffered deep shock and pain when I found out that one of our workers had lied to us and been dis-honest with money. Around this time I read John 12:6 about Judas: "He was a thief; as keeper of the money bag, he used to help himself to what was put into it." This ministered to me in a most unusual way. When I realized that even the greatest leader, Jesus, faced the same problem, I was comforted—and comfort is one of the greatest antidotes to bitterness.

(2) Peter viewed this episode as being part of God's plan. Verse 16 literally reads, "Brothers, it was necessary for the Scripture .... [concerning Judas] to be fulfilled." God was sovereign in what happened. Not only had he permit-ted it, he had also anticipated it and intended to use it for some good purpose. Romans 8:28 is indeed true: "In all things God works for the good of those who love him, who have been called according to his purpose." If betrayal is going to be turned into something good in our lives, then bitterness is unnecessary. We will indeed have sorrow and pain over a brother or sister who has moved away from us and (from our perspective) done something wrong. But, because

---

40. Gooding, *True to the Faith*, 44.

that wrong action was accommodated in God's ultimate plan for our lives and will be converted into an instrument of blessing, we have no reason to be angry. We have strength to forgive this person and look forward to life with hope and joy. The sorrow and the pain may remain, but the bitterness is gone.

Of course, these are not ideas many people like to entertain. We would rather nurse our wounds and grudges. That gives us an excuse for our anger, even though theologically the anger is unwarranted. Besides, deep down we have a desire to show this person how much he or she has hurt us. That is our "Christian" way of getting justice for what has happened to us. In other words, many choose to ignore the truth of God's sovereignty and remain in the gloomy world of bitterness. The message to us is: Let the experience of pain that Christ had comfort us, and let the knowledge of God's sovereignty enable us to look at the pain with gratitude and hope.

Choosing leaders and making decisions today. Each of the five points about decision-making given in the "Bridging Contexts" section is significant for us. They should remain high on our agenda during times of selecting leaders and making decisions, though they are easy to forget. Recently I met the national head of one of our larger denominations shortly after he returned from an important committee meeting of a powerful world Christian body. He told me how surprised he was to find that at the meeting there seemed to be no spiritual dimension in the decision making. It had become so politicized that politics rather than a yearning to know God's will ruled their deliberations. Such a state does not develop suddenly. It happens gradually, as little by little spiritual principles are overlooked or rejected—sometimes through sheer neglect and sometimes in the interest of expediency.

Two of the five principles in the selection of leaders listed above merit special mention. (1) The first is the place of prayer in choosing leaders. When the process of selecting leaders is saturated in prayer, the spirit of yearning to know God's will unconsciously influences the process, so that the chances of acting according to that will are much greater. Today, many churches and groups have fine-tuned their procedures for selecting leaders. They have a list of necessary qualifications; such a list is acceptable, as long as the qualifications are biblical.[41] Note that qualifications were listed for the appointment of Matthias too; this provides a process of eliminating unsuitable candidates. But often seeking God's guidance in prayer is a mere formality, not a vitally important aspect of the selection process. A random sampling

---

41. Sometimes, however, we bring extrabiblical, social qualifications, which may disqualify biblically qualified candidates for leadership. My fear is that often qualified and gifted Christians from among the poor are eliminated because they do not meet with some of these social requirements, such as educational requirements.

of churches and groups I am familiar with has revealed to me that this is far too often the case.

(2) There is a need to know, beyond the external qualifications, on how the person's heart is. If the apostles, who had been relatively close to these two candidates for at least two or three years (depending on what is meant by "John's baptism" in v. 22) needed this divine special guidance regarding the heart of the person, how much more do we when we make a selection. Written applications, interviews, personality profiles, and recommendations do help, but they can also fail to reveal what is in the heart.

We must be careful in making choices of leaders. One thing I always look for is whether the applicant has been part of a close community that practices spiritual accountability over a considerable period of time. Usually in such a fellowship one's heart is revealed, and the inability to be part of such a group may indicate a serious spiritual malady. But these groups have been getting less common in the church today, being replaced by short-term groups that are more in keeping with our culture but which give much less opportunity for true spiritual accountability.[42] However, the recent phenomenal growth of the Promise Keeper movement, with its program of accountability groups, may be signaling a welcome return to the biblical pattern of spiritual accountability.

---

42. For an exposition of this understanding of community, see my *Reclaiming Friendship*.

Acts 2:1–13

W HEN THE DAY of Pentecost came, they were all
together in one place. ²Suddenly a sound like the
blowing of a violent wind came from heaven and
filled the whole house where they were sitting. ³They saw
what seemed to be tongues of fire that separated and came to
rest on each of them. ⁴All of them were filled with the Holy
Spirit and began to speak in other tongues as the Spirit
enabled them.

⁵Now there were staying in Jerusalem God-fearing Jews
from every nation under heaven. ⁶When they heard this
sound, a crowd came together in bewilderment, because each
one heard them speaking in his own language.⁷Utterly
amazed, they asked: "Are not all these men who are speaking
Galileans? ⁸Then how is it that each of us hears them in his
own native language? ⁹Parthians, Medes and Elamites; residents of Mesopotamia, Judea and Cappadocia, Pontus and
Asia, ¹⁰Phrygia and Pamphylia, Egypt and the parts of Libya
near Cyrene; visitors from Rome ¹¹(both Jews and converts to
Judaism); Cretans and Arabs—we hear them declaring the
wonders of God in our own tongues!" ¹²Amazed and perplexed, they asked one another, "What does this mean?"

¹³Some, however, made fun of them and said, "They have
had too much wine."

Original Meaning

THE SECOND CHAPTER OF ACTS introduces three
of the most important keys to the entire book:
the fullness of the Spirit (vv. 1–13), the evangelistic ministry of the church (vv. 14–41), and the
community life of the believers (vv. 42–47). Each of these keys will occupy
a full study in this commentary.

The fulfillment of Christ's promise of the Holy Spirit appropriately takes
place during a Jewish harvest festival, Pentecost (v. 1). This term (derived
from the Gk., *pentecoste*, fiftieth) comes from the fact that the festival is celebrated on the fiftieth day after the Passover.¹ It was one of the three Jewish

---

1. The Pharisees and Sadducees had different systems regarding when to start counting the fifty days (see Ferguson, *Backgrounds*, 524). Pentecost is called the Feast of Weeks

pilgrimage festivals, when individuals were to appear before the Lord with gifts and offerings (Ex. 23:14–17); it celebrated the end of the barley harvest and the beginning of the wheat harvest.[2] It is appropriate that the event that was going to propel the gospel to the ends of the earth took place at a time when people from the ends of the earth were in Jerusalem.

We are not supplied specific details of the house (see v. 2) where the followers of Jesus met, neither are we told who was included in the "all" that were together when the Spirit descended (v. 1). Some manuscripts add "the apostles" here, but these are secondary manuscripts. The great fourth-century Bible expositor, John Chrysostom, thought that the one hundred and twenty of 1:15 were there,[3] and this view is popular today.

The wind and fire that accompanied the gift of the Spirit (vv. 2–3) are common biblical symbols for the activity of the Spirit. The Greek and Hebrew words for "Spirit" can also mean "wind" and "breath." In the valley of dry bones, wind and breath come and give life to dried-up bones. After that the Lord said, "I will put my Spirit in you and you will live" (Ezek. 37:1–14). According to Jesus, the blowing of the wind "illustrates the mysterious operation of the Spirit in effecting new birth"[4] (cf. John 3:7–8). In both cases the wind was a symbol of regeneration.

In the prediction of baptism with the Holy Spirit by John the Baptist, the wind (by implication) blows the chaff away (Luke 3:16–17). This is a symbol of judgment. Similarly, fire in this same prediction, which burns up the chaff, is a symbol of judgment. In other words, like the coming of the gospel message (2 Cor. 2:15–16), the coming of Spirit means life to some and judgment to others (as we will see with Ananias and Sapphira, Acts 5:3, 9).

Moreover, fire is also a symbol of the powerful presence of God, as both the fire at the burning bush (Ex. 3:2–5) and the pillar of fire at night (Ex. 13:21–22) indicate.

The separation of the tongues of fire "to rest on each of them" (v. 3) "seems to suggest that, though under the old covenant the divine presence rested on Israel as a corporate entity and upon many of its leaders for special purposes, under the new covenant, established by Jesus and inaugurated at Pentecost, the Spirit now rests on each believer individually."[5] This does

---

in the Old Testament (Ex. 34:22; Deut. 16:10) because it occurs seven weeks after the Passover.

2. In time it became a popular time for baptisms in the Christian church. The white dress of the candidates gave rise to the name Whitsunday (White Sunday) in Christian tradition ("Pentecost," *BEB*, 2.1639–40).

3. Chrysostom, "Homilies on Acts," 25.

4. Harrison, *Interpreting Acts*, 58.

5. Longenecker, "Acts," 270.

not negate the importance of the corporate relationship with God, as Paul's letters amply demonstrate. But from now on, the corporate arises out of a personal relationship with God through the Holy Spirit. This is in keeping with the prediction through Jeremiah that in the new covenant the law will be written on the hearts (Jer. 31:33).[6]

Two things happened to the disciples after the Spirit came: They "were filled with the Holy Spirit" and "began to speak in other tongues" (v. 4). The "tongues" are different from those described in 1 Corinthians 12—14 because, unlike there, "God-fearing Jews" from the Diaspora were able to understand what was being said. They exclaimed, "We hear them declaring the wonders of God in our own tongues!" (Acts 2:11). The gift of tongues generally seems to have been used for praising God (see 1 Cor. 14). But this particular manifestation of the Spirit, in languages understood by the people, was most appropriate here since those who heard it were eager to listen to the preaching of the gospel. At the start of what may be called "the era of the Spirit," he assisted in the work of witness in a way that depicts the gospel going to the ends of the earth. The sign fit in with the Spirit's role in enabling the church's worldwide witness (Acts 1:8). As a result, about three thousand people were "added to their number that day" (2:41).

Those who heard the praise of God in their own languages were devout Jews[7] "from every nation under heaven" (v. 5). The list of nations given in verses 9—11 suggests that Luke "was speaking, as the biblical writers normally did, from his own horizon, not ours, and was referring to the Graeco-Roman world situated round the Mediterranean basin, indeed to every nation in which there were Jews."[8]

The Greek for "staying in Jerusalem" could lend itself to the interpretation that only residents of Jerusalem are intended since these words are often used for permanent habitation. Howard Marshall has argued, however, that this expression does not need to exclude pilgrims from outside the holy city, especially since "residents of Mesopotamia" are mentioned in 2:9.[9] True, there would have been many Jews of the dispersion resident in Jerusalem,

---

6. Others feel that the "all" (v. 1), "whole" (v. 2), and "all" again in verse 4, used at the start of the process described here, suggest "that the Spirit's outpouring on the church as a body precedes its filling of the individual" (V. Verbrugge, in a letter to the author).

7. The word translated "God-fearing" (*eulabes*, see also 8:2) is different from those used in Acts for Gentile "God-fearers" (*eusebes*, see 10:2, 7, and *phoboumenos ton theon*, 10:2, 22; 13:16).

8. John Stott, *Acts*, 63.

9. I. H. Marshall, "The Significance of Pentecost," *SJT* 30 (1977): 357; cited in Wolfgang Reinhardt, "The Population Size of Jerusalem and the Numerical Growth of the Jerusalem Church," *BAFCS*, 4.261.

seeing that "it was the wish of pious Jews of the dispersion to spend their last days on the soil of the holy land and to be buried there."[10] But there is also evidence from Josephus and others that large numbers of pilgrims came to Jerusalem for the Feast of Pentecost.[11]

In amazement the people point out that those who are speaking are "Galileans" (v. 7a). "Inhabitants of Jerusalem regarded Galilee as a backward locale (cf. Acts 2:7), peculiar first of all because of its dialect (Matt. 26:73), in which laryngeal sounds were swallowed."[12] Once again God had broken earthly stereotypes of greatness and chosen people not held in high esteem in society in order to lead in a historic event (see 1 Cor. 1:26–31). Three times we are told that the disciples spoke in the people's "own language" (cf. vv. 6, 8, 11).[13] This refers to the vernacular languages of the people rather than to the Greek that the Jews of the dispersion would have known.[14]

Verses 12–13 give the two reactions of those who heard the faithful proclamation of God's word by the apostles. Some were touched and wanted to know more, asking, "What does this mean?" (v. 12). Others rejected the message and ridiculed what was said, indicated by the allegation, "They have had too much wine" (v. 13). The word translated "wine" means "sweet wine," which is normally "new wine." Yet this was not the time of the year for new wine. Some have suggested, therefore, that Luke was making a historical error here.[15] Bruce, however, points out that "there were means of keeping wine sweet all the year round" and even quotes an ancient recipe that gives a method of doing this.[16]

It is surprising that, in the face of such a spectacular miracle, some should mock what they saw. But as we will see below, this is in keeping with the theology of rejection that is clearly present in Scripture. As J. A. Alexander points out, however, "it was this frivolous aspersion, rather than the serious inquiries of the devout Jews, that gave occasion to the great apostolical discourse which follows."[17]

---

10. Harrison, *Apostolic Church*, 49.

11. See Reinhardt, "Population Size," 262–63.

12. R. Riesner, "Galilee," *DJG*, 253.

13. A different word is used in verse 11. But Bruce says that there is no significant distinction between the two words (*Acts: Greek Text*, 116).

14. Greek was the universal language of the time and it was likely spoken extensively in Palestine; the disciples themselves probably knew this language (John E. Stambaugh and David L. Balch, *The New Testament in Its Social Environment* [Philadelphia: Westminster, 1986], 87).

15. E.g., Barrett, *Acts*, 125.

16. Bruce, *Acts: Greek Text*, 119.

17. Alexander, *Acts*, 57.

Bridging Contexts

THE SIGNIFICANCE OF **Pentecost.** The experience of Pentecost is the key that unlocks the book of Acts. But what does it say to us today? (1) Note that, strictly speaking, this was not the birthday of the church. Richard Longenecker points to the fact that the word "church" (*ekklēsia*) takes several different meanings in the Bible. If we take it to mean "the body of Christ" and "an instrument of service" used by God for his redemptive purposes, then the church was in existence before Pentecost. Longenecker goes on to explain what did become new. (a) "The relationship of the Spirit to the members of the body of Christ became much more intimate and personal at Pentecost (. . . John 14:17)." (b) "At Pentecost a new model of redemption was established as characteristic for life in the new covenant—one that, while incorporating both individual and corporate redemption, begins with the former in order to include the other."[18] Pentecost made religion into much more of a personal experience with Christ through the Holy Spirit than before.

(2) Pentecost also signaled that we as believers have a new power for ministry. In our study of 1:1–11 we saw the importance of the Holy Spirit for Christian ministry. There are many parallels between Luke's description of the beginning of Christ's public ministry in Luke 4 and the beginning of the church's public ministry in Acts 2.[19] We must have God's anointing if we are to serve him (cf. comments on 1:1–8). Related to this is the fact that Pentecost brought to the church a new power for witness. Christ predicted this in 1:8, and Luke demonstrates the truth of this through the mighty wind and fire, the miraculous speech, Peter's fearless message, and the unprecedented response to his message. The rest of the New Testament gives other ways in which the Spirit's power is manifested in our lives (e.g., Rom. 8, which describes how the Spirit gives us victory over sin and life to our mortal bodies). But the great emphasis of Acts is the power we receive to proclaim the gospel.

(3) Pentecost also signals the breaking of barriers that have separated the human race since Babel, with the formation of a new humanity in Christ. In other words, Pentecost reverses what happened at Babel. In fact, as Conrad Gempf has shown, something greater happened. In a reversal of the scattering that took place at Babel, the Jewish pilgrim festivals, like Pentecost, brought people from the far corners of the earth to worship God. What is new here is that from now on, people would not need to come back to some central place to worship God—and in the Hebrew tongue. Rather, they could go

---

18. Longenecker, "Acts," 271.
19. Willimon, *Acts,* 31.

to the far corners of the earth and worship God in their own languages. Moreover, people no longer need to build up to the heavens in search of the significance they lost when they were thrown out of the garden of Eden. God has now sent his Spirit down to us and lifted our experience to a new level of significance. "Babel and Eden are not 'undone' as much as they are redeemed and their negative effects nullified."[20]

Pentecost, then, tells us that we, today, can have an intimate experience of God and can manifest power in ministry. Moreover, the barriers that divided the human race have been broken so that a new humanity is on the way to being created.

Tongues as a sign. It seems clear that speaking in tongues was a regular, if not the usual, sign of the coming of the Spirit in Acts (2:4; 10:46; 19:6). But the sign mentioned in Acts 2 seems to be different to that discussed in 1 Corinthians 12 and 14, for the language there was not understood by the people. Peter Wagner reports of several missionaries who have been given this gift of speaking in the unknown tongue of the people among whom they were ministering.[21]

In light of its three occurrences in settings where people received the Spirit, it is not surprising that many consider tongues to be the necessary sign of the baptism with the Holy Spirit. Yet the fact that many who give obvious evidence of being filled with the Spirit have not spoken in tongues should make us wary of insisting on tongues as the necessary sign, especially since nowhere in the Bible is it clearly stated that tongues must accompany Spirit baptism. Note that the tongues many refer to as the sign of their experience in the Spirit is of the unintelligible type described in 1 Corinthians 12–14, not the understandable tongues described in Acts 2. It is, however, a gift that has lifted many Christians to a new level of intimacy, joy, and power in their experience of God. Over this we should rejoice.

The reality of rejection. We expressed surprise that so clear a demonstration of God's power as that which took place at Pentecost could have elicited a mocking response (v. 13). But rejection of the gospel is a theme found throughout Acts. Beginning with the story of Judas's defection in the chapter 1, this theme appears in all but chapters 3 and 10—two chapters that give incomplete stories completed in chapters 4 and 11 respectively and which contain the rejection theme. Therefore, it is important for us to anticipate rejection and not be disillusioned when it comes. If everyone is pleased with what we do, we have probably not been truly faithful to God. The

---

20. Gempf, "Acts," 1071.
21. Wagner, *Spreading the Fire*, 86.

gospel and God's truth are so radically different to the thinking of the world that those who follow him should expect some to oppose them.

The form the rejection takes in our passage is significant, because it presents a common approach to God's message. In the face of unmistakable evidence of God's power, some attribute it to wine! Jesus encountered a similar type of criticism when his opponents said he was doing his miraculous work through the power of Beelzebub (Mark 3:22). This ridicule occasioned a severe discourse by Christ on the nature of his enemies' unbelief, climaxing in his statement about the unforgivable sin (3:23–30).

The Bible contains an advanced theology of this type of rejection, especially relating to Jewish rejection of God's message. When God called Isaiah, he told him that not only would some reject his message, but some would also be confirmed in their chosen path of blindness and rebellion because of his message (Isa. 6:10):

> Make the heart of this people calloused;
>> make their ears dull
>> and close their eyes.
> Otherwise they might see with their eyes,
>> hear with their ears,
>> understand with their hearts,
> and turn and be healed.

Jesus himself indicated that some would respond to his parables in this way (Matt. 13:11–15). According to Paul, the apostles are "the smell of death" to some and "the fragrance of life" to others (2 Cor. 2:16). Thus, when rebellious people in Acts 2 see the Pentecostal phenomena and hear Peter preach, their rebellion is intensified. Their mocking response reminds us that whenever we follow God faithfully, we will face rejection.

INTIMACY WITH GOD and joy in worship. As noted above, Pentecost has opened the door for us to have an intimate and supernatural experience of God. To many, however, even within the evangelical fold, Christianity is restricted to entering the kingdom through a rational acceptance of the truth of the gospel, followed by their labor to live according to the Bible. This is indeed an important ingredient to Christianity. But Pentecost and its working out in Acts tells us that there is "something more." The greatest contribution of the Pentecostal movement (and the Wesleyan Holiness movement that preceded it) is that it gave back to the church the importance of a subjective experience of Christ through the Holy

Spirit in one's personal life and in corporate worship.[22] At Pentecost, when the disciples were filled with the Spirit, they began "declaring the wonders of God" (v. 11). When we sense, through experience, that "God has poured out his love into our hearts by the Holy Spirit, whom he has given us" (Rom. 5:5), our hearts are filled with joy, and this joy expresses itself in praise.

Singing, of course, is one of the supreme expressions of our joy over the intimacy we have in Christ. Just as love songs express the joy of human love, Christian songs express the joy we have in our love relationship with God. John Wesley has said, "Singing is as much the language of holy joy as praying is of holy desire." Paul connects singing directly with the fullness of the Spirit in Ephesians 5:18–20, presenting it as an outflow of such fullness: "Be filled with the Spirit, speaking to one another in psalms and hymns and spiritual songs, singing and making melody with your heart to the Lord" (NASB). "Speaking," "singing," and "making melody" are participles in the Greek related to the imperative, "be filled." Christians, then, must constantly seek to recapture what Pentecost signified: vibrant intimacy with God and joyous worship that ensues from it.

The Reformed tradition has emphasized the majesty of God and the awesomeness of worshiping such a great and transcendent God. This key biblical emphasis, it is true, may be lacking in some branches of the Pentecostal movement. But the great contribution of the Pentecostal movement was to bring back the heart and soul into worship, especially into Western Anglo-Saxon worship (Afro-Caribbean worship seems to have been able to preserve this in a most meaningful way).

One danger of an emphasis on subjective experience in worship, however, is that it can satisfy people so much that they neglect important Christian disciplines of day-to-day life, such as striving after personal and social holiness and mastering the Scriptures. It is possible for Christians to worship God with what seems to be deep intimacy on Sunday, and then to behave in unchristian ways in their workplaces on Monday (e.g., adopting unethical business methods and exploiting labor). They concentrate so much on subjective experience that they neglect the hard work of pursuing a Christian mind that informs their lives and vitally influences the decisions they make and the way they behave.

Yet this abuse of something good should not cause us to refrain from seeking it. Nor must we think that using our minds in worship and devotion

---

22. For a scholarly fruit of this emphasis, see Gordon Fee, *God's Empowering Presence: The Holy Spirit in the Letters of Paul* (Peabody, Mass.: Hendrickson, 1994), which shows how central to the letters of Paul is his teaching on the Spirit. Fee points out that this factor has often been overlooked by earlier scholars (1).

is in some way superior to using the heart. Paul serves as a powerful example of a thorough Christian intellectual who also had ecstatic, subjective experiences with God (e.g., 2 Cor. 12:1–6). In fact, the great truths of the gospel on which a Christian intellectual meditates can be the springboard for spiritually and emotionally uplifting experiences, as the doxologies in Paul's letters indicate (Rom. 11:33–36).

A heartening feature in the recent revival of vibrancy in worship is that it has not been confined to groups generally characterized as Pentecostal or charismatic, with whom it originated. In most renewal movements in the history of the church, what began as a distinctive of one group soon went mainstream and raised the quality of life in the entire church. One of the most meaningful and joyous experiences of worship I have had was at the Bethlehem Baptist Church in Minneapolis, pastored by a well-known Reformed preacher, John Piper, who has written extensively from his Calvinistic perspective. What especially thrilled me at this service was observing how the Calvinistic emphasis on the transcendence and majesty of God was harmonized with the Pentecostal emphasis on intimacy with God and vibrancy in worship.

I must add here that many evangelical churches are now emphasizing the entertainment aspect of worship by having well-rehearsed performances at their worship services. Top quality music and drama does befit the worship of our supreme and glorious God. The detailed and extensive instructions in the Old Testament regarding worship (e.g., in Exodus and Leviticus) give evidence of the fact that God does desire beauty and quality in worship. But while quality can be an expression of spirituality, it can never be a substitute for it. All Christians should give due attention to having quality in worship. But more importantly they must ensure that the Holy Spirit has ample opportunity to fill the service with the sense of God's presence and to lead the people to a deep experience of God. I fear that sometimes what we aim at is to entertain people through our quality. This can be an effective means of attracting people in our entertainment-oriented society, but it should never so consume our efforts that it becomes a substitute for seeking God's fullness in worship, as reflected in the Pentecostal experience in Acts.

Experiencing Pentecostal power today. We have said that the heart of the power of Pentecost in Acts is power for ministry. This power, however, is not the power of a magician that can be called up according to the will of the Christian. In fact, even in the era of the Spirit, Christians are susceptible to frustrating experiences of many kinds (Rom. 8:18–25), over which they have no power. As I write this book, I have to submit to five- to eight-hour power cuts each day, which severely curtails my writing plans. But that is the lot of everyone in our country, from which I cannot immune myself.

We suffer, we feel weak and get sick, we have sorrow, and finally we die. But in our ministry there will be power. A dear friend I know was used powerfully in the area of the miraculous during a time when his wife and, for a time, he were sick physically.

The way the power of Pentecost for ministry is expressed in our lives depends, among other things, on the spiritual gifts we have received (see 1 Cor. 12). Believers do not have all of these gifts accessible to them all the time. This is particularly true of the power to perform miracles; those who have that gift will also be given the faith that enables them to pray boldly for a miracle. But those who do not have the gift of miraculous powers can still pray in faith during times of need and be surprised to see God answer their prayers. At its heart, the power of Pentecost is an experience of the immediacy of God. God is indeed with us, and we can experience his nearness and powerful enabling to minister in the Spirit.[23]

The breaking of barriers. We have already seen that Pentecost overcame the effects of Babel. We saw how when the disciples praised God, they did not do so in the Greek language, which most of the people knew. Instead, they praised God in the vernacular dialects of these people. The significance of this work of the Spirit, in a world torn by cultural disharmony, has been presented powerfully by British Baptist pastor Roy Clements.[24] He notes how important to people their culture is. Different movements have tried to create a single world order, but in doing so, "they are implicitly imperialistic, involving the domination of one culture over another." Even with Islam, the unity that is forged is dominated by Arab culture and language.

But, as Clements goes on to way, "culture refuses to be dominated in that way." He asks: "Is there a power that can unify the divided nations of the earth without subjugating them? Is there a way of making people one, without at the same time making them all the same?" To which he answers: "It is precisely that sort of unity which the Holy Spirit brings. And he declares his intention in the matter right at the beginning, on the day of Pentecost, by the miracle he performed."

Clements' point is that

the Pentecostal tongues were a pointer to the way in which the Holy Spirit was going to break down social barriers and create an unprecedented kind of internationalism. Unlike the imperialisms of men, the Spirit had no ambition to homogenize the peoples of the world into a uniform Christian culture.

---

23. See Jack Deere, *Surprised by the Power of the Spirit* (Grand Rapids: Zondervan, 1993).

24. The following quotes are taken from Roy Clements, *The Church That Turned the World Upside Down*, 20–23.

Instead, the Spirit created "a new kind of social identity altogether"—the "fellowship of the Holy Spirit." Thus, in the book of Acts we see the growth of "one church in diverse cultures." All of this looks forward to the day when there will be a "a great multitude that no one could count, from every nation, tribe, people and language, standing before the throne and in front of the Lamb" (Rev. 7:9).

Pentecost, then, gives us a hint of how the revolutionary breaking of social and other barriers by the gospel will work out in practical life. The implications are immense. As we take the gospel to the peoples of the world, we should not expect people to subject themselves to a language like English (which is today what Greek was in the first century). We need to learn the heart language of people and to share the gospel with them in that language. All the advances in technology are no substitute to the hard work of identifying with a culture and learning to understand and appreciate its distinctives—hard work indeed in a culture that values efficiency so highly and tries so hard to eliminate frustration.

Yet while we work hard to present the gospel in culturally appropriate ways, we should never isolate any Christians from the church in the rest of the world. We must show them that they are part of a large worldwide family, who share a deep unity in diversity that will outlast all human barriers until we go to our heavenly home, where people from all cultures will be at home.

Most of the members in the church my wife and I attend are converts from Buddhism. They usually find translations of Western hymns difficult to sing. When I lead worship in church, I try to use at least one hymn translated from English, though I usually choose a hymn that fits our style of music, where the drum is the most important instrument. The reason for choosing a translated hymn is so that our people will realize that they are part of that worldwide family called "the body of Christ." We have a westernized English language congregation that meets in our church as well. And we regularly have combined services. These are difficult services to plan; they call for hard and creative thinking if we want to avoid boredom. But the risk is worth taking, given the need to affirm that we are one despite our cultural differences. All of this applies to the multicultural societies in the West too.

The use of "Galileans" to help usher in the era of the Spirit is also a sort of breaking of barriers. It shows that when God chooses to do something marvelous, he does not necessarily wait till a person high in earthly esteem comes along. He does use such people, of course, as we see with God's using Paul. But he is not limited to them. The key to usefulness is the fullness of the Spirit, and the Spirit can bring life to anyone he chooses, provided that he or she is open to this enlivening.

We who live in this era of the Spirit should develop the dual discipline of disregarding the social and economic background of people when thinking of their potential and of looking at them through the eyes of faith. We must envision the possibilities of grace in their lives as the Spirit exercises his power over them. This difficult discipline is challenged by the prejudices we imbibe from our cultures and by the humiliation we receive when people we believe in fail to live up to their potential. But it is fed by the unmistakable evidence from Scripture and from history that God can use people, whom the world wrote off as useless, to be his mighty servants.

Are tongues for today? We have argued that tongues was probably the key sign of the filling of the Holy Spirit in Acts, but that the Scriptures do not suggest it was the inevitable sign of this filling. Is speaking in tongues valid for today? Some answer this with a firm "No," based on Paul's statement in 1 Corinthians 13:8—10: "But where there are prophecies, they will cease; where there are tongues, they will be stilled; where there is knowledge, it will pass away ... but when perfection comes, the imperfect disappears." Many of them claim that tongues ceased with the close of the apostolic age[25] or with the completion of the canon of Scripture.[26]Numerous scholars have countered the arguments for this "cessationist" view.[27] In my estimation, the strongest case can be made for the view that the "perfection" that will make tongues and prophecy unnecessary will be achieved when Christ returns. Tongues has not disappeared from the church after the apostolic age. Note the conclusion of church historian Cecil M. Robeck Jr.: "Speaking in tongues has always been in the Church, although with varied levels of expression and acceptance."[28]

Unfortunately, tongues has been the focal point of much division in the church, especially since the Pentecostal movement burst onto the scene at the turn of this century. Far too many have taken one of two extreme positions: that all Christians should practice this gift, or that no members of their group or church should practice it. We should beware of both charismania (an overemphasis on charismatic gifts) and charisphobia (a fear of charismatic gifts), and always ask ourselves this question: Do I have all that God wishes for me to enjoy? We must leave it to God to give us what gifts he desires for

---

25. Benjamin B. Warfield, *Counterfeit Miracles* (Edinburgh: Banner of Truth Trust, 1918, reprint 1972); cited in C. M. Robeck Jr., *ISBE*, 4.872.

26. Walter J. Chantry, *Signs of the Apostles: Observations on Pentecostalism Old and New* (Edinburgh: Banner of Truth Trust, 1976); cited in Robeck, *ISBE*, 4.872.

27. See D. A. Carson, *Showing the Spirit: A Theological Exposition of 1 Corinthians 12—14* (Grand Rapids: Book, 1987), 76—72; Jack Deere, *Surprised by the Power of the Spirit*; Gordon D. Fee, *God's Empowering Presence*, 204—8; idem, *1 Corinthians*, NICNT (Grand Rapids: Eerdmans, 1987), 642—46.

28. Robeck, *ISBE*, 4.874.

us. Though it is legitimate to ask God for gifts we would like to have (1 Cor. 12:31; 14:1), we should not insist on receiving gifts that the Lord (who sovereignly decides what gifts to give us [1 Cor. 12:11; Eph. 4:7]) has not assigned to us.

Responding to rejection. There can be no doubt that if we proclaim God's truth today, we too, like Jesus and the first disciples, should expect rejection and misrepresentation. Jesus said, "Remember the words I spoke to you: 'No servant is greater than his master.' If they persecuted me, they will persecute you also" (John 15:20). When people reject what we say, our tendency is to ask, "What is wrong with me?" While that is always an appropriate question to ask, it is also important to remember that there will always be people who reject God's message. If we do not remember this, we may become so upset by such people that our ministry to the receptive will also be affected.

As a youth worker I sometimes speak at evangelistic gatherings, where some in the audience are not only hostile to what I am saying but also poke fun at it. Once I had a section of the audience start clapping a minute or two after I started, indicating that it was time for me to stop! I must try to not permit such reactions to deprive others of the life-giving message of Christ that I am presenting.

Such rejection can also make us bitter. We reason: "After all I am sacrificing to share the good news with these people, look at the way they treat me. They are unworthy of my love." We might end up hating them and becoming bitter inside. This can especially happen after we face mockery, which is often more painful than outright rejection. For when people reject what we say, we know that at least they have considered us important enough to merit a serious response. Mockery, however, indicates that we are being treated with disdain. We must learn the discipline of anticipating such responses and of refusing to let them make us bitter and discouraged.

Acts 2:14–41

❧

THEN PETER STOOD up with the Eleven, raised his voice and addressed the crowd: "Fellow Jews and all of you who live in Jerusalem, let me explain this to you; listen carefully to what I say. ¹⁵These men are not drunk, as you suppose. It's only nine in the morning! ¹⁶No, this is what was spoken by the prophet Joel:

¹⁷"'In the last days, God says,
     I will pour out my Spirit on all people.
   Your sons and daughters will prophesy,
       your young men will see visions,
       your old men will dream dreams.
¹⁸Even on my servants, both men and women,
     I will pour out my Spirit in those days,
     and they will prophesy.
¹⁹I will show wonders in the heaven above
     and signs on the earth below,
     blood and fire and billows of smoke.
²⁰The sun will be turned to darkness
     and the moon to blood
     before the coming of the great and glorious day
         of the Lord.
²¹And everyone who calls
     on the name of the Lord will be saved.'

²²"Men of Israel, listen to this: Jesus of Nazareth was a man accredited by God to you by miracles, wonders and signs, which God did among you through him, as you yourselves know. ²³This man was handed over to you by God's set purpose and foreknowledge; and you, with the help of wicked men, put him to death by nailing him to the cross. ²⁴But God raised him from the dead, freeing him from the agony of death, because it was impossible for death to keep its hold on him. ²⁵David said about him:

"'I saw the Lord always before me.
     Because he is at my right hand,
     I will not be shaken.
²⁶Therefore my heart is glad and my tongue rejoices;
     my body also will live in hope,

²⁷because you will not abandon me to the grave,
nor will you let your Holy One see decay.
²⁸You have made known to me the paths of life;
you will fill me with joy in your presence.'

²⁹"Brothers, I can tell you confidently that the patriarch David died and was buried, and his tomb is here to this day. ³⁰But he was a prophet and knew that God had promised him on oath that he would place one of his descendants on his throne. ³¹Seeing what was ahead, he spoke of the resurrection of the Christ, that he was not abandoned to the grave, nor did his body see decay. ³²God has raised this Jesus to life, and we are all witnesses of the fact. ³³Exalted to the right hand of God, he has received from the Father the promised Holy Spirit and has poured out what you now see and hear. ³⁴For David did not ascend to heaven, and yet he said,

"'The Lord said to my Lord:
"Sit at my right hand
³⁵until I make your enemies
a footstool for your feet."'

³⁶"Therefore let all Israel be assured of this: God has made this Jesus, whom you crucified, both Lord and Christ."

³⁷When the people heard this, they were cut to the heart and said to Peter and the other apostles, "Brothers, what shall we do?"

³⁸Peter replied, "Repent and be baptized, every one of you, in the name of Jesus Christ for the forgiveness of your sins. And you will receive the gift of the Holy Spirit. ³⁹The promise is for you and your children and for all who are far off—for all whom the Lord our God will call."

⁴⁰With many other words he warned them; and he pleaded with them, "Save yourselves from this corrupt generation." ⁴¹Those who accepted his message were baptized, and about three thousand were added to their number that day.

Original Meaning

PETER, NO LONGER afraid to own his Lord, stands up to speak to those gathered to witness the amazing phenomena that had been manifested (v. 14). But he stands up "with the Eleven," which suggests that the other apostles are backing him. Ministry is almost always done as a team in Acts.[1] But there may have been a deeper reason for all of them to stand up. The vacancy of the twelfth person, who had to be a witness to the resurrection, had been filled just prior to Pentecost. Peter's speech will hinge upon the fact of the resurrection. When he says, "We are all witnesses of the fact" (2:32), he must have been referring to the Eleven standing beside him.

Robert Mounce presents what can be considered the common apostolic gospel (*euangelion*) or *kerygma*, containing three basic features found in Peter's speech:

(1) a historical proclamation of the [I would add "life and ministry" here] death, resurrection and exaltation of Jesus, set forth as the fulfillment of prophecy and involving man's responsibility; (2) a theological evaluation of the person of Jesus as both Lord and Christ; (3) a summons to believe and receive the forgiveness of sins.[2]

Explaining the Phenomena (2:14–21)

PETER LAUNCHES HIS message by connecting with his audience through something they can relate to: the mockers' statement that they are drunk (v. 15). This is a wise method to win the attention of his audience insofar as it relates to something that the people are curious about. He points out the unlikeness of the charge: "It's only nine in the morning!" (v. 15).[3] Then he points to the real reason for the surprising phenomena they have witnessed: the fulfillment of a prophecy by Joel (Joel 2:28–32) that all devout Jews have been longing to see fulfilled (Acts 2:17a). At that time Peter may not have fully understood the full implications of what was meant by "all people" upon whom the Spirit will be poured out. But with hindsight Luke, who records this, knows that it includes Gentiles.

The expression "last days" in this prophecy includes two distinct periods; the start of the second one is separated from the start of the first by a long time. But in a way typical of the prophetic perspective, these two events are juxtaposed side by side by the prophet Joel. What the people are witnessing is the "beginning"[4] of the last days, when people of all types and ages will prophecy (vv. 17b–18). At the "end"[5] of the last days will be cosmic

---

1. See the comments on Acts 3.
2. Robert H. Mounce, "Gospel," *EDBT*, 474.
3. Peter's words translate literally, "It is only the third hour of the day" (NASB). According to our system of reckoning time, that is 9.00 A.M.
4. Marshall, *Acts*, 74.
5. Ibid.

disturbances (vv. 19–20; cf. Rev. 6:12–14; 8:5, 7; 20:9), which will herald "the great and glorious day of the Lord" (v. 20b)—the day of judgment at the end of the world. For believers, this will not be a time to dread, for "everyone who calls on the name of the Lord will be saved" (v. 21).

Peter incorporates tongues here loosely under the idea of prophecy. This must be because the apostles are speaking here in recognizable languages, which is like prophecy in that it edifies the church (see 1 Cor. 14:1–5, 39).[6] In the Old Testament the coming of the Spirit on persons for special purposes is often accompanied by their prophesying (Num. 11:26–29; 1 Sam. 10:6–12). The Jews came to believe that "with the passing of the last of the writing prophets in the early post-exilic period the spirit of prophecy had ceased in Israel." But they "expected that with the coming of the Messianic age there would be a special outpouring of God's Spirit, in fulfillment of Ezekiel 37, and that prophecy would once again flourish."[7] Peter is telling the people that this age of fulfillment for which they have been eagerly waiting has dawned. This point about fulfillment of prophecy was a key aspect of the *kerygma* of the early church.[8]

The Miracles and Death of Christ (2:22–23)

PETER'S PRESENTATION OF the gospel begins with a reference to the miracles of Christ as evidence that he was accredited by God (v. 22). Since Luke is only giving a summary of the speech,[9] presumably Peter speaks at some length about Christ's ministry.[10] He points out that the hearers know these facts. In his Gospel, Luke quotes Jesus as saying: "But if I drive out demons by the finger of God, then the kingdom of God has come to you" (Luke 11:20). Here too his miracles are presented as evidence that God has accredited him.

Next, Peter presents the death of Christ as having been caused by the audience, but also as being "by God's set purpose and foreknowledge" (v. 23). We see here, as often in Scripture, the paradox between divine providence and human responsibility (4:27–28). While God planned for Christ to die on the cross, those who carried out this act were responsible for it. The idea that this was God's plan was far from Peter's mind when he first heard about

---

6. Gary V. Smith, "Prophet; Prophecy," *ISBE*, 3:1004. By contrast, the tongues described in 1 Corinthians 12–14 were unintelligible without an interpreter and were primarily for private edification (see comments on 2:1–11).

7. Longenecker, "Acts," 271.

8. See the influential book of C. H. Dodd, *The Apostolic Preaching and Its Developments* (New York: Harper & Row, 1964 reprint), 7–31.

9. See the discussion on the speeches of Acts in the Introduction.

10. Note how in his speech in Cornelius's house Peter makes the same point, but there he outlines the career of Christ in more detail (10:37–39).

Christ's impending death (Matt. 16:22). But with the teaching of Jesus, especially through his explanations after the resurrection (Luke 24:27, 45–46), he realized that all of this was part of God's plan. For this reason the Gospels often report that Christ's death was according to God's plan, having been predicted by the prophets (Luke 18:31; 24:25–26, 46). This is also a common theme in the evangelistic preaching of Acts (2:23; 3:18; 8:32–35; 13:27, 29).

This affirmation that the cross was a preplanned redemptive act of God was the Christian response to the fact that a crucified Messiah was a stumbling block to the Jews (see 1 Cor. 1:23). As Gordon Fee puts it, to the Jews "Christ Crucified is a contradiction in terms, of the same category as 'fried ice.'"[11] The first Christians must have thought hard about how to respond to this stumbling block in their evangelism with the Jews, and they came up with this strategy of presenting it as a triumph that God had planned from the beginning.

The Resurrection (2:24–32)

THE RESURRECTION OCCUPIES nine verses of Peter's sermon. The language of verse 24 is graphic. The Bible often refers to the resurrection as an act of God ("God raised him"), which is in keeping with the fact that it was God's accreditation of the person and work of Christ. "Freeing him from the agony of death" literally reads, "when he had loosed the pangs [*odin*] of death."[12] The word *odin* usually denoted the pains of childbirth. The next statement, "It was impossible for death to keep its hold on him," clearly shows that Peter is using the resurrection as a validation of Jesus' life and ministry. Because he is Messiah, he *cannot* remain dead. G. Bertram describes beautifully what Peter is saying: "The abyss can no more hold the Redeemer than a pregnant woman can hold the child in her body."[13]

In verses 25–28 Peter quotes Psalm 16:8–11, where David anticipates a resurrection. Then he goes on to argue that, since David did not rise from the dead, this passage must be referring to David's great Son, Jesus (vv. 29–31). Longenecker explains how the apostles followed the exegetical precedent set by Jesus in interpreting Psalm 110 as a messianic psalm (cf. Mark 12:35–37) as well as Psalm 16 (which has similar phrases). Presumably Jesus referred to this psalm in his post-resurrection explanations (cf. Luke 24:44). Peter clinches his argument for the resurrection with his claim: "We are all witnesses of the fact" (Acts 2:32).

---

11. Gordon D. Fee, *The First Epistle to the Corinthians*, NICNT (Grand Rapids: Eerdmans, 1987), 75.

12. C. K. Barrett, *Acts*, 127.

13. G. Bertram, "ὠδίν," *TDNT*, 9:673.

The Exaltation (2:33–35)

PETER NEXT STATES that Jesus has been exalted to the right hand of the Father and connects the event of Pentecost with this exaltation. Jesus received the Holy Spirit from the Father and has poured out what they have just seen and heard (v. 33). While we often speak of the ascension of Christ, the scriptural term *exaltation* may be a more appropriate word since it implies the significance of the event. In the New Testament the resurrection and exaltation of Christ are held in close association with each other, almost as if they constituted a single event. Note Peter's words here: "This Jesus God raised up again.... Therefore having been exalted to the right hand of God ..." (vv. 32–33, NASB).[14]

After his resurrection, Jesus met the disciples often, but we are not told how and where he spent the rest of his time. Was he already, in a sense, exalted? What we do know is that in his recording the ascension, Luke "was describing the cessation of the resurrection appearances of Jesus—'an acted declaration of finality.'"[15] He did appear in his exalted state one more time to Paul on the road to Damascus—an event that was more like a resurrection appearance than a vision (1 Cor. 15:8). G. E. Ladd feels that the resurrection appearances "were condescensions of the glorified Christ to convince them that he was really alive again."[16]

As with the resurrection, Peter gives evidences for the exaltation of Christ. (1) He appeals to their experience of the Holy Spirit, which is proof that Jesus has indeed gone to heaven and sent the one he promised (v. 33). (2) He quotes from another Davidic psalm (Ps. 110) and, as before (vv. 29–31), claims that what David said there cannot apply to him: "David did not ascend to heaven" (vv. 34–35). This quotation also gives us a clue as to what Christ is doing now in his exalted state: He is seated at the right hand of God and bringing to pass the complete defeat of his enemies. The phrase "The Lord said to my Lord" is significant. While the same word is used in the Greek both times for "Lord," the Hebrew of Psalm 110:1 reads, "*Yahweh* said to my *Adonai*." Peter sees this as God speaking to Jesus, who is David's Lord.

Lord and Christ (2:36)

PETER'S NEXT STATEMENT represents the second major feature of the apostolic *kerygma*: a theological evaluation of the person of Jesus. The words with

---

14. Note especially Phil. 2:8–9. The resurrection of Christ is not mentioned in this Christological hymn. Rather, immediately after mentioning Jesus' death, Paul refers to the exaltation: "He humbled himself and became obedient to death—even death on a cross! Therefore God exalted him to the highest place and gave him the name that is above every name."

15. Ladd, *Theology*, 370. The words in single quotes are from C. F. D. Moule, "The Ascension," *ExpTim* 68 (1956–57): 208.

16. Ladd, *Theology*, 371.

which he begins his major affirmation, "Therefore let all Israel be assured of this," are appropriate considering the convincing way he has argued his case up to now. His conclusion is clear: "God has made this Jesus, whom you crucified, both Lord and Christ."

Peter claims first that Jesus is "Lord." With the resurrection and exaltation of Jesus, the disciples now fully understand the implications of who he is. G. E. Ladd comments on the use of the word *kyrios* (Lord) in Acts: "It is amazing to find the term used of both Jesus and God. Not only is Jesus, like God, *kyrios;* the term is used both of God and the exalted Jesus in practically interchangeable contexts."[17] In this speech *kyrios* is used for Jesus in ways that were used for God in the LXX (see vv. 20–21); moreover, Jesus as Lord has taken on divine functions, such as pouring out the Spirit (v. 33) and being the object of faith (v. 21). Note how in verse 36 Jesus is called Lord while in verse 39 God continues to be called Lord. Ladd concludes:

> Here in the earliest Christology of the primitive church are the beginnings of Trinitarian theology, although they are not reflected upon. Implicit in the recognition of the Lordship of Jesus is the acknowledgment of his essential divinity.[18]

Thus, the *kerygma* of the early church included the Lordship of Christ; intimately associated with that was the reign of Christ, to which Peter has just referred (v. 34). Jesus is now enthroned and "has become the one by whom Jesus will bring under control every rebellious power in the world."[19] In his next speech Peter will say, referring to this same exalted reign, "He must remain in heaven until the time comes for God to restore everything, as he promised long ago through his holy prophets" (3:21). Here is the answer to the disciples' question about whether Christ will "restore the kingdom to Israel" (1:6). He will restore not only Israel, but everything. The process he began with his exaltation will climax in the great consummation, after "he has put all his enemies under his feet" and "God may be all in all" (1 Cor. 15:25, 28).[20]

The title "Christ" (i.e., Messiah, Anointed One) points to the hope of Israel for a deliverer. The early church understood the deliverance that Christ brought as being primarily a deliverance from sin and its effects rather than the political deliverance that the Jews were anticipating. In other words,

---

17. Ibid., 375. This is also true of the Luke's Gospel, where the word is used at least 39 times for Jesus.

18. Ibid., 377. See also R. N. Longenecker, *The Christology of Early Jewish Christianity* (London: SCM Press, 1970).

19. Ladd, *Theology*, 376.

20. See 1 Cor. 15:24–27, which describes the rule of the exalted Christ until that time.

while the title "Lord" emphasizes the sovereign kingship of Jesus, the title "Christ" emphasizes the salvation he brings.

A Summons to Repent and Receive Forgiveness (2:37–40)

THE THIRD FEATURE of the apostolic *kerygma* is a summons to respond to the message. It comes as a result of the inquiry of the audience, who, "cut to the heart," ask, "Brothers, what shall we do?" (v. 37). Peter gives two stipulations and promises two blessings. They must repent and be baptized, and they will receive the forgiveness of sin and experience the Holy Spirit. As Lord, Jesus demands repentance and baptism, which is an outward expression of allegiance to him. As Savior, he offers the unmerited gift of forgiveness. There is no separation of the Lordship of Christ from his role as Savior here.

In this story, as in every story of conversion, the grace of God fills us with wonder. In his message, Peter has reminded these people that they put Jesus to death. Now this same Jesus offers them salvation. Peter is showing them how they can appropriate Christ's plea on the cross for their forgiveness. David Gooding describes this "amazing grace" as follows:

> They had murdered God's Son; he was offering them his Spirit. They had crucified the second person of the Trinity; he was offering them the third. They had thrown God's Son out of the vineyard in the hope of inheriting the vineyard themselves; now he was inviting them to receive God's Spirit not just into their vineyard but into their very hearts, to be their undying life, to be the earnest and guarantee of an infinite and imperishable inheritance.[21]

Some have understood the statement, "Repent and be baptized, every one of you, in the name of Jesus Christ for the forgiveness of your sins" (v. 38), as implying that baptism is a necessary requirement for salvation. But that interpretation reads too much into the text. In the home of Cornelius, those present received the Spirit and spoke in tongues before they were baptized (10:44–48). Bruce says, "It is against the whole genius of biblical religion to suppose that the outward rite would have any value except insofar as it was accompanied by the work of grace within." He points to the similar situation in 3:19, where "the blotting out of the people's sins is in direct consequence of their repenting and turning to God. ... Nothing is said about baptism, although it is no doubt implied (the idea of an unbaptized believer does not seem to be entertained in the New Testament)."[22] Peter's message concludes with a more intense appeal to the will than before, including warning and pleading (v. 40).

---

21. Gooding, *True to the Faith*, 55.
22. Bruce, *Acts*, NICNT, 70.

The Response to the Message (2:41)

THE AMAZING RESPONSE of three thousand baptisms illustrates Jesus' promise that with his going away and the Spirit's coming, the disciples will do even greater works than he did (John 14:12). Some scholars have doubted the accuracy of the high figures of converts in Jerusalem; they maintain that it is unlikely that so many would have been converted in a city that did not have a large population. This interpretation has been based on population figures for Jerusalem ranging between 25,000 to 30,000.[23] Recent studies, however, show that a population "figure of 60,000 to 120,000 seems realistic, and even the higher end of this scale [is] not impossible for the 30s of the 1st century."[24]

CHRISTIANITY IS CHRIST. It has been often said that "Christianity is Christ." Peter's message at Pentecost gives us an indication why we can make such a claim. Every step in Christ's career opens the door to some facet of the faith and practice of the Christian.

This passage gives the first evangelistic sermon of the New Testament church. In terms of results it was eminently successful. When we realize the amount of space Luke devotes to this sermon, we can assume that he intended it as a model of evangelistic preaching in the early church. We can therefore expect to learn much about evangelistic preaching here.[25] Each of the following points is vital in the Christian gospel and forms the basis of our proclamation. Our message too must focus on Christ.

- Jesus' incarnation and ministry made it possible for him to be our Savior (v. 22). It showed that he was not a mere man; he was indeed God's answer to the human dilemma.
- His death on the cross achieved salvation (v. 23).
- His resurrection confirmed the efficacy of and validated his work (vv. 24–32).
- His exaltation made it possible for him to send the Holy Spirit, who actualizes this salvation in our daily lives (vv. 33, 39).

---

23. See Joachim Jeremias, *Jerusalem in the Times of Jesus*, trans. by F. H. and C. H. Cave (London: SCM, 1969), 84.

24. See Wolfgang Reinhardt, "The Population Size of Jerusalem and the Numerical Growth of the Jerusalem Church," *BAFCS*, 4:237.

25. Leighton Ford uses this sermon as a model for public evangelism in his influential book, *The Christian Persuader: A New Look at Evangelism Today* (New York: Harper & Row, 1966), 92–139.

- His present exalted state confirms his Lordship and messiahship and represents his reign, during which he will defeat all rebellion to God (vv. 34–36).
- His second coming will consummate his work (not explicitly stated, but implied in v. 35).
- In view of who Jesus is and what he has done, our salvation depends on him (vv. 36, 38). Our receiving of salvation involves admitting our need through repentance and accepting Jesus as Savior and Lord. It results in our reception of the Holy Spirit and is expressed in baptism in his name (v. 38).

Beginning with real questions. Peter began his speech by answering a real question being asked by the audience about the languages they were hearing (v. 15). This pattern we will see in every sermon in Acts. The evangelists do not launch into a proclamation of the gospel out of the blue, but begin with something the audience can relate to. Often, as here, the launching pad is a question they had about a miracle they have just seen (see also 3:12–16; 16:11–14). Sometimes, as in Athens, it is a felt need that the audience has expressed (17:22–23). Our evangelistic preaching too should start where people are, so that they can identify with our message. From there we can take them to the basic message we want to communicate.

The life of Christ and the evangelistic message. Peter began his exposition of the gospel by describing events out of the life of Christ. The life of Christ is a crucial resource in evangelism. As the name "Gospel" suggests, the first four books of the New Testament are actually evangelistic tracts. "Strictly speaking they are not biography, but testimony. They bear witness to Christ and to the good news of his salvation. Therefore the authors select, arrange and present their material according to their purpose as evangelists."[26] Concerning his Gospel, John writes, "But these are written that you may believe that Jesus is the Christ, the Son of God, and that by believing you may have life in his name" (John 20:31).

In addition, in evangelism we are asking people to follow Jesus as Lord. Should we not tell people something about the nature of this person whom we are asking them to follow? And what better way to tell them about Jesus than to describe his life on earth? In other words, the life of Christ and the content of the four Gospels should be key features of our evangelistic message.[27]

The accreditation theme and persuasion. A key to understanding Peter's speech is to grasp the fact that he was attempting to show the Jews from

---

26. John Stott, *Understanding the Bible* (Glendale, Calif.: Regal, 1976), 113–14.
27. For a discussion of using the life of Christ in evangelism see my *Supremacy*, 75–80.

Scripture and from events that had taken place (especially the resurrection) that the gospel of Christ has been validated and accredited as true. He attempted to show incontrovertible evidence that Jesus is indeed the Messiah they were looking for. That Peter was successful in this attempt is evidenced by the amazing response to his message.

The phenomena that the people witnessed received confirmation through the prophecy of Joel (vv. 17–21). Jesus himself was accredited by miracles, wonders, and signs (v. 22) and by his resurrection (vv. 24–31, 34–35). The resurrection, in turn, was buttressed by the fact that the eleven people standing with Peter were eyewitnesses of it (v. 32), by the predictions about him in Scripture (vv. 25–28, 34), and by the coming of the Holy Spirit with the accompanying manifestations of his power (v. 33). All this evidence gave Peter the confidence to say that the one they crucified is "both Lord and Christ" (v. 36).

This emphasis on evidence and accreditation fits in with the practice of persuasion in evangelism in Acts, which we will examine in our study of 17:1–15.

The death of Christ as a victory. Christ's death was a stumbling block to the Jews. The apostles responded to this issue by presenting it as a victory that had been planned by God. It was not the unfortunate defeat of a good man who had no power to save himself from such a death.

The New Testament is clear in this portrayal of the victory of Christ through his death. In his trial and crucifixion, Jesus marched on, amidst pain and humiliation, as a strong man who had the situation under his control! When he introduced himself to the guards in the garden, for example, they drew back and fell to the ground. He took time in the middle of his arrest to heal the ear of the high priest's servant and to exhort Peter about the uselessness of using the sword. He also reminded Peter that twelve legions of angels were available for him to use if he wished to go free. He told the high priest about his return on the clouds from heaven. He told the women who were weeping for him not to do so, but rather to weep for themselves. From the cruelly painful cross he pronounced salvation to a thief, asked God to forgive his crucifiers, and made arrangements for his mother's maintenance. Finally, he raised a cry of triumph, "It is finished."

In the same way, in our witness for Christ today, we should seek to present Christ's death not as a defeat or a great tragedy but as a triumph.

The reign of Christ. The reign of the exalted Christ, climaxing in the consummation when he will "restore" all things (cf. Matt. 17:11; Acts 3:21), was a regular feature of the apostolic *kerygma*. In the Roman empire, the famous affirmation was "Caesar is Lord." When the Christians called Christ "Lord," they were affirming that he was their king. The allegiance of the Christians to Christ was soon to be severely tested by the authorities—first in Jerusalem and finally in Rome itself. Belief in Christ's sovereignty must have done much to sustain these believers as they faced the terror of opposition from their rulers. Interestingly, the first time they faced opposition, their prayer was an extended meditation on the sovereignty of God (Acts 4:24–28). This sovereign reign of Christ must be emphasized in our evangelism today too.

The personal appeal. An important feature of Peter's message was its personal appeal. Peter did not hesitate to bring about conviction of personal sin. He reminded the people of their involvement in killing Christ (vv. 23, 36). This message caused the people to be "cut to the heart" and elicited the response, "Brothers, what shall we do?" (v. 37). Peter called on them to repent and be baptized, so that they might receive forgiveness of sins (v. 38). The apostle then combined pleading and warning in his statement: "Save yourselves from this corrupt generation" (v. 40). There was no skirting over the fact of sin in the lives of the hearers. The chart on "Evangelistic Preaching in Acts" in the Introduction shows that this emphasis on sin and repentance was a consistent theme in the evangelism of the early church. It must be so today too.

Peter's transformation. Finally on principles we glean from the Pentecost story, I turn to the amazing transformation that took place in Peter's life. When Peter had been warned of impending temptation, he felt confident of his ability to be faithful to Christ (Mark 14:27–29). But at the crucial moment of trial, not only did he deny his Master, he even began to curse and swear (Matt. 26:69–75). Yet Jesus went out of his way to restore this disciple, who was grief-stricken over denying his Master. Once restored, he gave himself to prayer in anticipation of the promised blessing of the fullness of the Spirit. Once that came to him, he was irrepressible, and God used him as the human instrument to usher in the great era of the church. This pattern has been repeated over and over in the history of the church and is still awaiting repetition.

BEGINNING WITH THE **questions of our audience.** Unlike the New Testament evangelists, who invariably started their messages with questions that their audience was asking, evangelists and witnesses today sometimes start by talking about questions they feel people should be asking. True, it is our responsibility to lead people to come face-to-face with questions they should be asking. But if we start with those questions, they may never listen to us, because they may not be interested in them. We must start with questions that they are really asking; then, having won their attention in this way, we can lead them to the questions they should be asking.

Finding people's questions and making the connection between them and the gospel is an art we must develop. It helps to study and meditate over the issues people face and to pray about them, yearning to see them come into line with God's thinking. An even more important key is our personal ministry, which enables us to interact with people and thus informs our minds about how best to reach them. Failure may be an important aid here. We ask, "Why couldn't I get through to him or her?" Such questioning teaches us a lot about how to minister to people. We can then extend to our public ministries what we have learned through personal ministry.

Using the life of Christ in evangelism. For many years in this century, evangelicals were reluctant to use the life of Christ in evangelism. This was in part a reaction to the liberal view that the heart of the Christian gospel was the example of Christ and not the salvation won through the atoning, substitutionary death of Christ. Evangelicals used Paul and the theological statements of John as their basic sources of evangelistic material. They were afraid of presenting the example of Jesus lest people think that salvation is achieved through following his example (i.e., salvation by works). Recently, however, there has been a change in this—a change that is surely in keeping with the Scriptures—for, as we have shown above, the Scriptures themselves use the life of Christ in evangelism.[28]

The life of Christ offers a great evangelistic appeal to our generation. This is evidenced by the unprecedented effectiveness of the film *Jesus*, distributed worldwide by Campus Crusade for Christ. I have seen Buddhists stand in the open air through the entire three hours that it takes to screen this film. Some refused to leave even when it started to rain. We are living in an age when many are disillusioned with their leaders and have come to believe that it is impossible for good people, people of integrity, to succeed in life. Most good people appear to them as unsuccessful in life and they wonder whether goodness and success can be combined. To this generation, groping to find a model of success that does not contradict the voice of conscience, we present Jesus: the good person, the perfect person, who started a movement so effective that in three centuries the mighty Roman empire had bowed its knee to him.[29]

Some who may be first repelled by the idea of a blood sacrifice needed to win the salvation of humanity (e.g., Buddhists, who oppose any form of killing animals) may become receptive to the gospel by observing the life of

---

28. It is interesting, however, that the records of Paul's speeches in Acts do not mention his using the life of Christ. In his letters, however, are places where key theological implications are drawn from the life and example of Jesus (e.g., Phil. 2:1–11; 1 Tim. 3:16).

29. On this see my *Supremacy*, 58–65.

Jesus. My wife and I have worked with Buddhists, who were first attracted to the Christian way because of the life of Jesus and who later came to understand the liberating good news of salvation from sin through his atoning death. Missiologists have observed that Muslims too, who object to the idea of a prophet like Jesus being crucified, are immensely attracted to his life.[30] Bishop Stephen Neill has pointed out that recent Muslim biographies of the prophet Mohammed have toned down some of his less agreeable features and presented him as a more Christ-like figure. This, says Neill, is evidence of the appeal of Christ's life to Muslims.[31] Thus, the life of Christ can, and in fact does, open those resistant to the gospel to hear and accept other aspects of the gospel to which they may have first been resistant.

The value of accreditation today. Acts gives a high place to the accreditation of the gospel through eyewitnesses of the events surrounding Christ's life. This truth is particularly important today because many view Christianity only in subjective terms—in terms of the wonderful experience they have had (see comments on 1:1–8). A subjective experience of the risen Christ is an important key to understanding the nature of Christianity, and it has sometimes been neglected by evangelicals who regarded themselves as being very orthodox in their theology. Such an attitude is a betrayal of biblical Christianity. But so is an attitude that emphasizes experience so much that it neglects the objective facts of the Christian message.

Paul discussed practical experience extensively in 1 Corinthians. But when he came to describing the essence of the gospel he had preached to the Corinthians (1 Cor. 15:1)—the gospel by which they were saved (15:2)—he listed the sequence of events surrounding the death and resurrection of Jesus (15:3–7). He particularly stressed the appearances of the risen Christ (15:5–7). This was so important because, as he stated later, if Christ has not been raised, "our preaching is useless and so is your faith . . . your faith is futile; you are still in your sins" (15:14, 17).

No one can deny that many of the subjective experiences of Christianity have been duplicated by others. Recently we have seen Muslims, Jews, and New Agers all claiming to have had "born again" experiences. Moreover, Christians can go through dark periods, implying perhaps that non-Christians are better off than them. But our faith is not founded on our experiences; it is founded on the rock-solid facts of what Jesus has done on our behalf.

Craig Blomberg has said that "no religion stands or falls with a claim

---

30. See ibid., 79–80.

31. Stephen Neill, *Crises of Belief* (London: Hodder and Stoughton, 1984), 90 (North American Edition, *Christian Faith and Other Faiths* [Downers Grove, Ill.: InterVarsity Press]).

about the resurrection of its founder in the way that Christianity does."[32] Yet it may be true that not many people today come to Christ primarily because of a conviction about the objective truths of the gospel. In my informal surveys, I have discovered that most people come to Christ attracted by the fact that he meets their felt needs—things like Christ's love and concern for individuals (especially seen in his dying for them on the cross), his power to heal, his ability to take away guilt, his comfort, and his control of the future. Only occasionally do I hear people saying that it was the resurrection that attracted them.

Consequently, the resurrection is not popular in evangelistic preaching today. It seems so out of step with the way people are thinking that we are tempted to leave it out of our presentation and to bring it up only later on, in the follow-up process. A quick look at some of the popular evangelistic counselor training materials in use today or the basic guides to helping people make a decision for Christ reveals that the resurrection does not have the important place it should have in our evangelism.

When people come to Christ in search of an answer to a felt need, they will be on an unstable footing unless they are quickly grounded in the truths of the gospel. They will find that Christ may not immediately answer a felt need the way they expect him to. He may not heal them at once from sickness or remove a difficult problem. I have seen recent converts to Christianity wilt under this strain and, in their desperation, go to other sources of help, such as medicine men, spirit channelers, mediums, astrologers, devil dancers, and shrines to supposedly powerful gods and saints. After twenty-one years of evangelistic ministry with non-Christians, I have come to the conclusion that most people *come* to Christ in order to have a felt need met, but they *stay* with Christ because they have come to believe that the gospel is true.

For these reasons, it would be wise for us to follow the example of the evangelists in Acts, who did not shrink from using the resurrection as the proof of the validity of their message (17:31) even though it met with strong negative reactions (as in Athens, 17:32). We must also remember that there are still people who find the evidence for the resurrection so compelling that they seek to know what their response to it should be. Of course, this also brings to us the challenge of presenting this message in a suitable way.

This emphasis on the facts of the gospel is particularly important in our pluralistic, postmodern age, where truth is viewed as something subjective. Pluralism denies that there is such a thing as absolute truth. Instead, truth is what people have discovered through their experience. It cannot be what

---

32. Craig Blomberg, *The Historical Reliability of the Gospels* (Downers Grove, Ill.: InterVarsity, 1987), 77.

Christians claim, something once-for-all revealed through certain saving acts of God. Hinduism is a pluralistic religion and in many ways the mother of the New Age movement, which is one of the most visible forms of modern-day pluralism. In Hinduism religious stories are vehicles that carry religious principles. To many devoted followers of Krishna it does not matter whether Krishna lived or not.

Bishop Lesslie Newbigin, formerly a missionary in India, mentions a conversation he had with a devout and learned teacher of the Hindu missionary movement, the Ramakrishna Mission. "I have never forgotten the astonishment with which [this Hindu] regarded me when he discovered that I was prepared to rest my whole faith as a Christian upon the substantial record concerning Jesus in the New Testament." To this person "it seemed axiomatic that such vital matters of religious truth could not be allowed to depend upon the accidents of history."[33]

Since pluralism views truth as subjective, it can take good points from all religions without attributing absolute uniqueness to any particular one. This is how the pluralist Mahatma Gandhi was able to hold Christ in such high esteem while rejecting his claims to uniqueness. He took from the life and teachings of Jesus those principles he found useful without bothering about those features of the Gospel records that seemed to suggest that Christ was unique. He downplayed the historical importance of the Gospels and therefore rejected those features he found offensive.[34]

But the Gospels give no room for such an approach to the life of Christ. They were written as history; they present Jesus as supreme, as the unique bearer of absolute truth, who won the salvation of humankind through his death and resurrection. Yet because pluralists regard the Gospels as subjective reflections of the early Christians rather than historical documents, they can reject their absolute claims as subjective musings, arising out of the experiences of people who had come to view Christ as their Lord. This is why one of the most important points in response to pluralism is the evidence for the objective historicity of the Gospels.[35]

The death of Christ as a victory. Just as the death of Christ was a stumbling block to the Jews in the first century, it remains a stumbling block to many today. We live in an age where the appearance of strength and of being in control is important. Leaders, especially candidates for political office, hire specialists to help project an image that they are "on top of things."

---

33. Lesslie Newbigin, *The Finality of Christ* (Richmond: John Knox, 1969), 50.

34. For Gandhi's views on Christ, see M. M. Thomas, *The Acknowledged Christ of the Indian Renaissance* (London: SCM, 1969), 193–236.

35. On this issue see my *Supremacy*, 21–24, 85–98.

Thus, we should not be surprised if contemporary people find repulsive the idea that the person who claims our allegiance meekly submitted to so ignoble a fate as death by crucifixion. As mentioned earlier, the idea of a crucified Messiah was a contradiction in terms to the Jews. This is why there is such a strong emphasis in the speeches of Acts and in the Gospels on the death of Christ as planned by God and as a victory rather than the unexpected defeat of a good man.[36]

The Muslims respond to the idea of Christ's death on the cross in a manner similar to the Jews and find it impossible to accept that one they regard as a prophet died in this way. So they propose alternate explanations to the story of the cross. A prominent Buddhist writer in Sri Lanka once told me that he regarded Christ as a failure because he was defeated by the very wickedness he sought to combat.

But Jesus was no weakling as he went to the cross. Rather, he manifested incredible strength, which people today try so hard to have. Using professionals to make one look good does not enable someone to feel good, for deep inside is that gnawing sense of insecurity that one cannot adequately face the challenges of life, especially the challenge of death. But in Jesus we see a man who was everything a leader wishes to be—one who did not fear any problem and had the strength to face any eventuality. Are not such people the happiest on earth—those who do not fear either life or death? Thus, Jesus' death can be a potent evangelistic tool today. The more one studies him, the more one sees he was not a weakling but a source of great strength.

Furthermore, Jesus died his cruel death out of a commitment to us. In our selfish world, people suffer much from the effects of people who have broken their trust, who forsook them when the going got tough. By contrast, we proclaim the truth that the love of Christ for us exceeds our highest imaginations.

Let's remember too what the cross achieved—the salvation of the world. Jesus was no failure, for he founded what can properly be called the most influential organization in the history of the world—the church. And the church has as its symbol, a cross! The favorite name given to the triumphant Christ in heaven in Revelation is Lamb,[37] indicating that his triumph was achieved when he was slain. Indeed, as Paul says, "having disarmed the powers and authorities, he made a public spectacle of them, triumphing over them by the cross" (Col. 2:15). We must remove misconceptions about the cross and show people what the cross really means—the greatest triumph in the history of the human race.

---

36. On this see my *Supremacy*, 149–53.
37. "Lamb" is used 28 times of Christ in Revelation.

Proclaiming the reign of Christ today. One of the major obstacles that many have to becoming a Christian is the fear of reprisals—from other gods, from religious leaders, from government authorities, and from family, community and friends. They fear curses, persecution, ridicule, and discrimination. I know many Buddhists and Hindus who are convinced of the truthfulness of Christianity but who will not become Christians because of such fears. We need to show them that the only one really to fear is the supreme Lord of the universe, who will conquer all rebellion against him. The safest thing to do is to align ourselves with him.

When the church was asked not to preach in the name of Christ, they concluded that even though the authorities were able temporarily to show their power, ultimately they would have to bow to the will of God (cf. 4:25–28). Far too many people are so afraid of present threats that they ignore eternal threats. But we must show the world that the only one we ought to fear is the one who has the keys to eternity (Luke 12:4). We must proclaim the sovereign reign of Christ.

The reign of Christ is another feature of the evangelistic message that evangelicals have neglected in this century. This may again be because it seemed to take away from the emphasis on grace and because liberals used it in a way that devalued grace. Giving postmillennialism an unbiblical twist, liberal theologians anticipated that human progress would cause the evolution of an ideal society, when Christ's rule would be fully realized. This hope was, of course, discredited by two devastating world wars.[38] It is our hope that the idea of Christ as king will now make its return to the basic gospel proclaimed by the evangelical church.

Making the personal appeal today. Peter did not skirt the issue of the personal responsibility of his audience. He accused them of sin and called them to repent. There is some discussion today about whether it is essential to talk about sin in every evangelistic setting. Some feel that the opportunity to be heard will be lost if they make strong statements about sin. When John Wesley went to an area, he had a strategy of preaching "the law" so as to bring about the conviction of sin before emphasizing the gospel. "At our first beginning to preach at any place, after a general declaration of the love of God to sinners and his willingness that they should be saved, to preach the law in the strongest, the closest, the most searching manner possible; only

---

38. Classic statements of the liberal position are found in Albrecht Ritschl, *The Christian Doctrine of Justification and Reconciliation* (1870–1874; trans. reprinted by Clifton, N.J.: Reference Book, 1966), and Adolf von Harnack, *What Is Christianity?* (London: Ernst Benn, 1958 reprint). For a recent analysis of this approach, see Peter Toon, *The End of Liberal Theology: Contemporary Challenges to Evangelical Orthodoxy* (Wheaton: Crossway, 1995).

intermixing the gospel here and there, and showing it, as it were, afar off."[39] Once people had been convicted of sin through the preaching of law, he went on to emphasize grace.

This method is disputed today. Many prefer to hold back any emphasis on sin until the person's interest has been won. It is therefore possible that sin will not be even mentioned in the public meetings of some ministries today. It is true, of course, that one must be sensitive to one's audience and adapt the unchanging message to it. But in so doing, we must ensure that those who come under the influence of any evangelistic ministry must at some time be confronted with the seriousness of sin and its consequences. We should not ask one to accept Christ as Savior until he or she has been told that this step involves repenting from sin, and that salvation is primarily salvation *from sin*. Thus, the attempt to bring conviction about sin, to warn about judgment, and to call people to repentance ought to be standard elements today, as they were in Acts.[40]

Jesus did not fear losing his audience by his hard sayings. In fact, he indicated that sometimes his teaching in parables was intended to close the minds of some while opening the minds of others (Mark 4:10–12). This sharp edge in our preaching will help people to realize that when they come to Christ, they are leaving sin behind and beginning a new life—one that includes a new lifestyle. If this is not clear, coming to Christ will, for many, not be the radical turnaround that the Bible states that it is. Unfortunately, there are indications that many members of evangelical churches today have not understood Christianity in this way.

A. Skevington Wood writes, in a study of John Wesley's message, "Christianity is optimistic about grace, but pessimistic about human nature." Such statements may not sit well with the way many think today. But unless we emphasize both features, we will seriously misrepresent the gospel and proclaim an anemic brand of Christianity.[41] So, while we remain sensitive to felt needs in our preaching as described earlier, we also remain alert to warn people of the seriousness of sin.

While there was an appeal to personal sin in Peter's message, there was also an appeal to the personal benefits of salvation: forgiveness of sins, the experience of the Holy Spirit, and a promise that extends to one's children as personal blessings that come with the gospel. The bulk of Peter's message, of course, argued for the validity of the Christian gospel. But from that

---

39. From John Wesley, *Letters*, (London, 1931), 3:82. Quoted in A. Skevington Wood, *John Wesley: The Burning Heart* (Grand Rapids: Eerdmans, 1967), 242.
40. See 2:23, 36–38, 40; 3:13–15, 19, 23, 26; 10:42–43; 13:40–42; 14:15; 17:30–31.
41. Wood, *John Wesley: The Burning Heart*, 230.

foundation arose an offer of the personal blessings of salvation. Here is the biblical combination again—objective facts that give the foundation for blessed subjective experiences (see comments on 1:1–8).

The gospel is not something simply to be discussed. It is a message that demands a personal response, and we must always work towards provoking such a response, even if it means warning people and pleading with them (v. 40).

Transformed servants of God. Stories like that of Peter's transformation have been repeated over and over in the history of the church. In 1935 Blasio Kigosi, a schoolteacher in Rwanda, Central Africa, was deeply discouraged by the lack of life in the church and the powerlessness of his own experience. He followed the example of the first Christians and closed himself for a week of prayer and fasting in his little cottage. He emerged a changed man. He confessed his sins to those whom he had wronged, including his wife and children. He proclaimed the gospel in the school where he taught, and revival broke out there, resulting in students and teachers being transformed. They were called *abaka*, meaning people on fire. Shortly after that, Blasio was invited to Uganda, to share with the leaders of the Anglican church there. As he called leaders to repentance, the fire of the Spirit descended again on the place, with similar results as in Rwanda.

Several days later, Blasio died of fever. His ministry lasted only a few weeks, but the revival fires sparked through his ministry swept throughout East Africa and continue to the present. Hundreds of thousands of lives have been transformed over the decades through this mighty East African revival. It all began with a discouraged Christian setting himself apart to seek the fullness of God's Spirit.[42]

---

42. Shenk and Stutzman, *Creating Communities*, 31–32.

Acts 2:42–47

🝆

THEY DEVOTED themselves to the apostles' teaching and to the fellowship, to the breaking of bread and to prayer. 43Everyone was filled with awe, and many wonders and miraculous signs were done by the apostles. 44All the believers were together and had everything in common. 45Selling their possessions and goods, they gave to anyone as he had need. 46Every day they continued to meet together in the temple courts. They broke bread in their homes and ate together with glad and sincere hearts, 47praising God and enjoying the favor of all the people. And the Lord added to their number daily those who were being saved.

 THE DESCRIPTION OF the events on the day of Pentecost ended with the spectacular statement that three thousand people were "added to their number" (2:41)—the result of the first evangelistic message of what may be called the era of the Spirit. Verses 42–47 describe the community life of the young church. We are first told that "they [presumably the new converts] devoted themselves" to what the church provided for their follow-through care (v. 42). Next is a description of the miraculous ministry of the apostles (v. 43), followed by a more general description of the community life of the whole church ("all the believers," vv. 43–47).

Follow-Through Care of the Converts (2:42)

THERE WAS IMMEDIATE, regular follow-through[1] care of the first converts in the early church. The verbal expression "they were devoting themselves to" (lit. trans.) covers four activities. "Devoting" (*proskartereo*) is the same word as is used in connection with the persistent devotion of the disciples to prayer in 1:14 (translated "constantly" there). This word occurs six times in Acts.[2] "The meaning is that they continued in faithful adherence to the newly formed

---

1. I prefer the expression "follow-through care" to the more commonly used "follow-up," as the former stresses that this is a personal ministry rather than a mechanical process dependent on materials and techniques.

2. See 1:14; 2:42, 44; 6:4; 8:13; 10:7.

community."[3] The word is used often with the idea of "persisting obstinately in" something—a meaning that is appropriate here.[4]

(1) The first feature is "the apostles' teaching." Considering that Jesus spent so much time teaching the crowds and his inner band of followers, it is not surprising that teaching had an important place in the early church. Jesus himself instructed his disciples to teach obedience to those who had been baptized (Matt. 28:20). What is surprising is that, while Luke's Gospel contains many descriptions of the content of Jesus' teaching, nowhere in Acts are we given a clear description of what was taught to the new believers. From the Gospels and Acts we can say that it likely included explanations of the nature of salvation, the person and work of Christ, the commands of Christ and other features of the Christian life, and the message of the kingdom.[5]

(2) The word *koinonia,* which Luke uses for "fellowship," is a favorite word of Paul's, though this is the only time it appears in Luke's writings.[6] Its basic idea is sharing, but it is used also to denote intimacy and fellowship in general. It is used for "the fellowship of the Holy Spirit" (2 Cor. 13:14) and also for our participation in the blood and body of Christ when we partake of the cup and the bread at the Lord's Supper (1 Cor. 10:16). Paul speaks of the pillars of the Jerusalem church giving him and Barnabas "the right hand of fellowship" (Gal. 2:9) as a sign of their accepting them as legitimate servants of Christ. In secular Greek the word was used for the sharing of possessions (cf. 2 Cor. 9:13). We should be cautious about using different occurrences of any word in the Bible to arrive at a general meaning of it, as words take different meanings according to the context in which they appear. But the nineteen occurrences of *koinonia* in the New Testament suggest that the church used this word for the unique sharing that Christians have with God and with other Christians.

(3) "The breaking of bread" has a definite article before bread, causing some to render it "the breaking of the loaf" (see also Luke 24:35) and to distinguish it from "the breaking of bread" (without the definite article) in verse 46 (see also 20:7, 11; 27:35; 1 Cor. 10:16; 11:23–24). They claim that verse 42 refers to the Lord's Supper while verse 46 refers to ordinary meals.[7] But

---

3. Barrett, *Acts,* 164.

4. Ibid., 162.

5. For a summary of the possible content of teaching in the early church, see Harrison, *Apostolic Church,* 165. Harrison's material is from C. H. Dodd, *Gospel and Law: The Relation of Faith and Ethics in Early Christianity* (New York: Columbia Univ. Press, 1951), 252.

6. Some have claimed that this word was coined or given a completely new meaning by the church. But this is incorrect. This word appeared commonly in the classical writings to refer to, among other things, a close bond among people. See *NIDNTT,* 1:639–41.

7. Harrison, *Acts,* 74.

this difference may not be so significant. This phrase "was a technical expression for the Jewish custom of pronouncing the blessing and breaking and distributing the bread at the beginning of a meal."[8] Others maintain that this phrase in Acts refers to the daily fellowship meals, which were separate from the continuation of the Last Supper (which, they claim, was first observed only annually at Passover time). These meals are said to have developed into the Agape (or love feast) and only later were they incorporated with the Last Supper to become the Lord's Supper (see 1 Cor. 11:20–21).[9]

We prefer the view of scholars like Bruce, Murray Harris, Polhill, and Marshall, that the phrase "breaking of bread" in Acts refers to the Lord's Supper, which was probably part of the ordinary fellowship meals as described in 1 Corinthians 11. As Paul's traveling companion, Luke would have been aware of this practice in the churches of celebrating the Lord's Supper and having fellowship meals together. It would have been confusing to his readers if he mentioned the breaking of bread without meaning the Lord's Supper.

Bruce, quoting Rudolph Otto,[10] has argued that it is the symbolism of broken bread in connection with the breaking of Christ's body in death that makes this action significant. This is why there are at least twelve references to the breaking of bread in the New Testament.[11] Note also that the other three features mentioned in 2:42—teaching, fellowship, and prayer—are spiritual activities, which suggests that this fourth one—the breaking of bread—is also a spiritual activity (i.e., the Lord's Supper).

(4) The final feature in verse 42 literally reads, "and to the prayers" (see NRSV). The phrase could refer to prayer during the set times of the Jerusalem temple, which the disciples attended (3:1; cf. 2:46; 22:17). But there were also times when they prayed on their own (1:24; 4:24; 12:12). The prayer life of the early church was founded on the teaching about prayer in the Old Testament as practiced by the Jews of the time. Did the early Christians use the Lord's Prayer during these times? We cannot be sure. We do know that by

---

8. Murray J. Harris, "Baptism and the Lord's Supper," In God's Community: Essays on the Church and Its Ministry, ed. David J. Ellis and W. Ward Gasque (Wheaton: Harold Shaw, 1978), 21.

9. G. F. Hawthorne, "Lord's Supper," ZPEB, 3:978–86; E. Earle Ellis, The Gospel of Luke, New Century Bible (London: Marshall, Morgan and Scott, 1974), 250; Oscar Cullmann, Early Christian Worship (London: SCM, 1966), reprinted in Robert E. Webber, ed., The Complete Library of Christian Worship; vol. 1, The Biblical Foundations of Christian Worship (Peabody: Hendrickson, 1993), 318–19.

10. Bruce, Acts, NICNT, 73, quoting R. Otto, The Kingdom of God and the Son of Man (London, 1943), 315.

11. See Matt. 26:26; Mark 14:22; Luke 22:19; 24:30, 35; Acts 2:42, 46; 20:7, 11; 27:35; 1 Cor. 10:16; 11:23–24.

the second century they were using it. In fact, the manual of church life called the Didache[12] recommended the use of the Lord's Prayer three times a day.[13]

The great contribution of Jesus to the Christian understanding of prayer was his intimacy with God, whom he called "Father" (Mark 14:36). He taught his disciples also to share this intimacy, and even the Gentile Christians used the characteristic Aramaic word that he used, "Abba," when addressing God (Rom. 8:15; Gal. 4:6). This new understanding of intimacy with God would have been actualized in their experience through the coming of the Holy Spirit at Pentecost. The fourth-century Bible expositor John Chrysostom defined prayer as "conversation with God."[14]

The Community Life of the Church (2:43–47)

THE DESCRIPTION OF follow-through care of the new converts gives way to a description of the community life of the whole church. This is the first of at least eight summaries found in Acts that describe that life and say how it led to the growth of the word of God or of the church.[15]

First we are told about the "awe" that everyone was filled with and about the ministry of miracles performed by the apostles (v. 43). "Everyone" here could refer both to the believers and to outsiders who saw and heard what was happening in the church. These people could sense that God was at work. The miracles could also be signs to the Jews that the new age they were looking for was dawning. In the book of Acts such signs are closely connected to the evangelistic ministry of the church.[16]

The practice of sharing possessions in the early church (2:44–45) will be discussed in more detail in our study of 4:32–35. Property was sold according to need; the imperfect tense in the verbs here suggests this very thing. Thus, we do not have here a case of enforced sharing, as in communism. Nor was it a once-for-all disposal of all private property in the church. The important point is that the fellowship touched the pocketbook too!

Next we are told that the early believers went to the temple (v. 46a), just as Jesus did. They tried to remain within the Jewish fold; that attitude to

---

12. The Didache is variously dated from somewhere in the end of the first century to the late second century.

13. Didache, 8:2–3; in Apostolic Fathers, 259.

14. From his Homilies in Genesis (30:5); quoted in Everett Ferguson, "Prayer," Encyclopedia of Early Christianity, ed. Everett Ferguson (New York and London: Garland, 1990), 744.

15. See 4:32–35; 5:12–16; 6:7; 9:31; 12:24; 16:5; 19:20.

16. For evidence for this see Gary S. Greig and Kevin S. Springer, ed., The Kingdom and the Power (Ventura, Calif.: Regal, 1993), 359–92.

Judaism prevailed among Christians in Judea throughout the New Testament era (see 21:26). Paul generally first went to the Jewish synagogue when his mission took him to a Gentile city. Stephen, however, attempted to show that the temple was no longer necessary (ch. 7). Soon the church was to declare that it was not necessary for a Gentile convert to become a Jew (ch. 15).

According to what we argued above, the breaking of bread mentioned in verse 46 included both the Lord's Supper and fellowship meals. That there were such meals in the first church is confirmed by the statement, "they ... ate together with glad and sincere hearts." House fellowships were common in the early church; later they developed into "house churches." In Corinth there seem to have been times when the whole church met "probably ... in the large house of one of the wealthy Christians in the city."[17] At this time unbelievers were also present (1 Cor. 14:23). But there were also smaller churches that met, for example, in the house of Aquila and Prisca (1 Cor. 16:19).[18]

Eating together "with glad ... hearts" can be an important expression of fellowship in any culture, and in the early church it had an important place (v. 46b). The believers also had "sincere hearts" when they met. The word translated "sincere" can mean single-minded devotion, the absence of pretense, or simplicity and generosity. Bruce thinks the context favors generosity.[19] While it is difficult to decide on the exact meaning here, we can confidently say that it signifies an openhearted attitude, where there is no pretense and performance in the way the believers behaved. The joy came from the heart, because people were not trying to impress anyone. They had developed an attitude toward each other that enabled them to truly enjoy each other.

When God's people come together and enjoy fellowship, "praising God" is the natural result (v. 47a). True fellowship focuses on God and helps people to remember the good things he has done, which, in turn, causes praise. Such fresh and powerful community life would win the admiration of people outside the church. And this is what happened in Jerusalem too, for the early Christians enjoyed "the favor of all the people" during their first few weeks (v. 47a).

In the meantime the church grew numerically[20] (v. 47b). Luke never writes that these new conversions took place primarily through the preaching of the

---

17. David Prior, *The Message of 1 Corinthians*, BST (Downers Grove, Ill.: InterVarsity, 1985), 250.

18. See also Rom. 16:5; Col. 4:15; Philem. 2. It is interesting that the church era began in a home (Acts 2:2); that the first group of believers from the Gentile world met Christ in a home (10:27–48), and that in Corinth when the doors of the synagogue were closed to Paul and his team, they went to a house (18:7).

19. Bruce, *Acts: Greek Text,* 133.

20. In our discussion on 4:4 we will see the significance of numbers in terms of the results of evangelistic activity.

apostles. The favor that all the believers had among the people would have given opportunity for them to give the reason for the obvious transformation evident in their lives. Personal witness through word and life added to the impact of the miraculous signs and the public preaching and resulted in a comprehensive evangelistic outreach.

But it was "the Lord" who "added to their number." Ultimately, God is the evangelist.[21] Paul wrote, "I planted the seed, Apollos watered it, but God made it grow. So neither he who plants nor he who waters is anything, but only God, who makes things grow" (1 Cor. 3:6−7). God does use our efforts and our techniques, but we must ensure that we are in the place where he can use us and that our techniques are acceptable to him. As more people "were being saved," they were added to the Christian community.[22]

Bridging Contexts

COMPLETENESS IN COMMUNITY life. This passage gives us a picture of early Christian community life. Each of the things the new Christians practiced are given often in the Scriptures, especially in the New Testament letters, as essential aspects of the Christian living. For this reason we will use this passage to teach us about effective community life. The first thing that we see is the completeness of their community life. There was care of the new believers (v. 42), the various elements of worship (vv. 42, 47), evangelistic outreach (vv. 43, 47), caring for the material needs of each other (v. 45), oneness in spirit (v. 44), and joyful informal fellowship in homes (v. 46). Would that we too might have such comprehensiveness in our community life!

Immediate follow-through care. The immediate involvement of new believers in regular follow-through care (v. 42) reminds us of the importance of making plans for this when organizing an evangelistic program. Follow-through care is implied in the Great Commission, which, in Matthew, includes baptism and teaching (Matt. 28:19). We do not know whether the early church had made plans for follow-through care before the day of Pentecost. But they knew they had to do it, and the way they got down to it is an admirable example to us.

Christianity is community living. The follow-through care was done within the context of "the fellowship" (v. 42). In addition to being devoted to the Lord, fellowship is something Christians are devoted to (v. 42), even though

---

21. See David F. Wells, *God the Evangelist: How the Holy Spirit Works to Bring Men and Women to Faith* (Grand Rapids: Eerdmans, 1987).

22. Bruce, *Acts: Greek Text*, 133.

it has a lower level of authority over their lives. From what follows (v. 46) we can assume that the early believers met in different homes for the equivalent of what we call "growth groups," "cell groups," or "discipleship groups."

I still remember my surprise when, as a young volunteer in YFC, I read in the first "follow-up guide" we used that the most important thing in the first few days after conversion is fellowship with other believers. As a lover of the Bible and a firm believer in its primacy for faith and practice, I felt that the Bible should have been mentioned here rather than fellowship. But soon I learned that new believers usually get to learn the importance of the Bible through the fellowship. The Bible is a strange book to many new believers. When they see others who have reached out to them in love studying the Bible, teaching it, quoting it, applying it, and describing its importance for life, they realize that they themselves need to get down to a study of the Scriptures. In the fellowship they will also get a feel for how the Bible is studied. Soon they themselves become people who "correctly handle . . . the word of truth" (2 Tim. 2:15).

According to the Bible the entire Christian life, including spiritual growth, battling sin and Satan, and serving God, are intended to be done in community. The passages in Ephesians, for example, that describe these things are all in the plural, suggesting that we do them along with others. Unfortunately, we may miss that emphasis because the plural "you" that appears in Greek in Ephesians and elsewhere is not immediately evident in English Bibles. One key aspect of fellowship that helps us grow in the faith is spiritual accountability (implied in v. 44 but clearer in 4:32–5:11). Hebrews 10:24 describes such accountability: "Let us consider how we may spur one another on toward love and good deeds."

Nowhere is it stated that Christians should continue to meet daily as they did in the first days of the Jerusalem church (v. 46). Considering the responsibilities one has in family life and in witness and vocation in society, it may not be a good idea for Christians to have a program in church every day of the week. History has shown that usually at the start of a revival there are daily meetings. After that it tapers off into a less frequent but regular pattern. Certainly it is helpful for new believers to be with Christians daily until they are more stable in their faith.

Community life is an integral part of the basic Christian life because Christianity is by nature a community religion. Paul says, "In Christ we who are many form one body, and each member belongs to all the others" (Rom. 12:5). So we get together not only because it is helpful, but also because we are a vital part of the body of Christ. In the preface to one of his earliest collections of hymns that he compiled for the Methodists, John Wesley wrote, "The Gospel of Christ knows no religion but social; no holiness but social holiness."[23] The body of Christ is incomplete without us, and we are incomplete without the body of Christ. Community life is not an option for a Christian, but a basic aspect of Christianity.

Teaching. The first activity of follow-through care mentioned is "the apostles' teaching" (v. 42). Teaching was so important to the life of the church that when Paul gave Timothy a list of qualifications for elders, the only ability-related qualification mentioned was the ability to teach (1 Tim. 3:2). All the other qualifications had to do with the behavior, character, and reputation of the person.

The "apostles' teaching" would have been particularly important in the early church because of their special relationship to Christ and his promise to them that the Holy Spirit "will guide [them] into all truth . . . and . . . will tell [them] what is yet to come" (John 16:13). With time the church developed a comprehensive body of teaching, so that Paul told the Ephesian elders that he had given them "the whole will and purpose of God" (20:27).[24] At the end of his life he urged Timothy, "What you heard from me, keep as the pattern of sound teaching, with faith and love in Christ Jesus. Guard the good deposit that was entrusted to you" (2 Tim. 1:13–14). Later the church came to recognize that certain books with connections to the apostles best represented that "good deposit," and the canon of the New Testament came into being. The New Testament along with the Old Testament has become the basis for our teaching today. A key, then, for follow-through care today is to teach people the Bible.

The Lord's Supper as a means of follow-through care. The Lord's Supper is also mentioned among the basic things done with and for the new believers (v. 42). Most Christian traditions have come to understand the Lord's Supper as a means of edification for believers, though there are differences among churches about the details and extent of its value. Paul said that this meal is a proclamation of that which lies at the heart of the Christian gospel, the death of Christ (1 Cor. 11:26).

Does this suggest, then, that the Lord's Supper would be helpful in confirming new believers in the faith and helping them grow in grace? This is a provocative question, for new believers are often prevented from participating in the Lord's Supper until they are baptized and/or confirmed, which may take place several months after conversion. Should we then permit new Christians to participate in the Lord's Supper before baptism and/or confirmation in churches where these take place some time after conversion? This

---

23. "Social" here refers to Christian fellowship; John Wesley, "Preface," *Hymns and Sacred Poems* (1739).

24. Bruce's translation in *Acts,* NICNT, 391.

is difficult to determine from this passage alone since the believers were baptized soon after they repented and believed. But it seems clear that, according to the Bible, we are incorporated into the body of Christ when we exercise saving faith (see Eph. 2), and that the Lord's Supper is a characteristic activity of those belonging to the body of Christ (1 Cor. 10:17).

Prayer. We have already said how important prayer is to the life of the church. What verse 42 reminds us is that we must get people into the life of prayer soon so that it becomes natural to them. They must imbibe it into their lifestyle by participating in its vibrant use in the life of the church.

Are signs and wonders for today? Should we expect to see signs and wonders in our ministries today, just as people did in the apostolic age (v. 43)? Some feel that such activity ceased after the apostolic period.[25] Others feel that their importance diminished after the apostolic period. Still others, however, actively promote the use of signs and wonders today.[26] This is too complex a debate to enter into here. My view is that there is sufficient evidence in Acts to indicate that miraculous occurrences were an important part of the evangelistic and pastoral life of the church and that there is insufficient evidence for the view that they were intended to cease following this era.[27]

We would do well to heed D. A. Carson's reminder that we do not have evidence of Jesus' going somewhere specifically to hold a healing service.[28] We must also bear in mind, however, that the early church asked God in a time of crisis to act "to heal and perform miraculous signs and wonders" (4:30). These were God's confirmation of the message preached (14:3). Our conclusion is that ministries that express God's miraculous power are valid for today. But we should be careful about making that the primary function of any ministry, though individuals within a ministry may have this as their primary gift.

The importance of hospitality. Hospitality is a key theme in Luke-Acts. Acts manifests several types of hospitality, one of which—having Christians

---

25. The classic statement of this view is in Benjamin B. Warfield, *Counterfeit Miracles* (Edinburgh: Banner of Truth Trust, 1918, reprint 1972).

26. See John Wimber and Kevin Springer, *Power Evangelism* (San Fransisco: Harper and Row, 1986); idem, *Power Healing* (San Fransisco: Harper and Row, 1987).

27. For a comprehensive defense of the view that miracles are for today, see Gary Greig and Kevin Springer, *The Kingdom and the Power*; Jack Deere, *Surprised by the Power of the Spirit* (Grand Rapids: Zondervan, 1993). For the opposite viewpoint, see Thomas R. Edgar, *Satisfied by the Promise of the Spirit* (Grand Rapids: Kregel, 1996). For a study of four views on this issue, see Wayne Grudem, ed., *Are the Miraculous Gifts for Today: Four Views* (Grand Rapids: Zondervan, 1996).

28. D. A. Carson, "The Purpose of Signs and Wonders in the New Testament," *Power Religion: The Selling of the Evangelical Church?* ed. Michael Scott Horton (Chicago: Moody, 1992), 99.

over for food, fellowship, and worship—appears here (v. 46).[29] The risen Christ made himself known to his disciples and taught them at the meal table (Luke 24:35, 41–43; Acts 1:4). Once he himself prepared and served a meal to his disciples (John 21:9–14). And when he chose a symbol to help his followers remember his work of redemption, he turned to the supper motif (Luke 22:13–20). Christ's Last Supper was part of a festival meal; today, there is a meal-type fellowship that characterizes the celebration of the Lord's Supper.

In the post-ascension life of the church, we find references to the Upper Room (where the disciples were staying, 1:13) and to the house where they were on the day of Pentecost (2:2). Moreover, "*koinonia* at table becomes the socio-religious hallmark of the young Jerusalem church (2:42, 46)."[30] One scholar has named this first group of residential believers "the Lukan banquet community."[31] Mary the mother of John Mark opened her house for the fellowship (12:12–17). At the end of Acts, as at the start (1:4), we find two references to hospitality, this time by Paul the prisoner (28:17, 30–31). We know that later the church had fellowship meals that they called "love feasts" (Jude 12; cf. 2 Peter 2:13).

It is probable that the house was an evangelistic center too. The Bolivian theologian Mortimer Arias describes the habit of house fellowship in Acts as "centripetal mission or evangelization by hospitality." He argues that this is a factor in the proclamation of the gospel that we need to take far more seriously.[32] We know that in Corinth, when Paul was driven out of the synagogue, he went to the home of Titius Justus (Acts 18:7). We can assume that the houses where the evangelistic outreach took place became house churches. In fact, until the middle of the third century, Christians usually gathered in homes (Rom. 16:23; Col. 4:15; Philem. 2).[33] These were key centers of Christian fellowship, and they can be so today as well.

Sincerity, joy, and praise in fellowship. As mentioned above, the early Christians developed an attitude toward each other that enabled them to truly enjoy each other, especially when they met for meals (v. 46). The early church, of course, followed the example of Jesus, who enjoyed his meals so

---

29. For the other types see the index at the back of the book.

30. John Koenig, *New Testament Hospitality* (Philadelphia: Fortress, 1985), 89.

31. J. Navone, "The Lukan Banquet Community," *Bible Today* 51 (1970): 155–61; cited in ibid., 89.

32. Mortimer Arias, "Centripetal Mission or Evangelization by Hospitality," *Missiology: An International Review* 10 (1982): 69–81; cited in Koenig, *Hospitality,* 106.

33. On house churches see, Robert Banks, *Paul's Idea of Community: Early House Churches in Their Historical Setting* (Grand Rapids: Eerdmans, 1988); Del Birkey, *The House Church: A Model for Renewing the Church* (Scottdale, Pa.: Herald, 1988).

much that he was accused of being "a glutton and a drunkard" (Luke 7:34). He broke the stereotype of a religious person in whose presence others were not supposed to have fun. One of the keys to enabling this was sincerity, which gave rise to an openhearted fellowship. Today, too, we should encourage enjoyment in our fellowship groups.

In the house groups time was given for praise (v. 47). In a similar manner, praise should be constantly heard when we get together in our groups.

Can we also enjoy favor with outsiders? The early Christians also enjoyed the favor of the people outside the church (v. 47), which is often the case with a new work of God. Unfortunately, such favor does not always last for long, for those who admire the life of Christians soon come to realize the implications of their message. They realize they are being challenged to make a decision about adopting Christianity and rejecting their own cherished religion. Vested interests of some powerful groups become jeopardized. Thus, admiration is replaced by fear and opposition. This happened in Jerusalem especially as a result of the ministry of Stephen. Note 8:1: "On that day a great persecution broke out against the church at Jerusalem, and all except the apostles were scattered throughout Judea and Samaria."

However, in the midst of it all, the radiant testimonies of Christians will leave their mark, even with people hostile to Christianity. This is apparently the effect that James (the Just), the brother of Jesus, had on the people of Jerusalem. But he too was martyred in A.D. 62. Josephus writes that this verdict was not popular with the people. Later stories of uncertain accuracy speak eloquently of James's exceptional life of godliness.[34]

THE CHALLENGE OF **immediate follow-through care.** Experience in evangelistic ministry shows that during the first few days after a commitment has been made to Christ, Satan will do all he can to ensnare new believers into his traps. They will face doubts regarding what has happened to them and be tempted to sin, sometimes even succumbing to it. This will make them fear that they do not have the strength to make it spiritually. Then they will face persecution and ridicule. They will become discouraged over the behavior of other Christians, and sometimes even become discouraged with God since he does not seem to answer their prayers. They may get entangled in the cares and attractions of the world and may trip and fall. These and a host of other factors will challenge the com-

---

34. See F. F. Bruce, *Peter, Stephen, James and John: Studies in Non-Pauline Christianity* (Grand Rapids: Eerdmans, 1979), 114–19.

mitment they have made. Thus, like newborn babies, new believers need special care during the first few days of their spiritual life.

Usually, however, those involved in organizing a big evangelistic campaign are so drained of their energy at the end of it that they need some rest, and the follow-through process gets delayed. This can be disastrous to the lives of babes in Christ. For this reason it is important that plans for "neonatal care" be made before the birth of the babies and that this process of follow-through care occurs immediately after the evangelistic program. John Wesley considered this so important that he is reported to have said, "I determined not to strike in one place where I could not follow the blow." The organized system he developed to conserve the fruit is considered one of the secrets of the long-term effectiveness of the Wesleyan Revival.

Community living in an individualistic age. People today are so individualistic that the biblical idea of community seems strange to them. We live private lives without interference from others. We will open up certain segments of our lives to certain people because that is a necessary part of living in society. But that comes nowhere close to the biblical ideal of devoting ourselves to the fellowship (v. 42) and having "everything in common" (v. 44). If we have emotional problems, for example, we go to a professional therapist who is not part of our regular social contacts and who helps us in a detached manner. In this way we find solutions for our problems without having others invade our lives and disturb our privacy.

The idea of commitment to a community is alien in this culture, characterized by transient relationships. People change spouses readily when one relationship becomes undesirable and/or another becomes desirable. People regularly change jobs for advancement and convenience and often go to work for a competitor they once worked at overtaking. The idea of twenty- or thirty-year veterans in an institution is regarded as a relic from a past era. People move homes all the time so that the chances of being committed to a community is minimized. One unifying factor of a community is the teams that represent it in sports. But these sports teams often have players from outside who come not because of any commitment to the community but because of the attractiveness of the package of payments and benefits.

In earlier times residents of a neighborhood had to depend on each other in order to survive. Now such need is minimized so that sometimes no one even knows that a person who lived alone next door has died until there is obvious evidence of the death (such as mail and newspapers accumulated outside the house, or a foul smell emanating from it).

Yet we as human beings are communal beings. We cannot find real fulfillment in life unless our community life is meaningful. Therefore groups, both within and outside the church, that encourage strong community life often experience growth. I once expressed to an eminent British Christian sociologist, Alan Storkey, my sense of despair over the fact that people no longer seem to need the church. I told him that television and the availability of services for needs that the church once met has taken away from people the need for being deeply involved in a Christian community. He told me that we should view this as an opportunity facing the church. Life without community creates a deep void in people's lives, which the church can fill admirably if we would get down to truly practicing Christian community.

It is a well-established fact, for example, that many so-called psychological problems are solved best within the context of a caring community.[35] This type of community is also a great help in keeping Christians morally pure. The joy, enrichment, and security that come from a caring community outweigh by far the pain and inconvenience that come with getting close to people. So the time is ripe for Christians to present to the world a community that is radically different from the existing social structures of society.

In spite of this need for a prophetic presence, however, churches seem to be aping the prevailing structures in society rather than challenging them. Professionalism, not spiritual compatibility, governs the hiring practices of many Christian churches and groups. Much of the reflection on management and organizational life that is taking place in the church today uses as its basic material concepts derived from the business world, where the culture of individualism reigns. People change churches and groups with the same frequency evident in the rest of society. The rate of divorce in the Western church is not much different from the rest of society, and our churches in the East seem to be catching up with their counterparts in the West.

Many strategists within the church are asking for paradigm shifts in our organizational life. But the paradigms they recommend are primarily those found in the business world. We should rather be searching the Scriptures with an open mind, uncluttered by preconceived notions, to see whether we have lost some of its teachings on community life. The Scriptures are usually used today not to derive truth but to reinforce or illustrate truth derived from secular management studies.

Consider some of the essential differences between business ventures and the church. In business the philosophy of competitiveness clashes at many points with the Christian teaching regarding the oneness of all the body of Christ. The business model works through paid workers whereas the church is essentially a volunteer movement. The business model is driven by a profit motive whereas the church is driven by the empowering of the Spirit and by

---

35. See my *Reclaiming Friendship*, 146−48. Here I have drawn on Gary Collins, *How to Be People Helpers* (Santa Ana, Calif.: Vision House, 1976), 58−59.

a desire to see God glorified. In business the strong thrive ("the survival of the fittest") whereas in the church the weak are used not because of their natural ability but because of God's power.

I believe that there is much we can learn from the business world as those in it strive to achieve success in a world created by God. But we must always be restrained by the fact that there are major differences in the goals and the methods of these two spheres. If we do not remember that, our churches are going to be run like businesses. Thus, we urgently need to reexamine the principles governing our community life in light of what the Scriptures say about it. We must explore more fully the implications of the devotion to the fellowship that Christians practiced in the first century. The book of Acts is a great place to start such a study.

Desire for teaching as an evidence of conversion. The value of and challenges to a teaching ministry today are dealt with in other studies of this commentary.[36] Let me say here that openness to being fed by the Word is key evidence that one is truly regenerated. Many people come to Christ to have a felt need met because they hear that the God of the Christians is a prayer-answering God. In their eagerness to be blessed by this God, they go through the motions of "making a decision." Since the possibilities of prayer attracted them to Christ, they may give a high place to prayer. But how do we know that the seed of eternal life is germinating in them? If there is such a seed, it will hunger for the nourishment of the Word. Peter states this principle by using a metaphor from human life: "Like newborn babies, crave pure spiritual milk, so that by it you may grow up in your salvation" (1 Peter 2:2).

The Lord's Supper and follow-through care today. The Roman Catholic Church gave an interpretation of the Lord's Supper as a means of grace that was almost a means of salvation. In reaction the Protestants of the low church and evangelical traditions may have gone too far in discounting the significance of the Lord's Supper as a means of growth in the Christian life. While focusing on remembrance and thanksgiving, we may have ignored the power of its symbolism in helping us understand and internalize what really happened at Calvary. In reacting to an overemphasis on the presence of Christ in the elements (transubstantiation), we may have forgotten that Christ is indeed present at this communion meal in a special way (1 Cor. 10:16).

If the Lord's Supper is so important to our spiritual growth, should we not open it up for new believers? This is a problem because, unlike in the early church, new believers are usually not immediately baptized today. Many churches offer the Lord's Supper only to those who have expressed their solidarity with the people of God through baptism. But baptism is delayed until

---

36. See the studies on 1:1–8; 6:1–7; 17:1–15; 20:1–38.

suitable instruction has been given. Roland Allen, in his influential book *Missionary Methods: St. Paul's or Ours?* has demonstrated that Paul's strategy was to baptize people and introduce them to the Lord's Supper immediately after conversion. The bulk of the "teaching followed, it did not precede, baptism. For baptism, apparently, very little knowledge of Christian truth was required."[37]

Practices associated with the Lord's Supper are an intimate part of the heritage of many churches. Often these have emerged after much struggle and pain, and so churches are touchy about any changes being made in connection with them. But it may be worth reconsidering whether it is wise to delay the entry of new believers into the Lord's Table—up to as much as a year after conversion. In the early church the table was opened to converts immediately after conversion.

Another tradition worth reconsidering is that of infrequent celebration of the Lord's Supper. Some churches have it only two times a year. In some denominations this infrequency arose out of a lack, during their early years, of ordained people who could do the rounds of the different churches and give communion. Later that established the practice of the denomination for the Lord's Supper. This was clearly not the practice of the early church.

Ministering in the miraculous. The early Christians prayed for signs and wonders to accompany their ministry (4:30) for, as Acts shows, such signs won the attention of those uninterested in the gospel. As we seek to make evangelistic inroads into non-Christian groups, it is appropriate for us to pray that God will reveal himself in some unmistakable way. This does not mean that miracles should be confined only to the evangelistic setting. True, the miracles of Jesus had an evangelistic function in giving support to his claims.[38] But at other times he performed them because of his compassion.[39] Moreover, some miracles were also performed on believers.[40] The Gospels and Acts show that miracles did not necessarily trigger faith in everyone and that what was most important is that people heard the message of the gospel. But miracles also did help in opening people's minds to hear this good news.

The evangelistic value of a ministry of miracles is well expressed in the response of Sergius Paulus to Paul's ministry in Paphos. When he saw the power of God as Paul struck the false prophet Elymas with blindness, "he believed, for he was amazed at the teaching about the Lord" (Acts 13:12). The teaching about the Lord had been faithfully done; the miracle helped orient Sergius Paulus in the direction of accepting this teaching.

---

37. Roland Allen, *Missionary Methods: St. Paul's or Ours?* (Grand Rapids: Eerdmans, repr. 1962), 95 (see esp. 81–94).

38. See Matt. 11:2–5; Mark 2:8–11; John 10:37–38; 14:11; 20:30–31.

39. See Matt. 14:14; 15:32; 20:29–34; Mark 1:41.

40. Probably Matt. 8:14–15; Acts 9:36–41; 20:9–12.

The gospel facts must always have the supreme place in our ministries. The message communicated by miracles is by no means the total gospel. It proclaims some aspects about God: for example, that God is powerful and worthy of attention, and that he can get involved in people's lives. Miracles are not an essential norm for biblical evangelism. But they are a means commonly used by God. Unfortunately, today we have the situation of a sign-mania on the part of some Christians and a sign-phobia on the part of others.

We must always remember that God sovereignly gives gifts to his children. As a result, we must not demand that each minister of the gospel and each church have ministries that work in the miraculous realm. However, I think one reason why many do not see the miraculous in their ministries is that they simply do not have the faith to believe that God can use them in this way. Some prefer not to have these gifts, while others do not feel constrained to ask God to give such gifts. It may be true that the giving of these gifts is often linked to the openness of people to them. But we know of several people who received such gifts without ever wishing for them or asking for them. Our passion should be for having all that God wishes for us— nothing more, nothing less. Towards that end we pray.

Unfortunately, the abuses of "power ministry" today are many.[41] But that should not deter us from engaging in it. It is a practice modeled by the apostles in Acts. We should never fear to be biblical. Only when this is done in an unbiblical way do abuses arise.

House fellowships today. Today most growing churches have found house fellowships as an effective means of nurture and evangelism. Effective large churches (e.g., the Full Gospel Church in Seoul, Korea; new churches in South America) have found in the house fellowship the ideal place for nurture and intimate fellowship to grow. Many of us are aware of how the church in China thrived and grew through their house churches in what is numerically probably the largest church growth in this century—and that was at a time when meeting together was illegal. In the busy West and the urban areas of the world, where it is difficult for people to find time to come to church more than once a week, neighborhood fellowships meeting at times convenient to the members could begin to take a more and more significant role.

Informal fellowship like this takes away pretense and helps people to be themselves. This in turn opens the door to deep sharing. It also helps the many lonely people in today's competitive and fast-moving society to find a place where they are loved and accepted. The home is also a suitable place for evangelism because non-Christians who feel uneasy about entering a church may feel more at home in a friend's house. Home fellowships also give

---

41. On this see my *Supremacy*, 81–84.

people not gifted in public ministry an opportunity for effective ministry for the kingdom.

Yet today many Christians are reluctant to host others in their homes.[42] An American pastor, Donald Bubna, surveyed Christians to find reasons for this reluctance. The two main reasons he found were: (1) having guests frightens some prospective hosts, and (2) some felt their home furnishings were too modest or inadequate. Others said they were too busy, the expense of showing hospitality was too great, and the tension and exhaustion from getting the house cleaned and the food prepared was too much for them.[43]

Bubna suggests that the most common reasons for the reluctance to host others stem from pride. "To be ashamed of our furniture or afraid of serving an inadequate meal can best be described as pride." The same point is made by Karen Burton Mains, who writes, "True hospitality comes before pride."[44] It has "nothing to do with impressing people, but everything to do with making them feel welcome and wanted." Mrs. Mains is a pastor's wife, and many church activities were held in her home. For years it seemed as if she "did nothing but clean up after people." After each group left, she had to get the house back into shape so that it would be ready for the next group. Yet she was not a housekeeper by nature. Sometimes she delayed cleaning up the house if company was not expected. On one such day someone from the church came to visit her. The house was in a mess. Let Mrs. Mains tell what happened:

> Hospitality before pride . . . I reminded myself dismally. Determined, I welcomed the woman with warmth, invited her into the unsightly rooms and refused to embarrass her with apologies. I consciously let go of my pride. [The visitor's response amazed her.] "I used to think you were perfect," she said, "but now I think we can be friends."

This story is not intended to provide an excuse for keeping an untidy house. Rather, it is to show that the key to hospitality is not our performance as housekeepers and cooks but an openhearted friendship that makes people feel welcome and wanted. The fellowship is the main thing. The food is secondary, as Jesus tried to show Martha (Luke 10:38–42).

Sincerity, joy, and praise in fellowship. The importance of gladness and sincerity in Christian fellowship cannot be overestimated. As indicated above, Jesus himself set the precedent for this (see Luke 7:34). When the Creator

---

42. Much of what appears below is found in my *Leadership Lifestyle: A Study of 1 Timothy* (Wheaton: Tyndale, 1985), 69–71.

43. Donald Bubna, *Building People Through a Caring Sharing Fellowship* (Wheaton: Tyndale, 1978).

44. Karen Burton Mains, *Open Heart—Open Home* (Elgin, Ill.: David C. Cook, 1976).

came into the world, even though he came as a man of sorrows, he had a place for fun in his life, for he was the complete person, and fun has a place in human completeness. In our hedonistic world, it is so important to remember that God is the Creator of our capacity for pleasure. If so, this capacity can be completely satisfied only in his way. The "life . . . to the full" that Christ gives (John 10:10) involves the fulfillment of our capacity for pleasure as well. This involves enjoyment in community with gladness and sincerity (v. 46) in a way different to the unreal acting we see often. This acting may appear as pleasurable, but in reality it is hollow and hypocritical.

The entertainment industry works hard at catering to the capacity for pleasure in us. Unfortunately, much of the means they use violate our essential humanity in seeking to elicit pleasure through what the Bible regards as sinful.[45] When we violate our essential humanity, while we may get a temporary "kick" of pleasure, we will be left unfulfilled and empty. Today's church is challenged to demonstrate a holy, happy fellowship.

The evidence, however, is that even Christians have succumbed to the lure of sinful pleasure afforded by the world. Some find it difficult to sit through a beautiful movie because their minds have been numbed by repeated doses of sex and violence. More and more people are retreating into a private world of pleasure through the use of videos, cable TV, video games, and the Internet. But human beings are by nature gregarious. When people taste the beauty of joyous fellowship, they will be confronted with a more pleasurable source of joy than their private world of "media" pleasure. They will be encouraged to seek a better way.

How can we ensure that praise has a high place in the agenda of our small groups? The most important requirement is separating time for it. Some of the praise will be offered at specially set-aside times, using hymns and prayers. Then when people are given the opportunity to share testimonies of what God has done to them, praise will result.

Praise is a factor that lifts the spirits of people who live under pressure because of challenges they face in life. They come to an environment that focuses on God; they listen to testimonies and sing songs that remind them of eternal realities that do not change. They receive a lift so that they too can praise God. Praise is a discipline we must learn to cultivate when we meet. It is so easy to let the challenges the group faces and the study time to so fill the program of our small groups that we can neglect praise.

---

45. For graphic evidence of this see, Michael Medved, *Hollywood Versus America* (Grand Rapids: Zondervan, 1992).

Acts 3:1-26

ONE DAY PETER and John were going up to the temple at the time of prayer—at three in the afternoon. ²Now a man crippled from birth was being carried to the temple gate called Beautiful, where he was put every day to beg from those going into the temple courts. ³When he saw Peter and John about to enter, he asked them for money. ⁴Peter looked straight at him, as did John. Then Peter said, "Look at us!" ⁵So the man gave them his attention, expecting to get something from them.

⁶Then Peter said, "Silver or gold I do not have, but what I have I give you. In the name of Jesus Christ of Nazareth, walk." ⁷Taking him by the right hand, he helped him up, and instantly the man's feet and ankles became strong. ⁸He jumped to his feet and began to walk. Then he went with them into the temple courts, walking and jumping, and praising God. ⁹When all the people saw him walking and praising God, ¹⁰they recognized him as the same man who used to sit begging at the temple gate called Beautiful, and they were filled with wonder and amazement at what had happened to him.

¹¹While the beggar held on to Peter and John, all the people were astonished and came running to them in the place called Solomon's Colonnade. ¹²When Peter saw this, he said to them: "Men of Israel, why does this surprise you? Why do you stare at us as if by our own power or godliness we had made this man walk? ¹³The God of Abraham, Isaac and Jacob, the God of our fathers, has glorified his servant Jesus. You handed him over to be killed, and you disowned him before Pilate, though he had decided to let him go. ¹⁴You disowned the Holy and Righteous One and asked that a murderer be released to you. ¹⁵You killed the author of life, but God raised him from the dead. We are witnesses of this. ¹⁶By faith in the name of Jesus, this man whom you see and know was made strong. It is Jesus' name and the faith that comes through him that has given this complete healing to him, as you can all see.

¹⁷"Now, brothers, I know that you acted in ignorance, as did your leaders. ¹⁸But this is how God fulfilled what he had foretold through all the prophets, saying that his Christ would

suffer. ¹⁹Repent, then, and turn to God, so that your sins may be wiped out, that times of refreshing may come from the Lord, ²⁰and that he may send the Christ, who has been appointed for you—even Jesus. ²¹He must remain in heaven until the time comes for God to restore everything, as he promised long ago through his holy prophets. ²²For Moses said, 'The Lord your God will raise up for you a prophet like me from among your own people; you must listen to everything he tells you. ²³Anyone who does not listen to him will be completely cut off from among his people.'

²⁴"Indeed, all the prophets from Samuel on, as many as have spoken, have foretold these days. ²⁵And you are heirs of the prophets and of the covenant God made with your fathers. He said to Abraham, 'Through your offspring all peoples on earth will be blessed.' ²⁶When God raised up his servant, he sent him first to you to bless you by turning each of you from your wicked ways."

LUKE HAS JUST given a summary description of the community life of the young church (2:42–47). Included in that description was the fact that "many wonders and miraculous signs were done by the apostles" (2:43). Of these many miracles Luke mentions one that received much publicity and triggered a series of events involving serious opposition to the gospel. This story ends in 4:31 with the disciples' prayer in response to the decree banning evangelism.

The Lame Man Healed (3:1–10)

THE STORY BEGINS during one of the daily visits (2:46) that Christians made to the temple (3:1). This visit was at 3:00 P.M., one of the Jewish times of prayer (the other two being 9:00 A.M. and 12 noon). As was common at entrances to places of worship, a man crippled from birth was begging at the temple gate called Beautiful (v. 2).¹

Following his plea for money, "Peter looked straight at him, as did John" (v. 4). The reference to John alongside Peter, even though John plays no significant role in this story, has puzzled some commentators. Some suggest that the inclusion of John is an addition to the story, perhaps to provide two wit-

---

1. There is no unanimity about the identity of this gate. See the discussions in Williams, *Acts*, 66; Barrett, *Acts*, 179–80.

nesses for the trial before the Sanhedrin later on. But, as Howard Marshall points out, the appearance of both apostles in this episode is in keeping with the fact that Peter and John were associates and that the early Christians were in the habit of working in pairs.[2] The addition of John's name in verse 4, where it is almost an afterthought, may indicate that, though Peter was the prominent member of the team, John had an important role. Luke seems to alternate between the mention of both Peter and John and of Peter alone in this chapter.

Peter's memorable words to the beggar (v. 6) indicate that they were in touch with the power of Jesus. "The name of Jesus" signifies his authority here. The name in Semitic thought "expresses the very nature of [a person's] being. Hence the power of the person is present and available in the name of the person."[3] Marshall reminds us that "Jesus himself had no need to appeal to a higher authority such as the name of God."[4]

Peter's Speech (3:11–26)

THE EXUBERANT RESPONSE of the healed cripple gives prominence to the miracle, and that in turn becomes a launching pad for Peter's speech. Many features typical of evangelistic speeches to Jews in Acts appear here.

> Although both the Pentecost speech and the temple speech call to repentance, review the story of Jesus, and cite Scripture, they are complimentary rather than simply repetitive. Different aspects are emphasized and new perspectives are introduced, broadening the picture of Jesus' significance for the people of Jerusalem.[5]

The people's astonishment over a miraculous happening provides the launching pad for the speech. A new feature is Peter's serious effort to deflect glory from himself and John. He asks why the people are staring at them "as if by our own power or godliness we had made this man walk" (v. 12). Peter then refers to "the God of Abraham, Isaac and Jacob, the God of our fathers" (v. 13a)—a description relevant to his Jewish audience. The miracle is presented as glorifying the one they "handed . . . over to be killed" and "disowned" (vv. 13b–14).

Peter makes significant Christological statements in this speech. As at Pentecost, the "name" of Jesus receives emphasis; Acts 3–4 have eight references to it.[6] Longenecker sees this as significant because "the Name (*to onoma*)

---

2. Marshall, *Acts*, 87.
3. Longenecker, "Acts," 294.
4. Marshall, *Acts*, 88.
5. Tannehill, *Narrative Unity*, 58.
6. See 3:6, 16; 4:7, 10, 12, 17, 18, 30.

was a pious Jewish surrogate for God and connoted his divine presence and power."[7] The speech begins and ends with the expression of Jesus as God's "servant" (vv. 13, 26). This directs us back to the messianic servant of Yahweh in Isaiah 42–53. The Septuagint uses the same word (*pais*) in those passages. Jesus is also called "the Holy and Righteous One" (v. 14), "the author of life" (v. 15), and "a prophet like [Moses]" (v. 22, citing Deut. 18:15, 18–19). As at Pentecost, he is called "the Christ" (v. 20).

The death of Christ is again given as a fulfillment of prophecy (v. 18), and again God is said to have raised up Jesus (v. 15), with the apostles being witnesses of the resurrection (v. 15). Jesus is the one appointed or designated as their Messiah (v. 20; cf. 2:36). This reminds us of Romans 1:4: "who through the Spirit of holiness was declared with power to be the Son of God by his resurrection from the dead: Jesus Christ our Lord." The resurrection was something like an ordination of Christ, when he was confirmed on earth for who he really is.

Peter refers to the fulfillment of Old Testament promises when he says that times of refreshment will come as a result of their repentance (v. 19). This was part of the Jewish hope. But Peter clarifies that this will come only when God sends the Christ following their repentance and cleansing (v. 20). This anticipates to the second coming of Christ. Thus, while the messianic age has dawned, it has not yet been consummated. In the present age, "he must remain in heaven" (v. 21a; cf. 2:33–35), but only until the time of the final restoration promised by the prophets (3:21b). The noun used here (*apokatastasis*, "restoration") is from the same root as the verb in the disciples' question about God's restoring the kingdom to Israel (*apokathistano*, 1:6).

Jesus extends that restoration from Israel to all things, but it will happen at the end of time when God will be "all in all" (1 Cor. 15:28). We can assume that these are all parts of Jesus' teaching about the kingdom and that they were included in Paul's teaching about the kingdom (Acts 19:8; 20:24; 28:31). Thus, we find two points of eschatology in this evangelistic sermon. On the positive side is the promise of the restoration of all things (3:19–21); on the negative side is the threat that those who do not listen to Jesus will be completely cut off (v. 23).

The use of the second person plural "you" here is significant. At the start of his speech Peter clearly places responsibility for the death of Christ on his audience (vv. 13–14). In the middle of his speech he gets conciliatory by saying that he knows they "acted in ignorance" (v. 17). He ends his speech on a positive note, reminding them that they are "heirs of the prophets and of the covenant" (v. 25) and that God's servant was sent first to bless them via

---

7. Longenecker, "Acts," 296.

repentance (v. 26). Just prior to that, however, he issues a strong warning about those who do not listen being cut off (v. 23). This warning is in the third person because it becomes real only if they reject the message. This message, then, is not an abstract and detached discourse on the Christian gospel. It is an urgent plea that pulsates with the need for personal response.

Peter cites many blessings to the audience. He reminds them of the promise of universal blessedness made to Abraham (v. 25). As Isaiah promised before (Isa. 43:25), their sins will "be wiped out" (Acts 3:19). Barclay reminds us that "ancient writing was on papyrus and the ink had no acid in it. It therefore did not bite into the papyrus like modern ink, but simply lay on top of it. To erase the writing a man simply wiped it away with a wet sponge."[8] One of the blessings of the resurrection is that people will be turned from their wicked ways (v. 26). This is in keeping with the many promises of the Old Testament regarding the new covenant, where God himself will give people the ability to keep the law (Jer. 31:31–33; Ezek. 11:19; 36:26). Repentance and forgiveness will also result in "seasons of refreshment . . . from the presence of the Lord, that he may send him who has been designated as your Messiah—namely Jesus" (v. 20).[9] We have already seen the blessings to come in connection with Christ's consummating history (v. 21).

OUR PASSAGE GIVES us a description of the typical evangelistic ministry among Jews in the early church. As we seek to apply it to today, we will particularly look for principles of ministry that we too can follow.

Team ministry. Through the alternation of the use of Peter and John and Peter alone in this passage, we have a good example of the team ministry of the evangelist Peter. This style is found throughout Acts. When Jesus sent out his twelve apostles and the seventy disciples, they were sent out two by two (Mark 6:7; Luke 10:1). When Peter rose to speak on the day of Pentecost, he "stood up with the Eleven" (Acts 2:14). When he talked of his witness, he said, "We are witnesses of this" (3:15; cf. 2:32; 5:32). Peter was not a lone voice; he had a ministry team backing him when he spoke. Peter and John ministered as a team after this incident too (8:14). When Peter went to the home of Cornelius on his historic visit, he took six brothers with him (10:23; 11:12).

When the first missionary team for Gentile evangelization was commissioned, the Holy Spirit wanted two people set apart (13:2). When this team

---

8. Barclay, *Acts*, 35.
9. Bruce's translation in *Acts*, 82–83.

broke up, both Paul and Barnabas took others along to form their own teams (15:39–40). We know that Paul almost never traveled alone. He had his traveling Bible school, where he trained "interns" like Timothy and Titus. Even when Paul went to Rome as a prisoner, Luke was with him (27:2). In his last letter written from prison, Paul asked Timothy to join him quickly and to bring Mark along (2 Tim. 4:9, 11).

Only in exceptional cases, such as Philip the evangelist, do we see ministry performed alone in the New Testament. Even in Philip's case we cannot be sure he went to Samaria alone, for other disciples may have gone there with him when they were scattered. (It seems clear, however, that he was alone when he met the Ethiopian eunuch.) Jesus, of course, always had his disciples with him, unless he wanted to be alone in prayer. In other words, we can safely say that in the Bible, working in teams is the normal style of ministry.[10] We are not always told how the teams operated as far as the responsibilities of the members are concerned. Paul asks that Mark be brought to him "because he is helpful to me in my ministry" (2 Tim. 4:11). Presumably the teams worked according to the giftedness of the members as described in 1 Corinthians 12.

Deflecting glory from the evangelist. We have noted how Peter made a serious effort to deflect glory from himself. People often associate power with the instrument of miraculous occurrences. If not, they at least say that this person was used because he is a holy or great person. Peter vigorously refuted the idea that the healing of the crippled man was done through their power or godliness (v. 12). Instead, it was done "by faith in the name of Jesus," and even that faith "comes through him" (v. 16). Luke does not say whose faith is being referred to. He perhaps deliberately leaves that question open so that the focus will be entirely on Christ.[11]

Peter and Paul both try to deflect glory from themselves elsewhere in Acts (10:26; 14:14–15). This is a refreshing change from what Luke describes in his Gospel, where the disciples began disputing among themselves as to which one was the greatest (Luke 9:46; 22:24). They have finally heeded Jesus' warning that "everyone who exalts himself will be humbled, and the one who humbles himself will be exalted" (Luke 14:11; 18:14; cf. 9:48; 22:26).[12]

A complete message. Luke records a large number of the features of a good evangelistic message. Peter identifies with his audience in that the message starts by answering questions in the people's minds about the miracle. The heavy use of Jewish terms for God and for Christ, the references to

---

10. Much of the material above is from my *Reclaiming Friendship*, 36–37.
11. Polhill, *Acts*, 132–33.
12. Cf. Tannehill, *Narrative Unity*, 53.

their national hopes and aspirations, and the appeal to their Scriptures also demonstrate his effort to identify with the audience. The message has explanation (vv. 12−16), accusation (vv. 13−15), exposition (vv. 13−15, 18, 21−22, 24−26), conciliation (v. 17), appeal (vv. 19, 22), promise (vv. 19−22, 24−26), and warning (v. 23). Finally, the frequent use of the second person plural brought the message straight home to the hearers.

While the message was personalized and direct in its application to the hearers, the bulk of the space was given to explanation, exposition, and promise. The *content* of the gospel is most important. That is something we can easily forget in our efforts to be relevant. The use of warning and accusation shows us that there is a negative side to our presentation too. The gospel is always good news. But for that good news to be relevant we must often present the bad news of people's sin and warn them of its consequences.

A significant feature in the evangelistic sermons in Acts is the primacy of a person's relationship with God. While human aspirations and problems are dealt with and are often the launching pad for evangelism, ultimately what matters is what God has done in Jesus for humankind and how individuals respond to that. What attracts a person to Christ may be the answer Christ provides for a problem he or she has. That is natural, and therefore the apostles often started with questions people had. But they used those questions as stepping stones for presenting the foundational truths of the gospel, which are what ultimately matter. Soon in the evangelistic process or in the process of follow-through care, people must realize what these unchanging foundational truths of the gospel are.

A rounded or holistic ministry. Peter's complete message was the result of a ministry that was rounded in terms of emphases and activities. It started by dealing with a human need, evidenced in a person they encountered on the street. This led to a miracle and then to a sermon, which was strong on intelligent argumentation, using concrete evidence from Scripture and experience for the truthfulness of Christianity. The message consisted primarily of a rational case for the truthfulness of Christianity. People usually come within the sound of the gospel in order to avail themselves of the power of God for personal needs. But they stay because they know Christianity is the truth. Therefore the evangelistic message proclaimed by the "miracle worker" Peter also focused strongly on the truthfulness of Christianity. Like Stephen and Paul, Peter was a miracle-working apologist.

A powerful ministry. A complete message and rounded ministry is ineffective without spiritual power. Peter and John exhibited this power when they commanded the man to walk (v. 6). They were clearly in touch with God's power. We must always ensure that all our ministry is done in the power of the Spirit. Those without the gift of healing may not have the boldness to make the same type of statement that Peter made, resulting in the healing. But all ministry should be done in the power of the Spirit.

TEAM MINISTRY TODAY. The value of team ministry today cannot be overstressed. Ecclesiastes 4:9–12 gives four benefits of teams:

- Greater fruitfulness: "Two are better than one, because they have a good return for their work."
- Help in times of personal failure: "If one falls down, his friend can help him up. But pity the man who falls and has no one to help him up!"
- Warmth of affirmation in times of need: "Also, if two lie down together, they will keep warm. But how can one keep warm alone?"
- Strength to face attacks: "Though one may be overpowered, two can defend themselves. A cord of three strands is not quickly broken."[13]

Recently we have seen clergy with prominent ministries fall into serious sin. Many have noted that they did not have any group to which they were accountable. The pitfalls of a traveling ministry are well known. Traveling ministers often stay in hotels, which cater to the sexual gratification of traveling businessmen. After a tiring day of ministry, when we are emotionally and spiritually drained and have no strength for serious activity like studying or writing, it is easy to watch something unclean on TV in the privacy of the hotel room. No one knows about it. But several such incidents can leave us seriously polluted and vulnerable to more serious sin.

Some prominent ministers never travel alone, though not all of us can afford this luxury. Even then, it would be good for us to make sure that we have the backing of a team. I send out a prayer letter to a few people before every trip I make so that they will pray for me at every stage of my journey. I always request prayer for personal purity. On my return I report to my colleagues on how I fared, especially in my TV watching.

Ideally we should be staying in homes, which will help us identify with the people among whom we are ministering. This was how it was done in the early church (see discussion on 9:43). In Bible times the inns were likewise morally and hygienically unclean. I have also found it personally helpful to ask for a roommate who will effectively be my teammate when I am doing high pressure ministry, such as Bible expositions at a large conference. I was greatly ministered to at an Urbana missions conference, where I taught

---

13. I have elaborated on these points in my *Reclaiming Friendship*, 38–42, 132–45.

the Bible, through the friendship of American missions pastor Paul Borthwick, who volunteered to be my roommate.[14]

Deflecting glory from ourselves. Not only did Peter and John not go after glory, they strongly resisted it when it came unsolicited. How alien this is in a culture that places so much emphasis on appearance. Politicians hire organizations to make them look good in public. We see people unashamedly bragging about their achievements on TV. It is even common to hear Christian leaders talking at length about their achievements.

John the Baptist reflects the biblical attitude when he said, "He [Jesus] must become greater; I must become less" (John 3:30). A good principle to help us overcome the pitfalls arising from the temptation to win glory for ourselves is not to risk lifting up ourselves. Instead, we should concentrate on lifting up others and especially lifting up God. We can leave it to God to lift us up when he thinks it is fitting to do so.

We frequently find Paul lifting up his younger colleagues. He mentions their names along with his in the opening of his letters (1 Cor. 1:1; 2 Cor. 1:1; etc.). He writes glowing tributes of people like Timothy so that the church may accept them (2 Cor. 8:6–24; Phil. 2:19–24). The only times that Paul vigorously defended his own position was when the gospel was at stake and false teachers were questioning his credentials in their efforts to lead people away from the true gospel (see 2 Corinthians and Galatians). He did, of course, present his ministry as an example for others to follow (see Acts 20:17–35).

When we realize that none of us deserves the ministry we have been given and that we have our ministry only because of God's mercy (2 Cor. 4:1), it becomes difficult to take any glory for ourselves. We should be so thrilled that God has given us this call that we should focus on giving him all the glory. And when we realize how he lifts us up, we should be so filled with joy and gratitude that we give ourselves to lifting up others. This is why many famous but humble servants of God, such as evangelist Billy Graham and Bible scholar F. F. Bruce, are also known for the way they have encouraged and praised other Christian ministries and ministers. This was brought home to me a few days ago as I watched Billy Graham being interviewed by Larry King. I was amazed at the many good things he said about so many people.

Proclaiming a complete message today. Peter's presentation of the gospel had a completeness to it. Conscientious heralds of the good news need to work hard at incorporating different features of the gospel in their presentation. In Bible times, when this message was given to Jews, nothing was

---

14. For a discussion on team ministry in an itinerant context, see comments on 15:36–16:10.

said to introduce God since the listeners already had a basic understanding of God. But Paul's messages to Gentile audiences began with that topic before Jesus was presented (14:15–17; 17:23–29). This becomes significant today when presenting the gospel to "post-Christian" Western audiences and to non-Christians all over the world.

There are some features here that we may find difficult to incorporate into our message. In a world so interested in enjoying life in the here and now, the prospect of the Lord's return and the judgment are not easy to proclaim. It is the same with the call to convict people of their sin. Without ignoring these features of the gospel, as we are tempted to do, we should work hard at using our creativity to find convincing and attractive ways to present these truths.[15]

We also noted that though we may begin our proclamation with the felt needs of people, soon in the process of evangelism people should realize what the unchanging truths of the gospel are. People must be led to understand who God is, what he has done, especially through Christ, how we can receive his salvation, and how we can enjoy a relationship with him. This is why many churches use a historic creed as the base for their courses in preparing people for baptism, confirmation, or church membership.

If people are not aware of the foundational factors of the gospel, so basic to Christianity, they are headed for a warped Christian experience and will experience problems in weathering the storms of life. Those who see Christianity primarily as an answer to personal problems will find it difficult to continue in the path of obedience when they see no immediate solution to their problems. By contrast, one whose life is founded on the eternal realities of the gospel knows that even in the darkest night, those realities remain unchanged. There is a security that enables them to face the crisis and to realize that it is not as big as it may seem. God remains on the throne, so we trust him and do all we can to obey him, fully knowing that he will look after us.

In each culture people usually focus on one part of human experience and ignore others. Today's world finds a high place given to feelings. But if this dethrones truth about God from the supreme place in our lives, we are destined to unfulfillment, for feelings are too brittle an area of human life to build our security on. The Earl of Shaftesbury was a great social reformer in Britain, who did a great service to the nation by championing the cause of the oppressed in this newly industrialized nation. On his twenty-seventh birthday he pledged himself in writing to seek two things: the honor of God and the happiness of human beings; and he let his life be used by God to achieve these two things. But he always had his order right. Thus he said, "All

---

15. For a discussion on proclaiming judgment today, see my *Crucial Questions about Hell* (Wheaton: Crossway, 1994; orig. ed.: Eastbourne: Kingsway, 1991).

life is reduced to a transaction between the individual soul and the individual Savior"; and, "My faith is summed up in one word, and that is Jesus." With such an attitude we will not go wrong.

Thus, in the many problems and opportunities of our lives and ministries, let us never forget what is most important: who God is, what he has done for us in Christ, and how we should respond in obedience. In order to keep that uppermost in the church, may that also be uppermost in the procedure we adopt to incorporate people into the church—evangelism.

A rounded or holistic ministry. As noted above, the ministry of Peter and John, along with Paul and Stephen, exercised a threefold ministry of apologetics, evangelistic preaching, and healing. Often today different churches major on different aspects of the evangelistic challenge. Some are strong on miracles and weak on persuasion through the truth of Christianity. Others are excellent on theology and apologetics but weak on praying for the needs of non-Christians and presenting the miraculous power of God as an attractive feature of the gospel.

Would that there were more scholars in the church who also exercised some of these sign gifts. This could help us avoid the unhealthy extremes of arid and dull scholarship on the one hand, and fiery, uncontrolled sign-mania on the other. Yet, while we would like to have people like this in the church, nowhere is it said that this combination is the expected norm. That is, we cannot take a principle from this passage that everyone working in the miraculous must also be outstanding apologists. But when we do have this combination, we praise God for an unusual gift and wish for more of it to be manifested in the church.

True, if such persons were found in the church, some might look down on them as generalists, who have no significant contribution to make to the progress of the kingdom. It is sobering for us, living in an age of specialists, to note that often great doctrinal and evangelistic progress in the church in the New Testament era and, for that matter, right through history, was through the thinking and active ministry of generalists (e.g., Augustine, Luther, Calvin, and Wesley). Augustine was actually reluctant to go into pastoral ministry because of his desire to specialize in contemplation and theology. But he was "conscripted" to the pastorate against his will by the church in Hippo while on a visit to that city—and he stayed on there as a pastor-theologian for almost forty years.[16] These great theologian-practitioners were, of course, following the example set by their Master, Jesus.[17]

---

16. See my *Supremacy*, 42–43, which gets the story from David Bentley-Taylor, *Augustine: Wayward Genius* (Grand Rapids: Baker, 1980), 57–58.

17. On the integration demonstrated in the ministry of Jesus, see my *Supremacy*, 39–44; Stephen Neill, *The Supremacy of Jesus* (London: Hodder and Stoughton, 1984), 51–69.

In our age efficiency has become such an important factor that generalists are bound to experience frustration. It seems like a waste of time for a brilliant preacher, who preaches to a large congregation each Sunday and to thousands more through radio and TV, to spend many hours in the home of a dying member of his church. Thus, we have ministers of visitation to do that work. Similarly, a seminary professor, who is producing brilliant works of theology, may consider it a waste of time to spend an hour or two counseling with a depressed student who is doing badly. So seminaries have specialists in counseling to handle this type of challenge. Specialists from such an environment may produce impressive results, but they will lack the penetrative insight that can truly impact a culture with the truth of God. Such insight is born through the coupling of involvement in the lives of people and of careful study of the truth.[18]

The oft-quoted difference between efficiency and effectiveness is helpful to remember in our pragmatic age: Efficiency is doing a thing right, whereas effectiveness is doing the right thing. Ministers who will take up the cross of frustration and fatigue that may accompany a commitment to integrating the various disciplines will model effective and penetrative proclamation of truth. True, we have no scriptural or historical warrant for the claim that we do not need or should not use specialists. The church has been served with distinction by effective specialists, who were, however, not so specialized as to neglect human need when they encountered it. What we do not need are those unhealthy specialists who are so concerned with their particular disciplines that they do not bother to integrate that with human need. A sensitivity to human need is a corrective to the excesses of unhealthy specialization. The great theologian Karl Barth preached with some frequency to inmates in the Basel prison—which he referred to as "my favorite pulpit."[19]

A powerful ministry. We must never forget that all the work in the early church was done in the power of the Spirit. In our comments on 1:1-8 we reflected on the importance of the fullness of the Spirit for ministry. Peter's words in verse 6 expressing his economic poverty but commanding the crip-

---

18. For a discussion on Francis Schaeffer's attempts at integration and the criticism about his being a "generalist," see Gene Edward Veith, "The Fragmentation and Integration of Truth," and Lane T. Dennis, "Francis Schaeffer and His Critics," in *Francis A. Schaeffer: Portraits of the Man and His Work*, ed. Lane T. Dennis (Westchester: Crossway, 1986), 29–49, 101–26, respectively. Other chapters present Schaeffer as a social reformer, an evangelist, a counselor, a host to young people with questions about the faith, and a man of prayer.

19. Karl Barth, *How I Changed My Mind* (Richmond, Va.: John Knox, 1966), 71–72; cited in David L. Mueller, *Karl Barth*, Makers of the Modern Theological Mind (Waco, Tex.: Word, 1972), 45.

pled man to walk remind us that far more serious than economic poverty is spiritual poverty. An economically poor church that is able to harness the power of God is actually a rich church.

It is sad that with the increase of riches, dependence on God and consequently spiritual power often become less. It is unfortunately possible to use things that money can buy, such as a wonderful gymnasium for the youth and a grand pipe organ for worship, to have an impressive program and mask spiritual poverty. Economic poverty is sometimes a gift, for it forces us to look to God for strength. It is said that the theologian Thomas Aquinas (1225–1274) once called on Pope Innocent II when the latter was counting out a large sum of money. The Pope remarked, "You see, Thomas, the church can no longer say, 'Silver and gold have I none.'" Aquinas replied, "True, holy father, but neither can she now say, 'Rise and walk.'"[20]

---

20. Cited in Bruce, *Acts*, NICNT, 77–78.

Acts 4:1–22

✹

THE PRIESTS AND the captain of the temple guard and the Sadducees came up to Peter and John while they were speaking to the people. ²They were greatly disturbed because the apostles were teaching the people and proclaiming in Jesus the resurrection of the dead. ³They seized Peter and John, and because it was evening, they put them in jail until the next day. ⁴But many who heard the message believed, and the number of men grew to about five thousand.

⁵The next day the rulers, elders and teachers of the law met in Jerusalem. ⁶Annas the high priest was there, and so were Caiaphas, John, Alexander and the other men of the high priest's family. ⁷They had Peter and John brought before them and began to question them: "By what power or what name did you do this?"

⁸ Then Peter, filled with the Holy Spirit, said to them: "Rulers and elders of the people! ⁹If we are being called to account today for an act of kindness shown to a cripple and are asked how he was healed, ¹⁰then know this, you and all the people of Israel: It is by the name of Jesus Christ of Nazareth, whom you crucified but whom God raised from the dead, that this man stands before you healed. ¹¹He is

"'the stone you builders rejected,
which has become the capstone. '

¹²Salvation is found in no one else, for there is no other name under heaven given to men by which we must be saved."

¹³When they saw the courage of Peter and John and realized that they were unschooled, ordinary men, they were astonished and they took note that these men had been with Jesus. ¹⁴But since they could see the man who had been healed standing there with them, there was nothing they could say. ¹⁵So they ordered them to withdraw from the Sanhedrin and then conferred together. ¹⁶"What are we going to do with these men?" they asked. "Everybody living in Jerusalem knows they have done an outstanding miracle, and we cannot deny it. ¹⁷But to stop this thing from spreading any further among

the people, we must warn these men to speak no longer to anyone in this name."

¹⁸Then they called them in again and commanded them not to speak or teach at all in the name of Jesus. ¹⁹But Peter and John replied, "Judge for yourselves whether it is right in God's sight to obey you rather than God. ²⁰For we cannot help speaking about what we have seen and heard."

²¹After further threats they let them go. They could not decide how to punish them, because all the people were praising God for what had happened. ²²For the man who was miraculously healed was over forty years old.

CHAPTER 4 MARKS the beginning of resistance to evangelism in the life of the church, a feature that has been true of her life during the twenty centuries that followed! Here, as at the outset of the ministry of Jesus, the Jewish people in general seem to have been favorable towards the church while the authorities are beginning to express hostility.

Peter and John Arrested (4:1–4)

THE WORD FOR "people" (*laos*) appears five times in a generally positive light just before and after Peter's temple speech. As in the case of Jesus (Luke 19:47–48; 20:19; 21:38; 22:2), the popularity of the church with the people prevented the authorities from taking action against it. But soon, as with Jesus, the tide changed, so that by the time of Stephen's death, the people also seem to have turned against the church. By the time of Paul's arrest in Jerusalem, references to *laos* suddenly reappear (21:28, 30, 36, 39, 40), and the people cry for his death (21:36; 22:22). Chapter 4 records the first imprisonment in Acts; the book ends with Paul in prison. But God ultimately accomplishes his purposes, whether through imprisonment or miraculous release.[1]

Peter is seized by the priests (possibly the chief priests, who were all Sadducees), the captain of the temple guard (a powerful person who commanded the temple police force), and the Sadducees. They were particularly disturbed about the message of the resurrection (v. 2). To say that Christ rose would buttress the Pharisees' teaching regarding the resurrection, which the Sadducees rejected. The trial, however, was before the whole Sanhedrin, which at that time consisted of "a mixture of the Sadducean nobility (priestly

---

1. Many of the insights in this paragraph are from Tannehill, *Narrative Unity*, 59–60.

and lay) and pharisaic scholars."[2] They are deeply concerned, for "many who heard the message believed, and the number of men grew to about five thousand" (v. 4). This growth is phenomenal, considering that women and children are not included in this accounting.[3]

Before the Sanhedrin (4:5–12)

THE NEXT DAY Peter and John are brought before the Sanhedrin (v. 6; cf. v. 15). Annas, who was actually the senior ex-high priest, and his son-in-law Caiaphas, the reigning high priest, are there. They had participated in the trial of Jesus some weeks before, but their hopes of getting rid of Jesus were short-lived. In a typical question that authorities ask when their position is threatened, they demand to know the source of the apostles' "power" and "name" (i.e., authority, v. 7). Though they felt they had the authority over religious matters in the nation, they had neither power nor authority comparable to what these uneducated laymen had. In contrast to them is Peter, who has not only performed a miracle but who is now also "filled with the Holy Spirit" (v. 8). This is one of several instances in Acts where God's servants are filled with the Holy Spirit in order to face a special challenge.[4] We often call this anointing.

Though the disciples are technically on the defensive, they switch to an attacking position in their response to the Sanhedrin's question.[5] Peter replies, "It is by the name of Jesus Christ of Nazareth, whom you crucified but whom God raised from the dead, that this man stands before you healed" (v. 10). Then he cites Psalm 118:22, which became a favorite text in the early church: "He is 'the stone you builders rejected, which has become the capstone'" (v. 11).[6] Israel is probably intended in this psalm. "But, as so often in the New Testament, God's purpose for Israel finds its fulfillment in the single-handed work of Christ."[7]

Then comes a proclamation of the absolute uniqueness of Christ as the only means of salvation (v. 12). The meaning of "saved" here has been debated, especially since the same Greek word (*sozo*) is used in verse 9 with the meaning "healed." But the meaning here is closer to the way it is used in

---

2. W. J. Moulder, "Sanhedrin," *ISBE*, 4:332.

3. Cf. comments on 2:41, where we showed that the objections to the high figure of converts, based on earlier figures of the population of Jerusalem, have been countered by more recent research.

4. See 4:31; 7:55; 13:9.

5. Bruce, *Acts*, NICNT, 93.

6. See Mark 12:10–12; Eph. 2:20; 1 Peter 2:7.

7. Bruce, *Acts*, NICNT, 93.

2:40 (salvation from this perverse generation) and 2:47 (attachment to the people of God). Peter is referring here to a broader meaning than simple deliverance from sickness or birth defect (which may also be included here). He is talking about a change of status from being rebels to being accepted among God's people.

Warned and Discharged (4:13–22)

THE MEMBERS OF the Sanhedrin are "astonished" at the courage of Peter and John, for they are "unschooled, ordinary men" (v. 13a). The word translated "unschooled" (*agrammatos*) carried the meaning "illiterate" in some papyri. But that is clearly not the meaning here or in John 7:15, where the word is used for Jesus. In this latter text it expresses surprise "that he could teach and discuss subjects which normally were beyond the scope of those who had not received a rabbinical education."[8] That seems to be the sense here as well. The word translated "ordinary" (*idiotes*) refers to "a person who has not acquired systematic information or expertise in some field of knowledge or activity," thus yielding the meaning of layman or amateur.[9]

In other words, though Peter and John are professionally unqualified, they are boldly conducting their own defense with great eloquence before this august assembly. The Sanhedrin already knows that these men have been with Jesus. But this performance reminds them afresh how they have been influenced by Jesus, who also "taught . . . as one who had authority" (Mark 1:22). Jesus' ministry once prompted the Jews to ask (John 7:15), "How did this man get such learning without having studied?" We can add to this Luke's mention that Peter was filled with the Spirit here (Acts 4:8). Luke is thus describing effective ministry in the New Testament era: speaking out of the fullness of the Spirit and out of a knowledge of the Scriptures. The apostles have a boldness that comes from confidence about their message and empowerment by the Spirit.

After ordering Peter and John to leave the Sanhedrin, the Jewish leaders discuss the dilemma they are in, especially since no one can deny that an "outstanding miracle" had been performed (v. 16; cf. also v. 21: "They could not decide how to punish them, because all the people were praising God for what had happened"). The only thing they can do is to command Peter and John "not to speak or teach at all in the name of Jesus" (v. 18). The two apostles reply that they must obey God and "cannot help speaking about what we have seen and heard"—words that have inspired persecuted Christians throughout the history of the church (vv. 19–20).

---

8. Bruce, *Acts: Greek Text*, 153.
9. Louw and Nida, 329.

"What [they] have seen and heard" (i.e., the works and words of Jesus) was a message worthy of proclamation to the whole world. Loyalty to God and the nature of the message combine to give compelling reasons to disobey the command of the Sanhedrin. The question of civil disobedience is an important one today and will be discussed in our treatment of 5:29. Such is the dilemma of the Sanhedrin that even so bold a proclamation of defiance cannot bring about a punishment. All they can do is to threaten the apostles further and release them (v. 21).

THE IMPORTANCE OF **numbers**. In verse 4 we encounter another of the numbers-related references to the growth of the church in Acts (see 2:41, 47; 5:14; 11:24). This implies that God is interested in numbers, though not as a badge of success, for that would yield a triumphalist attitude alien to the gospel. God's interest in numbers is because they represent people who have been rescued from damnation and granted salvation. The individuals who make up the five thousand are beloved persons for whom Christ died. A minister, visiting a family in his congregation, noticed many children in the house. He asked the mother, "How many children do you have?" She began to count off on her fingers, "John, Mary, Lucy, David. . . ." The minister interrupted, "I don't want their names, I just asked for the number." The mother responded, "They have names, not numbers."[10] Numbers are important because they represent people.

The indispensability of suffering. We often hear people say that they would like to get back to the book of Acts and have a church just like that. But the view many have of this church is a romantic one. They think of a church that saw many miracles, much conversion, amazing unity, and Spirit-filled leadership. They forget that Acts also describes the troubles the church faced from within itself and without. The most consistent trouble mentioned is persecution.

After chapter 3 only three chapters in Acts do not mention persecution. This suggests that persecution may be a necessary part of the Christian life. Paul confirms this, "Everyone who wants to live a godly life in Christ Jesus will be persecuted" (2 Tim. 3:12). Jesus himself said, "'No servant is greater than his master.' If they persecuted me, they will persecute you also" (John 15:20). The truth of God is too radical for all people to respond to it passively. Some will oppose it and others will ignore it, but, thank God, some will take

---

10. John T. Seamands, *Daybreak: Daily Devotions from Acts and Pauline Epistles* (privately published in Wilmore, Ky., 1993), Jan. 17.

it to heart. Acts, then, challenges us to anticipate suffering as an indispensable ingredient of obedience to Christ.

Opposition from the religious leaders. The powerful people in Jewish society in New Testament times asked Peter and John, "By what power or what name [authority] did you do this?" (v. 7). Today too "the powers that be" will ask this of God's faithful servants. They are often people without many earthly credentials (v. 13), for as Paul said, "Not many of you were wise by human standards; not many were influential; not many were of noble birth. But God chose the foolish things of the world to shame the wise; God chose the weak things of the world to shame the strong" (1 Cor. 1:26–27). The "wise" and the "strong" do not usually take this shame passively. They use their wisdom and strength to fight God's people. Thus, as in Acts 4, when a new move of God appears that expresses his power and authority, it is often the ecclesiastical hierarchy that opposes it.

A new definition of significant service. In the eyes of the members of the Sanhedrin, Peter and John were not people from whom they expected something significant. Therefore, they expressed surprise, since Peter and John were unschooled, ordinary laymen. Several important indicators of significant service emerge in this passage.

- *An anointing with the fullness of the Spirit* (v. 8).
- *Courage* (v. 13). The noun translated "courage" (*parresia*) and its corresponding verb (*parresiazomai*) appear twelve times in Acts—generally in close association to preaching the gospel to Jews.[11] The death and resurrection of Christ and his uniqueness as the source of salvation were offensive to the Jews, but the early Christians had the inner motivation to persist in this work. In today's society we need a similar courage as we face similar challenges.
- *The desire to use every opportunity to share the message of the gospel.* Peter and John were being tried before a council, but their aim was not just to get off the hook. They used the opportunity to declare the gospel. This became a hallmark of Christian witness in Acts and in the history of the church. The gospel is such urgent news that we must use every opportunity we have; indeed, we must seek opportunities to get the message across.
- *The nearness and similarity to Christ that Peter and John exhibited.* Peter and John spoke with the boldness of Jesus, they performed miracles like Jesus, and they knew the Scriptures as Jesus knew them. The Sanhedrin took note that they had been with Jesus and presented that as the explanation for their unusual behavior (v. 13).

---

11. Barrett, *Acts*, 233.

- *Loyalty to God.* Peter and John chose to obey God even if it meant incurring the wrath of the most powerful people of the time (vv. 19–20).

- *Confidence over the gospel.* Peter and John said that they had no choice but to share what they had "heard and seen" (v. 20)—the facts about the life, death, resurrection, ascension, and teaching of Christ (see 3:14–15). This was the heart of the basic *kerygma.* When we witness for Christ, we are witnessing to these objective facts. Unlike the apostles, we were not there when these events occurred, but we believe that they took place as recorded in the Gospels. The Gospels give us an impression that Jesus is unique and that the events of his life are of eternal consequence to the whole world. We believe this record, and thus twenty centuries later we can also affirm the uniqueness of the message of Christ.

The absence of formal theological education. The need for theological education, which usually appears in today's criteria for selection of church leaders, is missing from this list. In fact, it is specifically stated that Peter and John lacked such education (v. 13). This raises the question as to whether formal theological education is necessary for usefulness in ministry. This will be discussed in some detail below.

One way to salvation. An aspect of the apostles' confidence over the gospel is the concept that belief in the name of Jesus is the only way to salvation (v. 12). This is a biblical principle stated throughout the New Testament, though it is hotly contested in this pluralistic age.

NUMBERS AND GROWTH **today.** In the Bible numbers are important because they represent people for whom Christ died. This approach to numbers stands in contrast with the triumphalist approach. If we are concerned primarily about numbers, we may be tempted to use wrong means to win people. We may lower our standards by watering down the gospel, not doing proper follow-through care, or not insisting on holiness. We may add unbiblical features to our gospel or indulge in sheep-stealing, evangelistic bribery, or manipulation. Some consider these acceptable methods to use in the marketplace and in society in general. Recently my wife and I listened to an audio version of a best-selling book on husband-wife relationships, which recommended methods of winning one's spouse over that sounded like dishonest manipulation.[12] Living in such an environment,

---

12. John Gray, *Men Are from Mars, Women Are from Venus* (New York: HarperCollins, 1993).

we may be tempted to accept such means as acceptable to make our churches grow numerically.

But when we use such methods, we can easily end up with fat but unhealthy churches. This is a danger in the megachurches of today. They can have members who get lost in the crowd and do not really partake in Christian community. I know of some churches that have a policy of dividing and starting a daughter church the moment they get to a certain size (e.g., four hundred members), in order to maintain the family atmosphere that is essential to Christian fellowship. The early church overcame these pitfalls and ensured spiritual accountability by having the members break up into smaller house groups (2:46) and by observing strict discipline in the church (5:1–11). Effective megachurches must have numerous small groups, which are the real local churches where true Christian fellowship and accountability are practiced.

Some churches reject any emphasis on numbers, saying that we are called to be faithful, not successful, and that God wants quality, not quantity. There is truth to this. Some are called to work in resistant fields, which need a faithful witness for a considerable period of time before people open up to the gospel. Once it opens up, there may be a huge harvest. I have heard about one saintly missionary who worked faithfully in an area for two decades without any visible conversions. After his death another missionary replaced him and experienced a remarkable turning to the Lord. When the people were asked why they had not come to Christ during the lifetime of that great missionary, they replied that the missionary had told them that Christians are not afraid of death and that they needed to see him die before they could accept his message. An overemphasis on numbers would have caused this man to become discouraged and give up.

On the other hand, thinking about many people coming to Christ is part of our faithfulness, for Christ has commanded us to go to all nations and bring as many as we can to salvation. Paul manifested this perspective when he wrote, "I have become all things to all men so that by all possible means I might save some" (1 Cor. 9:22). Many groups who claim that they are being faithful and committed to quality are not willing to change their styles of ministry and do things that they are uncomfortable with so as to reach as many as possible. Naturally, then, they do not see much growth. But that is not because of faithfulness. Rather, they are being unfaithful to the Great Commission, which calls for incarnational evangelism, of making ourselves nothing (Phil. 2:7), and of going into the world in the same sacrificial way as Jesus did (John 20:21). Their faithfulness is to their tradition, not to the gospel of Christ.

Suffering in an aspirin age. If, as we said, suffering and persecution are indispensable features of Christianity, why are so many Christians not suffering and being persecuted today? Is it because they have not taken up the cross of Christ? As the cross is what we suffer because of our commitment to Christ, all Christians should be suffering for Christ. Yet it is possible to avoid this suffering by refusing to take a stand for Christ when we should. In this pluralistic age it is considered against proper etiquette and politically incorrect to insist on the validity of one's views when it comes to certain issues, especially moral and religious issues. We as believers must not adopt such an attitude since we know that the light of Christ is opposed to the darkness of the world.

Here are some Christian beliefs and practices that can arouse hostility today: evangelism with conversion in view; insistence that practicing homosexuality and abortion and consuming pornography are wrong; a pattern of showing active love and compassion to homosexuals, AIDS patients, prostitutes, outcasts, and other people shunned by the church; opposition to all forms of injustice and exploitation; and insistence that doctrines that contradict the clear teachings of the Bible are heresies and must be rooted out of the church. When faced with wrong ideas and practices, some do nothing to express their opposition. They want to be known as nice people, and they will certainly not be persecuted. Yet as someone has said, "Nice guys have no cutting edge." They do little eternal service to humanity.

Thus, we must not fear persecution. Rather, we must seek to be faithful and guard against the temptation to tone down our gospel so that we too become respectable and avoid persecution. Many older, established churches have done this. They have downplayed the uniqueness of Christianity and beliefs that go against the grain of this pluralistic society. They have, as a result, been able to maintain their respectability in society, but they have lost their power and vitality. They have stopped growing, and their places as standard-bearers of the kingdom have been taken by others. Some conservative churches have stopped opposing injustice and maintained their respectability with the authorities, but by so doing they have betrayed Christ.

That suffering is a basic ingredient of the Christian life is confirmed by the fact that it occurs so often in the Bible. When Paul described both the justified life and the Spirit-filled life in Romans, he immediately went on to deal with the problem of suffering, which is an inherent part of that life (Rom. 5:3–5; 8:17–39). Luke has a significant summary of Paul's teaching during the last lap of his first missionary journey: "Then they returned to Lystra, Iconium and Antioch, strengthening the disciples and encouraging them to remain true to the faith. 'We must go through many hardships to enter the kingdom of God,' they said" (14:21b–22). The call to suffer must be a basic part of the follow-through care of new converts (see comment on 14:22).

We must remember that Jesus predicted what the disciples encountered in this episode. Shortly before his death he told them that they would stand before councils and rulers (Mark 13:9) and would be given the words to speak at such times (13:11). The fact that it had been predicted so accurately must have been a source of both comfort and strength to them. If new believers are not warned about and prepared for suffering, they may get disillusioned when they face it and wonder whether they have been deceived by those who led them to Christ. This is especially important since much of evangelistic proclamation today focuses on the blessings of salvation, such as eternal life, forgiveness, freedom, joy, peace, healing, significance, and purpose. Too many people view Christianity without including the blessing of suffering. Indeed, in the Bible suffering is presented as a blessing (Rom. 5:3–5; Phil. 1:29–30; James 1:2–4).

We live in an age that gives much attention to mastering the art of avoiding suffering. We live in what may be called an "aspirin generation," which views pain and suffering as calamities that are to be avoided at all costs. In this climate, Christians are tempted to avoid the cross through disobedience. We must help redeem suffering, so that Christians will learn to think biblically about it and anticipate the rich harvest of blessing that it yields. That will remove a lot of the "sting" of suffering. Then Christians can follow the biblical admonition to "consider it pure joy ... whenever you face trials of many kinds" (James 1:2).

Facing opposition from religious leaders. Often when there is a special move of God in the church, the religious leaders are the ones who oppose it. They are the ones in authority, but these upstarts seem to be having more authority with the people, and the new movement has unprecedented popularity. This places the leaders in a dilemma, and usually they respond by stamping down their authority and appealing to tradition to proscribe or criticize the movement. Some of the greatest opponents of renewal movements within the church have been its leaders.

We must, therefore, not be overly disillusioned when criticism and persecution come our way from those who should be encouraging us the most. Parents, whose children's lives are transformed for the better through a youth movement, may oppose the movement as they fear that their authority will be undermined and their hypocrisy exposed. Our best efforts may be discounted on technicalities by those who do not like what we say or are threatened by our message. For example, a powerful message through song, drama, or speech may be discounted because it took too long. To our acts of deepest sacrifice selfish motives will be attributed.

When the sixty-six-year-old Methodist leader Thomas Coke (1747–1814) announced that he had been called by God to take the gospel to Ceylon (now Sri Lanka), people accused him of being senile and of trying to build his personal kingdom. But he persisted and left for Ceylon with a band of young missionaries. He died before he reached our shores. But the young missionaries, inspired by his vision, came and preached the gospel, and people like me are in the kingdom as a fruit of their labors.[13]

Significant ministry today. Each of the six features of significant service we listed above is significant today. Perhaps *an anointing with the fullness of the Spirit* (v. 8) is the most important indicator, for in all significant service God is the one who does the work. Many prominent ministries may result in being burned up as wood, hay, and straw at the Day of Judgment (1 Cor. 3:11–15). It is possible to judge a ministry by the volume, status, and the prominence of the work it does. This can seduce us into giving ourselves to so much busy activity that we ignore the primary task of ensuring that God's anointing is with us. We may even use our work to cover up a sense of spiritual inadequacy.

The second and third features were *courage* (v. 13) and *the desire to use every opportunity to share the gospel message.* Though the gospel was offensive to the Jews, the first Christians had the inner motivation to persist in this work. In an effort to maintain respectability, we can be tempted to jettison some of the aspects of the gospel that are offensive to the world. This happened in Sri Lanka after it received independence from the British in 1948. Many within the established churches maintained their respectability with the Buddhist hierarchy by refusing to insist on the uniqueness of Christianity. One of the results has been a loss of fire in these churches, and with that also a loss of members. A key to maintaining a vibrant witness in an environment hostile to the gospel is courage.

Enthusiastic Christians are sometimes criticized for the foolhardy way in which they present their witness and sometimes turn people away from the gospel. Yet many of those who level these criticisms do no witnessing themselves. I have seen many people converted through witnesses with a lot of boldness and not much wisdom. An effective witness will not emerge from one who has never ventured to speak up for Christ.

Many factors can help those who lack boldness to witness. One is the realization of the urgency of the gospel—that people are lost without Christ. Another is prayer—asking God to give us opportunities for witness and to help us when the opportunities arise. A third is involvement in a witnessing community. Though we may be afraid to speak when alone, the presence of another Christian with us can increase our courage (note how Jesus sent his disciples out two by two). Even when we are alone, the knowledge that we belong to a witnessing community that expects its members to witness acts as a motivation to take the first steps in a witnessing situation—and the first steps are often the hardest.

---

13. John Vickers, *Thomas Coke: Apostle of Methodism* (Nashville: Abingdon, 1969), 343–52.

All this may give the impression that we are under a huge bondage that mandates a bold witness even though we do not want to witness. All I can say in response to that is that though I am often afraid to witness boldly, and though my witness is sometimes triggered more by a sense of duty than of love for the individual, I have always felt a great joy whenever I have witnessed. Is not this a means by which the love of God flows through us? Are we not sharing the greatest news there is to share? Ultimately, it is not a burden; it is a sheer delight!

The fourth characteristic is the *nearness to the Spirit of Christ*. This comes by spending time at the feet of the Master—learning from his Word, praying, and going out with him to serve. We tend to become like those with whom we spend extended time. A girl came to her pastor and said that she thought she was filled with the Spirit, but she did not see the fruit of the Spirit in her life. He asked her what type of devotional life she had. She said, "Hit and miss." He asked, "Do you have your meals that way?" She said, "I did once, and I nearly lost my health." She got the message! If she wanted to be like Jesus, she had to be with Jesus.

Coupled with spending time with Jesus should be a deep desire to be like him (Phil. 3:10—14). This is the aspiration that Jesus advocated in the Beatitudes: "Blessed are those who hunger and thirst for righteousness, for they will be filled" (Matt. 5:6). Such aspiration comes from a passion for Christ. Count Nicholas von Zinzendorf (1700–1760), the founder of the Moravians, had as his motto: "I have one passion only: It is he! It is he!"

The fifth characteristic of significant service is *loyalty to God*, even at a risk to personal safety. H. G. Wells has said, "The trouble with so many people is that the voice of their neighbors sounds louder in their ears than the voice of God."[14] William Barclay refers to a tribute once paid to the Scottish reformer John Knox (1514–1572): "He feared God so much that he never feared the face of any man."[15] An incident from the life of D. L. Moody well expresses the attitude we should have. When he was young, an Irish friend named Henry Varley told him, "Moody, the world has yet to see what God will do with a man fully consecrated to him." Moody was startled by the statement. He kept thinking about it for days. He reasoned: "A man! Varley meant *any* man. Varley didn't say he had to be educated, or brilliant, or anything else. Just a *man*. Well, by the Holy Spirit in me, I'll be that man."[16] This is passion: loyalty to God.

The final characteristic is *confidence over the gospel*, which comes through our confidence in the Gospel records of the life and work of Christ. When

---

14. Barclay, *Acts*, 41.
15. Ibid.
16. John Pollock, *Moody: A Biographical Portrait* (Grand Rapids: Zondervan, 1963), 99.

one's belief in the trustworthiness of this record goes, along with it goes belief in the uniqueness of Christ. This is how "Christian" pluralists today can sustain their doctrine. They believe that the record of the life, work, and teaching of Christ in the Gospels contains subjective reflections of devotees of Christ, not historically accurate records. In this way they are able to discard the teachings that present the uniqueness of Christ by claiming that Jesus himself did not say such things.

We must always distinguish between testimony and evangelism. Testimony is a powerful tool in evangelism. The healing of the cripple helped the witness of Peter and John by being evidence of what God had done. Today, too, testimony is effective in commending Christ. It is difficult to argue against (vv. 14, 16), and it opens doors for the proclamation of the gospel. But testimony is *not* the gospel. The gospel primarily has to do with what Jesus did in history for the world and how it can impact us today. Note that people of other faiths may be able to have experiences similar to ours, but in no other faith do we find Christ. Roy Clements says, "Testimony is telling people what Jesus has done for me in my personal experience, but evangelism is telling people what Jesus has done for the world in history."[17]

Is theological education necessary for preaching? The fact that uneducated laymen like Peter and John were used so powerfully makes us ask the question whether theological education is really necessary for a preaching ministry. There is likewise a great line of preachers in the history of the church who did not have any formal education—for example, powerful early Methodist preachers like Billy Bray, and in more recent times people like Charles Spurgeon, D. L. Moody, Campbell Morgan, "Gypsy" Smith, and A. W. Tozer. The so-called Third World has a host of powerful preachers who are not known outside their own nations because they do not write books and thus go unnoticed by the Western Christian media. Those people, however, are mighty in the Scriptures. Anyone who seeks to be used of God should be a careful student of the Word—but you do not need to go to seminary for that.

Seminaries, however, can be a great aid to the church. We must not forget that Peter and John were discipled (or mentored) by Jesus. He taught them through his life and teaching, so that when the Sanhedrin heard them, they took note that they had been with Jesus. They lived with him for three and one-half years—more credit hours of study than a basic seminary degree! Paul did the same thing with his "traveling Bible school," where he taught his younger assistants.

And this is what a seminary should seek to do: to have teachers who will mentor students by being with them and teaching them, just as Jesus did

---

17. Clements, *The Church That Turned*, 56.

with his disciples. If teachers fail in this regard, then the seminary fails in its task of preparing men and women for ministry. Some teachers do little personal work, though a seminary is rife with students needing personal counsel. Though the heart of ministry is working through committed teams, these teachers do not model team ministry in the way they relate to other members of the faculty. This type of seminary we do not need. A seminary where the teachers truly mentor the students can become a great asset to the church by sending out effective men and women.

As I think of my seminary experience, the thing that stands out most is the effect the lives of my professors had on me. Their godliness, their commitment to careful scholarship—especially the care they showed in the study of the Scriptures—their honesty, the time they gave to counsel and pray with me, their refusal to accept shoddy arguments, their commitment to excellence, and their letting me accompany them when they went out to preach have all left an abiding influence on my life.

When I arrived in Pasadena, California, for graduate studies, with fear and trembling I phoned the advisor assigned to me for my studies, Dr. Daniel Fuller. He had sent me a stern letter about the academic requirements for the course I was pursuing (Th.M. in New Testament). Thus, I was not eagerly looking forward to working with him! He came to the campus a few minutes after I called, talked with me—more about myself than about the studies I was to do—and prayed with me. His academic demands were high, but so was his concern for my personal welfare. He became a father to me, and his personal concern for me persists to this day.

No other name? Peter's claim that salvation is only through the name of Jesus (4:12), grates against the prevalent pluralistic mood in society. The church has responded to this in different ways. The first response is *pluralism*. Theologians like John Hick and Paul Knitter hold that while Christ may be unique to Christians, his is not an absolute uniqueness that applies to adherents of other faiths. They put Christ on par with the founders of other religions and claim that Christianity and the other faiths are "equals in the universe of faiths."[18] The pluralist denies that Acts 4:12 can be applied to all persons.

The second response is called *inclusivism*. While accepting the basic proposition that all those who are saved are saved only through the work of Christ,

18. John Hick, *God and the Universe of Faiths* (London: Macmillan, 1973); idem, *An Interpretation of Religion* (New Haven, Conn.: Yale Univ. Press, 1988); idem, "Whatever Path Men Choose Is Mine," *Christianity and the Other Religions*, John Hick and Brian Hebblethwaite, eds., (Philadelphia: Fortress, 1980); John Hick and Paul Knitter, eds., *The Myth of Christian Uniqueness* (Maryknoll, N.Y.: Orbis, 1987); Paul Knitter, *No Other Name? A Critical Survey of Christian Attitudes Toward the World Religions* (Maryknoll, N.Y.: Orbis, 1985).

they add that Christ can save through means other than explicit belief in the gospel. To put it in theological language, Christ is the ontological[19] ground of salvation—that is, salvation is grounded in Christ—but his gospel is not necessarily the only epistomological[20] means of salvation—that is, salvation does not necessarily require the knowledge of Jesus' name.

This approach was pioneered by Roman Catholic theologians like Karl Rahner and Raimundo Panikkar and popularized by Hans Küng. They extended the Catholic view that salvation is through the sacraments (like baptism and the Eucharist) to include the "sacraments" of other religions, like almsgiving and meditation. They claimed that in each case Christ is the one who saves these devotees of other religions. They are called "anonymous Christians," and their faiths are called the "ordinary" ways to salvation whereas the gospel is the "very special and extraordinary" way to salvation.[21] A modification of this approach has been seen in the Protestant orbit through the writings of Sir Norman Anderson and, more radically, of John Sanders and Clark Pinnock, who state that those who repent of their sin and place their trust in what they know to be God do indeed exhibit what the Bible describes as saving faith.[22]

The traditional view is called *exclusivism* or *particularism*, which holds that explicit faith in Christ is a necessary implication of the verse that only in the name of Jesus is salvation found. This has been argued by scholars such as Ramesh Richard, Ronald Nash, D. A. Carson, Douglas Geivett, and Gary Phillips. They show that the Bible in general teaches that explicit faith in Christ is necessary for salvation and that Acts 4:12 necessarily implies that

---

19. Ontology is the "study of being"; the word comes from a participial form of the Greek word "to be" (Ernest Weekley, *An Etymological Dictionary of Modern English* [New York: Dover, 1967], 1010).

20. Epistemology, the "study of knowledge," is derived from the Greek *episteme*, "knowledge" (ibid., 518).

21. See Hans Küng, in *Christian Revelation and World Religions*, Joseph Neuner, ed. (London: Burns and Oates, 1967), 52–53; Karl Rahner, "Christianity and the Non-Christian Religions," *Christianity and the Other Religions*, Hick and Hebblethwaite, eds., 52–79; idem, *Theological Investigations*, vol. 5, *Later Writings* (London: Darton, Longman, and Todd, 1966); Raimundo Panikkar, *The Unknown Christ of Hinduism*, rev. ed. (Maryknoll, N.Y.: Orbis, 1981).

22. See Sir Norman Anderson, *Christianity and the World Religions* (Downers Grove, Ill.: InterVarsity, 1984), 137–61; Clark Pinnock, *A Wideness in God's Mercy: The Finality of Christ in a World of Religions* (Grand Rapids: Zondervan, 1992); idem, "Acts 4:12—No Other Name Under Heaven," *Through No Fault of Their Own: The Fate of Those Who Have Never Heard*, ed. William W. Crockett and James G. Sigountos (Grand Rapids: Baker, 1991), 107–15; idem, "An Inclusivist View," *More Than One Way? Four Views on Salvation in a Pluralistic World*, ed. Dennis L. Okholm and Timothy R. Phillips (Grand Rapids: Zondervan, 1995), 95–123; John Sanders, *No Other Name: An Investigation into the Destiny of the Unevangelized* (Grand Rapids: Eerdmans, 1992).

too.[23] We should also mention that some, like Lesslie Newbigin, prefer an attitude of *agnosticism* on this issue. Such scholars do not want to venture into speculations about the results of the final judgment and refuse to answer the question of whether those who have never heard the gospel can be saved.[24]

It is beyond the scope of this book to go into a detailed study of this controversial issue.[25] Pinnock's main argument on Acts 4:12 is that it does not address the issue of what will happen to those who have not heard the gospel. He says that exclusivists read into this text the doctrines that they hold but which are not implied in this text: "I would claim the silence of the text in defense of my interpretation. It does not demand restrictive exclusivism."[26]

This view calls for some response.[27] The first half of verse 12, "Salvation is found in no one else" could perhaps be confined to an ontological interpretation, if considered alone. But the second part seems to eliminate that interpretation: "for there is no other name under heaven given to men by which we must be saved." The word "must" in the second part is related to the "name." Peter is saying that everyone in the world *must* be saved only by the name of Jesus. The word "must" (*dei*) emphasizes necessity; a response to this name is needed.

Ten of the thirty-two occurrences of the "name" of the Lord in Acts appear in Acts 2–4. In all those except 4:12, it is clear that conscious acknowledgment of the name is implied. This is equally true for most of the other occurrences in Acts. In his speech at the temple prior to his arrest, Peter said, "By faith in the name of Jesus, this man whom you see and know was made strong. It is Jesus' name and the faith that comes through him that has given this complete healing to him, as you can all see" (3:16). Thus, we can conclude with Geivett and Phillips that here Peter "is indicating what must be acknowledged about Jesus before one can be saved."[28]

---

23. Ramesh Richard, *The Population of Heaven* (Chicago: Moody, 1994); Ronald Nash, *Is Jesus the Only Savior?* (Grand Rapids: Zondervan, 1994); D. A. Carson, *The Gagging of God: Christianity Confronts Pluralism* (Grand Rapids: Zondervan, 1996); R. Douglas Geivett and W. Gary Phillips, "A Particularist View: An Evidentialist Approach," *More Than One Way?* 213–45. For an earlier treatment from this perspective see my *The Christians Attitude Toward World Religions* (Wheaton: Tyndale, 1987).

24. Lesslie Newbigin, *The Open Secret* (Grand Rapids: Eerdmans, 1978), 196; see also John Stott's views in David L. Edwards and John R. W. Stott, *Essentials: A Liberal-Evangelical Dialogue* (Downers Grove, Ill.: InterVarsity, 1988), 327.

25. For contemporary discussions on the different views, see Okholm and Phillips, *More Than One Way?* and Crockett and Sigountos, *Through No Fault of Their Own.*

26. Pinnock, "Acts 4:12—No Other Name Under Heaven," 112.

27. For more complete treatments, see Geivett and Phillips, "A Particularist View," 230–33, and Richard, *The Population of Heaven,* 55–60.

28. Geivett and Phillips, "A Particularist View," 232–33.

A common objection to this uncompromising affirmation of the absolute uniqueness of Christ is that it is sheer arrogance to maintain this in light of the treasures of religious insight that are found in other faiths. In response, we must say that arrogance has to do with attitudes of individuals and that those who understand the gospel cannot possibly have an arrogant attitude. To accept the gospel is to admit that we cannot help ourselves and that Christ alone can help us. In other words, to accept the gospel we must rid ourselves of arrogance. When we find this salvation, we are filled with gratitude to God for what he has done. Arrogance focuses on oneself while gratitude focuses on someone else. We dare not say that we are better that anyone else, for we know that we do not deserve salvation. But we dare to say that Jesus is the only way because we know that he can perform the impossible task of saving unworthy persons like us. We conclude with a statement by the Dutch missiologist, Hendrik Kraemer (1888−1965):

> Inspired by this biblical realism, the attitude toward non-Christian religions is a remarkable combination of downright intrepidity [that is, daring or courage] and of radical humility. Radical humility because the missionary and through him the Christian Church is the bringer of a divine gift, not something of his making and achievement; and what he has received for nothing. Downright intrepidity, because the missionary is the bearer of a message, the witness to a divine revelation, not his discovery, but God's act.[29]

---

29. Hendrik Kraemer, *The Christian Message in a Non-Christian World* (Grand Rapids: Kregel, 1969 [reprint of 1938 ed.]), 128.

Acts 4:23-31

ON THEIR RELEASE, Peter and John went back to their own people and reported all that the chief priests and elders had said to them. ²⁴When they heard this, they raised their voices together in prayer to God. "Sovereign Lord," they said, "you made the heaven and the earth and the sea, and everything in them. ²⁵You spoke by the Holy Spirit through the mouth of your servant, our father David:

> "'Why do the nations rage
>   and the peoples plot in vain?
> ²⁶The kings of the earth take their stand
>   and the rulers gather together against the Lord
>   and against his Anointed One.'

²⁷Indeed Herod and Pontius Pilate met together with the Gentiles and the people of Israel in this city to conspire against your holy servant Jesus, whom you anointed. ²⁸They did what your power and will had decided beforehand should happen. ²⁹Now, Lord, consider their threats and enable your servants to speak your word with great boldness. ³⁰Stretch out your hand to heal and perform miraculous signs and wonders through the name of your holy servant Jesus."

³¹After they prayed, the place where they were meeting was shaken. And they were all filled with the Holy Spirit and spoke the word of God boldly.

Original Meaning

WE NOW LOOK at the response of the early church to the proscribing of evangelism, their supreme task (4:21). The apostles, upon release from the authorities, went back to "their own people and reported" (v. 23) what had happened. This section describes the response of the early church to this new threat as well as the assurance they receive from the Lord.

Praying Together (4:23-24a)

IN VERSE 23, there is no unanimity about who is meant by "their own people" (*hoi idioi*). It is sometimes translated as "their companions" (NASB).[1] It is probably a smaller company rather than the whole church.

---

1. Bruce, *Acts*, NICNT, 97.

The immediate response of this group is to pray (v. 24). Though only one prayer is given, Luke says, "They raised their voices together." It is unlikely that, as some have suggested, they prayed the same thing under divine inspiration. I prefer the interpretation of the nineteenth-century commentator J. A. Alexander, that one person prayed and "the whole company gave audible assent" to what he said. It was a common practice in biblical times to express assent by saying "Amen." Deuteronomy 27:15–26 gives a recitation of the Levites, which elicited twelve "Amens"—one after each affirmation.[2] Quietly saying something like "Amen" or "Yes, Lord" helps a person to concentrate better and participate more fully in the prayer of someone else.

The word translated "together" is one of Luke's favorite words, *homothymadon*.[3] We noted earlier the question whether this word should take the strong meaning "with one accord," which is its etymological meaning, or a milder form "together," which is how NIV translates it.[4] Whatever the meaning, the word indicates a unity among the Christians as they prayed.

Affirming God's Sovereignty (4:24b–28)

MOST OF THIS prayer is a reflection on the sovereignty of God. Even the way God is addressed, "Sovereign Lord," is significant. This translates a single word, *despotes*, used here rather than the more usual word *kyrios*. *Despotes* was used for the relation of a master to his slave. Classical writers used it for someone who had absolute powers, and it is from this use that we get the English word "despot." Josephus says it was used in connection with confessing Caesar as lord.[5] The Greeks sometimes used it for their gods, and the LXX uses it a few times for God. In the New Testament it is used three times each for God[6] and for Jesus,[7] indicating that the Christians found it a helpful, though not common, designation.[8]

The content of the prayer shows the wisdom of the translation "sovereign Lord." When this title is put together with the Christians' affirmation that God is Creator (v. 24b), we see that his sovereignty over creation is being proclaimed. The implication is that the One who created the world is more powerful than those whom he created. Therefore, nothing can thwart his plans.

---

2. Alexander, *Acts*, 163–64.

3. Of its twelve occurrences in the New Testament, eleven are in Acts.

4. See comments on 1:14, where this word also appears in the context of prayer.

5. Josephus, *Wars* 7 (cited in *NIDNTT*, 1:345).

6. See Luke 2:29; Acts 4:24; Rev. 6:10.

7. See 2 Tim. 2:21; 2 Peter 2:1; Jude 4.

8. For the use of *despotes* in the LXX and the NT see Karl H. Rengstorf, "δεσπότης," *TDNT*, 2:46–49.

The prayer goes on to assert how God's sovereignty has been revealed in history. First comes a quotation from Psalm 2:1–2 about the power of those who are opposed to God (vv. 25–26). There is a note of cynicism here. The word translated "rage" is used in "late Greek writers, primarily of the neighing of high-fed, spirited horses."[9] William Barclay comments, "They may trample and toss their heads; in the end they will have to accept the discipline of the reins."[10] The great thrusts of evil are the work of one whose power is limited. Satan is on the loose, but he is on a leash. Moreover, these people may have great plans, but they are "in vain" (*kenos*). This word means "empty things."

Verse 26 continues with the theme of opposition to God by presenting the general principle that throughout history, the powers of this world have stood against the cause of God and of Christ. Verse 27 cites the death of Christ as a specific application of this principle. At that time there was an unprecedented joining of all the powerful forces. Herod and Pilate, who had been enemies before the day of the trial, became friends. So what chance did Jesus have? It seemed like a great defeat. The people even scoffed at him and made jokes to his face. But God foresaw the evil and planned to do something good out of it (v. 28). He used it to do the greatest thing that ever happened in the history of humanity: He won its salvation.

Verses 24–26 are saturated with Scripture. This is typical of many spontaneous prayers in the Bible (e.g., Jonah in Jonah 2; Mary and Zechariah in Luke 1). Scripture had been stored in the minds and hearts of biblical people, ready to be harnessed in times of need.

Two Requests (4:29–30)

AFTER THAT EXTENDED reflection of God's sovereignty, these believers give only one passing reference to their problem (v. 29)! Earlier they had reflected on the phenomenon of opposition to the work of God. But that was in order to demonstrate that history shows that opposition is always used by God to fulfill something good. When we gaze at our sovereign God, we need only to glance at our problems. The request they make is not for wisdom, protection, or favor with the authorities. All these are appropriate petitions, of course. But this prayer is for the ability to be obedient to Christ's command to them to preach the gospel.

The second request of the disciples is that God will show his power through "miraculous signs and wonders" (v. 30). It is significant that the only two requests in this prayer have to do with evangelism, which has just been

---

9. Bruce, *Acts: Greek Text*, 157.
10. Barclay, *Acts*, 42.

outlawed! These people have a consuming passion for evangelism, and the only practical things that come to mind in this time of crisis are related to fulfilling the evangelistic task.

God's Response to the Prayer (4:31)

IN THE OLD TESTAMENT the shaking of a place (v. 31) was a sign for a theophany, that is, a manifestation of God in a visible form (Ex. 19:18; Isa. 6:4). I. Howard Marshall says, "It would have been regarded as indicating a divine response to prayer."[11] It was God's way of indicating that he was present there and would answer the prayer. Next, "they were all filled with the Holy Spirit." This is not a fresh baptism, but a fresh filling.[12] This is another instance in Acts where filling does not describe the characteristic of a person, but a special anointing. As in most of these cases, the result of the filling is proclamation. G. Campbell Morgan believes that "the new filling was intended to prevent the development of incipient fear."[13] Certainly when we experience God in a fresh way, one of the first things we receive is courage. The revelation of God makes us affirm with Paul, "If God is for us, who can be against us?" (Rom. 8:31).

Thus, it is not surprising to find verse 31 ending with the announcement that the believers "spoke the word of God boldly." The same words are used here as in the prayer for boldness in verse 29. Luke uses the imperfect tense for "spoke." In other words, as Bruce suggests, they "continued to declare the word of God with freedom of speech."[14]

WE HAVE ALREADY said that prayer is an important feature in Acts. Our passage gives us the longest prayer recorded in Acts. Presumably Luke intends this to be an example of prayer, especially of prayer in a time of crisis. The prayer ends with the seal of God's approval (v. 31). The features we see in this prayer should therefore be relevant to us today as we too face trials. Several key points emerge from this passage regarding praying in times of crisis.

Strength to face suffering. Three keys gave strength to the disciples in this crisis. (1) The first is united fellowship. The disciples were in one accord as they prayed (vv. 23–24a). The fellowship of the believers is a key theme

---

11. Marshall, *Acts*, 107.
12. Bruce, *Acts*, NICNT, 100.
13. G. Campbell Morgan, *Acts*, 135.
14. Bruce, *Acts*, NICNT, 98.

in Acts, and we need not be surprised that this comes to the fore in a time of crisis. As Daniel shared and prayed with his friends when he heard of King Nebuchadnezzar's intent to kill all his wise men (Dan. 2:17), Peter and John shared and prayed with their own people when their supreme task was made illegal. Later, when Peter was in prison at night, "the church was earnestly praying to God for him" (Acts 12:5).

We noted earlier that the individualism of contemporary society has caused us to lower our standards of fellowship. One of the saddest results of this is that it leaves us ill-equipped for crises. The apostles shared what happened and prayed together. Three things can strengthen us today as well: We meet with our colleagues—"our own people"—who know us and are committed to us, we share our situation with them, and we pray together.

(2) The next major key giving strength to the disciples is the sovereignty of God, which was the primary focus of the prayer (vv. 24b–28). Because God is sovereign over the events of history, we have nothing ultimately to fear if we are obedient. That truth should give us hope and courage amidst crises.

(3) The final key comes from the fact that this prayer is saturated in Scripture (vv. 24b–27), as were the spontaneous prayers of Jonah (Jonah 2:2–9), Mary (Luke 1:46–55), and Zechariah (1:68–79). Scriptures hidden in the heart can minister to us in our times of need. In a crisis, we often do not have time to refer to the Scriptures to see how they can address our situation. The words of the Bible need to be stored in our hearts so that we can draw on them in a crisis. Like the animals that store food during the summer for the cold season, we too must spend time in God's Word as a daily habit. Then when crises hit, that Word hidden in the heart will minister to us. David said, "I have hidden your word in my heart that I might not sin against you" (Ps. 119:11).

The Christians in Acts were saturated in Scripture. The Bible figured in their discussions before they made decisions (1:20); it formed the heart of their sermons (2:14–41) and of their defense when brought to trial (7:2–50). From their reserves of Bible knowledge they could draw out passages that spoke to situations they faced. All in all there are about two hundred references to the Old Testament in Acts, either by direct quotation, synopsis of a passage, or allusion to some event.[15] The early Christians challenge us to be similarly saturated in Scripture.[16]

The two requests. Following their gaze at God, the problems facing these believers received only a glance, while their major request had to do

---

15. Coleman, *Master Plan of Discipleship*, 105.

16. It is ironic that though the early Christians did not own individual copies of the Bible, unlike Christians today, their knowledge of the Scriptures seems to have been so much more complete than that of today's believers.

with obedience (v. 29). Today too obedience to God should be our primary concern when we face crises.

But what do we do with the second request of these believers—for signs and wonders to accompany their ministry (v. 30)? In our discussion of 2:42–47 we sought to establish the validity of a ministry of signs and wonders. But should we pray such a prayer today? Several objections can be brought to this. One is that signs and wonders ceased with the apostolic age. But we have said that this does not seem to stand the scrutiny of Scripture.

Another objection is that the reappearance of signs and wonders in recent years in the church has resulted in many abuses and in the obscuring of the heart of the gospel in evangelistic ministry. But as we noted earlier, abuse of a biblical principle is no cause for us to be afraid of the right use of it.

Still others might say that signs and wonders are relevant with uneducated and simple-minded people, but do not work with sophisticated people. In Acts, however, even sophisticated people became open and finally responded to the gospel through the medium of signs and wonders. Note Sergius Paulus, the Roman proconsul, who is described as "an intelligent man" (13:7) and is said to have come from a distinguished family.[17] Moreover, Paul healed the father of "Publius, the chief official of the island" of Malta, which opened the door for a healing ministry in the island (28:7–9). Then and now influential and powerful people have become receptive to the gospel through the prayers offered for them in a time of need, when they faced a situation that they could not control. So we too can pray the prayer of the apostles that if it pleases God, he will open the hearts of people to the gospel through the performing of some miracle among them.

God assures his troubled servants. What should we make of the shaking of the place after the prayer (v. 31)? This is an event that is not repeated in Acts (though what happened on the day of Pentecost had some similarities). It was a sign to the disciples of the presence of God (cf. also Ex. 19:18; Isa. 6:4). But we should also remember that on one occasion God did not reveal himself to a troubled servant of his through a wind, a fire, or an earthquake, but through "a gentle whisper" (1 Kings 19:11–13). God can use various means to speak to our troubled souls in order to indicate that he is with us.

God does not have to act in this way. But he knows how much strain we can take, and at crucial times he comes to us with a revelation of himself that calms our troubled minds. He did this through a vision to Paul when he faced much opposition in Corinth, which reassured him and urged him to keep on ministering there (18:9–10). This must have been a great encouragement to the apostle, for he stayed there "for a year and a half, teaching

---

17. Bruce, *Acts*, NICNT, 248.

them the word of God" (v. 11). After Paul's arrest and trial on his last visit to Jerusalem, he had a vision of the Lord that told him that he would testify in Rome (23:11). At a crucial time during the disastrous voyage by ship to Rome, an angel stood beside him at night and encouraged him (27:24). We can certainly glean an abiding principle from these instances that God often assures his servants in times of crisis.

 THIS PASSAGE HELPS those who are going through a difficult time. In 1983, just after the worst riot we had in the twenty-year ethnic conflict in Sri Lanka,[18] the first message I preached was on this passage. In the past few years this passage more than any other text in the Bible has sustained me and given me the courage to persevere.

How fellowship helps in times of crisis. Like Peter and John we too must develop the discipline of going to our "support group" in times of crisis (v. 23) for strength. (1) When we meet with our colleagues (cf. "their own people" in v. 23) who know us and are committed to us, we will receive great strength and courage from knowing that we are not alone. When we are under attack, it is easy to get discouraged and to lose our boldness and compromise by not being totally obedient to our call. It is also easy to act rashly, creating unnecessary problems to the cause of the gospel. The strength of community helps overcome these temptations.

It is therefore important that workers under threat or facing opposition be undergirded by companions in Christ. If they are working in distant areas, people should go to them regularly, or they should be expected to come regularly to where there are other colleagues. This may seem to be a waste of time and money, but in the long run it is worth it.

(2) When we share our situation with our support group, we can unburden ourselves to them. How sharing clears the air! It helps us to look at problems rationally. When we keep it to ourselves, we can become so overwhelmed by the emotional influences of the situations that we cannot think straight about the problems. But when we share it with others, we are forced to think things through; otherwise, our colleagues will not be able to understand what is going on.

(3) When we are together with our support group, we can spend time praying together. The significance of partnership in a crisis is not only the strength that we give each other; being together also causes us to motivate

---

18. The conflict is related to the demand for a separate nation by sections of the minority Tamil community.

each other to seek God, who is the source of our strength. When we are alone, we can be so engulfed by our problems that we lose sight of the sovereignty of God. Being with fellow believers helps us to direct our attention to God because he is the reason for our being united to each other.

As noted above, the word *homothymadon* implies that the early Christians were united in this time of crisis. Maintaining this unity is a key way to prepare for crises that we will encounter. Sometimes at our staff meetings I find the staff reluctant to pray. This is unnerving for me as their leader, but I have come to regard this as a sign of health. The staff who refuse to pray will not permit a hypocritical situation of praying as if there were no problems, when there are actually serious problems that need to be ironed out. Of course, we must then take the initiative to do something about these problems. If we are unable to pray together because of disunity, we must struggle with the causes of disunity until we can come to a situation of unity that enables us to pray. We meet the people concerned and confront them with the things that bother them. The day we get used to living with such problems without confronting them is the day when a deadly cancer has infected the body. It will do its work of destruction and cause spiritual death.

Crises can often break marriages and destroy the peace of churches. The individuals were not united with each other, but they were able to hide this from public view until troubles came. Then the weakness of the relationship was revealed as people began to fight over how to respond to the crisis or they blamed each other for the crisis. But if there is unity before the crisis, usually the crisis helps to deepen such unity. If, however, crises reveal a lack of unity, leaders realize they must take remedial steps, with the result that unity is deepened.

How a vision of God's sovereignty helps in times of crisis. The perspective of God's sovereignty, the major theme of the prayer in these verses, is perhaps the most important teaching that Christians need to have in times of crisis. When we are going through a crisis, the enemy seems so powerful and his schemes so well planned that we feel weak in comparison. Christians serving God in difficult and unreached areas feel like this sometimes, especially when opponents of the gospel use the authority of the ruling powers to attack them. Those working in inner cities, with drug addicts and with abused children, in remote areas, and in the business world have all testified to this sense of powerlessness. But they do not need to be discouraged. Evil may seem to have won the day, but history will show that God used that temporary loss to further the agenda of the kingdom.

We see a dual perspective in this prayer. It takes into account the full force of the enemy—and let's face it, the enemy is powerful. We would do well to know the forces that attack us and to anticipate their moves. Shortsighted "positive thinking" will not do. Biblical positive thinking takes into account the enmity of the evil one to the things of God. There will be suffering, and it may be quite severe. But God will turn it into good. While the prayer takes evil into account, before and after that accounting is a description of God and his ways. Evil is a reality, but God is a deeper and more powerful reality.

Thus, we have courage to be obedient even to death, for we know that obedience leading to death will be used as a stepping-stone for victory by God. The disciples did not know here what was in store for them. What in fact did happen was that the persecution intensified. Stephen was martyred, and after that the people were scattered (8:1). But great progress took place for the cause of the gospel.[19] God proved his sovereignty by making the suffering Christians not just conquerors but more than conquerors!

Therefore, the most important thing to bear in mind in a crisis is the sovereignty of God. An envoy from the Pope once met Martin Luther and threatened him with what would follow if he persisted in his course. He warned him that in the end all his supporters would desert him. "Where will you be, then?" he asked. Luther replied, "Then, as now, in the hands of God."[20]

For these disciples a vision of sovereignty seemed to have come at once. But for other biblical characters it came only after a time of grappling (see the book of Job; Ps. 73; Jer. 15). We must not rest until that vision comes to us. At such times what we know of God (i.e., our theology) must address our experience with the truth of sovereignty, even though that truth may seem to run counter to what we are experiencing. This is what the psalmist did in Psalm 42−43. Three times we find the refrain, "Why are you downcast, O my soul? Why so disturbed within me? Put your hope in God, for I will yet praise him, my Savior and my God" (Ps. 42:5, 11; 43:5). The psalmist is addressing his experience with what he knows of the sovereignty of God. To those who grapple in this way God will give a revelation of himself that leaves them stronger in their trust in him.

In 1874 a French steamer collided with another ship and sank, with almost everyone on board being drowned. A Christian woman on the ship, Mrs. Spafford from Chicago, was saved by a sailor who found her floating in the water, but her four children died in this accident. Her husband, Horatio Spafford, was not on the ship and received a telegram from Wales from his wife with the words, "Saved alone." Two years later he wrote a hymn in commemoration of the death of his children.

---

19. See the discussion on 7:54−8:4.
20. Barclay, *Acts*, 42.

When peace like a river, attendeth my way,
  When sorrows, like sea billows, roll,
Whatever my lot, Thou has taught me to say,
  It is well, it is well with my soul.[21]

Spafford had learned to apply the principle of God's sovereignty to every situation he faced.

We should add that belief in God's sovereignty does not give us immunity from fear. Fear is a natural human emotion in the presence of danger. But when we experience such fear, we should address it with our belief in God's sovereignty, which will enable us to concentrate on obedience without compromising and choosing an easier path. By taking fear into consideration we can also act wisely under pressure. Christians do not need to be foolhardy in their response to danger and unnecessarily cause trouble for themselves through such folly.

Bible Christians. We have a great challenge today to develop men and women of the Word, who can face crises with the strength that Scripture hidden in them can give. The early Christians were what John Wesley liked to call the early Methodists: Bible Christians. Actually they were following the example of their Master, Jesus, who in the Gospels referred to the Old Testament at least ninety times.[22] The attitude we are talking about was well expressed by Charles Spurgeon: "It is blessed to eat into the very soul of the Bible until at last you come to talk in scriptural language, and your spirit is flavored by the words of the Lord, so that your blood is bibline and the very essence of the Bible flows through you."[23] Spurgeon said in one of his sermons, "Be walking Bibles."[24]

I think the biggest crisis facing the evangelical church today is a spiritually weak leadership. We wilt when crises come. We act without adequate spiritual strength in the face of conflict, criticism, hardship, persecution, and temptation. We say we accept the Bible's authority, but in a crisis that authority seems to be forgotten so that we act in unbiblical ways. A major cause for this may be that the average Christian leader does not give time for diligent daily study, meditation, and application of the Word. If that is so, we are in serious trouble, for if our leaders exhibit this deficiency, what can we expect from the members of the church?

---

21. W. J. Limmar Sheppard, *Great Hymns and Their Stories* (London: Lutterworth, 1945), 40–41.

22. Robert E. Coleman, *The Mind of the Master* (Old Tappan, N.J.: Revell, 1977), 54. This expands to 160 when one counts duplication in parallel accounts.

23. E. W. Bacon, *Spurgeon: Heir to the Puritans* (Grand Rapids: Baker, 1967), 109.

24. Charles Spurgeon, *Spurgeon at His Best*, compiled by Tom Carter (Grand Rapids: Baker, 1988), 22.

The priority of obedience in times of crisis. We noted that the first request that the disciples made was for boldness in being obedient to Christ's command. This is because in any time of crisis, the supreme battle we have is the battle for obedience. No evil power can thwart God's marvelous plan. The only way this can happen is by our disobedience—by our not doing what we should do or not saying what we should say. Our obedience depends on availing ourselves of God's enablement for living the Christian life. If we do that, God will give us victory. The biggest enemy is not our circumstances or the wickedness and injustice of the world; rather, it is our own proneness to disobedience. D. L. Moody is reputed to have said that he had more trouble with D. L. Moody than with any other person he had met.

A colleague of mine once went with two volunteers in the eastern part of Sri Lanka for a weekend of ministry. During this time they were caught in the midst of an unexpected flare-up of the conflict in our land. Their host died of gunshot injuries, and all three were hospitalized with head injuries. They called us and requested us to come and bring them back. It was not safe for them to use public transport. We wondered how we could do that. Youth for Christ had only one vehicle—a van, quite new at that time. People said we should not take the van, for it could get taken by force by militants on the dangerous route. Some asked me and a colleague of mine not to go since, if something happened to us, Youth for Christ would be in serious trouble.

While we were deciding what to do, my stomach was tight with tension. After much prayer and discussion, we decided that my colleague and I would go to that area in our new van. The moment the decision was made, it was as if a huge burden was lifted off me. The tension was gone, for we had prayed and discerned what we thought was God's will. Now there was nothing to fear. The trip turned out to be a pleasant one, which helped build a deep tie between those we brought home and me.

How God's assurance helps in times of crisis. We said that God often reassures the faithful when they encounter crises. God does not always act in this way. Sometimes he lets us be subjected to long silences, which some have called "the dark night of the soul." Though it may be difficult to go through these periods of silence, they ultimately deepen our faith. Yet in a time of crisis it is right for us to seek his face as the disciples did here. In one such time David said, "One thing I ask of the LORD, this is what I seek: that I may dwell in the house of the LORD all the days of my life, to gaze upon the beauty of the LORD and to seek him in his temple" (Ps. 27:4). When David sought God in his house at time of crisis, he was probably "looking for the divine word or action that would satisfy the longing in his heart."[25]

---

25. Willem A. VanGemeren, "Psalms," *EBC*, 5:245.

God has his way of confirming to his children that he knows what is happening and that he is involved in the situation. Usually this confirmation comes when we are seeking God in prayer. I have often found that it comes during my devotional time, in the form of a clear message from the Word relating to the situation I am facing. I am delightfully surprised at the providence of God in getting me to read a passage appropriate to what I am going through.

At other times God's assurance comes through something that happens to us: We read or hear something that speaks specifically to us; someone gives us a gift of money in a time of serious financial crisis; someone says a word of encouragement during a time of deep discouragement; God gives us a glimpse of how he has used us at a time when we feel useless. God can even use a miraculous means like a dream, a vision, or a prophetic utterance. Whatever the means, God uses it to comfort us and help us to persevere along the path of obedience.

Two workers who belonged to a missions movement Youth for Christ helped start had seen many people turn to the Lord in an unreached area. One day they were badly assaulted by people of the majority community. When we told the police about this, they took no notice. They even chided our landlord for renting his house to Christians. The workers and new believers felt weak and vulnerable. One day I got a phone call from one of the workers to say that an armed gang was going to the homes of the believers in the middle of the night and threatening them. It was a Saturday, and I told my colleague that I would come in time for the Sunday worship service.

As I was preparing for the service that evening, something made me ask God for a special visitation upon those people. When I went to that village, I found the people shaken by the events. During the worship time I felt urged to repeat my prayer for some intervention from God that would calm these troubled people. That intervention came as I was about halfway through my sermon. A policeman walked in and asked me to come out. Outside was the police chief for the entire region. He told me that he knew about us and about the trouble we had been through. He told us not to be afraid, for they would look after us. I was amazed, considering their earlier hostile response. I went back to the people and told them about my prayer asking God to speak to them and about how God had just spoken through the police chief. The people were so thrilled that we felt we needed a time of praise before I could proceed with my sermon! God had spoken to assure his troubled children.[26]

---

26. For more on the blessings of God's intervention in times of discouragement, see the comments on 18:1–22; 21:37–23:11; 27:1–28:15.

Acts 4:32-35

ALL THE BELIEVERS were one in heart and mind. No one claimed that any of his possessions was his own, but they shared everything they had. [33]With great power the apostles continued to testify to the resurrection of the Lord Jesus, and much grace was upon them all. [34]There were no needy persons among them. For from time to time those who owned lands or houses sold them, brought the money from the sales [35]and put it at the apostles' feet, and it was distributed to anyone as he had need.

FOR A SECOND time Luke describes the quality of the radical sharing that the first Christian community practiced (see 2:44–45). This time he describes it in greater detail. The fact that he mentions this issue twice suggests we should regard it with some importance.

Luke first presents what was at the heart of the practice of sharing—a deep unity (v. 32a). In the Gospels the disciples often quarreled among each other and had to be corrected by Jesus (Luke 9:46–47; 22:24–27); but in Acts the Twelve are a unified group (2:14; 5:29; 6:2–4), and this unity now spreads to the entire church. This is often the case: When the leaders are united, it helps the members to be united too.

"One in heart and mind" (*kardia kai psyche mia*) describes a comprehensive unity. As John Wesley put it, "Their loves, their hopes, their passions joined."[1] What joined them was not simply a common affiliation to the church. There was a spiritual unity and a unity of passionate commitment to a mission. Therefore, right in the middle of this description of unity we find what looks like an interpolation regarding the witness of the apostles (v. 33). Community life is never an end in itself; a vibrant community is a community in mission.

Included in this unity was the sharing of possessions among the believers. They did not consider their possessions as their own, but "shared everything they had" (v. 32b). This sharing extended to material possessions. As a result "there were no needy persons among them." But for that to happen, some costly sacrifices had to be made by some believers who sold their lands and houses (vv. 34–35).

---

1. Wesley, *Explanatory Notes*, 408.

This practice of selling land and giving it to the church has been called Christian communism. But it is different to communism in two ways. (1) It was an entirely voluntary renunciation of wealth. Unlike Communism and the Qumran community of the first century, the sharing of property was not legislated. In fact, Peter told Ananias regarding the land he sold, "Didn't it belong to you before it was sold? And after it was sold, wasn't the money at your disposal?" (5:4). The implication is that believers did not have to sell their land or give all their proceeds to the church.

(2) Private ownership continued in the church. Acts 12:12 mentions the house of Mary the mother of John Mark. Earlier we were told that people met in each other's homes for meals (2:46). Thus, what is mentioned here is not a renunciation of all private property by everyone in the church. David Gooding points out that "the phrase 'those who owned lands or houses' [v. 34] is describing people we would call nowadays 'landlords' or 'property owners.'"[2] Brian Capper thinks that what happened was that the wealthier members, like Barnabas, who had extra land and possessions, sold some and gave the proceeds so that the poor could be looked after.[3] In this way they were following the advice of John the Baptist, who said, "The man with two tunics should share with him who has none, and the one who has food should do the same" (Luke 3:11).

There are five verbs in the imperfect tense in verses 34—35. The imperfect describes continuous action in the past. In other words, this selling of land is something that took place regularly.[4] The NIV rendering ("from time to time") attempts to express this idea. In other words, whenever there was a need, those who owned land asked themselves whether the Lord wanted them to sell this land. Some did and then gave the proceeds to the leaders to distribute wherever there was a need. I do not think this was an easy decision to make. But some did make it, and the result was the elimination of poverty in the church.

The apostles administered these funds during the early days of the church, but with the appointment of seven men to serve tables in 6:1–6, such administrative responsibilities were delegated to others. Barrett sees the record of the practice of placing things at a person's feet as a Lucanism. Luke mentions it three times in connection with offerings brought to the apostles (4:35, 37; 5:2; cf. 7:58). It "emphasizes the authority of the apostles,"[5] while Marshall thinks it "suggests some kind of legal transfer expressed in formal language."[6]

---

2. David Gooding, *True to the Faith*, 93.

3. Brian Capper, "The Palestinian Cultural Context of Earliest Christian Community of Goods," *BAFCS*, 4:340–41.

4. F. F. Bruce, *Acts: Greek Text*, 132.

5. C. K. Barrett, *Acts*, 255.

6. I. H. Marshall, *Acts*, 109.

UNITY OF HEART and mind. Paul insists that the unity of heart and mind described here (v. 32) was the norm for Christian community life: "Make my joy complete by being like-minded, having the same love, being one in spirit and purpose" (Phil. 2:2). We must strive for such unity with utmost dedication: "Make every effort to keep the unity of the Spirit through the bond of peace" (Eph. 4:3). The desire to obey and please God is a key ingredient of such unity: "May the God who gives endurance and encouragement give you a spirit of unity among yourselves as you follow Christ Jesus, so that with one heart and mouth you may glorify the God and Father of our Lord Jesus Christ" (Rom. 15:5—6).

What is described is a passionate unity or a unifying passion. This characteristic is communicated by one of Luke's favorite words, *homothymadon*, translated "with one mind" or "with one accord" in the earlier translations but "together" in some newer translations (NIV, NRSV). E. D. Schmitz describes this word as signifying a "unanimity . . . not based on common personal feelings but on a cause greater than the individual."[7]

Christian sharing and possessions. Mammon has always been a key obstacle in the spiritual life (1 Tim. 6:10). Since fellowship is a spiritual reality, this aspect needs to be ironed out at the beginning of a church's life. That is why Luke mentioned this concept in his first summary description of the community life in the church (2:44—45). Today too we should be looking at what it means to extend oneness of heart and mind to our possessions.

Keeping the priority of evangelism. Verses 32 and 34 are about the sharing of possessions. But sandwiched between them is a verse about evangelism (v. 33). Why this detour? Because community life is never an end in itself. Harrison comments: "Maintenance of the group was not the primary consideration. . . . Above all, this was a witnessing community, and for this reason they enjoyed 'much grace' from the Lord."[8] It is easy for a movement to concentrate so much on consolidation after its initial growth that evangelism loses its place of priority.

Luke guards against giving any impression that there was any period when the early church did not evangelize. Acts 1 gives the commission as it came from the lips of Jesus (1:8), and in the same chapter Peter tells the believers that Judas's replacement had to be a witness of Christ's resurrection (1:22). Every chapter of Acts (except ch. 27) says something about evangelism. This first church history textbook is essentially a history of evangelism.

---

7. E. D. Schmitz, "Unanimity," *NIDNTT*, 3:908. See also comments on 1:14; 4:24.

8. Harrison, *Interpreting Acts*, 98.

The redistribution of wealth. The practice in the early church of sharing possessions through the redistribution of wealth has not been viewed
favorably by many contemporary Christians. Capper gives three reasons for
this sentiment. (1) Some extreme Anabaptist groups derived the basis for
their radical community life from our text. (2) Socialist thinkers over the last
hundred years used this passage in defense of their views on the organization of the state. (3) Many scholars have a negative assessment of Acts as a
historical source and suggest that this sharing never really happened—that
Luke created an ideal community, not a real one.[9]

It is true that some Greek writings present an ideal model. Plato in his
Republic presented such a utopian society, and many scholars have insisted that
this type of community was alien to Palestinian society. The force of this argument has been reduced considerably by the discovery, through the Dead
Sea Scrolls, of a strong model of radical sharing in the Essene communities.
This had been recorded by historians like Philo, Pliny, and Josephus. But
"our information about this practice was substantially augmented by the discovery of *The Rule of Community* (1QS) from Cave 1 at Qumran, which contains the legislation which governed the practice of the community of
goods."[10] We might also point out that Luke does not describe a utopian
society, for the next chapters tell us about the sin of Ananias and Sapphira
(5:1–11) and about the Hellenic Jews who grumbled about the inequitable
distribution of food (6:1–6).

Others scholars have claimed that Acts records an experiment in community living that failed. They say that some of the early Christians were starry-
eyed idealists, who were generous to a fault. They were so enthusiastic about
giving that they unwisely sold their possessions so that the Christians were
without their regular sources of income. One critic says, "The trouble in
Jerusalem was that they turned their capital into income, and had no cushion
for hard times, and the Gentile Christians had to come to their rescue."[11]

In answer to these critics, we must mention that there is not the slightest
hint in Acts that the sharing of these early Christians was a mistake, even
though when Luke wrote about this practice, he was aware of the financial
difficulties of the church at Jerusalem. Luke mentions this practice twice in

---

9. Capper, "Community of Goods," 356.

10. See Capper, "Community of Goods," 327. For an elaboration of this point see ibid.,
326–35. For other arguments on the historical reliability of this account, see ibid., 324–27;
Gonzales, *Faith and Wealth: A History of Early Christian Ideas on the Origin, Significance, and Use of
Money* (San Francisco, Harper & Row, 1990), 80–81.

11. J. A. Zeisler, *Christian Asceticism* (Grand Rapids: Eerdmans, 1973), 110; cited in Ronald
J. Sider, *Rich Christians in an Age of Hunger: A Biblical Study* (London: Hodder and Stoughton,
1977), 91.

Acts, and the first time, after describing the community life, he writes, "And the Lord added to their number daily those who were being saved" (2:47). Note the statement in the present passage: "With great power the apostles continued to testify to the resurrection of the Lord Jesus, and much grace was upon them all" (4:33). This was a powerful and healthy church.

There is also evidence that this practice was followed even after the New Testament era.[12] In other words, succeeding generations of Christians did not view this pattern as a mistake. Justin Martyr (c. 100–165) wrote of the Christians in the second century, "We who valued above all things the acquisition of wealth and possessions, now bring what we have to a common stock, and communicate to [share with] every one in need."[13] The second-century pagan Greek satirist Lucian of Samosata (c. 115–200) describes Christians as ethical but easily duped by charlatans. In his tale *The Passing of Peregrinus*, he writes of them:

> They show incredible speed whenever any such public action is taken [the arrest of Christians]; for in no time they lavish their all. . . . They despise all things indiscriminately and consider them common property. . . . So if any charlatan and trickster, able to profit by occasions, comes among them, he quickly acquires sudden wealth by imposing upon simple folk.[14]

While rejecting the naive simplicity reflected here,[15] this quote shows that Christian sharing and generosity were still making an impact on outsiders in the second century.

Moreover, the poverty in the Jerusalem church was not caused by this attitude of sharing. There were many reasons for this poverty. The Jerusalem church began with many poor people. Fisherman and peasants migrating from Galilee would find earning a living difficult in the capital city. Moreover, "since many Jews returned to Jerusalem to die, it is likely that the church had a higher proportion of older converts."[16] Possibly persecution took the form of economic discrimination.[17] Christians likely did not have access to the Jewish system of supplying the needs of people like widows. Finally,

---

12. See Gonzales, *Faith and Wealth.*

13. *The First Apology*, 14. *Ante-Nicene Fathers*, eds. Alexander Roberts and James Donaldson, American ed. (Grand Rapids: Eerdmans, 1996 reprint of New York: Scribner's, 1908–11), 1:167.

14. Lucian of Samosata, *The Passing of Peregrinus*, 13. Cited from the Loeb Classical Library ed. in Boring, *Hellenistic Commentary*, 313–14.

15. See below on "Giving to a central fund."

16. Peter H. Davids, "New Testament Foundations for Living More Simply," *Living More Simply*, ed., Ronald J. Sider (Downers Grove, Ill.: InterVarsity, 1980), 57.

17. Ibid.

Jerusalem's economic situation was in bad shape in the first century, having deteriorated through constant famines and shortages and continued unrest (see Suetonius, Tacitus, and Josephus).[18]

What principles are there in this section that we can follow in today's world? At different times Christians have practiced a radical community by fully giving what they owned into a common pool, out of which personal needs were then met. Many Roman Catholic orders that adopted a monastic lifestyle in the Middle Ages operated like this. Anabaptist groups, such as the Amish and the Hutterites, also followed this type of Christian communism. In the sixteenth century the Hutterites, who began in Moravia in Europe, grew to about 25,000 through their farm colonies known as *Bruderhofs*. Amish groups are still found in North America. Different groups of sincere Christians still exist that decide God has called them into a community to share in a radical community of goods, yet they do not insist on this for everyone. They see it rather as a specialized call.

It is true, of course, that if wealth becomes a hindrance to one's spiritual life, we may be required to renounce it, as the rich young ruler was asked to do (Luke 18:22). We should also not forget that Jesus himself said, "Sell your possessions and give to the poor" (12:33). Thus, while an important Christian practice is described here, we should be careful about using it to make absolute rules about sharing property that apply to all Christians. Rather, we should see this as a challenge to us regarding our attitude toward each other in the body of Christ and our attitude toward wealth. We should not regard anything we have as belonging exclusively to us but as belonging primarily to God; as his stewards, he expects us to use it wisely. We should ensure that there is no one in need in the body of Christ.

A great majority of Anabaptists today do not follow the way of a radical community of goods but, in the words of an Anabaptist scholar, "Possessing many of the same ideals, they have preferred to live and do business in society. Yet they hold private property as a sacred trust to be shared both within and outside the church family in many forms of relief work and mutual aid."[19] Thus, often when disaster strikes, the Mennonites (who are Anabaptists) are among the first to volunteer their services and expertise. They have developed a lifestyle that has been fashioned by Paul's advice regarding the rich: "Command them to do good, to be rich in good deeds, and to be generous and willing to share" (1 Tim. 6:18).

Giving to a central fund. In the early church money was given to a central fund, out of which it was disbursed to the needy (vv. 34b—35). I do not

---

18. Gonzales, *Faith and Wealth*, 81.
19. Faw, *Acts*, 57.

think we can make a rule that this is the only method to give to the needy. Sometimes we may give gifts directly to needy persons. But in keeping with our conviction that the narratives of the Bible can give examples that inspire us,[20] we may view this practice as an example given for our inspiration.

MAINTAINING A UNIFYING **passion today.** While being one in heart and mind is considered the usual model for Christian community life, it is not easy to maintain in today's individualistic society. We do not like having anyone "pry" into our personal lives, which would be necessary if the model shown in Acts were to be followed. For this reason many have lowered their standards and settled for a functional unity that comes more from secular management studies than from God's Word. People agree to work according to a plan, even through they may not be "one in heart and mind" with it. But can we jettison this biblical model so easily? Given the fact that there are so many commands to this model of unity, we should not be satisfied by lowering our standards.

This is an area where the church needs to be countercultural. In a society where people deny the community orientation that is part of human nature in order to protect their privacy, close Christian community life may be one of the most important prophetic messages we can give the world. No one cannot deny one's essential humanity without sooner or later feeling a void inside. The church must present itself as the group that can adequately fill this thirst for community in the heart of the human being.

But such deep unity is not easy to maintain. If our standards are high, our expectations from each other will also be high. Consequently the pain of disappointment will also be high. I believe this is a primary reason why people have lowered their standards of what to expect from Christian community. It is too painful to try to be one in the way the Bible describes unity. But the great blessing of completeness in life, motivation to holiness and excellence, and security that comes from those to whom they are accountable await those who attempt this.

I see five key biblical requirements needed to maintain a biblical level of unity. (1) Individuals must crucify themselves. This is clearly taught in Paul's great passage on unity (Phil. 2:1–11), where Christ's humiliation is presented as the model for our lifestyle if we are to maintain unity within the body. True, at times small annoyances will confront us; at such times a crucified self uses long-suffering. As Paul said just prior to urging the Ephesians to maintain the

---

20. See the section on, "Applying the Book of Acts Today," in the Introduction.

unity of the Spirit, we must "be patient, bearing with one another in love" (Eph. 4:2). When we are hurt in a conflict situation, crucified selves follow Paul's admonition: "Be kind and compassionate to one another, forgiving each other, just as in Christ God forgave you" (4:32).

One of the biggest hindrances to maintaining unity is hurt individuals who, in their efforts to solve a problem, give vent to their hurts. This may take the form of a battle for justice or truth, but is actually a battle to retrieve a hurt ego. A crucified self does not insist on its own way (1 Cor. 13:5). It should be willing to compromise on nonessentials for the greater good.

When self has been crucified, then we can follow Paul's injunction, "Submit to one another out of reverence for Christ" (Eph. 5:21). Paul uses the verb "submit" twenty-three times in his letters. F. F. Bruce says, "Reciprocal submission is a basic element in Christian ethical tradition."[21] This is hard to envision in our individualistic age, where terms like *submission* imply that one's individual freedom is being jeopardized.

Many Christians refer to abuses of this principle of submission to eliminate it completely from their lives. They do not feel a church has any right to makes demands on members. They choose which church they will join and choose to leave it when "it does not meet their needs." Such people will not get the benefit of deep fellowship from any church and will not receive the security and enrichment that comes from spiritual accountability. We must not allow abuses of the principle of submission to cause us to miss out on the great blessings that come from it.

(2) Leaders should make maintaining this unity one of their primary responsibilities. Paul's admonition in Ephesians 4:3, "Make every effort to keep the unity of the Spirit through the bond of peace," is particularly applicable to leaders. I think the biggest challenge I have had in leading Youth for Christ in Sri Lanka for twenty-one years has been that of attempting to maintain this principle, especially among our leaders. It is easy to get so engrossed in fulfilling our mission that we ignore or postpone dealing with matters of unity in the body. But that is suicidal, for such issues will emerge; when they do, they usually emerge as huge conflicts, sometimes even resulting in people leaving the group.

You cannot force a person to walk in the light. But if he or she does not, you know that no true fellowship is possible with that person (1 John 1:7). The leader's task is to pray and act so that everyone walks in the light with each other. (Incidentally, working towards this goal has often resulted in the onset of revival in the church.) Perhaps the most dangerous hindrance to unity that

---

21. Quoted in Leon Morris, *Expository Reflections on the Letter to the Ephesians* (Grand Rapids: Baker, 1994), 182.

can come from a leader is for him or her to take sides when cliques form and rivalries appear. Leaders must resist the tendency to lower their standards of unity and settle for less than a body life with one heart and one mind.

(3) Believers, especially team members, should meet often to share openly. The picture we get from the Gospels about Jesus' band of disciples is that of a group who spent a lot of time traveling, worshiping, talking, ministering, and learning together. It is when we "walk in the light" that "we have fellowship with one another" (1 John 1:7, NASB). But such openness of fellowship takes time to forge and maintain.

In this busy world we must find time for what we consider important—including regular meetings. Leaders should insist that such meetings take place. Each team member may be so engrossed in his or her particular mission that they lose sight of the importance of meeting with other members. Leaders should insist that these meetings be a priority by others on the team. Through them spiritual accountability can be forged. One of the greatest dangers in Christian ministry today is that many leaders are not accountable to anyone spiritually. We have developed good systems of financial and ministerial accountability by which our financial and ministerial activities are monitored, but we have forgotten the need for spiritual accountability.

The leaders should set a tone that allows people to share openly. This is well expressed in the "bands" or little companies that John Wesley set up for members in the early Methodist movements. Because of the sensitive nature of what was discussed at these meetings, he separated the men and women in these groups. He made the following rules:

> In order to "confess our faults one to another," and pray one for another that we may be healed, we intend, (1) To meet once a week, at the least. (2) To come punctually at the hour appointed. (3) To begin with singing or prayer. (4) To speak each of us in order, freely and plainly, the true state of our soul, with the faults we have committed in thought, word, or deed, and the temptations we have felt since the last meeting. (5) To desire some person among us (thence called a Leader) to speak his own state first, and then to ask the rest, in order, as many and as searching questions as may be, concerning their state, sins, and temptations.[22]

(4) Christian fellowship is essentially a spiritual unity in Christ. "Encouragement from being united with Christ" (Phil. 2:1) enables us to be "likeminded, having the same love, being one in spirit and purpose" (2:2; cf. Eph.

---

22. Robert G. Tuttle Jr., *John Wesley: His Life and Theology* (Grand Rapids: Zondervan, 1978), 278–79.

4:3). One of the ways to maintain this spiritual tie is to practice those things that will help deepen it. Through these we enjoy unconsciously what unites us, and that makes us realize that our differences are inconsequential.

We can mention several activities that confirm us in our unity in Christ. (a) *Worship and prayer* come to mind first. Acts consciously presents the connection between unity and prayer in 1:14 and 4:23.[23] Matthew 18:19–20 speaks of people agreeing in prayer and coming together in Christ's name, which will result in Christ's special presence. (b) Next is *a common commitment to the truths of God's Word.* The result of ministry of the Word by apostles, prophets, evangelists, pastors, and teachers in the church is that "we all reach unity in the faith and in the knowledge of the Son of God and become mature" (Eph. 4:13). (c) Romans 15:5–6 shows how *commitment to a common mission fosters* unity: "May the God who gives endurance and encouragement give you a spirit of unity among yourselves as you follow Christ Jesus, so that with one heart and mouth you may glorify the God and Father of our Lord Jesus Christ." An evangelistic passion certainly becomes a motive for unity, as Jesus said in his high priestly prayer: "May they be brought to complete unity to let the world know that you sent me and have loved them even as you have loved me" (John 17:23).

I will never forget a meeting of the Younger Leaders Committee of the Lausanne Committee for World Evangelization that I attended in Stuttgart, Germany. We had gathered to organize "Singapore '87: The Lausanne Younger Leaders Conference." Each one there was a leader in his or her own right. We came from different ecclesiastical traditions and had strong convictions about how the conference should be run. On the first few days it seemed as if we could not agree on anything, and the arguments became heated. Toward the end of the meeting, we had serious doubts whether we could even make the conference work.

On the last day our leader, Canadian Brian Stiller, led us in an extended time of worship. Hardly any decisions had been made regarding the conference. But we worshiped God for two to three hours. Our worship consisted of testimony, ministry of the Word, praise through prayer and song, and intercession. We all sensed that God had done something among us. We affirmed what had made us one and that God had knit our hearts together in a most wonderful way. In the few hours that remained, we were able to cover a volume of work much greater than what we did during the first few days of grappling. I believe the Lord richly blessed the conference, and the wonderful ties of friendship that developed among the committee members

---

23. Depending on how we understand the meaning of *homothymadon* used in these two verses.

remain to this day. It was to me one of the sweetest experiences of the glory of the body of Christ that spans the globe and brings people of such diverse personalities and cultures into one happy family.

(5) The final key to maintain a biblical level and quality of unity is that of striving for agreement over a course of action. Acts 15 gives us a good illustration of this. When some men from Judea came to Antioch and brought theological confusion about the place of circumcision in the Christian's life, Paul and Barnabas immediately took the long trip to Jerusalem. The church there summoned what is now known as the Jerusalem Council. Different groups were able to present their viewpoints. Under the statesmanlike leadership of James the council was able to come up with a solution that everyone agreed with (15:25–28).[24] Luke reports the solution on the controversy about the neglect of Grecian widows in a similar way (6:5).

Often in our hurry to get about our business, we are impatient to grapple for such unity. This is a near-sighted strategy, for the resulting lack of unity stunts growth, affects spiritual vitality, and hampers the fruitfulness of the group.

Extending oneness to our possessions. How believers view their possessions is an important aspect of Christian fellowship. Usually when we think of fellowship, we think of spiritual unity, of good relationships existing within the community, and of the sharing of good feelings towards each other. But the characteristically Christian word for fellowship, *koinonia*, means much more than that. Historian Justo L. Gonzales has shown that in the Bible, *koinonia* and its related words have the meaning of partnership as well.[25] Thus, we need to rethink our understanding of Christian fellowship in the light of what the New Testament records. True fellowship includes the attitude "this is not my own" to what one possesses. True accountability must involve our finances as well as other aspects of our lives.

Many people today do not like to talk to others about their finances; rather, they guard this area as if it is no one else's business but their own. They do not want to be accountable to others about what they spend their money on. This is especially true when there are big differences in the economic situation within a community. If there are rich and poor in the same community, the rich might be embarrassed about how they spend their money while their poor brothers and sisters barely struggle to survive.

---

24. In 15:24 the word *homothymadon* is used with the unmistakable meaning of "being of one mind."

25. Gonzales, *Faith and Wealth*, 82–83. The examples he cites include the business partnership between Peter and the sons of Zebedee (Luke 5:10), our sharing in Christ's sufferings (Phil. 3:10), our sharing in the body and the blood of Christ in the Lord's Supper (1 Cor. 10:16), and the giving and receiving of financial support between Paul and the Philippians (Phil. 4:15).

But refusal to share this aspect of our lives immediately lowers the level of fellowship. The poorer believers feel distant from the others, so that they do not have a sense of ownership of the enterprise. They may be tempted to be dishonest in using church funds. Satan may tempt a poorer employee of a Christian organization with thoughts like this: "How unfair it is for that person to be so rich while you are so poor—and both of you work for the same organization."

I was once speaking to a leader of a Christian movement where there is a wide disparity between the salaries of different staff members. This person said that they have found it almost impossible to trust poorer people, especially in the area of finances. One of the best antidotes to this is an attitude of openness about all things, including possessions. In such a situation it is difficult for a dishonest person to survive; he or she will either change or leave the organization.

Most business organizations keep the salary book private and secret, and many Christian groups have adopted this approach. But that hinders the oneness we have from extending to material possessions, which will greatly reduce the depth of oneness. We must remember that Jesus' team had a common purse (John 12:6; 13:29). The fact that the treasurer was dishonest does not negate the fact that Jesus considered such oneness about finances advisable for his team.

Of course, in order to be open about such things, it is essential that even the wealthy adopt a relatively simple lifestyle and avoid what others consider unnecessary extravagance. That is so hard for many people to do. They reason, "This is my hard-earned money. What I am spending it on is not sinful. I see no reason why I should not spend it this or that way." This attitude breaks down the fellowship and makes the community much less powerful in terms of its eternal impact. By adopting a simple lifestyle, we are not stumbling blocks to poorer Christians, and by so doing we make true partnership possible.

Giving evangelism priority today. It is difficult in this age of specialization to integrate the various aspects of the Christian life into one church. As a result, we have churches that have become specialists in one particular area. The New Testament presents a church that tried to be faithful in all the areas of the call of God.

We noted that Acts is essentially a history of evangelization in the first few decades of the Christian era. When I studied church history in seminary, the focus was more on doctrinal controversies and the progress of doctrine. Important as that is, the primary factor in church history should always be the progress of evangelization. Kenneth Scott Latourette was right on the mark when he entitled his monumental seven-volume history of the church, *A History of the Expansion of Christianity*.[26]

It is the task of a leader to ensure that a movement "keeps the main thing the main thing." Sometimes for a consolidation stage in a movement people who are good managers are chosen to replace the retiring visionary pioneer. This may be a wise move. But if the manager has no passion for evangelism, a slow rot can gradually convert the movement into a machine and finally make it into a monument.

This focus on evangelism will help maintain unity in the church. Albert Lee, who directs Youth for Christ in Singapore, has said that the church has many generals and that generals exist by battling. Thus, if they are not battling Satan for the expansion of the kingdom, they will end up battling themselves. All too often leaders' meetings in churches that have lost their evangelistic passion become an unbearable test of patience because hours are spent battling matters that are of little consequence in connection with the growth of God's kingdom. If we feel a passion to get the message to the lost and if we have crucified self, we will not waste time arguing over inconsequential things.

Sharing personal possessions today. "There were no needy persons among them" (v. 34). Paul wrote, "Our desire is not that others might be relieved while you are hard pressed, but that there might be equality" (2 Cor. 8:13). Relative equality is a goal every Christian should strive for. I use the term *relative* because people's spending can vary according to their culture and responsibilities. But we must strive to have a situation where there are no needy people in the church. Thus, Christians should not decide on their lifestyle by looking at their peers in society, but rather after looking at the needs of the believers around them.

A Christian may save funds over a considerable period of time to buy something or do an improvement on her house. Others may think this is an essential expenditure. But then she may find that a fellow Christian has an urgent need that should be met, and she may decide to give these funds to her friend. There is a great freedom and joy that comes from such a lifestyle that is rich in giving rather than in using for oneself.

Sadly, we cannot say that there are no needy people in the church today. But often we do not know the needs of fellow Christians. The economically

---

26. Kenneth Scott Latourette, *A History of the Expansion of Christianity*, 7 vols. (1937–1945, reprint Grand Rapids: Zondervan, 1970). Latourette's work was a step in the right direction. We must, however, not forget Wilbert Shenk's pertinent criticism about many church histories emerging from the West: "In the West, the history of the churches in Asia, Africa, and Latin America is generally subsumed to be a subcategory of Western mission history" ("Toward a Global Church History," *International Bulletin of Missionary Research*, 20 [April 1996]: 50).

poor and rich often go to different churches. People like to be comfortable in church (I do not know from where in the Bible they got that idea!), so they go to churches with a majority of people like themselves. Some even go through an elaborate process of shopping for a church that they will be comfortable with. In New Testament times there was a cultural diversity in the church.[27] Admittedly, that led to problems, such as in Acts 6:1–6, when the Hellenists complained against the Hebraic Jews. But they did not divide the church as a result; instead, they sought to solve the problem as it surfaced.

A great enrichment and a sobering effect await us if we worship and commune in an economically integrated church. We will be struck by the needs of others and realize how much of our expenditure is unnecessary and perhaps even sinful in light of the needs of others. That will force us to be generous. If we do not share, our fellowship with the needy will be hindered. It may also make us upset about the causes of poverty and drive us to do something about it.

This is how the Methodist revival resulted in so much social transformation. In the small groups of early Methodism the poor began to talk about their working and living conditions. The more wealthy members were appalled and did something to change that situation. This also drove them to be committed to a relatively simple lifestyle. John Wesley said in a letter to the Commissioner of Excise, replying to an inquiry about undeclared plate silver: "Sir, I have two silver teaspoons at London, two at Bristol. This is all the plate silver I have at present, and I will not buy any more while so many around me go hungry."[28]

A vital awareness of the needs of the poor through fellowshiping with them also influences our priorities for church life. Roy Clements says that the early church father Ambrose, bishop of Milan (c. 339–397), "rebuked the church of his day for the amount of money spent on beautifying its church buildings, while neglecting the service of the poor." Ambrose is reputed to have said, "A slave redeemed at the church's expense is a far better decoration for the Holy Communion table than a golden chalice."[29]

Giving does not become a major sacrifice when we realize that God owns our possessions. A good example of this attitude toward possessions is described by Juan Carlos Ortiz. When pastors first began to preach the message of discipleship in their church in Buenos Aires, many members brought the titles to their homes and apartments to give to the church. The leaders did not know what to do with this money. After six months of praying about this, they called

---

27. See David A. Fiensy, "The Composition of the Jerusalem Church," *BAFCS*, 4:213–36.

28. From John Wesley's *Letters*, 1776, cited in *The Daily Wesley*, ed. Donald E. Demaray (Anderson, Ind.: Bristol House, 1994), 299.

29. Clements, *The Church That Turned the World Upside Down*, 44.

the people and told them that they have decided to return everyone's real estate. "The Lord showed us that he doesn't want your empty houses," they said. "He wants a house with you inside taking care of it. He wants … everything ready—for him. He also wants your car, with you as the driver." But they added, "Just remember, though, that it all still belongs to him."

Ortiz says that now all houses are open. "When visitors come to our congregation, we don't say, 'Who can take these brothers into your house.' We don't ask; we command because the house is already given to the Lord. And the people thank the Lord that he lets them live in his house." [30] I still think it is a good thing to ask, since some may be more ready to have someone in their house than others at a given time. But the principle is clear: If we say that our possessions belong to the Lord, we should act as if they do.

Now I am aware of some who say that if the poor would only work harder, they would make it without needing the help of others. I suppose that would be possible in an ideal society. But we live in a society where many need a push to get started. They simply do not have the opportunities or the motivation because of the environment they have grown up in. This is why in the Bible there are elaborate instructions on how the weak should be looked after as well as stirring challenges to help the needy.

The recent collapse of the economies of communist countries and of rigidly socialist welfare states shows how important it is to encourage personal initiative. It is easy to foster a destructive welfare mentality among the poor when relief is doled out indiscriminately. But this is not possible in the type of Christian community the Bible is talking about. Here the unity is such that everyone feels he or she is a vital part of the movement. It is not a case of rich donors helping poor people who think the rich owe it to them. Rather, it is the case of a community where everyone grows together as equals and contributes vitally with their unique gifts for the common good. Some give money while others give nonmaterial gifts.

Some years ago the governments of many countries began to do what the churches did in terms of social welfare. As a result churches reduced their social programs. But in recent years governments are allocating less funds for welfare programs. This means that the church (and other "volunteer organizations") will once again have to take on a prominent role in helping the needy within and without the church.

Advantages of giving to a central fund. While giving to a central fund is not an invariable rule, there are some advantages in this method. (1) It avoids the unhealthy sense of obligation that a receiver can develop toward

---

30. Juan Carlos Ortiz, *Disciple: A Handbook for New Believers* (Orlando: Creation House, 1995), 36.

a donor. In countries with distinct classes, it is often difficult for a poor believer to regard a rich Christian as an equal. The receiver may develop a sense of obligation to a donor that prevents the two of them from acting as equals in the community of faith. Besides, this type of giving often makes "the poor too much dependent on a few rich individuals."[31]

(2) If the administrators of the common fund are faithful and wise stewards of God's money, they will ensure that the money is used responsibly. Often we respond to a need we see according to our emotional feelings at the time. That may occasionally be helpful. But sometimes money goes to the wrong people or in the wrong way because the giving was not preceded by careful consideration of some necessary factors. Sometimes the best way to meet a need is not to give relief but to help the person tackle the *cause* for the need. For example, it may be better to give a person capital to get started on a trade than to give him food. The trade will help him to earn money to feed himself and his family. As the common proverb says, "If you give a man a fish, you feed him for a day; if you teach him how to fish, you feed him for a lifetime." A responsible group that considers such issues carefully will therefore be a better initial recipient of our donations than a needy individual.

Lest we miss the challenge of this passage to us, I will conclude this study with a description of the church's care for the poor that comes from the second or third century:

> Be solicitous about their maintenance, being in nothing wanting to them; exhibiting to the orphans the care of parents; to the widows the care of husbands; to those of suitable age, marriage; to the artificer, work; to the unable, commiseration; to the strangers, a house; to the hungry, food; to the thirsty, drink; to the naked, clothing; to the sick, visitation; to the prisoners, assistance ... to the maiden, give her in marriage ... to the young man, assistance that he may learn a trade and may be maintained by the advantage arising from it.[32]

---

31. Gooding, *True to the Faith*, 93.

32. *Constitutions of the Holy Apostles*, 4.1.2. Quoted in Thomas C. Oden, *Classical Pastoral Care, Crisis Ministries* (Grand Rapids: Baker, 1994), 4:145. "The *Constitutions* are a collection of church canons compiled between 350–400 A.D. probably of second and third century, and chiefly Syrian, origin" (ibid., 196).

Acts 4:36–5:11

JOSEPH, A LEVITE from Cyprus, whom the apostles called Barnabas (which means Son of Encouragement), ³⁷sold a field he owned and brought the money and put it at the apostles' feet.

⁵:¹Now a man named Ananias, together with his wife Sapphira, also sold a piece of property. ²With his wife's full knowledge he kept back part of the money for himself, but brought the rest and put it at the apostles' feet.

³Then Peter said, "Ananias, how is it that Satan has so filled your heart that you have lied to the Holy Spirit and have kept for yourself some of the money you received for the land? ⁴Didn't it belong to you before it was sold? And after it was sold, wasn't the money at your disposal? What made you think of doing such a thing? You have not lied to men but to God."

⁵When Ananias heard this, he fell down and died. And great fear seized all who heard what had happened. ⁶Then the young men came forward, wrapped up his body, and carried him out and buried him.

⁷About three hours later his wife came in, not knowing what had happened. ⁸Peter asked her, "Tell me, is this the price you and Ananias got for the land?"

"Yes," she said, "that is the price."

⁹Peter said to her, "How could you agree to test the Spirit of the Lord? Look! The feet of the men who buried your husband are at the door, and they will carry you out also."

¹⁰At that moment she fell down at his feet and died. Then the young men came in and, finding her dead, carried her out and buried her beside her husband. ¹¹Great fear seized the whole church and all who heard about these events.

Original Meaning

THUS FAR WE have seen the church in a positive light, faithfully and effectively facing crises and challenges both from within and from without. Now Luke gives us an instance in which sin manifested itself within the church; he tells us how the church dealt with this situation.

The Generosity of Barnabas (4:36–37)

AFTER DESCRIBING THE spirit of sharing in the church (4:32–35), Luke gives good and bad examples of this sharing. The good example is Barnabas, who must have been singled out because he will play a key role in the unfolding events of Acts. His willingness to give up his land harmonizes with his unselfish style of enabling others, which we see elsewhere in Acts.

Joseph, a man from Cyprus, was given the nickname Barnabas, translated in the NIV as "Son of Encouragement" (4:36). It was common in Semitic languages to use "son" (*bar*) to indicate a person's character.[1] The exact meaning of Barnabas, however, is not easy to arrive at. It seems to mean "son of prophecy" (*bar* means "son of" and *nabi* means "prophet"). The NIV translates the Greek word *paraklesis* as "encouragement," a word that can mean encouragement but also consolation or exhortation. Perhaps we should translate Luke's definition as "Son of Exhortation." Barnabas "probably earned his new name through effective preaching and teaching."[2]

Being a Levite from Cyprus, Barnabas was from the large groups of Hellenistic Jews who migrated back to Jerusalem. He must have been from a wealthy background, for the mother of his cousin Mark had a house large enough to accommodate a prayer meeting for "many people" (12:12). Since, according to the Old Testament, Levites were not to own land, the plot he sold may have been his burial place.[3] Or perhaps "the Pentateuchal regulations prohibiting priests and Levites from holding landed property seem to have become a dead letter by this time."[4]

The Deception of Ananias and Sapphira (5:1–11)

THE BAD EXAMPLE of sharing is that of Ananias and Sapphira, who sold their property but kept back some of the money for themselves (5:1–2). "Kept back" (Gk. *nosphizo*) literally means pilfer, embezzle. It is interesting that Luke uses this word, for what this couple technically kept back was part of their own money. *Nosphizo* appears again in the New Testament only in verse 3 and Titus 2:10 (where it is translated "steal"). The LXX uses this word for Achan, who kept some of the booty from the spoils of war that had been devoted to God (Josh. 7:1). There, as here, the sin met with a severe punishment. The rarity of the word in the New Testament suggests that Luke deliberately drew on the language of the Old Testament.[5] In any case, wrong use of our possessions is a serious sin in God's sight.

---

1. G. M. Burge, "Barnabas," *DPL*, 66.
2. "Barnabas," *BEB*, 264.
3. Barrett, *Acts*, 260.
4. Bruce, *Acts*, NICNT, 101.
5. D. J. Williams, *Acts*, 96.

But Peter discerned what was happening. Was this through the expressions of guilt on the faces of these two, as some have suggested? More likely it was a direct prophetic revelation from God.[6] Five important truths emerge from Peter's words to Ananias in 5:3. (1) Satan had so filled and controlled Ananias's heart that he was carried away in his actions.

(2) Satan's activity does not remove culpability from Ananias. Verse 3 attributes the act to Satan's infilling, but verse 4 places responsibility for his action squarely on Ananias.

(3) The most serious thing Ananias did was to lie to the Holy Spirit, not keep back part of the money. Later Peter said that he could have done whatever he wanted with his money (v. 4).

(4) When we lie to the church, we lie to the Holy Spirit. We see the developing theology of the church here. In 5:11 we find the first of twenty-three times that the word *ekklesia* appears in Acts.[7] Saul/Paul finds out later that when he persecuted the church, he was persecuting Jesus (9:4). Later he expresses the treasured teaching that the church is the body of Christ (1 Cor. 12:27; Eph. 4:12; 5:23).

(5) Since giving everything was not mandatory (v. 4), the particular desire that Satan had filled Ananias and Sapphira with was the desire for recognition by the church. They lied to win the same sort of esteem that Barnabas had won in the church.

Ananias first and then Sapphira fell down dead following Peter's forthright condemnation (5:5, 10). One can imagine how surprised the bystanders must have been as they saw Peter, probably not a rich man, rebuking the rich giver of a large contribution. But whoever the person and however big the gift, sin is sin, and it has to be dealt with decisively. We are not told the biological cause of these two deaths. Some scholars do not accept the biblical record that they died immediately. They claim such an event is not in keeping with the spirit of Christianity. Rather, so these scholars say, the first deaths in the Christian community came as a shock to the believers, since they thought no one would die in the new age that had dawned. Thus, this story was created to conclude that these deaths were a judgment of God. But there is not a single hint in the text that this was what happened. Whatever the cause, the important thing is that the church saw it as God's judgment on the couple for their deceit.

The result of the death of Ananias is that "great fear seized all who heard what had happened" (5:5b). Luke repeats this affirmation at the end of the

---

6. Earle E. Ellis, *Prophecy and Hermeneutic in Early Christianity: New Testament Essays* (Grand Rapids: Eerdmans, 1978), 129.

7. Some Greek manuscripts have it in 2:47, but that seems to be an explanatory addition by a scribe (see Metzger, *Textual*, 305).

story (5:11). In other words, the fear resulting from judgment is a key aspect of the story. This was a fear of displeasing God that comes from a knowledge of his holiness and the consequences of our sin.

LUKE, UNDER THE inspiration of the Holy Spirit, includes this episode so as to show to his readers God's response to serious sin in the life of the community. Of the many sins that presumably surfaced in the life of the church, Luke chose this one since it was the sin on which God performed such a drastic judgment. We do well to pay close attention to what happened and to look for warnings and instructions for our lives.

A perfect church? The first thing that strikes us is that the church in Acts was not a perfect church, which has been true of the church throughout its history. But the early church, under Peter's leadership, immediately dealt with the problem they faced. Because of that, this episode did not hinder its growth. Immediately following this episode is one of the many summaries of the life of the early church (5:12–16), describing a vibrant group of people with the apostles performing miracles, believers being held in high esteem, and the church increasing. Clearly, then, how the apostles responded to this crisis should be a model for us to follow.

The use of possessions. The wrong use of money is a serious sin in God's sight. William Willimon observes that "a surprisingly large amount of the Book of Acts deals with economic issues within the community."[8] When we add to this the many references in Luke's Gospel that have to do with the use of money,[9] we realize how important this issue is for Luke. Jesus said, "How hard it is for the rich to enter the kingdom of God!" (Luke 18:24). Paul said, "For the love of money is a root of all kinds of evil. Some people, eager for money, have wandered from the faith and pierced themselves with many griefs" (1 Tim. 6:10). If money has so much power to lead us astray, then we should be teaching and preaching much about the dangers of wealth.

The specific sin relating to possessions that Ananias and Sapphira committed was lying about their use. This area remains a pitfall to many today. A key to the answer to this problem is what was talked about in the previous section: being one in heart and mind even about possessions (4:32). That is, we should be open about our possessions within the Christian community, in order to help us avoid many of the pitfalls relating to the use of money.

---

8. Willimon, *Acts*, 52.
9. See Luke 7:41–43; 10:29–37; 12:16–21; 16:1–8, 19–31; 18:14, 18–23; 19:11–27.

Can Satan fill our hearts? Satan "filled [Ananias's] heart" (5:3). There is nothing to say that Ananias and Sapphira were not believers. D. J. Williams points out that many of Satan's activities in the Bible are with believers.[10] This filling is not the same as demon-possession, where people have little control over their activities. Peter Wagner lists the following alternate ways of describing this filling: "demonic oppression," "demonic affliction," or "demonization."[11] The term *demonization* is gaining popularity today, referring to Satan's influence on both believers and unbelievers.[12]

Demonization is what happened when "Satan entered Judas" prior to his betrayal of Jesus (Luke 22:3). This word also leaves room for varying degrees of satanic influence on different people. According to Tim Warner, "spiritual 'possession' clearly implies ownership and would seem to include the control of one's eternal destiny. In either case it would be impossible to be owned and controlled by Satan and have a saving relationship with Christ at the same time."[13] By contrast, "demonization" denotes the occurrence in the lives of Christians when Satan gets them so obsessed with an idea or course of action that they get carried away and are blinded to the consequences. That seems to be what is happening here.

Lying to win esteem. Ananias's goal was to win the esteem of the church. The danger of doing that is real today. It is serious because it causes us to be dishonest with ourselves. A key to receiving God's grace is acknowledging our need of him; an attitude of pride can close the door that permits God's grace to enter our lives.

When Jesus gave his kingdom manifesto in the Sermon on the Mount, his first four Beatitudes say virtually the same thing: "The poor in spirit," "those who mourn," "the meek," and "those who hunger and thirst for righteousness" (Matt. 5:3–5) are united in not hiding their helplessness and in accepting their need for God. In Christianity all power comes through grace—undeserved, unmerited favor. The one thing that can hinder grace is pride—the sense that we deserve the blessings we get and the refusal to accept our faults. If we try to put on a show of being what we are not, we destroy our chances for growth by blocking the grace of God.

Untruthfulness also hinders fellowship in the body—a key theme in 4:32–5:11. John said, "But if we walk in the light, as he is in the light, we have fellowship with one another" (1 John 1:7). Thus, lying is a deadly cancer

---

10. Williams, *Acts*, 100.

11. Wagner, *Spreading the Fire*, 149.

12. Peter H. Davids, "A Biblical View of the Fruits of Sin," *The Kingdom and the Power*, ed. Gary S. Greig and Kevin N. Springer (Ventura, Calif.: Regal, 1993), 118–20.

13. Timothy M. Warner, *Spiritual Warfare: Victory Over the Powers of This Dark World* (Wheaton: Crossway, 1991), 80.

that can destroy the life of a body. When people are untrue, they cannot be genuine. The result is that spiritual superficiality sets in.

Dealing decisively with sin. As one who spends a considerable amount of time and energy raising funds, I encounter Peter's action with mixed feelings. Would I do the same as Peter did if I knew that a big donation coming our way was tainted by sin? This text tells me that I should. God's holiness and the fact that holiness is most important in people's lives tell me that I must deal decisively with sin. That is a key lesson we glean from this story (actually this is an aspect of the fellowship spoken of in 4:32). If we are to be of one heart and one mind, then we must confront sin when it appears in the body.

Does God judge like this today? Why does God not judge sin today in the way he did with Ananias and Sapphira? What we see here is a typical example of the full expression of the powers of the new age, which are usually reserved for the final day of the Lord.

Let's look at an analogous situation. Today we face sickness, though after the day of the Lord there will no longer be sickness. Yet sometimes in the present age God acts miraculously and shows his power over sickness by ways beyond what we know to be natural. In a similar vein, today when Christians sin against the body, they lose their peace, the body loses its power, and the blessing of God is withheld. But God does not always show his full feelings about it publicly. He did do that, however, during key revelatory periods. At the start of Israel's life in the Promised Land, he showed for all time—through the judgment that followed Achan's sin (Josh. 7)—what he thinks about deception. At the start of the life of the church, he again showed—by his judgment on Ananias and Sapphira—what he thinks about deception. We may not see such judgment today, but God has told us once and for all what he thinks of such sin.

We must note too what the Bible says about the judgment at the final day: "And I saw the dead, great and small, standing before the throne, and books were opened. Another book was opened, which is the book of life. The dead were judged according to what they had done as recorded in the books" (Rev. 20:12). On that day there are going to be a lot of surprises, for Jesus says, "What you have said in the dark will be heard in the daylight, and what you have whispered in the ear in the inner rooms will be proclaimed from the roofs" (Luke 12:3).

Does this mean that those who are saved will be lost because of what they have done since their conversion? The church has struggled with this issue for nearly twenty centuries. But biblical people on both sides of this divide accept certain truths. (1) Paul teaches that one who has built on the wrong foundation may be saved on the last day but will have all his or her work burned up and will just barely make it into the kingdom, "only as one escaping through the flames" (1 Cor. 3:12–15). (2) Jesus said, "Not everyone who says to me, 'Lord, Lord,' will enter the kingdom of heaven, but only he who does the will of my Father who is in heaven" (Matt. 7:21). If those who do not enter the kingdom did not lose their salvation, then they were never saved at all. But they were in close contact with the truth; therefore, the judgment on them will be severe—certainly more severe than for those who never heard the gospel (cf. Luke 12:47–48).

Fear in the community. The fear of God and of the consequences of sin is a major theme of this story (5:5, 11). Paul told Timothy that elders "who sin are to be rebuked publicly, so that the others may take warning" (1 Tim. 5:20). Public rebuke gives people a sense of the seriousness of sin, and that in turn acts as a deterrent to sin. The New Testament often talks about living with a fear of the consequences of sin and of displeasing God: "Therefore, since we are receiving a kingdom that cannot be shaken, let us be thankful, and so worship God acceptably with reverence and awe, for our 'God is a consuming fire'" (Heb. 12:28–29). A sobriety should mark our behavior as we heed the words of Paul: "Therefore, my dear friends, as you have always obeyed— not only in my presence, but now much more in my absence—continue to work out your salvation with fear and trembling" (Phil. 2:12).

FACING IMPERFECTIONS IN **church.** A man is said to have come to Charles Spurgeon, seeking his help in finding a perfect group of God's people. Spurgeon told him that if he found such a group, he should not join it, for if he did, it would no longer be perfect.[14] We saw that even the vibrant church of Acts had its share of problems. There is both a comfort and a challenge to us as we face trouble within the community.

In a situation of sin, we sometimes ask, "How could this happen in our community after we tried so hard to be biblical in our body life?" We can take *comfort* from knowing that the first church (and even Jesus' inner circle of the Twelve) faced such problems. The *challenge* comes from the fact that the early church dealt with the problem immediately. We are often tempted to ignore such problems and hope that they will clear up or at least not come to the surface. But when we do that, we let a deadly cancer into our community life that will eat into its spiritual vitality. We must deal with our imperfections the moment we face them.

Recovering the biblical attitude toward possessions. I think I am correct in saying that if a survey were taken about all the possessions-related preach-

---

14. Cited in Harrison, *Interpreting Acts,* 103.

ing from evangelical pulpits today, we will find more teaching on the promise of wealth than on the dangers of wealth. That goes against the entire tenor of the New Testament. Certainly the Old Testament contains teachings about the promise of wealth. The biblical attitude is for the righteous to regard their wealth as a blessing from God, provided, among other reasons, for their enjoyment (1 Tim. 6:17).

But we must remember that some of the promises of prosperity in the Old Testament have been given as part of the covenant blessings to Israel (e.g., Deut. 28). Craig Blomberg says this about such wealth, "Frequently that wealth is tied up with the land or the temple in ways that do not carry over into a New Testament age that knows no sacred piece of geography or architecture (John 4:24)." He also observes that many of the Old Testament promises of wealth to the righteous and industrious are from the wisdom literature (Ps. 112; Prov. 12:11; 13:21; 21:5). But the wisdom literature also says that it is better to be poor than rich through ill-gotten gains (Ps. 37:16–17; Prov. 15:16–17; 16:8; 17:1). "These contrasting emphases caution against absolutizing any one particular proverb; wisdom literature after all provides only generalizations of what is often true, and some statements are descriptive rather than prescriptive."[15] Moreover, both the Old and New Testaments contain numerous warnings about the dangers of wealth and advice on how to use wealth responsibly and charitably. That should be the primary emphasis in Christian teaching about wealth.

William Willimon cites the point made by Ernest Becker that "as belief in God and other traditional sources of immortality eroded in Western culture, money assumed a god-like quality in our lives, our ticket to enduring significance in the face of death."[16] Willimon shows how even though we say that we cannot take our possessions with us, we try to perpetuate our name. "We endow a chair at the university or have a pew named for us at church." Becker has called money "our 'immortality ideology,' our modern means of insuring that even if I must die my name, my family, my achievements, my power will continue after I have gone." Jesus, on the other hand, told the story of the rich fool (Luke 12:13–21), "the one who assumed that his possessions gave him god-like security against the invasions of mortality."[17] It is sad to see that the church has unashamedly brought over this ideology and pandered to it in its preaching.

One reason why the dangers of this are not seen is that we have ceased to insist on the way of the cross as the only way for a Christian to live.

---

15. Craig L. Blomberg, "Wealth," EDBT, 814.

16. Ernest Becker, The Denial of Death (New York: Free Press, 1973); cited in Willimon, Acts, 53.

17. Willimon, Acts, 53.

Countless Christians have forsaken the path of the cross. In Jesus' words, "they are choked by life's worries, riches and pleasures, and they do not mature" (Luke 8:14). In their desire for more wealth they may adopt unethical business practices or may not treat their employees in the way that they would have others treat them (Matt. 7:12). They may not share their possessions, as the Jerusalem and Macedonian Christians did (2 Cor. 8:1–5). They may rob God of his tithes and offerings (Mal. 3:8).

Not only do we fail to urge them to repent, we sometimes even ask them to take leadership in the church because of their high position in society. We need more teaching, preaching, and practicing in the church of the biblical attitude to wealth. It is the way of the cross, and that is the only option for Christian living.

The core sin of Ananias and Sapphira was their pride and deceit about the use of funds. Sadly this remains a major problem in the church today. Many of the recent scandals in the church have been about use of funds. It is easy, especially for Christian workers, to hide the truth about their financial situation. Sometimes this becomes outright deception. We may give people a wrong impression about our needs by not telling the whole truth about what we earn. We may receive help based on a wrong perception of our true needs. It is possible to raise funds for the same project from different sources without people knowing that many have been approached. Thus more funds may be received than are needed for the project, resulting in those extra funds being diverted to something else without the donors' knowledge. Or funds can be used for purposes other than that for which they were given.

It is equally possible for Christians to lie about money in their dealings in society. We can falsify tax returns, for example. I once sold some land using a Buddhist real estate agent. I told him that we must put the exact price of sale in the deed of purchase. He was surprised and told me of eminent clients of his who did not do this. It is common to undervalue the deed and pass some money "under the table" so that less tax is paid. Later I found out that a well-known Christian leader was among his clients. I told him that my God would not be pleased if I did that. Ultimately that is the reason why we must be truthful. Our holy God wishes us to be truthful even though society may think it unnecessary.

One of the best ways to avoid the pitfalls relating to possessions is to have people to whom we can be accountable about our use of money. It is wise for us to share with our accountability partners even significant personal gifts we have received. They can be a check to us that will help us avoid the snares of materialism and deception that are always looming near to us. Most of the recent funds-related scandals in the church could have been avoided if those involved had been completely open to a responsible person about their income and use of funds.

The demonization of Christians. We must be careful lest we let Satan fill us as Ananias and Sapphira did. This is how people we least expect end up having extramarital affairs. They never intended to have an affair. But they gave into the first steps of temptation, and after that they had little control over themselves. Obsessed with desire, they lost sight of reality and risked their happiness, their family, their ministry, and their reputation. Proverbs 7 talks about a young man who is seduced by a woman. He was in the wrong place at the wrong time. He gave into those first steps of seduction. After that he lost control over himself: "All at once he followed her like an ox going to the slaughter, like a deer stepping into a noose till an arrow pierces his liver, like a bird darting into a snare, little knowing it will cost him his life" (Prov. 7:22–23).

This happens in areas other than sex. It can happen with our obsession to hide a truth about ourselves, with our plans to teach a lesson to someone who hurt us, with our desire to clear our name, with our ambition to succeed in our career, or with our passion to put on a show of being something we are not (cf. Ananias and Sapphira). A drug addict who is wonderfully converted may, in a time of discouragement and spiritual weakness, give in to his old habit "just once." But that one opening triggers a process that sends him spiraling down to his old life.

When people are demonized, others are surprised to find them acting in ways so uncharacteristic of themselves. Who would have thought that Peter would be cursing and swearing that he did not know Jesus (Mark 14:71)? But Jesus had warned him: "Simon, Simon, Satan has asked to sift you as wheat" (Luke 22:31). It is believers whom Satan is after. So we must always seek to "be self-controlled and alert," for we know that our "enemy the devil prowls around like a roaring lion looking for someone to devour" (1 Peter 5:8).

When a person acts in a seriously unbalanced and uncontrolled way, it is appropriate to ask whether there may be spiritual, physical, and psychological explanations for their behavior. When we do so, we are not denying the reality of Satan or of the person's responsibility for his sins. What Satan does is to exploit those spiritual, psychological, or physical states to get hold of the person. When we minister God's healing to those people, we need to deal with these issues as well. The former drug addict may have been neglecting his devotions. The person who suffers from an uncontrollable temper may have a chemical imbalance that needs treatment. The person in an extramarital affair may be a victim of childhood sexual abuse, which has left wounds that need emotional healing. Similarly, if the person has been demonized, we may need to pray with that in view.

Rooting out untruthfulness. We have talked of the dangers of deceit in the body—a theme that must constantly occupy the mind of a leader. In Youth for Christ we work primarily through young volunteers who have met Christ through our ministry. Most of them are from other faiths. They do not know Christian etiquette well, they have a lot of zeal, and they sometimes lack in wisdom. Consequently, their actions can give YFC a bad name. When I visit our different centers, I usually teach the volunteers and staff as my top priority. One of the things I try to emphasize on every visit goes like this:

> In YFC we do not expect the volunteers not to make mistakes. We are willing to pay the price of those mistakes. Even though they may give us a bad name, we do not regard them as serious. But there is one thing we regard as deadly serious: lying. When people are not truthful with themselves, there is a hindrance so that God cannot work with them to help them. They are on a dangerous path.

I think this emphasis on the need for honesty has helped keep our movement relatively free from integrity problems. Unfortunately, we have found that people who have lied to and deceived us can survive for unexpectedly long periods without their deception surfacing. But sooner or later it will surface, and at that time people either have to change or leave.

The sin of trying to show that we are something when we are not is a major problem today because our society places such a high value on appearance. We want things to look good whether or not they are. Seeking recognition, we may choose to adorn our testimonies with exaggerations and lies. People are "blessed" by the testimony, so we keep using it, even if there may be doubts about its truthfulness. I remember a situation when a spectacular Christian autobiography became a best-seller. Then it became known that much of the book was in fact fictional. The publishers, being committed to Christian standards of integrity, recalled the book, at considerable cost to themselves. But later another publisher took on this book and published it as a fictional biography! Appearance can make us lose our hatred for sin, and market forces can cause us to be blinded to the holiness of God.

I also know of situations where people have known that a leader was guilty of sin. He denied it, for if it was true, it would have required the church taking unpleasant measures. So the church chose to ignore it, and the leader remained in the church. Such a hindrance to revival can cause spiritual death in the church. But in a culture where appearance is so important, a church like this can exist and even thrive. Yet it thrives as a child of its culture, not as a representative of the kingdom of God.

Our reluctance to deal decisively with sin. If there is true fellowship in a Christian community, then when sin appears in the body, it will be confronted. If we feel somebody is lying, we must question him or her about it.

However, Peter has been criticized for being uncharitable and missing the spirit of the gospel in the way he treated Ananias and Sapphira. These critics say that he did not treat people the way God treated him after he denied Christ. This is typical of the way some people react to church discipline. "Is there no forgiveness in Christianity?" they ask, and they condemn the church that disciplines its members.

In addition, other churches are ready to welcome and use those who have been thus disciplined. This can act as a deterrent to disciplining: Church leaders know that if they discipline their members, they may lose many to the church down the street! The story of Ananias and Sapphira teaches us what God thinks of the priority of purity in the body of Christ.

If sin has not been dealt with decisively, the chances of healing for the one who has sinned are greatly reduced. It has been my sad experience to encounter many Christian workers who fell into serious sin with sex or money. Some of them did not make a total confession and therefore did not go through the humiliating process of church discipline. Sometimes this was because another group took this person on and short-circuited the recovery process. These people went back into ministry, and some of them seemed to resume effective ministries. I know of one such person through whom many miracles were performed. But then they faced the same temptation again—and again they succumbed.

Many factors make such people susceptible to another fall. The freedom of forgiveness and walking in the light is not there to protect them. Though they have been serving the Lord, they do not have the joy of salvation that David so eagerly sought (Ps. 51:12). Thus, the joy of the Lord is not there as a deterrent to sin; the person has become used to living without it. The memory of the pain that takes place through disciplining is not there either; that too acts as a deterrent. Paul said of an offender within the church: "Hand this man over to Satan, so that the sinful nature may be destroyed and his spirit saved on the day of the Lord" (1 Cor. 5:5). Once you have experienced the pain and humiliation of thoroughgoing discipline, you will do everything to avoid going through it again. When temptation hits you again, you will resist it like the plague!

Fear in a "feel-good age." The idea of going through life fearing both God and the consequences of sin seems unattractive in our age where people are so devoted to good feelings. Fear is considered a bad feeling, and therefore people think it is wrong. If the Bible views living in fear favorably, we must reflect on it if we are going to convince people of the relevance and attractiveness of the Christian way in today's society. Actually, fear is a friend that alerts us of the danger of sin. But we live in a world where many think that enjoyment is possible primarily through what the Bible calls sin (e.g., through sex outside marriage or through enjoying violence). People who think in this way consider fear as a spoiler of fun and of good feelings.

They are wrong. The only way to truly enjoy life is to live it in the way ordained by the Creator of joy. Joy is a key theme in the Bible, and just as the world pursues it, Christians can indeed legitimately pursue joy within the context of our relationship with God. But the pleasures of sin are fleeting (Heb. 11:25). We cannot fight against the way we were made to live and truly enjoy life. When we violate our humanity, we condemn ourselves to a life without true joy, in spite of any temporary joy that is available through sin.

Some might say that temporary joy through sin is better than a life of fear and trembling. I respond that this fear and trembling is the gateway to lasting and truly satisfying joy. When we fear the holiness of God and the consequences of sin, we avoid sin. But we do not turn from sin into a vacuum; we embrace life to the full (John 10:10). We do not spend the rest of our days wishing that we could have had the experience of the sin we avoided. We are glad that we escaped that enslavement and are now "free indeed" (John 8:34–36). We are glad that God freed us to enjoy him, for he is not only holy, he is also loving. The Bible says that God delights in us (Ps. 147:11) and that we delight in him (43:4). When we run away from sin, we run into the arms of one whom we love and delight in and who loves us and delights to give us joy. We say with David, "You have made known to me the path of life; you will fill me with joy in your presence, with eternal pleasures at your right hand" (16:11).

Thus, the fear of displeasing God and of the consequences of sin does not take away the enjoyment of life. It is rather the gateway to true enjoyment. Fear, then, is our friend.

Acts 5:12–42

THE APOSTLES PERFORMED many miraculous signs and wonders among the people. And all the believers used to meet together in Solomon's Colonnade. ¹³No one else dared join them, even though they were highly regarded by the people. ¹⁴Nevertheless, more and more men and women believed in the Lord and were added to their number. ¹⁵As a result, people brought the sick into the streets and laid them on beds and mats so that at least Peter's shadow might fall on some of them as he passed by. ¹⁶Crowds gathered also from the towns around Jerusalem, bringing their sick and those tormented by evil spirits, and all of them were healed.

¹⁷Then the high priest and all his associates, who were members of the party of the Sadducees, were filled with jealousy. ¹⁸They arrested the apostles and put them in the public jail. ¹⁹But during the night an angel of the Lord opened the doors of the jail and brought them out. ²⁰"Go, stand in the temple courts," he said, "and tell the people the full message of this new life."

²¹At daybreak they entered the temple courts, as they had been told, and began to teach the people.

When the high priest and his associates arrived, they called together the Sanhedrin—the full assembly of the elders of Israel—and sent to the jail for the apostles. ²²But on arriving at the jail, the officers did not find them there. So they went back and reported, ²³"We found the jail securely locked, with the guards standing at the doors; but when we opened them, we found no one inside." ²⁴On hearing this report, the captain of the temple guard and the chief priests were puzzled, wondering what would come of this.

²⁵Then someone came and said, "Look! The men you put in jail are standing in the temple courts teaching the people." ²⁶At that, the captain went with his officers and brought the apostles. They did not use force, because they feared that the people would stone them.

²⁷Having brought the apostles, they made them appear before the Sanhedrin to be questioned by the high priest. ²⁸"We gave you strict orders not to teach in this name," he

said. "Yet you have filled Jerusalem with your teaching and are determined to make us guilty of this man's blood."

²⁹Peter and the other apostles replied: "We must obey God rather than men! ³⁰The God of our fathers raised Jesus from the dead—whom you had killed by hanging him on a tree. ³¹God exalted him to his own right hand as Prince and Savior that he might give repentance and forgiveness of sins to Israel. ³²We are witnesses of these things, and so is the Holy Spirit, whom God has given to those who obey him."

33When they heard this, they were furious and wanted to put them to death. ³⁴But a Pharisee named Gamaliel, a teacher of the law, who was honored by all the people, stood up in the Sanhedrin and ordered that the men be put outside for a little while. ³⁵Then he addressed them: "Men of Israel, consider carefully what you intend to do to these men. ³⁶Some time ago Theudas appeared, claiming to be somebody, and about four hundred men rallied to him. He was killed, all his followers were dispersed, and it all came to nothing. ³⁷After him, Judas the Galilean appeared in the days of the census and led a band of people in revolt. He too was killed, and all his followers were scattered. ³⁸Therefore, in the present case I advise you: Leave these men alone! Let them go! For if their purpose or activity is of human origin, it will fail. ³⁹But if it is from God, you will not be able to stop these men; you will only find yourselves fighting against God."

⁴⁰His speech persuaded them. They called the apostles in and had them flogged. Then they ordered them not to speak in the name of Jesus, and let them go.

⁴¹The apostles left the Sanhedrin, rejoicing because they had been counted worthy of suffering disgrace for the Name. ⁴²Day after day, in the temple courts and from house to house, they never stopped teaching and proclaiming the good news that Jesus is the Christ.

THE THEME OF the triumph of the gospel amidst adversity, which began in chapter 4, continues here. Each time God intervenes and the gospel moves forward. The first time that opposition from the authorities threatened the progress of the gospel, God intervened by shaking the place where the disciples were and giving them a special anointing with his Spirit (4:31). That emboldened them to speak the word of God boldly. Then, when the purity of the church was threatened from within, God intervened through the prophetic insight of Peter, which resulted in judgment (5:1–11). This is followed by an effective miraculous and evangelistic ministry (5:12–16). When trouble comes again from the authorities, God intervenes again, this time through a Jewish authority named Gamaliel (5:17–41). Our passage ends with a report that public and personal evangelism went on incessantly (5:42).

Continuing Power (5:12–16)

THE FEAR THAT came on the people as a result of the deaths of Ananias and Sapphira (v. 11) did not reduce the evangelistic effectiveness of the apostles. They continued to minister in the miraculous (v. 12) and to reap an evangelistic harvest (v. 14). Their ministry in the miraculous intensified (vv. 15–16). The sick stayed out on the streets just to have Peter's shadow to fall on them, and people were coming from neighboring towns as well. This is the nearest we have in the Bible to a modern-day healing campaign. Luke may be suggesting that the intensifying of signs and wonders indicated God's approval of the painful act of purifying the church in 5:1–11.

The emphasis on miracles, however, did not result in a situation where the gospel was cheapened and large numbers came into the church only for miracles. Though Christians were held in high esteem, people were reluctant to join the church (v. 13). They realized that "the awesome power of the Spirit that judges also demands commitment and responsibility."[1] Still, "more and more men and women believed in the Lord and were added to their number" (v. 14). The church did not lower its standards in order to win the lost.

The Apostles Arrested, Tried, and Beaten (5:17–40)

IT IS NOT surprising that, with such spectacular ministry by the apostles, the Jewish leaders "were filled with jealousy" (v. 17). The success of the apostles upset the peace that reigned in the community as these leaders lost their power and control over the people. They had to respond with a corresponding show of power. As often happens, they used political power to attack the church rather than spiritual power (v. 18). Yet their plans are foiled through an angelic rescue (v. 19).

Angels appear often in Acts, giving directions (8:26; 10:3) or words of encouragement (27:23), delivering God's people from prison (5:19; 12:7–11), and judging the wicked (12:23). Here the angel not only delivers the apos-

---

1. Polhill, Acts, 164.

tles from prison but also encourages them in fulfilling their call by giving a fresh commission (v. 20). He knows that they might be tempted to compromise their witness in this situation. Thus the commission is clear: "Go, stand in the temple courts," the very center of the Jewish faith, and "tell the people the full message," that is, "holding nothing back (out of fear, or tact?)."[2]

In instances of threat and danger in Acts, the key word from God concerns boldness in witness (4:29–31; 18:9–11; 23:11). Three times in this passage the evangelistic ministry of the apostles is described with the verb "teach" (*didasko*, vv. 21, 25, 28).[3] There must have been a major emphasis on the content—the truth—of the gospel. Truth is communicated through what the Bible describes as preaching and teaching.

In the meantime, the meeting of "the full assembly of the elders" (i.e., the Sanhedrin) is ready to begin, but the prisoners are missing (vv. 21–23). The puzzled officials are then informed that they "are standing in the temple courts teaching the people" (vv. 24–25). The captain of the temple guard[4] himself goes to rearrest them. It is ironic that those who probably had wanted to stone the apostles for blasphemy are now afraid that they themselves will be stoned by the people.[5] Consequently, "they did not use force" (v. 26b). This time all the apostles are brought before the Sanhedrin to be questioned by the high priest (v. 27). They are accused of disobeying the orders to stop teaching and of making the Jewish hierarchy "guilty of this man's blood" (v. 28). It is possible that they said this because they were fearing a popular uprising.[6]

"Peter and the other apostles" (v. 29) reply to the Sanhedrin. Presumably, "Peter was the spokesman for the group ... with the others in some way indicating their agreement"[7] (cf. 2:14). The Christian community is solidly unified. Peter's opening statement about obeying "God rather than men" (5:29) is reminiscent of his closing statement during his previous trial (4:19–20); he is willing to die rather than disobey his Lord. Later he will say that the Holy Spirit is "given to those who obey him" (v. 32). His obedience gives him a credibility that qualifies him later on to write to the church about obedience (see 1 Peter 1:2, 14, 22; 3:1, 6; 4:17).

The response given to the Sanhedrin is recorded in summary form here. Once again the apostles do not give what would be expected of a defense at

---

2. Barrett, *Acts*, 284.

3. This verb also appears in v. 42, but it seems there to refer to what is traditionally known as teaching, that is, the instruction of believers (see the comments on that verse).

4. A high official (see the comments on 4:1).

5. Polhill, *Acts*, 167.

6. Barrett, *Acts*, 288.

7. Longenecker, "Acts," 320.

a trial. Rather, they witness to the facts of the gospel (vv. 30–32; cf. 4:8–12). The *kerygma* is even more clearly explained here than in chapter 4.

- As always, Peter gives an introduction arising from the particular situation (v. 29). The apostles are responding to the question of the high priest about their defiance of his order not to teach in the name of Jesus (v. 28).
- Next the facts of Christ are presented, beginning with, "The God of our fathers raised Jesus from the dead" (v. 30a). The words "from the dead" have been added by the NIV translators, though this may not be the intended meaning. The expression "the God of our fathers" reminds the hearers of the great acts of God in Israel's history. Peter may be proclaiming that God has raised up Jesus as the Messiah, just as he had raised up other deliverers throughout Israel's history.[8]
- Then comes a reference to Jesus' death: "whom you had killed by hanging him on a tree" (v. 30b; cf. also 10:39; 1 Peter 2:24). The idea of hanging on a tree probably alludes to Deuteronomy 21:23, which pronounces a curse for one who hangs on a tree. The early Christians applied this text to the death of Jesus. By the time Peter wrote his first letter he had developed the theological significance of the tree more fully: "He himself bore our sins in his body on the tree, so that we might die to sins and live for righteousness; by his wounds you have been healed" (1 Peter 2:24). Paul developed this theme further: "Christ redeemed us from the curse of the law by becoming a curse for us, for it is written: 'Cursed is everyone who is hung on a tree'" (Gal. 3:13; cf. Acts 13:29). Before Jewish audiences (for whom the cross is a scandal), the apostles typically did not hide Jesus' death but presented it as a triumph of God planned long ago.
- If verse 30a does not refer to the resurrection, then the resurrection is not mentioned in Luke's summary of this speech. It is, however, implied in Peter's next statement about Jesus' exaltation: "God exalted him to his own right hand as Prince and Savior" (v. 31). How important the exaltation was to early Christian preaching (2:33–35; 3:20–21; 4:11), and how strange is our comparative neglect of this theme in our evangelistic preaching!
- Next comes the offer of salvation. As a result of Jesus' exaltation, not only forgiveness but also repentance is given by Christ (v. 31b). Repentance is triggered through the hearing of the Word, which brings the conviction of sin. But this act is not done by our own efforts; the grace to repent is given by Christ (v. 31b). Though Calvinists and Arminians may differ over the possibility of resisting the saving grace of God,

8. Williams, *Acts*, 109.

they will agree, if they seek to be biblical, that the ability to respond to grace is a gift from God.

- Peter then buttresses his points about Christ by claiming, "We are witnesses of these things" (v. 32a). This is unique to the apostles. But as we noted in our study of the sermon in Acts 2, we too can have the same confidence of the apostles if the facts recorded in the New Testament about Christ and his resurrection are historically true. We believe that there is sufficient evidence for that claim.
- Finally, Peter insists that the Holy Spirit is also a witness and that he has been given to those who are obedient (v. 32b). In other words, the Spirit's witness is made through believers. As F. F. Bruce puts it, the disciples were "indwelt and possessed by the Spirit to such a degree that they were his organs of expression."[9]

The fury and wish for capital punishment of the Sanhedrin (v. 33) is tempered by the comments of Gamaliel (vv. 34–40). He was the greatest teacher of his era and was considered the embodiment of Pharisaism. The apostles' miracles and escape from prison presumably made him suspect that God might indeed be blessing this new movement. Therefore he advocates caution and restraint. He is confident that God will sovereignly show in history whether this movement is of him or not. Gamaliel feared that by opposing it, they may be opposing God himself (vv. 38–39). Bruce has shown that this advice is a reflection of sound Pharisaic doctrine. The rabbis believed that "men may disobey God, but his will would triumph notwithstanding. The will of men was not fettered, but what they willed would be overruled by God for the accomplishment of his own purposes."[10] This advice persuades the Sanhedrin to drop their intentions of capital punishment, but it does not prevent a sound flogging of the apostles (v. 40).

After the Beating (5:41–42)

INCREDIBLY, THE APOSTLES rejoice over their flogging, because "they had been counted worthy of suffering disgrace for the Name" (v. 41). This is an oxymoron:[11] The disgrace was an indicator of their worth, so they felt honored by the dishonor! "Their suffering allowed them to demonstrate their loyalty" to Christ.[12] We see here a new dimension in the exposition on suffering, a major subtheme of Acts: To suffer for Christ is an honor that causes joy.

---

9. Bruce, *Acts*, NICNT, 113.

10. Bruce, *Paul*, 50–51. Bruce cites the words of Josephus (*Antiquities* 13.172; 18.13) and of the later rabbis Aquiba (*Pirqé Abôt* 3:19) and Yohanan (*Pirqé Abôt* 4:14).

11. That is, the bringing together of contradictory terms.

12. Arrington, *Acts*, 63.

Our passage closes with the report of the incessant witness of the church (v. 42). Luke may be employing a Greek rhetorical construction called chiasm (inverted parallelism) here. This is the arrangement of the parallel members of a literary unit to form an a-b-b'-a' arrangement:

> a in the temple courts
> > b and from house to house
> > b' teaching
> a' and proclaiming

If this is the case, the proclamation was done in the temple courts and the teaching from house to house. Since this report of incessant evangelistic activity comes immediately after the report of the beating that the apostles received, it seems as if Luke wants to point out that, far from reducing evangelism, the beating resulted in increased evangelistic intensity.

Bridging Contexts

IDENTIFICATION, HOLINESS, AND **power in evangelism.** The background for the effective evangelism described in verse 14 is significant. Peter had presented an unpleasant message of judgment on Ananias and Sapphira, which resulted in their deaths and in great fear coming on everyone (5:3–11). Because of this awesome holiness that characterized the life of the church, we are told that "no one else dared join them, even though they were highly regarded by the people" (v. 13). Nevertheless, Luke goes on to say, "more and more men and women believed in the Lord and were added to their number" (v. 14). This should give us courage to persevere in presenting the unpleasant aspects of the faith, just as Peter did.

Our identification with people's needs brings us close to them, but our holiness separates us from them. The end result of holiness is a restlessness among people as they realize we are different from them. Some will keep their distance (v. 13), some will oppose us (vv. 17–18), but some will be attracted to the difference and will respond to the prompting of the Holy Spirit by turning away from their past life in repentance to receive eternal life from Christ (v. 14).

The expression of God's holiness also led to his power manifested in the church through healings (vv. 15-16). A church that is pure but is powerless is an unattractive church. Along with an emphasis on God's holiness we must always see to it that there is also the experience of the fullness and power of the Spirit. This theme appears so often in Acts that it bears repeating. By contrast, a church that emphasizes the power of God but has no corresponding holiness reaps a scandalous dishonor to Christ. Thus, a threefold emphasis of identification (meeting people at their point of need), power (ministering in the power of the Spirit), and holiness (expressing God's hatred for sin) must characterize our evangelistic ministries.

Miraculous deliverances. This passage gives us an instance of a miraculous deliverance through the medium of an angel (vv. 19–20). This does not always happen in our lives. What we learn from this passage is that God *can* deliver us if he wishes; *our* task is to obey his call. That is what we must concentrate on and leave the rest in the hands of God.

Shadrach, Meshach, and Abednego expressed this attitude when King Nebuchadnezzar threatened to throw them into the fiery furnace if they refused to obey him. He told them, "Then what god will be able to rescue you from my hand?" (Dan. 3:15). The three men replied, "If we are thrown into the blazing furnace, the God we serve is able to save us from it, and he will rescue us from your hand, O king" (3:17). But knowing that God may not do this, they added, "But even if he does not, we want you to know, O king, that we will not serve your gods or worship the image of gold you have set up" (3:18). Miraculous deliverance or not, our primary responsibility is to be obedient to God.

Obeying God rather than human beings. Can we make an abiding principle out of Peter's proclamations that the apostles are willing to disobey the authorities in order to please God (4:19; 5:29)? Many Christians have abused these verses by claiming that their selfish desires were God's will and have disobeyed authorities in order to satisfy those desires. Yet there are plenty of scriptural examples of acceptable disobedience. In addition to Shadrach, Meshach, and Abednego (cf. above), Daniel refused to stop praying to Yahweh when it became illegal (Dan. 6). Yet we must be cautious about coming to absolute rules from statements that may in fact be limited in application by their particular contexts. We should look to all Scripture for guidance.

The Bible does command us to be subject to governing authorities. Peter himself says, "Submit yourselves for the Lord's sake to every authority instituted among men: whether to the king, as the supreme authority, or to governors, who are sent by him to punish those who do wrong and to commend those who do right" (1 Peter 2:13–14). This teaching is given in more detail in Romans 13, where Paul says that governing authorities have been established by God and we should therefore submit to them (Rom. 13:1–2). He specifically mentions the giving of taxes, revenue, respect, and honor (13:7). Even though Paul had suffered an unjust punishment from the state in Philippi (Acts 16:37), he sought to work within the structure of government. He may have even tried to win for Christianity a place as a legally accepted religion (*religio licita*).[13] A. A. Rupprecht has pointed out that "underlying all of Luke's narrative is ... Paul's careful adherence to the Roman law."[14]

---

13. David W. J. Gill, "Acts and Roman Religion," *BAFCS, Graeco-Roman Setting,* 2:98–103.
14. A. A. Rupprecht, "Legal System, Roman," *DPL,* 546.

By the time Revelation was written, however, the state had become hostile to God and his people (see Rev. 13), so that John expresses a different attitude toward the state.[15] John Stott shows that in Romans 13, "the God-ordained purpose of the power they [that is, government authorities] have been given is to promote good and punish evil." Stott asks, "What shall we do, then, when they use it rather to punish good and promote evil?" He answers, "We must resist. 'Civil disobedience' is a biblical concept." Stott argues that "since the state's authority has been delegated to it by God, we are to submit to it right up to the point where obedience to the state would involve disobedience to God. At that point it is our Christian duty to disobey the state in order to obey God."[16] Everett Harrison sees significance in the fact that in Romans 13, "Paul avoids saying that the Christian is to obey the state; instead, he says, 'Be subject' (13:1, 3).... This leaves room for the superior relationship, the ultimate authority, as alone worthy of implicit obedience."[17]

Incessant evangelism. This whole passage pulsates with the urgency of the evangelistic task. The apostles are arrested for evangelizing (v. 18). But after their miraculous release the angel tells them to go to the center of Jewish religion, the temple, and proclaim "the full message"; they are not to give in to the temptation to compromise it (v. 20). The divine encouragement to persist in witness in spite of threats is a recurrent theme in Acts (4:31; 18:9–10; 23:11). This not only shows how important witness is, but also that people need constant encouragement, for it is easy to lose passion for evangelism, especially in the face of opposition.

When the apostles are rearrested and asked to explain their actions, they use the opportunity to proclaim the message, not try to secure a release (vv. 29–39). This method of witness has been used throughout history. Christianity is a religion with a message, a message so important that it simply must be shared to all who live on earth. God's salvation in Christ is the answer of the Creator of the world to its basic problems. If it is that urgent, then every human being should be told this good news. Thus, when people bring us to trial for preaching, we must explain God's message. Both Stephen and Paul did this when they were brought to trial (7:2–53; 24:25; 26:2–29).

Evangelism also influences our attitude toward success on earth. From Acts it is clear that suffering is an essential feature of effective evangelism. In this passage the suffering of shame (flogging is a humiliating experience)

---

15. Harrison, *The Apostolic Church*, 81–89.

16. John R. W. Stott, "Christian Responses to Good and Evil: A Study of Romans 12:9–13:10," *Perspectives on Peacemaking: Biblical Options in the Nuclear Age* (Ventura, Calif.: Regal, 1984), 52.

17. Harrison, *Apostolic Church*, 83. How this works out in daily life will be discussed in the "Contemporary Significance" section.

because of faithful witness is an honor worth rejoicing about (v. 41). What the world considers as failure we may consider as success if it furthers the cause of evangelism and, as here, demonstrates our loyalty to Christ. We must always look at life with evangelistic eyes and be incessantly involved in evangelism. Even if we are brought to trial, we must use it as an opportunity to witness for Christ. If we are dishonored because of evangelism, we can view that dishonor as a great honor.

Gamaliel's wisdom. For twenty centuries the church has been grateful to Gamaliel for his advice (vv. 35–39). God used it to help the church continue its work of evangelism. This prominent Pharisee advised caution about condemning people (v. 35). He faced the situation from the perspective of God's sovereignty (v. 39) and regarded seriously the possible evidences of God's stamp of approval upon the church (vv. 38–39). He expressed fear that the Sanhedrin's decision might go against God's will through their zeal for their own interpretation of the truth (v. 39). All these are principles that we can use today.

But should we always follow the principle that if a group succeeds in the long run, it must be of God? Not always. Scripture contains many essential truths. If a movement contradicts those truths, it is wrong even if it grows. God may not be the one causing its success. It may be Satan, or brilliant strategizing, or the fact that this group addresses the felt needs of the people. The recent growth of the Jehovah's Witnesses and the Muslims does not indicate God's approval of those movements, for they refuse to accept basic tenets of God's revelation.

Of course, every movement on earth will have its shortcomings. We ourselves are often guilty of errors of judgment. Thus, we do not oppose a movement simply because we do not agree on all beliefs and practices. But if it contradicts *basic* truths, we must oppose it, even though it may grow rapidly and show evidence of miraculous power and wholesome living.

We should add here that there is an attitude that Gamaliel expressed toward the gospel that we clearly should not follow. He did not make a commitment about Christ. Instead, he waited to see what would happen. As far as we know, Gamaliel himself died waiting to see whether the Christian movement was really of God. The call of the gospel is to respond to God's voice today (2 Cor. 6:2; Heb. 3:7, 15; 4:7).

A GOSPEL WITHOUT **holiness or power.** Some have argued that presenting unpleasant truths of the gospel to an unbeliever can be deferred until the follow-through process; we must win a hearing first and only present these truths. There is some truth in this, for even the evangelists in Acts started their proclamation with some common ground that the people generally agreed with—some point of contact. But before we ask people to accept the gospel, they need to know those aspects of the essential gospel that may be unpleasant to them. Otherwise they may feel cheated that they were not shown the "fine print" before they entered into a covenant with God. The holiness of God and his hatred of sin are important aspects of the gospel, and they cannot be eliminated from the basic message. As our passage shows, the Jerusalem church exhibited both the awesome holiness of God—which provoked fear among outsiders—and the power of God—which made the gospel attractive to outsiders.

The results of preaching the gospel without the holiness of God in recent times have been tragic. We see people who claim to have had a born-again experience but who continue in the sins of their past life. I remember reports of a prominent publisher of pornography publicly claiming to be born again, but he did not give up producing pornography. We cannot, of course, automatically blame the church for this. But the fact that people living such flagrant lives of public sin can even claim to be born again may indicate that something is wrong in the understanding of being born again that the church is projecting to the world.

The most common objection to Christianity among the Buddhists in Sri Lanka is that we have a cheap religion. Christians, they say, can live any life of impurity and then receive forgiveness and happily go back to their impure life. That some famous preachers have done just that and that our newspapers have given those stories wide coverage have not helped.

The reason why evangelicals have been slow to battle exploitation and prejudice can in part be traced to a neglect of the holiness of God and its implications in our evangelistic preaching. We ask people to come to Christ to receive forgiveness of sins, but we do not ask them to repent of social sins such as prejudice against race, class, caste, and gender. Nor do we ask them to repent of sins of injustice, such as exploiting employees. We do not like to talk about personal sins like lying and greed. As a result, people accept a Christianity that is neutral on such matters. They enter into the fellowship of the church and become identified as Christians even though they continue to do things that bring disrepute to the name of Christ. We are seeing this in countries torn by ethnic or religious strife, where many supposedly devout Christians express attitudes toward those of the other side that are decidedly contrary to the spirit of Christianity.

Clearly in Acts the emphasis on God's holiness and its implications did not hinder the evangelistic effectiveness of the early church. Billy Graham stated at one of the International Conferences for Itinerant Evangelists in Amsterdam that when he started preaching about the Lordship of Christ, many felt that less people would respond to the appeal to commit their lives to Christ. But he did not find that to be so. If anything, there was an increase in the proportion of people who responded to the invitation.

On the matter of God's power, when groups lose the experience of that power, they have only their identification with the people as a means of attracting them to Christ. As a result, they lower their standards and do not insist on holiness, claiming that this is necessary if they are to attract people. But the ministry of Jesus and of the early church show that we do not have to become sinners to attract sinners. Jesus paid the price of such identification, for he was accused of being a sinner himself because he moved so closely with them. But he never lowered his principles. He did go to the home of Zacchaeus—to the surprise of many. But, by the end of the visit, Zacchaeus was a changed man (Luke 19:1–10). Yet we must not forget that it was Jesus' reputation (probably as a wonder-working rabbi) that made Zacchaeus eager to see him. Identification, holiness, and power make a great combination!

Today we are seeing a strange phenomenon in the church: People are expressing the power of God in their ministries through healing and other manifestations of miraculous gifts while living ungodly lives. How can this be? My tentative answer is to conclude that ministry gifts can become part of our personality and can express themselves for some time even after we have strayed personally from God. In an analogous manner, I have seen this with the gift of preaching, where gifted people who fell into serious sin still showed their giftedness for a time after their fall. But they cannot go on with this deception for long. Soon the fruit of a spiritually dry experience will become evident in their preaching.

Whatever the explanation, the fact that an ungodly person can express miraculous powers through his or her ministry does not mean that God accepts that ministry (see 1 Cor. 13:1–2). At the last judgment, Jesus will say, "I never knew you. Away from me, you evildoers!" to people who prophesied, drove out demons, and performed miracles in his name (Matt. 7:22–23). It is easy to be fooled by the display of power of such people and to ignore their ungodliness. This is happening a lot today, as we are blinded from seeing the long-term damage that results from their ministries because of the temporary results that are exhibited. When that person is exposed for who he or she really is, God will be dishonored. Then people will not only reject the minister but also the message, even if it was a correct message. I shudder to think of the judgment that awaits teachers who are a stumbling block to others (James 3:1).

American theologian Carl F. H. Henry wrote a seminal book in 1948, *The Uneasy Conscience of Modern Fundamentalism*, which signaled a change in attitude among evangelicals toward the social aspects of Christian holiness. In it he wrote, "We must confront the world *now* with an ethics to make it tremble, and with a dynamic to give it hope."[18]

Why sometimes no miraculous deliverance? If God can deliver us as he did Peter and John, why does he not deliver us all of the time? Many have grappled with this factor, and reports of God's deliverance sometimes discourage such people as they ponder the question of why God has not acted to prevent their pain. Just the day before writing this, I went to the home of a YFC volunteer who was arrested, having been falsely accused by a vindictive ex-employee in the organization where he works that the volunteer had links with a terrorist organization. As I prayed with his wife and mother, I was reminded about how the church first reacted to the news of the proscribing of evangelism—they reflected deeply on the sovereignty of God over history (Acts 4:24—28). That was the great hope of the church in Acts. Whatever befell them, because God was sovereign, he would use it to achieve some glorious purpose of his.

Even the martyrdom of Stephen and the ensuing persecution became an occasion for the scattering of the seed of the word of God (Acts 8:1—4).[19] It helped inaugurate the missionary program of the church, which occupies one of the most exciting places in the history of the world. Jesus said in connection with his own sufferings that he could have called twelve legions of angels to rescue him, but did not because through his death he was going to fulfill what the Scriptures prophesied (Matt. 26:53—54).

God does not will for us to be immune to the frustration that is a part of life in this fallen world (Rom. 8:18—25). But we know that even if we experience pain in this world, we will be more than conquerors through Christ in every situation we face (8:37), so that everything is turned for the good (8:28). In other words, when we go through an experience where God does not deliver us from pain and hardship, we must affirm that he can do it but has chosen not to since he has something better to achieve through our suffering. When we examine God's seeming inaction in times of crisis in this light, we can feel honored that he has called us to suffer for him, and we can look expectantly to the form that his "over-conquering" (cf. 8:37) is going to take—a form that will even surpass the triumph of a miraculous deliverance. If God can save us and does not, it is only because he has some greater good in mind.

Civil disobedience. Some important criteria need to be followed in practicing any civil disobedience responsibly. D. J. E. Attwood presents two sit-

---

18. Carl F. H. Henry, *The Uneasy Conscience of Modern Fundamentalism* (Grand Rapids: Eerdmans, 1948), 60 (italics his).

19. See our comments on 8:1—4.

---

uations that might warrant civil disobedience: "1. when believers are required to deny their faith in Christ, or explicitly disown their Lord; and 2. when the state has required Christians to take part in an action which is in clear conflict with their Christianly informed conscience." Peter's action comes under the first of these situations, as the refusal to witness is equivalent to denying the faith. Attwood goes on to cite criteria to help us make a decision:

> 1. All democratic and constitutional means must genuinely be exhausted. It is far preferable to persuade people by democratic argument. [That is what the great apologists of the early church did.] ...
> 2. Civil disobedience should be open and public. [This point is perhaps not necessary when it comes to verbal witness that could be done in private.] It should be submissive to arrest and punishment, ready to take responsibility for its illegal actions. 3. It should strongly prefer non-violent methods, some would say it must insist on non-violence. 4. Actions of civil disobedience should display a good knowledge of the law, and a full respect for it. 5. Actions should be appropriate to the cause. 6. Civil disobedience should have a specific and realistic end in view. It should not be designed or undertaken in ways that are politically counter-productive.

Attwood's conclusion is: "Fundamentally it remains only an extreme form of protest and persuasion, and it is not a form of coercion."[20]

Actions like breaking what we consider "a ridiculous speed limit," refusing to pay "unreasonable" taxes, and bombing abortion clinics do not qualify according to the criteria just mentioned. Two more helpful cautions come from John and Paul Feinberg. (1) While morality dictates disobeying the government, prudence suggests how we should do it.[21] Paul always used his mind to come up with the wisest way to respond to situations where his convictions clashed with those of the authorities. (2) We must remember that we are members of a spiritual community, the church. Therefore "counsel and prayer with other members of the body of Christ are advisable not only when planning strategy for representing God in society, but also when the option of acting beyond the law presents itself."[22] There are heroic stories in the film world of vigilantes who battle alone for justice. In real life, it is much more prudent to act in community.

In spite of these cautions we must remember that there will probably be disagreement within the church about the precise action one should take in

---

20. D. J. E. Attwood, "Civil Disobedience," *NDCEPT*, 234.

21. John S. and Paul D. Feinberg, *Ethics for a Brave New World* (Wheaton: Crossway, 1993), 402.

22. Ibid., 405.

certain situations. The classic example of this is Dietrich Bonhoeffer's participation in a plot against Hitler. Many Christians consider this a heroic decision, while others see it as opposed to the teachings of the Bible. Another example is the ethics of smuggling Bibles and Christian literature into "restricted access countries." Some have considered this a necessary means of getting the gospel to nations that prohibit the publication and distribution of Christian literature.[23] Others have felt that Christians should work within the legal limits of a nation and, when possible, negotiate with the restrictive governments to have the laws relaxed. God has used both groups of people for his glory.

Similarly, many sincere Christians in China feel they should work within the "official" Three-Self Patriotic movement despite the way the Communist government controls and uses it. Others view such involvement as compromise and work within the "illegal" house churches. Christians have also disagreed on the levels and means of participation in a war, especially when there is compulsory military conscription, bringing in the idea of "conscientious objector." Some solved the problem by serving in military hospitals and other humanitarian divisions that did not involve participation directly or indirectly in battle.

The Bible leaves room for disagreement among Christians on issues where there can be no single binding position. Scriptural examples of such issues are dietary habits (Rom. 14), the observing of sacred days (Rom. 14), and the consuming of food offered to idols (1 Cor. 8). On these issues Paul cites important guidelines, such as "each one should be fully convinced in his own mind" (Rom. 14:5). He cautions against a judgmental or superior attitude toward those who hold different views (14:1–4, 13) and against acting in ways that become a stumbling block to weaker Christians (14:13–16; 1 Cor. 8:9–13). These are areas where we must not force our opinions on others. According to Paul, "So whatever you believe about these things keep between yourself and God" (Rom. 14:22). Our actions should come from the overall aim Paul gives: "Let us therefore make every effort to do what leads to peace and to mutual edification" (14:19).

Having said this, we must also say that in the face of blatant injustice and oppression we cannot acquiesce to an attitude of silence because there is no unanimity in the church about how we should deal with the problem. This is what some Christians did during the atrocities committed by the Nazis.

Evangelistic passion. The early church was clearly focused on evangelism, using every opportunity and paying whatever price was necessary to further

---

23. See Brother Andrew with John and Elizabeth Sherrill, *God's Smuggler* (Lincoln, Va.: Chosen Books, 1970).

that cause. When they went to the courts, their primary concern was not winning a case; it was furthering the cause of the gospel. We too must look at situations of persecution as opportunities to share the gospel.

I was once traveling by train to a distant mission station in Sri Lanka at a time that Christianity had come in under attack because many poor Buddhists were coming to Christ. Christians were being falsely accused in the newspapers of buying up converts by offering financial incentives. I was seated next to a Buddhist who presented these typical arguments. In my response to him, I denied the charges, stating that the press was distorting the facts by, perhaps, using an isolated incident. Then I told him that Christians believe that this world has been created by the supreme God, who seeing the mess that it is in, presented in Christ the solution to this mess. We therefore regard it as the most important news in the world. Because we believe that, it is essential that we share it with the world, however much we suffer and are maligned for it. I used the opportunity to explain why and how it was the answer of the Creator to the world. My hope was that this Buddhist would not only understand why we evangelize, but that he would also be challenged by the fact that the gospel was the answer to *his own* need.

Evangelistic passion also caused the apostles to rejoice when they were flogged for evangelizing. They rejoiced because the earthly dishonor was to them actually a high honor. Consequently, the beating did not discourage evangelistic activity; it only propelled it forward with greater intensity (v. 42). This understanding of honor is why some Christians in the early centuries desired martyrdom and many rejoiced in it, though they may not have desired it. When Ignatius of Antioch in Syria was martyred around A.D. 107, he prayed, "I thank you, Lord and Master, that you have deemed to honor me by making complete my love for you in that you have bound me with chains of iron to your apostle Paul."[24]

Iranian Christian leader Mehdi Dibaj spent nine years in prison for his faith and was murdered in 1994, six months after his release from prison. One of his prison guards once asked him, "Does Jesus Christ know that He has someone in this prison who loves Him?" He replied, "Jesus Christ our Lord has millions of people who love Him and who wish to sacrifice their lives for Him. I too wish I was one of them." After relating this, Dibaj wrote, "How sweet it will be if one day my life is sacrificed for him."[25]

Such attitudes are not natural to us. Usually when we are ridiculed in public or punished for the gospel, we get angry and resentful—in part, per-

---

24. Duane W. H. Arnold, compiler and trans., *Prayers of the Martyrs* (Grand Rapids: Zondervan, 1991), 4.

25. Mehdi Dibaj, *Bound to be Free with the Suffering Church*, ed. Jan Pit (Tonbridge, Kent: Sovereign World, 1995), 153.

haps, because we think that we should look victorious in public. It is clear that there were long periods when biblical heroes looked anything but victorious. But they were propelled by the vision of God's ultimate victory and the belief that their temporary defeats were contributing to winning a great victory for the kingdom. These are important attitudes we must develop in relation to the gospel, especially as they are difficult to sustain in a culture that is so committed to the need to look good in public.

These attitudes did not come naturally to the apostles either. Calvin says, "It must not be thought that the apostles were so stolid as not to feel ashamed, and even to suffer from a sense that they had been wronged; for they had not discarded nature completely. But when they thought over the cause, joy got the upper hand." Calvin agrees that most of us do not think in this way: "Hardly one in a hundred understands that the ignominy of Christ is superior to all the triumphs of the world." Thus he says, "For that reason we must think about this sentence more earnestly."[26] The question we must constantly ask ourselves is, "How important to us is the gospel of Christ and honor of his name?"

---

26. Calvin, *Acts*, 155.

Acts 6:1–7

IN THOSE DAYS when the number of disciples was increasing, the Grecian Jews among them complained against the Hebraic Jews because their widows were being overlooked in the daily distribution of food. ²So the Twelve gathered all the disciples together and said, "It would not be right for us to neglect the ministry of the word of God in order to wait on tables. ³Brothers, choose seven men from among you who are known to be full of the Spirit and wisdom. We will turn this responsibility over to them ⁴and will give our attention to prayer and the ministry of the word."

⁵This proposal pleased the whole group. They chose Stephen, a man full of faith and of the Holy Spirit; also Philip, Procorus, Nicanor, Timon, Parmenas, and Nicolas from Antioch, a convert to Judaism. ⁶They presented these men to the apostles, who prayed and laid their hands on them.

⁷So the word of God spread. The number of disciples in Jerusalem increased rapidly, and a large number of priests became obedient to the faith.

Original Meaning

ACTS 4:32, 34 challenged us with a church where "all the believers were one in heart and mind" and among whom "there were no needy persons." In chapter 6 we see problems in both these areas. Every group of Christians that tries to practice true community will sooner or later encounter problems in the very areas of their strength in community life. But this section provides answers too, for the early church faced the problem squarely as soon as it surfaced.

The Problem (6:1)

JEWISH SOCIETY HAD a system to help needy widows. Probably the isolation that resulted when these people became Christians made these sources less accessible to them. Grecian widows were particularly needy as they were not native Judeans and did not have relatives to care for them. A lot of older couples came to die in Jerusalem so that they could be buried there.

There has been much discussion about who exactly the "Grecian Jews" were. The traditional view since John Chrysostom (c. 347–407) has been that they were Greek-speaking Jews while the Hebraic Jews spoke Aramaic. In spite of other suggestions, scholarly consensus seems to be going back to this view.[1] Probably these people grew up in the Diaspora, outside Palestine. Such cultural differences also resulted in differences in attitude and outlook.[2]

Almost certainly the Grecian widows were not deliberately discriminated against. The cause of the problem was the increase in the number of disciples (v. 1a). In an active and expanding movement it is possible for less prominent people not to be noticed. But that is still wrong. The Old Testament has many clear and specific regulations to ensure that socially depressed people like widows, orphans, and aliens are not overlooked. When a system is instituted such problems are minimized.

Problems among different ethnic and cultural groups have been common in the church. Barclay thinks that in Jewish society the Hebraic Jews looked down on the Grecians.[3] Longenecker thinks that pre-Christian prejudices may have reasserted themselves in the church. All of this contributed to the complaining that took place in the church.[4] The word translated "complained" (*gongysmos*) is an unpleasant word, used in the LXX for the murmuring of the Jews against Moses in the desert (Ex. 16:7; Num. 14:27). The church was now in danger of splitting. The problem might aggravate if it was not handled sensitively.

The Solution (6:2−6)

THE APOSTLES DID not focus attention on the complaining attitude toward the leadership. Nor did they talk about the priority of the spiritual and the relative unimportance of earthly food, as some may have done. There was a genuine problem, and the best way to quell doubts about prejudice was to solve the problem first. Thus, the apostles made an administrative decision. Thereby they not only averted a serious crisis of disunity, but also led the church to take a significant leap forward in terms of organizational structure. Though Luke does not use the word "deacon" here to describe the Seven,[5] this decision laid the foundation for the diaconal order, which, while taking different forms in the history of the church, has rendered great service in mediating Christ's love to needy people. Barclay observes, "It is extremely

---

1. David A. Fiensy, "The Composition of the Jerusalem Church," *BAFCS*, 4:235.

2. For a helpful discussion on the identity of these two groups see Longenecker, "Acts," 327−30.

3. Barclay, *Acts*, 52.

4. Longenecker, "Acts," 329.

5. The related noun *diakonia*, translated "distribution" in the NIV, is used in verse 1. *Diakoneo*, translated "wait on," appears in verse 2. Both these words refer to the serving of food. But in verse 4 *diakonia* is used in connection with the ministry of the Word.

interesting to note that the first office-bearers to be appointed were chosen not to talk but for practical service."[6]

The procedure adopted in choosing the Seven is instructive. The complaint came from the Grecians, "so the Twelve gathered all the disciples together" (v. 2). The entire group was given the task of choosing seven officials (v. 3). The apostles insisted that their own main task was to concentrate on "the ministry of the word" (v. 4 adds "prayer"). Therefore seven people had to be chosen to oversee the work of distributing food (vv. 2–3). The choice of seven may have been to correspond to "the Jewish practice of setting up boards of seven men for particular duties."[7]

The apostles laid down three qualifications for these men—"men of good repute" (REB) and "full of the Spirit and wisdom" (v. 3a). We do not know how these seven were selected. "Choose" (*episkeptomai*) means "look out for."[8] Since the word sometimes means "visit," J. A. Alexander thinks that the members were to "visit, or inspect with a view to discovering the necessary qualifications."[9] In any case, once the choice was made, the apostles said, "We will turn this responsibility over to them" (v. 3b). Chalmer Faw is probably right in suggesting that what happened was that the new leaders were "nominated by the group but appointed by the apostles."[10]

"This proposal pleased the whole group," and they chose seven men, all of whom have Greek names. This does not necessarily mean that they were all Hellenists, since "most Jews in the ancient world had three names—a Jewish, a Greek, and a Roman name—and used one or the other depending on the occasion."[11] But there are other reasons to conclude that "all seven appear to have been Hellenists."[12] We know for sure that Nicolas was a Hellenist, since he was a "convert to Judaism"; Stephen was one too, for his ministry was in a Hellenistic synagogue (6:9). Below we will discuss the wisdom of appointing Hellenists among the Seven.

The disciples then "presented these men to the apostles, who prayed and laid their hands on them" (v. 6). There we see the beginnings of church leaders laying hands on believers and commissioning them for specific tasks. The church has developed various orders of worship for such functions and given them names, such as commissioning, ordination, and induction services.

---

6. Barclay, *Acts*, 52.
7. Marshall, *Acts*, 126.
8. Bruce (NICNT) and Barrett translate it this way.
9. Alexander, *Acts*, 243.
10. Faw, *Acts*, 87.
11. Grant R. Osborne, "Hellenists," *BEB*, 1:961.
12. Bruce, *Acts*, NICNT, 121.

The Outcome (6:7)

LUKE IS EAGER to show that this administrative change did not reduce the evangelistic fervor of the church. So he adds another of his reports of evangelistic effectiveness (v. 7). The book of Acts is like a long hymn interspersed with refrains like this, which report on the spread of the church. Luke wants us to catch the spirit of this consuming passion for evangelism.

HOW CAN WE apply this passage? In a narrative book like Acts in some situations we can derive principles that apply to every situation in the Christian life. But in other situations, things happened that give us examples that may be helpful to remember, even though we cannot glean absolute principles from them. We need not think that every time we have a similar situation this is the only method to use. Here are two such examples from this passage.

- Acts outlines different methods of decision making in the church, and in this passage we find one such method. What is important here is that the leadership of the church led in this crisis and congregation had important input to give. This is a proper method to follow whenever decisions that affect the whole congregation are taken.
- We also see wisdom in the way the church handled the multicultural nature of her first constituency. But I do not think we can make an absolute principle out of how they acted in this situation.

In other words, as we apply this passage, we must note both types of material here: abiding principles and helpful examples. We now move to former.

Dealing with unity issues immediately and sensitively. While we can take comfort in the fact that the early church also had problems of disunity, we are challenged by the way these problems were immediately dealt with (cf. also the deception of Ananias and Sapphira, 5:1–11). Several factors could have prompted the apostles to shelve this problem without dealing with it right away. But they did deal with it, and the church took a great step forward.

The church used much sensitivity in the way they solved the problem. (1) Since this was a problem relating to a practice that affected the whole church, the entire group was involved in the solution. The principles were presented by the leaders (vv. 2–4), but their implementation involved the congregation: They did the choosing (v. 5). (2) Some, if not all, of those chosen for the distribution of food were Grecians (v. 5). There is much wisdom here, for they would know the needs of their own people best. (3) In solving this unity problem, the church took an administrative decision (vv. 3−6). Improper administration is often the cause of disunity and ill health in a church community. When important things that need to be done are overlooked, unease spreads among those who are affected.

Prayer and the ministry of the Word. Not all interpreters agree that it was a good idea for the apostles to take on the special responsibility to attend to prayer and the ministry of the Word. I have heard people say that this decision put a wedge between spiritual and the material, where the top leaders did the spiritual work and others did the less important material work. We must be careful about saying a mistake occurred here since at the end of this section, Luke reports that the church continued to be healthy and vibrant (v. 7). This is Luke's way of saying that God blessed the decision taken.

The idea that a mistake took place here arises from misconceptions about this passage. It does not say that prayer and the ministry of the Word are more important than the distribution of food. That is so only if we adopt an unbiblical separation of the sacred and the secular, which this passage does not adopt. This decision did not form a "spiritual elite."[13] Rather, the apostles affirmed that they had a primary calling and that they needed to exercise their spiritual gifts.

Nor does this passage say that the apostles prayed and ministered the Word to the exclusion of other ministries. They were not "pure" specialists. Paul's description of his ministry in Acts 20 shows that he did other things (20:34−35) besides preaching. Moreover, waiting on tables was not the only ministry that the Seven had. "It is clear that this was not their only role—perhaps not even their most important role. . . . This group was foremost in propagating the Christian message throughout Judea and the neighboring regions; it eventually launched the Gentile mission."[14]

Criteria for selecting administrative workers. Three criteria were important in the selection of officers to administer the distribution of food. They had to have a good reputation, to be filled with wisdom, and to be filled with the Spirit (v. 3). The responsibilities given to the Seven are like those we give to administrative workers in our churches today. When we appoint people to administrative posts in churches and other Christian groups, we too should look for these three important qualifications.

---

13. E. Stanley Jones (*The Word Became Flesh* [Nashville: Abingdon, 1963], 207) takes a different path in criticizing this decision by saying that by separating the sacred and the secular, the apostles lost their influence in the church. The result was that the Seven became the center of spiritual power in the church and the Twelve dropped out of the scene. This is reading too much into the text.

14. F. F. Bruce, *Peter, Stephen, James and John: Studies in Non-Pauline Christianity* (Grand Rapids: Eerdmans, 1979), 50.

A multicultural church. The Jerusalem church faced a serious problem in unity because of its multicultural composition. The conclusion of David Fiensy in a study of the composition of the Jerusalem church is that "the indications are that nearly all levels of society were represented. The church seems to have been a microcosm of the city."[15] The solution to the problem facing the church was not to divide and have separate churches—one for the Grecians and another for the Hebraists. Rather, they sought to ensure that the Grecians were cared for.

The multicultural nature of the church was preserved even in Antioch, where "the cosmopolitan population of [the city] was reflected in the membership of its church, and indeed in its leadership" (13:1).[16] "Eastern and western cultures were in contact and conflict [in Antioch]. The relationship between Jews and Gentiles in the church was debated and decided" here (Acts 15; Gal. 2:11–13).[17] Yet the early believers remained as a single church. Recent studies also show that the churches founded by Paul had a mixture of social levels in each congregation and reflected a fair cross section of urban society.[18]

Some have made too much of the separate cultural groups in the church in Jerusalem, using that as a precedent for having separate churches for different groups. Ernst Haenchen argues from chapters 6–11 that there was a cleavage in the church, even though Luke does not like to admit it since he was trying to present a picture of an ideal church. He claims that 8:1 implies this division when it says that all the believers except the apostles were scattered in the great persecution after Stephen's death—the Grecians left and the Hebraists stayed.[19] This is not at all certain. Indeed, would Luke distort facts simply in order to present an ideal church?[20]

John Polhill is nearer to the truth when he says, "There is no reason to picture a breach or separation in the total Christian community—only a sort of 'distancing' created by natural linguistic and cultural differences."[21] The multicultural nature of the New Testament church is worth emulating today.

---

15. Fiensy, "Composition of the Jerusalem Church," 4:213.

16. Stott, *Acts*, 216.

17. John E. Stambaugh and David L. Balch, *The New Testament in Its Social Environment* (Philadelphia: Westminster, 1986), 149.

18. Wayne A. Meeks, *The First Urban Christians: The Social World of the Apostle Paul* (New Haven: Yale Univ. Press, 1983), 51–73.

19. Haenchen, *Acts*, 266.

20. Peter Wagner adopts Haenchen's conclusion, even though I do not think he would agree with his point that Luke distorted the facts (*Spreading the Fire*, 182).

21. Polhill, *Acts*, 179.

SETTLING UNITY ISSUES **today.** Some leaders try to sweep problems like those faced in Acts 6 under the carpet because they do not want to face the humiliation that comes if such problems surface. Others attempt to force a unity through exercises of worship or external affirmations of unity, like picnics and hugs. Others are overcome by hurt in that, despite their good intentions and hard work, people attribute bad motives to them. Still others may feel offended by the attitude of the grumblers and focus on that attitude without solving the root of the problem. Such delays in dealing with problems usually aggravate situations and open the door for mighty explosions, which result in major church splits.

Christ's teaching on unity problems is clear: "If you are offering your gift at the altar and there remember that your brother has something against you, leave your gift there in front of the altar. First go and be reconciled to your brother; then come and offer your gift" (Matt. 5:23–24). Regardless of whether we think this brother is justified to be angry with us and whether he has been honorable in his actions or not, we must go to him immediately. So urgent is the issue that we should hold back at the altar a gift we have come to give. Elsewhere Paul said, "'In your anger do not sin': Do not let the sun go down while you are still angry, and do not give the devil a foothold" (Eph. 4:26–27). In family life and in community life, if we delay dealing with anger, we give the devil a foothold.

I live in a land of ethnic turmoil, where the church has members from both ethnic groups in the conflict. Often Christians do not talk about their problems with people of the other race; they keep their prejudices and complaints to themselves and discuss them only with people of their own group. They are polite and friendly when they meet those of the other group, but there is an undercurrent of anger, which occasionally surfaces. When we act in this way, we cease to be a healing community in our land. Christians must constantly be on the alert to the danger of unchristian prejudices reappearing in the church and deal with them decisively when they arise. We know that God is bigger than the problem and that what unites us is deeper than what divides us; thus, we must have the courage to face up to the problem squarely.

Making administrative changes. In the early years of a movement, needs can be met through the memory and observation of the leaders. But as the movement grows (v. 1), memory and observation can be taxed beyond a certain level, demanding a new structure to ensure that these needs are met. People may look back to the early days when all these administrative requirements were not there and conclude that new requirements demonstrate a breakdown of trust within the movement. "Why do we have to fill all these forms; don't they trust us anymore?" they ask, and they long for the early days. But structures are designed to serve an organization, and they must change according to its needs. Sometimes new structures and policies are needed to ensure that important things do not get overlooked.

What we must always ensure in any change is that the original vision and passion of the movement be maintained. This is a key responsibility of the leader. The new structures must always be kept in a subsidiary position. One sure way to check whether a rotting process has begun in a group is to see what topics predominate in discussions when the leaders meet. If maintenance of structures has overtaken mission as the major topic, we know that rot has set in. Luke shows that the new structure did not muffle the vision. After describing the organizational changes, he reports on how the church continued to grow (v. 7).

Leadership and prayer. Why and how do leaders give priority to prayer? Four points can be made here. (1) God is the ultimate leader of any Christian group. The earthly leaders represent him as his agents on earth. If they are to do so adequately, they must be attuned to him. And there is no better way for that to happen than by spending time with him in prayer and in the study of the Word. As we do so, his nature becomes implanted in us and we become godly. We think his thoughts and can thus lead as he would lead.

Sometimes when we are concerned about the lack of godliness in our churches, we look for a program that will help raise the spiritual life of the people. As a result, we organize prayer meetings, seminars, and revival meetings. While these may help, more important is the renewal of godliness in the life of the leadership. The Scottish minister Robert Murray McCheyne (1813–1843) died before he was thirty years old, and his short ministry was punctuated by severe illness. But it had a powerful impact on Scotland. He once made a statement that perhaps gives the key to his effectiveness: "My people's greatest need is my personal holiness."

Jesus also presents prayer as the secret of power in ministry. In answer to the disciples' query about their failure to drive out an evil spirit from a boy, Jesus said, "This kind can come out only by prayer" (Mark 9:29). Someone has said that the wind of the Holy Spirit blows according to his will. Our job is to set the sails of our boats in a direction that can catch this wind. This is what happens when we pray: We become attuned to God and receive what used to be called unction or the "plus of the Spirit" in our ministries.

A side effect of living a life of prayer is that others are challenged to be prayer warriors. How important this ministry is in this busy world where people are easily tempted to drop extended times of prayer from their schedules! Observing Jesus at prayer prompted the disciples to ask him to teach them to pray: "One day Jesus was praying in a certain place. When he finished, one of his disciples said to him, 'Lord, teach us to pray, just as John taught his disciples'" (Luke 11:1). In response Jesus taught them the Lord's Prayer.

(2) Leaders have a priestly function in that they must pray *for* the movement and the people they lead. The prophet Samuel said, "As for me, far be it from me that I should sin against the LORD by failing to pray for you" (1 Sam. 12:23). James says, "The prayer of a righteous man is powerful and effective" (James 5:16). Given the power of prayer, then, the most important thing a leader can do is to pray for his or her people. Jesus gave the lead here. He spent long hours, sometimes entire nights, in prayer. A significant portion of that time must have been spent in intercession. The only time the Gospels record him speaking about his own prayer life is in these words: "Simon, Simon, Satan has asked to sift you as wheat. But I have prayed for you, Simon, that your faith may not fail" (Luke 22:31–32a).

Moses spent forty days and forty nights in prayer interceding for his people and pleading to God to have mercy on them after they had sinned grievously (Deut. 9:18). We know how Joshua's army floundered in battle when Moses slacked in praying for it (Ex. 17:9–13). Paul mentions praying for his recipients in ten of his thirteen letters. The biblical evidence, then, is undeniable that one of the most important tasks of leaders is to pray for their people.

(3) Leaders pray *with* those they lead. This includes pastoral prayers through visiting people at home, in the hospital, and at special events in their lives (James 5:14–15). Many Christians can look back to a time of need in their lives when they were visited by a pastor who prayed with them and mediated God's strength through their presence and prayer. The leaders get to know their people through these visits; this greatly enhances the relevance of their preaching.

(4) Leaders should *lead* the community in prayer, as the apostles did when the Seven were chosen (v. 6). In Scripture, leaders often took the lead in calling the people to fast and pray.[22] Their commitment to prayer helped keep it as a priority in the movement. When people realize that their leader is in constant touch with God, almost unconsciously the level of prayer is raised in the movement. Some years ago I had the privilege of spending a sabbatical teaching at Gordon-Conwell Theological Seminary in the United States. I served in the missions department, led by Dr. J. Christy Wilson Jr. Whenever I talked to him about a need or concern, he would immediately say, "Let's pray about it," and then immediately led in prayer. That habit has left an indelible impression on my life. It challenged me to be more of a leader in prayer.

---

22. See 2 Chron. 20:3; Ezra 8:21.

Leadership and the ministry of the Word. God is the real leader of any Christian group. The leader's primary task is to guide the movement along the will of God, which is most comprehensively recorded in the Bible (2 Tim. 3:16–17). Thus, one of a leader's main responsibilities is to teach people the Word. For this reason, when Paul lists the qualifications for overseers in the church, the only ability related requirement he cites is that the person must be "able to teach" (1 Tim. 3:2; cf. 2 Tim. 2:2). The other fifteen requirements have to do with maturity, character, and reputation.

Paul also describes the comprehensive way in which he taught the Ephesian Christians: "I have not refrained from setting before you the whole will and purpose of God" (Acts 20:27).[23] In a marvelous way the entire Bible harmonizes to give us the full breadth of God's revelation. To miss out on some sections of the Bible is to miss out on key aspects of God's truth. The New Testament assumes the foundation of the Old Testament and does not repeat a lot of what is found there. How important to have our people learn the full truth of God's Word!

If we are to give people such a balanced diet, we ourselves must be fed on such a diet. That is why it is so important for every Christian leader to read the whole Bible through in a given time. The two outstanding textbooks on preaching by John Stott and D. Martyn Lloyd-Jones both recommend that a leader go through the Bible in a year; both also mention the Bible Reading Calendar prepared by Robert Murray McCheyne.[24] Slower readers may need to use another system that takes a longer time. When our lives have been influenced by all of Scripture, our ministries will also be influenced by the whole will and purpose of God.

Though the idea of studying the Word diligently may not be much in vogue today, this is an essential discipline for long-term effectiveness in ministry. One of the side effects of this discipline is that we are refreshed. The ministry, like all people-helping professions, can greatly strain the mind and body. It has been said that "'burn-out' may be more common in professions and business posts with a strong vocational element."[25] It has certainly become a serious problem in the Christian ministry.[26] One key to avoiding this is

---

23. Bruce's translation, *Acts*, NICNT, 391.

24. D. Martyn Lloyd-Jones, *Preaching and Preachers* (Grand Rapids: Zondervan, 1971), 172; John R. W. Stott, *I Believe in Preaching* (London: Hodder and Stoughton, 1982), 183 (US edition, *Between Two Worlds: The Art of Preaching in the Twentieth Century* [Grand Rapids: Eerdmans., 1981]). This "Calendar" is reproduced in full in Kent Hughes, *The Disciplines of a Godly Man* (Wheaton: Crossway, 1991), 230–39.

25. G. Davies, "Stress," *NDCEPT*, 817.

26. See Archibald Hart, *Coping with Depression in the Ministry and Other Helping Professions* (Dallas: Word, 1984); Donald E. Demaray, *Watch Out for Burnout* (Grand Rapids: Baker, 1983).

time spent lingering in God's Word. David said, "The law of the LORD is perfect, reviving the soul" (Ps. 19:7).

We constantly face wounds as people reject our advice, attribute bad motives to our actions, or fail to "make it" despite out best efforts. Many in ministry today are bitter over the way they have been treated after all the sacrifices they made. One of the best ways of healing after receiving blows from a hostile world is to spend time in the Word. The psalmist says, "If your law had not been my delight, I would have perished in my affliction" (Ps. 119:92). The Word also refreshes us as a source of great joy and pleasure. Just as entertainment refreshes us, so does the Word, but with much deeper and longer-lasting fruits. In Psalm 119 the psalmist claims nine times to delight in some aspect of the Word.

The leader's call is not only to know and teach the Word but also to apply it to the challenges that people face. The letters of the New Testament are essentially applications of God's truth to the challenges faced by their addressees. We are called to do the same today. To do this we must know both the Word and the world. Our knowledge of the latter comes by reading and viewing news, literature, and the arts and by observing what is happening around us. John Wesley was walking with one of his preachers when they came upon two women quarreling, using forceful language. The preacher suggested that they walk on, but Wesley checked him: "Stay, Sammy! Stay, and learn to preach!"[27]

How do we integrate what we learn from the Scriptures with what we learn of the world, and how do we apply the Word to the lives of our people? (1) *Reading.* When we read biographies and practical books, we learn how others respond to situations similar to those we face. (2) *Hard thinking.* We should put ourselves into the world of our people and see how the Scripture speaks to their experience. (3) I know of no better way than *practicing the art of application.* We do this in two ways. (a) We apply the Word to our own lives. (b) We do personal ministry and help others apply the Word to their lives. As we grapple with people's (including our own) situations by being with them, listening to them, counseling them, and praying for them, we are forced to examine and apply what we know from the Scriptures. Application is not a science we learn by study; it is a skill that we acquire through practice. It should become second nature to us.

I will go so far as to say that those who do not do personal ministry will most likely be poor appliers of Scripture. They will invariably apply Scripture only in a way that is relevant to themselves, and their challenges may be different to those of the person on the street. For this reason, in our own ministry we do not invite as speakers at our programs those who are not engaged in personal ministry.

---

27. W. T. Purkiser, *The New Testament Image of the Ministry* (Grand Rapids: Baker, 1970), 64.

Criteria for selecting administrative workers. The three criteria used in the selection of administrative workers in the early church were a good reputation, being filled with wisdom, and being filled with the Spirit. When we appoint officers in the church—for example, treasurers and administrators of various church projects—we ought to look for these three qualifications.

Of these three, the third seems most frequently neglected. We tend to put people into positions of leadership in administrative matters if they are administratively capable (i.e., if they have wisdom) and have a high place in society, regardless of whether their lives give evidence of the fullness of the Spirit. Thus, we end up with rich and influential people on boards and project committees, but people with few spiritual qualifications. They may indeed bring in money and other resources. But later we complain about the undesirable influence they have on the movement. This pattern has become a serious problem in evangelical relief organizations today.

This practice is wrong on three counts. (1) It reflects an unbiblical separation of the sacred and the secular. When we say that for "secular-type jobs," leaders do not need spiritual qualities, we are ignoring the fact that in the body of Christ everything we do is for the Lord. All service is spiritual in nature. Social service organizations that claim to be committed to holistic ministry should have holistic workers to do the work—those skilled in the project as well as having a vibrant relationship with God.

(2) Ignoring spiritual qualifications reflects a wrong idea of Christian community, the key of which is the spiritual unity we share as members of the body of Christ. As each person makes a contribution, the body of Christ moves forward. But we enter into this body through a spiritual tie with Christ. If we do not have such a tie, we cannot participate in body ministry.

(3) When we appoint unspiritual people to supposedly non-spiritual jobs, we forget that when people stay long in an organization, they often become senior staff, who, by virtue of their seniority, influence decisions that give the direction of the organization. It is better to wait until we can find the right people rather than do good work employing the wrong people. We may achieve a lot in terms of the volume of service, but in the long run it can take the church in a wrong direction.

Forging multicultural churches today. Does the multicultural nature of the New Testament church contradict the "homogenous unit principle," which, in its extreme form, advocates separate churches for separate groups?[28] We know that the Jerusalem church had two different language groups, which would have made a natural division. But the leaders did not divide the

---

28. For a discussion of this issue, see Lausanne Committee for World Evangelization, *The Pasadena Consultation—Homogenous Unit*, Lausanne Occasional Papers, No. 1 (Wheaton: Lausanne Committee for World Evangelization, 1978).

church. True, many of the church meetings were in houses, and presumably each of these groups operated in one language. But when the whole church assembled, the two groups met together. Beyond doubt the distribution of food was centralized.

In evangelism it is, I admit, usually beneficial to target a specific audience by presenting the message in a way that is particularly relevant to it. For this reason, we may need to have special strategies to reach the poor and the rich, the Jews and the Muslims, the Spanish-speaking and the English-speaking. But that betrays everything the Bible speaks about the unity of the body of Christ and about how Christ breaks barriers if we encourage major separations of congregations according to cultural divisions. In Corinth Paul strongly condemned the division of churches according to interest groups with the piercing question, "Is Christ divided?" (1 Cor. 1:13).

Jesus told his disciples that the unity of Christians is a key to bringing the world to believe in Christ (John 17:21). Indeed, the breaking of human barriers is a key ingredient of the Christian message (cf. Eph. 2:11–22), and our failure to demonstrate it a key hindrance to evangelistic effectiveness with non-Christians. Many Buddhists have, sometimes sincerely and sometimes critically, brought up this issue when I have talked to them about Christ. Often the Muslims present the "brotherhood of Islam" as the answer to the segregation of Christianity.

We are desperately in need of a more powerful demonstration of our unity today. On the one hand, people should usually worship God in their heart language; on the other hand, they should affirm their unity in Christ despite cultural divisions and should develop the discipline of being enriched by other cultures.

We will face three major obstacles if we try to have multicultural churches. (1) Today's pragmatism always looks at success in terms of measurable results. Christ would have us reach as large a number of people as we can (cf. comments on 4:1–22). Having monocultural churches, so many claim, helps achieve this rapidly. But biblical principles should take priority over "the success principle."

(2) Today's society also tries hard to avoid pain and unpleasantness, and multicultural churches usually experience pain as a result of misunderstandings and cultural insensitivity. Yet the benefits of multicultural churches are immense. We can learn much from each other. We can understand the problems of other types of people (e.g., the poor) better and thus help solve them if they are in our congregations.[29] We can demonstrate that Christ can make

29. In a recent book (*Church: Why Bother?* [Grand Rapids: Zondervan, 1998]), Philip Yancey explains in great detail why he will never join a church that does not have cultural and economic diversity.

people one. This is an important message in a world broken by ethnic, caste, and class strife.

(3) Established Christians are often unwilling to change practices in their church in order to welcome converts. Forms of worship, styles of music, the time of the worship service, and so on may need to be adjusted to accommodate non-Christians so that they will feel at home and be served better. Many Christians say they are committed to evangelism, but they do not want to pay the price of bringing in an evangelistic harvest. In actuality, they want to be comfortable. But God has not called us to comfort but to witness to everyone about Jesus Christ.

In other words, we need to explore how best to apply the biblical principle of the unity of the body amidst diversity. While we may need separate congregations because of language barriers, we can still have them as part of one "church." We can meet together for worship and fellowship occasionally, even though such meetings may be tedious even after careful and creative planning. The church where I worship has two congregations—one English-speaking and the other Sinhala-speaking. We meet once a quarter for a combined, bilingual service. The Sinhala-speaking congregation to which we belong has educated members and illiterate members, wealthy members and desperately poor members. About 75 percent of them are converts from Buddhism. My wife and I cherish the enrichment that has come to us through having as close brothers and sisters people who are so culturally different from us.

There was great wisdom in the early church's selection of some or all of the officials from the Grecian community. They knew well the needs and sensitivities of the aggrieved group. Often outsiders do not know how people of another group think, especially regarding things they are particularly sensitive to. Knowing this is important when dealing with minority groups or groups that have felt badly treated in the past. Sometimes those of other groups feel surprised that after all they have done, these people are still upset. They may have done a lot, but they may not have been sympathetic to sensitive areas.

This can be a serious problem in relations between Christian donors and receivers and between Christians from minority and majority communities. Some who desperately want the help offered by the powerful group willingly swallow their pride and remain silent. Others, who value their identity and principles, will speak up and are then unfortunately accused of being prejudiced and bitter. Many in the so-called "Third World" remain distressed that many well-meaning Christians in the West find it difficult to sense this problem and do something about it.

The response of the early church gives us several keys that will help solve this problem. They developed a listening ear that took the opinions of the other group seriously. They accepted responsibility for the error of overlooking the needs of the neglected group. They took immediate remedial action and included the people in finding a solution to the problem. And they appointed people from the aggrieved party to help administer the program where the problems had cropped up. There is much wisdom here for Christians interested in missions and in forging relationships with believers of other cultures.

Acts 6:8-7:53

❧

NOW STEPHEN, A man full of God's grace and power, did
great wonders and miraculous signs among the people.
⁹Opposition arose, however, from members of the
Synagogue of the Freedmen (as it was called)—Jews of Cyrene
and Alexandria as well as the provinces of Cilicia and Asia.
These men began to argue with Stephen, ¹⁰but they could not
stand up against his wisdom or the Spirit by whom he spoke.

¹¹Then they secretly persuaded some men to say, "We have
heard Stephen speak words of blasphemy against Moses and
against God."

¹²So they stirred up the people and the elders and the
teachers of the law. They seized Stephen and brought him
before the Sanhedrin. ¹³They produced false witnesses, who
testified, "This fellow never stops speaking against this holy
place and against the law. ¹⁴For we have heard him say that
this Jesus of Nazareth will destroy this place and change the
customs Moses handed down to us."

¹⁵All who were sitting in the Sanhedrin looked intently at
Stephen, and they saw that his face was like the face of an
angel.

⁷:¹Then the high priest asked him, "Are these charges true?"

²To this he replied: "Brothers and fathers, listen to me! The
God of glory appeared to our father Abraham while he was still
in Mesopotamia, before he lived in Haran. ³'Leave your country
and your people,' God said, 'and go to the land I will show you.'

⁴"So he left the land of the Chaldeans and settled in Haran.
After the death of his father, God sent him to this land where
you are now living. ⁵He gave him no inheritance here, not
even a foot of ground. But God promised him that he and his
descendants after him would possess the land, even though at
that time Abraham had no child. ⁶God spoke to him in this
way: 'Your descendants will be strangers in a country not their
own, and they will be enslaved and mistreated four hundred
years. ⁷But I will punish the nation they serve as slaves,' God
said, 'and afterward they will come out of that country and
worship me in this place.' ⁸Then he gave Abraham the
covenant of circumcision. And Abraham became the father of

Isaac and circumcised him eight days after his birth. Later Isaac became the father of Jacob, and Jacob became the father of the twelve patriarchs.

⁹"Because the patriarchs were jealous of Joseph, they sold him as a slave into Egypt. But God was with him ¹⁰and rescued him from all his troubles. He gave Joseph wisdom and enabled him to gain the goodwill of Pharaoh king of Egypt; so he made him ruler over Egypt and all his palace.

¹¹"Then a famine struck all Egypt and Canaan, bringing great suffering, and our fathers could not find food. ¹²When Jacob heard that there was grain in Egypt, he sent our fathers on their first visit. ¹³ On their second visit, Joseph told his brothers who he was, and Pharaoh learned about Joseph's family. ¹⁴After this, Joseph sent for his father Jacob and his whole family, seventy-five in all. ¹⁵Then Jacob went down to Egypt, where he and our fathers died. ¹⁵Their bodies were brought back to Shechem and placed in the tomb that Abraham had bought from the sons of Hamor at Shechem for a certain sum of money.

¹⁷"As the time drew near for God to fulfill his promise to Abraham, the number of our people in Egypt greatly increased. ¹⁸Then another king, who knew nothing about Joseph, became ruler of Egypt. ¹⁹He dealt treacherously with our people and oppressed our forefathers by forcing them to throw out their newborn babies so that they would die.

²⁰"At that time Moses was born, and he was no ordinary child. For three months he was cared for in his father's house. ²¹When he was placed outside, Pharaoh's daughter took him and brought him up as her own son. ²²Moses was educated in all the wisdom of the Egyptians and was powerful in speech and action.

²³"When Moses was forty years old, he decided to visit his fellow Israelites. ²⁴He saw one of them being mistreated by an Egyptian, so he went to his defense and avenged him by killing the Egyptian. ²⁵Moses thought that his own people would realize that God was using him to rescue them, but they did not. ²⁶The next day Moses came upon two Israelites who were fighting. He tried to reconcile them by saying, 'Men, you are brothers; why do you want to hurt each other?'

²⁷"But the man who was mistreating the other pushed Moses aside and said, 'Who made you ruler and judge over us? ²⁸Do you want to kill me as you killed the Egyptian

yesterday?' ²⁹When Moses heard this, he fled to Midian, where he settled as a foreigner and had two sons.

³⁰"After forty years had passed, an angel appeared to Moses in the flames of a burning bush in the desert near Mount Sinai. ³¹When he saw this, he was amazed at the sight. As he went over to look more closely, he heard the Lord's voice: ³²'I am the God of your fathers, the God of Abraham, Isaac and Jacob.' Moses trembled with fear and did not dare to look.

³³"Then the Lord said to him, 'Take off your sandals; the place where you are standing is holy ground. ³⁴I have indeed seen the oppression of my people in Egypt. I have heard their groaning and have come down to set them free. Now come, I will send you back to Egypt.'

³⁵"This is the same Moses whom they had rejected with the words, 'Who made you ruler and judge?' He was sent to be their ruler and deliverer by God himself, through the angel who appeared to him in the bush. ³⁶He led them out of Egypt and did wonders and miraculous signs in Egypt, at the Red Sea and for forty years in the desert.

³⁷"This is that Moses who told the Israelites, 'God will send you a prophet like me from your own people.' ³⁸He was in the assembly in the desert, with the angel who spoke to him on Mount Sinai, and with our fathers; and he received living words to pass on to us.

³⁹"But our fathers refused to obey him. Instead, they rejected him and in their hearts turned back to Egypt. ⁴⁰They told Aaron, 'Make us gods who will go before us. As for this fellow Moses who led us out of Egypt—we don't know what has happened to him!' ⁴¹That was the time they made an idol in the form of a calf. They brought sacrifices to it and held a celebration in honor of what their hands had made. ⁴²But God turned away and gave them over to the worship of the heavenly bodies. This agrees with what is written in the book of the prophets:

> "'Did you bring me sacrifices and offerings
>   forty years in the desert, O house of Israel?
> ⁴³You have lifted up the shrine of Molech
>   and the star of your god Rephan,
>   the idols you made to worship.
> Therefore I will send you into exile' beyond Babylon.

⁴⁴"Our forefathers had the tabernacle of the Testimony with them in the desert. It had been made as God directed Moses, according to the pattern he had seen. ⁴⁵Having received the tabernacle, our fathers under Joshua brought it with them when they took the land from the nations God drove out before them. It remained in the land until the time of David, ⁴⁶who enjoyed God's favor and asked that he might provide a dwelling place for the God of Jacob. ⁴⁷But it was Solomon who built the house for him.

⁴⁸"However, the Most High does not live in houses made by men. As the prophet says:

⁴⁹"'Heaven is my throne,
      and the earth is my footstool.
   What kind of house will you build for me?
      says the Lord.
   Or where will my resting place be?
⁵⁰Has not my hand made all these things?'

⁵¹"You stiff-necked people, with uncircumcised hearts and ears! You are just like your fathers: You always resist the Holy Spirit! ⁵²Was there ever a prophet your fathers did not persecute? They even killed those who predicted the coming of the Righteous One. And now you have betrayed and murdered him—⁵³you who have received the law that was put into effect through angels but have not obeyed it."

WHEN WE CONSIDER the space Luke gives to Stephen (which includes the longest speech in Acts), we realize the important place he had in the history of the early church—and not just because he was the first martyr. He presented to the church some radical implications of the gospel, especially about the temple. It is particularly significant that Luke gives him so much emphasis when, as F. F. Bruce has pointed out, "Luke, in both parts of his work, reveals a much more positive attitude to the temple than Stephen does."¹ This is a case for the historical reliability of this record, which many are skeptical about.² "These chapters are a real

---

1. F. F. Bruce, *Peter, Stephen, James, and John: Studies in Non-Pauline Christianity* (Grand Rapids: Eerdmans, 1979), 53.

2. For more arguments for the historical reliability of this passage, see D. J. Williams, *Acts*, 129.

hinge in the story of the early church"[3] since they show that Christianity and Judaism are really two different religions. They provide a transition between the Judean phase of Acts and the non-Judean phase, and a link between Peter (the apostle to the Jews) and Paul (the apostle to the Gentiles).

The Man Stephen (6:5, 8–10)

STEPHEN MUST HAVE been an outstanding person because Luke mentions six features of his character and ministry in 6:5–10. (1) He was "a man full of faith" (6:5). As David Williams points out, "His faith was not different in kind from the faith that all Christians have, but exceptional in the extent to which he was willing to trust Christ, to take him at his word and to risk all for Christ's sake."[4] This was a key requirement for one who blazed new trails for the gospel. Many opposed him. Probably even people within the church would have preferred for him to take a more cautious approach. But Stephen saw certain implications in what the Bible taught and what Christ did, and he was willing to risk all for the truth of those implications.

(2) He was "full . . . of the Holy Spirit" (6:5). This statement is found in the context of a listing of the Seven. This need not have been mentioned, since all of the Seven had to be filled with the Spirit (6:3). Possibly there were some like, Stephen and Barnabas (11:24), who so exhibited the power of the Spirit that when people observed them, they were struck by this fact, and it is thus given special mention. Verse 8 confirms this by saying Stephen was "a man full of God's . . . power." This feature manifested itself as he "did great wonders and miraculous signs among the people."

(3) He was "a man full of God's grace" (6:8). Since this phrase comes just before the external manifestation of God's power, we can assume that it refers to the way God was manifested internally. Thus, Bruce and Longenecker think that what is intended by the use of "grace" here is "spiritual charm" or "winsomeness."[5] This is a possible meaning of the word used here (*charis*).[6] Stephen had let God's grace impact him so much that it had made him a gracious person. Of course, graciousness does not mean weakness, and later we see him thundering accusations against the Jews (7:51–53). But it does mean that Stephen was able to act in a Christlike way under provocation.

(4) The opponents who debated Stephen were "members of the Synagogue[7] of the Freedmen" (v. 9). They came from four places: Cyrene and

---

3. Gempf, "Acts," *NBCTCE*, 1076.

4. Williams, *Acts*, 119.

5. Bruce, *Acts: Greek Text*, 185; Longenecker, "Acts," 334.

6. Luke uses *charis* in this way in Luke 4:22 and Acts 4:33.

7. Some have understood this verse as referring to more than one synagogue, and the figures suggested range from two to five synagogues. The NIV is probably correct in under-

Alexandria, cities in upper Africa, and Cilicia and Asia, provinces in Asia Minor. The most important town in Cilicia was Tarsus, Paul's hometown. Did Paul (Saul) worship in this synagogue? We cannot be sure, but we know that he was involved in Stephen's death. He may have, however, preferred a synagogue using Hebrew, for he calls himself a Hebrew (2 Cor. 11:22; Phil. 3:5). The most important town in Asia was Ephesus (cf. also the seven churches in Asia, Rev. 2–3). Freedmen (*libertinos*[8]) were probably the descendants of those who had been liberated from slavery or imprisonment. This synagogue "might well have owed its origin to Jews who had been taken as prisoners of war to Rome in the time of Pompey (63 B.C.)" and were later liberated.[9] This was clearly a Hellenist synagogue and may be the one to which Stephen himself once belonged.[10]

(5) and (6) The last two features of Stephen's character relate to his preaching: "They could not stand up against his wisdom or the Spirit by whom he spoke" (6:10). "Wisdom" (*sophia*) appears only four times in Acts (6:3, 10; 7:10, 22). It was an "inspired wisdom" (REB), in that the Spirit gave Stephen the words to speak, in keeping with the promise of Christ, "For I will give you words and wisdom that none of your adversaries will be able to resist or contradict" (Luke 21:15).

According to Jewish and Old Testament ideas, wisdom refers to one's "approach to life, arising out of life in the covenant bestowed by God." It was "regarded as the gift of God."[11] Luke follows this idea in his use of the word "wisdom."[12] We see it in Stephen's speech, which is saturated in Scripture and applies Scripture to the challenges arising from the gospel. Speaking out of the Jewish worldview, using Jewish Scripture, and inspired by the Spirit, Stephen speaks in a way that cuts to the heart of their thinking, and they cannot answer him. In the previous study we talked of the ability to apply Scripture to the challenges one faces as a key to an effective ministry of the Word. Stephen brilliantly exemplifies this ability.

Stephen Charged (6:11–15)

AFTER FAILING TO silence Stephen through debate, the Jews try to silence him through the law. They persuade certain people to make accusations

---

standing it as one synagogue with freedmen from all four places. See Bruce, *Acts: Greek Text*, 186–87.

8. A transliteration from the Latin *libertinus*.

9. F. W. Danker, "Synagogue of the Freedmen," *ISBE*, 2:360.

10. Williams, *Acts*, 124.

11. J. Goetzmann, "Wisdom," *NIDNTT*, 3:1030.

12. Ibid.

against him (6:11), which allows them to take him to the Sanhedrin (6:12) with this charge: He "never stops speaking against this holy place and against the law" (6:13). This is elaborated with a claim that he said that Jesus "will destroy this place and change the customs Moses handed down to us" (6:14). Bruce explains that when Judea became a Roman province in A.D. 6, capital punishment was allowed only by the decree of the Roman governor, except for offenses by word or deed against the sanctity of the temple. In such situations, the Sanhedrin was allowed to pronounce and execute the death sentence. They had tried to convict Christ in this way but failed. As a result, they took him to Pilate. With Stephen, however, they succeeded.[13]

The Sanhedrin observes that Stephen's "face was like the face of an angel" (6:15). Today too we sometimes hear people say that when they heard someone speak, that person's face seemed to radiate with the glow of God. David Williams points out that Luke has given a "description of one whose communion with God was such that something of the divine glory was reflected in him." He reminds us that "oddly, the same had been said of Moses (Exod. 34: 29ff.; cf. 2 Cor. 3:12–18)." Both "bore the mark of having been with God. And yet Stephen was accused of 'speaking against Moses and against God.'"[14]

Stephen's Speech (7:1–53)

STEPHEN'S FAMOUS SPEECH has been called his "defense," but, as Bruce points out, "it is not a speech for the defense in the forensic sense of the term." That is, it is not "calculated to secure an acquittal before the Sanhedrin." Rather, it is "a defense of pure Christianity as God's appointed way of worship."[15] It uses Scripture as a base, which is also the source of authority of Stephen's audience. It is, as we will see, a case of true biblical contextualization.

Stephen argues his points from Israel's history as recorded in the Jewish Scriptures. He stresses three major themes.

1. The activity of God is not confined to the geographical land of Israel. God spoke to Abraham in Mesopotamia (7:2–3) and Haran (7:4). He blessed Joseph in Egypt (7:9–16). He spoke to Moses in the desert near Sinai during the incident of the burning bush (7:30–34). He performed wonders and signs in Egypt, the Red Sea, and the desert (7:36), and he also gave his people the law at Mount Sinai (7:38).

2. Worship acceptable to God is not confined to the Jerusalem temple. The burning bush was holy ground, and Moses had to remove his sandals

---

13. Bruce, *Peter, Stephen*, 52–53. Some interpreters, however, think that what happened to Stephen was more a lynching than a legal punishment through the due process of law.

14. Williams, *Acts*, 125–26.

15. Bruce, *Acts*, NICNT, 130.

there (7:33). Moses encountered God in Mount Sinai and was given living words (7:38). The tabernacle was a suitable place of worship for the people of Israel (7:44–46). Stephen concludes that "everything necessary for pure worship was available to the people in the wilderness, before they ever entered the Holy land."[16] The Jewish Scriptures testify that God does not dwell in houses made by human beings (7:48–50). Actually, as Bruce says, "Solomon's action [of building the temple] is deprecated" (see 7:47–50). As "the Most High does not live in houses made by men" (7:48), Stephen is implying that "to announce the suppression or destruction of the temple was not to commit blasphemy or sacrilege against God, because God was independent of any temple."[17]

3. The Jews have constantly rejected God's representatives. Joseph was rejected by the patriarchs (7:9). Moses was rejected when he tried to intervene in a quarrel between two Jews (7:26–29), and yet this Moses was sent as Israel's deliverer (7:35). The message of Moses they rejected and instead erected a golden calf (7:39–43). Stephen climaxes his message in vigorous language by claiming that Israelite history is a history of rejection (7:51–53). It is possible that Stephen has to end his talk abruptly at this point because his audience has become so restive.

There is little about Jesus and a lot about Moses in this speech. This is understandable since the charge against Stephen is about his rejecting Moses' teachings (6:11, 14). Stephen points to one significant thing that Moses said to the Israelites about Jesus: "God will send you a prophet like me from your own people" (7:37). The other two references to Jesus are both in verse 52: The Jews "even killed those who predicted the coming of the Righteous One," and they "betrayed and murdered him."

Stephen's final words of accusation (7:51–53) may make us wonder what has happened to his angelic face. After all, when we think of an angel, we think of a sweet, gentle person who has no place for wrath and judgment. This idea, however, does not come from Scripture, for some of the angels in the Bible are agents of judgment.[18] Stephen is like Christ here. Though Jesus radiated the love of God as no one did, he also expressed God's wrath against hypocrisy and sham, especially in his denunciation of the Pharisees (Matt. 23:13–23).

The ministry of Stephen helped blaze new trails for the gospel, which has earned him the title "radical." He opened the door theologically for the world mission of the church. We do not know whether he himself realized this, but

---

16. Bruce, *Peter, Stephen*, 54.
17. Ibid., 54–55.
18. See Gen. 19:1–13; 2 Sam. 24:16–17; 2 Kings 19:35; Acts 12:21–23.

he freed Christianity from the temple and therefore from Judaism. A short time later the church concluded that one does not have to be Jewish first in order to be Christian. Though Stephen ended his life an apparent failure, though he did not live to see the fruit of his theologizing, God revealed later that his ministry had borne great fruit. The trail he blazed was later followed by Paul—the one who approved of his death (8:1) and kept the clothes of those who stoned him (7:58), but who later became the apostle to the Gentiles. The link between Stephen and the writer of the letter to the Hebrews has also been discussed much.[19] Stephen is also considered the precursor of the later Christian apologists, especially those who defended Christianity against Judaism.

BALANCED CHRISTIANITY. LUKE must surely have intended his readers to take special note of the character of Stephen, for he gives us so many glimpses of his character and ministry in chapters 6–7. We should seek to emulate these features. Interestingly, though he is known as a radical because he fearlessly blazed new trails for the gospel, when we look at his personality and character as portrayed in Acts, what stands out is his biblical balance. While we may think of a balanced Christian life as an insipid life of moderation in everything we do, a biblically balanced life is a radical life, where we follow a revolutionary Lord in everything we do. Balance refers to totality in obedience, not moderation. Thus, we will look at Stephen's life and ministry to learn how to have combinations of scriptural characteristics that usually do not seem to go together.

In our study of Peter in Acts 3:1–26, we looked at the phenomenon of a miracle-working apologist, as Stephen also was. Related to that is Stephen's combination of inspiration and wisdom. This combination is well expressed in Luke's comment that his opponents "could not stand up against his wisdom or the Spirit by whom he spoke" (6:10). On the one hand, this inspired wisdom is a gift of God; on the other, it comes from the application of the Scriptures to the challenges one faces. In other words, we must know the Scriptures and apply them relevantly to the challenges before us.

As a result, people will be confronted with the truth of God. Paul describes this call when he says: "We demolish arguments and every pretension that sets itself up against the knowledge of God, and we take captive every thought to make it obedient to Christ" (2 Cor. 10:5). Today we give the term *apologetics* this ministry. But apologetics is not dry intellectual discourse.

---

19. See especially T. W. Manson, *The Epistle to the Hebrews: An Historical and Theological Reconstruction* (London: Hodder and Stoughton, 1951), 25–46.

As Stephen's ministry shows, true apologetics must be done in the power of the Spirit. We must all seek to possess such "knowledge on fire."

Biblical radicalism. As God used Stephen to lead the church along a radically new path, Stephen's life and ministry will help us see the qualities required of those whom God calls to blaze new trails for him. His radicalism not only led him to fearlessly proclaim truths that were unpalatable to his audience, it also led him to thunder accusations against them. Consequently, his opponents severely opposed him and even gnashed their teeth at him (7:54). But in the midst of it all Stephen expressed the graciousness of God (6:8).

We can note a series of contrasts between Stephen's attitude and that of his accusers. When false accusations were made against him, "his face was like the face of an angel" (6:15). When the people were gnashing their teeth at him in fury (7:54), he was filled with the Holy Spirit and had a clear vision of Christ (7:55). While they stoned him fiercely, he prayed to God asking that their sin be excused (7:60). While we may not be called to be "specialist radicals," the gospel is by nature so radical that all serious Christians will sooner or later find themselves challenging people in the way they think and act. Stephen shows us that when we face opposition in such situations, we should remain winsome.

It is important to note that Stephen's radicalism had the Scriptures as its source and authority. What he said sprang from the Old Testament and the teachings of Jesus. In that sense, though what he was saying was revolutionary, it was not new. He did not create new truth; he discovered truth already taught explicitly or implicitly in the Scriptures and the teachings of Christ. If we approach the Bible with an open mind, we will find that it will make us also into radicals, for God's truth always has something radical to say to this fallen world. Given our limitations, we will always fall short of fully apprehending the truth of the Bible. Thus, we will constantly discover fresh truth if we are open to learning from Scripture. But the world, and even the church, will oppose what we discover and communicate. Yet even the prospect of death did not deter Stephen from communicating his radical scriptural message.

Radicals often express their message in anger to an obstinate people. This was true of Stephen, but he exemplified the unusual combination of an angelic face and angry accusation of the Jews for rejecting God's ways. If our hearts burn too with the things that are close to the heart of God, we will become angry at people's disdain for the ways of God. But at such times we must reflect both the holiness and the love of God.

Biblical contextualization. Stephen's speech is an example of biblical contextualization. Contextualization takes place when we make our message relevant to the context in which we present it. Stephen spoke from the Jewish Scriptures. He obviously knew his audience well, and he spoke in a way that was relevant to them. But the gospel was so revolutionary in nature that unless they were willing to repent of their past ways and take the radical step of conversion, they had to oppose him. Each generation of Christians must seek ways to make the gospel relevant to their communities without compromising its content.

Stephen's key themes. We might be tempted to neglect the three themes of Stephen's speech since we no longer need to be freed from the confines of Judaism. But they contain important and helpful aspects of Christian theology. The issue of God's activity not being confined to the geographical land of Israel has, to my knowledge, not been a problem in the church since Stephen's time. However, the idea of Christendom that has influenced much of the thinking on the relationship between state and church in Europe a few centuries ago can be seen, at least in spirit, as contradicting Stephen's emphasis (see below).

The other two issues have had more direct application to the church through the centuries. While no Christians claim that true worship can only be done at the Jewish temple, we have at different times come up with our own "Jerusalem temples." There has been an almost magical veneration of some places as holy ground. The writer of the letter to the Hebrews also pursued this theme. He emphasized that while in the era of the old covenant the high priest was needed and regular sacrifices had to be made in the temple, now the eternal sacrifice of Jesus has made those unnecessary (Heb. 9–10). Christ opened the door to a new and living way, where we can approach the throne of God with confidence (10:19–20; see 4:16). We therefore do not need a temple anymore. Paul later wrote that we are the temple of God, in whom God himself dwells (1 Cor. 3:16–17; 6:19).

Stephen's third point (that the Jews have always rejected God's representatives) contains a warning for all of us who claim to be God's chosen people. We too can end up opposing God's chosen vessels; indeed, the history of the church shows that Christians have been as bad at this as the Jews of old were.

THE CHALLENGE OF **balanced Christianity.** In our age, when specialization has gone to an extreme in almost every sphere of life, Stephen's balance has much to say to us. He sought to be obedient in *all* areas of life and thus exhibited combinations that we sometimes think do not go together. We are so influenced by pragmatism that we may look at specific things a person can achieve without thinking about other areas of his or her life. Take the example of a wonderful singer who is a poor wife and mother because of an uncontrollable temper. We might use her in an evangelistic rally, claiming that her private life does not necessarily impact her public singing. Or we might excuse a brilliant apologist for not being faithful in attending worship every Sunday, saying that he has a lot of study to do. Or we may leave biblical reflection to the teachers among us and look to the creative people to come up with new ideas for our programs.

Stephen's life shows us that it is possible, and indeed essential, for Christians to be balanced. Singers must be patient at home. Apologists must be faithful about participating in worship. Creative people must be men and women of God's Word. Biblical balance refers to total obedience. Such totality will force us to avoid unhealthy excesses. For example, we cannot neglect our families, because obedience to Christ includes caring for our families.

Acquiring inspired wisdom. If we are to have inspired wisdom so that opponents of the gospel will not be able to "stand up against [our] wisdom or the Spirit by whom" (6:10) we speak, we must work both at our message and our lives. We must outthink and outlive those who oppose the gospel. I can think of at least five requirements in this regard. (1) We must know the Scriptures. (2) We must know the people to whom we minister and the way they think. (3) We must be able to let the Scriptures speak penetratingly to the issues our audience faces. This comes through careful reflection, as we look for ways to make the connection between the world of the Bible and the world of our audience. (4) We must ensure that there is no hindrance to the infilling of the Spirit in our lives. We must be vessels fit for the Master's use, purified of ignoble things and prepared to do any good work (2 Tim. 2:20–21). (5) We must, through prayer, make sure that we are in tune with the mind of the Spirit.

How to become winsome radicals. The call to be winsome radicals, like Stephen, is an important challenge facing Christians today. If we are faithful to God, we are sure to face anger and opposition from within and outside the church. We will be treated unjustly, and many will attribute unworthy motives to what we do. Our "true worth" will not be recognized, and perhaps we too will end out lives as Stephen did—as apparent failures. How can we remain winsome under such circumstances?

To be sure, many radicals are anything but winsome. They are cynical and angry people, whose worthwhile messages may go unheeded because of their disagreeable disposition. Cynicism may have reached epidemic proportions in the church as a reaction to the predominance of appearance (looking good) that leaves room for hypocrisy (appearance without substance) to thrive.

Stephen's life shows us how to maintain winsomeness is a hostile world. He was "a man full of God's grace" (6:8). Whatever people may do to us, however severe their sins against us may be, we must be able to affirm the supremacy of grace—that God's grace "superabounds" (lit. trans. of *hyperperisseuo* in Rom. 5:20 and *hyperpleonazo* in 1 Tim. 1:14) over all sins and situations. We must affirm the principle that God will work good through what we have experienced because we "love him" and "have been called according to his purpose" (Rom. 8:28). We must be able to say, as Joseph said to his brothers who had treated him so badly, "You intended to harm me, but God intended it for good to accomplish what is now being done, the saving of many lives" (Gen. 50:20). We will need to battle in the presence of God, as the psalmists did (Ps. 73), until we know that he has comforted us and that the vision of superabounding grace has overcome our bitterness. Then, having tasted of the comforting grace of God, we will be able to minister this grace to others (2 Cor. 1:3–7).

Stephen clearly achieved his winsomeness through his contact with God. Evidence of this intimate relationship abounds in Acts 6–7. His communion with God seemed to deepen as the viciousness of the opposition deepened. When he was brought to trial, so close was his tie with God that his face looked like that of an angel (6:15). When he is then described as being filled with the Spirit, he had a vision of Christ and began to say the same things that Jesus said at his death (vv. 56, 59–60). The evangelist D. L. Moody once told his friend, Bible expositor G. Campbell Morgan, "Character is what a man is in the dark."[20]

The key to maintaining winsomeness under pressure is maintaining our tie with God, as Stephen did. We must develop the discipline of seeking God and his beautiful face first (Ps. 27:4) whenever we are attacked, so that we can always operate out of an experience of grace. Then grace will make us gracious, and we will become winsome radicals. Millions of Christians, by not waging a war against bitterness, have missed out on the opportunities to radiate God's grace through winsomeness and charm.

With this winsomeness Stephen had the face of an angel and expressed God's wrath against sin. Sometimes we hear people say, "He's such a saint, he never gets angry." This is because we have come to value an understanding of tolerance that is far from the biblical lifestyle. True, in the past we may have seen uptight religious people who were unpleasant to be around because they were always ranting and raving against evil. Nothing pleasant came from their lips. We must surely avoid this extreme, but we must also avoid the opposite extreme.

---

20. Jill Morgan, *A Man of the Word: Life of G. Campbell Morgan* (Grand Rapids: Baker, 1972 reprint), 93.

I have come to realize that my failure at times to get angry over wrong is a reflection of my fallenness rather than by godliness. I may have often sinned against my children and colleagues by not expressing wrath concerning things in their lives that dishonored God. When we do not show anger against our children when they do wrong, we may be opening the door for serious insecurity in their lives. Unconsciously we may be sending them the message that their wrong actions are not serious enough to merit an angry response. That in turn communicates the idea that they are not significant enough to be taken seriously. Many such children grow up to be delinquents, and through their wrong deeds try to grab the attention they were deprived of in their childhood.[21]

How the Scriptures can make us radicals. In our discussion of biblical radicalism, we pointed out that Stephen's radicalism had Scripture as its source and authority. In the same way we too, because of the radical nature of God's truth, will become radicals if we take the Scriptures seriously today.

This can happen in four ways. (1) We can *rediscover truths* that have been hidden from us because of theological, cultural, historical, or other blinds. Stephen had to remind his audience of what the Bible said about the temple. These were truths that had been obscured through years of tradition. The evangelical church has recently rediscovered similar truths—for example, the biblical use of the whole body in worship, resulting in dance and the use of the hands. Another has been the importance of worship as an end in itself rather than as a means of evangelism or teaching. Helpful in this process is learning from people of other traditions who may not be hampered by the blinds we have. For example, evangelical authors like A. W. Tozer, who helped the evangelical church rediscover biblical spirituality and worship,[22] have found much inspiration from Roman Catholic spiritual writers.[23]

(2) We can see *implications* in what the Bible says, which will open the door to radical ideas. Stephen concluded that the temple was not necessary by drawing implications from what the Old Testament said about God. In a similar vein, the Bible does not give an explicit prohibition of slavery. But about two hundred years ago, Christians in Britain realized that what the Bible said about the worth of individuals clearly contradicted the form of slavery that was practiced in the British Empire. Thus, they fought it on scriptural grounds. In this century Christians in our part of the world have been realizing this about casteism and class prejudice.

---

21. On this, see James Dobson, *Hide or Seek* (Old Tappan, N.J.: Revell, 1974), 81–88.

22. See the discussion on worship below.

23. See A. W. Tozer, ed., *The Christian Book of Mystical Verse* (Harrisburg, Pa.: Christian Publications, 1963).

(3) The Bible can become a radical book when we try to *apply it* in a thoroughgoing manner. Stephen had the audacity to point the finger and say "you," and to thunder accusations against his opponents as he applied the truths he expounded. Similarly, in a world torn by war, when we apply what the Bible says about loving our enemies, we may end up taking radical courses of action. Thoroughgoing application is one of the most "dangerous" aspects of preaching. Christians, especially those in the evangelical tradition, like to hear doctrinally sound messages. Many appreciate our preaching on unpleasant topics like hell and judgment. But what if we apply some of the teachings to areas that are not considered "kosher" by evangelicals? They may accuse us of meddling rather than preaching.

(4) We can be radical in *the form in which we express* Christianity. Christians get used to ways of worshiping God and communicating the gospel. But some of the ways we are "comfortable with" may be hopelessly irrelevant if we want to reach the lost around us. True Christian love drives us to do things with which we are uncomfortable so that we can reach our contemporaries (see 1 Cor. 9:19–23). Others who see these new ways of communication may become upset and oppose them. When George Frideric Handel performed his oratorio *Messiah* for the first time in Dublin, Ireland, it was warmly received. But when he brought it to England, the reception was lukewarm. Lord Shaftesbury says in his *Memoirs*, "Partly from the scruples some persons had entertained, and partly from not entering into the genius of the Composition, this Capital Composition was but indifferently relish'd."[24] The words were from Scripture, but the style of music and the place it was performed (the concert hall) did not sit well with many.

If Scripture drives us to radicalism, we must not be surprised if our best efforts at obedience to God go unappreciated. Ours is a market-oriented culture, and the church has been heavily influenced by this. Markets thrive on popularity, but radical things are rarely popular, at least at the start. For this reason we may shy away from biblical radicalism. We may avoid writing a book that we know will not sell well, even though that book contains a message the Lord wants his church to have. We may avoid preaching a sermon that people will not like. We may avoid talking about a scriptural truth that will be opposed by influential people.

The perspective of God's sovereignty should help us be faithful. If we do "not become weary in doing good . . . at the proper time we will reap a harvest if we do not give up" (Gal. 6:9). The reaping in Stephen's case took place after his death. But he was faithful. Thus, undaunted by the world's

---

24. Cited in Christopher Hogwood, "Introduction," George Frideric Handel, *Messiah: The Wordbook for the Oratorio* (New York: HarperCollins, 1992).

fascination for quick results, the Christian remains faithful to the eternal will of God. "The world and its desires pass away, but the man who does the will of God lives forever" (1 John 2:17).

Becoming biblical contextualizers.[25] Stephen contextualized his message by adapting it to his audience without toning down its radical nature. In contextualizing the gospel today, we must present it so that our audience understands it and does so in a way that is relevant to them and grabs their attention. We may use language and practices that our audience already uses, if are consonant with scriptural measures of judgment. But we must not tone down our message and leave out things that are unpleasant. Neither may we add things that are alien to or contradict the Scriptures, for then contextualization becomes syncretism. When that happens, people end up accepting what we say and remain perfectly happy as Buddhists, Hindus, or secularists. Or people may become Christians but retain some of their practices that are contrary to Christianity. That is, they may continue to be pornographers, adulterers, or racists, or to consult the astrology page in the newspapers each morning.

Missiologist Paul Hiebert has popularized the term *critical contextualization* to refer to a biblical way of doing this.[26] We must study people and their culture as well as biblical teachings that relate to their ideas and practices. We must then come up with a message and a lifestyle that is relevant, understandable, and inviting to their situation. This message will challenge their culture through God's principles. When that happens, some who do not want to change will be provoked and oppose the Word. But others will accept what we say and be transformed by Christ.

Sacred space? It is true to say that at different times in the history of the church, Christians have neglected the teaching of Stephen that there is no special place (such as the Jerusalem temple) to worship God. Believers have fought battles, for example, over the place of the altar in worship. On one extreme are the Roman Catholic, Orthodox, and "high church" Anglican (Episcopalian) traditions, who have the holy altar depicting the presence of God in the sanctuary. On the other extreme are the Brethren Assemblies, who call their places of worship gospel halls. These halls have the pulpit in the middle, depicting the primacy of God's Word.

The Reformers were surely correct in battling what may be called the sacralizing of space. There is no place in the New Testament for holy places where people go on pilgrimage, expecting merit to accrue to them by being

---

25. For more discussion on contextualization see the studies on 17:16–34 and 19:8–41.

26. Paul G. Hiebert, "Critical Contextualization," *Missiology* 12 (July 1987): 287–96; reprinted in *The Best in Theology*, vol. 2, J. I. Packer, ed. (Carol Stream, Ill.: Christianity Today, n.d.).

there. The popularity of these places even today may be traced to a lack of an intimate knowledge of God resulting from not having the confidence to freely enter his throne, which the new covenant opened for us (Heb. 4:16; 10:19–20).

There has been a trend recently, even in some Roman Catholic circles, to use church buildings for "secular" purposes when they are not being used for worship. Considering the cost of buildings and the valuable space they take, this may be a helpful contemporary extension of the principles for which Stephen battled.[27]

The eighteenth-century revival carried a trend begun with the Reformation even further by helping break down the traditional sense of a parish— a geographical area under the control of a priest. John Wesley spoke of the whole world as being his parish.[28] Until then, the parish had been a key unit of Christendom, where the countries had their state churches—Anglican in England, Presbyterian in Scotland, Reformed in the Netherlands, and Lutheran in Scandinavia and some German territories.[29] The extreme expression of this idea was the Christianizing ambitions of countries like Spain and Portugal, whose missionaries went along with the colonial armies as they conquered the nations that became their colonies.[30] All this seems to contradict the spirit of Stephen's appeals to desacralize space and to free the gospel from nationalist exclusivisms.

While the Protestant, especially the evangelical, movement can be credited with combating the unbiblical sacralizing of space, it may have gone too far in emphasizing intimacy with God to the exclusion of honoring the holiness of God. We must remember that the same letter that speaks of confidence in entering the throne of God also asks us to "worship God acceptably with reverence and awe, for our 'God is a consuming fire'" (Heb. 12:28–29). We cannot throw away completely this Old Testament emphasis, which, as we saw, is in the book of Hebrews as well. The psalmist says, "Worship the LORD in the splendor of his holiness; tremble before him, all the earth" (Ps. 96:9).

In order to do this well in this busy world with all its distractions, we may find that a building conducive to concentrating on God is a great aid to wor-

---

27. See the discussion in F. Debuyst, "Architectural Setting (Modern) and the Liturgical Movement," The New Westminster Dictionary of Liturgy and Worship, ed. J. G. Davies (Philadelphia: Westminster, 1986), 44–45. This article refers to a book by J. G. Davies entitled The Secular Use of Church Building (1968).

28. I am indebted to my colleague at Colombo Theological Seminary, Dr. Charles Hoole, for this insight.

29. See David J. Bosch, Transforming Mission: Paradigm Shifts in Theology of Mission (Maryknoll, N.Y.: Orbis, 1991), 274–75.

30. See ibid., 214–36.

shiping him with reverence and awe.[31] It is heartening to see that many within the evangelical movement have seen this need for a renewed emphasis on worship and are writing and advocating a fresh return to finding what A. W. Tozer called "the missing crown jewel in evangelical Christianity."[32]

God's people opposing his representatives. Stephen's indictment of the Jews as opposing those whom God sent with his message should cause us sober reflection. This is especially so since the history of the church has so many instances of Christians being out of step with what God is doing, either opposing the very people who were pleasing God or siding with those who were championing unbiblical standards. Let me cite three examples:

- When William Carey attempted to place before a meeting of Baptist ministers the challenge of missions, he is said to have been rebuked by a senior minister with the words, "Sit down young man! When God chooses to convert the heathen he will do it without your aid or mine!"[33]

- When the sixty-five-year-old British Methodist leader Thomas Coke announced that he was planning to take a missionary team to Ceylon (now Sri Lanka), a famous churchman, Dr. Edward Pusey, wrote accusing him of trying to build an empire. Coke "was known," said Pusey, "to be ambitious, affecting high titles of honor, to which he had no claim."[34]

- When Hitler began his radical nationalistic program, many Christians joined him. Moreover, many not only in Germany but also throughout the world kept quiet when they heard about the atrocities being committed against the Jews.[35]

I think a major reason for this scandalous record within the church is that Christians often want to be comfortable; thus, they resist change. Christianity,

---

31. On the value of a holy place see Ronald Allen and Gordon Borror, *Worship: Rediscovering the Missing Jewel* (Portland: Multnomah, 1982), 47.

32. A. W. Tozer, *Whatever Happened to Worship?* ed. Gerald B. Smith (Camp Hill, Pa.: Christian Publication, 1985), 7. See also Allen and Borror, *Worship;* Marva J. Dawn, *Reaching Out Without Dumbing Down: A Theology of Worship for the Turn-of-the-Century Culture* (Grand Rapids: Eerdmans, 1995); Robert Webber, *Worship Is a Verb* (Waco, Tex.: Word, 1985); idem, *Worship Old and New* (Grand Rapids: Zondervan, 1982); Warren W. Wiersbe, *True Worship: It Will Transform Your Life* (Nashville: Oliver-Nelson, 1986).

33. Kellsye M. Finnie, *William Carey: By Trade a Cobbler* (Eastbourne: Kingsway Publications, 1986), 32. Finnie says that whether this statement was indeed made has not been confirmed.

34. John Vickers, *Thomas Coke: Apostle of Methodism* (Nashville: Abingdon, 1969), 344.

35. See Robert G. Clouse, Richard V. Pierard, and Edwin M. Yamauchi, *Two Kingdoms: The Church and Culture Through the Ages* (Chicago: Moody, 1993), 560–62.

however, can never coexist with comfort. Human thoughts are too far from God's, and the world is in so much trouble that the nearer we get to God's way of thinking, the more uncomfortable we will become. Evangelicals often called themselves conservatives because they are faithful to the faith once for all delivered to the saints (Jude 3). Yet the conservative mentality is often associated with an unwillingness to change and accept the mistakes one has made. Biblical Christians must always be open to change because they know how far they are from the ideals of God. We must be open to self-criticism[36] and remember that this self-criticism will often come through people who have discovered something from the Word that the rest of us had neglected. May we welcome such prophets, rather than persecute them. And may we humbly open ourselves to correction.

---

36. Willimon, *Acts*, 63.

Acts 7:54–8:4

W HEN THEY HEARD this, they were furious and gnashed their teeth at him. ⁵⁵But Stephen, full of the Holy Spirit, looked up to heaven and saw the glory of God, and Jesus standing at the right hand of God. ⁵⁶"Look," he said, "I see heaven open and the Son of Man standing at the right hand of God."

⁵⁷At this they covered their ears and, yelling at the top of their voices, they all rushed at him, ⁵⁸dragged him out of the city and began to stone him. Meanwhile, the witnesses laid their clothes at the feet of a young man named Saul.

⁵⁹While they were stoning him, Stephen prayed, "Lord Jesus, receive my spirit." ⁶⁰Then he fell on his knees and cried out, "Lord, do not hold this sin against them." When he had said this, he fell asleep.

⁸·¹And Saul was there, giving approval to his death.

On that day a great persecution broke out against the church at Jerusalem, and all except the apostles were scattered throughout Judea and Samaria. ²Godly men buried Stephen and mourned deeply for him. ³But Saul began to destroy the church. Going from house to house, he dragged off men and women and put them in prison.

⁴Those who had been scattered preached the word wherever they went.

THIS SECTION OF Luke's account of the history of the early church gives the aftermath of Stephen's speech, both for Stephen and for the church as a whole. Stephen was stoned to death as a result of his powerful witness to Jesus Christ, and the church as a whole began to feel the effects of Jewish opposition to the fledgling Christian movement.

Stephen's Vision (7:54–56)

WITH HIS ACCUSATION against the Jewish people (7:51–53), Stephen brings his speech to an (abrupt?) end. Predictably, the reaction is bitter (7:54). Yet the next verse starts with one of the many glorious "buts" found in the Bible, signaling a change in the direction or tone of events. The Greek literally says of Stephen, "But being filled with the Holy Spirit...." (7:55a). The word "being" (*hyparchōn*, not translated in the NIV) means here "to be in a state, normally with the implication of a particular set of circumstances."[1] Stephen had been filled with the Holy Spirit throughout his Christian life, and this fullness did not leave him at his time of crisis. It intensified into a special anointing, opening the door to a vision of God's glory and of Christ (vv. 55b–56). As F. F. Bruce points out, "It was the Spirit of prophecy that took possession of him now."[2] Here is another instance where God comes with a special revelation of himself to comfort the faithful in their time of deep crisis.[3]

Stephen's vision is filled with deep significance.[4] At his time of shame and apparent defeat he "saw the glory of God" (7:55b). He also saw Jesus and exclaimed, "Look ... I see heaven open and the Son of Man standing at the right hand of God" (7:56). This is the only New Testament occurrence of the title "the Son of Man" outside the Gospels.[5] Stephen's statement reminds us of a similar statement made by Jesus to the same court only a few months before. The high priest had asked him, "Are you the Christ, the Son of the Blessed One?" and Jesus had replied, "I am. And you will see the Son of Man sitting at the right hand of the Mighty One and coming on the clouds of heaven" (Mark 14:61–62). For that Jesus was adjudged guilty of blasphemy and worthy of death (14:63–64).

Now Stephen is, as it were, challenging that judgment by affirming that Jesus is indeed the glorious Christ and is now at the right hand of God. The Sanhedrin had no choice but to condemn Stephen too, unless they were willing to say they were wrong about their verdict on Jesus. This vision must have given Stephen courage. He is not wrong in the path he has taken. This cause will triumph, as proclaimed in the psalm that the early Christians valued so much: "The LORD says to my Lord: 'Sit at my right hand until I make your enemies a footstool for your feet.' The LORD will extend your mighty scepter from Zion; you will rule in the midst of your enemies" (Ps. 110:1–2). Stephen's vision confirms their interpretation of that psalm.

Why is Jesus *standing* and not seated, as the other Scriptures declare? Many explanations have been given for this shift. I agree with the many

---

1. Louw and Nida, 150.
2. Bruce, *Acts: Greek Text*, 210.
3. See also 4:30–31; 7:55–56; 18:9–10; 23:11; 27:23–24.
4. I am indebted to Bruce for much of what I have written on these verses. His whole discussion is well worth reading. *Acts*, NICNT, 154–57.
5. Bruce points out that the expression in Rev. 1:13 and 14:4 is not the title "the Son of Man," but "one like a son of man," that is, a human figure (*Acts*, NICNT, 154).

commentators today[6] who argue that Luke intends Jesus' standing "as a witness or advocate in Stephen's defense."[7] Jesus had said, "I tell you, whoever acknowledges me before men, the Son of Man will also acknowledge him before the angels of God" (Luke 12:8). In keeping with that promise, as Stephen is rejected by earthly courts, he finds Jesus acting as his advocate and testifying on his behalf. But Jesus is also the Judge, whose judgment alone matters from the eternal perspective. Therefore, there is nothing to fear. Rejection by his own people, the Jews, would have been hard to bear, but acceptance by that greatest of Jews, great David's greater Son,[8] more than compensates for the pain.

Also confirmed in this vision is what Stephen had been arguing for in his speech. Bruce comments:

> The presence of the Son of Man at God's right hand meant that for his people a way of access to God had been opened up more immediate and heart-satisfying than the temple could provide. It meant that the hour of fulfillment had struck, and that the age of particularism had come to an end. The sovereignty of the Son of Man was to embrace all nations and races without distinction: under his sway there is no place for an institution which gives religious privileges to one group in preference to others.[9]

Stephen's Death (7:57–60)

WITH DRAMATIC CRISPNESS Luke describes how the angry audience acts in haste to put Stephen to death. When they add these words about the vision of Jesus to his damaging statements about the temple, they have no choice but to kill him for blasphemy—just as they had killed Jesus. Their covering of their ears (7:57) must have been a characteristic response to blasphemy. They wish "to shut out his words lest God come and consume them for listening to such blasphemy."[10] Stephen is dragged out of the city for stoning (7:58a) in keeping with the command to "take the blasphemer outside the camp . . . and . . . stone him" (Lev. 24:14). Luke mentions Saul at this point

---

6. E.g., F. F. Bruce, *Acts*, NICNT, 154; E. F. Harrison, *Interpreting Acts*, 136; C. F. D. Moule, "From Defendant to Judge and Deliverer: An Enquiry into the Use and Limitations of the Theme of Vindication in the New Testament," *Studiorum Novi Testamenti Societas*, 3:47, quoted in Harrison, *Acts*, 136; Richard Longenecker, "Acts," 350–51; I. Howard Marshall, *Acts*, 149.

7. Bruce, *Acts*, NICNT, 156.

8. See Luke 1:32–33.

9. Bruce, *Acts*, NICNT, 157.

10. Polhill, *Acts*, 208.

(Acts 7:58b), in keeping with his habit of introducing major characters of his book in a narrative before they come into prominence (cf. 4:36–37; 6:5).

Stephen's last words are surprisingly close to two of the last words of Jesus just before he died. He asks God to receive his spirit (7:59; cf. Luke 23:46) and not to "hold this sin against" his killers (Acts 7:60; cf. Luke 23:34). Only Luke mentions the two parallel statements of Christ. Presumably he wants his readers to note the similarity. As we will see below, he has entered into the fellowship of sharing in Christ's sufferings.

The Church Scattered (8:1–4)

THE DEATH OF Stephen gives a new impetus to the anti-Christian forces with which Saul is now prominently associated (8:1a). A great persecution arose that day, "and all except the apostles were scattered throughout Judea and Samaria" (8:1b). The fact that the apostles "could stay on in Jerusalem (no doubt along with other Christians) confirms the suspicion that it was mainly Stephen's group which was being attacked."[11] The apostles may also have stayed on in Jerusalem because they felt it was "their duty to stay at their post."[12]

Stephen was buried and mourned over by "godly men" (8:2). The adjective "godly" (*eulabes*) is usually used of Jews. We cannot be sure whether Luke means Jewish Christians[13] or pious Jews other than believers, who deplored the injustice committed.[14] The language used for mourning suggests loud and deep mourning, which later rabbinic literature (the Mishnah) considered inappropriate for the burial of people condemned to death by the Sanhedrin.[15] If Christians are meant here, Stephen was certainly a deeply loved person (understandable, considering his unique character). If non-Christian Jews are meant, this mourning indicates how much some Jews regretted what had happened. Whatever the reason, it is comforting to find that in a culture where an honorable burial was a much valued feature, the first Christian martyr received such a burial.

Luke is not reluctant to describe the pre-Christian vehemence of his later friend Saul/Paul (8:3). I live in a land of turmoil and am often concerned for what our children might think about our decision to stay and serve an evangelistic organization here. Thus, I have naturally wondered what those Christian children would have felt like as they fled their homes in fear or saw their

---

11. Marshall, *Acts*, 151.

12. Bruce, *Acts*, NICNT, 162.

13. Bruce, *Acts: Greek Text*, 215.

14. Stott, *Acts*, 145. Longenecker thinks it may refer to Jews who were open to the Christian message ("Acts," 355).

15. Longenecker, "Acts," 355.

parents dragged off to prison. What has happened to the victorious Christ and the power of his resurrection? Why does God remain inactive, even dormant, while they suffer?

Acts keeps unfolding its deep theology on the subtheme of suffering as the book proceeds. God is not dormant; he actually feels the pain that Saul inflicts (see 9:4). For the moment, Luke gives us a glimpse of the victory God is going to win out of this seeming tragedy: "Those who had been scattered preached the word wherever they went" (8:4). As Everett Harrison writes, "The people went as missionaries more than as refugees." He points out that "Luke could have used the general term for scattering but chose instead to use a word [*diaspeiro*] that means to scatter as seed is scattered on the ground."[16] This word is connected with the Jewish dispersion. Perhaps Luke is conscious of a new dispersion coming into being.

With the benefit of hindsight, Luke sees great significance in these events. In fact, when he describes the preaching of the gospel to Gentiles for the first time outside Palestine, he says that the ones who did this were "those who had been scattered by the persecution in connection with Stephen" (11:19). Luke deliberately associates Stephen and the persecution with this important development in the church, which Barclay calls "one of the greatest events in history."[17]

LUKE UNDOUBTEDLY HAD several reasons for giving Stephen so much prominence in Acts. In the previous study we discussed three of them: the example of balanced Christianity that one sees in his life, the model of godly radicalism and contextualization in his ministry, and the important place his message had in the development of Christian doctrine. The present passage shows the way Stephen and the early churches faced persecution. Suffering is one of the major subthemes of this book.[18] It is reasonable, therefore, to conclude that Luke is describing the suffering of Stephen and the church and their response to it in order that his readers might glean lessons on how Christians should face suffering.

Suffering and fullness. Stephen's experience of the Spirit's fullness in preparation for death (7:55) gives us a fresh insight into the nature of that fullness. It is given here to help a faithful Christian face suffering. This theme receives extended treatment in Romans 8, the great chapter of Paul that

---

16. Harrison, *Interpreting Acts*, 139.
17. Barclay, *Acts*, 88.
18. See the index at the back.

describes the Spirit-filled life. The second half of that chapter is devoted to the experience of the Spirit amidst suffering (Rom. 8:17–39).[19]

Stephen's anointing with the Spirit's fullness took the form of a vision of God's glory and of the exalted Christ in his role as advocate in heaven. Through it Stephen received strength to face his painful ordeal triumphantly. On many other occasions in Acts when God's servants suffered for the gospel, God revealed himself in some recognizable way that gave them the courage to go on (4:31; 18:9; 23:11; 27:23–24). We can conclude that God, knowing how much we can endure, gives us his strength in our times of need, which boosts our spirits and spurs us on to obedience, even to obedience leading to death. In a similar way God fulfilled this promise in the life of Paul when no relief from suffering came to him: "My grace is sufficient for you, for my power is made perfect in weakness" (2 Cor. 12:9).

Sharing in Christ's sufferings. We noted in the "Original Meaning" section Stephen's two statements that are similar to what Luke records Jesus as saying at his death (7:59–60). When we compare Luke's records of the deaths of Jesus and Stephen, the tie between them is too close to be coincidental. Stephen is accused of a similar charge made against Christ: offense against the temple (Matt. 26:61; Mark 14:58).[20] In a remarkable fulfillment of a prophecy made by Christ at his trial (Luke 22:69), Stephen receives a vision of the Lord Jesus at the right hand of God. Both Jesus and Stephen are taken out of the city to be killed. As they die, they say similar things. Not only has Jesus come close to Stephen, Stephen has, in the process, become like Jesus. Paul speaks of desiring these same two things: "the fellowship of sharing in his sufferings [and] becoming like him in his death" (Phil. 3:10). Stephen has, in effect, entered into the fellowship of sharing in Christ's sufferings.

The Bible's teaching on this doctrine is a natural extension of the doctrine of our union with Christ. Christ is a suffering Savior, and if we are to be truly one with him, we too must suffer. There is a depth of union with Christ that comes to us only through suffering. But not only do we share in his sufferings, *he shares in our sufferings*. The exalted Christ, sharing in the glory of God, is not deaf to our cries of pain as we suffer; he himself suffers with us when we suffer. Paul came to understand this on the road to Damascus when he heard Jesus say, "Saul, Saul, why do you persecute *me*?" (Acts 9:4). Saul had been hitting the church, but Christ had been feeling the pain!

Thus, in our times of suffering we can affirm by faith, "This is going to bring me closer to Jesus. Therefore it is a blessing."

Suffering and evangelism. As noted above, Luke implies that Stephen's death and the persecution that followed served the cause of the gospel in

---

19. I like to give this passage from Romans the title "Spirit-Filled Suffering."

20. This accusation, however, does not appear in Luke's Gospel.

being a catalyst in getting the message out (8:4; 11:19). In the previous study, we saw that Stephen's ministry opened the door *theologically* for the world mission of the church (by showing that the temple was not necessary). Now it opens the door *circumstantially* for world missions, for it catapults missionaries out of Jerusalem into other geographical areas mentioned in the Great Commission. We can glean here a principle that is always true, insofar as other passages also suggest it: God uses persecution and suffering to advance the gospel. Writing to the Philippians about his imprisonment, Paul said, "Now I want you to know, brothers, that what has happened to me has really served to advance the gospel" (Phil. 1:12).

Perhaps the strongest affirmation of this belief is Colossians 1:24–25: "Now I rejoice in what was suffered for you, and I fill up in my flesh what is still lacking in regard to Christ's afflictions, for the sake of his body, which is the church. I have become its servant by the commission God gave me to present to you the word of God in its fullness." This curious statement seems to imply that Christ's sufferings are incomplete, an idea Paul would vehemently oppose. But while Christ's sufferings are complete in winning our salvation, the reception of this salvation is incomplete. Before Jesus comes again, there must be the "birthpangs of the Messiah," which is an Old Testament and Christian idea.[21]

The church (which is one with Christ) must encounter some of these birthpangs. We know that the coming of Christ is intimately linked with the preaching of the gospel to all nations; only after this has been completed will the end come (Matt. 24:14). While the suffering of Christ is complete, the reception of its blessings is not complete. To put it another way propitiation is complete but propagation is incomplete. For this to happen there is a "quota of suffering"[22] that must be borne. Paul says in Colossians 1:24 that he rejoices in taking on that quota. The point, then, is that suffering is an essential ingredient of effective evangelism and ministry.

SPIRIT-FILLED SUFFERING. STEPHEN'S experience of a special anointing with the Spirit's fullness in the midst of suffering challenges many prevalent notions of that fullness. We usually relate that fullness to some ministry activity, such as preaching, healing, or prophesying,

---

21. On "birthpangs of the Messiah," see Peter O'Brien, "Colossians," *NBCTCE*, 1266; idem, *Colossians, Philemon* (WBC 44; Waco, Tex.: Word, 1982), 78–81.

22. The idea of a "quota of suffering" is from C. F. D. Moule, "The Epistles to the Colossians and to Philemon," *The Cambridge Greek New Testament Commentary* (London: Cambridge Univ. Press, 1968), 76–77.

or to an ecstatic personal spiritual experience, such as speaking in tongues. While that is certainly valid, we must not forget that the Spirit's fullness is also given to prepare us for suffering, which is such an important part of the life of obedience. God is powerfully at work both when the sun shines brightly and when the dark clouds loom over us.

We must, therefore, develop a theology of the fullness of the Spirit in the darkness. Such a teaching is not easy to grasp in this sensual, hedonistic world, which is afraid of suffering and does so much to avoid it. Yet the Bible tells us to anticipate suffering rather than avoid it. If we have a theology of the fullness of the Spirit in the darkness, we will eagerly seek the blessings we know God will give us through the darkness.

I believe the Spirit's fullness in the darkness is so important for our spiritual health that God permits us to go through dark times in order that he can fill us afresh. Many preachers will testify that some of their best experiences of the freedom of the Spirit in preaching came during times of deep pain in their lives. I have found personally that before a major assignment that I know will be a drain on me spiritually (such as speaking at a large conference), I often encounter some major crises. I have now come to recognize these as God's gifts to draw me nearer to him. Struggling with such crisis increases my dependence on him, which is a key to opening us to an experience of God's fullness. The Japanese evangelist and social reformer Toyohiko Kagawa (1888–1960) once thought that he was going blind. He described what he felt like in this way: "The darkness, the darkness is a holy of holies of which no one can rob me. In the darkness I meet God face to face."[23]

The vision of God's glory and Christ's exaltation must have done much to encourage Stephen. Rejection by one's own people is always hard to face. But when we realize that God is on the throne and that he is for us, we can find courage and even joy amidst our pain. The story is told of a Christian martyr smiling as he was being burned at the stake. His persecutor was annoyed by that smile and asked him what there was to be smiling about. He replied, "I saw the glory of God and was glad."

Amidst our pain we will wonder whether it is worth suffering for the gospel. At such times we ought to "fix our eyes on Jesus, the author and perfecter of our faith, who for the joy set before him endured the cross, scorning its shame, and sat down at the right hand of the throne of God" (Heb. 12:2). With such a vision we can run with perseverance the race that is set before us, refusing to give up when the going gets tough and divesting ourselves of unnecessary earthly weights that so easily entangle us (12:1).

---

23. Cited in James S. Stewart, in *Classic Sermons on Suffering*, compiled by Warren W. Wiersbe (Grand Rapids: Kregel, 1984), 92.

Suffering and the pursuit of pleasure. Can we sustain the biblical idea that suffering is a blessing in a hedonistic society, which is bent on a relentless pursuit of pleasure and avoidance of suffering? Not unless we rediscover true Christian hedonism.[24] Because God is the Creator of all things, we also know that he is the source of purest and fullest pleasure (for he created pleasure). The greatest pleasure is to know God intimately. As David said, "You have made known to me the path of life; you will fill me with joy in your presence, with eternal pleasures at your right hand" (Ps. 16:11). Our pursuit of the highest pleasure, therefore, is a pursuit of union with God in Christ. And one of the deepest aspects of that union is sharing in the fellowship of Christ's sufferings. Paul said, "I want to know Christ . . . and the fellowship of sharing in his sufferings, becoming like him in his death" (Phil. 3:10). As Peter O'Brien has pointed out, the Greek here implies that sharing in Christ's sufferings is an aspect of knowing Christ.[25]

The question, then, is how important knowing Christ is to us. If it is our consuming passion, we will not resent suffering because amidst the pain we have the underlying assurance that it is leading us to achieve our deepest ambition in life. John and Betty Stam were missionaries in China who were martyred by the communists in the 1930s while they were still in their late twenties. John Stam once said, "Take away everything I have, but do not take away the sweetness of walking and talking with the King of glory!" Those who find such joy in their union with Christ will find that suffering is indeed a blessing, for it leads them to greater depths of the greatest pleasure one can know. We need to redeem pleasure from the stranglehold of emptiness to which the world has condemned it.

Suffering and ministry today. Not only does suffering deepen our tie with Christ, it also enhances the effectiveness of our ministry, especially the ministry of evangelism. This again is a message that ought to be emphasized in a world that seeks to avoid pain. For example, much is being written today about the dangers of stress.[26] But we must never forget that a certain type of stress is necessary and helpful for effective ministry—the stress of taking on the pain of our people. Did not Paul say, "I face daily the pressure of my concern for all the churches" (2 Cor. 11:28)? Note too his stress over the wayward Galatians: "My dear children, for whom I am again in the pains of childbirth until Christ is formed in you, how I wish I could be with you now and change my tone, because I am perplexed about you!"(Gal. 4:19–20).

---

24. The expression "Christian hedonism" is from John Piper's book, *Desiring God: Meditations of a Christian Hedonist* (Portland: Multnomah, 1986).

25. Peter T. O'Brien, *The Epistle to the Philippians*, NIGTC (1991), 402–3.

26. I have been particularly helped by the writings of Dr. Archibald D. Hart, such as, *Adrenalin and Stress* (Dallas: Word, 1991).

The truth is that what we suffer increases our credibility in ministry. Paul can tell the Galatians, "Finally, let no one cause me trouble, for I bear on my body the marks of Jesus" (Gal. 6:17). Such credibility opens the door for us to exhort people with some authority. Paul told the Ephesians, "As a prisoner for the Lord, then, I urge you to live a life worthy of the calling you have received" (Eph. 4:1). Exhortation has gone out of fashion today, and one wonders whether that situation would change if Christian ministers were willing to suffer more.

It is, however, in evangelism that the power of suffering is best illustrated. The North African Christian writer and apologist Tertullian (c. 160–225), addressing the rulers of the Roman empire, said, "Kill us, torture us, condemn us, grind us to the dust.... The more you mow us down the more we grow, the seed is the blood of Christians."[27] A similar statement comes from an Anglican bishop from Uganda, Festo Kivengere. Speaking in February 1979, on the second anniversary of the death of his archbishop, Janani Luwum, he said, "Without bleeding the church fails to bless."[28]

This century has seen a lot of persecution and martyrdom of Christians. Dr. Paul Carlson may have been correct when he told the Congolese believers before his martyrdom that more believers have died for Christ in this century than in all the previous centuries combined.[29] But associated with the persecution is great effectiveness in evangelism, as the amazing growth of the church in China in the past half-century proves. The rapid growth of the church in Sri Lanka in the past fifteen years and the rise of persecution have gone hand in hand. Speaking on persecution in Sri Lanka at the World Congress on Evangelism in Berlin in 1966, my father said that the question to ask is not, "Why are we being persecuted?" but, "Why are we not being persecuted?" That situation changed after the church started taking obedience to the Great Commission more seriously. Evangelism provokes persecution while persecution energizes evangelism.

If we are obedient to Christ, even if we live in countries where there is relative freedom for Christians, we will face suffering of some sort—even if it is the suffering of tiredness or of pressure out of a concern for people. It may be the hurt that comes from people who disappoint us even though we refuse to give up on them. It may mean being betrayed by people we trusted. It can take the form of persecution for sharing Christ with non-Christians

---

27. Tertullian, *Apology,* ch. 50; cited in Stott, *Acts,* 119.
28. Ibid.
29. Cited in James and Marti Hefley, *By Their Blood: Christian Martyrs of the Twentieth Century* (Milford, Mich.: Mott Media, 1979), 589. This book gives a stirring account of twentieth-century martyrdom.

who do not want to hear the gospel, or for telling Christians things that they do not like to hear.

Obviously, all the above things can be easily avoided. We can avoid tiredness by not responding in love to a need of someone else. We can avoid the pressure of concern for people by not taking things pertaining to their lives as a personal responsibility. We can avoid the hurt of disappointment by not having such high hopes for people. We can avoid betrayal by not trusting people and investing in them. I fear that much thinking on Christian ministry tends in the direction of helping us avoid such pain. Such patterns indicate that the church has lost the biblical understanding of suffering and pain as something glorious.

Today we have a lot of therapy for sufferers. While this may be helpful, more helpful is a theology of suffering. Even with all the therapy we cannot avoid or escape suffering. In fact, by trying to avoid or escape suffering we may become disobedient to God's will. A theology of suffering will take the bitter sting out of it. It will help us to maintain joy in the midst of it and turn the suffering into something constructive for the kingdom.

Acts 8:5–25

❧

PHILIP WENT DOWN to a city in Samaria and proclaimed the Christ there. ⁶When the crowds heard Philip and saw the miraculous signs he did, they all paid close attention to what he said. ⁷With shrieks, evil spirits came out of many, and many paralytics and cripples were healed. ⁸So there was great joy in that city.

⁹Now for some time a man named Simon had practiced sorcery in the city and amazed all the people of Samaria. He boasted that he was someone great, ¹⁰and all the people, both high and low, gave him their attention and exclaimed, "This man is the divine power known as the Great Power." ¹¹They followed him because he had amazed them for a long time with his magic. ¹²But when they believed Philip as he preached the good news of the kingdom of God and the name of Jesus Christ, they were baptized, both men and women. ¹³Simon himself believed and was baptized. And he followed Philip everywhere, astonished by the great signs and miracles he saw.

¹⁴When the apostles in Jerusalem heard that Samaria had accepted the word of God, they sent Peter and John to them. ¹⁵When they arrived, they prayed for them that they might receive the Holy Spirit, ¹⁶because the Holy Spirit had not yet come upon any of them; they had simply been baptized into the name of the Lord Jesus. ¹⁷Then Peter and John placed their hands on them, and they received the Holy Spirit.

¹⁸When Simon saw that the Spirit was given at the laying on of the apostles' hands, he offered them money ¹⁹and said, "Give me also this ability so that everyone on whom I lay my hands may receive the Holy Spirit."

²⁰Peter answered: "May your money perish with you, because you thought you could buy the gift of God with money! ²¹You have no part or share in this ministry, because your heart is not right before God. ²²Repent of this wickedness and pray to the Lord. Perhaps he will forgive you for having such a thought in your heart. ²³For I see that you are full of bitterness and captive to sin."

²⁴Then Simon answered, "Pray to the Lord for me so that nothing you have said may happen to me."

²⁵When they had testified and proclaimed the word of the Lord, Peter and John returned to Jerusalem, preaching the gospel in many Samaritan villages.

WITH ACTS 6 a new phase began in the history of the church as God prepared her to take the gospel to the whole world. Stephen's ministry prepared the church theologically by freeing Christianity from the Jerusalem temple. His death and the persecution that followed propelled witnessing Christians out of Jerusalem. The present chapter contains two key steps in this direction—the conversion of Samaritans and of an Ethiopian. Chapter 9 records the conversion of Paul, the apostle to the Gentiles; chapters 10–11 record the conversion of Gentiles in Caesarea and Antioch. Then in chapter 13 a full-blown Gentile mission begins with the commissioning of Paul and Barnabas. In chapter 15 a major theological breakthrough occurs as the church agrees that Gentiles do not need to become Jews first before they become Christians. In other words, each chapter records an exciting new phase in the program of fulfilling the Great Commission.

Samaritans Receive the Spirit (8:5–17)

AMONG THE SCATTERED witnesses from Jerusalem was Philip, who went to Samaria and "proclaimed the Christ there" (v. 5); we are not told which city. There is no unanimity among scholars about the origins of the Samaritans, but they seem to have been descendants of Jews of the northern kingdom who intermarried with foreign people. They were not regarded as Gentiles by the Jews, but as part of "the lost sheep of the house of Israel."[1] Their religion was based on the Pentateuch, though their Pentateuch was different in a few places to the one we are familiar with. They were awaiting a future deliverer (*ta'eb* or restorer) in keeping with the promise of Deuteronomy 18:15–19 about the coming of a prophet like Moses (cf. the Samaritan woman in John 4, who referred to the hope of the coming Messiah, John 4:25). Philip seems to have built on this hope when he preached the Messiah there. It was a bold step he took since bad feelings existed between Jews and Samaritans.

We see here again how ministering in the miraculous opened the door for the hearing of the gospel. Verse 6 establishes a direct link between the miracles

---

1. Marshall, *Acts*, 153.

and the fact that the Samaritans "all paid close attention to what [Philip] said." Signs served to enhance the preaching of the word as the more important element in evangelism.[2] This verse contains one of thirteen occurrences of the word *semeion* in Acts, usually translated "miraculous signs." This is a good word to use for miracles since it means "an event which is regarded as having some special meaning."[3]

Philip "preached the good news of the kingdom of God and the name of Jesus Christ" (v. 12). "Preached good news" translates the single word *euangelizo*. The two expressions "the kingdom of God" and "the name of Jesus" (or expressions similar to them) are used often in Acts[4] as a summary of the gospel. "Great joy" resulted from Philip's ministry (v. 8), though we are not told the exact reason for the joy. Was it the result of conversion or of so many people being healed? I am reminded of my trips to the north of Sri Lanka, where the security forces (consisting primarily of people of my race) are at war with rebels from the Tamil race who live there. I am supposedly in enemy territory, but for me and, I believe, for my Tamil brothers and sisters too, there is great joy. In a joyfully powerful way, ministry in "enemy territory" demonstrates the power of the gospel to break down human barriers.

Luke then introduces Simon the sorcerer, a man who performed great works through his magic and had a big following (vv. 9–11).[5] He was amazed by what he saw in Philip's ministry, and he too "believed and was baptized" (v. 13). As the story proceeds, however, it becomes apparent that his belief was superficial. This is one place in the Bible where the meaning of "believe" falls short of saving faith (cf. James 2:19–20). Not all who profess faith in Christ are true believers. Some are so attracted to something they see in the church, which does not come to the heart of the gospel, that they are blinded from truly understanding the gospel.

Peter and John are sent from Jerusalem to check out what has happened in Samaria (v. 14). It is a situation where a second generation leader is doing the work that Jesus and the apostles have been doing, and the role of the apostles shifts from initiation to verification.[6] When the apostles arrive, they pray "for them that they might receive the Holy Spirit, because the Holy Spirit had not yet come upon any of them; they had simply been baptized into the name of the Lord Jesus" (vv. 15–16). After their prayer, the Spirit descends on the Samaritans (v. 17).

---

2. The primacy of God's word in Philip's ministry is indicated in Luke's report that "the apostles in Jerusalem heard that Samaria had accepted *the word of God*" (8:14, italics added).

3. Louw and Nida, 443.

4. See Barrett, *Acts*, 408.

5. Simon is called Simon Magus in postapostolic writings—Magus being a word given for people who practice sorcery. According to these writings he led many people astray.

6. Tannehill, *Narrative Unity of Luke-Acts*, 2:102–4.

We are not told how Peter and John knew that the Holy Spirit had come on the Samaritans. There must have been some external manifestation, such as speaking in tongues, that gave unmistakable evidence. This passage has been a storm center in Bible study for a long time. Is the pattern of a baptism with the Holy Spirit subsequent to conversion something always followed by God, or is this a special situation here? We will examine this shortly.

Regardless of what biblical theology we derive about the reception of the Holy Spirit, this section contains another important truth: It is providential that through the ministry of leaders from the Jerusalem church the Samaritans received the Spirit. It helped maintain the unity of the early church. Animosity toward Jerusalem among the Samaritans had deep historical roots. They were refused a share in rebuilding the Jerusalem temple (see Ezra 3:7–4:5), so they erected a rival temple on their hill, Gerizim. The Judean ruler John Hyrancus destroyed this temple and conquered Samaria in the second century B.C. When the Romans conquered Palestine in 63 B.C. they liberated Samaria from Judean control.[7] The importance of this issue to Samaritans becomes clear in that the first thing the Samaritan woman talked about when she realized that Jesus was "a prophet" was the temple issue (John 4:19–20).

With such a background it was appropriate for the Jerusalem leaders to have a big part in blessing the new Samaritan Christians. It helped them begin their life as Christians with an attitude of warm love toward their traditional enemies. Perhaps somewhere in this process, they repented of their attitudes of animosity toward Jerusalem.[8] For the Jerusalem Christians too, it was important that the authenticating sign of the conversion of the Samaritans took place when the apostles were there and through their mediation. Accepting Samaritans to their fold also involved some major attitude shifts on their part. Therefore, clear evidence that God was in these events was necessary.

Simon's Misplaced Religion (8:18–24)

SIMON IS ATTRACTED by what happened through laying on of hands by the apostles (v. 18a). He is not interested in his own receiving the Spirit; what he wants was the ability to lay hands on people with similar results (v. 19). His offer of money for this ability (v. 18b) evokes a strong response from Peter (v. 20). Peter's point is that this is a gift that God gives sovereignly; we human beings cannot manipulate him into giving us what we desire. That is what happens in Simon's magic kingdom, not in God's righteous kingdom.

Peter tells Simon that he has "no part or share in this ministry, because [his] heart is not right before God" (v. 21). The word translated "ministry" is *logos*

---

7. Bruce, *Acts: Greek Text*, 164.
8. Gooding, *True to the Faith*, 145.

and thus may mean gospel (lit., "word"). Peter is likely saying that Simon has no share "in the blessings of the gospel."[9] This and the verses that follow show that Peter views Simon as still being unregenerate.[10] The important thing, says Peter, is to have one's heart right before God. Without that there is no point of even talking about abilities.

After calling Simon to repent (v. 22), Peter explains his condition to him: "For I see that you are full of bitterness and captive to sin" (v. 23). The word "bitterness" (lit., "gall of bitterness") comes from Deuteronomy 29:18, where the influence of those who led the Israelites to follow other gods is described as a "root among you that produces such bitter poison." Hebrews 12:15 warns, "See to it that no one misses the grace of God and that no bitter root grows up to cause trouble and defile many." Peter may be referring to the potential that Simon has of causing much damage to the church—which (according to tradition) is what happened. If so, Peter's statement reflects his desire to rid the church of this evil influence. The Greek can also mean that Simon is filled with a bitter poison—the idea communicated by the NIV rendering.[11]

Simon is a good example of misplaced religion. He believed and was baptized, but it was obviously an inadequate belief. He sought God's power without any apparent interest in developing a relationship with God. In verse 24 he gives Peter an inadequate reason to pray for him. He does not express a desire to be right with God; rather, he wants Peter to "pray to the Lord for me so that nothing you have said may happen to me" (v. 24). That is, he wants freedom from punishment rather than the true freedom that God gives.

The Apostles Evangelize in Samaria (8:25)

THE STORY ENDS with Peter and John "preaching the gospel in many Samaritan villages" on their return journey to Jerusalem (v. 25). The lead taken by the junior person Philip is followed by the senior leaders. It is heartening to see the same John, who had earlier asked Jesus whether to call down fire on some Samaritan villages (Luke 9:51–55), now preaching the gospel to them.

SECOND-GENERATION LEADERS. Up to 6:6 the original apostles play the prominent role in Luke's record of the life of the church. But at 6:7 the emphasis shifts to a second generation of leaders, like Stephen, Philip, and Paul. Chapter 9 describes the conversion of Paul,

---

9. Marshall, Acts, 159.

10. Bruce, Acts, NICTC, 223.

11. See Williams, Acts, 158, for a discussion of these two options.

whose ministry dominates the rest of Acts. In fact from now on, except for the pioneering work by Peter in the home of Cornelius, these newer leaders are the standard-bearers of the advance of the kingdom. As we noted above, they become the initiators while the apostles become verifiers. In a beautiful sequence Peter and John follow the lead given by Philip and preach the gospel in many Samaritan cities (8:25).

We can detect a certain hesitancy to change among the older established leaders, which is natural. Thus, when there is an evangelistic harvest in Samaria by Philip, Peter and John are sent to check things out. Peter later resists the message to go to the home of Cornelius (10:9–23). When Paul tries to join the Christians in Jerusalem, he is accepted only after Barnabas intervenes before the apostles on his behalf (9:26–27). When the gospel is preached later in Antioch among Gentiles, the Jerusalem authorities send Barnabas to check out what has happened (11:19–24).

The good thing is that in each of these four instances of groundbreaking changes within the church, the apostles accept the changes after giving them due consideration. Our passion for obedience to God and his ways should make us careful about naively accepting every change that comes along without examining them. But it is our passion for obedience that also enables us to accept the changes even though we may sometimes be uncomfortable with them. In this way we not only encourage healthy change and growth in the church, we also help develop new and creative leadership. The abiding principle we learn from this is that good leaders are open to change that comes from younger creative people and, after giving it proper thought, encourage such change and even learn from it.

Knowing that the Holy Spirit has been received. What has been called the Samaritan Pentecost clearly involved the reception of the Spirit at some time subsequent to the Samaritans' conversion (vv. 15–17). The question of whether this is a pattern for all Christians is an issue on which there is no unanimity in the church. We have grappled with this problem in the first study in this commentary (see 1:1–8); thus, we will not go through the points here again.

Let me summarize by saying that those who believe that the baptism with the Spirit is generally an experience subsequent to conversion see this passage as buttressing their view. Those who hold that the baptism with the Spirit takes place at conversion hold that this was a special circumstance because it was the Samaritans who were involved. Since they were not considered full Jews, unmistakable evidence of their acceptance into the messianic community was needed. Hence, they were given a recognizable, subjective experience when Peter and John placed their hands on them (v. 17), which confirmed to the Jewish Christians that Samaritans were also now included among the new people of God. In other words, the Samaritan Pentecost should not be considered normative as the way of receiving the baptism with the Spirit.

I am reluctant to come down one way or the other on this issue, since both views have sound arguments. But at least this passage shows that a felt experience of the Spirit (vv. 17–18) is common, if not the norm, for Christians. This is sometimes overlooked by those who hold that baptism with the Spirit is an initiatory fact that takes place at conversion. This may be a result of their overly rational approach to conversion and saving faith. There was tangible evidence that the Samaritans had indeed been saved. Paul says, "The Spirit himself testifies with our spirit that we are God's children" (Rom. 8:16). Some confine this entirely to witness through Scripture. But even the witness through Scripture has a subjective element that convinces readers that the passage speaks to them. We can say that the Bible presents, as a norm for Christian experience, the possibility of having some sound evidence and assurance that we have received the Spirit.

The importance of unity in the body of Christ. We noted above that the involvement of Peter and John with the Samaritans helped maintain the unity of the church. We do not have here a case of centralized control from the Jerusalem church. Centralized control is a phenomenon that does not seem to appear in Acts, though it was found in the later church through centers like Rome and Constantinople. The unity of the whole body of Christ is important to God. When the book of Ephesians waxes eloquent on the beauty of the unity of the body of Christ, it is talking about the church universal, not the local church situation. It is important that Christians affirm this unity rather than retain the fiercely independent spirit so common today.

Miraculous but wrong. Simon represents a person who had miraculous powers but was dangerously wrong in what he did. He must have done many things for people that appeared to have helped them temporarily. This is why he had such a big following. The Bible predicts that this phenomenon of wonder-working false messiahs will become more and more prominent as the end draws near (Matt. 24:24; 2 Thess. 2:9). This section of Acts therefore warns us that the presence of wonder-working power does not mean that the power wielded is God's power. Peter is forthright in his denunciation of Simon, though subsequent history does not seem to indicate that he ever repented of his sins and came to God.

Money and power. Peter's strong response to Simon's attempt to buy power with money should make us sit up and take note, for it is a serious issue. This can be a dangerous trap both for Christian ministers and for persons who come to them with requests. Thus, it must be dealt with forcefully. (1) It is dangerous for the minister because all of us are vulnerable to temptation in the area of money.[12] After Elisha refused to take a gift from Namaan, his servant Gehazi tried to exploit Namaan's gratitude in order to make some money. Elisha pronounced a judgment on him that resulted in his getting the same leprous condition Namaan had (2 Kings 5:15–27).

(2) The practice of giving gifts for divine favors is dangerous to the givers because it can detract them from the most important thing in life—to have their hearts right before God (v. 21). The word "simony" has entered the English language through this incident; it refers "to the attempt to secure ecclesiastical office or privilege through monetary means."[13] When money and power combine, there are many pitfalls that can cause great damage in the lives of individuals and in the church as a whole.

ENCOURAGING SECOND-GENERATION LEADERS. The example of Peter and John in not only accepting but also learning from and following the lead given by Philip is a challenge to all leaders today. There is a lot of talk today about passing the baton to a new generation of leaders. Pioneer leaders are sometimes reluctant to do this. Actually, passing the baton is not something that happens when a leader comes close to retirement age. It is the result of an attitude that is cultivated early in one's leadership—the willingness to learn, especially from younger creative people.

After giving new ideas and trailblazing efforts due consideration, those that are valid should not only be approved but also encouraged. Sometimes we as older leaders ignore or delay looking at new efforts. We may be busy with existing programs, we find the new effort too different from what we are used to, or we feel threatened by the drive of the young initiators. The result is that creative leaders lose their motivation, become angry rebels, or just leave.

True, we should not naively accept every new idea that comes along. Examining a new work, as Peter and John do in this story, is important. This ensures that errors are avoided and helps bring the benefit of mature wisdom to the young person's plan. Such analysis also can become a source of encouragement to the young person. If we simply hand over responsibility to younger leaders and do not offer our assistance, they may soon be discouraged for they will face problems along the way that could have been eased by the input of mature people.

---

12. Money is presented in Acts as a factor in the evil acts attributed to Judas (1:18), Ananias and Sapphira (5:1–11), the owners of the soothsaying girl (16:16–19), and Demitrius the silver worker (19:24–27) (see Tannehill, *Narrative Unity*, 106).

13. Polhill, *Acts*, 220. He writes: "Were the term fully based on Simon's behavior, it would be extended to cover any attempt to manipulate God for personal gain."

Many groups flounder after their first-generation leadership ages because they have not cultivated creative younger leadership. They have depended so much on the pioneer leaders and their creative energies that they have not prepared for the next stage of the movement. Younger leaders should do their pioneering while benefiting from the wisdom and encouragement of the older leaders. In the early church the pioneer leaders regarded innovative advances from a new generation of leaders as important. Therefore, not only did they encourage them, they also learned from them and followed the lead they gave.

Knowing that we have received the Holy Spirit. We said that some want to confine the "witness of the Spirit" regarding our salvation entirely to the work of the Spirit in and through Scripture. The primacy of Scripture is a needed emphasis especially because there has been so much abuse of the experiential aspects of the Christian life. People have used certain experiences as a norm and insisted that those who have not had such experiences are either not saved or are missing out on a basic aspect of Christianity. We must not insist on experiences that the Bible does not insist on. Moreover, sometimes people have claimed that dubious experiences are genuine without looking for other biblical criteria for true conversion. The Bible is always the ground on which we stand. Every decision we make and attitude we have must be in harmony with Scripture.

Yet the Bible does speak of a warm spiritual experience of God as a norm for the Christian life. If we downplay the subjective aspects of Christian assurance, we become unbiblical. Unfortunately, this is what many biblical studies on the doctrine of assurance do. They focus on what the Bible describes as being steps to salvation and assure all who have followed those steps that they are saved. They leave out the biblical teaching of the evidence of salvation through experience. We need to recover biblical balance in our thinking regarding the evidential value of Christian experience.[14]

Fostering unity in the church universal. Unity of the body of Christ is important to God, and we should be looking at ways to foster this unity. While it is true that we live in a global village, there is much animosity between the peoples of different nations and groups—north verses south, rich

---

14. For classic treatments of the experiential aspect of Christianity from Calvinist theologians, see Jonathan Edwards, *A Treatise Concerning Religious Affections* in *The Works of Jonathan Edwards* (Edinburgh and Carlisle, Pa.: Banner of Truth Trust, reprint), 1:234—343 (a modern version of this has been edited by James M. Houston, entitled *Religious Affections: A Christian's Character Before God* [Minneapolis: Bethany]); D. Martyn Lloyd-Jones, *Enjoying the Presence of God*, ed. Christopher Catherwood (Ann Arbor, Mich.: Servant, 1991). Others who have written helpfully on the experiential aspects of Christianity include John and Charles Wesley and Blaisé Pascal.

versus poor, Western versus non-Western, American versus British, black versus white, Jew versus Arab, one ethnic group versus another ethnic group, hierarchical versus egalitarian; these are all divisions we face in the world, and they have entered into the life of the church as well. A person may aggravate the problem by denying that there is a problem, which sends a message to the other party that this person is insensitive to their feelings.

In such an environment we must constantly be aware that people have been hurt or have feelings of animosity acquired from their upbringing. Huge cultural differences do not solve the problem. We must be aware of these differences, especially if we are from a group that has been viewed as powerful (e.g., rich, white, educated, male, Western, or majority). One way in which unity can be encouraged is by missionary exchange. When the Samaritans were blessed by the Jerusalem leaders, they would have automatically felt good about the church in Jerusalem.

Missionary exchange works out of the belief that each group has something to contribute to the other. Peter and John obviously learned something new from their Samaritan visit, for they preached in Samaritan villages on their way back. We are all servants of one another. The model of the patronizing missionary should never have existed, and it certainly should not be tolerated today. In our study of the Antioch church, we will see how this unity is fostered by that church's helping with the needs in the Jerusalem church (11:28–30).

Opposing false miracle workers. With the current interest in spirituality within and without the church, people like Simon, who had power to help people, will likely gain respect in society at large. It is easy for Christians to fall into the trap of following society here. Many people with dynamic and magnetic personalities attract those who are looking for stability and security in a confused world. William Willimon writes of how Christians all too often resort to "mushy affirmations of popular practices" with statements like, "Even though I disagree with some of Simon's techniques, he does draw a lot of people and he does do a lot of good."[15] Most often we stay away from committing ourselves in public about these things.

But the danger of their influence is real. It is amazing to see the things that Christians will resort to when they are desperate. If they see no answer to an urgent prayer request, they may go to another "source" for help because many tell them that this source is good for that particular problem. Jesus said that even the elect will be deceived by miracle-working false christs (Matt. 24:24). Such people may not realize that in doing so, they are opening themselves to the terrible wrath of God. Consequently, we must expose

---

15. William H. Willimon, *Acts*, 70.

these powers for who they are—surely an unpopular thing to do in this pluralistic age.

I once spoke to a "Christian" devotee of the popular guru Satya Sai Bäba, shortly after our Youth for Christ magazine had run an article exposing Sai Bäba. He told me that, given the many evidences of this man's power, we may have done a foolish and risky thing by publishing this article. It would have been safer for us to remain silent rather than commit ourselves in this manner. Sri Lanka's most famous painter testifies to the tranquillity and freedom from materialism and immorality that came to him as a result of an encounter with Sai Bäba. All this seems wholesome in our depraved society, and thus it attracts people looking for a moral alternative to the vice around us. This is all the more reason why we should guide people by telling what God thinks about these supposedly "holy people."

Sensitive people often realize after a time that all is not as beautiful as it seems with the person to whom they are devoted. Some see him paying special attention to the rich, who reward him handsomely for his services. Some see actions of his that are not in keeping with his claims. This may begin a process that results in their liberation from the spell of the "holy person's" hold over their lives.[16]

Traps relating to money and power. The influence of the methods of magic on people is so strong that they are willing to give substantial gifts to holy men and women who will pray for them. These gifts spoil the minister and are of no help to the giver; they must be resolutely rejected. By not rejecting such gifts many ministers today have compromised their ministries through opulent lifestyles. Moreover, there is the danger of viewing as more important those who have a lot of money and of neglecting the poor who, according to the Bible, should be objects of special concern. We may also soft-pedal our moral teaching to avoid embarrassing a donor.

Giving money can spoil the giver too. By giving big gifts, the rich may think they have fulfilled their religious obligations and can now live any way they want. I see this happening a lot today. People who live dishonest and immoral lives are often generous when it comes to giving to religious causes. They apparently think that they can compensate for their sin by giving gifts to religious activities. We would help them more by refusing their gifts and by using the opportunity instead to tell them what is most important in life.

It is sad that simony is taking place in the church today too—people using money to buy influence. I have heard of candidates for a bishopric who spend a significant amount of money on their campaigns. They give gifts

---

16. This is what happened to Tal Brooke, once one of Sai Bäba's chief Western disciples. See his *Lord of the Air* (Eugene, Ore.: Harvest House, 1990).

to people and arrange holidays and sumptuous meals for them. Peter would strongly condemn all of this; as we noted above, verse 23 suggests that his strong words to Simon are aimed at ridding the church of his evil influence.

But we avoid acting like Peter because we are afraid of the consequences of opposing powerful people or of disturbing the peace of the church. Thus, we allow people who practice simony to be elected to office in the church. We also allow those whose hearts are not right with God to endow the church with their wealth without ever confronting them about their spiritual poverty. These are serious cancers that can bring speedy death to the church. May we pray earnestly over these abuses of money and power and rise up to pay the price of seeking to purify the church of them.

Acts 8:26–40

NOW AN ANGEL of the Lord said to Philip, "Go south to the road—the desert road—that goes down from Jerusalem to Gaza." ²⁷So he started out, and on his way he met an Ethiopian eunuch, an important official in charge of all the treasury of Candace, queen of the Ethiopians. This man had gone to Jerusalem to worship, ²⁸and on his way home was sitting in his chariot reading the book of Isaiah the prophet. ²⁹The Spirit told Philip, "Go to that chariot and stay near it."

³⁰Then Philip ran up to the chariot and heard the man reading Isaiah the prophet. "Do you understand what you are reading?" Philip asked.

³¹"How can I," he said, "unless someone explains it to me?" So he invited Philip to come up and sit with him.

³²The eunuch was reading this passage of Scripture:

"He was led like a sheep to the slaughter,
and as a lamb before the shearer is silent,
so he did not open his mouth.
³³In his humiliation he was deprived of justice.
Who can speak of his descendants?
For his life was taken from the earth."

³⁴The eunuch asked Philip, "Tell me, please, who is the prophet talking about, himself or someone else?" ³⁵Then Philip began with that very passage of Scripture and told him the good news about Jesus.

³⁶As they traveled along the road, they came to some water and the eunuch said, "Look, here is water. Why shouldn't I be baptized?" ³⁸And he gave orders to stop the chariot. Then both Philip and the eunuch went down into the water and Philip baptized him. ³⁹When they came up out of the water, the Spirit of the Lord suddenly took Philip away, and the eunuch did not see him again, but went on his way rejoicing. ⁴⁰Philip, however, appeared at Azotus and traveled about, preaching the gospel in all the towns until he reached Caesarea.

THE PREVIOUS SECTION showed how Philip spread the gospel among the Samaritans. In the present section God has new work for his pioneering evangelist. The Spirit moves him to spread the message about Jesus to a foreigner, who worked in the palace of a pagan queen.

The story of the conversion of the Ethiopian eunuch occupies about the same amount of space as the story of Philip's ministry in Samaria (8:5–25). There is no unanimity about where the evangelist was when the angel of the Lord asked him to go south to a desert road (southwest of Jerusalem, v. 26). Was he still in Samaria, which is north of Jerusalem and therefore far away from that road? Was he in Jerusalem? Or had he by now settled in Caesarea, where he went after this episode and where we find him many years later (21:8)? We cannot be sure.[1] In this vividly written piece Luke is not interested in specifics of geography. Rather, he wants to show how God directly led Philip to do something significant.

Philip immediately obeyed this somewhat strange command. And the God of surprises shocked him with the appearance of an Ethiopian (v. 27). He is called a "eunuch" (*eunochos*); there is disagreement among scholars as to whether he was literally a eunuch, for this word was used also for trusted workers of a royal court. If he was a eunuch, he may have been restricted from full participation in the worship of the Jerusalem temple, for Deuteronomy 23:1 prohibits castrated people from entering the assembly. Isaiah 56:4–5, however, promises an everlasting name within the walls of God's temple for faithful eunuchs. What we know for sure is that he was a high official—something like the finance minister—in Ethiopia.

Ethiopia (Cush in the Old Testament) corresponds to what is known as Nubia. It encompasses parts of what is now southern Egypt and northern Sudan. In ancient literature the Ethiopians were considered as living in the ends of the earth.[2] In other words, with the gospel going to the Samaritans and then to the Ethiopian, it was going to the last two geographical spheres of the Great Commission as given in Acts 1:8. Luke does not mention the religious background of the Ethiopian. He had come to the Jerusalem temple to worship and had a copy of Isaiah with him—not something easy to obtain in those days. This suggests that he may have been a God-fearer or a proselyte.[3]

---

1. For the view that the Greek of verse 26 may suggest that Philip was in Jerusalem at the time, see Williams, *Acts*, 160.

2. Tannehill discusses this point and cites the relevant literature on it (*Narrative Unity*, 108–9).

3. See Longenecker, "Acts," 363.

Only the most well-to-do had chariots in those days,[4] but the Ethiopian was in one, reading from the prophet Isaiah (v. 28). Considering the high standing of this official, it would have required some boldness for Philip to obey the Spirit's command to go to the chariot (v. 29). Since people almost always read aloud in those days,[5] Philip heard him reading—one of the favorite messianic passages of the early church. Philip's question about whether the eunuch understood what he was reading got the response he needed to share the good news with him: "How can I . . . unless someone explains it to me?" (vv. 30b—31).

The passage the eunuch was reading (Isa. 53:7—8) talks of the unjust humiliation and sufferings of the Lord's servant (Acts 8:32—33). His question about the identity of this servant (v. 34) becomes a launching pad for Philip's telling "him the good news[6] about Jesus" (v. 35). The Ethiopian must have had with him the rest of Isaiah 53 too, where the substitutionary nature of Jesus' death is presented. Matthew and John specifically apply Isaiah 53 to Jesus' healing ministry,[7] whereas Luke presents Isaiah 53 as being fulfilled in the sufferings of Jesus.[8] After a survey of Jewish interpretation of the Suffering Servant passages, Longenecker concludes that "while the individual elements for a suffering conception of the Messiah may have been in process of being formed in certain quarters, a doctrine of a suffering Messiah was unheard of and considered unthinkable in first century Jewish circles generally."[9] Yet in the church these passages became important messianic texts because Jesus applied these songs to himself.

It is the Ethiopian who suggests baptism when they come to some water (v. 36). Philip may have discussed baptism with the Ethiopian, or he may have already known about it because it was the initiatory rite for Gentiles who converted to Judaism. Philip takes another bold step in baptizing the eunuch (v. 38). Considering all the signs of divine leading he had received, Philip must have been convinced of the genuineness of this conversion, even though not long before he had baptized Simon, whose professed conversion turned out to be fake. Thus, just a few moments after the eunuch's decision for Christ, Philip baptizes him.

Philip is then taken away suddenly by the Spirit of the Lord. But the newfound joy of the Ethiopian cannot be dampened by his disappearance (v. 39).

---

4. Keener, *BBC*, 346.
5. Bruce, *Acts*, NICNT, 175.
6. "Told . . . the good news" translates an aorist form of *euangelizo*.
7. See Matt. 8:17 on Isa. 53:4 and John 12:38 on Isa. 53:1.
8. See Luke 22:37 on Isa. 53:12; cf. Longenecker, "Acts," 365.
9. Ibid.

We do not hear of him again in the Bible, though Irenaeus, writing in the second century, says that he became a missionary to the Ethiopians.[10] Philip next appears in Azotus, some twenty miles north of Gaza, and continues traveling north, preaching incessantly until he reaches Caesarea (v. 40). It is there that we find him again about twenty years later, now the father of four unmarried prophetesses (21:8). Luke, who probably visited him on this occasion,[11] describes him as "Philip the evangelist"—a most appropriate title for one who was so mightily used in evangelism.

THE IMPORTANCE OF **and guidelines for personal evangelism.** As we think about applying this passage today, many may say that because they are not specialist evangelists like Philip, this passage has little to teach them. But one of the important truths of Acts is that the prominent preachers and theologians of the early church were also personal evangelists. Philip is a good example. In the first part of this chapter he has a public ministry that allows him to bear the title given him by Luke: "evangelist" (21:8). But here he is a *personal* evangelist.

The British scholar and evangelist Michael Green believes that Luke's primary reason for including the story of Philip and the Ethiopian was to teach the value of personal, one-on-one evangelism and to give guidelines on how it should be done.[12] This story shows how important personal evangelism is, insofar as a key preacher in the church is taken on a long journey in order to share the gospel with just one person. And note that the episode is given the same amount of space as the record of the conversion of large numbers in Samaria.

When Paul later refers to his ministry to the Ephesian elders, he speaks both of public and personal ministry (20:21). After listing the many occasions in Acts that public evangelists are involved in personal evangelism,[13] Robert E. Coleman writes, "Clearly the Book of Acts wants us to realize that these early leaders were no less astute in personal evangelism than they were in formal preaching."[14] Michael Green lists the well-known Christians in the

---

10. Irenaeus, *Against Heresies*, 3:12 (*The Ante-Nicene Fathers* [Grand Rapids: Eerdmans, reprint 1996]), 1:433. Longenecker says, "We do not know whether he only inferred that from this account or whether he had independent knowledge about it" ("Acts," 366).

11. Acts 21:8 is in one of the "we" passages of Acts.

12. Michael Green, *Evangelism in the Early Church* (Grand Rapids: Eerdmans, 1970), 225.

13. See Acts 3:1–16; 8:9–24, 26–40; 13:6–12; 16:13–15, 16–18; 16:19–40; 18:1–4, 7–8, 24–28; 19:1–7; 27:9–44.

14. Coleman, *The Master Plan of Discipleship*, 90.

sub-apostolic church who were converted through personal witness or became personal witnesses. Justin Martyr, for example, was converted through the witness of an old man and then led Tatian to the Lord. The great intellectual Origen worked with sensitivity, tact, and persistence until Gregory was converted.[15] These leaders, of course, were following the example of Jesus.[16]

Much of the evangelism in the early church was done by laypeople who shared their faith wherever they went. This is implied in Acts 8, where Luke says that all except the apostles were scattered (8:1), and that "those who had been scattered preached the word wherever they went" (8:4). The public preachers stayed at home while laypeople went out and witnessed for Christ.

This model is seen in Ephesus, where Paul had discussions daily for two years in the lecture hall of Tyrannus. The result was that "all the Jews and Greeks who lived in the province of Asia heard the word of the Lord" (19:10–11). Coleman explains what happened: "The apostle was in the city teaching and setting an example of witnessing before the church, but the real evangelizing of the area came through those persons Paul was discipling, who in turn were reaching others."[17] Michael Green reaches this conclusion: "Above all how the early church grew [was] by personal evangelism."[18]

We must look at this passage in order to learn about personal evangelism. The way Philip witnessed to the Ethiopian serves as an example. We can learn from this expert evangelist about personal witnessing because the principles that emerge from this encounter are applicable to all Christians who seek to witness for Christ (see the "Contemporary Significance" section).

The calling of an evangelist. In Acts 8 Philip lives up to his title "evangelist" (cf. 21:8). All of us are called to evangelism and should contribute, through our personal witness and other ways, to the total witness of the body to which we belong. But some are specially called to be evangelists (Eph. 4:11; 2 Tim. 4:5). This calling remains needed today too. We need to recognize this call and encourage those who respond to it.

In passing let me mention that the Ethiopian was reading while traveling. John Wesley, who read while traveling, makes the observation: "It is good to read, hear, seek information even in a journey. Why should we not redeem all our time?"[19] I do not think that we can derive an abiding principle about

---

15. Michael Green, *Evangelism in the Early Church*, 224–29.

16. The personal evangelistic ministry of Jesus has been the subject of many studies. See esp. Robert E. Coleman, *They Meet the Master* (Fort Lauderdale: Christian Outreach, 1973); *The Master's Way of Personal Evangelism* (Wheaton: Crossway, 1997); also G. Campbell Morgan, *The Great Physician: The Method of Jesus with Individuals* (Old Tappan, N.J.: Revell, 1937).

17. Coleman, *Master Plan of Discipleship*, 92.

18. Michael Green, *Acts for Today: First Century Christianity for Twentieth Century Christians* (London: Hodder and Stoughton, 1993), 110.

19. John Wesley, *Explanatory Notes*, 426.

reading while traveling from this passage. But a lot of traveling occurs today, and bookstores in airports are generally busy. In our mobile culture, we can use our travel time well by reading good books.

 THE IMPORTANCE OF **personal evangelism.** There is no doubt about the value of lay personal witness as a means of church growth today. Laypeople come in contact with non-Christians in a way that paid church workers do not. They can identify with their fellow students or fellow workers in a more natural way than professional Christian workers. If we are going to reach the lost world for Christ, they are surely a key. But to be successful, church leaders, especially preachers (like Philip), must give the lead. They must show the importance of personal evangelism by demonstrating it in their lives. And just as Luke recorded this story for posterity, preachers today can tell Christians in their preaching, teaching, and conversing about their experiences in witnessing. In this way personal evangelism is upheld as a basic part of the Christian lifestyle.

We all know how we can let opportunities for witness slip past us. Keeping personal witness high on our topics of discussion helps us to be vigilant and to use these opportunities when they present themselves.

Guidelines for personal evangelism. Let us now examine the guidelines for personal evangelism that are apparent in this passage.

Witness as obedience. The first truth that leaps out of this passage is Philip's obedience. When God asked him to go to the desert road, he went even though the command seemed an odd one (vv. 26–27). When he was asked to go to the chariot and stay near it, he obeyed again (vv. 29–30a). Through his obedience the Lord opened a door to an evangelistic situation.

We often hear it said that a key to personal witness is "Spirit-led boldness." Some claim that they do not have this boldness and therefore cannot witness. In reality, much of Christian witness inspired by Spirit-led boldness begins with a decision to be obedient to the call to witness. If we take that first step of obedience, the Spirit will guide us and equip us with boldness. We often miss out on opportunities to witness simply because we do not take the first step to turn a conversation into a witnessing situation.

I can think of several situations where I talked about many things with an individual and missed opportunities along the way to make the conversation into a witnessing situation. I recognize too that the basic problem was my disobedience to the promptings of the Spirit. But I also know of other situations where I did use the opportunities—and how joyous was the result, for there are few things as thrilling in life as talking to someone about the Savior!

Obedience to the Great Commission and to the promptings of the Spirit is the key that unlocks the release of the Spirit into our lives and transforms us into being witnesses with Spirit-led boldness.

Witness across cultures. Personal evangelism can take place across cultures. We do not know much about Philip's background. But we know enough of the Ethiopian that he was very different from the Christian Jew, Philip. He was probably a black-skinned African of a high standing, who had servants attending to him as he traveled in his chariot.

Cross-cultural evangelism and the related topic of contextualization are popular topics of study in the church today. This is an exciting development, for it teaches people to respect cultures, to be sensitive to others, and to be relevant in their witness. But there is a danger that with all this missiological study, the priority of personal witness is downplayed and evangelism becomes a complex procedure beyond the reach of ordinary people. The facts of history are that simple Christians can share Christ with people who are different from them by simply loving them and by being humble and sensitive to their needs.

A servant girl from Israel influenced her master, Namaan, the commander of the army of Aram, to seek contact with the God of the Israelites and to experience his healing (2 Kings 5). Philip led a high Ethiopian official to Christ. A desperately poor servant filled with the joy of the Lord had a marked influence on a theology student at Oxford University, John Wesley, who knew nothing of his joy and freedom.[20] In India today we are hearing of some "high" caste Brahmins, who are usually resistant to the gospel, coming to Christ through the witness of Christian servants working in their homes. When an opportunity comes to talk to someone about Christ, we must pray for guidance, be aware of our shortcomings, and launch out into loving witness about our Savior.

Hearts are prepared by God. Philip discovered that the Ethiopian had been prepared by God before he even spoke to him. We too can expect this as we share Christ with others. As we share, we are often surprised to find that the person with whom we are talking has been prepared by God for the encounter. This doesn't always happen, of course, but it happens often enough for us to realize that God can lead us to people whom he has already prepared to listen to what we have to say. We are just one link in what God is doing in that person's life.

Leighton Ford, in his excellent book on personal evangelism, *Good News Is for Sharing*, reports how a young pastor friend of his was used to lead a hardened criminal in a county jail to Christ. This man told the preacher,

---

20. Ingvar Haddal, *John Wesley: A Biography* (Nashville: Abingdon, 1961), 28–29.

"Now preacher, don't get the big head because I have accepted Christ. You are just the twenty-fifth man." On asking what that meant, the pastor was told that at least twenty-four others had witnessed to him about Christ and that his conversion was the effect of all of these together.[21] God was at work before the pastor came on the scene.

Start often with their questions. Philip started his gospel presentation from where the Ethiopian was, that is, with the question whether the eunuch understood what he was reading (vv. 30b–31). Then Philip gave the eunuch an opportunity to ask another question (v. 34). From that point, Philip took him to where he should be in terms of knowing the facts of the gospel. We should always look for such bridgeheads to share the gospel with people.[22]

This principle is relevant to public evangelism as well (cf. our study of 17:16–34). In both types of evangelism, we must start where people are and lead them to where we hope they will go. Often people are not interested in the questions we think that the gospel answers. This is particularly true of postmodern society, where people may not consider themselves to be interested in finding the truth, to be in need of a supreme God, or to be guilty of sin. Thus, we may need to start with what they recognize as needs (i.e., their felt needs) and then show them what Christianity has to say about those needs. From there we can lead them to recognize a need for Christ and his salvation.

About 75 percent of those who attend our church are converts from Buddhism or Hinduism (with two from Islam). Almost all came into contact with Christianity through friends telling them that God could solve some problem they had. These believers brought them to a Christian meeting where the problem could be discussed or prayed over. Gradually they became aware of the heart of the gospel and eventually trusted in Christ for salvation.

A witness based on Scripture. Philip's witness was based on the Scriptures (v. 35a). Much discussion is taking place today on the role that Scripture has in evangelism among non-Christians who have no background in the Bible. When I was a seminary student in the United States, I wrote to a Buddhist who had studied with me at the university in Sri Lanka, asking her to read the Gospel of John. I felt bad that I had not adequately witnessed to her and hoped that this would create an interest. But she stumbled over the first few verses, about the Word becoming flesh, and did not go beyond that! She wrote back that the Bible was an unintelligible book. In the Ethiopian's case God had led him to just the right passage. In the same way we too can choose suitable passages from an understandable version and give those to non-Christians.

---

21. Leighton Ford, *Good News Is for Sharing* (Elgin, Ill.: David C. Cook, 1977), 49.
22. See also the studies on 16:11–40 and 18:2–11.

In the mission ministry that Youth for Christ in Sri Lanka started, we have done this in many Buddhist villages. Teams of volunteers visit these unreached villages, taking with them attractively produced tracts with relevant portions of Scripture. We have an address at the back of the tract that they can write to if they are interested. And from those who write in we have found a nucleus for ministry in these areas. The work has become so large that it is now an independent church-planting ministry. In the West it may not be that easy to get people interested in the Bible, but the principle of arresting people's attention through strategically chosen and attractively produced Scriptures still applies. The medium of communication, however, may need to be much more sophisticated. There is a humanly unexplainable power in the Word when it is appropriately presented to hungry people (Isa. 55:10–12).[23]

Our presentation of the gospel must always be based on Scripture. We may decide not to quote Scripture verbatim with people who do not accept its authority, but the ideas we present must spring from Scripture. This is what Paul did in Athens (Acts 17:22–31). I have found it helpful to tell some of those to whom I am talking that such and such is what the Bible says on a particular issue. It comes as an aside, but it shows these people that the Bible has some wise and relevant things to say. Even though we may not use the exact words of a Bible translation, the ultimate goal we have in personal evangelistic communication is to have the person accept the truth of the gospel.

Jesus is the theme. The main theme of Philip's witness was Jesus (v. 35b). E. Stanley Jones was an American missionary with an effective evangelistic ministry among the Hindu intellectuals of India. Regardless of where he started in personal or public speaking, he always ended with Christ. Our message is Jesus, and everything about Christianity revolves around who Jesus is and what he has done. W. H. Griffith Thomas aptly entitled his heart-warming book on the supremacy of Christ, *Christianity Is Christ*.[24] Jesus himself said that he is "the way and the truth and the life" (John 14:6). In that pithy statement are found truths the depth of which the human mind is incapable of plumbing.[25] We must "offer them Christ," as John Wesley used to say. If this is so, then one way to prepare for personal evangelism is to deepen our intellectual and experiential knowledge of Christ.

---

23. Such portions are published in attractive form by groups like the Bible Society and Scripture Gift Mission.

24. W. H. Griffith Thomas, *Christianity Is Christ* (Canaan, Conn.: Keats, 1981 [repr. of 1949 ed.]).

25. I have made an attempt at explaining the gospel using that statement as a base in *Supremacy*.

Aim at a response. The Ethiopian realized that he needed to respond to Philip's message. Thus, when they came to some water, he suggested baptism (v. 36). We are not told how Philip brought him to this point, but here, as in all the evangelistic situations in Acts, a response is implied. Similarly, in all our witness we must have in mind the goal of a response to the gospel. This is not popular in our pluralistic society. People have accepted dialogue as a suitable way to discuss religion. But the end of such dialogue is mutual enrichment. The evangelism of Acts, by contrast, always aims at a response.

It is possible for us to confine our conversations with non-Christians to discussions on religion, where we present what Christianity says about a certain topic. This is indeed a good beginning, but it is not evangelism.[26] We should also not stop with only answering the questions that people ask. Rather, we must always look for an opportunity to bring people to the biggest and most important question of all: "What will you do with Jesus Christ?" This does not mean that every time we talk to a non-Christian about Christ, we must press for a decision. While we desire that, we may sense that the situation is not ripe for a response, so we end hoping that someday this person will be led to Christ, even if it is through person number twenty-five.

Baptism at once? Philip baptized the Ethiopian immediately after his conversion to Christ (vv. 36–38). Was he ready for immediate baptism? Can we be so sure of people today? After all the miraculous leading that Philip had received from God, he must have realized that this conversion was a genuine one, in which God had led right along. As a result, he baptized the eunuch at once.

We may not always have such an assurance. Some people profess a conversion without understanding that a total giving of one's life to God is involved. We have found, for example, that when some Hindus and Buddhists in Sri Lanka accept Jesus Christ, they intend him to be a help to them alongside their other gods and ways of life. They pray a typical prayer of commitment, but they have no intention of giving up their Buddhism or Hinduism. There are similar situations in the West, where people take on the "born-again" badge without any intention of repenting from their past life. I do not know of any Scripture that prohibits us from delaying baptism. Sometimes we may need to wait until a person has shown some signs of conversion and until some basic instruction about Christianity has taken place.

Yet Philip's trust in God's work in the Ethiopian's life continues to challenge us, especially since this came shortly after the baptism of Simon in Samaria, who had not genuinely converted to Christianity. Matthew Henry's words are instructive here: "If some hypocrites crowd into the church, who

---

26. For a discussion of dialogue see the study on 17:1–15.

afterwards prove a grief and scandal to us, yet we must not therefore make the door of admission any straiter than Christ has made it; they shall answer for their apostasy, and not we."[27] I must confess that I do not feel that the church has fully come to grips with the fact that in Acts, immediate baptism seems to have been the norm. I wonder whether the reasons for delay today are more pragmatic than scriptural.[28]

Encouraging evangelists. Because the primary work of those called to be evangelists is with people outside the church, Christians may not recognize their value and not give them the support they need. I know of many evangelists who spend far too much time trying to raise their support. It would be much better to have local churches commission evangelists to go where God leads them (within or without the church). The churches can then give them the backing and accountability they need. An interdenominational evangelist may find it more appropriate to work outside the confines of one local church. Such persons should have a good group to back them. Evangelists especially need support because evangelism is a spiritually draining work and because Satan is active to trip them, seeing that they are directly invading his territory.

I close this study with a quotation from the great Bible scholar and specialist on Acts, F. F. Bruce. Towards the end of his autobiography, he writes:

> For many years now the greater part of my time has been devoted to the study and interpretation of the Bible, in academic and non-academic settings alike. I regard this as a most worth-while and rewarding occupation. There is only one form of ministry which I should rate more highly; that is the work of an evangelist, to which I have not been called.[29]

This is, of course, a subjective opinion, not a biblical affirmation, for the Bible teaches the equal importance of all the gifts in the body (1 Cor. 12). But I trust it will give encouragement to the evangelists among us.

---

27. *Matthew Henry's Commentary on the Whole Bible in One Volume*, ed. by Leslie F. Church (Basingstoke, Hants: Marshall Pickering, 1960 ed.), 466.

28. On this see Roland Allen, *Missionary Methods: St. Paul's or Ours?* 81–99.

29. F. F. Bruce, *In Retrospect: Remembrance of Things Past* (Grand Rapids: Eerdmans, 1980), 311.

Acts 9:1–31

ﻬ

MEANWHILE, SAUL WAS still breathing out murderous threats against the Lord's disciples. He went to the high priest ²and asked him for letters to the synagogues in Damascus, so that if he found any there who belonged to the Way, whether men or women, he might take them as prisoners to Jerusalem. ³As he neared Damascus on his journey, suddenly a light from heaven flashed around him. ⁴He fell to the ground and heard a voice say to him, "Saul, Saul, why do you persecute me?"

⁵"Who are you, Lord?" Saul asked.

"I am Jesus, whom you are persecuting," he replied. ⁶"Now get up and go into the city, and you will be told what you must do."

⁷The men traveling with Saul stood there speechless; they heard the sound but did not see anyone. ⁸Saul got up from the ground, but when he opened his eyes he could see nothing. So they led him by the hand into Damascus. ⁹For three days he was blind, and did not eat or drink anything.

¹⁰In Damascus there was a disciple named Ananias. The Lord called to him in a vision, "Ananias!"

"Yes, Lord," he answered.

¹¹The Lord told him, "Go to the house of Judas on Straight Street and ask for a man from Tarsus named Saul, for he is praying. ¹²In a vision he has seen a man named Ananias come and place his hands on him to restore his sight."

¹³"Lord," Ananias answered, "I have heard many reports about this man and all the harm he has done to your saints in Jerusalem. ¹⁴And he has come here with authority from the chief priests to arrest all who call on your name."

¹⁵But the Lord said to Ananias, "Go! This man is my chosen instrument to carry my name before the Gentiles and their kings and before the people of Israel. ¹⁶I will show him how much he must suffer for my name."

¹⁷Then Ananias went to the house and entered it. Placing his hands on Saul, he said, "Brother Saul, the Lord—Jesus, who appeared to you on the road as you were coming here—has sent me so that you may see again and be filled with the

Holy Spirit." [18]Immediately, something like scales fell from Saul's eyes, and he could see again. He got up and was baptized, [19]and after taking some food, he regained his strength.

Saul spent several days with the disciples in Damascus. [20]At once he began to preach in the synagogues that Jesus is the Son of God. [21]All those who heard him were astonished and asked, "Isn't he the man who raised havoc in Jerusalem among those who call on this name? And hasn't he come here to take them as prisoners to the chief priests?" [22]Yet Saul grew more and more powerful and baffled the Jews living in Damascus by proving that Jesus is the Christ.

[23]After many days had gone by, the Jews conspired to kill him, [24]but Saul learned of their plan. Day and night they kept close watch on the city gates in order to kill him. [25]But his followers took him by night and lowered him in a basket through an opening in the wall.

[26]When he came to Jerusalem, he tried to join the disciples, but they were all afraid of him, not believing that he really was a disciple. [27]But Barnabas took him and brought him to the apostles. He told them how Saul on his journey had seen the Lord and that the Lord had spoken to him, and how in Damascus he had preached fearlessly in the name of Jesus. [28]So Saul stayed with them and moved about freely in Jerusalem, speaking boldly in the name of the Lord. [29]He talked and debated with the Grecian Jews, but they tried to kill him. [30]When the brothers learned of this, they took him down to Caesarea and sent him off to Tarsus.

[31]Then the church throughout Judea, Galilee and Samaria enjoyed a time of peace. It was strengthened; and encouraged by the Holy Spirit, it grew in numbers, living in the fear of the Lord.

Original Meaning

THE CONVERSION OF Saul of Tarsus has been considered one of the most crucial events in the history of God's dealing with humanity. This man will dominate the rest of the book of Acts and, as the apostle to the Gentiles, lead the way in taking the gospel to the ends of the earth. The account of Saul's conversion appears three times in Acts (see also 22:3–21; 26:12–18). Keener has pointed out that while in classical literature reports of messages given to messengers were generally repeated verbatim on their delivery, there was a preference for variation in reporting in the rhetorical style of Luke's day. This made repeated narratives more interesting to read.[1] Willimon observes that "only an event of greatest importance would merit such repetition by an author whose hallmark is brevity and concision."[2]

Saul's Vehemence (9:1–2)

SAUL'S LATER FRIEND and partner, Luke, uses strong language to express the vehemence with which Saul persecuted Christians (v. 1), but that is something Saul himself did in his own descriptions of his pre-Christian behavior (see 26:11; Gal. 1:13). In these excesses Saul was departing from the attitude of his esteemed teacher Gamaliel and of the Pharisees in general, who were characterized by caution and leniency in the administration of justice.[3] But, as Bruce points out, just as "Stephen saw the logic of the situation more clearly than the apostles, Saul saw it more clearly than Gamaliel." Both Stephen and Saul had realized that the new order and the old were incompatible. Whereas Stephen argued, "The new has come; therefore the old must go," Saul's point was, "The old must stay; therefore the new must go."[4] The root of this was his zeal (Phil. 3:6), especially his zeal for the traditions of his fathers (Gal. 1:14). The idea of a crucified Messiah was an impossibility, according to Saul's thinking. And when Stephen proclaimed that the temple was no longer necessary, all this was too serious to be ignored; it had to be stopped.

The Sadducees were, according to Josephus, more heartless in their judgments than the Pharisees,[5] and it may not have been natural for a loyal Pharisee like Paul to go and request letters from the Sadducean high priest (v. 2). This is an indication of the extremes he was willing to go in attempting to stamp out this menace.

Saul left for Damascus to seek out people "who belonged to the Way." The designation "the Way" (*he hodos*) was probably applied to the church by the Christians themselves.[6] As a designation for the church it appears six times, only in Acts, and probably indicated that they viewed themselves as following

---

1. Keener, *BBC*, 347.

2. Willimon, *Acts*, 74.

3. See E. P. Sanders, *Judaism: Practice and Belief, 63 BCE–66 CE* (London: SCM, and Philadelphia: Trinity Press International, 1994), 419–20. Sanders uses evidence from Josephus and other sources.

4. Bruce, *Paul*, 70.

5. From Josephus, *Antiquities* 20; cited in Sanders, *Judaism*, 419.

6. Haenchen, *Acts*, 320. The Qumran community also described itself as "the Way" (*NIDNTT*, 3:941–42).

the true way in the larger Jewish community.[7] Damascus was an old city, with a long history of being controlled by different national powers. Tens of thousands of Jews lived there, and it had several synagogues (cf. Luke's "synagogues" in v. 2).

The Last Post-Resurrection Appearance (9:3–9)

As Saul approaches Damascus, he hears a voice and sees a bright light. The double vocative, "Saul, Saul" (v. 4), is reminiscent of the way God's voice was heard often in the Old Testament.[8] The light Saul sees (v. 3) must have been strong, for it is around noon when he encounters it (22:6; 26:13). It would have reminded him of the Shekinah glory of God in the Old Testament. This accounts for Saul's question, "Who are you, Lord?" (v. 5). *Kyrios* can mean both "Lord" and "sir," but considering the circumstances of the light from heaven and the calling of his name, Saul must have realized that he was in the presence of the Lord God.

The voice from heaven asks a simple question: "Why do you persecute me?" (v. 4). In response to Saul's question about who is speaking to him, the voice replies, "I am Jesus, whom you are persecuting." In other words, while Saul was hitting the church, Jesus has actually been feeling the pain! Paul later expounds in depth about the church as the body of Christ (1 Cor. 12; Eph. 3–5).

The use of the human, earthly name "Jesus"[9] (v. 5) "rather than a divine title would have put everything into focus for Saul," says Harrison. "Jesus of Nazareth was alive. His disciples had been right after all in proclaiming his resurrection from the dead."[10] The evidence was too compelling to reject any longer. Saul had been coming to Damascus "to arrest all who call on your name" (cf. v. 14). In the Old Testament "calling on the name" is a standard description of prayer to God. He had heard Stephen call on the "Lord Jesus" as he was dying (7:59). All this was blasphemy to Saul, and it had to be stopped! Now as he is on his way to do just that, he is jolted into the realization that Jesus is indeed alive.

Saul's conversion has been given physical and psychological explanations that seek to downplay the idea that a revelation of Jesus caused this huge turnaround. Some say that it was caused by something like "the extraordinary enhancement of illumination experienced by epileptics." Bruce dismisses this view by showing that this is more revolutionary and long term than can be

---

7. Polhill, *Acts*, 234.

8. See Gen. 22:11; 46:2; Ex. 3:4; 1 Sam. 3:4 LXX; cited in Beverly Roberts Gaventa, *From Darkness to Light: Aspects of Conversion in the New Testament* (Philadelphia: Fortress, 1986), 57–58.

9. Acts 22:8 has "Jesus of Nazareth."

10. Harrison, *Interpreting Acts*, 159.

explained by such a phenomenon. It was "a total conversion . . . of will, intellect, and emotion which dictated the abiding purpose and direction of his subsequent life and activity."[11]

Others claim that Saul was a person in turmoil. The radiant testimony of Stephen had left him deeply troubled, and the way he overcame this was by being fanatical about his opposition to Christianity. Psychologist Carl Jung thought that Paul's fanaticism is typical of "individuals who are compensating secret doubts."[12] Some decades ago scholars under the influence of the psychoanalytic movement read Romans 7 into the Acts accounts and claimed that Saul was troubled by his inability to keep the law fully, and that his persecution of the church was an expression of his intense inner conflict.[13] But, as G. E. Ladd points out, in Paul's own testimony he "paints no background of distress, despair or wavering in his Jewish convictions."[14] Paul felt that he was faultless in terms of legalistic righteousness (Phil. 3:6b), that he persecuted the church out of zeal (3:6a), and that he was acting in ignorance and unbelief (1 Tim. 1:13).

We will later show that Christ's statement, "It is hard for you to kick against the goads" (26:14), does not refer to Paul's battling his conscience. Rather, Saul was spiritually blinded by wrong convictions until a greater light caused him to become spiritually enlightened, though physically blinded. The evidence is suddenly now too overwhelming. He has to accept "the Way." "The change that occurred that day was initiated not from within but from without."[15]

This passage records the last of the post-resurrection appearances of Jesus. Paul calls this a "vision" in 26:19, but it is more than a typical vision, for his companions also see the light (22:9) and hear the sound (9:7). In his list of post-resurrection appearances Paul says, "and last of all he appeared to me also, as to one abnormally born" (1 Cor. 15:8). The words "as to one abnormally born" literally translates "as if to the miscarriage." It can mean, therefore, that Paul is saying "as to one born too early." Actually he was the last to be "born," but he may be emphasizing that he did not have the usual gestation period of being with Jesus for three years. In that sense this was a

---

11. Bruce, *Acts,* NICNT, 183.

12. C. G. Jung, *Contributions to Analytical Psychology,* trans. H. G. and C. F. Baynes (1945), 257; cited in Williams, *Acts,* 123.

13. A. C. McGiffert, *A History of Christianity in the Apostolic Age,* rev. ed. (New York: Charles Scribner's Sons, 1906), 119–209; cited in Gaventa, *Darkness to Light,* 53.

14. Ladd, *Theology,* 404.

15. Harrison, *Interpreting Acts,* 158. See S. Kim, *The Origin of Paul's Gospel* (Grand Rapids: Eerdmans, 1982); A. F. Segal, *The Apostolate and Apostasy of Saul the Pharisee* (New Haven, Conn.: Yale Univ. Press, 1990).

premature birth.[16] But by placing it alongside the other post-resurrection appearances, Paul says that it was as objective an appearance as those recorded in the Gospels. Bruce says, "If Paul uses the same language of his own experience as of the experience of Peter and the others, it is to suggest not that their experience was as 'visionary' as his but that his was as objective as theirs."[17]

The words "rise and enter" (lit. trans. of *anastethi kai eiselthe*, v. 6) "reflects once more the language of the Septuagint, where *anistemi* frequently introduces divine commissions (e.g., Gen. 21:18; 31:13; 1 Kings 17:9; Jon. 1:2)."[18] That a commission is included here is implied by the words "you will be told what you must do" (v. 6; cf. also v. 15). In 26:16−18 Paul reports that he received a commission as part of his encounter with Christ, and in 22:15 that it was communicated by Ananias. This is typical of Luke's style of introducing a concept and developing it later.[19]

Paul later describes his having seen the risen Christ as part of his qualification for apostleship (1 Cor. 9:1), along with his receiving a specific commission from Christ; both these elements are met through the Damascus experience. Paul describes elsewhere what he received in Damascus: "Through him and for his name's sake, we received grace and apostleship to call people from among all the Gentiles to the obedience that comes from faith" (Rom. 1:5). James the Lord's brother also seems to have qualified for apostleship through a similar encounter with Christ (see 1 Cor. 15:7; Gal. 1:19).

An influential study by K. Stendahl claims that Paul's Damascus experience was a call to be a missionary to the Gentiles, not a conversion.[20] Since then there has been a shift in emphasis from looking at this event as a commission rather than a conversion. Indeed, the accounts in Acts emphasize the call because of Luke's purpose in describing the Gentile mission. But in Paul's letters when he describes this experience, he emphasizes not the call but the contrast between his former life in Judaism and his present life in Christ (Gal. 1:13−17; Phil. 3:4−9). Paul's radical break with Judaism and change in life in Acts can be explained *only* in terms of conversion. We conclude that while the emphasis in Acts is on the call, it also includes a conversion.[21]

In Damascus the blinded Saul follows the most intense type of fast, spending three days without eating or drinking (v. 9). People engaged in such fasts

---

16. This explanation is from Craig Blomberg, *1 Corinthians*, NIVAC (Grand Rapids: Zondervan, 1994), 297.

17. F. F. Bruce, *1 and 2 Corinthians*, NCBC (Grand Rapids: Eerdmans, 1971), 142.

18. Gaventa, *Darkness to Light*, 59.

19. Ibid., 66.

20. K. Stendahl, *Paul Among Jews and Gentiles* (Philadelphia: Fortress, 1976).

21. For a concise discussion on this debate see, J. M. Everts, "Conversion and Call of Paul," *DPL*, 156−63.

only if they were repenting or seeking God's face. Both are involved here (cf. v. 11, where Ananias is told Paul is praying).

Ananias's Ministry to Paul (9:10–19a)

ANANIAS WAS A wise choice to help Saul at this time for "he was a devout observer of the law and highly respected by all the Jews living there" (22:12). As with Peter and Cornelius (10:1–23), God's arrangements are confirmed by a double vision (vv. 10, 12).[22] Visions occur often in Acts when God intervenes to direct the church into some new thing.[23] The Greek of 9:11b–12 begins with "for behold" (*idou gar*)—an expression used to announce that "something surprising follows, something worthy of note (cf. Luke 1:44, 48; 2:10; 17:21)."[24] As Gaventa points out, "In this instance two developments account for the *idou gar*: (1) Saul is praying, and (2) Saul saw Ananias come so that he might be healed."[25]

"Straight Street" (v. 11) is still identifiable today. "The present *Darb al-Mustiqim* ('Straight Street'), otherwise known as *Suq et-Tawileh* ('Long Bazaar'), probably follows the line of that ancient street."[26] Saul is described to Ananias as "a man from Tarsus" (v. 11), which Paul later describes as "no ordinary city" (21:39). Tarsus was a fortified trading center even before 2000 B.C. It was the principal city of Cilicia, the most southeasterly part of Asia Minor (in present-day southern Turkey). It was a city of great culture.[27] Though Saul was born there, he was "brought up" in Jerusalem (22:3), but he would have had some acquaintance with Greek culture, which would have prepared him to be the apostle to the Gentiles.[28]

Ananias's protest is understandable, considering all that Saul had done to the "saints[29] in Jerusalem" and had been planning to do in Damascus (vv. 13–14). But his willingness to obey immediately, after the Lord's explanation (vv. 15–16), is commendable. So is his magnanimous act of "placing his hands on Saul" and addressing him as "brother Saul" (v. 17). According to the Lord's description to Ananias of his plans for Saul, the latter will go to "the Gentiles," "their kings," and "the people of Israel" (v. 15). The order, though different from that in the commission Jesus gave (1:8), is significant. It "moves

---

22. Marshall, *Acts*, 171. Marshall, however, calls these dreams.

23. Polhill, *Acts*, 253. See 9:10, 12; 10:3, 17, 19; 11:5; 16:9–10; 18:9; 27:22–26.

24. Gaventa, *Darkness to Light*, 61.

25. Ibid.

26. Bruce, *Steps*, 13.

27. Most of the details on Tarsus are from ibid., 6–8.

28. See the arguments of Sir William M. Ramsay, *The Cities of St. Paul* (New York: Armstrong, 1908), 88; cited in Harrison, *Interpreting Acts*, 162.

29. On "saints" see comments on 9:32.

from those who receive Paul's preaching (Gentiles) to those who hear without receiving (kings) to those who reject it (sons of Israel)."[30]

Right at the start of his spiritual pilgrimage, Saul is informed that he will suffer for the name of Jesus (v. 16). Suffering is a basic aspect of following Christ. But before Paul experiences this cross, he will experience Christ's power: Ananias says that he has come so that Paul "may see again and be filled with the Holy Spirit" (v. 17). Though there is no record that he was filled with the Spirit, we have no reason to doubt that this happened.

Early Attempts at Ministry (9:19b–25)

AT ONCE SAUL launches out on a preaching ministry in the synagogues of Damascus (v. 20). Later he wrote that new converts should not be leaders in the church (1 Tim. 3:6), but the fact that he preached did not mean he was a leader. Besides, unlike most new converts, Saul was already well versed in the Scriptures. His message was "that Jesus is the Son of God." Bruce observes: 'The proclamation of Jesus as the Son of God represents an advance on the way in which his messiahship has been proclaimed thus far in Acts." The Old Testament saw the ideal king of the future, the Messiah of David's line, as the Son of God (Ps. 2:7).[31] This is why the high priest asked Jesus, "Are you the Christ, the Son of the Blessed One?" (Mark 14:61). The people are baffled by this sudden change in Saul (v. 21). But Saul grows in his eloquence as a herald of and an apologist for Christ (v. 22), "proving that Jesus is the Christ."

Verse 23 finds Saul in Damascus "after many days had gone by." His trip to Arabia and his return to Damascus (see Gal. 1:17) must have occurred during this time—probably doing both meditating and preaching. He spent almost three years in Arabia.[32] Arabia was ruled by the Nabateans at the time, and Damascus may have been either part of it or bordering it. Predictably, opposition arose, and the persecutor Saul becomes the persecuted—with the Jews conspiring to kill him (vv. 23–24). Saul had to make an unceremonious exit from Damascus in a basket (v. 25). In 2 Corinthians 11:32 Paul says that he had to leave Damascus in this way because the governor under the Nabatian king Aretas was guarding the city in order to arrest or kidnap Saul. In other words, both the Jews and the Arabs were now after him! Perhaps this governor wanted to arrest him since he had done something in Arabia that he did not like—such as preaching![33]

---

30. Gaventa, *From Darkness to Light*, 63.

31. Bruce, *Acts*, NICNT, 190.

32. While this is not obvious in the NIV rendering, it seems to be the correct interpretation.

33. On this see Bruce, *Acts*, NICNT, 191–92.

Finally to Jerusalem (9:25–30)

In GALATIANS 1 Paul makes much of the fact that he did not go to Jerusalem until three years after his conversion. This fact was evidence that he had received his commission as an apostle directly from Christ, not from Christian leaders in the holy city. It must have been an emotionally stirring time for Saul as he returned to the city he loved, where he had grown up, and where he had been such an eminent success. He could assume his former associates would shun him. But how difficult it must have been for him to find that when he tried to join the disciples, "they were all afraid of him" (v. 26). Their reaction was understandable, considering the terror he had inspired and the wounds he had inflicted on them. Was it not a well-known strategy for spies to infiltrate the inner ranks by faking commitment to a cause?

Another of the great "buts" of Acts introduces God's solution to the problem as Barnabas takes him, not just to the disciples, but to the apostles themselves (v. 27). He tells them Saul's story. According to Galatians 1:17–18, Paul met only the two key apostles, Peter and James. Luke's reference to "the apostles," therefore, should be interpreted as "a generalizing plural."[34] Paul spent fifteen days with Peter (Gal. 1:18). Most translations render *historeo* in that verse as "get acquainted with," but the word means "visit, with the purpose of obtaining information."[35] We can imagine that, when a new apostle spent fifteen days with an older apostle, they did more than discuss the weather![36] Saul would have been filled in on many of the details regarding the life and words of Christ. Peter must have told Saul about the special post-resurrection appearance to him that is mentioned in 1 Corinthians 15:5.

Saul gets busy in Jerusalem, "speaking boldly" and debating for the Lord (vv. 28–29). But the Jews try to kill him, and he makes a hasty exit to Caesarea en route to his birthplace, Tarsus.[37] He next appears in Acts several years later, still in Tarsus (11:25).

The Church Remains Healthy (9:31)

THIS SECTION ENDS with the report of a healthy church (v. 31). We note that, though there is no specific record in Acts of any ministry in Galilee, there was a church there. This is to be expected, considering how many followers Jesus had in Galilee. The church now enjoyed a time of relative calm, which is true of most evangelistic communities that face persecution: There

---

34. Ibid., 193.
35. Louw and Nida, 453.
36. Daniel P. Fuller, in an unpublished commentary on Galatians.
37. Galatians says he went to Syria and Cilicia. Tarsus is in Cilicia and Syria is on the way.

are periods of respite from serious opposition. The numerical growth of the church continued, for there is never a respite from the work of evangelism.

CONVERSION. THE ENGLISH word "conversion" comes from the Latin *convertere*, meaning "to turn around."[38] The equivalent Greek word, *epistrophe*, appears only once in the New Testament (Acts 15:3), though the NIV translates as "convert" words that literally mean "proselyte," "neophyte," and "firstfruits." Related verbs like "to turn" (*epistrepho*) and synonyms such as "repentance," "regeneration," and being "born again" appear often.[39]

Paul's conversion is sometimes described as a typical biblical conversion. But it has many atypical features. It was triggered by a post-resurrection appearance of Christ. It was a sudden turnaround in direction with no evidence that he had been moving toward Christianity (as is the case with most converts). His was a conversion like that of C. S. Lewis, who said, "I gave in and admitted that God was God and knelt and prayed: perhaps, that night, the most dejected and reluctant convert in all England."[40] The last thing Saul ever intended to do was to become a Christian. But he was, in his own words, "grasped by Jesus Christ" (Phil. 3:12).[41] In the features given below, however, his conversion is typical of biblical conversions.

Features typical of biblical conversions. (1) Conversion comes as a result of a divine initiative. Jesus initiated the encounter that resulted in Paul's conversion (vv. 3–6). Paul had no qualms about admitting that he did nothing to merit salvation. On the contrary, he was, in his words, "the worst of sinners" (1 Tim. 1:16). But, he goes on to say, he was shown mercy so that he might be an example of the unlimited patience of God. Thus, no one can boast of salvation as something he or she has achieved or deserved (Eph. 2:9). Paul explains the process of conversion in a way reminiscent of his own experience when he says, "For God, who said, 'Let light shine out of darkness,' made his light shine in our hearts to give us the light of the knowledge of the glory of God in the face of Christ" (2 Cor. 4:6).

---

38. Ernest Weekley, *An Etymological Dictionary of Modern English* (New York: Dover, 1967), 1:357.

39. Hugh T. Kerr and John M. Mulder, *Famous Conversions* (Grand Rapids: Eerdmans, 1994), ix.

40. C. S. Lewis, *Surprised by Joy: The Shape of My Early Life* (New York: Harcourt, Brace & World, 1955), 228–29.

41. This is the rendering of Peter O'Brien, in *Commentary on Philippians*, NIGTC (Grand Rapids: Eerdmans, 1991), 417.

(2) There is a personal encounter with Christ (vv. 4–6). We all meet Jesus in different ways; but if we are converted, we have met him and entered into a personal relationship with him. Jesus said that eternal life is to know God and Jesus Christ (John 17:3). D. A. Carson comments on this verse, "Eternal life is not so much everlasting life as personal knowledge of the Everlasting One."[42]

(3) Paul surrendered to the Lordship of Christ. While the word *kyrios* in verse 5 can mean either "Lord" or "sir," there is no doubt that what we have here is a deep surrender of Saul's life to Christ. This is evidenced by his total fast for three days, indicating that until he completed the process that began on the road, he was not going to cease from his intense quest for God. Such surrender is indeed the norm for all followers of Jesus. Paul's later radical calls to discipleship imply nothing short of total surrender to the Lordship of Christ. Roy Clements says he does not "use the phrases 'decided for Christ' or 'committed to Christ,' though decision and commitment are certainly involved. . . . Conversion is at root not a decision, nor a commitment, but a surrender to the supreme authority of Jesus."[43]

(4) We see the important place of the body of Christ in the conversion process. While Paul was eager to show that the gospel he received had not been taught to him by any human but was given by the Lord himself (Gal. 1), others in the body of Christ played an important role in his conversion and early Christian life. Through baptism he was incorporated to this body (Acts 9:18). Then he "spent several days with the disciples in Damascus" (v. 19). The thing that stands out in our passage is the role of the two encouragers, Ananias and Barnabas. Probably the first words Saul heard from a Christian after his conversion were, "Brother Saul" (v. 17). Stott says, "It must have been music to his ears." The archenemy of the church was welcomed as a brother; the dreaded fanatic was received as a member of the family.[44] Lloyd Ogilvie muses, "Imagine laying your hands on someone who you know had been on his way to arrest you!"[45] There you see the love of the encourager reaching out to a new believer in spite of his past.

Barnabas shows two other traits of an encourager in the body. He takes the risk of introducing the ex-adversary to the inner circle of the church leaders (v. 27a). If Saul was indeed a spy, this would have been the opportunity he was waiting for. But Barnabas acts on his trust of Saul and takes this risk. Moreover, he tells these believers the story of Saul—of his conversion and his witness (v. 27b). He represents the junior man before the senior people. All new believers would benefit greatly from such encouragement.

---

42. D. A. Carson, *The Gospel According to John* (Grand Rapids: Eerdmans, 1991), 556.

43. Clements, *The Church That Turned*, 137.

44. Stott, *Acts*, 176.

45. Ogilvie, *Acts*, 170.

(5) Though Saul's conversion is individual, it is not individualistic. Gaventa points out that he "is not converted in order to savor the experience but in order to witness."[46] Thus, along with his conversion came a commission to witness. Though we may not receive a specific commissioning to apostleship as Paul did, all Christians are called to be witnesses for Christ. Once we come to him, we become his ambassadors (2 Cor. 5:20) and have the responsibility and high privilege of representing him on earth and communicating his message to the world.

Suffering and discipleship. At the start of his pilgrimage, Saul is informed that he will suffer for the name of Christ (v. 16). This became a standard aspect of discipleship teaching in the early church, for Jesus' basic call to discipleship was to a cross (e.g., Matt. 10:38; 16:24). While Saul encountered more sufferings than many other obedient Christians, we must remember that suffering for Christ is a normal part of Christianity and it should come into standard introductions to Christianity for new believers.[47]

The significance of the Damascus experience. Paul's conversion has been viewed by the church as a unique event. An eighteenth-century English statesman, George Lyttleton, expressed the immense importance of the Damascus Road experience when he wrote, "The conversion and apostleship of St. Paul alone, duly considered, was of itself a demonstration sufficient to prove Christianity to be a divine revelation."[48] Why is this so?

In the New Testament the apostles had a special place as revelatory spokesmen. The Old Testament prophets spoke through direct inspiration so that they could say, "This is what the LORD says." This phenomenon stopped four hundred years before the birth of Christ, and the Jews had a complete canon of the Hebrew Bible. With the coming of Christ this level of verbally inspired revelation became a reality again. Jesus said, "The words I say to you are not just my own. Rather, it is the Father, living in me, who is doing his work" (John 14:10b). His promise that the Holy Spirit "will teach you all things" (14:26) and will "guide you into all truth" (16:13) was fulfilled in the teaching of the apostles. Because they had seen the risen Christ and had been commissioned by him, they were in a unique position. They led the church after Jesus' ascension and before the New Testament canonical books were accepted as authoritative. They were revelatory spokesmen, just like the Old Testament prophets.

Paul was eager to show that he did not depend on human instruments to receive his basic message (Gal. 1) since, as an apostle, he also was a revela-

---

46. Gaventa, *From Darkness to Light*, 92.

47. The significance of this has been discussed in the study on 4:1–22 and 14:1–28.

48. G. Lyttleton, *Observations on the Conversion and Apostleship of St. Paul* (London, 1747), paragraph 1; cited in Bruce, *Paul*, 75.

tory spokesman. Note his claim for verbal inspiration in 1 Corinthians 2:6–13, which climaxes with these words: "This is what we speak, not in words taught us by human wisdom but in words taught by the Spirit, expressing spiritual truths in spiritual words."

This is why Paul could claim absolute authority for his teachings. He said, "If anyone does not obey our instruction in this letter, take special note of him. Do not associate with him, in order that he may feel ashamed" (2 Thess. 3:14). Again, "But even if we or an angel from heaven should preach a gospel other than the one we preached to you, let him be eternally condemned!" (Gal. 1:8). He separated his personal opinions from the teaching of the Lord when speaking about the complex subject of marriage (1 Cor. 7:10, 22). Daniel Fuller says, "The absolute authority that Paul ascribed to his teaching should not be charged off as the rantings of an eccentric egotist but should be taken as a sober recognition of the fact that in all his teaching, none other than Jesus Christ, the Son of God, is speaking."[49]

Paul's extreme zeal for the traditions of the fathers (Gal. 1:14) took him to Damascus to arrest followers of a religion that contradicted these traditions. On the way he had an encounter with Jesus and received a commission that took him on a completely opposite path. He became the apostle to the Gentiles. As an apostle he knew he was the bearer of verbally inspired truth. We today can read his letters, which form more than a quarter of the New Testament and give to them the authority we would accord to the words of Christ himself.

 **THE SIGNIFICANCE OF divine initiative in salvation.** In our study of Acts 4:12 we noted that our inability to do anything for our salvation should cause us to be humble; no genuine Christian has any reason for arrogance. When someone asked Mahatma Gandhi what he thought about E. Stanley Jones, Gandhi replied, "He's a good man, but he's too proud of his religion." When Jones was told about this, he said that Gandhi was right according to his own convictions. To Gandhi salvation was the result of hard work. Earning salvation was as difficult as trying to empty an ocean of water with one's hands. According to such a scheme, anyone who says that he or she is assured of salvation will be justly called arrogant.

But according to the Christian scheme, salvation is a gift of God; we do not deserve it and it is freely given to us by God, who takes the initiative by

---

49. Daniel Fuller, *Hermeneutics* (Pasadena, Calif.: Fuller Theological Seminary, 1974), VIII-13.

seeking us and bringing us to himself. In other words, we have no grounds for feeling superior to anyone. This truth we must demonstrate in an age when Christian belief about full assurance of salvation is considered arrogant by pluralists, who see the pursuit of salvation as something generated from within.

Another significant inference from the fact that God takes the initiative to save the least likely people, such as Saul the persecutor, is that we cannot pronounce anyone hopeless as far as conversion is concerned. As we face irreligious people or the followers of New Age thinking or any other religion, we may think that they are impossible to bring to Christ. As Paul said in 1 Timothy 1:16, the fact that the worst of sinners could be converted is a sign that the least likely people can be saved. Such realities should encourage us to dream about, pray for, and work toward the conversion of resistant people and enemies of the gospel.

Leading people to personal encounter with Christ. Our task as witnesses is to lead people to Jesus so that they will encounter him as their Savior and Lord. We may discuss religion, argue for the truth of it, and seek to persuade people about its relevance and power. But the end that we aim at is to introduce people to Jesus. This is why it is advisable to help those who are ready to accept the Christian way to pray a prayer of seeking salvation. We may have them repeat words after us. However we do it, our aim is to lead them in this encounter with Christ to talk personally to him.

We must never take it for granted that all to whom we minister have a personal relationship with God. My mother led me to such an encounter when I was a religious fourteen-year-old, who was already knowledgeable of the Scriptures and active in church. When I was in seminary, a fellow student who had been nurtured in an evangelical background testified in class that he had encountered Christ for the first time a few days before. The Emmanuel Methodist Church in Madras, India, was finding it difficult to maintain its property because it had a small congregation. They were preparing to sell some of the property when someone suggested to the pastor, an American missionary, to have some revival meetings in the church. He invited a Baptist preacher, very different to him in theology and outlook, to preach at these meetings. On the first night when that preacher invited those who wanted to be born again to come forward, the first one to go up was the pastor of the church! He met Christ personally, and his ministry was so transformed that the church became and still is, a few decades after his retirement, one of the great centers of Christian witness in India.

The importance of surrender. Christians have debated whether presenting the Lordship of Christ is an essential part of the gospel presentation. Some are afraid it will take away from the primacy of grace to say that for salvation one must submit to the Lordship of Christ. This pitfall will be avoided if we realize that everything we do, even exercising saving faith, is done because of God's initiative and enabling. Not to present the need for total surrender to Christ is to present a gospel without a key aspect of Christianity. Those who respond to a gospel that did not present the necessity of surrender may feel as if they have been tricked into accepting a gospel without having been shown "the fine print" about what a Christian commitment implies.

The place of encouragers today. We can imagine Saul's despair, loneliness, and disappointment when other Christians rejected him. He later expounded deeply about the "in Christ" existence, according to which earthly barriers are broken because we are one body in Christ. Yet the members of that body did not trust him. How many bright new Christians face such loneliness and disappointment! It can lead to despair and bitterness. But God often provides a way of healing in the form of an encourager. Would that there were more Ananiases and Barnabases in our churches!

The risk Barnabas took was immense. Was Saul a spy? His fiery enthusiasm and outspoken boldness would have provoked negative reactions in some of the more sober elders. Who is this young upstart, who goes to extremes in everything he does? He must be an unbalanced individual, for once he was violently opposing Christianity and now he is vigorously defending it. Yet Barnabas stuck his neck out to support Saul. He was willing to take that risk. When we glorify risk-taking today, most often we do so about our personal exploits. Here is another type of risk-taking: accepting new people and pushing them forward. This is Christian risk-taking. Because Christianity is a religion of love, some of our greatest exploits are ventures of love. Taking the risk of believing people is one such venture.

Barnabas also encouraged Saul by telling the apostles Saul's story. In order to be able to do this, he had first listened to that story. Often leaders are so interested in telling their own story that they have no time to listen to those of others. By telling the apostles Saul's story, Barnabas acted as a public relations man for the junior person. Normally public relations work is done for leaders by the juniors, but here that order is reversed. Paul often did the same sort of things in his letters. He gives, for example, glowing tributes of younger, lesser-known people, such as Titus and Timothy (e.g., 2 Cor. 8:16–24; Phil. 2:19–24).

Avoiding the trap of individualistic conversion. Given the great blessings that come from conversion, it is possible to place so much emphasis on these that converts forget that they are people under a commission. For Saul conversion and commission went together. We must teach converts about Christian service and get them active the moment they come to Christ.

The conversion of the great Indian evangelist Sadhu Sundar Singh (1889–1929) was remarkably similar to that of Saul. He too was a young man who vehemently opposed Christianity until he had a vision of Christ that transformed his life. When his family members, who were Sikhs, realized that the conversion he professed was not a passing fancy, they poisoned him and sent him away from home. He landed at the doorstep of the home of a pastor, desperately ill. The doctor who saw him gave up hope that he would recover. "But as he lay, there came to him the profound belief that God had not called him out of darkness to die without witnessing to his faith in Christ, so he began to pray with all his remaining powers."[50] He recovered and launched out on a life of witness. Donning the garb of an Indian holy man, he traveled the length and breadth of India barefoot, preaching the gospel. This earned him the name "the apostle of the bleeding feet," for his feet, unprotected from the hostile elements, sometimes bled. His realization as he lay dying was that he was "saved to tell others" the gospel.

God's redemptive acts and the pluralist attitude. The notion of the absolute authority of Paul's writings goes against the grain of the contemporary mood. Modern-day pluralists hold, like the Hindus held for centuries, that truth is subjective. They place little stock in historical events like the commissioning of Paul. To them ideas are important, not events. Events may illustrate ideas, but they do not win salvation and endow a person with authority.

As we look at Scripture, we see that God's approach to salvation is through events. Theologians speak of "salvation history" and of "the God who acts." The Bible teaches that God acts decisively through key redemptive events, such as the Exodus, the giving of the law, the Conquest, the incarnation and life of Christ, his death, his resurrection, his ascension, Pentecost, the conversion/call of Paul, and the second coming of Christ. We must seriously reflect on these basic dealings of God with humankind if we are to be biblical in this pluralistic age. We must see that Christianity is based on objective historical events.

---

50. Rebecca Parker, *Sadhu Sundar Singh: Called of God* (Madras: Christian Literature Society, 1918), 16.

Acts 9:32–43

A S PETER TRAVELED about the country, he went to visit
the saints in Lydda. [33]There he found a man named
Aeneas, a paralytic who had been bedridden for eight
years. [34]"Aeneas," Peter said to him, "Jesus Christ heals you.
Get up and take care of your mat." Immediately Aeneas got
up. [35]All those who lived in Lydda and Sharon saw him and
turned to the Lord.

[36]In Joppa there was a disciple named Tabitha (which, when
translated, is Dorcas), who was always doing good and helping the poor. [37]About that time she became sick and died, and
her body was washed and placed in an upstairs room. [38]Lydda
was near Joppa; so when the disciples heard that Peter was in
Lydda, they sent two men to him and urged him, "Please come
at once!"

[39]Peter went with them, and when he arrived he was taken
upstairs to the room. All the widows stood around him, crying
and showing him the robes and other clothing that Dorcas
had made while she was still with them.

[40]Peter sent them all out of the room; then he got down on
his knees and prayed. Turning toward the dead woman, he
said, "Tabitha, get up." She opened her eyes, and seeing Peter
she sat up. [41]He took her by the hand and helped her to her
feet. Then he called the believers and the widows and presented her to them alive. [42]This became known all over Joppa,
and many people believed in the Lord. [43]Peter stayed in Joppa
for some time with a tanner named Simon.

*Original
Meaning*

PETER'S VISIT TO "the saints" (*hagioi*) around Palestine indicates that he had a pastoral role throughout the church (v. 32). We can imagine him
teaching, encouraging, correcting, and counsel-
ing the believers and leaders on these visits. *Hagios* (lit., "holy person"; one
of Paul's, though not Luke's, favorite words for Christians) appears three
times in chapter 9 (four times total in Acts to mean "saints": 9:13, 32, 41;
26:10). The New Testament always uses the word for a group rather than for
an individual believer. It is not a designation given to a special class of people,

so that the emphasis is not on saintly character, as it became in later centuries. Rather, the term is used "with reference to the group of believers who belong to God as his own."[1] This fits in with a basic meaning of "holy" being separateness. Separated as God's own people, saints must follow the laws of his kingdom. In other words, saintly character is implied in the designation.

Among the many healings performed through Peter's ministry, Luke mentions two here—those of Aeneas and Tabitha. Aeneas was from Lydda (vv. 32–33), twenty-five miles northwest of Jerusalem, and Tabitha was from Joppa (v. 36), thirty-five miles northwest of Jerusalem. Joppa was the sea port of Jerusalem (modern Jaffa, a suburb of Tel-Aviv). Aeneas had been relatively inactive for eight years because he was a paralytic (v. 33) whereas Tabitha had been extremely active in the service of the needy (v. 36).

With both healings Peter clearly places the emphasis on Christ as the healer. The first time he says, "Jesus Christ heals you" (v. 34); the second time, before speaking, "he got down on his knees and prayed" (v. 40). After Aeneas's healing we are told that "all those who lived in Lydda and Sharon saw him and turned to the Lord" (v. 35).[2] After Tabitha's healing Luke says that "many people believed in the Lord" (v. 42). We do not know whether Aeneas was a Christian, but Tabitha certainly was; this fact indicates that miracles in the church were performed not only on unbelievers but also on believers.

Tabitha, "who was always doing good and helping the poor" (v. 36b), had died. Great haste was needed in bringing the message to the apostle Peter and in getting him to come to Joppa from Lydda (a distance of ten miles). A body was normally buried before sundown on the day of death. But Peter made this journey on foot right away to help the lady who had helped so many presumably insignificant people. Upon arrival, he was confronted by a moving scene of widows weeping and showing things that Tabitha had made for them (v. 39). Peter, who was there when Jesus had raised Jairus's daughter, followed some of his procedures here. He sent the mourners out (v. 40; cf. Mark. 5:40). He probably spoke in Aramaic, and his words, probably *"Tabitha koum(i)"* (Acts 9:40), differed in only one letter to Jesus' words, *"Talitha koum(i)."*[3]

Peter stayed on in Joppa in the house of Simon the tanner (9:43). In the Babylonian Talmud[4] appears the statement: "Woe to him who is a tanner by trade."[5] It was a demeaning trade in Jewish eyes, for strictly speaking, tanners were ceremonially unclean since they handled dead animals. A tanner's shop

---

1. F. E. Hamilton and R. L. Harris, "Saints," *ZPEB* 5:217.

2. "All" is a hyperbole referring to a large number of people.

3. Bruce, *Acts*, NICNT, 199.

4. A compilation of rabbinic teaching and interpretation made during the third through sixth centuries A.D.

5. *Kiddushin* 82b; cited in J. C. Trevor, "Tanned ... Tanner," *ISBE*, 4:726.

had to be in the outskirts of town because of the bad odor that came from it; Simon's home was by the sea (see 10:6).

In this whole passage there is no record of any preaching, though it must have been done. The focus is on service. In the next chapter Luke will refer to Cornelius's acts of charity (10:2).

 **MIRACULOUS HEALING FOR believers.** The healing of Tabitha (vv. 36–41) shows that healing ministry can occur in a pastoral setting, that is, outside the evangelistic setting, where it generally occurs in Acts. It is also interesting that though there would have been Christian leaders and people of prayer in Joppa, the believers asked for Peter to come a distance of at least ten miles and pray for Tabitha. In this time of emergency the church looked for help from the person with the special gift of healing. There was nothing wrong in this, which suggests that today too we can go for prayer in times of crisis to those with special gifts in our area of need.

James outlines the proper procedure in his letter, which leaves us with no doubt that in times of sickness we can call specially gifted people to pray for the need: "Is any one of you sick? He should call the elders of the church to pray over him and anoint him with oil in the name of the Lord. And the prayer offered in faith will make the sick person well; the Lord will raise him up" (James 5:14–15).

In this instance in Acts 9, a dead believer is miraculously raised. This is probably what happened later when Paul raised Eutychus (20:7–12). Can this happen today too? Jesus did it, the apostles did it, and there is no prohibition to Christians in later ages praying for the dead. We must, of course, remember that death is God's gateway to ultimate triumph, and many wonderful Christians, like Stephen and James in Acts, were not spared "untimely" deaths. Therefore, we must have considerable discernment and sensitivity before praying for the raising of the dead. But submission to Scripture prohibits me from saying that we should never pray in this way.

Serving the needy. Luke gives special emphasis to the acts of kindness of Tabitha by mentioning them twice in this passage (vv. 36, 39). Presumably Tabitha had the spiritual gifts of service and acts of mercy (Rom. 12:7–8). But kindness is a quality that all Christians should have (1 Cor. 13:4; Gal. 5:22). Considering Luke's special mention of Tabitha's kindness, we can conclude that she is a model for all Christians. This passage reminds us that, however important evangelism may be, kind deeds for the needy must never be overlooked. The urgency of this is well expressed in the sudden ten-mile journey that Peter took to pray for Tabitha. The top leaders of the church also seem to have distinguished themselves in the art of servanthood!

Various passages of the New Testament contain instructions about a special concern for the needy. Indeed, Acts shows how the Christians shared their possessions so that the needy would be looked after. James 1:27 says, "Religion that God our Father accepts as pure and faultless is this: to look after orphans and widows in their distress and to keep oneself from being polluted by the world." Paul made special mention to Timothy of arrangements for the care of widows (1 Tim. 5:16). Yet it is in the Old Testament, the Bible of the first Christians, that this theme is dealt with comprehensively (esp. in Deuteronomy). We can safely say that caring for the needy is an essential aspect of the Christian lifestyle.

Hospitality to preachers. Verse 43 records the second of the four types of hospitality described in Acts: having traveling servants of the Lord over to stay in the homes of believers. Peter's stay in the home of Simon the tanner is one of many instances of this type of hospitality in Acts.[6] This was a standard practice in the early church, partly because inns were morally unsuited for Christians. After describing the moral and hygienic degradation of taverns and inns in those days, Everett Ferguson writes:

> The moral dangers at the inns made hospitality an important virtue in early Christianity (Rom. 16:23; 1 Pet. 4:9; 2 John 10; 3 John 5–8; Heb. 13:2; 1 Clement 10–12; *Didache* 11–13) because of the needs of missionaries and messengers of the churches and other Christians who happened to be traveling . . . The churches provided an extended family, giving lodging and assistance for the journey.[7]

This is a good practice to follow today as well. There are, of course, hygienically clean hotels today. But morally they can still be snares for traveling Christians, especially if they are alone, as we will show below. Thus the same need that existed in the early church exists today, prompting the suggestion that we give the practice of hosting traveling ministers in the homes of Christians more emphasis today.

Contemporary Significance

PRAYING FOR SICK **believers.** There is considerable controversy in the church today about whether, when someone is sick, we should have special people like Peter pray over him or her. Obviously, this practice is endorsed in Scripture. Yet I have heard people say, "Why

---

6. See also 10:48; 16:15; 18:3, 18, 26; 21:8, 16; cf. 28:7. The other three types are discussed in the studies on 2:46; 10:1–33; and 18:26. See the entry on hospitality in the index.
7. Ferguson, *Backgrounds,* 82.

should you go to special people? Don't we all pray to the same God? Why not just go to the people in your own church?"

I believe that we should go first to our own local church (cf. James 5:14–15). If we choose to go to someone else, our church should know about it. It is unfortunate that some church leaders get angry when their members go outside for help, so that it has to be done secretly. This did not seem to have happened with the leaders in Joppa when Peter was called. The fact remains that although all church leaders should pray with their sick, some have gifts of healing and/or faith that enables them to pray in faith that results in healing and glory to God (1 Cor. 12:9).

I have personally prayed with countless sick people over the years. Perhaps there have been some (unspectacular) healings along the way. But I have friends who are able to pray with a faith that I do not have. One of these friends is an illiterate person, whose only way to study personally the Scriptures is to meditate on what he has heard because he cannot read. But when he prays there is great faith, and God answers his prayers wonderfully. We have come to recognize that he has the gift of healing.

I think, however, that we should beware of what may be called "panic praying," where people go from place to place seeking special prayers. That may be an expression of our lack of faith in the sovereign will of God. I know of people who cannot settle down to any abiding Christian service because they keep going from one prayer meeting to another, seeking prayer for their problems. There are times when we may find that the answer we hope for is not forthcoming. On such occasions we will need to adopt the attitude of Paul, who, after pleading three times for release from his thorn in the flesh, was told to depend on the sufficient grace of God that perfects strength in weakness. Instead of panicking, Paul gladly boasted about his weakness (2 Cor. 12:9).

At such times we should affirm that the answer we want has not come because God has something better in store for us (Rom. 8:28). God does not have to answer our prayers in the precise way as we ask. Sometimes he may have a better plan that will take us through what may look like a disaster. Though we cannot understand what we are going through, we can remain at peace, for we trust God and know that he will do what is best for us.

Perhaps a word should be said about the possibility of raising the dead today. There have been reports of this happening in different parts of the world today. I met a missionary working with a tribal group in India who told me that among this group in the past few years, there have been seven cases of bringing dead people back to life. When someone among them dies, the believers pray for about three-and-one-half hours after his or her death. After that, if the person has not come back to life, the elders give the signal to prepare the corpse for burial.

Caring for the needy. As governments throughout the world are cutting welfare budgets these days, the church can once again expect to play a major role in caring for the needy. Tabitha's care for the needy is presented as a model to the church. I will go so far as to say that a good test of Christian character is how people treat those considered unimportant in society, especially when no one is looking. Those of us who are leaders should not be too influenced by special concern showed to us. The true test is whether special concern is shown to the needy. Many Christian women have distinguished themselves in God's kingdom by their service to the needy. Some were widows who may have not had much strength and means left. But they did what they could, and they left their mark in the lives of the people they touched.

Such concern may not be known to others because of the Christian principle of not letting the left hand know what the right hand is doing (Matt. 6:3). But frequently what they have done emerges at funerals. In Acts 9 the poor were openly expressing their sorrow over Tabitha's death. While eulogies from the rich and famous are impressive, words of gratitude from the poor and unknown are especially moving. The Earl of Shaftesbury (1801—1885) did much to improve the conditions of the poor and needy out of a Christian concern that was expressed in the arena of politics. When his coffin was being carried out of Westminster Abbey, a poor laborer in tattered garments, but with a piece of crepe sewed on his sleeve, was heard to say, "Our Earl's gone! God A'mighty knows he loved us, and we loved him. We shant see his likes again."[8]

The blessings of staying in homes. As in the first century, there are moral dangers in staying in today's hotels. Therefore, also as in the first century, it may be advisable for traveling Christians to stay in the homes of believers rather than in hotels. After a busy day of ministry, which can be emotionally and spiritually draining, usually we are unable to go to bed at once. It is easy to sit before the television and keep flipping from channel to channel, imbibing unedifying material. One may even be tempted to watch R- or X-rated adult shows that are sometimes even shown without a fee, especially at night. Extramarital affairs among traveling members of Christian ministry teams have become sufficiently common to force the church to ask hard questions about drastic changes in customs associated with ministerial travel. As a result, I strongly feel that we give more emphasis to staying in the homes of believers.

(1) The most frequently heard objection to staying in homes of Christians when traveling is how tiring it can be to spend time talking with the hosts. I think we used to call this fellowship! But today we strictly regulate fellow-

---

8. J. C. Pollock, *Shaftesbury—The Poor Man's Earl* (London: Falcon Booklets, 1961), 3.

ship so that we can control it according to our well-planned schedules. Long conversations with our hosts are one of the best ways to identify with the people to whom we are ministering. We get to know things about these people that we may not find out by other means, and thus we can be more relevant in our ministry.

(2) We may also have opportunities for personal ministry, which is a key to freshness in ministry. Staleness is one of the common pitfalls of an itinerant ministry. A person who travels a lot often loses freshness because of lack of deep contact with people. Staying in homes is a great way for incarnational identification with people. True, staying in homes may be inconvenient. But incarnational ministry has never been and never will be convenient. But it adds depth to ministry. While it can be helpful to learn about the people by reading up on them, it can never be a substitute for incarnational closeness with the people.

(3) I have also found that I am usually greatly enriched by my hosts. They teach me so many things about life, about the struggles that laypeople have in their places of work, about their opportunities for service, and so forth. Moreover, our hosts can back us spiritually through their prayers and concern. Traveling people are particularly in need of prayers, especially since they are far away from their network of spiritual support. So the loss of sleep as a result of conversation is more than compensated for by the enrichment that comes through these conversations.

Unfortunately, the church has elevated some people to superstar status, which can make it uncomfortable for potential hosts. My first response to this objection is that there are no superstars in Christianity. The greatest person in the kingdom is the servant. Traveling preachers and artists, however famous they may be, are also servants, because that is the leadership lifestyle of Christianity. We must never allow anyone to elevate them to any higher status; to do so is dangerous to their spiritual well-being.

Peter is a model for us here. When he heard about the death of a church member, he dropped everything and rushed ten miles on foot (!) in order to bring healing to this woman. Then he stayed in the home of a tanner for a number of days. He certainly seemed to be freed from the celebrity syndrome! He had learned his lifestyle from the servant Jesus, who, on his way to the parallel event in Jairus's home, stopped and sought out the woman who had touched the hem of his garment in the midst of a milling crowd (Mark 5:21–34). We are first and foremost servants of the people. When we travel on speaking tours, we are not celebrities; rather, we are servants of the pastor and the members of the congregation, servants of the driver who picks us up, servants of the enthusiastic young person whose long testimony eats into our sermon time, servants of the little child whose cries disturb our message.

Acts 10:1–33

AT CAESAREA THERE was a man named Cornelius, a centurion in what was known as the Italian Regiment. ²He and all his family were devout and God-fearing; he gave generously to those in need and prayed to God regularly. ³One day at about three in the afternoon he had a vision. He distinctly saw an angel of God, who came to him and said, "Cornelius!"

⁴Cornelius stared at him in fear. "What is it, Lord?" he asked.

The angel answered, "Your prayers and gifts to the poor have come up as a memorial offering before God. ⁵Now send men to Joppa to bring back a man named Simon who is called Peter. ⁶He is staying with Simon the tanner, whose house is by the sea."

⁷When the angel who spoke to him had gone, Cornelius called two of his servants and a devout soldier who was one of his attendants. ⁸He told them everything that had happened and sent them to Joppa.

⁹About noon the following day as they were on their journey and approaching the city, Peter went up on the roof to pray. ¹⁰He became hungry and wanted something to eat, and while the meal was being prepared, he fell into a trance. ¹¹He saw heaven opened and something like a large sheet being let down to earth by its four corners. ¹²It contained all kinds of four-footed animals, as well as reptiles of the earth and birds of the air. ¹³Then a voice told him, "Get up, Peter. Kill and eat."

¹⁴"Surely not, Lord!" Peter replied. "I have never eaten anything impure or unclean."

¹⁵The voice spoke to him a second time, "Do not call anything impure that God has made clean."

¹⁶This happened three times, and immediately the sheet was taken back to heaven.

¹⁷While Peter was wondering about the meaning of the vision, the men sent by Cornelius found out where Simon's house was and stopped at the gate. ¹⁸They called out, asking if Simon who was known as Peter was staying there.

¹⁹While Peter was still thinking about the vision, the Spirit said to him, "Simon, three men are looking for you. ²⁰So get up and go downstairs. Do not hesitate to go with them, for I have sent them."

²¹Peter went down and said to the men, "I'm the one you're looking for. Why have you come?"

²²The men replied, "We have come from Cornelius the centurion. He is a righteous and God-fearing man, who is respected by all the Jewish people. A holy angel told him to have you come to his house so that he could hear what you have to say." ²³Then Peter invited the men into the house to be his guests.

The next day Peter started out with them, and some of the brothers from Joppa went along. ²⁴The following day he arrived in Caesarea. Cornelius was expecting them and had called together his relatives and close friends. ²⁵As Peter entered the house, Cornelius met him and fell at his feet in reverence. ²⁶But Peter made him get up. "Stand up," he said, "I am only a man myself."

²⁷Talking with him, Peter went inside and found a large gathering of people. ²⁸He said to them: "You are well aware that it is against our law for a Jew to associate with a Gentile or visit him. But God has shown me that I should not call any man impure or unclean. ²⁹So when I was sent for, I came without raising any objection. May I ask why you sent for me?"

³⁰Cornelius answered: "Four days ago I was in my house praying at this hour, at three in the afternoon. Suddenly a man in shining clothes stood before me ³¹and said, 'Cornelius, God has heard your prayer and remembered your gifts to the poor. ³²Send to Joppa for Simon who is called Peter. He is a guest in the home of Simon the tanner, who lives by the sea.' ³³So I sent for you immediately, and it was good of you to come. Now we are all here in the presence of God to listen to everything the Lord has commanded you to tell us."

Original
Meaning

ACTS 10:1–11:18 IS the longest single narrative in Acts (sixty-six verses). Because of its great length we will divide our treatment of this narrative into two studies. The space given suggests that the events surrounding Cornelius's conversion were important to Luke. The centurion's vision is described four times (vv. 3–6, 22, 30–32; 11:13–14) and Peter's twice (vv. 9–16; 11:4–10), and Peter alludes to the events again at the Jerusalem Council (15:7–11). As we see the events unfolding in Acts, we realize that this episode is a crucial step in the progress of the church in fulfilling the Great Commission.

This narrative has often been organized into seven different scenes, and we will follow this analysis here. This first study will cover the first four scenes of the narrative.

Scene One: Cornelius's Vision (10:1–8)

CORNELIUS LIVED IN Caesarea (v. 1), a seaport on the Mediterranean coast that was rebuilt by Herod the Great and named after Caesar Augustus. It was the center of the Roman administration of the province of Palestine and "served as a showpiece for Roman culture";[1] it even had a temple dedicated to Caesar. The Jews hated Caesarea, calling it "the daughter of Edom," and "would often speak of it as though it were no part of Judea."[2] The population there had more Gentiles than Jews. According to Josephus, riots between these two groups sparked off the Jewish war against Rome in A.D. 66.[3] Josephus also claims that the entire Jewish population of 20,000 in Caesarea was massacred in A.D. 66.[4]

Cornelius was a centurion, which means that he was nominally in command of a hundred Roman soldiers. Centurions generally appear in a positive light in the New Testament. The first Gentile to whom Jesus ministered in the Gospels was a centurion, and it was in connection with his faith that Jesus said, "I say to you that many will come from the east and the west, and will take their places at the feast with Abraham, Isaac and Jacob in the kingdom of heaven" (Matt. 8:11). It was a centurion who said at the cross, "Surely he was the Son of God!" (27:54).

Cornelius "and all his family were devout and God-fearing" (v. 2). There is some debate today about the meaning of the designation "God-fearer." It is usually held that God-fearers were those who attended the synagogue and honored Jewish laws and customs but had not been incorporated into the Jewish community (i.e., become proselytes) through circumcision. But the view that "devout" and "God-fearing" may not have been strict technical terms is becoming more accepted now. Instead, the word "sympathizer" is used.[5] After a lengthy discussion, Barrett sums up as follows:

---

1. "Caesarea," *The Biblical World*, ed. Charles F. Pffeifer et al. (Grand Rapids: Baker, 1966), 154.

2. Williams, *Acts*, 184.

3. Josephus, *Antiquities*, 20.8.7–9; *Wars of the Jews* 12.13.7;14. 4–5; in Josephus, *Complete Works*, 422–23; 483–84.

4. Josephus, *Wars of the Jews*, 2.18.1; in Josephus, *Complete Works*, 492.

5. E. P. Sanders, *Judaism: Practice and Belief; 63 BCE–66 CE* (London: SCM Press, and Philadelphia: Trinity Press International, 1992), 265. See ibid., 519 n. 34 for references regarding the recent debate.

What is important is (a) that some Gentiles were attracted to Jewish ethics, theology and worship, but did not become proselytes; (b) that in some places (one!) they formed a recognized and valued element in the synagogue community, though the degree of their religious attachment is not specified and remains unknown; (c) that such Gentiles presented a great opportunity to Christian evangelists; (d) that Luke was aware of this.[6]

Luke gives two features about the piety of Cornelius: his generosity to the needy and his regular prayer (v. 2). These represent the God-ward and person-ward sides of religion as taught in the Scriptures (Mic. 6:8; James 1:27; 1 Peter 4:7–11). Cornelius had a vision "at about[7] three in the afternoon" (lit., "the ninth hour," v. 3). This was one of the three traditional Jewish times of prayer, and Cornelius later tells Peter that he was praying at the time (v. 30).

Here we have another occurrence in Acts of direction through a vision[8] and through the action of an angel.[9] Luke uses a strong word (*emphobos*) to describe Cornelius's reaction of fear (v. 4). Often in biblical instances of human contact with the spirit world, godly people responded with fear and God gave them words of reassurance. Bruce points out that the angel's words, "Your prayers and gifts to the poor have come up as a memorial offering before God" (v. 4), are full of sacrificial terminology. "Cornelius' acts of piety and charity had ascended into the divine presence like incense or the smoke of a sacrifice."[10]

The angel tells Cornelius to summon Peter from Joppa (vv. 5–6).[11] His message says nothing about what will happen as a result of his coming. The mention of Peter's staying in the house of Simon the tanner may have come as a surprise to Cornelius, as this was not a highly esteemed trade.[12] Despite the lack of details, Cornelius obeys immediately (vv. 7–8). As head of his delegation he sends a soldier who was both in sympathy with the mission ("devout") and close to him ("[one] of those who were in constant attendance upon him," NASB).

Scene Two: Peter's Vision (10:9–16)

PETER, THE ONE to whom the keys of the kingdom were given (Matt. 16:19), is again chosen to open another important door for the gospel—as he did

---

6. Barrett, *Acts*, 501.
7. See comments on 1:15 for Luke's use of "about" when referring to numbers.
8. See comments on 9:10.
9. See comments on 5:19.
10. Bruce, *Acts*, NICNT, 204.
11. On Joppa see comments on 9:36.
12. On tanners see comments on 9:43.

with the Jews on the day of Pentecost and with the Samaritans a short while later. We find him in Joppa, where he will disregard his prejudices, obey God by traveling to Caesarea, and open the door for Gentiles to respond to the gospel—the very thing that Jonah resisted in the same city (Jonah 1:3). He goes to the roof of the house he is staying at around noon to pray (v. 9, not one of the prescribed Jewish times for prayer). The flat roofs of Palestine, approached by an outdoor flight of steps, were common places of prayer in biblical times.[13] It was a good place to pray during the daytime as it was separate from the activity of the house, and the sea breeze and an awning helped cool the place.

Peter receives a vision, given at a time when he was hungry, in which he sees a sheet that "contained all kinds of four-footed animals, as well as reptiles of the earth and birds of the air" (v. 12). The entire animal world is symbolized, and clean and unclean animals are included. Peter receives a command to "kill and eat" (v. 13), which would be unacceptable for him as a Jew, as some of the animals were not kosher (suitable for Jews to eat).[14] His answer, "Surely not, Lord!... I have never eaten anything impure or unclean" (v. 14), contains a contradiction: He makes a categorical refusal to obey one whom he calls "Lord" (*kyrios*). The use of "Lord" suggests that he had recognized the voice as being divine.[15]

Some have said that this statement may mean that Peter assumed God was testing him to see whether he would be faithful to the law. Barrett thinks "that Luke (or Peter, if the narrative does in fact go back to him) failed to see the logical implication of what was said."[16] We feel it is probable that this was an outburst characteristic of Peter. He was revolted by the command and refused to obey, even though God may have been the one giving it to him. We must remember that for the Jews "the dietary laws are not a matter of etiquette or peculiar culinary habits. They are a matter of survival and identity."[17]

The answer Peter receives clearly brings God into the picture: "Do not call anything impure that God has made clean" (v. 15). The adjective and verb translated "impure" (*koinos, koinoo*, lit., "common") appear five times in chapters 10–11. In verse 15 it appears as a present imperative with the negative (*me koinou*), which makes it a prohibition. J. H. Moulton translates it, "You must stop considering it as common."[18] Later, Peter's disciple Mark, after report-

---

13. See 2 Kings 23:12; Neh. 8:16; Jer. 19:13; 32:29; Zeph. 1:5.

14. On "kosher" food laws, see Lev. 11 and Sanders, *Judaism*, 214–17.

15. Marshall does not think it is necessary to imply that Peter is referring to a divine being. The word *kyrios* can also mean "sir" (*Acts*, 185).

16. Barrett, *Acts*, 507.

17. Willimon, *Acts*, 96.

18. J. H. Moulton, *A Grammar of New Testament Greek* (Edinburgh: T. & T. Clark, 1908), 1:125; cited in Robert Hanna, *A Grammatical Aid to the Greek New Testament* (Grand Rapids: Baker, 1983), 208.

ing on the discourse of Jesus on clean and unclean objects (Mark 7:5–23), would make an editorial comment stating, "In saying this, Jesus declared all foods 'clean'" (7:19b). Perhaps this vision helped Peter understand the implications of that discourse of Jesus. The impact of the vision on Peter is heightened by its repetition two more times (v. 16).

Peter will soon realize that he may not consider any group of people common or unclean either (v. 28). Scholars disagree on whether food laws were indeed abrogated by this vision. Some think, however, that the vision dealt primarily with food laws rather than with interaction with Gentiles.[19] Polhill points out that "this is to overlook the fact that the two are inextricably related. In Lev. 20:24b–26 the laws of clean and unclean are linked precisely to Israel's separation from the rest of the nations." Bruce writes, "The animals in the vision are parabolic of human beings: Peter is being prepared to accept Cornelius' invitation to visit him."[20]

Scene Three: Peter Meets the Messengers (10:17–23a)

CORNELIUS'S MESSENGERS STOP at Simon's gate (v. 17), and the Holy Spirit instructs Peter to go with the men (vv. 19–20). While we are told that the Spirit spoke to Peter, we must note that Peter was in a fit state to receive a communication from God. Luke says he was "wondering about the meaning of the vision" (v. 17) and "thinking about the vision" (v. 19). The word translated "thinking" (*dienthymeomai*), which appears only here in the Bible, means "to think about something thoroughly and/or seriously." Louw and Nida say it is used to indicate intensity of thought.[21] While God led Peter clearly, he was earnestly seeking to find God's will.

Peter's bold step of inviting "the men into the house to be his guests" (v. 23a) introduces an important emphasis in this passage, that of hospitality.[22] "It was easier for a Jew to have Gentiles stay with him than for a Jew to stay with Gentiles. Nevertheless, this kindly act was a great step forward for Peter."[23]

Scene Four: Peter and Cornelius Meet (10:23b–33)

IN KEEPING WITH the regular practice in the early church, Peter takes some brothers rather than go on this assignment alone (v. 23). Cornelius seems to have been certain about the time Peter would come (four days after he saw

---

19. Polhill, who makes this point, does not identify these scholars (*Acts*, 255).

20. Bruce, *Acts: Greek Text*, 256.

21. Louw and Nida, 350.

22. Beverly Roberts Gaventa, *From Darkness to Light: Aspects of Conversion in the New Testament* (Philadelphia: Fortress, 1986), 113.

23. Williams, *Acts*, 189.

the vision, v. 30), for Peter finds "a large gathering of people" at the house (v. 27). Cornelius shows great humility for a centurion for, like the centurion whom Jesus encountered (Luke 7:6), he "fell at [Peter's] feet in reverence" (v. 25). But Peter will have none of this, as such reverence is reserved only for God (v. 26). Such acts of reverence to respected people were not unusual in the Near East in those days. In fact, it was "typical of the welcome a hero receives in the Greek novel."[24] But Peter will not risk anything that might suggest that he is accepting the type of respect that is due to God alone.

Peter's discovery, as he explains to his audience, is the pivotal message of this whole passage: "God has shown me that I should not call any man impure [*koinos*] or unclean" (v. 28). Earlier we noted that *koinos* means "common." Here it has the idea of "being ritually unacceptable either as a result of defilement or because of the very nature of the object itself."[25] A big shift has taken place in Peter's thinking, for he now realizes that no longer are the typical Jewish distinctions among people significant. They have been rendered void once and for all. In this episode Jew and Gentile have come together (cf. v. 28, as well as the repeated use of the prefix *syn* ["together with"] in compound words in this scene).[26]

Rarely does an evangelist find as receptive an audience as Peter found here (v. 33). The stage is set to move to the next scene: the proclamation of the gospel.

Bridging Contexts

NO "COMMON" PERSONS. The major theme of this section is the breaking of old distinctions that divided people. The hope that Gentiles will also share in the blessings of God is a clear theme in the Old Testament. It gains prominence first in the call of Abraham (Gen. 12:3) and is a thread that runs throughout the Old Testament,[27] reaching its zenith in the Servant Songs of Isaiah (Isa. 42:1–17; 49:8–12). Peter O'Brien has shown that Paul viewed his call in terms of the fulfilling of these Old Testament promises of blessings to the Gentiles.[28] Acts has already recorded the begin-

---

24. Gaventa, *Darkness to Light*, 116. She refers to the *Ephesian Tale* 1.1.3; 2.7; 12.1 in M. Hadas, *Three Greek Romances*, (Indianapolis: Bobbs Merrill, 1964).

25. Louw and Nida, 537.

26. Gaventa, *Darkness to Light*, 116. Five of these *syn*-compound words occur a total of six times here: *synerchomai*—went along (vv. 23, 27); *syngkaleo*—called together (v. 24); *syngenes*—relatives (v. 24); *synantao*—met (v. 25); *synomileo*—talking with (v. 27).

27. See Isa. 2:1–4; 66:18–22; Mic. 4:1–3; Zech. 2:11; 8:20–23; 14:16.

28. Peter O'Brien, "Paul's Missionary Calling Within the Purposes of God," *In the Fullness of Time: Biblical Studies in Honour of Archbishop Donald Robinson*, ed. David Peterson and John Prior (Homebush West, NSW: Lancer, 1992), 131–48.

nings of the fulfillment of these promises through the conversions of the Samaritans, the Ethiopian, and of Paul (who would be the apostle to the Gentiles).

Before the church was to fulfill this role, she had to shed some of the exclusivism connected with Judaism. Stephen had showed that the temple was unnecessary. Now God shows the church that the Jewish idea that anyone not conforming to their national standards of purity could not be saved is no longer valid. These purity laws may have been needed at one stage of the history of God's people. But it was now no longer necessary for Gentiles to conform to these regulations.

Peter describes his discovery with two great statements: "God has shown me that I should not call any man impure or unclean" (v. 28); and "I now realize how true it is that God does not show favoritism" (v. 34). The next great step would be the Jerusalem Council, when the church would officially accept the principles that Peter learned through this episode (ch. 15). The belief that emerged is summarized in Paul's declaration, "There is neither Jew nor Greek, slave nor free, male nor female, for you are all one in Christ Jesus" (Gal. 3:28; cf. Col. 3:11). Paul was to explain later that the breaking of barriers among humans is a direct result of the death of Christ (Eph. 2:13–16; cf. 2 Cor. 5:14–17; also John 10:15–16).[29]

Is this relevant to us today? After all, most Christians today are Gentiles, so that the specific issue facing the church in Acts does not apply to us. While the specific issue may not apply to us, the general principle certainly does. "God does not show favoritism" (v. 34); that is, in the kingdom of God we may not categorize people according to their background. This principle is urgently in need of reiteration in every age, including ours (see below).

An attitude of repentance. When Peter realized that he had been wrong about his earlier prejudices, he readily admitted that in his conversation with Cornelius (v. 28). When he preached to the crowd, he again publicly confessed the lesson he had learned: God shows no favoritism (v. 34). This attitude of willingness to accept and repent of past prejudices goes a long way in healing relationships ruptured through prejudice; it also opens a ministry for the repentant leader with those he once viewed in a wrong way.

How God makes his will known. Through the Cornelius episode God led the church to take a great step forward in understanding his ways. Could we not learn something from this episode about how God leads individuals and the church into new exciting paths of obedience? Certainly we cannot find principles here that work in every situation of guidance. But as we observe God at work here, we may learn principles that are important to us today.[30]

---

29. For an exposition of this, see my *Supremacy*, 195–201.
30. See the discussion on "Applying the Book of Acts Today" in the Introduction.

Yet the means used here have caused some to discount the practical importance of this passage. Haenchen says of this passage, "The presence of God may be directly ascertained. But here faith loses its true character of decision, and the obedience from faith which Luke would have liked to portray turns into something utterly different: very nearly the twitching of human puppets."[31] Yet, as Tannehill points out, "the narrative presents a more sophisticated and complex account of humans discerning the will of God than Haenchen thought."[32] The visions and special divine messages "are best called divine promptings because they are incomplete in themselves. They require human action or reflection."[33]

Grappling with what we are uncomfortable. In verses 17 and 19 Peter was grappling intensely regarding the meaning of the vision when the Holy Spirit spoke to him. At first Peter vehemently refused to be open to change, as is expressed by his cry, "Surely not, Lord!" (v. 14). He had strong convictions. But when he sensed that God was indeed teaching him something new, he seriously considered the implications of the vision. Thus, both divine guidance and Peter's willingness to grasp what God was showing him combined to produce a change in his thinking, even though it was something he was uncomfortable with. A passion for obedience makes God's servants open to changes with which they may at first be uncomfortable.

God found in Peter a person who was open to living with the uncomfortable. That helped him to be open to God's surprises. This openness is seen earlier in that he stayed in the home of a tanner (see comments on 9:43). Peter had already left his "comfort zone" because of his commitment to ministry, and this made him open to more of God's revelations.

God speaks when we are at prayer. The revolutionary message to Peter came while he was engaged in private prayer (v. 9). God spoke to Cornelius also when he was in prayer (v. 30). This conforms to a pattern found in both of Luke's volumes: God used prayer time as an occasion to lead people to new avenues of ministry.[34] This is perhaps to be expected. God, who wishes two-way communication with his children, will find our times of prayer, when we are attuned to him, as suitable occasions to break through to us.

Evangelistic hospitality. We have already seen two features of hospitality in Acts.[35] Here we see a third feature: having non-Christians over in our

---

31. Haenchen, *Acts,* 362.

32. Tannehill, *Narrative Unity,* 131.

33. Ibid., 128.

34. See Luke 3:21–23; 6:12–16; 9:18–22, 28–32; 22:39–46; Acts 1:14; 10:3–6, 9–18; 13:1–3.

35. Having believers over for fellowship and meals and having traveling Christians staying in our homes (see the discussions of 2:46 and 9:43). The fourth type of hospitality, having Christians over who have a special need, is described in the study of 18:26.

homes (as Peter had the Romans stay over at Simon's home, v. 23), and being in the homes of non-Christians (as Peter did in the home of Cornelius, vv. 25 and 48).[36] Paul also did this in Rome, where for two years he stayed in his own rented house, welcoming all who came to see him, preaching the gospel, and teaching about Jesus (28:30–31). Also, when Paul was shipwrecked on Malta, he stayed in the home of "Publius, the chief official of the island" (28:7). We may call this evangelistic hospitality.

GIVING UP OUR **prejudices**. That Peter needed a drastic message from God to get rid of his prejudices about distinctions among people suggests that even mature Christian leaders may occasionally need a major paradigm shift in order to come into line with God's thinking. Peter's initial response to the command in the vision (10:14) is typical: "Surely not, Lord! I have never eaten anything impure or unclean." As J. A. Alexander points out: "Even [divine] authority was not sufficient to break the force of prejudice and habit." The thought behind Peter's statement is, "I cannot do it now because I never did it before."[37] But to such thinking comes God's message: "Do not call anything impure that God has made clean" (v. 15).

The particular person whom God asked Peter to meet was a top official of the army of occupation in the hated capital of Palestine. Often even Christians find such people difficult to accept. Living in a land of ethnic strife and struggling with the question of feelings for one's race and the other's race in a time of conflict, I have come to realize that prejudice is often one of the last things that is touched by the process of sanctification. For example, it is not uncommon to find supposedly devout Christians becoming unreasonably adamant in their opposition to a child of theirs marrying a Christian from a race under which they have suffered so much.

Recently when expounding the book of Galatians, I looked for an example that would illustrate how powerfully Christ breaks barriers (Gal. 3:28) and how Christians sometimes do not accept that. This is what I came up with. There is an eminent Christian couple in leadership in the church—he a university professor and she a specialist physician. They have a son who is a wonderful Christian. He falls in love and wants to marry a young woman who is also a wonderful Christian. But her mother is a prostitute and drug addict, and she does not know who her father is. How will the parents of this young man

---

36. See also our comments on 10:48.
37. Alexander, *Acts*, 394.

react? Will they oppose it because of her background? Naturally, they will want to warn their son about conflicts that may arise because of differences in background. But because Christ has broken all barriers, background should not be a reason to object to a marriage.

Often Christians have not wanted to break the barriers of caste, class, and race because it is inconvenient to do so. Sometimes believers do not bring up these issues, fearing that doing so will affect the evangelistic effectiveness of the church. At other times it seems advantageous to treat those different from them as inferior. Some Christians thought that it would spell national economic ruin to accept as equals slaves in the British Empire and then in North America. Even today, some think it will bring shame to them if their children marry outside race, class, or caste. Once some Christian parents in Sri Lanka were upset when YFC took their children to minister in what they considered outcast villages. The evangelical church in particular has such a bad record in the areas of prejudice and condoning race, caste, and class distinctions. Muslims are now exploiting this by proclaiming the brotherhood of Islam as an alternative to the prejudice of Christians. And Islam is growing with converts from Christianity among peoples who were once treated inferior by other Christians.

It is beyond the scope of this book to detail how we can remedy this problem in the church. I will only list a few essential things we must do if we are to rid the church of this terrible malady of prejudice.

- We must help people understand the nature of Christian identity, which does not depend on human distinctions. When people realize that they are accepted as significant and useful to the kingdom not because of any merit of their own but only because of the mercy of God, they also realize that they cannot look down on anyone. In what is most important to them, they are undeserving recipients of glorious gifts. Prejudice, then, is an expression of insecurity and feelings of inferiority. If we do not feel secure and accepted in Christ, we need earthly things to make us feel important. One of those earthly things is the idea that we are superior to others. To one who has truly understood grace, such a position is an impossibility.

- We must teach and preach the biblical truths that combat prejudice regularly in our churches. Many so-called Bible-believing churches do not do this. This allows Christians to imbibe sinful attitudes from their environment without being told such attitudes are wrong.

- We must listen to the heart of those on the other side of an issue that divides people. Because this can be a painful exercise, Christians often keep to themselves feelings that deeply affect them. When YFC in Sri

Lanka began to work with the poor, we found that the first converts sometimes reacted angrily to the injustice that existed in society and in the church. Once they became Christians and realized their equality in Christ, their anger expressed itself even more forcefully than before, for now they saw the utter sinfulness of many who treated them as inferior. Listening to that anger was helpful to us in understanding a malady that has existed so fiercely in the society and the church in our land.

- We must confront prejudice when it appears in church and society and condemn it with holy zeal, as Paul did when Peter gave in to prejudice in Antioch (Gal. 2:11-13). This can be difficult, for vested interests are often touched in such situations. It also can earn us the reputation of being traitors to our own people.
- We must stand up for and pay the price of helping people of the "other" group. This too can be costly in terms of reputation and convenience. But it helps heal wounds within people who have been hurt. A Christian friend of the opposite race to mine in the conflict in Sri Lanka once told me that because Christians of my race had paid a great price to help him when he was hurt through the ethnic crisis, it is impossible for him to condone the destructive attitudes of violence and animosity that so many of his race have.
- The next key—an attitude of repentance—appears in our passage, so we will examine it with greater depth.

An attitude of repentance. An attitude of repentance on the part of leaders will help heal relationships broken through prejudice and open a door for ministry for the repentant leader. David Gooding observes, "So very often it is the man who admits that he himself had to be corrected and to change his views who makes the most readily acceptable teacher of others."[38] The process of going through the turmoil of repenting of past attitudes helps create a sensitivity that is a key to identifying with others. I have found that upper-class people who have been most effective in ministry among the poor are those who have repented of their attitudes of class superiority. By contrast, those who say they are not prejudiced are often the most prejudiced and bigoted. We will struggle with prejudice all our lives. But if we let God's Spirit rebuke us of our wrong attitudes, we will have effective ministries among those who are different from us.

One of the things that public confession of prejudice or error does is to reduce destructive anger in people who have been discriminated against.

---

38. Gooding, *True to the Faith,* 178.

They respond to this confession with a sense that at least this person knows how they feel. In the ethnic crisis in our land one of the most frequently leveled accusations from both sides has been: "You just don't understand what we go through." We had a terrible riot in 1983, where many people of the Tamil race were badly harmed by Sinhalese rioters. The Sinhalese Anglican Bishop Lakshman Wickremasinghe was in England for a heart operation at the time. In his first sermon after his return to Sri Lanka, he used the words, "We have killed. ..." Even though he was not in the country at the time of the riot, he took responsibility for the members of his race. Needless to say, this bishop had a credibility with the Tamils that made him into an powerful instrument of peace.

We know it is not easy for leaders to retract publicly certain positions that they have advocated. Yet they must constantly be open to this personal humiliation that may be needed in order that the gospel can move forward. Our commitment to truth will help us persevere in making such drastic changes in our positions. Toward the end of his life the great theologian Augustine wrote a book entitled *Retractions*, in which he retracted things he had written earlier about which he had changed his mind.[39]

In a conflict situation often we can cause hurt without ever intending to do so. A wrong word slips out of our mouth to which a connotation is assigned that we never intended. While we never intended to hurt, the fact is that our words did hurt. And if we have hurt someone, we can apologize unreservedly without sticking to our position that we have been misinterpreted. Those who do this and refuse to apologize increase division without being agents of healing.

When Christians understand their status in Christ, it is not difficult for them to apologize. Their identity does not depend on their performance but on the acceptance they receive from Christ. Sin can hinder that acceptance. Therefore if they think that they have sinned, they will be eager to apologize, so as to ensure that they have their identity and security in Christ intact.

Grappling with things we are uncomfortable with. Unlike Peter, our stubborn hearts can close our minds and refuse to listen to God's promptings toward change. Making these changes is often difficult. On one occasion a radical change of philosophy was thrust upon us out of necessity in a certain area where the YFC ministry that I was leading was involved. I strongly opposed those changes, but we could find no other way out of our dilemma. I became ill as I grappled in my mind about this. I wrote my letter of resignation several times but never turned it in. But as I prayed about the issue, I

---

39. See David Bentley-Taylor, *Augustine: Wayward Genius* (Grand Rapids: Baker, and London: Hodder and Stoughton, 1980), 212.

was forced to accept that the thing I was resisting was a move of God. I had to release my will to God, at first rather reluctantly. As I look back now, I see those new moves as exciting ventures to which God has guided us.

Peter's openness to change was fueled by his being willing to do things he was uncomfortable with, such as living in the home of a tanner. There is a lot of talk about being on the cutting edge today. But for Christians cutting-edge ministry comes as a result of cutting-edge identification. Some great Christian advances are made not in the strategy meetings of our air-conditioned boardrooms but in the difficult and uncomfortable situations to which love for people takes us.

The place of prayer. Prayer gets us in tune with God and therefore receptive to his leading. At such times, God can speak to us. He may speak through a strong impression that comes into the mind while we are at prayer. He may speak through a message given in a prophecy-type utterance.[40] He may guide a leader of a group after a prayer time to say something that opens the door to something unusual. For example, Samuel Mills (1783–1818) led his four fellow students at Williams College, Massachusetts, during the now famous haystack prayer meeting and propelled North American Protestants into foreign missions.[41] In other words, prayer is a key to Christian planning methodology.

We should be warned that when we are seeking to discern God's will on an issue, we must never substitute dependence on direct communications from God for serious study of Scripture and of existing situations. Often God does not communicate his will to us directly because he wants us to grapple with the situation and with what the Scriptures say about it. This grappling can be an enriching experience that contributes to our growth to maturity. It helps give us a Christian worldview and develops what Harry Blamires calls "a Christian mind."[42] On such occasions there is a greater likelihood that the lessons learned will go deep into our minds, as they did here in Peter's mind.

It is significant that Peter went to pray at noon (v. 9). Though there are instances of devout people praying at this time (Ps. 55:17), it was not one of the prescribed times of prayer for the Jews. Peter was obviously a person of prayer, who looked for suitable times and places (like the rooftop) to pray. In our day when research and expert advice seem to be the keys to strategic

---

40. For a discussion of ways God speaks to us today, see Joyce Huggett, *Listening to God* (London: Hodder and Stoughton, 1986).

41. See David M. Howard, *Student Power in World Evangelism* (Downers Grove, Ill.: Inter-Varsity, 1970), 65–72 (see comments on this in the discussion of Acts 13:1–3).

42. Harry Blamires, *The Christian Mind* (London: S.P.C.K., 1963; Ann Arbor, Mich.: Servant, 1978).

planning, we must not forget that more primary is the key of leaders who know what it is to be silent before God. I have traveled with leaders who are so out of touch with the discipline of lingering in the presence of God that, even when they have the time in their travels, they find it difficult to stop and pray. Their workaholism has made them lose their thirst for prayer. Such people must not be permitted to be leaders of God's people.

The blessings of evangelistic hospitality. When non-Christians see Christians at close quarters through either the giving or the receiving of hospitality, they can observe things about Christians that they would not be able to see in any other way, and their false concepts will be corrected. Such hospitality also opens doors for informal opportunities of verbal witness. Along the way they may become attracted to the gospel. Thus, this type of hospitality is a valid way of evangelistic witness.

Some years ago we had staying in our home a Buddhist mother and her young daughter from a village where we had been ministering. The evangelists, realizing that the girl had what seemed like a serious heart condition, recommended that they take her to the capital city, Colombo, for treatment. The two of them stayed in our home for about two weeks, during which time tests were done and a decision was made to operate on her. A few nights before the young girl left for the hospital, she had a dream in which Jesus met her and told her not to worry because he would look after her. That morning she told her mother that she would like to become a Christian. The operation was successful, and a few months later I was at the service where both the mother and daughter were baptized.

On another occasion we had a young Hindu convert stay in our home with his mother after their home was burned down in riots between our race and theirs. She stayed with us for six months, but before she left she too was baptized as a Christian. Of course, not all such contacts become Christians. We have many Hindu neighbors for whose salvation we have yearned many years. One night during the same riots just mentioned, my wife kept about thirty of these Hindu women and children in our home while gangs from my race were attacking their race (I was ministering in Pakistan at that time). They were grateful for our expression of solidarity with them. But despite our efforts at witness, none of them has become Christian. Yet that will not influence our decision to have them again and again if the need arises.[43]

Of course there is inconvenience when people of different cultures come and stay in our homes. For this reason it is important that the decision to have them over becomes a family decision rather than one that is thrust upon the

---

43. Since originally writing this, I have found out that a couple belonging to this group has been wonderfully converted after leaving our neighborhood.

family by the father or mother. But I believe that the enrichment it brings outweighs the inconvenience.

Doors can also be opened for evangelistic witness when we live in homes of non-Christians, especially if these people are so despised by others that we would not be expected to stay with them. This was the case with Peter's staying in the home of Cornelius. The Maltose people are a mountain tribe in India that has had such a high mortality rate that they were expected to become extinct by 2025. They almost never bathe since they have no access to water. Consequently, the rest of society rejects them. People will not go near them because of the smell they emit. Missionaries from the Friends Missionary Prayer Band began a work among this tribe. They not only visited their villages, they even lived in their homes beside them.

By 1996, about 34,000 of the 85,000 people in this tribe had become Christians, and with the consequent change in lifestyle, there has been a significant drop in the mortality rate. The missionaries have paid a great price to reap this harvest. Four of them have died of the diseases that have been killing the Maltose: malaria, tuberculosis, and kalaarzar. One of them was the young son of Patrick Joshua, the leader of this mission. He had received his master's degree in social work and went to live among these people to help with their social reconstruction. After his death three other young people went in his place—a costly but precious harvest indeed, which included identification through the receiving of hospitality.

Evangelistic hospitality can also take place by inviting friends to our homes for meals or meetings. In recent years this method of evangelism has been effectively used by many churches through what they call cell groups or house churches.[44]

---

44. For practical guidelines on how to conduct such meetings, see John Chapman, *Dialogue Evangelism* (Sydney: Anglican Information Office, 1993).

Acts 10:34–11:18

THEN PETER BEGAN to speak: "I now realize how true it is that God does not show favoritism ³⁵but accepts men from every nation who fear him and do what is right. ³⁶You know the message God sent to the people of Israel, telling the good news of peace through Jesus Christ, who is Lord of all. ³⁷You know what has happened throughout Judea, beginning in Galilee after the baptism that John preached—³⁸how God anointed Jesus of Nazareth with the Holy Spirit and power, and how he went around doing good and healing all who were under the power of the devil, because God was with him.

³⁹"We are witnesses of everything he did in the country of the Jews and in Jerusalem. They killed him by hanging him on a tree, ⁴⁰but God raised him from the dead on the third day and caused him to be seen. ⁴¹He was not seen by all the people, but by witnesses whom God had already chosen—by us who ate and drank with him after he rose from the dead. ⁴²He commanded us to preach to the people and to testify that he is the one whom God appointed as judge of the living and the dead. ⁴³All the prophets testify about him that everyone who believes in him receives forgiveness of sins through his name."

⁴⁴While Peter was still speaking these words, the Holy Spirit came on all who heard the message. ⁴⁵The circumcised believers who had come with Peter were astonished that the gift of the Holy Spirit had been poured out even on the Gentiles. ⁴⁶For they heard them speaking in tongues and praising God.

Then Peter said, ⁴⁷"Can anyone keep these people from being baptized with water? They have received the Holy Spirit just as we have." ⁴⁸So he ordered that they be baptized in the name of Jesus Christ. Then they asked Peter to stay with them for a few days.

¹¹:¹The apostles and the brothers throughout Judea heard that the Gentiles also had received the word of God. ²So when Peter went up to Jerusalem, the circumcised believers criticized him ³and said, "You went into the house of uncircumcised men and ate with them."

⁴Peter began and explained everything to them precisely as it had happened: ⁵"I was in the city of Joppa praying, and in a

trance I saw a vision. I saw something like a large sheet being let down from heaven by its four corners, and it came down to where I was. ⁶I looked into it and saw four-footed animals of the earth, wild beasts, reptiles, and birds of the air. ⁷Then I heard a voice telling me, 'Get up, Peter. Kill and eat.'

⁸"I replied, 'Surely not, Lord! Nothing impure or unclean has ever entered my mouth.'

⁹"The voice spoke from heaven a second time, 'Do not call anything impure that God has made clean.' ¹⁰This happened three times, and then it was all pulled up to heaven again.

¹¹"Right then three men who had been sent to me from Caesarea stopped at the house where I was staying. ¹²The Spirit told me to have no hesitation about going with them. These six brothers also went with me, and we entered the man's house. ¹³He told us how he had seen an angel appear in his house and say, 'Send to Joppa for Simon who is called Peter. ¹⁴He will bring you a message through which you and all your household will be saved.'

¹⁵"As I began to speak, the Holy Spirit came on them as he had come on us at the beginning. ¹⁶Then I remembered what the Lord had said: 'John baptized with water, but you will be baptized with the Holy Spirit.' ¹⁷So if God gave them the same gift as he gave us, who believed in the Lord Jesus Christ, who was I to think that I could oppose God?"

¹⁸When they heard this, they had no further objections and praised God, saying, "So then, God has granted even the Gentiles repentance unto life."

IN THE PREVIOUS section we looked at the first four sections of the narrative surrounding the conversion of Cornelius and his family and friends. This passage gives us the last three scenes—Peter's speech to the group, the people's receiving the Holy Spirit and baptism, and Peter's defense of his actions in Caesarea before the authorities in Jerusalem.

Scene Five: Peter's Speech (10:34–43)

PETER'S SPEECH IS typical of evangelistic messages of Acts. Each speech is unique and relevant to the audience, but certain features are common to all of them. The audience in Cornelius's house consists of a unique type of Gentile in that they were God-fearers, who were familiar with the Jewish

Scriptures. Thus, for example, Peter was able to refer to the Jewish prophets (10:43). Paul did not do this either in Lystra and in Athens; there he began by describing who God is.

Verse 34 begins with words that literally mean, "And opening his mouth . . ." (NASB). This phrase is sometimes used to introduce a weighty utterance (cf. 8:35; Matt. 5:2)[1] and is appropriate here since Peter will announce the great discovery that he has made. Peter's first phrase (lit., "upon the truth") implies his surprise at realizing that "God does not show favoritism but accepts men from every nation who fear him and do what is right" (Acts 10:34—35). As in the other evangelistic messages in Acts, this introduction is unique and specific to the audience. It expresses a truth already implied by the early prophets, who "insisted that God's choice of Israel was an act of grace, not of partiality, and that it called for a response of obedient service, not of careless complacency."[2]

Jesus had already implied that he was bringing salvation to the Gentiles (John 10:16; 12:32). The Great Commission made taking the gospel to them a command (Matt. 28:19; Mark 16:15; Luke 24:47; Acts 1:8). But it took a special revelation before the full implications of these truths would be understood and practiced. Later Paul expounded on the new Christian attitude towards Gentiles with great clarity and vividness (2 Cor. 5:16; Gal. 3:28; Eph. 2:11—22).

Some scholars hold that Cornelius and his friends were already saved—that this is why they knew the message God sent through Jesus and the events surrounding his ministry (10:36—37).[3] These scholars also point to Peter's not mentioning repentance and conversion in his sermon and claim that the main result of his visit was that these Gentile Christians were baptized with the Spirit. But this interpretation seems unlikely. (1) The angel specifically told Cornelius, "He [Peter] will bring you a message through which you and all your household will be saved" (11:14). (2) The content of Peter's speech is typical of an evangelistic message. (3) The absence of a call to repentance and conversion may be because the message was interrupted by the descent of the Spirit. Or such a call may be implied in the statement made just prior to this descent: "Everyone who believes in him receives forgiveness of sins through his name" (10:43).

Peter introduces his message as containing "good news of peace through Jesus Christ" (10:36)—the "message God sent to the people of Israel." Peace was the content of God's basic promise to the Jews in the Old Testament. But

---

1. Bruce, *Acts: Greek Text*, 260.
2. Bruce, *Acts*, NICNT, 212.
3. Arrington, *Acts*, 112—13.

by describing Jesus as "Lord of all," Peter extends this blessing to Gentiles also. "'Lord of all' . . . was properly a pagan title of deity . . . but it was rebaptized by the early Christians to become an appropriate Christological title (cf. Col. 1:15–20)."[4] "Peace" here is a virtual synonym for salvation (Luke 1:79; 2:14; Eph. 2:17; 6:15); it "denotes not merely the absence of strife and enmity between man and God but also the positive benefits that develop in a state of reconciliation."[5]

Peter's speech here is the only evangelistic message in Acts where a summary of the ministry of Jesus is given (10:37–39a). At Pentecost Peter briefly mentioned that Jesus' miracles were God's accreditation of Christ (2:22). Here the ministry of Jesus is given in a more narrative style, as the opening comment suggests: "You know what has happened throughout Judea, beginning in Galilee after the baptism that John preached" (10:37). When we remember that Luke is probably recording a summary of the speech, we can assume that "in its actual delivery it would be amplified by the inclusion of examples of Jesus' works of mercy and power."[6]

In verse 38 Peter clearly attempts to show his audience that Jesus' ministry was accredited by God. It begins with "how God anointed Jesus of Nazareth with the Holy Spirit and power," and ends with "because God was with him." In between are the words, "and how he went around doing good and healing all who were under the power of the devil." These words remind one of Isaiah 61:1, which Luke cites Jesus as quoting when he began his ministry (Luke 4:14–22). Peter's point is that the life and miracles of Jesus demonstrate that Jesus was God's special messenger. Jesus himself had said, "But if I drive out demons by the Spirit of God, then the kingdom of God has come upon you" (Matt. 12:28). As in Luke's Gospel (Luke 4:18–19), the good deeds and miracles of Jesus are associated with his anointing by the Holy Spirit. This probably refers to what happened when the dove descended on Jesus at his baptism (3:22).[7]

After pointing out that the apostles were witnesses to what happened in the ministry of Christ (10:39a), Peter presents the death and resurrection of Jesus (10:39b–40). That death is described in typical fashion. Peter implicates the opponents of Christ and implies the curse of hanging on a tree: "They killed him by hanging him on a tree" (10:39). As in the other speeches, Peter stresses that God raised Jesus up.

---

4. Longenecker, "Acts," 393.

5. Marshall, *Acts*, 191.

6. Bruce, *Acts*, NICNT, 214.

7. Note that Christ or Messiah means "anointed one." On the significance of the anointing and use of Isa. 61:1 for the ministry of Jesus, see I. Howard Marshall, *The Gospel of Luke*, NIGTC (Grand Rapids: Eerdmans, 1978), 183.

Then the apostle goes on to explain the important place of a select band of witnesses to the resurrection. "He was not seen by all the people, but by witnesses whom God had already chosen—by us who ate and drank with him after he rose from the dead" (10:41). He had already talked about witnesses to the ministry of Christ (10:39a). Now Peter makes the point that the risen Christ was seen only by specially chosen witnesses. These witnesses were crucial to the future of Christianity and thus had to be chosen carefully. The behavior of the people in Jerusalem during the time of Christ's passion showed that they were not suitable for such a high privilege. Lenski says: "People, who in spite of all that they had seen and heard of Jesus had, nevertheless, refused to have faith in him, were unfit to be witnesses of his resurrection, and an appearance of Jesus to them would have increased their disbelief that much."[8]

A unique feature of Peter's sermon is the point that Jesus even ate and drank with the apostles after his resurrection (10:41). Luke's Gospel is the only one that records this fact (Luke 24:41–43), and to Luke it must have been one of the "many convincing proofs that he was alive" (Acts 1:3). "This emphasis would have been particularly important in preaching to Gentiles like Cornelius for whom the idea of a bodily resurrection was a new concept (cf. 17:18)."[9] It was valuable evidence for Jews too, "since in Jewish thinking angels and apparitions are unable to eat and drink, being without digestive tracts."[10]

Though many modern scholars would like to discount the historicity of such events, the evangelists of the early church thought it was important to give evidence for the fact that these events really happened. As in the speeches in Acts 2–3, Peter uses arguments to demonstrate the validity of the Christian gospel (cf. also the speeches of Paul and Stephen). As we pointed out in our study of Acts 3, the New Testament evangelists were both heralds of the good news and apologists. Many of them were also people through whom miracles were performed. So they were not specialists who concentrated only on one form of ministry.

Next Peter speaks of the commission the apostles received to proclaim Christ. Christ's command to them was "to preach to the people and to testify that he is . . . judge" (10:42). Two important words describe the evangelistic task here—"preach" (kerysso) and "testify" (diamartyromai). Kerysso emphasizes the forthright proclamation of the message. "Testify" comes from the context of a witness in a court of law. It carries two ideas: witness and solemnity. Nida and Louw define it as making "a serious declaration on the basis of presumed knowledge."[11] C. K. Barrett points out that because preach

---

8. Lenski, Acts, 426.
9. Polhill, Acts, 262.
10. Longnecker, "Acts," 393.
11. Louw and Nida, 413.

"has no independent object noun or clause to give it content ... it must probably be taken with [testify]."[12] Thus, both words describe the evangelistic task. *Preaching* shows that evangelism is a confident proclamation of important news; *testifying* points to the solemnity of the task—it is a matter of judgment and salvation—and to the fact that this is something that we have experienced and know to be true.

Here, as with Paul in Athens (17:31), Peter presents Jesus "as judge of the living and the dead" (10:42). Judgment is an essential part of the evangelistic message. It is an aspect of the Great Commission, even though it does not appear in the standard statements of the Commission in the four Gospels and Acts. This suggests that what we have in the New Testament is only a sampling of the comprehensive teaching about evangelism that Jesus gave after his resurrection.

In verse 43 Peter gives the scriptural authentication of the person and work of Christ: "All the prophets testify about him that everyone who believes in him receives forgiveness of sins through his name." This statement implies that Peter's audience will receive the forgiveness of sins if they respond by believing in Jesus. Unlike in his previous messages (2:16, 25–31, 34–35; 3:18, 21–26), Peter cannot elaborate on this element because the Holy Spirit falls on the people, which cuts short his message (10:44). That Peter had more to say is implied by his comment to the Jerusalem church: "As I began to speak, the Holy Spirit came on them" (11:15).

Scene Six: Gentiles Receive the Holy Spirit (10:44–48)

NOWHERE ELSE IN Acts does the Spirit come before baptism.[13] Later Peter explained to the Christians in Jerusalem that the way the Holy Spirit came on these people was "as he had come on us at the beginning" (11:15). It was accompanied by "speaking in tongues and praising God" (10:46). In spite of all the leading that God had given up to this point, Jewish believers are astonished that these Gentiles have received the Holy Spirit (10:45). With such unmistakable evidence that these Gentiles have indeed been converted, Peter does not hesitate to baptize them immediately (10:47–48). The specific reason he gives is clear: "They have received the Holy Spirit just as we have" (10:47). This was an argument from experience. Peter's point is: "They are having an experience just like the one we had, which we know was from God. So this too must be from God." The earlier specific guidance that Peter received must also have been significant in his coming to that conclusion. But those were experiential

---

12. Barrett, *Acts*, 527.

13. Beverly Roberts Gaventa, *From Darkness to Light: Aspects of Conversion in the New Testament* (Philadelphia: Fortress, 1986), 119.

too. This points to the role that experience plays in discerning God's ways. As we will see, it is not the only criterion for deciding what is true, but it is one contributing factor in the decision-making process.

With his scruples about table fellowship with Gentiles overcome, Peter seems to have accepted Cornelius's invitation for him to stay a few days (10:48). This gives time for the news of what Peter has done to travel to Jerusalem before he arrives there. The consternation of the Christians there must have been immense because not only had their leader baptized Gentiles, he was also having continuous table fellowship with them. The table fellowship, which is what Peter's critics objected to (11:3), indicated in a powerful way that Cornelius and company were indeed accepted into the Christian community.

Scene Seven: The Jewish Christians Approve (11:1–18)

A REVOLUTIONARY THING had happened in the life of the church, and the news about it spread through the church in Judea (11:1). When Peter arrived in Jerusalem, "those of the circumcision" (lit.) criticized him.[14] Luke is probably referring to the group within the church who required circumcision of all Gentile believers.[15] The only objection mentioned is that they "went into the house of uncircumcised men and ate with them" (11:3). It shows how important the issue of table fellowship was to Jews.

In response to the criticism Peter "explained everything to them precisely as it had happened" (11:4). Luke's report is an extended summary of chapter 10. This repetition "is an indication of the importance Luke attached to that story."[16] We will not go into Peter's speech here except to point out two elements. (1) The apostle stressed that he had with him "six brothers" (11:12), who could confirm everything that he was telling the leaders in Jerusalem.

(2) As Peter concluded his report, he commented that the Holy Spirit came on Cornelius and company "as [he] began to speak" (11:15). This suggests that he was unable to complete his talk. He clarified that the Holy Spirit came on them "as he had come on us at the beginning" (11:15)—that is, as at Pentecost. In verse 16 Peter recalled Jesus' promise of the baptism with the Holy Spirit. Just as this promise had been fulfilled among Jews at Pentecost, now it was being fulfilled among Gentiles. This was indeed a Gentile Pentecost!

With so much evidence of God's work, Peter dared not resist as he had done when he was told to eat unclean flesh in Joppa. He says, "So if God gave them the same gift as he gave us, who believed in the Lord Jesus Christ, who

---

14. Barrett translates it as "those who represented circumcision" (*Acts*, 532).
15. Polhill, *Acts*, 266.
16. Barrett, *Acts*, 533. See also his comment on this on p. 491.

was I to think that I could oppose God?" (11:17). The evidence was too great for further objections. The church then praised God and affirmed a new principle about God's dealings with humankind: "So then, God has granted even the Gentiles repentance unto life" (11:18).

For the moment the circumcision party is silenced. They will emerge again in chapter 15 when they see what large numbers of Gentiles have come into the church. Not everyone has undergone the permanent change of conviction that Peter has. They join in the praise now, but as they see the wider implications of this step, they will rise up again in protest.

"THE CORNELIUS FACTOR." The story of Cornelius is being used in the debate today about whether people can be saved without hearing the gospel. Some argue that Peter's statement in 10:34–35 ("I now realize how true it is that God does not show favoritism but accepts men from every nation who fear him and do what is right") shows that sincere seekers will be saved whether or not they hear the gospel.

This passage has clear features that disqualify it from being used to develop a doctrine of the possibility of those who have not heard the gospel being saved. (1) Though Cornelius was not a Jew in the full sense, he had heard and responded to the Old Testament message so that he is described as a God-fearer, who "prayed to God regularly" (10:2). Thus he is not typical of the people we refer to when we speak of "those who have not heard." Though he was not a Christian and these acts did not merit salvation, God did regard with value his groping for God (see 10:4) and saw an attitude that was close to saving faith. Proof that this was the case is that Cornelius accepted the gospel the moment he heard it from Peter.

(2) Even after he had expressed an attitude that comes close to saving faith, "God's response was not to save Cornelius by fiat, but to show him how he could learn of the appointed way."[17] In fact, the angel told Cornelius that Peter "will bring you a message through which you and all your household *will be saved*" (Acts 11:14). Only after they heard the message would salvation come to that house. Therefore, when Peter said that God "accepts men from every nation who fear him and do what is right," he does not mean that such people are saved because of this attitude. Rather, as Harrison points out, it shows "that they are suitable candidates for salvation.... Such preparation betokens a spiritual earnestness that will result in faith as the gospel is heard and received."[18]

---

17. Harrison, *Acts*, 176.
18. Ibid., 182.

What, then, does Peter mean when he suggests that God accepts right deeds (10:35)? According to some, it refers to acts that believing Gentiles commit *after* salvation; when they are saved, they will do these righteous deeds. This interpretation means that Cornelius will do such acts only after his salvation. But this chapter describes Cornelius's preconversion acts elsewhere (10:2, 4), which makes it likely that these are the acts spoken of in verse 35 as well. To me, the stress is on the attitude out of which these actions emerged—an attitude of fearing God. Cornelius did not think that these acts merited salvation. Rather, he did them out of humble devotion to God. God accepted these righteous deeds, but they did not save the centurion. God mercifully extended the offer of salvation to him through the preaching of the gospel.

From the fact that God revealed the gospel to Cornelius, a sincere seeker after God, we can conclude that he does reveal the truth about salvation to such sincere seekers. It would be perilous to build a doctrine of this nature based on one example. But we know that Jesus said, "Blessed are those who hunger and thirst for righteousness, for they will be filled" (Matt. 5:6). We can infer from this text that an unbeliever who thirsts after righteousness will be shown the way of salvation by God. The only way we know from Scripture that people can be saved is by responding to the gospel, which they have heard in an understandable way. Paul says, "'Everyone who calls on the name of the Lord will be saved.' How, then, can they call on the one they have not believed in? And how can they believe in the one of whom they have not heard? And how can they hear without someone preaching to them?" (Rom. 10:13–14). If God has chosen another way to bring salvation to people, he has not revealed it to us in his Word.

The life of Christ in evangelism. Peter's message is an important model for us in presenting the gospel to devout people who, like Cornelius, may know something about God but are ignorant of the saving gospel of Christ. Many features of this message have already appeared in the other speeches and have been discussed especially in our study of the Pentecost sermon (2:14–43). Of particular interest is Peter's stress on the life of Christ in this sermon (10:36–43).

Many scholars have pointed to the relationship between this speech and the Gospel written by Peter's disciple Mark. Bruce says, "The scope of the *kerygma*, as attested by this address of Peter's, is almost exactly the scope of Mark's Gospel."[19] Bruce gives the following features of similarity: "beginning with John's baptismal ministry, and going on to tell of Jesus' ministry in Galilee,

---

19. Bruce, *Acts*, NICNT, 212. See also Polhill, *Acts*, 261–62; David Williams, *Acts*, 191, 193; and C. H. Dodd, "The Framework of the Gospel Narrative," *Expository Times*, 43 (1932), 396ff., and *The Apostolic Preaching and Its Developments* (New York: Harper & Row, 1964), 46–47.

Judaea and Jerusalem, of his crucifixion and resurrection, followed by the insistence on personal witness and on the coming judgment, with the offer of forgiveness through faith in him here and now."[20] The second-century church father Irenaeus wrote this concerning the second Gospel: "Mark the disciple and interpreter of Peter, also transmitted to us in writing the things preached by Peter."[21] In our study of Peter's message on the day Pentecost (2:14—41), we saw the value of using the life of Christ in evangelism.

The place of witnesses. In this speech (10:39, 41), as in three other speeches (2:32; 3:15; 5:32), Peter testifies that there are witnesses to the events he describes (see also 1:22; 13:31). The testimony of the eyewitnesses was important to the Christians in the first century and is so for all generations. This is because Christianity is based on events surrounding Christ's sojourn on earth. Though we ourselves have not seen the risen Christ with our own eyes, our faith rests on the fact that he did rise from the dead and that a host of reliable witnesses attested this fact.

The place of judgment. Judgment was a key way in which God arrested the careless and disobedient Jews in the Old Testament. It was also an essential part of the message of Jesus, who spoke more about hell than anyone else in the Scriptures. Now we see that it was also a part of the evangelistic message in Acts (10:42). This suggests that it should be part of our message too. Elsewhere I have delved into the place that judgment should have in our preaching.[22] I have shown that Jesus did not speak about judgment primarily to inform people with details about what hell will be like. Rather, he did so to warn people so that they would repent, live righteous lives, and avert punishment.

Peter Toon has listed thirty-one different passages (not counting parallel passages) in the Gospels that contain warnings of hell.[23] The strategy of Jesus can best be described with his words in Mark 8:34—38. First there is a call to deny oneself, take up one's cross, and follow Jesus (8:34). Then Jesus says that those who attempt to save their life by rejecting Christ will end up losing it (8:35). Next he says, "What good is it for a man to gain the whole world, yet forfeit his soul? Or what can a man give in exchange for his soul?" (8:36—37). When he comes in glory, he will be ashamed of those who have been ashamed of him on earth (8:37). His point is that if people do not deny themselves, take up their cross, and follow him, they will be destroyed in the judgment.

---

20. Bruce, *Acts*, NICNT, 212—13.

21. Irenaeus, *Against Heresies*, 3.1.1, in *The Ante-Nicene Fathers* (Edinburgh: T. & T. Clark, and Grand Rapids: Eerdmans, 1996 reprint), 1:414.

22. See my *Crucial Questions About Hell* (Eastbourne: Kingsway Publications, 1991; and Wheaton: Crossway Books, 1994), ch. 12: "Why Should We Talk About Judgment," and ch. 14: "Proclaiming the Message of Judgment."

23. Peter Toon, *Heaven and Hell* (Nashville: Thomas Nelson, 1986), 29—46.

Creativity, criticism, and community. When Peter took the revolutionary step of baptizing those at Cornelius's home, he faced criticism from a segment of the church (11:2–3). This is natural, for those other Christians had not gone through the spiritual pilgrimage of discovery that Peter had before he came to accept Gentiles as full believers. Criticism is something any creative person who leads the church into new areas of obedience and ministry will face.

But when the church criticized Peter, he did not reject the church and go out working alone. Instead, he did everything he could possibly do to gain their approval. This is why he took six Jewish brothers with him (10:23; 11:12). He wanted them to witness what was happening and testify to the church about it. This is also why he "explained everything to them precisely as it had happened" (11:4). He wanted the community to accept what he had done, so that they would be united over this new direction the church was taking. That is what happened, for the members of the church "had no further objections and praised God" (11:18).

From the space Luke gives to the process of Peter's receiving the approval for what he had done, we can see how important these events are. Many facts are repeated. Thus, while this passage teaches that criticism from Christians is inevitable in creative ministry, it also teaches that we should regard the wider community, especially our critics, with utmost seriousness and work hard to win their approval for what we are doing.

THE GOSPEL REVEALED **to seekers after truth.** The history of missions has many examples of people like Cornelius, who, after sincerely seeking for God, have an opportunity to hear and respond to the gospel of Jesus Christ. One day in the early part of this century, a chief in Malaysia was repairing one of his wooden idols when he told his wife, "This is foolish. Here we are worshiping these wooden objects, but our hands are greater than they are. Surely there must be a higher Being, the God who created all of us. Let us worship him." So for twenty-five years they went into their prayer room every day and prayed to "the unknown God." One day a Christian missionary came along and introduced the chief and his wife to the Bible and to Christ. When they heard the good news, they rejoiced and said, "This is the true God we have been seeking all these years. We now believe in him."[24] This couple had responded to the light they

---

24. Reported in John T. Seamands, *Daybreak: Daily Devotions from Acts and the Pauline Epistles* (Wilmore Ky.: privately published, 1993), Feb. 16.

received through creation (see Rom. 1:19–20) and began a search that resulted in their hearing and accepting the gospel.[25]

We must also keep in mind the teaching of Paul that "there is no one who understands, no one who seeks God" (Rom. 3:11). In their natural state people are incapable of seeking after God, because of the heart of rebellion that sin has produced. To this is added the fact that "the god of this age has blinded the minds of unbelievers, so that they cannot see the light of the gospel of the glory of Christ, who is the image of God" (2 Cor. 4:4). Those who do seek after God, then, do not do so entirely by their own efforts but by the enlightening of their minds and the energizing of their wills by the Holy Spirit.

This activity has been described differently by different theological traditions. Even the Wesleyan tradition, where there is a greater emphasis on the human involvement in the process of salvation than in the Calvinistic tradition, has the doctrine of prevenient grace. Thomas Oden describes prevenient grace as "the grace that begins to enable one to choose further to cooperate with saving grace." He goes on to say that "by offering the will the restored capacity to respond to grace, the person then may freely and increasingly become an active, willing participant in receiving the conditions for justification."[26]

Proclaiming judgment today. That the message of judgment is not popular today is well known. It seems out of step with contemporary thought.[27] As theologian Donald Bloesch has said, "If anything has disappeared from modern thought, it is the belief in a supernatural heaven and hell."[28] This is the age of pluralism, which seeks to unite people of differing viewpoints.

But the message of judgment speaks of an irreversible division of people. Reincarnation is becoming more and more popular today, even in the West. It presents the opposite of the message of judgment—that people can keep improving through a series of births rather than have to account after death for what they have done with their lives. The memory of hellfire-and-damnation preachers who abused the doctrine of judgment may cause many to be cautious about bringing up the topic today. Moreover, the emphasis on human potential directly clashes with the idea that if we try to save ourselves

---

25. On the topic of those who have not heard, see the study on 4:1–22; see also my *The Christian's Attitude Towards World Religions* (Wheaton: Tyndale, 1987), pp. 119–46; William Crockett and James Sigountos, eds., *Through No Fault of Their Own: The Fate of Those Who Have Never Heard* (Grand Rapids: Baker, 1991).

26. Thomas C. Oden, *John Wesley's Scriptural Christianity* (Grand Rapids: Zondervan, 1994), 243.

27. What follows is a summary of some points in chapter 1, "The Decline of Hell," in my book *Crucial Questions About Hell.*

28. Donald Bloesch, *Evangelical Theology* (San Francisco: Harper & Row, 1978), 2:211.

by our efforts, we are headed for judgment. Besides, it simply does not feel good to talk about such "uncivil" topics as hell today.

In this environment of hostility to the idea of judgment, we are called to be faithful to the biblical message, which includes judgment. Yet we must remember that the sense that sin should be punished is present in all people. This is why even those who care little for morality, when confronted by a disgusting act like the sexual abuse of a minor, will exclaim, "That deserves to be punished." Our task is to resurface this sense in people that sin deserves punishment and to present Christ as the answer to that dilemma. I do not think the answer is to preach a whole series of sermons on hell. Rather, it is to include the aspect of judgment as one among many points as we argue for the validity of the gospel, just as Peter did here and Paul did in Athens.[29]

The portrayal of Christ as the supreme judge of all humanity counters a common misconception of Christ as a gentle and weak person, one who fails to win the respect of those in our generation who like to present themselves as being strong, self-sufficient people. They think of Jesus as being a crutch for weak people needing comfort and regard him as being of no use to them. What if we present him as the supreme Lord of all people, the weak and the strong, to whom all humanity will have to give an account at the end of time? The wise will heed such a warning and consider carefully the claims of Christ.

Creativity, criticism, and community. All who bring pioneering-type changes in the church—for that matter in any sphere of life—usually face criticism.

- When styles of music we are unfamiliar with are presented in church, many protest, saying it is irreverent, without really trying hard to understand why the changes have been made. We showed earlier how this happened when Handel's *Messiah* was first perfomed in England.[30]
- William Booth, founder of the Salvation Army, broke new ground for the church by going out to the poor, the alcoholics, and others considered undesirables in society. But respected and devout leaders of the church criticized him. Even the great evangelical politician the Earl of Shaftesbury, who was himself a champion of the rights of the poor, once announced that after much study he was convinced that the Salvation Army was clearly the Antichrist. Someone else even added that

---

29. For a full discussion on proclaiming judgment today see chapter 14, "Proclaiming the Message of Judgment," in *Crucial Questions About Hell.*

30. See the study of 6:8–7:53.

in his own studies, he learned that the "number" of William Booth's name added up to 666![31]

- When missionaries like E. Stanley Jones in India expressed solidarity with the Indian struggle for independence from Britain, evangelicals accused them of liberalism.
- Many immediately branded the Pentecostal revival as demonic because it did not square with their understanding of the place of some gifts of the Spirit in this dispensation.

Peter's actions show how important it is to take pains to get body approval for the directions we are moving in. How often we try to sidestep this difficult process. Many evangelicals who try out previously untried applications of biblical social concern are accused of espousing a social gospel and turning theologically liberal. Unfortunately, some end up theologically liberal because it is the liberals who welcome their new ideas. This is partly because they do not try hard to contend for their viewpoint with other evangelical leaders. It seems easier and more efficient to fulfill their vision alone or through a group that is more sympathetic to it. Prolonged fellowship with "liberals" and alienation from evangelicals, however, can easily lead us to jettison our evangelical convictions.

Making a serious effort to convince the church of a new position takes hard work and sometimes comes only after a long and tiring struggle. Modern day pragmatism, which does not have much place for commitment to long-lasting relationships, does not have patience for such a long struggle. They feel their agenda does not allow such a "waste of time." Thus, they simply leave the group and join a new one.

Given the individualism of our age, people place less emphasis on community ministry today. We are often too impatient to involve the Christian community in our ventures. We find it too time consuming to explain everything to them and to spend hours trying to get their support. Everyone seems to be so busy, and there are so many things to get done in the short time available to us. As a result, we have evolved a structure taken more from the secular business model, where leaders are put at the top of the organizational chart and are given the freedom to lead creatively, using others as consultants, but not having to submit to the rest of the body in spiritual accountability for their actions. People have got used to this structure, and they usually do not question a leader unless some serious problem emerges. If they do not like the

---

31. Bramwell Booth, *Echoes and Memories* (New York: George H. Doran, 1925), 27; cited in Warren W. Wiersbe and Lloyd M. Perry, *The Wycliffe Handbook of Preaching and Preachers* (Chicago: The Moody Press, 1984), 185.

leader's philosophy, they can simply go somewhere else. In Acts, by contrast, we find the church grappling with issues until they reached agreement.

The community orientation of the church in Acts, then, provides a huge challenge to the church in the twenty-first century.[32] The individualism of the society in which we live has influenced our thinking so much that we have jettisoned some of the principles of community solidarity seen in Acts. It may be possible to get quicker positive results from the individualistic method of ministry. But whether such success is success in God's sight is another matter. God's way of doing ministry is surely the way that involves the rest of the body to which we belong. And we must learn to do our work in God's way, however inefficient it may initially seem.

---

32. See also our discussions on 4:32–35; 15:25.

Acts 11:19–30

NOW THOSE WHO had been scattered by the persecution in connection with Stephen traveled as far as
Phoenicia, Cyprus and Antioch, telling the message
only to Jews. ²⁰Some of them, however, men from Cyprus and
Cyrene, went to Antioch and began to speak to Greeks also,
telling them the good news about the Lord Jesus. ²¹The Lord's
hand was with them, and a great number of people believed
and turned to the Lord.

²²News of this reached the ears of the church at Jerusalem,
and they sent Barnabas to Antioch. ²³When he arrived and
saw the evidence of the grace of God, he was glad and
encouraged them all to remain true to the Lord with all their
hearts. ²⁴He was a good man, full of the Holy Spirit and faith,
and a great number of people were brought to the Lord.

²⁵Then Barnabas went to Tarsus to look for Saul, ²⁶and
when he found him, he brought him to Antioch. So for a
whole year Barnabas and Saul met with the church and taught
great numbers of people. The disciples were called Christians
first at Antioch.

²⁷During this time some prophets came down from
Jerusalem to Antioch. ²⁸One of them, named Agabus, stood
up and through the Spirit predicted that a severe famine
would spread over the entire Roman world. (This happened
during the reign of Claudius.) ²⁹The disciples, each according
to his ability, decided to provide help for the brothers living in
Judea. ³⁰This they did, sending their gift to the elders by Barnabas and Saul.

THE OPENING WORDS of this section take us back
to 8:4, which has a similar opening. This suggests
that Luke is recording another new beginning,
parallel to what happened with the ministries of
Philip and Peter recorded in 8:4–11:18. Luke is reminding us that the scattering by the persecution in connection with Stephen was indeed the scattering of the seed of the gospel in God's plan.[1]

---

1. See comments on 8:4.

Gentiles Converted in Antioch (11:19–21)

THOSE WHO WENT to Phoenicia, Cyprus and Antioch shared the message with Jews only, but some from Cyprus and Cyrene shared the gospel in Antioch with Greeks[2] as well (v. 20). While Luke tells us where these daring spirits who took the lead in this great step forward in the life of the church hailed from, we do not know their names—possibly because there were no famous leaders among them and no one stood out as prominent.

Antioch in North Syria by the Orontes River was the largest of sixteen cities in the eastern Mediterranean bearing that name. They were so named because many kings of the Seleucid dynasty (who ruled the eastern part of Alexander the Great's empire after his death) bore the name Antiochus. With an estimated population of about 300,000[3] Antioch in Syria was the third largest city in the Roman empire, surpassed in population only by Rome and Alexandria. It was also the seat of administration of the Roman province of Syria. A large Jewish population lived there, estimates of which range from 22,000 to 65,000.[4]

Antioch had lax morals, especially owing to cult prostitution at a shrine in Daphne, five miles south of the city. Because it was an international commercial center, it was a cosmopolitan city. People were accustomed to innovations there. "They had their rough corners rubbed smooth, and traditional attitudes which were taken so seriously in a place like Jerusalem did not matter much."[5] According to Josephus, a large number of proselytes lived there.[6] In fact, one of the seven men chosen to serve tables in Jerusalem was Nicolas, a proselyte from Antioch (6:5). It was, then, an ideal place to be "the real birthplace of Gentile Christianity."[7] It remained an important center of Christianity for many centuries. It is now a part of Turkey and is called Antakya, with a relatively small population of about 40,000.

Encouragement from Barnabas (11:22–26)

THE PROBLEM WITH unknown people doing significant things is that they lack credentials for others to accept the validity of what they are doing. Therefore, a known and respected person was sent by the Jerusalem church

---

2. There is some question as to whether the original is *hellēnas*, which translates "Greeks" (as in NIV), or *hellēnistas* (as in the UBS4 text), which would read "Grecian Jews." For a discussion on why we choose Greeks here, see Longenecker, "Acts," 400–401.

3. J. McRay, "Antioch of the Orontes," *DPL*, 23.

4. Ibid.

5. Bruce, *Steps*, 21.

6. Josephus, *Wars of the Jews*, 7.3.3 (*Complete Works*, 591).

7. Bruce, *Steps*, 23.

to check out what was happening (v. 22). They made a wise choice in Barnabas, for he had distinguished himself as an encourager (4:36) and was known for his godliness (11:24). Moreover, he was a Jew from Cyprus, like some of those who had preached to Gentiles in Antioch. He would have a broader perspective than those who had never been abroad. It may be that he volunteered his services for this assignment.[8]

Barnabas's first response to seeing the evidence of God's grace in Antioch shows why he was given the name "Encourager." "He was glad and encouraged them all to remain true to the Lord with all their hearts" (v. 23). The word "encouraged" (*parakaleo*) should take the meaning "exhorted" here. What Barnabas urged was not just perseverance along the Christian way. Barrett translates it literally as "to continue with the Lord in the purpose of their hearts."[9] The discipline required for perseverance comes from a clinging love relationship with the Christ who loved them and gave himself for them.

The NIV unfortunately does not translate the first word of verse 24, *hoti*, meaning "because." That word connects Barnabas's ministry of encouragement (v. 23) to his Christian character as "a good man, full of the Holy Spirit and faith" (v. 24).[10] Paul ranks goodness above righteousness in Romans 5:7: "Very rarely will anyone die for a righteous man, though for a good man someone might possibly dare to die." It is a quality that inspires loyalty and commitment. It can mean generosity (Matt. 20:15), a quality that comes to the fore here with Barnabas's unhesitating acceptance of this new work. Sometimes it refers to good as opposed to bad, as in good fruit versus bad fruit in Matthew 7:17. In the parable of the sower in Luke, the good soil is said to refer to "those with a noble and good heart" (Luke 8:15). To sum up, when Luke uses "good" to describe Barnabas, he is describing someone with true Christian character, a man of integrity and wholesomeness.[11] That goodness was specially mentioned suggests that Barnabas "was outstanding for the Christian quality of his life."[12]

While Barnabas is the only one described as "a good man" in Acts, others, like the Seven (including Stephen), are likewise described as "full of the Holy Spirit" (cf. 6:3, 5). Barnabas was also "full of . . . faith," which probably means faith in God.

---

8. Bruce, *Acts*, NICNT, 226, citing M. Hengel, *Acts and the History of Earliest Christianity*, trans. J. Bowden (London: SCM, 1979), 101–2.

9. Barrett, *Acts*, ICC, 544.

10. Luke used the words "good man" (*aner agathos*) to describe Joseph of Arimathea too (Luke 23:50).

11. Harrison, *Interpreting Acts*, 194.

12. Marshall, *Acts*, 202.

Next follows a typical Lukan statement, that "a large crowd was added to the Lord" (v. 24b; lit. trans.).[13] The coming of the encourager/consolidator did not result in a reduction in evangelistic zeal and effectiveness. Soon, however, Barnabas realized that he needed help to adequately pastor this flock. Thus, he went in search of Saul and brought him back to help in a teaching ministry that went on for a whole year (vv. 25–26). The trip to Tarsus was about a hundred miles—a major undertaking.[14] About ten years must have elapsed[15] since Saul had left Jerusalem and gone to Tarsus (9:30). He himself says that he was in Syria and Cilicia (whose principal city was Tarsus) during this time (Gal. 1:21). There is every reason to believe, especially considering his comments in Galatians 1, that he was evangelizing during this time.[16]

Another reason why Antioch has a special place in the history of Christianity is that here "the disciples were called Christians first" (v. 26), a name that has prevailed. This was probably a name given by the Antiochene population; Christians used it of themselves beginning only in the second century.[17] In New Testament times, they preferred to use words like "disciples," "saints," and "brothers." In the New Testament only non-Christians (like Agrippa, 26:28, and the persecutors of Christians, 1 Peter 4:16) use the term. The Gentiles must have heard the believers speak so often of Christ that they supplied a suffix to the word "Christ"—thus, "Christians" (meaning "the Christ people"). The Jews would not have given them this name, since "Christ" is the Greek word for the title "Messiah," and the Jews did not accept Jesus as the Messiah.

A Gift to Jerusalem (11:27–30)

THE MESSAGE BROUGHT by the group from Jerusalem involved the use of prophecy, a gift that has a fairly prominent place in Acts[18] and Paul's letters. Prophecies took the form of understandable messages in the speaker's ordinary language (unlike tongues) given under the direct inspiration of God, that is, by the revelation of the Spirit. Often, as here, prophecy involved prediction of future events. Paul considered it to have high value (1 Cor. 12:28; 14:5, 24–25; Eph. 4:11), even something to be desired (1 Cor. 14:1, 39), for prophecies contained messages from God that edified Christians (1 Cor. 14:3). Agabus used this gift twice to predict future events (Acts 11:27–28; 21:10–11).

---

13. On the significance of numbers in church growth see comments on 4:4.
14. Keener, *BBC*, 354.
15. Bruce, *Paul*, 127.
16. See Bruce, *Paul*, 126–28; idem, *Acts*, NICNT, 227, n. 30.
17. Bruce, *Acts: Greek Text*, 274.
18. See Acts 2:17–18; 11:27–28; 13:1; 19:6; 21:9, 10–11.

Luke's comment that the famine "happened during the reign of Claudius" (v. 28), who reigned in A.D. 41–54, helps us place this visit of Paul and Barnabas at around A.D. 46, during which time, according to Josephus, there was a severe famine in Judea.[19] Scholars debate whether this visit of Paul to Jerusalem harmonizes with the one referred to in Galatians 2:1–10 as Paul's second post-conversion visit to Jerusalem "fourteen years later." The problem is that the first visit should be dated around A.D. 35; if the second visit was fourteen years later, it would be around A.D. 49, which would identify it with the Council of Jerusalem. We can harmonize the A.D. 46 date with the Galatians account only if we take the fourteen years Paul refers to as being fourteen years after his conversion (dated c. A.D. 33). He says he "went in response to a revelation" (Gal. 2:2), which would then be the prophecy of Agabus.[20]

That this young church gave a gift to the "mother" church in Jerusalem shows how the missionary spirit had caught on so soon in a church that would be the mother church of Gentile missions (vv. 29–30). What a quick reversal of missionary roles! The mother church in Jerusalem sends the gospel, and the daughter church in Antioch sends money to the mother church.

IN THIS PASSAGE Luke reports for us another significant step in the progress of the gospel to the ends of the earth. As he does so, he lets us observe some keys to vibrant community life that enabled the church to flourish. This is seen in the way the group of unnamed pioneers shared their faith in places to which they were scattered (vv. 19–21), in the way the church in Jerusalem reacted to the news of what was happening in Antioch (v. 22), in the way Barnabas acted in Antioch (vv. 23–26), and in the way the church in Antioch responded to the prophecy about a coming famine (vv. 27–29). These are important examples for us to follow. In keeping with our conviction that Acts gives us inspiring examples that we can follow,[21] we will look at this passage as an example of how God works through vibrant community life.

Unnamed pioneers. The first thing that strikes us is that we are not given the names of those who took the church forward to what Barclay calls "one

---

19. Josephus, *Antiquities*, 3.15.3; 20.2.5 (*Complete Works*, 84; 416).

20. This way we do not need to identify the second visit spoken of in Gal. 2 with the Jerusalem Council, as many do. For a brief defense of this view see Longenecker, "Acts," 405–6. For a more detailed defense, see F. F. Bruce, *The Epistle to the Galatians*, NIGTC (Grand Rapids: Eerdmans, 1982), 105–28.

21. See the discussion on "Applying the Book of Acts Today" in the Introduction.

of the greatest events in history"[22]—the first general[23] attempt at taking the gospel directly to Gentiles. We are only told where they hail from (v. 20), which suggests that no one emerged as prominent among them. This great work was done by a group of "ordinary Christians" who went and shared the gospel. In fact, much of the growth of the church must have happened through such people (see 8:1, 4)—as should be the case today.

Barnabas the encourager. Luke undoubtedly intends to present the qualities of Barnabas as an encourager in this passage. He had earlier said how this man had been given his new name, meaning "son of encouragement," by the apostles (4:36). Now Luke not only records how Barnabas encouraged the young church in Antioch (v. 23), he also gives the character traits that enabled this man to be such an effective encourager (v. 24). We will therefore use this passage to study the ministry of encouragement.

(1) Barnabas was glad when he "saw the evidence of the grace of God" (v. 23a). He must have seen many weaknesses and perhaps "many excesses of religious enthusiasm that would have shocked some people."[24] But he did not focus attention on these. Instead, he focused on the evidence of God's grace among them, and that made him glad. Biblical encouragers are easily gladdened.

(2) Barnabas encouraged perseverance in the people's relationship with Jesus (v. 23b). Just to know that the envoy from Jerusalem was happy would have been a great source of encouragement. But that was not enough. Encouragement is an active ministry, not just a passive acceptance of people. Thus, Barnabas encouraged (i.e., exhorted) them "to remain true to the Lord with all their hearts." By their speech and life encouragers urge others to go on in the life of faith without giving up.

(3) Luke then cites the character traits that made Barnabas an effective encourager (v. 24). Encouragers are "good" people—people of genuine Christian character. Those who live godly lives will encourage others to be godly. Encouragers are also "full of the Holy Spirit" (a theme discussed at length elsewhere in this book). In addition, encouragers are "full of . . . faith." Faith in God's provision gave Barnabas the courage to sell his land and give the proceeds to meet the needs of the poor (4:37). Faith in God's ability to change people gave him the courage to risk supporting Saul when the others were afraid of him (9:26–27). Here again faith in the possibilities of grace enabled Barnabas to look beyond the weaknesses he saw to focus on what God had done and could do in the life of the church in Antioch.

---

22. Barclay, *Acts*, 88.

23. The preaching to the Ethiopian and at the home of Cornelius were special events involving direct guidance from God.

24. Bruce, *Circle*, 17.

(4) Barnabas took a trip of about a hundred miles to recruit Saul to help him in his work (vv. 25–26). He had to be highly motivated to do that. Barnabas realized that the task was so big that he needed capable help. But Saul was probably more talented and educated than Barnabas. By getting Paul he was seriously jeopardizing his own position of leadership and prominence. But encouragers know that there are some things that others can do better than themselves, and they encourage such people to use their gifts within the context of the encouragers' own ministries.

The gift of prophecy. Like with the gift of tongues, the issue of whether the gift of prophecy, which Agabus exercised (v. 28), is valid for today continues to be a point of contention in the church. What we said in connection with tongues[25] applies here as well.[26] I see no adequate biblical reason for eliminating this gift from the life of the church.

Partnership in missions. The Antioch church developed a missionary attitude, which resulted in a reversal of missionary roles (vv. 27–29). The result is partnership in missions, where each church contributes to the other out of its economic, cultural, intellectual, or spiritual riches. Paul describes this partnership approach to missions when he reflected on the benefits of his proposed visit to Rome: "I long to see you so that I may impart to you some spiritual gift to make you strong—that is, that you and I may be mutually encouraged by each other's faith" (Rom. 1:11–12). This is the model of missions that we should strive for in every church.

THE VALUE OF **non-prominent Christians.** The fact that non-prominent Christians did such significant work for Christ reminds us that the famous are not necessarily the most significant or most important people in the church. The famous have gifts that put them into the limelight—and that is not wrong. But neither is it necessarily great. Some of the most significant work for the kingdom has been done by unknown witnesses who are obedient to Christ right where they are and where they do not attract much attention. Today we associate significance and greatness with newsworthiness. Much effort is made to make an event look newsworthy, and thus it has to be associated with names—such as the names of those who write best-selling books or head a big organization. These names attract the people in the media.

---

25. See comments on 2:1–13.

26. For comprehensive studies on the gift of prophecy see David E. Aune, *Prophecy in Early Christianity and the Ancient Mediterranean World* (Grand Rapids: Eerdmans, 1983); Wayne Grudem, *The Gift of Prophecy in the New Testament and Today* (Wheaton: Crossway, 1988).

I know of some people who write books simply to become newsworthy. Some even pay others to do most of the writing for books that will go under their name! All this is unnecessary, for our task is to be faithful to what God calls us to do. If that does not put our name forward on earth, that should not bother us, for our aim in life is not to get our name in the papers, but to hear the Master say, "Well done." It is the prospect of this reward that thrills true Christians.

Encouragers are easily gladdened. Some people see a new work and immediately compare it with their own work. This makes them feel threatened about their status, so they look at the shortcomings in the new work—and there will always be shortcomings. Focusing on those things, they end up criticizing the work. Such criticism may be valid, but it is ill-timed and done in the wrong spirit. Such people alienate themselves from the young, enthusiastic, and sometimes immature leaders. They forfeit their chance to influence them towards maturity.

There are many young enthusiastic Christians who have joined churches with a sincere desire to serve. They were not lacking in zeal, but they were lacking in wisdom and maturity. The potential of these youth who had so much to offer is lost from the church if they receive only criticism. Some give up trying and remain uninvolved. Others go elsewhere to serve, and the rest become bitter rebels. But wise encouragers see the good in the new movement, are pleased with it, and help it to grow and become stable.

Encouragers urge perseverance. Young enthusiastic Christians can cool off in their enthusiasm and commitment once the initial thrill of the new life wears off and they face disappointments and discouragement. At such times mature leaders are needed. They have weathered storms and are not surprised by problems. Because they have faith to handle crises, they can give stability to less experienced believers. This is one reason why we should have mature Christians involved in a new work—to help people persevere. We often take people who are young, committed, and enthusiastic and send them out to minister in difficult areas. Sometimes these people come to disastrous ends. In a crisis or a time of discouragement, they are alone, make rash decisions, or commit huge mistakes. Some fall into big sins as they are unequipped to face the strong temptations that come from Satan as they challenge his rule.

Encouragers have a calling to help people abide in Christ wholeheartedly (v. 23b). This involves teaching—which Barnabas and Saul did for a whole year in Antioch (v. 26). It involves being with people and urging them to persevere when they are in a challenging situation and may be tempted to compromise or give up.

This ministry of urging people to persevere is well expressed in a story I heard from a preacher years ago. His son was running a race, and the father was watching the race from near the final bend before the home stretch. When the son came to that spot, he was not in the lead. The father cried out as loud as he could, "Go!" The son recognized the father's voice, and this cry created a new determination, which helped him to increase his speed and win the race. We can be a shot in the arm to the faith and life of many people. When they are discouraged, we can help lift them up through words of encouragement. When they are committed, we can help them go deeper in their commitment.

Here is a new believer who had lost a battle against temptation and fallen into sin. She thought that there was little chance for her to succeed as a Christian. We sit and talk with her, reminding her of the promises of God to help people like her. She receives the strength to start walking with God again.

Or I think of the young preacher who comes to speak at a meeting. From his face we see something has gone wrong. We ask him about it, and he tells us about some big problems at his home so that he cannot prepare adequately for his talk. We assure him of the sufficient grace of God for such situations, lay hands on him, pray for him, and send him off for the meeting with fresh hope in the promises of God.

Here is a young evangelical with a passion for social justice and a sense of call to do something in this area. She is discouraged because she finds that few of her fellow evangelicals understood her passion. We talk with her and explore possibilities of how she can be involved constructively in such ministry, and we introduce her to people with whom she can work.

The character of an encourager. The first character trait we examined was *goodness*. Good persons refuse to break any principles to achieve their desired goals. They do not have ulterior motives of achieving some hidden agenda as they serve in the church or the world. When they are put in leadership, we can expect them to make unselfish and principled decisions. Good persons do not lie to suit their own purposes. They do not crush others in order to climb in society or manipulate people and situations for their own ends. They do not use people and then drop them when they no longer serve their purposes. They take responsibility for mistakes.

It is possible for people without integrity—people who are not good—to climb to leadership positions in the church today. Ours is a pragmatic generation, which seems to have a love affair with results. If a person produces results, we regard him or her as successful, and people without integrity can do well and succeed. Because the church is an entity in contemporary society, it is not surprising that this problem has hit the church. When motivated, capable, and ambitious people do supposedly great things, we can be so enamored by the results that we overlook their character flaws. Such people can build their empires and become prominent spokespersons for Christianity.

But when such people are discovered as having no integrity, Christ is dishonored. If bad people stand for the right message and win a hearing for this message, people may end up rejecting the gospel. At the beginning of this century liberalism posed a great threat to the church and nearly destroyed its vitality. At the end of this century worse results may come through the devastation caused by people who preach the evangelical message but lack personal integrity.

The seriousness of this problem surfaces in the growth of religions like Buddhism and Hinduism, which focus on self-effort. People of these religions object that Christianity, with its free offer of forgiveness for sins through grace, opens the door for irresponsible living. (This is one of the most common criticisms made against Christianity by Buddhists in Sri Lanka.) In answer we say that God not only forgives us, but he also gives us the strength to overcome sin. But if they accept that argument, they will examine the lives of Christians to see whether it really works. And if they do not see holiness in Christians, they will accuse us of making fraudulent claims. This is precisely what the former Indian President and Hindu philosopher Dr. Sarvepalli Radhakrishnan meant when he said, "Christians are ordinary people making extraordinary claims." This was also Gandhi's major objection to the Christian gospel.

Elsewhere we have discussed how important the *fullness of the Spirit* is to Christian ministry.[27] The third quality of encouragers mentioned here is *faith*. Both faith in God and faith in people are important for the ministry of encouragement. To encourage people you must believe in them, which is not easy to do today given the lack of integrity we encounter. If we become disappointed over people, we are tempted to refrain from trusting anybody. It is faith that helps us believe in people. Ultimately we put our belief not so much in people as in the promises of God—in the possibilities of grace in the lives of people. That vision of grace helps us to see beyond the gloom, to believe, and so to try to be agents of grace in the lives of others. We will not give up on people. We will pray for them and meet with them. We will urge them and rebuke them. And we will do so believing that God can make them into his mighty instruments.

Paul once wrote, "Timothy, my son, I give you this instruction in keeping with the prophecies once made about you" (1 Tim. 1:18). Based on some prophecies made about Timothy, Paul had a vision of what he could become. That vision led him to instruct Timothy so that he could become the person God wanted him to be. How we need to feed faith in our lives! Reading the Bible daily can help keep us from becoming cynics. Perhaps we question

---

27. See especially the comments on 1:1–8.

whether we can expect Christians to act as the Bible says Christians should act. Are we being impractical fools when we press for scriptural holiness? The promises in the Bible challenge our cynicism. They encourage us to believe that grace can indeed effect a profound change in people and make them Christlike. Believing in the possibilities of grace, we have courage to hope, pray, and work toward seeing these possibilities realized in our lives and in the lives of others.

Thus, the key to helping people stay close to Christ is the Christian character of the leader. This is in keeping with what Paul gives as the qualifications for leaders in the church. Out of the long list he gives in 1 Timothy 3:2–7 only one element has to do with ability (the ability to teach). The rest are about the maturity, character, and reputation of a leader. There are many things that we can do in ministry without godliness and the fullness of the Spirit. We can lead meetings, prepare and deliver messages, organize and implement programs, win elections, and head committees. But we cannot help people abide in the Lord. To produce godly people we too must be godly. To produce people of prayer we too must be people of prayer. To produce people who walk close to God we too must walk close to God.

The power of the life of a godly leader is still important even in this pragmatic age. Deep down people desire to be holy. But many have taken shortcuts, thinking that such a life will not be practical. But as the famous American evangelist of an earlier generation, Henry Clay Morrison, said, "God never fixed me up so that I couldn't sin. He fixed me up so that I couldn't sin and enjoy it." There is a yearning for godliness in the human heart. When people see that it is possible to be holy, they too are urged to pursue this path. This is why godliness and integrity have a way of pervading the fabric of movements led by godly leaders.

Encouragers enlist the help of capable people. Some leaders reluctantly accept help from other capable people because they know it is inevitable. Barnabas, on the other hand, took the initiative and personally made the long journey in search of the highly talented Saul. Because encouragers know there are others who can do some things better than themselves, they are not possessive of their status. They do not thrive on being worshiped as heroes, so they do not try to protect their flock from the ministries of other gifted leaders. Some leaders get upset when their people are thrilled about someone else's teaching. But encouragers are not defensive, always trying to prove their own abilities. They, like Barnabas, will prove the abilities of others.

Some leaders are willing to have young, inexperienced, and enthusiastic assistants but are threatened by capable colleagues. They are afraid that their position will be jeopardized. Such people are never happy. When any threat comes to their position, they lose control and act rashly. Take the example of a Christian couple who plan on being married. The couple asks a preacher from another church, who is a friend of theirs, to preach at the wedding. Their pastor becomes angry, resurrects a forgotten rule, and prevents this, or he expresses his anger in some other way. We should leave it to Christ to honor us and concentrate instead on honoring Christ and others. In 1 Samuel 2:30, God says, "Those who honor me I will honor." We can rest on that promise, realizing that the honor that comes from God is the only honor worth striving for.

The gift of prophecy today. I said that I see no adequate reason for rejecting the idea that the gift of prophecy can be operative today also. But I must also say that any messages given through the exercise of this gift should not contradict what God has already revealed in the Scriptures. Thus, for example, when a prophecy is given regarding the date of the Lord's return, it should be judged as inauthentic because it contradicts the clear teaching of the Scriptures (see comments on 1:1–8).

Why is it, then, that many churches do not seem to experience the operation of the prophetic gift? Unlike the gift of tongues, which is not necessary for public worship to be complete, Paul seems to suggest that prophecy is at least desirable, if not essential, in the community life of the church (1 Cor. 14). Wayne Grudem has pointed out that often the gift of prophecy is operating in churches without its being recognized as such.[28] For example, sometimes in a time of prayer someone may pray something that becomes an unusual means by which God directs the group. Or a speaker may say something he or she had not planned to say, which becomes a direct message from God to someone in the audience.

Forging missionary partnership. How can we forge a model of missionary partnership today? How can we break the donor-recipient barrier so that all segments of the church see themselves as capable and called to make significant contributions to the worldwide mission of the church? Two keys need emphasizing. (1) We must develop what can be called a "body of Christ" mentality. This was well expressed by the Indian Christian leader Sam Kamaleson, in a statement he made at the Urbana '70 Student Missionary Conference: The church "is not an organization but a supernatural organism: she feels, she throbs with vitality. In other words, when the church in the United States is pinched, the church in India must say, 'Ah, that hurts!'"[29]

Because of this mentality, the need of the church in Jerusalem became the responsibility of the church in Antioch. Some have called this the kingdom

---

28. Grudem, *Gift of Prophecy,* 254–58.

29. Samuel Kamaleson, "The Local Church and World Evangelism," *Christ the Liberator* (Downer's Grove, Ill.: InterVarsity, 1971), 158–59.

perspective—where our concerns are not only for our own programs but for the entire kingdom of God. Those with such a perspective think not only of their own work but also of the impact their activities have on the wider body. Leighton Ford speaks of the need to be kingdom seekers rather than empire builders.

(2) Another key that helped break the donor-receiver distinction in Antioch was the fact that the group without money was the mother church and the group with money was the daughter church. Today money rules much missionary strategy. Money is power in our society, and that myth has infiltrated into the thinking of the church. So the one with more money may feel superior and the one with less money inferior. Such attitudes make partnership impossible. But because the mother church was poor, the relationship between the churches in Antioch and Jerusalem was freed from this malady.

If we are to arrive at partnership today, we must free missions from the stranglehold of money. We must think in terms of sharing *everything* we have. Missionary giving can take place through prayer, ideas, spiritual gifts, and people, as well as money. The one who gives money is not greater than the one who contributes ideas or prays. Usually, however, we behave as if money is most important. In the partnership model, rich Christians can look for help in spirituality and community living from poor Christians since they know these two qualities tend to grow well in the soil of poverty. When the rich realize how important the spiritual and community life are to Christianity, they will not feel superior to the poor. When the poor realize that they are being treated as equals and that their contribution is highly valued, they feel confident of what they can offer. In such an environment missionary partnership will thrive.

Some missionary leaders complain that nationals are not emerging as leaders on the mission field. But the reason for this may be that the environment is not conducive to the development of national leaders. If the rich foreigner is considered superior, we can be sure that true leaders will scarcely emerge. Potential leaders will be either stifled or, more likely, move away. "Yes-men," that is, people hoping that some of the money will come their way, will stay. These people have no sense of ownership; they just want to grab what they can from the rich person. Naturally, therefore, you cannot hand the work over to them. Developing models of partnership, then, is a vital need for the church today.

Acts 12:1–24

❧

I T WAS ABOUT this time that King Herod arrested some who belonged to the church, intending to persecute them. ²He had James, the brother of John, put to death with the sword. ³When he saw that this pleased the Jews, he proceeded to seize Peter also. This happened during the Feast of Unleavened Bread. ⁴After arresting him, he put him in prison, handing him over to be guarded by four squads of four soldiers each. Herod intended to bring him out for public trial after the Passover.

⁵So Peter was kept in prison, but the church was earnestly praying to God for him.

⁶The night before Herod was to bring him to trial, Peter was sleeping between two soldiers, bound with two chains, and sentries stood guard at the entrance. ⁷Suddenly an angel of the Lord appeared and a light shone in the cell. He struck Peter on the side and woke him up. "Quick, get up!" he said, and the chains fell off Peter's wrists.

⁸Then the angel said to him, "Put on your clothes and sandals." And Peter did so. "Wrap your cloak around you and follow me," the angel told him. ⁹Peter followed him out of the prison, but he had no idea that what the angel was doing was really happening; he thought he was seeing a vision. ¹⁰They passed the first and second guards and came to the iron gate leading to the city. It opened for them by itself, and they went through it. When they had walked the length of one street, suddenly the angel left him.

¹¹Then Peter came to himself and said, "Now I know without a doubt that the Lord sent his angel and rescued me from Herod's clutches and from everything the Jewish people were anticipating."

¹²When this had dawned on him, he went to the house of Mary the mother of John, also called Mark, where many people had gathered and were praying. ¹³Peter knocked at the outer entrance, and a servant girl named Rhoda came to answer the door. ¹⁴When she recognized Peter's voice, she was so overjoyed she ran back without opening it and exclaimed, "Peter is at the door!"

¹⁵"You're out of your mind," they told her. When she kept insisting that it was so, they said, "It must be his angel."

[16]But Peter kept on knocking, and when they opened the door and saw him, they were astonished. [17]Peter motioned with his hand for them to be quiet and described how the Lord had brought him out of prison. "Tell James and the brothers about this," he said, and then he left for another place.

[18]In the morning, there was no small commotion among the soldiers as to what had become of Peter. [19]After Herod had a thorough search made for him and did not find him, he cross-examined the guards and ordered that they be executed.

Then Herod went from Judea to Caesarea and stayed there a while. [20]He had been quarreling with the people of Tyre and Sidon; they now joined together and sought an audience with him. Having secured the support of Blastus, a trusted personal servant of the king, they asked for peace, because they depended on the king's country for their food supply.

[21]On the appointed day Herod, wearing his royal robes, sat on his throne and delivered a public address to the people. [22]They shouted, "This is the voice of a god, not of a man." [23]Immediately, because Herod did not give praise to God, an angel of the Lord struck him down, and he was eaten by worms and died.

[24]But the word of God continued to increase and spread.

IN THE SEQUENCE that Luke is following in the unfolding drama of Acts, Gentile Christianity is gradually beginning to take center stage. In the middle of this growing emphasis is an insertion, as it were, that indicates that God is still active in the Jewish church. Acts 12 gives us a realistic picture typical of what seem to be tragedies and triumphs in the early church.

Herod, James, and Peter (12:1–19)

THIS TIME THE source of persecution is King Herod (Agrippa I), who makes James the first of the apostles to be martyred (vv. 1–2). This Herod was more popular with the Jews than the other Herods, possibly partly because his grandmother was a Hasmonean.[1] He is said to have "set himself sedulously

---

1. Members of the Hasmonean family instigated the Jewish revolt against the Greeks in 167 B.C.

to win and retain their goodwill."[2] When he realized that the Jews were pleased with the killing of James, he also had Peter imprisoned (v. 3a). This incident indicates how much the relationship between Jews and Christians in Judea had deteriorated from the earlier situation of "enjoying the favor of all the people" (2:47). We do not know whether the general public was in favor of the earlier persecutions. But this time, as the use of the general term *Jews* suggests, approval for James's death was widespread.

There is much irony in this chapter. According to Luke, the imprisonment of Peter took place "during the Feast of Unleavened Bread," that is, the Passover (v. 3b). At the time when the Jews were celebrating the deliverance of their nation through God's intervention, a herald of God's climactic act of deliverance was taken into custody to please the Jews. While they should have been celebrating a great salvation, they were hoping to inflict a great punishment on the representative of the Savior (v. 11).

To the gloomy picture of Peter in prison Luke adds the hopeful note of the church earnestly in prayer for him (v. 5). The word translated "earnestly" (*ektenos*) literally means "stretched out" and could thus mean continuous, in which case it carries a similar idea as it does in 1:14, which gave us the idea of prevailing prayer. But the idea of continuous or repeated prayer is already carried by the use of the imperfect tense for the verb "praying."[3] Luke's use of *ektenos* here, therefore, seems more like his use of this word in Luke 22:44, where it refers to Jesus' earnest prayer in the garden (see also Acts 26:7). This idea of earnestness (see NIV) comes from the idea of hands *stretched out* to God in fervent supplication. It gives the impression of wholehearted, urgent pleading to God. While Peter was fast asleep in prison in the middle of the night (the angel had to wake him—v. 7), the church was engaged in vigilant prayer for him.

The second instance of irony is the unbelief of Peter and the praying church that their prayers had been answered (vv. 9–11, 15). And this came after God had similarly released Peter from imprisonment on an earlier occasion—that time too through an angel at night (5:19–20). In fact, when the servant girl Rhoda was overjoyed over the answer to the prayers of the believers, they pronounced her out of her mind (vv. 14–15).

The statement "it must be his angel" (v. 15) reflects the Jewish belief in protecting and guiding angels, who "were sometimes thought to resemble the human beings they protected."[4] Thus the believers thought that Rhoda mis-

---

2. Bruce, *Acts*, NICNT, 233. Bruce cites an example of one of these attempts of his (see n. 4).

3. Williams, *Acts*, 212.

4. Barrett, *Acts*, 585. See ibid. for references from Jewish literature.

took Peter's guardian angel for Peter. The irony continues as Peter went on knocking while the believers argued among themselves (v. 16a). While the big iron gate of the prison opened with no effort to let Peter out (v. 10), he was unable to get past the gate of his own friend's home.

Though we do not know from whom Luke got these details, the record of Peter's anxious gesture of motioning with his hand for them to be quiet (v. 17) indicates "the authentic touch of an eyewitness."[5] Peter probably then went "underground so successfully that no one to this day has discovered for certain where he went."[6] Peter wanted James to be informed about what had happened, which suggests that he had already become an important leader in the church (cf. also Gal. 2:1–10). Because James was known to hold strongly to Jewish ways, he would not be in as much danger from the Jews as Peter was.

A third instance of irony is Herod's response to Peter's escape, which deflated his ego. He restored his image by having the guards executed (v. 19a). This extreme reaction is typical of people who seek popularity but are unexpectedly humiliated. Luke then says that Herod went to Caesarea (v. 19b). He begins verse 19b with the word "and" (*kai*), which means it is part of the same sentence about the executions of the guards. This suggests Herod may have left Jerusalem because of frustration over Peter's escape.[7]

Herod's Death (12:20–24)

HEROD'S DEFLATED EGO received a big boost at his conference with the desperate delegates from Tyre and Sidon, who, deprived of their food supply, resort to flattery to win him over (vv. 20–22). The account of this incident by Josephus supplements the sketchy account given here.[8]

- According to Luke, Herod was "wearing his royal robes" (v. 21); Josephus writes that he wore a garment made wholly of silver, which shone in a surprising manner when the rays of the sun touched it.
- Luke says that Herod's punishment was because he did not praise God when the flatterers shouted that his was the voice of a god (vv. 22–23). Josephus reports that "the king did neither rebuke them, nor reject their impious flattery."
- Josephus says that he had violent abdominal pains and died five days later, whereas Luke says, "Immediately . . . an angel of the Lord struck

---

5. Bruce, *Acts*, NICNT, 239. Among those suggested as Luke's informants are John Mark and Rhoda.

6. Ibid., 238–39.

7. Longenecker, "Acts," 413.

8. Josephus, *Antiquities of the Jews*, 19.8.2 (*Complete Works*, 412).

him down, and he was eaten by worms and died" (v. 23). This apparent discrepancy can be explained in that Luke applied the "immediately" to the striking down with sickness (which took place immediately), not to the dying (which took place five days later).[9]

We are not told the exact cause of the death; Longenecker suggests it may have been through infection by intestinal roundworms.[10] There is irony here too, for the man who was glorious on the outside was rotting of worms on the inside.

Immediately after the report of Herod's death Luke gives a report of the growth of the church he had brutally tried to suppress. The customary summary of growth in verse 24 ends the description in Acts of the Christian mission to the Jewish world.[11] The section closes on a positive note. The early popularity of the church has given way to hostility, but that does not hinder the forward march of the gospel. From the next chapter to the end of Acts, the focus will be on Paul and his missionary activity.

Bridging Contexts

RESCUE AND NO **physical rescue**. Often in applying this passage, we focus on God's deliverance of Peter in answer to fervent prayer (vv. 5–11) and ignore the nondeliverance of James, which resulted in martyrdom (v. 2). This is how I approached this passage for several years. But the fact that Luke has placed these two events side by side suggests that the two ways in which God's sovereignty is expressed—physical rescue and no physical rescue—should both be considered when thinking about God's help in times of trouble. What is common to these situations is that both Peter and James were faithful to Christ. Just as the disciples earnestly prayed for Peter's release (v. 5), we too have the freedom to pray earnestly for physical deliverance. But we must leave it to God to let his sovereignty over a situation be expressed in the way he regards best. What is most important is that, like James and Peter, we remain faithful and obedient to God regardless of the outcome of a crisis we face.

We know also that those who oppose the work of God will be judged, as Herod was (v. 23). Wicked leaders, like Herod, may look impressively invincible and hurt the church for a time. But, as Mary warned in the Magnificat, the proud will indeed be humbled (Luke 1:52–53). God always has the last

---

9. Williams, *Acts,* 218.

10. Longenecker, "Acts," 413.

11. Interestingly, the Greek of verse 24 is exactly the same as that of 6:7a (apart from the "and" at the start of 6:7a).

word. If this does not seem to be the case, it is because the last word has not yet been said. James was killed here, and Peter was killed some twenty years later. But the word of God continued, and will continue, to spread (Acts 12:24).

The power of earnest prayer. The sequence of verses 5 and 7 has often been repeated in the history of the church. It began with "so," followed by a gloomy report; then came a hopeful "but" and a report of saints at prayer; and that led to "behold" (*idou* at the beginning of v. 7; not trans. in NIV), followed by a report of God's intervention. Just as the words "constantly" or "prevailing" express the duration of powerful praying,[12] "earnestly" expresses the mood of powerful praying. It is true that we do not always receive the answers we ask for (cf. the contrast between James's death and Peter's release), but the Bible is clear that "the prayer of a righteous man is powerful and effective" (James 5:16).

Here, as in 1:14, community prayer is being described. We will, of course, always submit to God's will and accede to the fact that we do not always know what that will is. Jesus submitted to the will of God in the garden (Luke 22:42), but that did not prevent him from praying "earnestly" (22:44). Once we realize that prayer does change things, we can be bold to "storm the gates of heaven" with earnest prayer for God's intervention.

Peter Forsyth, in his classic book, *The Soul of Prayer,* has argued that there is a sense in which God's will is changed in answer to our prayers.[13] This is what happened after Moses' intense intercession for Israel, accompanied by a total fast for forty days and nights following the golden calf incident (Deut. 9:18). As a result of this prayer, "the LORD relented and did not bring on his people the disaster he had threatened" (Ex. 32:14; see Amos 7:2–6). Paul believed that through our prayers we can influence the course of history. He indicated this dual divine-human role as he contemplated his release from prison: "For I know that through your prayers and the help given by the Spirit of Jesus Christ, what has happened to me will turn out for my deliverance" (Phil. 1:19). He also saw the prayers of God's people as a key to the effectiveness of his ministry (2 Cor. 1:11; Eph. 6:19–20).

At the heart of such prayer is an intensity of Spirit that is well expressed by Paul's willingness to be cursed so that his people, the Jews, might come to Christ (Rom. 9:1–3). This desire gave rise to a prayer for Israel's salvation (10:1). He also expresses this intensity in his cry to the Galatians, "My dear children, for whom I am again in the pains of childbirth until Christ is formed in you, how I wish I could be with you now and change my tone, because I

---

12. See comments on 1:14.

13. P. T. Forsyth, *The Soul of Prayer* (Grand Rapids: Eerdmans, reprint of 1916 edition), 82–87.

am perplexed about you!" (Gal. 4:19–20). Through earnest prayer we can influence the course of history, for God powerfully answers such prayers.

The ministry of angels. The English word "angel," which appears seven times in this passage, comes directly from the Greek word for messenger (*angelos*).[14] Angels have a prominent role in Acts—directing people (8:26; 10:3–6), helping them in times of trouble (5:19–20; 12:7–10; 27:23), and acting as agents of judgment (12:23). Of particular interest is the statement of the Christians who said that the person at the door had to be "his [Peter's] angel" (v. 15). As noted above, this reflects the Jewish belief in guardian angels. Revelation 1–3 speaks of angels assigned as representatives of churches (see Rev. 1:20). When urging the people not to look down on "little ones," Jesus said, "their angels in heaven always see the face of my Father" (Matt. 18:10). Jesus may be saying here that there are special angels who represent the little ones in heaven. They will not go unnoticed because "the little ones matter to God."[15]

These few references are insufficient to build a full-blown doctrine about guardian angels, especially since the interpretation that Jesus' statement just mentioned refers to angels is disputed.[16] But we can be certain that one key role of angels is to help the saints (see Heb. 1:14).

GOD'S RESPONSE TO **prayers of rescue.** In times of trouble God's sovereignty can be expressed by rescue or no rescue. In the violence that has engulfed Sri Lanka over the past years we have seen five types of situations that Christians have encountered that can be applied to difficulties in general. (1) Some have experienced wonderful deliverances that can be explained only as miraculous interventions from God. There have been stories of bombs missing houses or not going off, of mobs suddenly turning away and avoiding the houses of God's servants. These certainly remind us that God can and does save his children in times of crises if it is his will.

(2) Others have gone through great crisis and earthly loss but remained so radiant with the love of Christ that they were powerful testimonies of God's sustaining grace. In a terrible riot in 1983 the home of Dr. Arul Anketell, who directs Hospital Christian Fellowship in Sri Lanka, was burned. When I met him for the first time after the event, he ministered the peace of Christ

---

14. See verses 7, 8, 9, 10, 11, 15, 23.

15. Leon Morris, *The Gospel According to Matthew* (Grand Rapids: Eerdmans, 1992), 465.

16. D. A. Carson thinks that the angels in Matthew 18:10 are the spirits of little ones who have died. "Matthew," *EBC*, 400–401.

to me rather than vice versa. He was a wonderful testimony of the sufficiency of God's grace.

(3) The faith of certain people was shattered by the problems they faced. Not only did they question why God allowed the tragedy and became engulfed in a cloud of gloom—both of which are natural—they also never recovered from the gloom. In bitterness of spirit they turned their back on God.

(4) Other people compromised their principles in order to avoid pain. For example, some Christians left the country by illegal means or by telling lies to visa officers at embassies.

(5) Finally, some who had not cared for the things of God, owing to their relentless pursuit of earthly success, were jolted into realizing the unreliability of earthly treasures as a means of security. They turned to God for security and succor and found him to be the answer to the aching void in their hearts.

Whatever experiences God's providence permits us to go through, our primary commitment should be to obedience. All the threats from the authorities did not cause the early church to pull back on its commitment to proclaiming the gospel. Peter saw wonderful deliverance through the intervention of God, while James faced death for Christ. But the early Christians persevered in obedience, knowing that if God is sovereign he would use their obedience to win a great victory for the kingdom.

This truth is well expressed in the story of the deaths of the five missionaries to the Auca Indians in the jungles of Equador. Steve Saint, son of the one of the five missionaries killed by these Indians in 1956, recently built an airstrip among those same people. He found out details about those deaths that had not previously been known. For example, the five missionaries had guns and could have easily shot and killed their assailants, but they refused to do so. This is what others had done to the Indians. Rather, the missionaries only shot into the air to frighten them. Shots had accidentally grazed and slightly injured two people, so they knew that the guns could kill them. But the missionaries had determined not to hurt anyone. And though it cost them their lives, they stuck to that decision obediently. The Aucas were struck by this decision, and that contributed much to their ultimate conversion to Christ.[17]

When these young men died, elements in the secular media, sometimes vehemently, criticized the whole missionary enterprise, especially missions among tribal peoples. But subsequent events have proved that God's sovereignty indeed won a mighty victory for the kingdom through their deaths. That does not mean, however, that victory is immediately obvious. In Acts,

---

17. Steve Saint, "Did They Have to Die?" *Christianity Today* (Sept. 16, 1996), 26—27. This article is from *Martyrs: Contemporary Writers on Modern Lives of Faith*, ed. Susan Bergman (San Fransisco: Harper San Fransisco, 1996).

for example, Stephen's death led to the growth of the church through the scattering of the seed of the word. But in James's case we see no obvious evidence of triumph. In our fast moving age we want immediate evidence to feel that the sacrifices we make are worthwhile. But God may reserve that revelation until we get to heaven, which will make it all the more glorious. Until then we persevere in patience and obedience.

We do not know what will happen to us. But we do know that whatever happens, the greatest challenge we face is the challenge to be obedient. The answer of Shadrach, Meshach, and Abednego to the furious king who was getting ready to kill them is instructive:

> O Nebuchadnezzar, we do not need to defend ourselves before you in this matter. If we are thrown into the blazing furnace, the God we serve is able to save us from it, and he will rescue us from your hand, O king. But even if he does not, we want you to know, O king, that we will not serve your gods or worship the image of gold you have set up (Dan. 3:16–18).

Because the Bible highlights both situations of miraculous deliverance and of triumphant fortitude amidst painful suffering, we must present both possibilities in our preaching and teaching. Of course there may be times when God gives someone an assurance of deliverance, as he did to Paul on his way to Rome that no one would die from the shipwreck (Acts 27:23–24). At such times we can act on that assurance. But that does not happen every time.

A constant refrain in Acts is that through all of the triumphs and seeming tragedies of life the word of God continues to spread (12:24). This growth has gone on unabated. The gospel, which began with such small beginnings in the first century, has now spread to the ends of the earth. The churches in Jerusalem and even in much of the areas of Paul's labors, it is true, have either disappeared or succumbed to nominalism. As Revelation 2–3 warns, when one church loses its vitality, its place as the standard-bearer of the kingdom will be lost. But that place will be taken by another. And unless we repent, we too can lose our places, just like the churches in Asia addressed in Revelation eventually lost their places to Islam. But God cannot be defeated by human unfaithfulness. The word of God will continue to spread until the "gospel of the kingdom will be preached in the whole world as a testimony to all nations, and then the end will come" (Matt. 24:14).

Praying earnestly. The English preacher Samuel Chadwick once said, "Intensity is a law of prayer.... There are blessings of the kingdom that are only yielded to the violence of the vehement soul."[18] He gives several exam-

---

18. Samuel Chadwick, *The Path of Prayer* (Kansas City: Beacon Hill, 1931), 68; quoted in Wesley L. Duewel, *Mighty Prevailing Prayer* (Grand Rapids: Zondervan, 1990), 76.

ples of this type of earnest prayer from the Bible: "Abraham pleading for Sodom, Jacob wrestling in the stillness of the night, Moses standing in the breach, Hannah intoxicated with sorrow, David heartbroken with remorse and grief."[19]

However, there are many features that discourage such earnestness today. A recent book on youth is entitled *A Generation Without Passion*—presumably in keeping with the pluralistic mood of the day, which is accepting of everything but passionate about nothing.[20] The present era is characterized by an overload of information and by many leaders, religious and otherwise, who have failed to live up to their claims. Such situations have fostered coldness, boredom, or cynicism. Contemporary society is also the era of entertainment, which has replaced passion as a means of attracting people in church and society. Passion can be a problem to people who have dropped out of charismatic groups in reaction to that emotionalism that was permitted to grow to uncontrolled excesses. Finally, many Christians have not had a vibrant experience of God. All these factors militate against the fostering of passion today.

In this environment people do not want to be passionate about anything. They play it safe spiritually. Such attitudes hinder earnestness in prayer. They will bring on the situation described by Samuel Chadwick when he said, "The crying need of the church is her laziness after God."[21] P. T. Forsyth has said that he believes the primary reason for disbelief in prayer among Christians is "the slipshod kind of prayer that men hear from us in public worship; it is often but journalese sent heavenwards, or phrasemaking to carry on."[22]

When we recover the biblical vision of God and his truth, we will recover biblical passion. If God is who the Bible claims he is and if what the Bible says about life is true, then we must face up to the implications of those truths. We must be inspired to dream great things and be horrified by what we see in our lives and in the church and world. Coldness, boredom, and cynicism melt at this twofold vision of the greatness of God and the sinfulness of his creation. Fired afresh by an ambition to see all that God wishes for us, we will be emboldened to pray earnestly towards that end.

This earnestness may express itself in prayer for a loved one, as in the prayer for Peter's release in Acts 12. It is seen in the prayers of parents as they agonize for their rebellious children, just as Monica agonized for years for

---

19. Chadwick, *Path of Prayer*, 81–82; quoted in Duewel, *Mighty Prevailing Prayer*, 76.

20. The above observation is taken from a talk on "Passion" given by Paul Borthwick to the staff of Youth for Christ in Sri Lanka.

21. Quoted in Duewel, *Mighty Prevailing Prayer*, 30.

22. Forsyth, *Soul of Prayer*, 81.

her son Augustine.[23] It is seen in prayers for the conversion of unbelieving spouses.[24] It may also express itself in prayers for church and nation. The Scottish reformer John Knox expressed this earnestness when he cried, "Give me Scotland or I die!" We end this section with a plea from the Scottish preacher Alexander Whyte: "Let every man put his passion into his prayers."[25]

The role of angels today. My first reaction to discussions about angels looking after us has usually been something like this: "That is kid's stuff. It was good for the Christmas story, but we live in the era of the Holy Spirit. The Spirit is the one who now ministers to us." But the ministry of angels is pronounced in Acts,[26] even with Acts' focus on the acts of the Holy Spirit. In other words, even in the era of the Spirit angels minister to us. God, who almost always works through some medium to send us help, can use angels for this. In the book of Acts he often did this in the lives not of little children, but of eminent apostles.

We too, therefore, should anticipate the ministry of angels on our behalf. The texts cited from Acts suggest that angels have an important ministry in the lives of Christian ministers. In other words, ministers too should take this doctrine seriously. Without any doubt God never lets us go through a crisis without preparing us adequately for it and providing for us to come out of it victoriously. We are reminded of the promise to Paul as he was troubled by his thorn in the flesh: "My grace is sufficient for you, for my power is made perfect in weakness" (2 Cor. 12:9). God always sends us sufficient help to see us through our most difficult times, and he sometimes does it through angels, as happened to Jesus after his temptations and before his death (Mark 1:13; Luke 22:43). We are reminded of the familiar verse in Psalm 91:11–12:

> For he will command his angels concerning you
> > to guard you in all your ways;
> they will lift you up in their hands,
> > so that you will not strike your foot against a stone.

John G. Paton, a Scottish missionary to the New Hebrides Islands in the South Pacific, was a heroic figure in recent missionary history. One night hostile tribesmen surrounded his mission headquarters, intent on burning it and killing Paton and his wife. The two of them prayed all through that terror-filled night, asking God to deliver them. When daylight came they were

---

23. See Ruth Bell Graham, *Prodigals and Those Who Love Them* (Colorado Springs: Focus on the Family, 1991).

24. See Duewel, *Mighty Prevailing Prayer*, 146–47, 178.

25. Alexander Whyte, *Lord, Teach Us to Pray* (New York: Harper, n.d.), 75; quoted in Duewel, *Mighty Prevailing Prayer*, 77.

26. See 5:19; 8:26; 10:3–7; 12:7–11, 23; 27:23.

surprised to see the attackers leave. A year later, the chief of the tribe was converted to Christ, and Paton had an opportunity to ask him what kept them from burning the house and killing them. The chief replied, "Who were all those men who were there with you?" Paton said, "There were no men there; only my wife and I." But the chief said that they had seen hundreds of big men in shining garments with drawn swords in their hands. They seemed to circle the mission station, so the tribesmen were afraid to attack.[27] Paton realized that God had sent his angels to protect them.

John Paton did not always experience God's provision in that way. His first wife died as a result of problems during childbirth. Seventeen days later the child also died. That happened early in his missionary career, and he had no one to comfort him. He even had to dig the graves for his wife and child. But he writes about that difficult time: "I was never altogether forsaken. The ever merciful God sustained me to lay the precious dust of my loved ones in the same quiet grave. But for Jesus, and the fellowship he vouchsafed me there, I must have gone mad and died beside that lonely grave!"[28] Jesus was there, and he gave sufficient grace—grace enough for him to stay on working among those people and reap a great harvest for the kingdom.

Sometimes angels are present in times that, unlike the two stories of Peter's deliverance in Acts, are times of apparent tragedy. I think of what Steve Saint found out about his father's death in the jungles of Equador: At the time they were being killed, the Auca Indians saw a multitude of angels in the sky and heard them singing. This played an important role in their eventual conversion to Christ.[29]

---

27. Cited in Billy Graham, *Angels: God's Secret Agents* (Waco, Tex.: Word Books, 1986), 3.

28. Cited in *Daily Readings from F. W. Boreham,* selected and arranged by Frank Cumbers (London: Hodder and Stoughton, 1976), 320.

29. Saint, "Did They Have to Die?" 26–27.

Acts 12:25–13:12

WHEN BARNABAS AND Saul had finished their mission, they returned from Jerusalem, taking with them John, also called Mark.

13:1 In the church at Antioch there were prophets and teachers: Barnabas, Simeon called Niger, Lucius of Cyrene, Manaen (who had been brought up with Herod the tetrarch) and Saul. 2While they were worshipping the Lord and fasting, the Holy Spirit said, "Set apart for me Barnabas and Saul for the work to which I have called them." 3So after they had fasted and prayed, they placed their hands on them and sent them off.

4The two of them, sent on their way by the Holy Spirit, went down to Seleucia and sailed from there to Cyprus. 5When they arrived at Salamis, they proclaimed the word of God in the Jewish synagogues. John was with them as their helper.

6They traveled through the whole island until they came to Paphos. There they met a Jewish sorcerer and false prophet named Bar-Jesus, 7who was an attendant of the proconsul, Sergius Paulus. The proconsul, an intelligent man, sent for Barnabas and Saul because he wanted to hear the word of God. 8But Elymas the sorcerer (for that is what his name means) opposed them and tried to turn the proconsul from the faith. 9Then Saul, who was also called Paul, filled with the Holy Spirit, looked straight at Elymas and said, 10"You are a child of the devil and an enemy of everything that is right! You are full of all kinds of deceit and trickery. Will you never stop perverting the right ways of the Lord? 11Now the hand of the Lord is against you. You are going to be blind, and for a time you will be unable to see the light of the sun."

Immediately mist and darkness came over him, and he groped about, seeking someone to lead him by the hand. 12When the proconsul saw what had happened, he believed, for he was amazed at the teaching about the Lord.

FROM 12:25 ON Paul dominates the book of Acts. Luke records the events that happened on the apostle's three missionary journeys, his arrest in Jerusalem, and his trials before governing officials. Luke ends his book with the story of Paul's journey to and arrival in Rome, including an exciting shipwreck in the Mediterranean Sea.

A Missionary Team Is Sent Out (12:25–13:3)

WHEN SAUL AND Barnabas returned to Antioch from Jerusalem, Barnabas's cousin (see Col. 4:10) John Mark was with them. We cannot be sure whether Luke is suggesting in Acts 13:1 that the same people were both teachers and prophets or whether these gifts resided in different people. Certainly Paul exercised both teaching and prophetic ministries, as we will see below.[1] Harrison distinguishes these two roles, explaining that the teacher provided basic information for living the Christian life, while the prophet provided special guidance from the Lord as needed. The former had a more sustained ministry, expounding the Old Testament and the traditions about the life and teachings of Jesus as handed down in the church. The prophet spoke in response to a distinct moving of the Spirit.[2] If the church was to be both responsible and creative, it needed both teaching and prophecy.[3]

The list of prophets and teachers (13:1) "symbolized the ethnic and cultural diversity of Antioch," a city with a "cosmopolitan population."[4] Barnabas is mentioned first, possibly because he was the leader of the group. He was a Jew from the Jerusalem church but was originally from Cyprus (4:36), an island west of Palestine. Simeon is a Jewish name, but he is called Niger, meaning black. Attempts to identify him with Simon of Cyrene have not been convincing. Bruce suggests that Niger was a "descriptive addition, given to him perhaps because he was an African."[5]

Lucius was from Cyrene, which was in North Africa (present-day Libya). Some have suggested that this is Luke, but that is unlikely. Manaen is a Jewish name. The NIV translates *syntrophos* as "had been brought up with" Herod the tetrarch, but it means foster brother or close friend from childhood.[6]

---

1. See the discussion on verses 9–11.

2. Harrison, *Interpreting Acts*, 214.

3. For an exploration of the prophetic ministry in relation to its creative content as in the ministries of the Old Testament prophets and Jesus, see Walter Bruggemann, *The Prophetic Imagination* (Philadelphia: Fortress, 1978).

4. Stott, *Acts*, 216.

5. Bruce, *Acts: Greek Text*, 292.

6. Barclay M. Newman Jr., *A Concise Greek-English Dictionary of the New Testament* (London: United Bible Societies, 1971), 175.

Bruce says that this title "was given to boys of the same age as royal princes, who were taken to the royal court to be brought up with them."[7] How strange that Herod should end up beheading John the Baptist and being involved in the trial of Christ, while Manaen became a leader of the church. Saul, an educated Jew originally from Tarsus, is mentioned last.

The Holy Spirit sent a message to this church, probably through one of the prophets there, which propelled it into a new era of missionary involvement. It happened "while they were worshiping the Lord and fasting" (13:2). "They" refers either to the prophets and teachers or to the whole church; the latter is more likely.[8] The word translated "worshiping" (leitourgeo) literally means "ministering." In classical Greek it was used for "doing public work at one's own expense." In the LXX this word group was "used almost exclusively for the service of priests and Levites in the temple." Twice Paul uses these words for help given to him (Phil. 2:25, 30). The noun appears in this sense in Luke 1:23, referring to Zechariah's service in the temple. In Acts 13:2 (the only other time one of these words appears in Luke-Acts) "the cultic meaning is completely spiritualized and applied to Christian worship in prayer."[9] The word for service seems to have fitted into the Christian understanding of worship and prayer.

The church's prayer was accompanied by fasting, both when the church received the message and when they sent off the missionary team (13:2–3). When Paul and Barnabas visited the churches they had established on the way back from this first missionary journey, they "appointed elders for them in each church and, with prayer and fasting, committed them to the Lord" (14:23). Fasting gives evidence of an "atmosphere of urgent desire"[10] in the church.

The sending-off ceremony with the laying on of hands was "an act of blessing in which the church associated itself with them and commended them to the grace of God (14:26)."[11] Thus, it was more a commissioning to a specific task than an ordaining to ministry. It is not surprising that at the end of the mission, Paul and Barnabas returned to the church in Antioch and gave a report of what happened (14:26–27). There must have been much more work to be done in Antioch. But God asked the church to release their key leaders for missions. To their credit the church did so, with no apparent hesitation. That is how important missions and obedience to the Spirit were.

---

7. Bruce, Acts, NICNT, 245.

8. Codex Bezae (D) adds pantes (all) after "prayed" in verse 3, which Bruce regards as "probably a true interpretation" (Acts: Greek Text, 294). This would mean that the whole church fasted, prayed, and sent them off.

9. The quotations are from K. Hess, NIDNTT, 3:551–52.

10. Harrison, Interpreting Acts, 216.

11. Marshall, Acts, 216.

Ministry in Cyprus (13:4–12)

VERSE 4 REMINDS us that the Holy Spirit is the one who ultimately sends his servants out. The first place of ministry for the missionaries was the area Barnabas came from, the island of Cyprus southwest of Antioch, to which they sailed from Seleucia, the port city of Antioch. They began their ministry in the northeastern city of Salamis, preaching first in a synagogue in keeping with the principle of going to the Jews first (Rom. 1:16). But they soon took a new step, directly approaching a Gentile official who sent for them (13:7).

Luke inserts a note that "John was with them as their helper" (13:5b). Some have suggested that the word "helper" here (*hyperetes*) has a restricted meaning similar to synagogue attendant (cf. Luke 4:20), so that Mark's responsibility was to care for the scrolls of the Scriptures along with a "sayings of Jesus" collection. But Luke uses this word in the broader sense elsewhere (Luke 1:2; Acts 5:22, 25; 26:16), which seems to be the meaning here.[12] As a resident of Jerusalem Mark may have had an eyewitness knowledge of events in the gospel story, especially relating to the Passion narrative, of which Paul would have availed himself.

The team next went to the provincial capital, Paphos, on the opposite (southwestern) side of the island. In the Roman empire "the peaceful and civilized provinces where no legions had to be quartered—about ten in number—were administered by the senate. A provincial governor had the title of proconsul (Acts 19:38), that is, 'in the place of consul' or functioning with the power of a consul in that *provincia*."[13] Cyprus was declared a senatorial province in 22 B.C.[14]

In Paphos Saul and Barnabas encountered a sorcerer, Bar-Jesus or Elymas, just as Philip and Peter did in Samaria. Like Simon in Samaria, Elymas faced a stern rebuke from the evangelist, because of his adverse influence on the proconsul of Cyprus, Sergius Paulus (13:6–11). Elymas presumably opposed Paul and Barnabas because their ministry jeopardized his standing with the proconsul. Such opposition to the gospel for selfish reasons is common in Acts.[15]

At this stage we are told that Saul "was also called Paul" (13:9), and from now on this is the name used in Acts (except when he relates the story of his conversion [22:7, 13; 26:14][16]). As a Jew he would have proudly borne the name of Israel's first king, Saul, who like him was from the tribe of Benjamin

---

12. Longenecker, "Acts," 419.
13. Ferguson, *Backgrounds*, 41.
14. M. N. Tod and R. A. Gwinn, "Cyprus," *ISBE*, 1:842.
15. See 5:17; 13:45; 16:19–21; 17:5; 19:25–28.
16. Here it is not *Saulos* but the transliterated Hebrew *Saoul* that is used.

(Phil. 3:5). Roman citizens had three names: a praenomen, a nomen, and a cognomen. The apostle's first two are not mentioned in the New Testament. Paul (*Paulos*, meaning "little") was his cognomen, and inscriptions show that often the cognomen of Jews sounded like their Jewish name, as is the case here. As Paul entered the Gentile phase of his ministry, he would have gone by his Roman name. Thus, the view that this name change resulted from his conversion is wrong.

Paul has severe words for Elymas (13:9–11). Luke is careful to say that he was "filled with the Holy Spirit" when he uttered them, indicating that this was not an error on Paul's part. It is an example of the use of the prophetic gift through which the apostle communicated a direct and specific word of judgment from God. Verse 12 attributes the belief of Sergius Paulus both to his seeing the miracle and being amazed at the teaching of the Lord. As we will see below, these factors present two key elements of effective evangelistic ministry.

A LEADERSHIP REFLECTING the diverse population. It is significant that the church in Antioch had such a culturally diverse leadership in keeping with the diversity of the population of the city (13:1). Did Luke mention the names and backgrounds of the leaders to highlight this diversity? We cannot make a binding principle out of this one text, but what happened in Antioch was certainly remarkable and may be an example worthy of emulation. I will go so far as to say that fostering leaders from different cultural backgrounds is a goal to work at in all churches that have a diversity in their membership.

Missionary sending. From this church's officially sending out "foreign missionaries" we can learn many important principles about the missionary involvement of churches. How the church came to recognize this call of God is instructive. Tannehill shows how three features in this passage are found in two other Lukan commissioning passages: "The beginnings of the missions of Jesus and the apostles are preceded by references to prayer (Luke 3:21; Acts 1:14), which provides opportunity for action of the Spirit (Luke 3:22; Acts 2:1–4), and the Spirit leads directly to mission (Luke 4:14; Acts 2:5–41)."[17] Prayer here is viewed as a service we do for God (13:2). To this is added fasting (13:2), which was also associated with the start of Jesus' ministry (Luke 4:2). Ralph Earle writes that fasting "emphasizes a state of unin-

---

17. Tannehill, *Narrative Unity*, 161.

terrupted concentration which made it possible to ascertain the will of the Lord. That is the main purpose and value of fasting."[18]

The message the church received was to release their best for missionary service (13:2), and their earnestness was such that they were willing to do so (13:3). This is typical of churches that have a missionary vision, churches whose main aim is more than survival or maintenance. Missions is so important to them that they willingly take steps that may seem harmful to the church in order for the missionary program to thrive. They have a corporate "others orientation."

Saul, of course, had already received a call from God to Gentile evangelism (cf. 22:15; 26:17). What happened here is that the church, having recognized this call, realized that this was the time for him to launch out into this task and commissioned the team to pursue it. "This event brings together the themes of personal call and congregational affirmation."[19] It is interesting that though verse 3 says the church "sent them off," the next verse says they were "sent on their way by the Holy Spirit." Ultimately the Holy Spirit is the key to the whole missionary enterprise.

Five words, then, characterize the missionary program of this church: prayer, fasting, guidance, release, and commissioning. These features come from an earnestness to know and obey God's will, which allows the Holy Spirit to superintend the whole process.

Harsh words in evangelistic settings? We may be surprised to find such harsh words being spoken to Elymas in an evangelistic setting (13:10–11). Lest we think that Paul made a mistake here, Luke assures us that he was filled with the Holy Spirit when he spoke (13:9). These words are in keeping with Jesus' harsh statement, "But if anyone causes one of these little ones who believe in me to sin, it would be better for him to have a large millstone hung around his neck and to be drowned in the depths of the sea" (Matt. 18:6). Elymas was trying to keep someone else from learning the way of salvation through "all kinds of deceit and trickery" (13:10). The salvation of Sergius Paulus was so valuable that this hindrance had to be rooted out. We too may at times need to speak and act strongly against those who try to keep others from the truth.

Evangelism through deeds and words. In our application of 2:43 we discussed how the conversion of Sergius Paulus is a good example of the place of signs and wonders in evangelism. He was "an intelligent man" (13:7), a provincial governor, and from other writings in that period we know that he hailed from "a family which rendered distinguished service to the empire in

---

18. Carter and Earle, *Acts*, 175.

19. Shenk and Stutzman, *Creating Communities*, 35.

the first and second centuries."[20] In other words, as some would say, he was not a naive simpleton who would be easily attracted to the supernatural, the type with whom miraculous ministry will be effective.

This passage shows, therefore, the combination of the various elements of an evangelistic ministry that results in belief. The proconsul believed when he "saw what had happened" (13:12). But that was not the cause of belief. The verse goes on to give the real cause of the belief: "for he was amazed [lit., being amazed] at the teaching about the Lord." Paul's teaching had been faithfully done; that was the foundation of belief. But the proconsul's heart was opened to receive this message through the miracle. It was a trigger for belief, a confirmation of the truthfulness of what was being said (see 14:3). The miraculous, then, was important because it directed people to the truth. Ministries that include the miraculous must ensure that there is also faithful proclamation of the gospel so that people respond to it rather than to miracles.

FOSTERING LEADERSHIP FROM **diverse backgrounds.** While it is helpful to have a leadership that reflects the backgrounds of the members of our churches, often this does not happen. Usually a powerful type of people (e.g., educated, wealthy, English-speaking, white) forms the majority of the leadership. Even if people from different backgrounds gain leadership positions, they are often those who have become culturally like the majority.

We ought to develop an environment that is conducive to developing leaders from groups not usually represented in leadership. One problem with doing this is a difference in the biblical qualifications for leadership and the world's qualifications. In the Bible the key qualifications are Christian character, reputation for godliness, and ability (giftedness) to lead. In the world, while ability is usually important, so are education and standing in society (wealth and cultural background). It is sad but true that in many churches most leaders and board members are rich and educated, even though there may be many poor members in those churches. To change this we need to do some serious thinking about the organizational culture that characterizes our groups. Those who meet the biblical criteria for leadership should be able comfortably to become leaders even though they may not meet worldly criteria.

When our ministry in Sri Lanka began to work with the poor, we decided we would work hard toward fostering ownership and leadership from among the poor. We had to make some important adjustments in order to do this.

---

20. Bruce, *Acts,* NICNT, 248.

Here the poor usually speak only the national languages (Sinhala and Tamil), not English. In fact, in some circles speaking in English is referred to as "wielding the sword," for it cuts off those who do not speak English. On the other side, rich and middle class people often joke about how those who are not good in English "murder the queen" (with broken English). Thus, we gave new importance to the national languages and spoke little or no English when we were among those who did not speak it. We wanted to avoid things that alienated them or reminded them of the sinful class difference.

We knew that a key to ownership is financial contribution. So we began to urge the poor to support our work financially. To encourage this we decided not to publicize large gifts, for that would give the poor a message that their gifts were less important. We sought to foster Jesus' "widow's mighty mite" approach to giving from the poor (Mark 12:41–44), so that the poor would realize that their contributions were significant (and they are!). When we realized that our salaries are paid in part by people who cannot afford two meals a day, we had to modify our attitude to lifestyle and expenditure. We dared not to spend such sacrificial gifts carelessly or extravagantly.

Gradually leaders began to emerge from among the poor. Adjustments then had to be made at the leaders' meetings. Formerly all the leaders spoke English. Now with people speaking three different languages, extra time had to be given for translation. Sometimes the leaders' meetings were held in Tamil, a language I do not speak, and I had to have someone seated next to me quietly translating what was being said.

With people from poor backgrounds in the leadership, our effectiveness in evangelism among the poor increased markedly. They had wisdom about these matters that the others did not. We began to appreciate and enjoy new types of humor. (Humor, an important part of youth ministry, is also culturally conditioned.) We were challenged by new models of godliness (e.g., those who could not read meditated daily on what they heard at the meetings instead of doing the customary Bible reading). We were challenged by the faith of illiterates who were unencumbered by our debilitating sophistication (e.g., one person who could not read had the gift of praying for healing). It was no sacrifice to change our customary forms of activity, for the enrichment that came as a result has been immeasurable.

This is just one example of the types of adjustments that need to be made to ensure that the church truly reflects its belief in the worth and equality of every group. Each organization or church needs to go through a similar pilgrimage of discovery in the art of integration. The church in many places has a poor record in doing this, and that has brought much dishonor to Christ. Islam, which claims to be the answer to "the segregation of the Christians," is growing rapidly today, especially in situations where there has been a history of segregation by Christians. This issue should be considered a major item in the priorities of any group that wishes to be God's faithful representatives on earth.

Earnest prayer and missions. The Antioch church demonstrated earnestness by their prayers and fasting. From the word Luke uses, we know that prayer is service we do for Christ. There are some who ask others to pray, claiming that their calling is to work. But in the Bible prayer is work (Col. 4:12–13). The Scottish evangelical preacher Thomas Chalmers (1780–1847) has said, "Prayer does not enable us to do a greater work for God. Prayer is a greater work for God."[21]

The history of missions is replete with great leaps forward that took place when people got together to pray. In the Haystack Meeting of 1806, some students from Williams College, Massachusetts, who had a concern for the spiritual welfare of their fellow students, met twice a week for prayer. Because they were ridiculed, they met outside the college in the countryside. One day five of them got caught in a storm and sought refuge under a haystack. While they waited there they prayed, and their special focus of prayer was the awakening of foreign missionary interest among students. Their leader, Samuel Mills, directed the discussion and praying to their own missionary obligation. He said that unless students dedicated their lives to foreign evangelism, the gospel would not be taken to places like Asia. He exhorted his friends with the words that later became like a watchword for them: "We can do this if we will."

After some discussion these five students offered their lives to foreign missions. This gave birth to the first student missionary society in America. The esteemed church historian Kenneth Scott Latourette has said, "It was from this haystack meeting that the foreign missionary movement of the churches of the United States had an initial main impulse."[22] Someone has described what was set in motion as "a golden chain stretching from the haystack meeting to the greatest student uprising in all history." Urgent prayer arising from a desire for all that God wishes makes us receptive to him and inspires a great leap forward in the history of the church.

Missions and costly release. The Spirit directed Barnabas and Saul to be set apart for reaching the lost. As we noted above, these were the top leaders of the church, and the young church in Antioch presumably had many needs. But when God calls, we must release even those we consider the most

---

21. Cited in *Living Quotations for Christians*, ed. Sherwood Elliot Wirt and Kersten Beckstrom (New York: Harper and Row, 1974), 177.

22. Kenneth Scott Latourette, *These Sought a Country* (New York: Harper and Bros., 1950), 67; from David M. Howard, *Student Power in World Evangelism* (Downers Grove: InterVarsity, 1970), 67. Many of the facts in this story are from Howard's book.

important and valued persons. That's how important missions is. One does not have to be brilliant (humanly speaking) to be a missionary. One has to be called, and God often calls "ordinary," unspectacular people to do special things for him (1 Cor. 1:26). But sometimes he sends the most talented. When brilliant people respond to the missionary call, we may say, "What a waste! Their audience will be uneducated, backward people. Why should the most brilliant go to them?" But throughout history God has called some of the brightest people in their generation to the mission field—for example, Henry Martyn, Stephen Neill, Lesslie Newbigin, and Stanley Jones.

Is this happening today too? I can think of many sharp people, young and old, who are on the mission field today. But I also see a hindrance to this happening. The church has been influenced by worldly standards of success, and going to the unreached is low on this status scale. The pastor of a church of 2,500 people may be considered a powerful person. If that person was called to go to the lost, he may at first have only two people in his church— himself and his colleague. For this reason many opt for the big church instead of answering God's call to missions.

Paul also encountered these wrong values in the church. Towards the end of his life he wrote that no one was with him in his trial because they all had deserted him (2 Tim. 4:16). Perhaps there was no status in associating with Paul. He himself often spoke of how he was, humanly speaking, abased. But today he is a hero and one of the most admired persons in the history of the world. Usually heroes are admired only from a distance, not when they are doing their great work. In their own time they were often regarded as fools or failures. Their heroism made them give up earthly glory, so that earthly people did not admire them.

May we not be reluctant to challenge all—the brilliant and the ordinary—to consider missions. And when such are called, may we release them wholeheartedly for this work. May we place missions high up in our list of priorities. As David Livingstone said, "God had only one son and he was a missionary." May we encourage those with an interest in missions. And may those who feel called to missions share this vision with their churches so that they can be sent away for this task by a group that is committed to them and will pray for them.

Paul's approach to Elymas in an age of tolerance. Ours is an age of tolerance, where pluralism mandates that since there is no absolute truth, different ideologies are equals in the universe of faiths. We cannot pronounce one wrong and the other right. This attitude is well expressed in the statement coming from the heir to the British throne about being "defender of the *faiths*" rather than "defender of the *faith*." (The king or queen of Britain is the titular head of the Church of England.) Today sorcerers, like Elymas, have equal status with ministers of the gospel in many surroundings. Governments want to be fair to all the ideologies represented by their citizens. In countries (like ours) where Christians are a minority, we appreciate that.

But let us remember that the church remains under the authority of a normative revelation. It therefore has a commitment "to contend for the faith that was once for all entrusted to the saints" (Jude 3). This task gains a high level of urgency when it views its mandate as being to "snatch others from the fire and save them" (Jude 23). If the gospel is indeed the only way to salvation, then our task becomes urgent—as urgent as it was to Paul when he said, "I am compelled to preach. Woe to me if I do not preach the gospel!" (1 Cor. 9:16).

Influenced by the pluralistic mood, many view evangelism as a mere exchanging of views among people of different ideologies. Instead, we should view the gospel we preach as holding the key to eternal salvation. If a father sees a man trying to peddle heroin to his little son, he will not seek to enter a discussion with the man on the merits and demerits of heroin or politely request him to stop doing that. He will take urgent and decisive action. If a mother sees her daughter about to accept an attractive piece of candy into which has been injected the deadly poison cyanide, she will not simply share her views on the subject. She will take urgent action. If a hotel employee discovers a fire in a room, realizes that the fire alarm has not gone off, and knows that hundreds of occupants might be killed, she does not calmly go her way, not wanting to disturb the sleeping people. She will take urgent action. If such drastic action is taken for temporal problems, how about a problem that has dire consequences for all eternity? One who loves humanity will not calmly stand by when he or she sees the eternal salvation of a person for whom Christ died jeopardized through the deception of a false teacher.

The place of miracles in conversion. When non-Christians are confronted with the message of Christ, most will at first have moral and cultural blocks to even considering it seriously. It is a costly message for it involves renouncing one's past life and embracing Christ as Lord. Thus, unless there is some compelling evidence that will move their hearts, people will not regard it as worthy of consideration.

God often uses actions of Christians—such as deeds of kindness, miracles, and blameless lives—to incline the hearts of people favorably toward the gospel. Once the heart is open, it is possible for the will to be oriented to accepting the gospel. People will be able to regard its teaching for what it is worth without their earlier prejudices and fears. They will realize it is something worth committing their lives to. Acts 13 emphasizes that both deeds and words are important elements in the evangelistic process. Though ultimately people put their trust in Christ based on the words they hear, deeds often act as a trigger to open them to considering the words.

Acts 13:13–52

FROM PAPHOS, PAUL and his companions sailed to Perga in Pamphylia, where John left them to return to Jerusalem. [14]From Perga they went on to Pisidian Antioch. On the Sabbath they entered the synagogue and sat down. [15]After the reading from the Law and the Prophets, the synagogue rulers sent word to them, saying, "Brothers, if you have a message of encouragement for the people, please speak."

[16]Standing up, Paul motioned with his hand and said: "Men of Israel and you Gentiles who worship God, listen to me! [17]The God of the people of Israel chose our fathers; he made the people prosper during their stay in Egypt, with mighty power he led them out of that country, [18]he endured their conduct for about forty years in the desert, [19]he overthrew seven nations in Canaan and gave their land to his people as their inheritance. [20]All this took about 450 years.

"After this, God gave them judges until the time of Samuel the prophet. [21]Then the people asked for a king, and he gave them Saul son of Kish, of the tribe of Benjamin, who ruled forty years. [22]After removing Saul, he made David their king. He testified concerning him: 'I have found David son of Jesse a man after my own heart; he will do everything I want him to do.'

[23]"From this man's descendants God has brought to Israel the Savior Jesus, as he promised. [24]Before the coming of Jesus, John preached repentance and baptism to all the people of Israel. [25]As John was completing his work, he said: 'Who do you think I am? I am not that one. No, but he is coming after me, whose sandals I am not worthy to untie.'

[26]"Brothers, children of Abraham, and you God-fearing Gentiles, it is to us that this message of salvation has been sent. [27]The people of Jerusalem and their rulers did not recognize Jesus, yet in condemning him they fulfilled the words of the prophets that are read every Sabbath. [28]Though they found no proper ground for a death sentence, they asked Pilate to have him executed. [29]When they had carried out all that was written about him, they took him down from the tree and laid him in a tomb. [30]But God raised him from the dead, [31]and for many days he was seen by those who had traveled with him from Galilee to Jerusalem. They are now his witnesses to our people.

³²"We tell you the good news: What God promised our fathers ³³he has fulfilled for us, their children, by raising up Jesus. As it is written in the second Psalm:

"'You are my Son;
today I have become your Father. '

³⁴The fact that God raised him from the dead, never to decay, is stated in these words:

"'I will give you the holy and sure blessings
promised to David.'

³⁵So it is stated elsewhere:

"'You will not let your Holy One see decay.'

³⁶"For when David had served God's purpose in his own generation, he fell asleep; he was buried with his fathers and his body decayed. ³⁷But the one whom God raised from the dead did not see decay.

³⁸"Therefore, my brothers, I want you to know that through Jesus the forgiveness of sins is proclaimed to you. ³⁹Through him everyone who believes is justified from everything you could not be justified from by the law of Moses. ⁴⁰Take care that what the prophets have said does not happen to you:

⁴¹"'Look, you scoffers,
wonder and perish,
for I am going to do something in your days
that you would never believe,
even if someone told you.'"

⁴²As Paul and Barnabas were leaving the synagogue, the people invited them to speak further about these things on the next Sabbath. ⁴³When the congregation was dismissed, many of the Jews and devout converts to Judaism followed Paul and Barnabas, who talked with them and urged them to continue in the grace of God.

⁴⁴On the next Sabbath almost the whole city gathered to hear the word of the Lord. ⁴⁵When the Jews saw the crowds, they were filled with jealousy and talked abusively against what Paul was saying.

⁴⁶Then Paul and Barnabas answered them boldly: "We had to speak the word of God to you first. Since you reject it and

do not consider yourselves worthy of eternal life, we now turn to the Gentiles. [47]For this is what the Lord has commanded us:

> "'I have made you a light for the Gentiles,
>> that you may bring salvation to the ends of the earth.'"

[48]When the Gentiles heard this, they were glad and honored the word of the Lord; and all who were appointed for eternal life believed.

[49]The word of the Lord spread through the whole region. [50]But the Jews incited the God-fearing women of high standing and the leading men of the city. They stirred up persecution against Paul and Barnabas, and expelled them from their region. [51]So they shook the dust from their feet in protest against them and went to Iconium. [52]And the disciples were filled with joy and with the Holy Spirit.

THE WESTWARD PROGRESS of the gospel continues as "Paul and his companions" sail northwest from Paphos in Cyprus to Perga in Pamphylia (v. 13). We are not told whether they preach in that city, though we know that they preached there on their return journey (14:25). Most of chapter 13 deals with the experiences of these evangelists in Antioch of Pisidia.

Preaching in Pisidian Antioch (13:13–41)

VERSE 13 RECORDS two interesting changes in the missionary team. (1) Paul seems to have taken the prominent role. Prior to this Barnabas was always mentioned first.[1] Now Barnabas is not even mentioned but is included as one of Paul's "companions." Hereafter, except in the description of the proceedings of the Jerusalem Council (15:12) and the letter it sent to the churches (15:25), the order is always "Paul and Barnabas."[2] This seems to be Luke's way of saying that Paul has taken over the leadership slot or at least the place of prominence.

(2) John Mark leaves to return home to Jerusalem. Paul later describes this departure as a desertion (15:38), but we are not told why he leaves. Is he homesick? Has he not planned to be away for so long? Does he find the rigors of travel, especially the prospect of a climb up the mountains to Galatia,

---

1. See 11:26, 30; 12:25; 13:1, 2, 13:7.
2. See 13:42, 43, 46, 50; 14:1, 3, 14, 20, 23; 15:2, 22, 35.

too hard on him? Does he resent the fact that his cousin Barnabas is falling into second place? Does he have problems with the bold approach to Gentiles that Paul is developing? We cannot be sure.

From Perga Paul and Barnabas travel inland and northward to the higher altitudes, and they minister in cities of south Galatia. They presumably took the paved Roman highway, the Via Sebaste, from Perga to Antioch.[3] Antioch of Pisidia was an important civil and military center of the Romans (v. 14), which lay about 3,600 feet above sea level. The city actually belonged to Galatia, but it was near Pisidia and thus got its name (as there was another Antioch in the same district).

In Galatians 4:13 Paul says that "it was because of an illness that [he] first preached the gospel" in this area. Sir William Ramsay suggests that Paul had caught malaria in the low-lying territory and went to recuperate in the higher altitudes of the north,[4] but we cannot be sure about this. One of the wealthiest business families of Antioch was the family of Sergius Paulus, the proconsul of Cyprus, who had been converted (13:5—12). It is not surprising, then, that an expert on the archaeology of the area, S. Mitchell, writes: "We can hardly avoid the conclusion that the proconsul himself had suggested to Paul that he make [Antioch] his next port of call, no doubt providing him with letters of introduction to aid his passage on his stay."[5]

As was their custom, Paul and Barnabas go to the local synagogue on the Sabbath, and they are invited to speak (vv. 14—15). We note that Paul addresses both Jews and God-fearers twice, using different designations each time (vv. 16, 26), and that the message is tailored to suit an audience with a background of knowledge about the Old Testament. While he covers some of the same ground in his historical survey of Israel's history as Stephen, his aim is different. Stephen wanted to demonstrate that the old era with the temple and the law of Moses had given way to the new. Paul's aim is rather to show how God's activity in history climaxed in the coming of Jesus. Thus he talks of how God worked with Israel in Egypt (v. 17a), in the Exodus (v. 17b), in the desert wanderings (v. 18), in the conquest of Canaan (v. 20), in the period of the judges (v. 20b), and during the time of Israel's first two kings, Saul and David (vv. 21—22). From there Paul jumps straight to Jesus the Savior, who came as one of David's descendants (v. 23). The implication here is that Jesus fulfills Jewish aspirations.

---

3. G. Walter Hansen, "Galatia," BAFCS, 2:384.

4. W. M. Ramsay, St. Paul the Traveler and Roman Citizen (London: Hodder and Stoughton, 1920), 94—97; cited in Bruce, Acts, NICNT, 251.

5. S. Mitchell, Anatolia: Land, Men and God's in Asia Minor, vol. 2: The Rise of the Church (Oxford: Clarendon, 1993), 7; quoted in Hansen, "Galatia," 386—87.

From that point on, Paul argues for the validity of his claim in verse 23 that Jesus is indeed the promised "Savior." John the Baptist had anticipated his coming (vv. 24–25). Paul's hearers possibly knew more about John than about Jesus.[6] After proclaiming that this message of salvation has been sent to them (v. 26), Paul proceeds to expound on the death of Christ with the characteristic apologetic presented to the Jews in Acts: He was innocent and his death fulfilled Old Testament prophecy (vv. 27–29). Then, as in Peter's Pentecost sermon, Paul gives an extended exposition of how the resurrection was witnessed by credible people and was in keeping with what the Old Testament said (vv. 30–37).

Following the exposition of the Christ event is an offer of forgiveness (v. 38) and justification (v. 39). Verse 39 contains ideas that are typical of Paul's letters: belief, justification, and the inability to be justified by the law of Moses. Stott adds to these references some others from elsewhere in the speech: death on the tree (v. 29), sin (v. 38), and grace (v. 43). After pointing out that Paul was addressing Galatians here, Stott observes that these ideas provided the foundation stone to his letter to the Galatians, which he would write a few months later. Stott observes that W. C. Van Unnik felt able to assert that "Luke has no understanding of the doctrine of justification by faith as the center of Pauline thought."[7] Stott, however, shows how this speech contradicts that assertion.[8] So we do not need to assume, as some do, that the Paul of Acts could not have written letters like Galatians and Romans.

Paul concludes his message with a quotation from Habbakuk (Hab. 1:5)—a warning of judgment to those who reject God's offer of salvation (Acts 13:41).

The themes of the displacement of people and God's choice are keys to Paul's sermon.[9] He speaks of the displacement of the nations and the choice of Israel (v. 19); the displacement of Saul and the choice of David (v. 22); the fact that "all the people of Israel" had to go through the sign of conversion to Judaism, baptism, if they were to avoid displacement (v. 24); the displacement of John by Jesus (v. 25); and the displacement of the Jews and the choice of Jesus (vv. 40–41; cf. vv. 46–48). Paul expresses God's plan of salvation for the world through the progress of history. Beginning with his salvation at the Exodus, he shows how God systematically kept unfolding his purposes until it reached its climax in the Christ event.

---

6. Gempf, "Acts," 1086.

7. Leander E. Keck and J. Louis Martyn, eds., *Studies in Luke-Acts* (Philadelphia: Fortress, 1980), 26.

8. Stott, *Acts*, 225–26.

9. Gempf, "Acts," 1086–87.

The Aftermath of Paul's Sermon (13:42–52)

PAUL AND BARNABAS are invited to speak the next Sabbath as well (v. 42). In the meantime, "many of the Jews and devout converts to Judaism" (*proseluton*) follow them. We can assume that Paul and Barnabas gave themselves to personal ministry with these contacts during the week: They "talked with them and urged them to continue in the grace of God" (v. 43). The last expression may not mean that they were converted; rather, they had become open to the grace of God working in their hearts, and they were now being urged to continue along that path.

The Jews probably did not expect to see nearly the whole city there on that day (v. 44). Their jealousy is aroused, and they oppose Paul's next message with abusive talk (v. 45). Paul and Barnabas respond to this by stating what became a feature of their ministry and of Paul's theology: They preach to the Jews first, but if their response is unworthy of eternal life, they go to the Gentiles (v. 46).[10] Paul backs that step from the Scriptures (v. 47). While he would have spoken with confidence on this occasion, this phenomenon of Jewish rejection of the gospel hurts him deeply and inflames his desire to yearn and pray for their salvation (Rom. 9:1–3; 10:1).

In Romans 9–11 Paul uses his great theological skill for a profound exploration of the implications of and reasons for this rejection. In fact, a part of Romans 9–11 is in some ways an exposition of Acts 13:47. The receptivity of the Gentiles was remarkable, considering the fact that the imperial cult (public worship of the emperor) was strong in Antioch. There was a temple of Augustus in the center as the city's most prominent building, and this cult dominated the city's daily life and annual calendar.[11]

The Gentiles receive Paul's word with gladness (v. 48a). The unusual expression "honored (*edoxazon*) the word of the Lord," (v. 48b) probably means "that they gave glory to the Lord for the word that they had heard."[12] After considerable emphasis on the human response to the gospel, both positive and negative, Luke redresses the balance by emphasizing God's foundational role in salvation: All those who believed "were appointed for eternal life" (v. 48c). "It is never merely a person's own choice that saves them, it is always God's love and mercy."[13]

The severity of the opposition to the gospel is such that the team has to leave town (vv. 49–50). Despite these problems the new believers are "filled with joy and with the Holy Spirit" (v. 52). As Paul and Barnabas leave the area,

---

10. Cf. 18:6; 22:21; 26:20; 28:28; cf. Rom. 1:16.
11. Hansen, "Galatia," 394–95.
12. Barrett, *Acts,* 658.
13. Gempf, "Acts," 1087.

they express their verdict on the Jews by shaking the dust off their feet (v. 51). David Williams points out that "strict Jews performed this symbolic action on entering the Holy Land from abroad, lest they be contaminated with the dust of profane places." Now, by doing it against Jews, Paul and Barnabas "declared them in effect to be no better than the pagans among whom they lived; these Jews were profane and no longer part of the true Israel."[14]

MORE KEYS TO the ministry of encouragement. Acts provides us with a fascinating picture of the way Barnabas served as an encourager to Paul and to Mark. This section gives three common experiences of encouragers. (1) Luke's reversal in the order of names (mentioning Paul's before Barnabas's from verse 13 on[15]) suggests that Luke wants to show that Paul had become the prominent partner in the team. Here is a common experience of encouragers—they exhibit a willingness to hand over leadership to a junior person, if that is best for the progress of the kingdom.

(2) Once Paul became the prominent partner, Barnabas was simply there while Paul did the preaching and teaching. If, as suggested in our discussion of 4:36, the name Barnabas means "Son of Exhortation," Barnabas was a good teacher. But good teachers who are encouragers will give the teaching slot to someone who may be a more effective teacher for a particular situation and simply be there as a team member.

(3) Barnabas was also an encourager to Mark, his cousin (Col. 4:10)—a fact that becomes evident when Paul decides not to take Mark along on a later journey, which led in turn to Barnabas's decision to separate from Paul and travel with Mark (Acts 15:37–39). Mark's decision to leave the team at Perga (13:13) must have been a source of sorrow for Barnabas. Encouragers face such blows, as some of those for whom they have high hopes fail to live up to their expectations.

The progress of history. In Paul's message, he showed how God systematically kept unfolding his purposes, beginning with the Exodus, until it reached its climax in the Christ event. Luke-Acts has a strong emphasis on the concept of the history of salvation. It rests on "the basic assumption that God works out salvation within a special history that is also a part of general world history." In his presentation, "Luke is intent to present the Jesus-event not as just another event in God's special saving history, but as *the* event in that history."[16] The hope of the Old Testament is fulfilled through what

---

14. D. J. Williams, *Acts*, 240.

15. In verse 13 Barnabas's name is not even mentioned.

16. J. Julius Scott Jr., "Theology of Luke-Acts," *EDBT*, 496.

happened as a result of Jesus' coming (Acts 2:16). We will show below that the practice of recounting God's progressive unfolding of his plan for the world in history can be a useful evangelistic methodology even today.

Emphasizing the content of the gospel in evangelism. In my fresh study of Acts for writing this commentary, one of the features that kept coming up is how important the content of the gospel is to evangelism. This is why Luke emphasizes it so often in Acts, as he does here at considerable length (vv. 16–41).[17] Christianity is essentially a religion of revelation, and Christians are the people of a book. Thus the content of the gospel and arguing for its validity are important to Christianity.

We see evidence of this in the way Paul argues for the validity and attractiveness of the gospel in his speech in Pisidian Antioch. This speech is a model of persuasive apologetics. The primacy of the content of the gospel to evangelism is also seen in how Luke describes the response to the gospel: The people "gathered to hear the word of the Lord" (v. 44). Those who accepted this word "honored the word of the Lord" (v. 48). "The word of the Lord spread through the whole region" (v. 49). Clearly the word of the Lord, God's truth revealed to humanity, was a primary aspect of the evangelistic process.

The Gentile converts in Antioch did not view Christianity only as an answer to some earthly personal problems of theirs. If that was their attitude, the expulsion of the missionaries from the city would certainly have taken away their joy. Instead, they viewed Christianity as the truth of God, and they were able to rejoice even after the team left (cf. v. 52). True, when people come to Christ, it may at first be in order to have a need met. But they stay on because they believe that the gospel is the truth. When we realize that this is the heart of the gospel, we have a security that can weather the storms of life. And we can even have joy amidst those storms.

ENCOURAGERS HAND OVER **leadership.** It must not have been easy for Barnabas to hand leadership over to Paul. Paul was in some ways his trainee. Barnabas was probably physically older than Paul—and certainly older spiritually. He was also probably more distinguished looking, for later the people of Lystra called Barnabas Zeus, the chief Greek god, and Paul Hermes, the spokesman of the god (14:12). Commenting on the exchange of leadership roles Bruce cites the rhymester,

---

17. For Luke's emphasis on the content of the evangelistic message, see 2:14–40; 3:12–26; 4:8–12; 5:29–32; 7:2–53; 8:32–35; 10:34–43; 13:16–41; 14:15–17; 15:7–11, 13–21; 16:31–32; 17:11, 22–31; 18:28; 22:3–21; 24:10–21; 26:2–27; 28:26–31.

It takes more grace than I can tell
To play the second fiddle well.[18]

This is a challenge that all leaders will face at some time. We must be willing to hand over our position if that will benefit the kingdom. And if we do so, we must make it easy for our successors. I am thankful to report that I have often seen this happen in Christian circles, where the senior leader stayed on as a fund-raiser or an advisor to the younger person and where the younger leader benefited from the senior person's experience without being threatened by his or her presence.

In order to let this transition take place smoothly, the senior leader may need to take definite steps in crucifying the flesh. The famous Bible teacher F. B. Meyer (1847–1929) often ministered at D. L. Moody's Northfield Bible Conference and always drew large crowds to his meetings. Then the younger Bible teacher G. Campbell Morgan (1863–1945) began to preach there, and his stirring Bible studies began to attract larger audiences than Meyer's. Meyer confessed to some of his close friends that he was sometimes envious of Morgan. But then he said, "The only way I can conquer my feelings is to pray for him daily, which I do."[19] This was a definite step he took to adopt a kingdom perspective over his loss of prominence in the hands of a younger preacher.

If Paul was the speaker, Barnabas must have listened while he spoke. Many top leaders today, given their busy schedules, might think it a waste of time to be listening to junior people preach. But one of the great privileges and joys of leadership is to just "be there" in order to encourage a younger person, as he or she does what we know we too could do very well. My seminary teacher and mentor, Dr. Robert Coleman, used to say that the glory of the teacher is to sit at the feet of the student and learn from him or her. I had the opportunity of preaching a few times when I was a student in seminary. That was a difficult task because in seminaries sermons are critiqued. Dr. Coleman would say, "I'll be there in the Amen corner"—and he always was. When I became nervous while preaching, all I had to do was to look in his direction and see his beaming face. That encouraged me to go on preaching with zeal.

Luke reverted to the old order of "Barnabas and Paul" in his report of the proceedings of the Jerusalem Council (15:12) and of the letter that the council sent to the churches (15:25). Barnabas was an esteemed senior leader in Jerusalem, and it was certainly more appropriate for him to take the lead

---

18. Bruce, *Circle*, 19.

19. W. Y. Fullerton, *F. B. Meyer: A Biography* (London: Marshall, Morgan and Scott, n.d.), 37.

role there rather than Paul. Paul apparently let that happen. In other words, leadership is not an inalienable right to which we cling tenaciously. It is rather a responsibility related to the agenda of the kingdom. That agenda is always more important than our personal prominence and status.

Encouragers are often saddened. In our application of 11:23 we noted that encouragers are easily gladdened. But here we see how the generous spirit of Barnabas received a painful blow when Mark left the team (13:13). Just as encouragers are easily gladdened, they are also often saddened. Some of those we invest in and hope for will not live up to our expectations and achieve the ambitions we have for them. This will bring disappointment and pain because we were genuinely ambitious for these people. It may also result in humiliation since we have taken the risk of backing these persons in public.

To avoid such pain, some leaders play it safe and never get close to people or take the risk of backing them. Sometimes cynicism and suspicion take over, which disqualifies them from the ministry of encouragement. They may avoid pain, but they also avoid having lasting fruit. Paul also experienced much pain and stress because of his deep commitment to people (2 Cor. 11:28–29; Gal. 4:19–20). But he also bore much fruit. We know, of course, that though the pain of Barnabas's commitment to Mark intensified later (15:37–39), his hopes about him were well founded as he became an even more prominent person in the history of Christianity than Barnabas as the writer of one of the Gospels. The pain of commitment, then, is well worth taking on, for though some do not make it, others do.

Using the unfolding of God's plan for humanity in evangelism. The unfolding of God's plan of salvation for humanity has been the basis for the outline of several important works in biblical theology.[20] Paul uses the same theme to construct an outline of his evangelistic preaching in Acts. This seems also to be the strategy Jesus used in his heartwarming explanation of the gospel on the road to Emmaus (Luke 24:27). I suggest that it is an appropriate method for constructing evangelistic messages today. In his message Paul showed how, through the vicissitudes of human history, God was working out his plan for his creation and that this plan reached its zenith in "the Christ-event."

---

20. Elmer A. Martens, *God's Design: A Focus on Old Testament Theology* (Grand Rapids: Baker, 1981); Daniel P. Fuller, *The Unity of the Bible* (Grand Rapids: Zondervan, 1992); Walter C. Kaiser Jr., *Toward an Old Testament Theology* (Grand Rapids: Zondervan, 1978); Erich Sauer, *The Dawn of World Redemption: A Survey of Historical Revelation in the Old Testament* (Grand Rapids: Eerdmans, reprint); idem, *The Triumph of the Crucified: A Survey of Historical Revelation in the New Testament* (Grand Rapids: Eerdmans, reprint); Geerhardus Vos, *Biblical Theology* (Grand Rapids: Eerdmans, 1954); Bruce K. Waltke with Charles Yu, *Old Testament Theology: The Making of the Kingdom of God* (Grand Rapids: Zondervan, forthcoming).

Many people fear for the world as they see it heading toward self-destruction, through moral degradation, war, or ecological irresponsibility. Many live in cynicism and despair as savior after savior fails to satisfy the human thirst for an eternally secure solution to the problems of life. The cyclic view of history, characteristic of Hinduism, which has greatly influenced the New Age movement in the West, adds to this sense of despair, for it does not see history headed for a goal or consummation. Paul's speech, by contrast, clearly shows that the Lord of the universe is not inactive, that he has not abandoned his creation and let it run its own course. Rather, God has acted according to a plan, which has been gradually unfolding. In Christ the desire of the ages is fulfilled. People looking for the meaning of history and thinking that they will have to concede that it is meaningless need not come to that gloomy conclusion. There is hope! The plan of the Creator of the universe is being worked out.

Such a message can bring hope to hopeless people. It can give security to listeners who come to realize that there may indeed be meaning to the puzzle of life. Tracing the hand of God in the history of the human race creates in some people a desire to join in with this most important process in the universe. For this reason, I often use Paul's approach of explaining the unfolding of God's program for the world in my evangelistic preaching with predominantly non-Christian audiences (usually beginning with the creation of the world).

I was part of a group that created a popular evangelistic Scripture booklet consisting of Genesis 1–12 and John. In between these two sections of Scripture, we included a brief summary of God's dealings with the human race between Abraham and Jesus, beginning with the creation of the nation of Israel and leading to the predictions about a coming Messiah by the prophets. It was presented in such a way as to show how God's purposes were fulfilled in history according to a plan, with Christ as the apex of this plan.

Through its experience in trying to reach unreached tribes with the gospel, the New Tribes Mission has developed a course, *Building on Firm Foundations*, that uses what they call the "chronological approach" to evangelism and to teaching believers. They offer a nine-volume set, in which two volumes are for evangelism and six are for teaching. Each series starts with the Old Testament and goes to the New Testament.[21] This approach may well be a key not only to reaching people in non-Christian countries but also in reaching the "post-Christian" West.

---

21. The story of how this was used in a tribe is vividly portrayed in two videos entitled, *"Ee-Taow"* ("It is true") and "Now We See Clearly."

Content-centered evangelism. There are three key factors in today's world that impede making the content of the gospel central to the evangelistic process. (1) The dominant philosophy of our age, pluralism, has given the idea of truth a severe bashing. Pluralism denies the importance of objective truth. In such an environment apologetics is regarded as inappropriate and even presumptuous. The pluralist says that truth is subjective—something we learn from our experience. There is therefore no absolute truth that comes from objective revelation. Instead of apologetics they propose dialogue—by which they mean an exchange of beliefs and experiences that will result in each one enriching the other.[22]

(2) We live in a technological and information era that concentrates so much on action and information that there is little time to think about ideas and truth. Sammy Tippit has said, "Perhaps one of the greatest needs of this generation is for thinking men and women. The advent of the computer has brought artificial intelligence into the world. Many Christians have ceased to be thinkers in an age of computers and television."[23] When people want refreshment, they go to something that will keep them active (like outdoor recreation) or that will numb their senses (like television). Preachers have an abundance of computer programs available that have done a lot of the thinking they would usually have done. While these have a place, nothing can replace meditation and hard thinking about truth. It is from such lingering with truth that effective apologetics and proclamation emerge. We should use the marvels of technology to make us efficient in doing things and gathering information so that we will have more time to think.

(3) Many Christian groups are oriented to experience. While this is not wrong and is, in fact, desirable, it must never dethrone truth. Sometimes experiences like healing or being slain in the Spirit can become so prominent that people do not associate the gospel with intelligent and demonstrable arguments. Many are not willing to work hard at studying the background of the audience and tailoring the message of what Christ has done for our salvation in order to be relevant, as Paul did. People fast and pray in order to receive the power of God—and that is vital for evangelism. But so is the power of being equipped with God's Word, which requires preparation time. For this power we must both pray and study.

In other words, we must exhibit the power of God's Spirit *both* in experience *and* in the world of thought. In this way we will have a balanced gospel

---

22. For critiques of this approach to truth, see Paul Helm, ed., *Objective Knowledge: A Christian Perspective* (Leicester: Inter-Varsity, 1987); Paul J. Griffiths, *An Apology for Apologetics: A Study in the Logic of Interreligious Dialogue* (Maryknoll, N.Y.: Orbis, 1991).

23. Sammy Tippit, *The Prayer Factor* (Chicago: Moody, 1988), 41; quoted in Paul Borthwick, *Feeding Your Forgotten Soul* (Grand Rapids: Zondervan, 1990), 96.

that can withstand the dry spells that will surely come, when God's hand seems withdrawn from us. Christians are not immune to such experiences. Those whose faith is founded on the truth will persevere, knowing that nothing can take away the truthfulness of the gospel. They will have the joy that the Christian disciples in Pisidian Antioch had despite the problems they faced (v. 52). But those whose faith is founded on experience will flounder when they encounter times of darkness. One would hope that at these times such people will stumble on the more secure and unchanging realities of Christianity.

It is not wrong, then, to attract people to Christianity by presenting them an attractive program that ministers to their felt needs. But that is not enough. We must get people to understand the glory of the truth of the gospel— something deeper and more lasting than experience. Then they will have joy in the gospel, a joy that can withstand the mysterious times of darkness in life.

In order to communicate this vision we must know in our own lives the joy of truth. We must take time to feed our minds with the truth and to meditate on it so that it will glow within us. As a result, those to whom we minister will, by observing us, also acquire a respect and appreciation for the truth. They will catch our enthusiasm over it. In the meantime we too will find ourselves refreshed and fed. This will help us remain fresh amidst the debilitating challenges of ministry.[24] John Stott has said, "Scripture comes alive in the congregation only if it has come alive in the preacher first. Only if God has spoken to him through the Word which he preaches will they hear the voice of God through his lips."[25]

---

24. See the "Contemporary Significance" section of 6:1–7, "Leadership and the ministry of the Word."

25. John R. W. Stott, *The Preacher's Portrait: Some New Testament Word Studies* (Grand Rapids: Eerdmans, 1961), 30.

Acts 14:1–28

AT ICONIUM PAUL and Barnabas went as usual into the Jewish synagogue. There they spoke so effectively that a great number of Jews and Gentiles believed. ²But the Jews who refused to believe stirred up the Gentiles and poisoned their minds against the brothers. ³So Paul and Barnabas spent considerable time there, speaking boldly for the Lord, who confirmed the message of his grace by enabling them to do miraculous signs and wonders. ⁴The people of the city were divided; some sided with the Jews, others with the apostles. ⁵There was a plot afoot among the Gentiles and Jews, together with their leaders, to mistreat them and stone them. ⁶But they found out about it and fled to the Lycaonian cities of Lystra and Derbe and to the surrounding country, ⁷where they continued to preach the good news.

⁸In Lystra there sat a man crippled in his feet, who was lame from birth and had never walked. ⁹He listened to Paul as he was speaking. Paul looked directly at him, saw that he had faith to be healed ¹⁰and called out, "Stand up on your feet!" At that, the man jumped up and began to walk.

¹¹When the crowd saw what Paul had done, they shouted in the Lycaonian language, "The gods have come down to us in human form!" ¹²Barnabas they called Zeus, and Paul they called Hermes because he was the chief speaker. ¹³The priest of Zeus, whose temple was just outside the city, brought bulls and wreaths to the city gates because he and the crowd wanted to offer sacrifices to them.

¹⁴But when the apostles Barnabas and Paul heard of this, they tore their clothes and rushed out into the crowd, shouting: ¹⁵"Men, why are you doing this? We too are only men, human like you. We are bringing you good news, telling you to turn from these worthless things to the living God, who made heaven and earth and sea and everything in them. ¹⁶In the past, he let all nations go their own way. ¹⁷Yet he has not left himself without testimony: He has shown kindness by giving you rain from heaven and crops in their seasons; he provides you with plenty of food and fills your hearts with joy." ¹⁸Even with these words, they had difficulty keeping the crowd from sacrificing to them.

¹⁹Then some Jews came from Antioch and Iconium and won the crowd over. They stoned Paul and dragged him outside the city, thinking he was dead. ²⁰But after the disciples had gathered around him, he got up and went back into the city. The next day he and Barnabas left for Derbe.

²¹They preached the good news in that city and won a large number of disciples. Then they returned to Lystra, Iconium and Antioch, ²²strengthening the disciples and encouraging them to remain true to the faith. "We must go through many hardships to enter the kingdom of God," they said. ²³Paul and Barnabas appointed elders for them in each church and, with prayer and fasting, committed them to the Lord, in whom they had put their trust. ²⁴After going through Pisidia, they came into Pamphylia, ²⁵and when they had preached the word in Perga, they went down to Attalia.

²⁶From Attalia they sailed back to Antioch, where they had been committed to the grace of God for the work they had now completed. ²⁷On arriving there, they gathered the church together and reported all that God had done through them and how he had opened the door of faith to the Gentiles. ²⁸And they stayed there a long time with the disciples.

CHAPTER 14 RECORDS further activities of Paul and Barnabas in south Galatia, where they visit the cities of Iconium, Lystra, and Derbe. At the end of this chapter, they retrace their route in Galatia and eventually sail back to Antioch. They report to the church there the great things that "God had done through them" (v. 27).

Ministry in Iconium (14:1–7)

ICONIUM (MODERN KONYA) was and still is an important junction along which the east-west road from Syria to Ephesus passed. It was about ninety miles southeast of Pisidian Antioch, and Paul and Barnabas continued on the Via Sebaste that brought them to Antioch. Lystra was less than twenty miles southwest of Iconium. The sixty-three miles from Lystra to Derbe was on unpaved track.[1] The story of how this chapter helped the great archaeologist Sir William Ramsay to come to believe in the trustworthiness of the New Testament is described in the Introduction.

---

1. G. Walter Hansen, "Galatia," *BAFCS*, 2:384.

Paul and Barnabas followed their "usual" practice of going first to the local synagogue (v. 1). Many Jews and Gentiles believed, which resulted in opposition from the Jews who did not believe (v. 2; cf. 13:50; 14:19; 17:5–9). But Paul and Barnabas persevered with the ministry of the word and of miracles (v. 3); the latter were a confirmation from God of the message preached. The confirmatory role of miracles is implied in the believers' request to God in 4:30 to send miracles to their ministry and is illustrated in the conversion of Sergius Paulus after Elymas was struck blind (13:12), but here it is explicitly stated. The gospel caused the city to be divided (v. 4), and a plot against Paul and Barnabas forced them to flee to Lystra and Derbe (v. 5).

Ministry in Lystra and Derbe (14:8–21a)

THE HEALING OF the cripple with which the account of the ministry in Lystra begins probably took place sometime after Paul and Barnabas had arrived in Lystra, for it is clear that by the time Paul was stoned, there were already believers in the city who went to his aid (v. 20). The report of the miracle has remarkable similarities to the healing at the temple gate (3:2–10). Both the subjects were born lame. Paul looked directly at the cripple, just as Peter and John did (14:9; cf. 3:4). Both men jumped up after being healed (14:10; cf. 3:8). Both are said to have had the faith to be healed (14:9; cf. 3:16). In both cases the preachers had to divert the attention from themselves to God (14:15; cf. 3:12).

Identification of Paul and Barnabas with Zeus and Hermes (vv. 11–12) is understandable, for "Zeus was the most widely worshipped God in Galatia. . . . [and] was often linked with other gods. In the territory of Lystra there are carvings and inscriptions which show Zeus accompanied by Hermes."[2] The frenzied response of the Lystrans may be traced to an ancient legend retold by Ovid (43 B.C.–A.D. 17) in his *Metamorphosis*. Zeus and Hermes once visited the Phrygian hill country disguised as ordinary men. They were turned away from a thousand homes where they sought lodging, but were finally taken in by an elderly couple into their humble home. The gods turned that house into a temple and destroyed all the houses that had rejected them.[3]

Paul and Barnabas could not understand what was being said by the people since they were shouting "in the Lycaonian language" (v. 11). This accounts for their delayed response to plans to offer sacrifices to them. When they found this out, their response was swift and typically Jewish (v. 14). "Jewish people were required to tear their clothes when they heard

---

2. Ibid., 393.
3. Ibid., 394. The story is reprinted in Boring, *Hellenistic Commentary*, 322–23.

blasphemy."[4] It was an opposite reaction to Herod when he was equated to a god (12:22–23).

Paul uses the situation to launch into a witness to the gospel, stating that he and Barnabas are presenting a much more sublime message than can be obtained from "these worthless things" (v. 15, i.e., either idols or the sacrifices being prepared). This is the first speech in Acts presented to an audience that has not been influenced by a Jewish synagogue and its beliefs. Thus, Paul has to start at the beginning with information that those influenced by biblical religion already knew. His approach is clearly to distinguish the Lord God from the pagan gods by pointing out that he is Creator of everything that there is (v. 15), whose influence as sustainer of creation is felt throughout the whole world (vv. 16–17). He is also the living God, who calls us to turn to him in repentance (v. 15).

But once again we find Jews opposing the ministry of Paul and Barnabas. This time they have traveled from Antioch, 110 miles away, and Iconium, 20 miles away, indicating the urgency with which they were ready to stamp out this work. In crisp language Luke reports an event that, when we think deeply about it, proves to be an amazing occurrence: "They stoned Paul and dragged him outside the city, thinking he was dead" (v. 19b; see 2 Cor. 11:25).

In my study of this verse I considered the psychological factor behind it (though avoiding psychologizing) by meditating on what it must have meant to be treated in this way.[5] What must Paul have felt as he was being stoned? The results of my meditation were shocking. We usually hurry through this passage to look for some devotional or theological application. But in order to enter into the spirit of Acts, it may help us to sense what the early Christians went through, for that will give a key to how the gospel went out in its first few decades. When a person is stoned until he becomes unconscious and is then dragged out of the city, perhaps deeper than the physical pain is the mental anguish and the pain of utter humiliation.

Yet at this dark hour, there is support from the new believers of Lystra, who "gathered around" Paul and "went back into the city," with him (v. 20). What a source of comfort this must have been to him.[6] He and Barnabas leave the next day for Derbe. The pain of being wounded and humiliated does not dampen enthusiasm for the mission God has given them. The message they preach in Derbe is still "the good news," even though it has caused bad experiences. The Lord blesses their efforts with "a large number of disciples"

---

4. Keener, *BBC*, 362.

5. See Robert A Traina, *Methodical Bible Study: A New Approach to Hermeneutics* (Privately published, 1952, subsequently published by Grand Rapids: Zondervan), 154–55.

6. In our application of 4:23–31 we discussed the comfort that fellow Christians bring in times of persecution.

(14:21), and there is no mention of opposition here. When we note Paul's faithful perseverance at great cost, we can perhaps understand his impatience with Mark, who deserted them at the start of this leg of their journey.

Return Visits to Churches and Antioch (14:21b–28)

THEIR RETURN JOURNEY took Paul and Barnabas through the three towns they had just ministered at: Lystra, Iconium, and Antioch (v. 21). They had been expelled from one of them (13:50) and had fled from the other two (vv. 6, 20). But this time they went in a new role in follow-through care of the converts rather than in pioneering evangelism. Four important truths are given about this ministry of follow-through care. (1) They strengthened the disciples (v. 22a).

(2) They exhorted (*parakaleo*) them to remain in the faith (v. 22b, lit.).

(3) They warned them about approaching hardship in a statement that implies that hardship is a necessary requirement along the path to the kingdom. It literally reads, "Through many tribulations it is necessary (*dei*) for us to enter the kingdom of God" (v. 22c). The word "many" (*pollon*) "expresses not mere quantity or number but variety."[7] This idea of variety in suffering is more clearly expressed in James 1:2, which uses the word *poikilois* ("various kinds of") with trials. The word for "trials" (*thlipsis*) means "trouble involving direct suffering."[8] Paul implies that Christians will not sail through trouble with consummate ease. Rather, they will struggle with difficult hardships of various kinds.

(4) Paul and Barnabas helped the new churches get organized by setting up a leadership team (v. 23). The leaders are called "elders" (*presbyteros*), a word that occurs sixty-six times in the New Testament. It was used originally for the Jewish leaders, and it occurs with this meaning in Acts (see 4:5, 8, 23; 6:12; etc.). Without explanation the word is suddenly used for the elders of the Jerusalem church in 11:30. The next use within a Christian context is the present passage, after which it appears in Acts eight more times to refer to the elders of the church and three more times to refer to the Jewish elders. The elders appointed by Paul and Barnabas are committed to the Lord, and once more the commissioning of leaders is accompanied by prayer and fasting (14:23b; cf. 1:24–25; 6:6; 10:9–16; 13:2–3).

The journey of Paul and Barnabas back to Antioch takes them through Perga, from where they had started their journey up to the mountains of southern Galatia. We do not know whether they had preached there on their earlier visit, but they definitely did so on this return visit (v. 25a). From

---

7. J. A. Alexander, *Acts*, 2:64.
8. Louw and Nida, 243.

there they went to Attalia and finally sailed back "home" to Antioch, having completed the task they were commissioned to do (v. 26). The church must have been thrilled to hear the report of their mission (v. 27) and happy that "they stayed there a long time with the disciples" (v. 28). The Greek word for "disciple" (*mathetes*, lit., "learner") has now become a favorite term to refer to Christians, appearing four times in this chapter (vv. 20, 21, 22, 28) and twenty-eight times in Acts (it appears over 250 times in the Gospels).

RESPONDING TO OPPOSITION. This chapter gives us several features about the opposition early Christians faced that can be instructive to us today. While many things have changed since the first century, there are many similarities between the way people opposed the gospel and its proclaimers then and the way they do so now. The way the church responded to opposition can also be instructive to us. (1) Just as the people of Iconium were divided over the gospel (v. 4), communities today can also become divided when we share the gospel with them. This is in keeping with the words of Christ, "Do not suppose that I have come to bring peace to the earth. I did not come to bring peace, but a sword" (Matt. 10:34).

(2) We see the powerful way in which a mob can be swayed from adoration to contempt in such a short time (vv. 11–19). The sudden change in the attitude of the mob is reminiscent of the change that took place in Jerusalem when the crowd that had welcomed him as they would a king (Luke 19:37–38), shouted, "Crucify him! Crucify him!" (23:21) less than a week later.

(3) We find these bold proclaimers of the gospel taking evasive action and fleeing from places of danger (v. 6; cf. v. 20). They were certainly not timid, for even after the Gentiles were stirred up and their minds poisoned (v. 2), Paul and Barnabas "spent considerable time there, speaking boldly for the Lord" (v. 3). But when staying on would do more harm than good, they left the area. Though Paul left Lystra, we know that the church there survived the ordeal so that he visited them on his way back (14:21), and then visited them again on his next missionary journey (16:1). He recruited his beloved assistant Timothy from there (16:1–3). Though he left the place, he seems to have made arrangements for the survival of the church. All this suggests that while boldness is a prerequisite for effective evangelism, there are times when wisdom suggests that we move away temporarily from an explosive situation.

Sensing faith to heal. Luke comments that Paul "saw that [the lame man] had faith to be healed" and that this was what made him call out to him to stand up (vv. 9–10). Apparently Paul had a special gift that enabled him to discern whether he should pray for healing or not. The fact that he decided to do so in this case because the man had the faith to be healed suggests that even Paul did not pray for the miraculous healing of every sick person he encountered.

Is an abiding principle to be gleaned from the fact that Paul prayed for the lame man only after he saw that he had faith to be healed? Can ordinary Christians also see this? Or is this an ability given to those who have received the gift of healing? I tend to think that Paul was given a special ability in keeping with his gift of miraculous healing. But that does not eliminate others without this gift from praying for healing. Spiritual principles operate with heightened intensity in those who have special gifts, but many of these principles are open to all believers. Those who do not have the special gift of faith also need to exercise faith in their daily walk with God. But they may not be called to lead God's people into special exploits where they launch out in faith to do the impossible. In the same way we may not sense faith the way Paul did here, and thus we may not at a public meeting suddenly call out to a lame person to stand up. But we still can pray for the sick.

Proclaiming the gospel to the totally unreached. This passage contains the first report of a message given to a group that did not have a preparatory influence from the Jewish faith (vv. 15–18). It gives us an important key to ministering with such a group: Begin at the beginning by explaining who God is. This principle and others appear in more detail in Paul's ministry in Athens (17:16–31). We will look at this topic in greater depth there.

Four features of follow-through care. Acts 2:42 gave four basic practices of follow-through care of new converts in the Jerusalem church: teaching, fellowship, the breaking of bread, and prayer. Luke's summary of what Paul and Barnabas did when they revisited the cities of Lystra, Iconium, and Antioch presents four more items in the process of follow-through care (14:21–23). Actually the first three items in this list can be considered amplifications of 2:42. "Strengthening" is what happened through all four items in 2:42, and the "encouraging" (exhortation) and warning about coming hardship in 14:22 can be included under "teaching" in the earlier list. The fourth feature in this list, the appointing of elders, was not necessary in the Jerusalem church because it already had the twelve apostles as its elders.

It is possible that the three points that follow the first feature—"strengthening" (v. 22)—describe *how* the strengthening was accomplished.[9] This brings us to Luke's statement "encouraging them to remain true to the faith." While the word used here (*parakaleo*) can mean encourage, the encouraging would have included exhortation. "Exhortation" is another way to translate

---

9. Barrett, *Acts*, 686.

parakaleo. Charles Carter explains that exhorting "was primarily hortatory, and its appeal was mainly to the emotions and will."[10] This activity reminds us of what Barnabas did when he came to the new church in Antioch: He exhorted them to adhere to the Lord with all their hearts (11:23). An aspect of this exhortation would be the warning about hardship (14:22b; cf. above), but they would have exhorted about other things as well.

The third feature of follow-through care here is warning the converts about hardship. Not only does Acts 14 tell us about the necessity of suffering, it also illustrates that by showing how Paul suffered. We referred earlier to the mental anguish and humiliation that Paul must have experienced when he was stoned and dragged outside the city of Lystra. Luke suggests that this message about suffering was an important part of his ministry of "strengthening the disciples and encouraging them to remain true to the faith," for immediately after he records their teaching: "We must go through many hardships to enter the kingdom of God" (v. 22b).

Hardship is a key ingredient of discipleship. Paul also teaches this in his letters (Phil. 1:28—30; 1 Thess. 3:3), and Jesus mentioned it in his basic call to discipleship (Luke 9:23—24). Acts 14:22 goes further, however, suggesting that suffering is a *condition* for entrance into the kingdom of God. Paul says the same thing in his letters: "We share in his sufferings in order that we may also share in his glory" (Rom. 8:17; see 2 Tim. 2:12).

The fourth feature of follow-through care is the appointing of elders. Because so much of the growth and life of the Christian takes place in community, it was necessary for Paul and Barnabas to ensure that the communities were well organized. Thus he appointed elders in these new congregations (v. 23). A comment of Paul to Titus shows that this was a practice consistently followed by Paul: "The reason I left you in Crete was that you might straighten out what was left unfinished and appoint elders in every town, as I directed you" (Titus 1:5). Shenk and Stutzman observe that "Paul never left his congregations with a lack of clarity as to who was in charge."[11]

As the word "elder" was already in use in the Old Testament and in Israel in the first century, "the office of the elder in the New Testament cannot be fully understood without the background of the Old Testament local elder, an office still functioning in New Testament Judaism."[12] The Old Testament elders had the "twofold task of judging and discipline generally, and of ruling and guiding the people in an orderly way."[13] In the New Testament the

---

10. Carter and Earle, *Acts*, 202.
11. Shenk and Stutzman, *Creating Communities*, 172.
12. Cornelis Van Dam, "Elder," *EDBT*, 198.
13. Ibid., 197.

same people who are called elders are also called bishops (*episkopos*). The two names are used interchangeably in Acts 20:17, 28 and Titus 1:5, 7. While the name elder points to the seniority of the person, bishop (meaning overseer) points to the role. We will discuss this role in greater detail in our study of Acts 20:1–38.

The plural is always used in connection with the appointment of leaders. While it is true that one person must emerge as the key leader in a group, biblical leadership operates in the context of a team. Paul uses the word used for the Jewish council of elders, *prebyterion* (Luke 22:66; Acts 22:5), for the gathering of the elders (1 Tim. 4:14). It is from this word that the ecclesiastical term *presbytery* comes.

Leadership and prayer. The process of appointing leaders was accompanied by prayer (v. 23), and we pointed to several instances where this has already happened in Acts. On two occasions the prayer was accompanied by fasting (13:2–3; 14:23). Once the prayer was for guidance in the choice of leaders (1:24–25); on three occasions God spoke about the mission of the leaders during a time of prayer (10:9–15; 13:2; cf. 9:11; 22:15); and four times the praying was during the commissioning or sending off time (6:6; 13:3; 14:23; 21:5). We can add to this list the times we find the people praying for the leaders (12:5, 12; 21:5).

Outside Acts too are many references to prayer for leaders. In eight of his letters Paul asks his readers to pray for him.[14] Before Jesus chose his twelve apostles he spent the whole night in prayer (Luke 6:12). The only time the Gospels refer to him speaking about his own prayer life, it was about his prayer for Peter (Luke 22:32). Paul says he prayed night and day for the young leader Timothy, whom he left in Ephesus (2 Tim. 1:3). In other words, not only should Christian leaders be people of prayer (see comments on 6:1–7), they should also be people who are prayed for. Prayer must back their selection, their commissioning, and their ministering.

WISDOM IN RESPONDING **to opposition.** This passage contains three keys to understanding and responding to opposition. (1) The first is a sad one, in that the gospel does sometimes divide communities. Well do I remember being at a Buddhist temple facing the wrath of the monks and their lay supporters in an area where we had started an evangelistic work. Our accusers said to us that they had lived in peace for

14. See Rom. 15:31; 2 Cor. 1:11; Eph. 6:19–20; Phil. 1:19; Col. 4:3–4; 1 Thess. 5:25; 2 Thess. 3:1–2; Philem. 22 (cf. Heb. 13:18–19).

so many centuries and that now we had come and ruined the peace of the community. And we knew that this was partly true. It was a hard accusation to take, for Christians seek to follow Paul's advice: "If it is possible, as far as it depends on you, live at peace with everyone" (Rom. 12:18). We who aim to be instruments of peace had become agents of disharmony.

In much of the discussions on social harmony today, evangelism with conversion as a goal is considered a major hindrance. In earlier generations, people viewed evangelism as taking the gospel to those who had forsaken the path of human righteousness.[15] But today we realize that the living religions of the world also advocate human righteousness. Thus, some view our evangelism as disrupting the harmony of religious people who pursue righteousness.

For this reason even some Christians are not enthusiastic about evangelism. They feel conversion is desirable, but if it is going to cause so much disruption to families and societies, they ought to downplay its importance. For example, some evangelists in Sri Lanka went to an area and won many Buddhists to Christ, provoking opposition to Christianity. Then other Christians, who were doing joint social projects with the Buddhist temple nearby, tried to discourage the evangelism because it was disrupting their program.

Yet when we realize the supreme worth of an individual and of his or her salvation, and when we realize that we are carrying the message of ultimate importance from the Creator to his creation, we are challenged to persevere despite the cost. When we take the gospel to primitive tribes, we are criticized for disrupting the "pristine beauty" of cultures that have not been affected by the ravages of modernization; but the message of the gospel is so important that we must take it to them. However, as Donald McGavran used to say, we must aim at conversion with minimum social dislocation.[16]

(2) We must also take into consideration the mood of the people, realizing that sometimes unnecessary harm can be done by our staying in a situation where a mob mentality has taken over and reason will not prevail. Note how twice in this chapter Paul and Barnabas leave an evangelistic situation because of the hostile environment. Boldness *and* wisdom combine to produce an effective evangelistic strategy. Because of the ethnic conflict in our land, there are some places where YFC works that I cannot visit, even though I would dearly like to go to those places. But if I go there, I would be putting my colleagues at risk. Similarly, we may sometimes need to let someone else do what we like to do if we sense that our presence there will not help.

---

15. I am calling this "human righteousness," which we know does not merit salvation in God's sight.

16. Donald McGavran, *Understanding Church Growth* (Grand Rapids: Eerdmans, 1970), 198–215.

(3) It seems that when Paul and Barnabas came back to these cities where opposition had developed, they came in a new role—to strengthen believers. This may be the role that foreigners have in certain sensitive missions situations: let the locals preach the gospel and train them to do it. Nevertheless, there are other times when the presence of a foreigner may be more effective in evangelism than that of a local. In our ministry we generally do not use Westerners for evangelism among the Easternized people, who speak only the local languages. But we have found music and drama teams and preachers from Western countries can be effective in evangelism with the Westernized youth of our land. All this indicates that we must be wise in our strategizing so that what is most effective will be done to get the gospel out.

Praying for healing today. Though every Christian may not have the special gift of healing, all of us can pray for the sick in faith. James gives us a general principle about healing that seems to apply to the ministry of those without the gift of healing: If someone is sick, "he should call the elders of the church to pray over him. . . . And the prayer offered in faith will make the sick person well; the Lord will raise him up" (5:14–15). James refers here to the faith of the elders of the church. Then he says something that extends beyond the elders to all members: "Therefore confess your sins to each other and pray for each other so that you may be healed. The prayer of a righteous man is powerful and effective" (5:16). Thus, the same principles that are expressed with spectacular intensity in the lives of those with special miraculous gifts are seen in the day-to-day life of the church in less spectacular ways. All of us should pray in our personal ministries for healing for the sick.

Giving exhortation its due place. In the exhortation that forms an important part in the follow-through and strengthening of believers, the need to prepare them to suffer in order to enter the kingdom is an essential ingredient (v. 22b). Paul's letters suggest that he and Barnabas exhorted these Galatian converts. They urged them to resist Satan and false doctrine, to put away the old lifestyle and put on the new lifestyle, to pray and give thanks always, to give primacy to love in all they do, and to have a biblical attitude to possessions. In order that Christians receive such exhortation early on, we should teach those parts of Scripture that lend themselves to these elements (e.g., the Ten Commandments; the Sermon on the Mount; the practical sections of Paul's letters, such as Rom. 12–15; Gal. 4–6; Eph. 4–6; the book of James).

Today some people shy away from exhortation, perhaps because of the influence of our pluralistic culture, which is skeptical of any dogmatic approach; because of the entertainment orientation that dominates much Christian proclamation today; or because of the loss of credibility of preachers through moral failures. Yet many sections of the Bible that teach believers are exhortational. Surely, then, Christian leaders should be exhorting Christians today.

Perhaps one way we can win back the credibility that will enable us to exhort freely is being examples of sacrificial living. When Paul talked to these Galatians about suffering, his message was credible since they had seen how he suffered for the gospel. Paul occasionally appealed to his sufferings when he wrote something difficult to accept (cf. Gal. 6:17). In Ephesians 4:1 he said, "As a prisoner for the Lord, then, I urge you to live a life worthy of the calling you have received." Being a prisoner gave him credibility to exhort people. Similarly, today, when our hearers know that we are truly committed people who have paid a big price because of our commitment, they have no choice but to take note of what we say.

Giving sufferings its place in discipleship. Like Paul, two of my colleagues have been painfully assaulted by the very people they were sacrificing to share the gospel with. Several of my colleagues have been assaulted by defense personnel just because they happened to be in a certain spot at a time the personnel were venting their anger. Others have spent nights in police cells, having being taken in as terrorist suspects for no other reason than the fact that their identity card indicated they were born in a place deemed as a terrorist breeding ground. They have all told me that the emotional pain of humiliation and the anger that welled up within them over the unjust way they were being treated were more difficult to endure than any physical pain or discomfort. Like Paul these colleagues had been model citizens. This is not the romantic death we think of when we hear the term *martyr*. It is sheer humiliation, which can cause great shame and anger.

Do all Christians go through such experiences of hardship today? Though our experiences may differ in detail, the clear testimony of Scripture is that all Christians must suffer in some way if they are true believers. Note Paul's words in 2 Timothy 3:12: "In fact, everyone who wants to live a godly life in Christ Jesus will be persecuted." In addition to persecution, general hardship will also be the lot of all Christians insofar as we will have to go through struggles (cf. v. 22). The struggle may be with temptation, sickness, economic reversal, a difficult neighbor, or the costliness of the stand taken for Christ.

Why then do some Christians not experience such hardships today? Perhaps those who taught them the basic principles of discipleship did not teach much on suffering. Thus when these believers should have embraced suffering for the sake of Christ, they avoided it. The preachers may not have taught much about it because they did not themselves have much experience in taking on the cup of suffering. Perhaps a reason why they have not suffered is that they are being disobedient to God. My point is that the cross of suffering is something that we take on through obedience or something that we can avoid if we wish.

Actually, one reason why the Galatian churches were able to survive even though the original evangelists stayed such a short time may have been the suffering they encountered. Churches born in suffering are strong churches. The converts are forced to thrust themselves upon God in earnest desire for his help, and that has a way of strengthening our faith and purifying our motives. While we all come to Christ seeking help for ourselves, some come out of motives quite alien to the heart of the gospel. Some come only for healing or even for the prospect of financial gain. When suffering comes, such may leave the church or lose their enthusiasm for Christ; or they may have an experience of going through the refiner's fire, through which their faith is strengthened and their motives purified.

A common reaction of Christians when they see a fellow Christian suffer is to look for something wrong that the sufferer has done. They seem to think that these persons are suffering because they have done something that is not in keeping with God's will. They may advise the sufferers or even rebuke them. If a person is tired because he has done God's work along with his job and family responsibilities, he is rebuked for working too hard. When a person is unpopular in the workplace for taking a stand for Christ, she is rebuked for being unwise. When someone gets assaulted and ends up in the hospital for trying to make peace in a conflict, he is criticized for trying to act like a messiah, not minding his own business. Those who should be encouraging sufferers end up discouraging them and adding to their pain.

These well-meaning rebukes can be helpful. Sometimes we may indeed be suffering because of our folly, and rebukes help us see that. Rebukes can sober us and force us to ask ourselves and others whether what we are doing is right. Such grappling always helps us to be wise in our behavior. Sometimes we may not change our course of action, but we may do what we are doing in a better way because of the criticism. Criticism can be a blessing.

We can, of course, avoid the cross of suffering, but usually only out of disobedience. If Paul had not preached when it was dangerous to do so, he would have avoided suffering. But he followed a Master who asked his followers to love their neighbors as themselves. Thus, he had to go out with the gospel, which met their deepest need. Similarly, if we remain quiet about Christ in our workplaces, we may avoid suffering. We can avoid fatigue if we refuse to assist our aging neighbor who is sick and in need of help. We can avoid inconvenience and pain if we refuse to care for the member of our small group who has had a nervous breakdown.

Paul could also have avoided anguish and stress if he had not troubled himself over the false beliefs of the Galatians (Gal. 4:19–20) and over the weaknesses and sins of other Christians (2 Cor. 11:28−29). Similarly, we too can reject or ignore someone who is going astray or is weak, saying that it is none of our business. Paul's listings of his hardships shows how inconvenient Christian ministry was to him. He spoke of "troubles, hardships and distresses ... hard work, sleepless nights and hunger" (2 Cor. 6:4−5). It is amazing how many Christians today consider convenience when deciding about what service they will be involved in. Should one who believes that the cross of suffering is basic to Christianity do that?

Those who miss the hardships of the cross will also miss the prizes of the kingdom. It was in connection with entrance into the kingdom that Paul presents the necessity of suffering (v. 22; see Rom. 8:17; 2 Tim. 2:12). But many Christians hardly think about the heavenly reward today. Certainly it is not one of the major motivating factors in their lives, the way the New Testament portrays it as being. After Jesus urged his disciples to lay up treasures in heaven, he said, "For where your treasure is, there your heart will be also" (Matt. 6:21). Paul said, "Set your minds on things above, not on earthly things" (Col. 3:2). That this is not true of many supposedly evangelical Christians shows how far we have moved from a biblical attitude toward life. In his memorable essay "Joy Will Come in Its Own Time," A. W. Tozer writes:

> Christ calls men to carry a cross; we call them to have fun in his name. He calls them to forsake the world; we assure them that if they but accept Jesus the world is their oyster. He calls them to suffer; we call them to enjoy all the bourgeois comforts modern civilization affords. He calls them to self-abegnation and death; we call them to spread themselves like green bay trees or perchance even to become stars in a pitiful fifth-rate zodiac. He calls them to holiness; we call them to a cheap and tawdry happiness that would have been rejected with scorn by the least of the Stoic philosophers.
>
> ... We can afford to suffer now; we'll have a long eternity to enjoy ourselves. And our enjoyment will be valid and pure, for it will come in the right way in the right time.[17]

Remember that the clear teaching about the inevitability of suffering comes in a section that describes the follow-through care of the new converts. This leads us to the conclusion that teaching on suffering should be considered part of the basic follow-through training given to new converts. Some years ago I was involved in a group that edited, for an international audience, a follow-through guide for young new believers produced by Singapore

---

17. A. W. Tozer, *Born After Midnight* (Harrisburg, Pa.: Christian Publications, 1959), 141−42.

Youth for Christ. The third of the eight studies in this guide is called "Strength in Difficulties."[18] A chapter like this should be included in all basic follow-through guides.

Leadership in the church. Sometimes we hear Christians proudly affirming that in their small groups, there is no one as a leader and all are equals. Leadership is actually not a factor that influences equality; rather, it is a matter of function. There is a lot of talk today about the "tall poppy syndrome" and how we like to "cut down to size" anyone who emerges as a leader. This is not a biblical idea for, according to the Bible, leaders have an important place in the life of God's people. For groups to be guided aright they must have leaders. The appointment of leaders was an important feature in the life of the early church. This is why their commissioning was accompanied by prayer and fasting (v. 23).

When the leaders operate as a team or a group of elders—which is what the Greek word *presbyterion* means—some of the abuses that can happen when a single individual has absolute authority can be avoided. We are not saying that any one system of church government is the only acceptable system. Advocates of each system can give scriptural reasons as to why they feel that theirs is "the scriptural system." Whatever system we adopt, we must have biblical principles in place. Among these are the principles that leadership is an important function in the church, which must be taken seriously and backed with prayer (see below), and that leaders should operate within the context of a team, not alone.

Saturating leadership with prayer. Every step of the leadership process should be accompanied by prayer. Prayer went into the selection of leaders in the New Testament. Today this should be the major strategy of choosing leaders. Those involved in the leadership selection process need to meet for extended times of prayer, possibly with fasting. This opens the selectors to the mind of God and increases the chances of the choices being in keeping with the will of God. It should be commonplace in Christian meetings, when a decision is being taken, to stop everything and give ourselves to earnest prayer for guidance.

During a time of sensitive deliberation a leader recently suggested to the highest body of a denomination that they should stop and pray; everyone seemed confused, not knowing what to do! This sort of automatic shifting from deliberation to prayer is something we should get used to. In addition, we should have special times for prayer when making important decisions. When an election or appointment is going to be held, we should write and

---

18. *Love Joy Peace*, International edition (Singapore: Singapore Youth for Christ, 1993), 13−18.

announce it far and wide, asking for prayer for guidance. Many people may ignore the appeal to pray; but some will pray, and "the prayer of a righteous man is powerful and effective" (James 5:16b).

Similarly, when we send people off on an assignment or when we commission, induct, or ordain them, the meeting should be saturated in prayer. Today's commissioning services are often public relations exercises with a little prayer included, and they are often followed by a time of refreshments. The biblical services were accompanied by fasting (13:2–3; 14:23) and were saturated in prayer (6:6; 13:3; 14:23; 21:5). Perhaps we should redesign our commissioning and ordination services to include these features.

Finally, leaders should ensure that people pray for them by asking for prayer for themselves and their ministries. Some leaders do not like to become so vulnerable as to make known their weaknesses and needs so that people can pray for them. I was at a service when a visiting minister took offense at the fact that the preacher conducting the service prayed for his health. He had been sick and was close to retirement. Perhaps he did not want to show that, like Paul, he was wasting away outwardly (2 Cor. 4:16)! But biblical leaders know that all of their ministry is done through God's mercy (2 Cor. 4:1). Therefore they should do everything they can to have that mercy mediated to them by the prayers of God's people. Some may laugh at them and others gossip about the weaknesses they acknowledged in their prayer appeal. But others will pray, and God will use those prayers both to help them overcome the darts that Satan flings at Christian leaders and to receive a powerful anointing from God for their ministries.

Acts 15:1–35

SOME MEN CAME down from Judea to Antioch and were teaching the brothers: "Unless you are circumcised, according to the custom taught by Moses, you cannot be saved." ²This brought Paul and Barnabas into sharp dispute and debate with them. So Paul and Barnabas were appointed, along with some other believers, to go up to Jerusalem to see the apostles and elders about this question. ³The church sent them on their way, and as they traveled through Phoenicia and Samaria, they told how the Gentiles had been converted. This news made all the brothers very glad. ⁴When they came to Jerusalem, they were welcomed by the church and the apostles and elders, to whom they reported everything God had done through them.

⁵Then some of the believers who belonged to the party of the Pharisees stood up and said, "The Gentiles must be circumcised and required to obey the law of Moses."

⁶The apostles and elders met to consider this question. ⁷After much discussion, Peter got up and addressed them: "Brothers, you know that some time ago God made a choice among you that the Gentiles might hear from my lips the message of the gospel and believe. ⁸God, who knows the heart, showed that he accepted them by giving the Holy Spirit to them, just as he did to us. ⁹He made no distinction between us and them, for he purified their hearts by faith. ¹⁰Now then, why do you try to test God by putting on the necks of the disciples a yoke that neither we nor our fathers have been able to bear? ¹¹No! We believe it is through the grace of our Lord Jesus that we are saved, just as they are."

¹²The whole assembly became silent as they listened to Barnabas and Paul telling about the miraculous signs and wonders God had done among the Gentiles through them. ¹³When they finished, James spoke up: "Brothers, listen to me. ¹⁴Simon has described to us how God at first showed his concern by taking from the Gentiles a people for himself. ¹⁵The words of the prophets are in agreement with this, as it is written:

16 "'After this I will return
    and rebuild David's fallen tent.
  Its ruins I will rebuild,
    and I will restore it,
17 that the remnant of men may seek the Lord,
    and all the Gentiles who bear my name,
  says the Lord, who does these things'
18 that have been known for ages.

19 "It is my judgment, therefore, that we should not make it difficult for the Gentiles who are turning to God. 20 Instead we should write to them, telling them to abstain from food polluted by idols, from sexual immorality, from the meat of strangled animals and from blood. 21 For Moses has been preached in every city from the earliest times and is read in the synagogues on every Sabbath."

22 Then the apostles and elders, with the whole church, decided to choose some of their own men and send them to Antioch with Paul and Barnabas. They chose Judas (called Barsabbas) and Silas, two men who were leaders among the brothers. 23 With them they sent the following letter:

The apostles and elders, your brothers,

To the Gentile believers in Antioch, Syria and Cilicia:

Greetings.

24 We have heard that some went out from us without our authorization and disturbed you, troubling your minds by what they said. 25 So we all agreed to choose some men and send them to you with our dear friends Barnabas and Paul—26 men who have risked their lives for the name of our Lord Jesus Christ. 27 Therefore we are sending Judas and Silas to confirm by word of mouth what we are writing. 28 It seemed good to the Holy Spirit and to us not to burden you with anything beyond the following requirements: 29 You are to abstain from food sacrificed to idols, from blood, from the meat of strangled animals and from sexual immorality. You will do well to avoid these things.

Farewell.

30 The men were sent off and went down to Antioch, where they gathered the church together and delivered the letter.

³¹The people read it and were glad for its encouraging message. ³²Judas and Silas, who themselves were prophets, said much to encourage and strengthen the brothers. ³³After spending some time there, they were sent off by the brothers with the blessing of peace to return to those who had sent them. ³⁵But Paul and Barnabas remained in Antioch, where they and many others taught and preached the word of the Lord.

"LUKE'S ACCOUNT OF the discussion regarding the relation of the Gentiles to the law of Moses forms the center of Acts both structurally and theologically."¹ Though the church in Jerusalem had accepted that Gentiles also could be saved (11:18), some believed that "the Gentiles must be circumcised and required to obey the law of Moses" (v. 5) in order to be saved (v. 1). We see from Galatians 2 and from the decree that came out of this council (Acts 15:29) that the issue of table fellowship between Jewish and Gentile Christians was also included in this controversy. The decision the church leaders took here would have far-reaching implications for the understanding of who a Christian is, especially in relation to the law of Moses.

Marshall writes, "Probably no section of Acts has aroused such controversy as this one or led to such varied historical reconstructions of the actual situation."² The traditional view has been that this chapter is describing the visit to Jerusalem that Paul talks about in Galatians 2:1–10. But there are problems associated with this view. Some reject the historicity of this chapter or say that it is chronologically out of place. One scholar has the events of verses 1–19 occurring at one time (the same as the events of 11:30 and Gal. 2:1–10) and those of verses 20–29 occurring at another time, in the absence of Paul.³ We follow scholars like Bruce, Marshall, and Longenecker in concluding that the theory that Galatians 2:1–10 describes the events of Acts 11:30 and that the Jerusalem Council took place later, fits in best with the evidence, though there are still problems.⁴ This places the council around A.D. 49.

---

1. Marshall, *Acts*, 242.

2. Ibid., 243–44.

3. D. R. Catchpole, "Paul, James and the Apostolic Decree," *New Testament Studies* 23 (1976–1977): 428–44.

4. For a defense of this view, see Bruce, *Acts*, NICNT, 283–85; Marshall, *Acts*, 244–47; Longenecker, "Acts," 444–47. See also the helpful charts in Scot McKnight, *The NIV Application Commentary: Galatians* (Grand Rapids: Zondervan, 1995), 88–89. For a defense of the traditional view that Galatians 2 describes the Jerusalem Council, see Kistemaker, *Acts*, 533–36.

Paul and Barnabas Go to Jerusalem (15:1–4)

THE EVENTS ARE sparked off by "some men [who] came down from Judea to Antioch" (v. 1). Verse 24 makes clear that they went "without [the] authorization" of the church leaders in Jerusalem. They must have significantly troubled the minds of the Christians in Antioch because they insinuated that the apostles and elders agreed with what they were saying. As is often the case, this heresy aimed at removing the scandal of Christianity. In Galatians 5:11, Paul writes: "Brothers, if I am still preaching circumcision, why am I still being persecuted? In that case the offense of the cross has been abolished." If Paul preached circumcision, there would be no scandal to Christianity. But since he preached that salvation occurs through no work of our own and only through the merits of the death of Christ, such a message was scandalous to the average Jew. The teachers from Judea were trying to remove this scandal.

The church realized that something serious was happening. As a result, Paul and Barnabas were brought "into sharp dispute and debate with them" (v. 2a). It became clear that the issue was so serious that a formal decision had to be taken by the church in Jerusalem. Thus, a team was sent under the leadership of Paul and Barnabas (v. 2b). On the way to Jerusalem they stopped over at the churches in Phoenicia and Samaria and reported on "how the Gentiles had been converted" (v. 3a). "This news made all the brothers very glad" (v. 3b), which seems to be the general response in Jerusalem as well (v. 4).

Settling the Issue of Salvation and the Gentiles (15:5–19)

THE JOY AT Paul and Barnabas's report was broken by objections regarding the circumcision issue from "some of the believers who belonged to the party of the Pharisees" (v. 5). Therefore, "the apostles and elders met to consider this question" (v. 6). We cannot be sure whether the whole church was present at this meeting (cf. vv. 12, 22). If so, the deliberation and decision rested with the leaders.[5] It is also possible that a second meeting was called in which the whole assembly gathered after the elders had discussed the issue. If the visit mentioned in Galatians 2:1–10 preceded the council, the issue had already been settled by Peter, James, and John, "those reputed to be pillars" (Gal. 2:9). Yet when the issue came up again, time was given for "much discussion" (v. 7). The theological controversy was not swept under the carpet and allowed to simmer; it was brought into the open and fearlessly discussed.

After the discussion Peter spoke up (v. 7). Oscar Cullmann has argued that Peter was at this council not as the leader of the Jerusalem church but as a missionary. James, clearly the president of this gathering, had taken over

---

5. Bruce, *Acts: Greek Text,* 335.

that leadership role. Cullmann suggests that Peter interrupted his missionary work to come for this meeting.[6] If this council met after the humiliating confrontation in Antioch where Peter was publicly rebuked by the younger Paul (Gal. 2:11–21), as we think it did, it is indeed creditable that Peter should be the first to get up and speak on behalf of Paul's side in the controversy. This is typical of the honorable commitment to God's truth rather than to personal preferences and prestige that characterized the attitudes and behavior of the leaders at this council.

Peter's main point was that the opening of the door of salvation took place through God's initiative. He referred to the conversion of Cornelius and his friends and pointed out that this whole event had been of God's choosing (v. 7). We know that Peter only reluctantly accepted God's teaching to him through the vision (10:14–15). "God, who knows the heart," confirmed that they had been truly saved "by giving the Holy Spirit to them, just as he did to" Peter and his company (15:8). As with Peter and the first disciples at Pentecost (2:2)—but unlike the converts after the Pentecost sermon (2:38)—there was no prior instruction given about receiving the Spirit. The Spirit just fell on them most unexpectedly "while Peter was still speaking" (10:44), as God's sign of acceptance.

Peter then explicitly stated the great truth that Paul later expounded in Ephesians 2:14–22—that God broke all barriers separating Jews and Gentiles; in purifying the Gentiles' hearts by faith, God "made no distinction between us and them" (Acts 15:9). With surprising candor Peter admits that the Mosaic law was "a yoke that neither we nor our fathers have been able to bear" (v. 10). Insisting that Gentiles keep the law is to "try to test God" (v. 10), a serious issue. Peter was saying that "to impose conditions on believers over and above those which God has required is to stretch his patience and invite his judgment."[7]

In verse 9 Peter affirmed that Cornelius and his company had been saved "by faith." In verse 11 he affirmed that salvation "is through the grace of our Lord Jesus Christ." It is significant that he said "that we are saved, just as they are." This implies that no Mosaic ritual is needed for the salvation of the Jews.[8] With this speech Peter bows out of the book of Acts. As far as Luke is concerned, as Martin Hengel says, "the legitimation of the mission to the Gentiles is Peter's last work."[9]

---

6. Oscar Cullmann, *Peter: Disciple-Apostle-Martyr*, trans. Floyd V. Filson (New York: Living Age Books, 1958 [repr. of 1953 ed.]), 49–50.

7. Ibid., 336.

8. Harold Dollar, *St. Luke's Missiology*, 97.

9. Martin Hengel, *Acts and the History of Earliest Christianity* (London: SCM, 1979), 125; cited in Bruce, *Acts*, NICNT, 291.

The next to speak are Barnabas and Paul,[10] who tell of "the miraculous signs and wonders God had done among the Gentiles through them" (v. 12). In Luke's writings signs and wonders have an authenticating function.[11]

James then makes his entrance. He is not introduced here or in 12:17, which records his first appearance in Acts, probably because he was a well-known figure in the early church.[12] From what he says and the way he says it, it becomes evident that he is now the leader of the church in Jerusalem. While not all scholars agree, this James is probably the brother of Jesus. He seems to have become the leader of the church in Jerusalem after the apostles were scattered (Acts 8). Peter wanted him to be informed when he left Jerusalem after his miraculous escape from prison (12:17). Paul mentions him first when listing the three pillars of the Jerusalem church, the others mentioned being Peter and John (Gal. 2:9).

Much is told about James in extrabiblical writings of the time. He was respected even among non-Christians, "largely because of his ascetic way of life and his regular participation in the temple services of prayer, where he interceded for the people and their city."[13] He was stoned to death in Jerusalem in A.D. 62, and many of the people were gravely shocked at this. "Some years later some ascribed the calamity which overtook the city and its inhabitants to the cessation of James' prayers on their behalf."[14] Bruce says that "the church's readiness to recognize his leadership was due more to his personal character and record than to his blood relationship to the Lord."[15] His role in the council is evidence of this character.

James's first statement (v. 14) is loaded with significance. When he refers to Peter, he does not use the name "Peter," as Luke did in verse 7. Peter is the Greek translation of the Aramaic Cephas, meaning rock, which is the name Christ gave him (John 1:42). James calls him *Symeon* or "Simeon" (NASB), which the NIV renders as "Simon."[16] In the Greek New Testament Peter is called Simon seventy-five times, twenty of which are in Luke's writings. But he is called Simeon only twice: here and in 2 Peter 1:1. The use of Simeon here probably shows James's "affinities with the Jewish Christians."[17]

Luke is eager to show that James is speaking here as a typical Hebrew. Yet this ardent Jew goes on to make a revolutionary statement: "God at first

---

10. We have already commented on the return to the order of having Barnabas mentioned first (see comments on 13:13–52).

11. See Luke 5:24; 7:19–22; Acts 14:3.

12. Tannehill, *Narrative Unity*, vol. 2, 186.

13. Bruce, *Acts*, NICNT, 239.

14. Ibid.

15. Ibid., 292.

16. Simon is the Hellenized spelling of the Hebrew name Simyon.

17. Robertson, *Word Pictures*, vol. 3, *Acts*, 229.

showed his concern by taking from the Gentiles a people for himself." In the Old Testament (LXX) the "nations" or "Gentiles" (*ethne*) stand in contrast to the "people" (*laos*), which usually refers to the Jews. Deuteronomy 14:2 says, for example, "You are a people [LXX *laos*] holy to the LORD your God. Out of all the peoples [LXX *ethne*, nations] on the face of the earth, the LORD has chosen you to be his treasured possession." In other words, the Israelites have been called out from the nations to be a people for the Lord God. James says the opposite: From *within* the nations God has taken a people for himself. As Tannehill says, "The speakers are making the important affirmation that Gentiles can be God's *laos* in the full sense that Israel is."[18]

In arguing for the full inclusion of Gentiles into the church Peter appealed to direct guidance and intervention from God, and Barnabas and Paul appealed to God's confirmation of their work through signs and wonders. James appeals to Scripture, showing that "the words of the prophets are in agreement with [*symphonousin*]" what has happened (v. 15). James quotes Amos 9:11–12[19] from the LXX[20] and sees its fulfillment in the Gentile mission. The exact meanings of some of the individual clauses in this paragraph are disputed, but the general sense is well summarized by Longenecker:

> In the end times, James is saying, God's people will consist of two concentric groups. At the core will be restored Israel (i.e., David's rebuilt tent); gathered around them will be a group of Gentiles (i.e., the remnant of men) who will share in the messianic blessings but will persist as Gentiles without necessarily becoming Jewish proselytes.[21]

James concludes that the church "should not make it difficult for the Gentiles who are turning to God" (v. 19)—perhaps referring to not requiring them to go through the painful (esp. for adults) step of circumcision. Below we will see how courageous a statement this is.

Fellowship Between Jewish and Gentile Christians (15:20–35)

ONCE THE ISSUE of the requirements for salvation has been settled, James brings up an important issue that impacts fellowship between Jewish and

---

18. Tannehill, *Narrative Unity*, 2:187.

19. There are phrases from other Old Testament Scriptures too that expand the meaning of phrases in the Amos passage. "After this I will return" (v. 16) is from Jer. 12:15 and "that have been known for ages" is from Isa. 45:21.

20. Longenecker has answered the objections of Haenchen ("Acts," 448) and others that the Hebrew James could not have used the LXX, and that therefore these are Luke's ideas, and not James's. He suggests the possibility that James was using a Hebrew variant of Amos 9:11–12 then current, and shows that it is plausible that such a variant existed (447).

21. Ibid., 446.

Gentile Christians. To many Jews maintaining their purity was an extremely important aspect of their survival and identity, especially when they were under foreign rule and had dispersed far and wide into Gentile territory. Thus, the issue of table fellowship with Gentiles and the consumption of non-kosher food was a serious issue.[22] But in the early church eating together was also an important element of community life (2:46). If there was going to be openhearted fellowship between the Jewish and Gentile Christians, there would have to be some sensitivity to Jewish scruples by the Gentiles. Thus, James proposes three prohibitions relating to food (v. 20). Two of these prohibitions (meat from animals killed by strangling and blood) had to do with the Jewish practice of draining the blood of animals before eating them.

The prohibition of sexual immorality (*porneia*) seems to belong to a different category from the rest, and it appears out of place in this list. Surely it goes without saying that sexual immorality is prohibited for Christians. I think that there was so much immorality in some of these places, like Antioch (which was notorious for its immorality),[23] that the churches were also affected by the immorality surrounding them. Therefore a special warning was necessary. Perhaps this prohibition was implying that immoral church members should not be extended the privilege of table fellowship with Christians (cf. 1 Cor. 5:9–11).[24] This explanation would then tie in this prohibition with the other three.

Bruce suggests that *porneia* may be used here in a more specialized sense of marriage between degrees of blood relationship or affinity expressly forbidden in Leviticus 18:6–18. It is used in this sense elsewhere in the New Testament (1 Cor. 5:1; possibly Matt. 5:32; 19:9).[25] In any case, James's concluding point in verse 21 was probably made to reassure the Christians who had come from the Pharisees and who wanted to see the Torah taught among the Gentiles. He says that this was already happening in the synagogues in every city each Sabbath.

The Jerusalem leaders decide to send some of their own people as a delegation bearing a letter from the council (v. 22). The letter to the churches takes on a conciliatory tone. The trouble caused by certain Christians from Jerusalem is condemned in uncompromising language (v. 24). The word translated "troubling" (from *anaskeuazo*) is "a military metaphor for plundering a town."[26] Barnabas and Paul are described in endearing and compli-

---

22. See the discussion in Dollar, *St. Luke's Missiology*, 151–58.

23. It had a shrine in Daphne nearby, where cult prostitution was practiced. See the comments on 11:19–21.

24. See Dollar, *St. Luke's Missiology*, 161.

25. Bruce, *Acts: Greek Text*, 342.

26. Ibid., 345.

mentary terms (vv. 25–26). The words describing the final position of the council are prefaced by words that show how unity had won the day after an intensely trying time in the church: "It seemed good to the Holy Spirit and to us" (v. 28).

This letter emphasizes the unity and unanimity of the church in this decision. Verse 25 says, "So we all agreed to choose some men and send them to you with our dear friends Barnabas and Paul" (cf. NASB, which translates more lit.: "It seemed good to us, having become of one mind, to select men to send to you ..."). The word translated "of one mind" (NASB) and "agreed" (NIV) is *homothymadon*, which often carries the idea of "unanimous."

Verses 30–35 describe a situation where joy and encouragement have replaced the uncertainty of a few days before. The hard work of the past days had indeed been worth the effort. The church had taken another important step in fulfilling the Great Commission.

THE FALSE TEACHING from Jerusalem. Nearly twenty centuries after the battles with the Judaizers were fought in the church, they may seem rather irrelevant to us. But they were important at the time and won for succeeding generations formulations of Christianity that clarified key issues about the nature of saving faith. The Jerusalem Council affirmed that Gentiles do not need to become Jews in order to be Christians. While that fact is no longer disputed, there are many things that we can learn from this passage regarding false teaching.

(1) As in the first century, the issue of people wanting to do something to earn salvation and the church adding to a list of conditions for salvation has been a continuing problem.

(2) The false teaching was powerful because the teachers came from the mother church in Jerusalem, probably claiming the support of the leaders there for their views.

(3) Just as the Judaizers tried to take away the scandal of the gospel, there have always been people who have tried to do this in their efforts to make Christianity more relevant to society.

(4) The church considered this teaching a grave threat and therefore dealt with it in great seriousness. Paul and Barnabas and their team made the long trip to Jerusalem to battle for the gospel. When the resolution was reached, the Jerusalem church sent some of their own leaders to the Gentile churches with an official letter to do all they could to offset the damage.

(5) Note too how the false teaching was combated. The incidents in Antioch "brought Paul and Barnabas into sharp dispute and debate with

them" (v. 2). But individuals were respected in the way the issues were discussed at the council. The Judaizers had a chance to say what they wanted to say, for Peter got up to speak only "after much discussion" (v. 7). Yet in the end, the letter to the churches was uncompromising in the way it condemned the false teachers (v. 24). The situation was too serious for polite acceptance of this teaching or for allowing it to stay alongside other teaching as an option, as would be the case in the pluralist model of theologizing. False teaching was roundly condemned after it had been shown to be wrong.

The prohibitions. The four prohibitions are mentioned three times in Acts (15:20, 29; 21:25), but apart from the one about sexual immorality the others do not appear in Paul's letters. In fact, Paul seems to have adopted a more liberal approach to the issue of food offered to idols in 1 Corinthians 8, which was written six or seven years after the council (c. A.D. 55), and perhaps in Romans 14, which was written eight years after the council (c. A.D. 56). We noted that these prohibitions were made more out of sensitivity for the scruples of the Jews than for theological reasons. Thus we can conclude that in applying this passage, we do not need to slavishly follow the prohibitions regarding food. But we do learn about the need to be sensitive to the consciences and scruples of our fellow believers.

This is the stance that Paul takes in his discussions in Romans 14 and 1 Corinthians 8. He recommends sensitivity to people's consciences, to the weaker brother, and to putting a stumbling block in the way of someone else. Our convictions must always be tempered by love. Love will make us do things that we have fought against legislating. If the gospel is not to be hindered, we will be magnanimous to the weak and to those we seek to win. It is interesting to find the same Paul, who fought so vehemently against legislating circumcision, having Timothy circumcised a short time after the council, before he allowed him to join them on a missionary journey (Acts 16:3). Here, however, the cause seems to have been to open doors for evangelism among unbelieving Jews rather than to appease believing Jews.

The issue of sexual immorality had to be brought up because the society in which the Gentile Christians lived was so pervaded with sexual immorality that the church had also been influenced by it. Isaiah admitted to being influenced by his environment when he said he was a man of unclean lips, who lived among a people of unclean lips (Isa. 6:5). In the same way the church can reflect in its life some of the sins that plague society. This clearly seems to have been the case in the church in Corinth, a city whose name had become "proverbial for licentiousness" partly because "it was a center of the worship of Aphrodite, the goddess of love."[27]

---

27. Bruce, *Steps*, 41.

The principle we glean from this prohibition is that if a church in a given area is particularly susceptible to a certain temptation, then in setting standards for that church, one should be particularly conscientious in mentioning that evil. This is relevant today as this very sin—sexual immorality—has become a serious problem in today's society.

Keys to theological debate within the church. This passage gives us an example of how the Lord led the people into a theological consensus after serious conflict and debate. As we experience such conflicts in the church, Acts 15 is an important passage for us to consider today. God led the early church through three major means. (1) He spoke through experiences. This includes Peter's experience with Cornelius (vv. 7–11) and the experiences of Paul and Barnabas through their ministry in the miraculous and in the conversion of Gentiles.

(2) James' speech gives a most important key in theological debate: the Scriptures. The experiences described earlier were all in harmony with Scripture (vv. 14–18).

(3) The generous Christian character of the leaders shines forth throughout this chapter. If the council took place after Paul's confrontation with Peter in Antioch, then we see Peter acting in a most honorable way. Paul had publicly rebuked him. But when truth is at stake, personal humiliations are forgotten. The leader Paul also let Barnabas take over the leadership role in speaking (his name is mentioned first in v. 12). And James advocated principles contrary to his own personal preferences. He remained a law-abiding Jew to the end, but he did not push that on others. The trouble in Antioch that had resulted in Paul's confronting Peter was after men from James had come there and influenced Peter (Gal. 2:12). How disappointed these men must have been when they found that the one they looked to as their leader spoke up for the other side. But Christian leaders do not take sides in a conflict. They battle over issues, not for sides.

The letter and the decree also show how the church was bending over backwards to make peace. Those who disrupted the churches are strongly condemned (v. 24), but the prohibitions show a sensitivity to Jewish scruples. Paul and Barnabas are commended for the work they have done (vv. 25–26), and Judas and Silas from the church in Jerusalem are sent along with the letter to reassure the Gentile Christians.

The end result of the conflict is something that we should all strive to have in our community life today: being of one mind (v. 25) and sensing that the Spirit and the community are agreed about the direction in which the church is headed. It came after much struggle, aided by the statesmanlike behavior of the leaders. But it came, and that is what we should aim at.

ADDING REQUIREMENTS FOR **salvation.** When the Reformers rediscovered the biblical insistence of salvation by faith, they realized that the church had almost completely obliterated this doctrine by adding other requirements for salvation, making it into a salvation by works. John Wesley had to rediscover this doctrine again since he had been trusting in his strict Christian discipline but found no assurance of salvation through it. Even today many people would like to do something so that they may feel satisfied that they have earned their salvation.

Religious peddlers are only too willing to accept the gifts that are given to them in order to merit a favor from God. This may be a trap that Satan uses to keep people from surrendering their lives to God. Many who are unwilling to entrust their lives to God to be Lord of their lives are nevertheless willing to give generous gifts for God's work. Many temples and shrines of other faiths and even some churches thrive on such giving. But we must resist such giving, for it keeps people from the way of faith.

The Judaizers in Jerusalem felt that Gentiles should become Jews if they were to become true Christians. Similarly, some early missionaries felt that converts to Christianity should take on the culture of their own homeland. While they may not have insisted on these things or taught them as conditions for salvation, people assumed that if they became Christians, they would have to take on the English, or German, or American culture, or whatever. Some knew that they would not be able to become leaders of the church if they did not speak the language of the missionary. Often the missionary was from the same country as the colonial rulers, who were imposing their culture in their colonies. Today will Hispanic Christians have to renounce some of their culture if they want to become leaders in churches dominated by Anglo-Saxons? Have we unwittingly made things we are comfortable with, but which are not taught in the Bible, into basic prerequisites for Christian involvement? It can easily happen, and we must constantly be on guard about bringing in extrabiblical requirements into the church.

The appeal of false teaching today. When false teachers came to Antioch, what they said could not be easily dismissed since they had come from the mother church in Judea. In the same way today teachers from reputed seminaries can come and cause great damage in the church by false teaching. This type of thing has happened in this century to many churches in the Third World, when liberal teaching came from the mother churches in the West, either through missionaries or through the seminaries where Third World ministers studied. It has caused havoc in older churches, resulting in spiritual death.

Just as the Judaizers sought to remove the scandal of the gospel, throughout the history of the church people have tried to remove the unpleasant aspects of Christianity. In the aftermath of the scientific revolution, many tried to divest Christianity of its miraculous element, since it did not harmonize with the so-called scientific worldview. Today, when pluralism and religious tolerance hold sway, people have tried to divest Christianity of its claim to uniqueness and its doctrine of eternal punishment.

In situations closer to what happened in Acts, some teachers have avoided the unpleasant doctrine of Christ's breaking human barriers and encouraged instead the growth of segregated churches or refused to speak up against racism. The message of integration in Christ is one of the most revolutionary features of Christianity in this world torn by strife. Those who proclaim it get into trouble with extremists. Consequently, many choose to play safe and ignore it, and Christians end up with racist attitudes. If there is no exposure to the Christian view on this issue, people will tend to go with the crowd in their racist thinking.

Opposing false teaching. We said that there was no tolerance of false teaching in this passage. This may sound strange to our ears in this age of pluralism, where opposing viewpoints are permitted to stand side by side and the formulators of new theology are praised for their creativity. But as Bishop Stephen Neill has pointed out, in Christianity there is "the awful and necessary intolerance of truth."[28] Christianity is a religion of revelation. We believe that God has spoken a definite and eternal Word to humanity. Any teaching contrary to that Word within the church must be rooted out with utmost urgency.

The practice of contending for the truth, of course, has been abused much in the past, especially when people brought in sharp personal attacks on those whom they were opposing. Therefore people nowadays shy away from such battles. But we can argue for truth without insulting people whose views we oppose. Heretics must not be allowed to continue to influence the church. Thus, when all else fails, disciplinary action must be taken against them, and that may mean excommunication (1 Tim. 1:19–20).

The practice of contending for the truth has also been abused when people have contended for things about which the Bible is not clear—for example, the time of Christ's coming and the exact interpretation of the signs regarding this coming. Our commitment is to truth, and if God has chosen not to show something clearly to us, we should not be afraid of being tentative in our understandings on that issue.

The New Testament church took immediate steps to attack the false teaching. This is the consistent pattern in Scripture. Galatians 2:11–13 relates

---

28. Stephen Neill, *Creative Tension* (London: Edinburgh House), 11.

how Peter vacillated in Antioch on the same issue of Acts 15 and withdrew from eating with the Gentiles. Paul says, "I opposed him to his face, because he was clearly in the wrong." There had been a public display of serious error by a top leader, so Paul had to confront him in public, because many would otherwise be led astray. We would like our Christian communities to be places without strife. Indeed, we are committed to peace (Rom. 12:8). But often troubles come that must be confronted head-on if the purity of the church is to be maintained.

If we do not confront these problems, we may be able to keep the peace for a time by ignoring the problem. But if we fail to confront serious issues at all, we plunge the church along a path downward, which is increasingly more difficult to arrest. Note how many denominations allowed people to remain in leadership after they departed from the truth. By the time they dealt with it, it was too late. As a result, the church had to develop a structure that allowed people with such views and practices to remain.

There is a warning for leaders here. It is painful to confront error in doctrine and behavior. But we must do it if we think about error as God does. And because of love for God and his church, we must be willing to confront the error and pay the price of it. This is painful, and often we come out of the battle with wounds that take time to heal. But should we not be willing to be wounded in order to maintain the purity of the church, which Christ bought with his own blood (20:28)? Christ himself said, "Love each other as I have loved you." But immediately after that he went on to describe what he meant by this love: "Greater love has no one than this, that he lay down his life for his friends" (John 15:12–13). We must be willing to lay down our lives for the church by confronting error and paying the price of that confrontation.

Sensitivity to others' scruples. The prohibitions developed by the Jerusalem Council show us that theological convictions aside, Christians should be sensitive to the scruples of those whose consciences are offended by certain practices. This is particularly important for people who have been recently "liberated" from a legalistic demand that others still hold. For example, once many evangelicals held to a strong prohibition of the consumption of alcoholic beverages. Now many have come to sense that there is no scriptural ground for such total prohibition. But they need to be sensitive to the scruples of those who still feel that total abstinence is the only suitable approach.

This is particularly significant in countries like Sri Lanka, where the other three major religions (Buddhism, Hinduism, and Islam) officially condemn the consumption of alcohol as a sin. In this context, it is wise for Christians to consider seriously how they can avoid being a stumbling block to those of other faiths vis-à-vis their attitude toward strong drink. Whereas earlier abstinence was considered as an evidence of the genuineness of one's conversion, now it is recommended as expedient in order not to be a stumbling block in the way of some people.

Sometimes we have the situation where those who have been "liberated" from a prohibition of the past become almost evangelistic in their promotion of this practice and even make things difficult for those who still hold to the old prohibition. This pattern of behavior contradicts the spirit of the Jerusalem accord, which was characterized by the willingness of Christians on both sides to make concessions on behalf of the other.

Prohibition of immorality today. We can apply the prohibition of sexual immorality directly to the present. As in Antioch (and Corinth) many today no longer consider immorality as evil. What Christians call immorality the society around us calls love. The power of the media is such that it is difficult to avoid the impact of this onslaught.

This problem is not confined just to cities known for licentiousness. It is a problem even in conservative Asian societies. These attitudes have even influenced the church. The extent of the problem in the United States is expressed by the results of a recent study claiming that 56 percent of single "fundamentalists" engage in sex outside marriage.[29] The pastor of a large evangelical church in North America told a friend of mine that about half the members of his church that get married there have already had sexual relations with each other. According to Gene Edward Veith Jr., polls suggest that whereas earlier if Christians indulged in sex outside marriage, there was a sense of shame and remorse over sin, which is missing in today's church. But Christians seem to have accepted that immorality is not as serious as was once thought.[30]

In this environment is the church taking a strong stand against immorality from the pulpit and in its disciplinary procedures? I don't think so. We do not recoil with the horror that Paul expressed when he wrote to the Corinthians about their permitting immoral people to remain in the church (1 Cor. 5). Many church leaders prefer to ignore these issues, saying that these are personal issues. If, as some have suggested (see above), the prohibition in our passage related to table fellowship, then it may be suggesting that we should not eat with Christians who persist in immorality—a Pauline teaching clearly mentioned in 1 Corinthians 5:9–11.

I believe that we should be warning our people about the dangers of the new lax attitude to immorality. Paul said that the sexually immoral and adulterers will not inherit the kingdom of God (1 Cor. 6:9–10). Today we seem so eager

---

29. Cited in Gene Edward Veith Jr., *Postmodern Times* (Wheaton: Crossway, 1994), 17.
30. Ibid., 18.

to increase our attendance at church that we leave these issues for another forum rather than the pulpit. That makes the pulpit what it was not in the Bible. We must take a firm stand against immorality when it is manifested in the church. Loving sinners Christianly involves the pain of thoroughgoing confrontation of sin, followed by faithful nursing during the time of healing.

Experience and Scripture in theological formulation. Scripture and experience both played a role in arriving at the doctrinal formulation that emerged from the Jerusalem Council. God spoke through the experiences of Peter, Paul, and Barnabas. But James showed that what they had experienced was in keeping with the Scriptures, so that it should become normative. The Scriptures are such a vast resource that we will never plumb its depths or scale its heights this side of heaven. There is always more to discover, and we are often hindered from knowing it by our lack of knowledge of all of Scripture or by our cultural blinds.

We can usually find our misunderstandings of Scripture by studying the Bible with an open mind or by hearing or reading the fruit of someone else's study of Scripture. We sometimes also discover this through an experience that opens our eyes to a hitherto neglected truth. Once we are open, we "diligently study the Scriptures" (John 5:39), examining them like the noble Bereans to see whether what we have been exposed to is true (17:11). Then we realize that what we thought was new was taught in the Scriptures all along without our being aware of it.

Sometimes, however, what we have experienced is not unmistakably taught in the Scriptures. If so, it cannot become normative to us. If such experiences do not contradict Scripture and if they can be seen as applications of principles taught in the Bible, then we can accept them as legitimate; but we must not insist on them for everyone. This has often happened in the church, that people had a particular experience that enriched their lives and did not seem to contradict Scripture. While it was legitimate for those who had this experience, it would have been wrong for them to insist on everyone having the same experience.

In other words, *Scripture is always our only standard for faith and practice.* But our experiences can help us see things in the Scripture to which we have been blind. John Wesley, actually talks of the quadrilateral—Scripture, tradition, reason, and experience—which influences the formulation of theology.[31] But the foundation, the ultimate source of raw material for constructing theology, is Scripture.

---

31. For a recent discussion of this see, Donald A. D. Thorsen, *The Wesleyan Quadrilateral: Scripture, Tradition, Reason and Experience as a Model of Evangelical Theology* (Grand Rapids: Zondervan, 1990).

Honorable leadership. Conflicts in the church today are often marred by a partisanship that reduces debate to the level of politicking. People take sides depending on their experiences. A person who has humiliated someone else must be opposed and humiliated in return. Though the issues discussed seem to be principles, deep down a hurt self is causing havoc in the church. How different Peter was! He refused to let the past humiliation in Antioch color his actions at the council. Instead, he spoke up on behalf of the cause of Paul and Barnabas even before they themselves spoke.

Leaders who have crucified self battle the tendency to let the humiliation of previous confrontations influence their actions. They fight the desire that wells up within to "teach that upstart a lesson," and their actions are determined only with the progress of the kingdom and the honor of God in mind. How many unpleasant situations in the church could have been avoided if hurt leaders had been a little more like Peter! So many of the flames of the so-called "battles over principles" are fanned by leaders who have not crucified the flesh. What goes as a battle for principles is really a clash of personalities.

We noted that James did not take sides in the conflict, and he went against his own preference. Wise leaders often have to do that. We may personally not like a certain kind of modern music that others feel is effective when working with a certain group of people. But we must not let our tastes influence what is best for the kingdom. We must instead work hard at acquiring a taste for this music so that we can spread the gospel more effectively.

James also did not consider loyalty to people who looked to him as their leader a factor that should affect whose side he would champion in the conflict. How politicized the church has become today! Acts speaks of a church where people were of one heart and one mind (2:44; 4:32). But in contemporary conflict situations, some Christians associate only with people on their side. Cliques form in the church, which view each other as competitors. People from one clique try to outmaneuver those from the other. Politics, rather than the overriding desire for the glory of God, rules in such situations.

Acts 14 records an event when party spirit was defeated and theology won the day. At the heart of it was godly leadership. Conflicts are often spurred on by leaders. They may place the responsibility for the angry actions upon the people and claim that the people are angry about what has happened. But it is the leaders who have influenced these people to act in this way. Ultimately the blame for conflict gone out of control lies with the leaders.

Coming to being of one mind. The church as it met in Jerusalem did not start with unanimity, but as the proceedings went on, some felt led to change their positions, so that unity emerged. There was serious discussion and urgent meetings, involving people having to travel long distances. The unity of the church is so important that such a price had to be paid. Would that we too could work like that in our communities.

Instead, we use the voting method today, which is (I admit) much quicker. But the problem with the voting method is that some people are always dissatisfied with the decision, and thus there is no unity as believers work on a given project. When problems come, those against the project say, "I told you this won't work" and become a discouragement to everyone. Campbell Morgan says, "An overwhelming majority often leaves behind it a minority disaffected and dangerous."[32] Other times the leader makes a decision and others are forced to comply out of respect for his or her position. But that means that there may be many who comply whose hearts are not in the course of action taken. The power of a united body is missing.

It takes much longer to arrive at a situation where the people are of one mind. Many are impatient with a consensus method of decision making, fearing that they won't get much done that way. But the price is worth paying in the long run. Even though it may take a longer time to reach a decision, when it is being executed, better results can be expected. Everyone will be enthusiastic about it and will be motivated to work hard to see it through. The loss of time caused by waiting for unanimity will be more than compensated for.

---

32. Campbell Morgan, *Acts*, 365.

Acts 15:36–16:10

S OME TIME LATER Paul said to Barnabas, "Let us go back and visit the brothers in all the towns where we preached the word of the Lord and see how they are doing." 37Barnabas wanted to take John, also called Mark, with them, 38but Paul did not think it wise to take him, because he had deserted them in Pamphylia and had not continued with them in the work. 39They had such a sharp disagreement that they parted company. Barnabas took Mark and sailed for Cyprus, 40but Paul chose Silas and left, commended by the brothers to the grace of the Lord. 41He went through Syria and Cilicia, strengthening the churches.

16:1He came to Derbe and then to Lystra, where a disciple named Timothy lived, whose mother was a Jewess and a believer, but whose father was a Greek. 2The brothers at Lystra and Iconium spoke well of him. 3Paul wanted to take him along on the journey, so he circumcised him because of the Jews who lived in that area, for they all knew that his father was a Greek. 4As they traveled from town to town, they delivered the decisions reached by the apostles and elders in Jerusalem for the people to obey. 5So the churches were strengthened in the faith and grew daily in numbers.

6Paul and his companions traveled throughout the region of Phrygia and Galatia, having been kept by the Holy Spirit from preaching the word in the province of Asia. 7When they came to the border of Mysia, they tried to enter Bithynia, but the Spirit of Jesus would not allow them to. 8So they passed by Mysia and went down to Troas. 9During the night Paul had a vision of a man of Macedonia standing and begging him, "Come over to Macedonia and help us." 10After Paul had seen the vision, we got ready at once to leave for Macedonia, concluding that God had called us to preach the gospel to them.

Original Meaning

AFTER THE JERUSALEM Council, Paul told Barnabas that he wanted to revisit the churches they had started on their first missionary journey (v. 36). Part of the reason for this visit was presumably also to deliver on the way the letter written by the council. This was to be Paul's second missionary journey.

The Team Breaks Up (15:36–40)

IN DISCUSSING THE idea of revisiting the churches with Barnabas, Paul disagrees with the suggestion that they take Barnabas's cousin Mark (Col. 4:10) along, "because he had deserted them in Pamphylia" (vv. 37–38). Though the word Luke uses for the resulting conflict is a strong one (*paroxysmos*), it does not give us a hint about who was right and who was wrong. That the team should have broken up because of this conflict is sad. Perhaps the pain of the public confrontation in Antioch after Barnabas went along with Peter (Gal. 2:13) had something to do with the severity of this conflict.[1] Longenecker suggests that Mark may have been "in some way responsible for inciting the Judaizers to action,"[2] which would have made Paul all the more wary of taking him on. But this too is not stated.

We agree with Marshall: "It is a classic example of the perpetual problem of whether to place the interests of the individual or of the work as a whole first."[3] It is encouraging to find out that later Paul and Barnabas seem to have become colleagues again (1 Cor. 9:6; Col. 4:10) and that Paul had not only come to appreciate Mark but also to depend on him so much that he asked for him to come to him towards the end of his life (2 Tim. 4:11; cf. Col. 4:10; Philem. 24).

The sovereignty of God as he works out his purposes even through human weakness is revealed as two teams now set out, and the area of the first missionary journey is divided between Paul and Barnabas. The latter goes to his native Cyprus with Mark (15:39), while Paul takes Silas and travels via Syria and Cicilia to South Galatia (15:40–16:1).

Silas was a leader in the church of Jerusalem (15:22) and a prophet who "said much to encourage and strengthen the brothers" in Antioch (15:32). This must mean he was an enthusiastic backer of Paul's program of Gentile evangelism. He was also a Roman citizen like Paul (see 16:37)—an asset in an itinerant ministry in the Roman empire. Silas is probably an abbreviation of the Latin Silvanus, by which he is called in the letters.[4] He is named as coauthor of the two Thessalonian letters. He "was probably the amanuensis employed in the writing down of 1 Peter, and responsible for its rather elegant Greek style"[5] (see 1 Peter 5:12).

Paul and Silas are commissioned and sent off by the church in Antioch (15:40), just as the earlier team had been sent off (13:3). There the commissioning included fasting, prayer, and the laying on of hands. The same

---

1. Bruce, *Acts*, NICNT, 302; Williams, *Acts*, 272–73.

2. Longenecker, "Acts," 454.

3. Marshall, *Acts*, 258.

4. See 2 Cor. 1:19; 1 Thess. 1:1; 2 Thess. 1:1; 1 Peter 5:12. The NIV renders both the Greek *Silouanos* in these verses and the Greek *Silas* elsewhere as Silas.

5. Bruce, *Circle*, 28.

may have been done here too. The commissioning is mentioned as being "commended . . . to the grace of the Lord." There is no mention of a similar send-off for Barnabas and Mark, but this may be because from now on Luke focuses on Paul's ministry. All ministry stems from God's grace, but grace is often mediated through the prayers, concern, accountability, and provisions of other Christians. The laying on of hands itself was intended to signify the mediating of God's blessing.[6] The church released Paul and Silas to the grace of God, but they would have pledged to do their part in continuing to mediate this grace.

The Macedonian Call (16:1–10)

ACTS 15:41 AND 16:5 indicate that the first leg of this journey by Paul and Silas was essentially one of "strengthening the churches." One aspect of this ministry was that "they delivered the decisions" of the Jerusalem Council "for the people to obey" (16:4).

In Lystra a well-spoken-of young man of mixed parentage, Timothy, becomes the newest member of the team (16:1–3). Paul's circumcising of him has received much discussion. It is alleged that the Paul of the letters, who spoke so strongly against circumcision, could not have done this, and therefore that the Paul of Acts may not be the authentic Paul of history. But we must remember that the Paul of Acts also considered the circumcision issue so important that he made the long trip to Jerusalem to battle the Judaizers. His battle was against insisting that circumcision was a condition for the full inclusion of the Gentiles among the people of God. Here the issue was qualifications for ministry. No church today asks for a theological degree as a necessary condition for membership, but many require this for entrance into the ministry.

Timothy needed to win the esteem of the Jewish Christians, and being circumcised would have given him openings in evangelizing Jews. If he had been a "full-blooded Gentile" Paul would not have insisted on circumcision, as we see with the Greek Titus, whom he took along to Jerusalem (Gal. 2:3). But Timothy was half Jewish, and it would be more appropriate for him to go through the painful process of full initiation into the Jewish community. Some accuse Paul of inconsistency, but Bruce reminds us of R. W. Emerson's statement about "foolish consistency" being the "hobgoblin of little minds, adored by little statesmen and philosophers and divines."[7]

The providence of God is obvious in this section, hindering Paul from doing what he wanted in order to be led to the place where God wanted him

---

6. "Laying on of Hands," BEB, 2:1317–18.

7. Bruce, Acts, NICNT, 304; from R. W. Emerson, "Essays on Self-Reliance," Essays, Lectures and Orations (London, 1848), 30.

to go (16:6–10). After ministering in Phrygia and Galatia[8] he wanted to go southwest to the province of Asia, probably to minister in Ephesus, the important capital of Asia, but "the Holy Spirit" prevented him (16:6). Then he traveled west to the border of Mysia and tried to go north to Bithynia, but again the Spirit—this time called "the Spirit of Jesus"—"would not allow them" (16:7). Paul had ministered in the east, he cannot go north or south, so he can only go further west and comes to the seaport Troas (16:8). There he has the vision with a call from Macedonia (v. 9) and concludes that "God had call[ed him] to preach" there (v. 10).[9] After this period of uncertainty about God's will, when the will is confirmed, Paul and his team get ready "at once" to go to Macedonia, and with that to a new horizon in the expansion of Christianity.

In verse 10 we have the first of the "we" passages of Acts,[10] suggesting to some that Troas may be where Paul first met Luke[11] or at least where they first began to travel together. Some have suggested that he joined the team in his capacity as a doctor (cf. Col. 4:14), which is possible, considering Paul's frequent ill health. Bruce says, "It is no exaggeration to say that Paul is the hero of Acts."[12] This could be because Luke got to know Paul intimately through being with him. He was the only one with Paul shortly before his execution in Rome (2 Tim. 4:11). But Luke also gives other leaders, like Peter and James, due place in Acts. In fact, as Bruce says, "Luke is a truly catholic writer; he knows that there are various strands in primitive Christianity, and he weaves them together in the interests of Christian unity—a cause obviously dear to his heart."[13] Traveling with Silas would certainly have helped Luke get the perspective of the Jerusalem church.

Bridging Contexts

THIS PASSAGE DOES not have any explicitly stated principles that can be unmistakably affirmed for today. But there are many human experiences with which we can identify and through which we see God at work. Therefore, this passage is instructive to us as we learn how to fight the good fight of faith. We can be grateful that Luke did not

---

8. For a discussion of what is meant by Phrygia and Galatia, see Longenecker, "Acts," 457.

9. Longenecker sees, in the progression from "the Holy Spirit" to "the Spirit of Jesus" to "God" "an unconscious expression of the early church's embryonic Trinitarian faith" ("Acts," 457).

10. See 16:10–17; 20:5–21:17; chs. 27–28.

11. An important Western variant of 11:28, which records an incident in Antioch, supplies the first "we" passage of any text of Acts (Metzger, *Textual*, 391). Colin Hemer says, "It is possible that this reading reflects an early tradition which connected Luke with that city" (*Acts*, 312).

12. Bruce, *Circle*, 42.

13. Ibid., 43.

gloss over crises in the early church and hide the weaknesses of its leaders. It was not an ideal church, with saints whose perfect lives leave us panting with frustration over our failures and imperfections. It was a church with people just like us but who nevertheless were available to God and were used to do great things for him. This passage demonstrates the truth of 2 Corinthians 4:7: "But we have this treasure in jars of clay to show that this all-surpassing power is from God and not from us."

The conflict. It is significant that after so many centuries of study, the church is still not sure who was at fault in the conflict between Paul and Barnabas. Interpersonal conflicts can be complex and difficult to unravel. It is encouraging to see that God works through this conflict. "But," as John Stott says, "this example of God's providence may not be used as an excuse for Christian quarreling."[14] Neither should we assume that such disruption is the norm when there is a disagreement among Christian leaders. It is an exception brought about by human error rather than by divine design.

But God is bigger than our problems, and he wills for his children to live in unity. Thus, we can hope for a resolution whenever there is a problem. That we may be unable to resolve it is because of stubbornness, error, or ignorance on the part of one or both sides of the conflict. Conflict is a fact of life in this fallen world, and sometimes conflicts in Christian relationships do end up unresolved.

Encouragers look with the eyes of hope. We cannot help observing the mentality of the encourager in Barnabas, as he refuses to give up on Mark (15:37–39). The younger Paul could not see the potential that Barnabas saw. And Barnabas's hopes were not unfounded, for Mark did live up to his expectations. The first desertion did not automatically mean continued desertions. Later, Paul came to value Mark, and he seems to have become an assistant to Peter, who sends greetings from "my son Mark" at the close of his first letter (1 Peter 5:13).

Mark was in all probability the writer of the second Gospel. Papias, bishop of Hierapolis around A.D. 130, states: "Mark having become interpreter of Peter, wrote down accurately whatsoever he remembered ... [of] the sayings or deeds of Christ." He describes how Mark "took special care" to write an accurate account.[15] The father of church history, Eusebius, in his *Ecclesiastical History* (A.D. 325), claims that Mark undertook this task in response to appeals from Christians who wanted a permanent record of what Peter had

---

14. Stott, *Acts*, 253.

15. See "Fragments of Papias," *The Ante-Nicene Fathers*, vol. 1, *The Apostolic Fathers with Justin Martyr and Irenaeus* (Edinburgh: T. & T. Clark; and Grand Rapids: Eerdmans, 1996 reprint), 154–55.

taught. Eusebius also presents the less well-attested tradition that "Mark is said to have been the first man to set out for Egypt and preach there the gospel ... and the first to establish churches in Alexandria itself."[16] There is no doubt, then, that Mark has a significant place in the history of the early church. "As a member of three intersecting circles in the early church, he provides an important link between Barnabas, Peter and Paul."[17]

The example of Barnabas's not giving up on Mark invites us also to look at people with the eyes of hope. Paul also seems to have developed this character, as we see him refusing to give up on people like Timothy and the Corinthians despite their weaknesses. Hope, then, is a key to the ministry of encouragement. This is not blind hope, of course, but hope that comes out of the possibilities of grace. In fact, when we encourage people who have failed in an area of their lives, our main message to them is not, "You can do it," but "He can do it in you."

Principles of itinerant ministry. This section establishes some key features about itinerant ministry in the early church. (1) The ministry was done in teams. After Paul and Barnabas separated, each took on another team member, Silas and Mark respectively, who accompanied them in their travels (15:39–40).

(2) Paul's team accomplished a twofold ministry. They first visited existing churches and strengthened them (15:41). Then they went to the unreached region of Macedonia, in an evangelistic ministry (16:10). Today too itinerant ministers can travel to strengthen churches and do evangelism.

(3) A local group commended the team "to the grace of the Lord" (15:40) as the team set off. This group backed the team and supported it (at least in prayer). We know that on the first missionary journey Paul's team was sent out by the church in Antioch (13:3) and that they returned there (14:27). Local support groups are also a great asset to itinerant ministers today.

The circumcision of Timothy. Circumcision was a painful experience for an adult in days before the use of anesthetics.[18] This is probably one reason why many Gentiles preferred to remain God-fearers without becoming full Jews. Yet in order for Timothy to win his credibility, he had to undergo the pain of this experience. Thus, soon after the battle to free the church of circumcision was won, Paul circumcised his young assistant (16:3). Leaders may need deliberately to take on things that will cause them pain but will give them credibility in ministry.

---

16. Eusebius, *The History of the Church from Christ to Constantine*, trans. G. A. Williamson, rev. and ed. Andrew Louth (London: Penguin, 1989), 49–50.

17. Bruce, *Circle*, 80.

18. See comments on 15:19.

In 1 Corinthians 9 Paul talks about how he took on many difficulties, even though he was free to live the way he wanted (1 Cor. 9:1). Talking about his legitimate right to support he writes: "But we did not use this right. On the contrary, we put up with anything rather than hinder the gospel of Christ" (9:12b). In this same chapter he expresses his passion for the gospel as follows: "Though I am free and belong to no man, I make myself a slave to everyone, to win as many as possible" (9:19). He goes on, "I do all this for the sake of the gospel, that I may share in its blessings" (9:23). With such commitment he could ask people like Timothy also to pay a price. Leaders who do not pay a price are usually unable to motivate others to such commitment. Paul not only insisted on costly discipleship for others, he modeled it in his own life.

Human planning and divine guidance. God's strange providence in the way he prohibited Paul from going to places where he wanted to go (16:6–8) shows us that, while it is right for humans to plan and have visions, those plans must be submitted to the will of God and be open to his veto. Proverbs 16:9 says, "In his heart a man plans his course, but the LORD determines his steps." Paul submitted to God's will and was also receptive to his voice. Though he had his plans, he always presented them to God, and God was able to get through to him with his will because of this submissive spirit. Note James 4:13–15:

> Now listen, you who say, "Today or tomorrow we will go to this or that city, spend a year there, carry on business and make money." Why, you do not even know what will happen tomorrow. What is your life? You are a mist that appears for a little while and then vanishes. Instead, you ought to say, "If it is the Lord's will, we will live and do this or that."

Just as Paul was guided by God after a period of uncertainty, we too can trust God to guide us if we earnestly seek his will. Paul says, "Those who are led by the Spirit of God are sons of God" (Rom. 8:14). We cannot, however, say for how long the time of uncertainly will last. Yet during those dark nights of the soul, God often does a work in us that does us great good.

WHEN WE FACE **conflicts.** While it is true that this passage does not give us an excuse to quarrel, it does give us comfort if we have disagreements that do not end in amicable resolutions. It also gives hope, for just at Paul and Barnabas got together after the heat of the conflict had died down, so can we. Therefore we must be sure that during the heat of a conflict we do not do or say things that complicate a final resolution. All too often when people are hurt and disappointed, they make public statements that are difficult to live down. Perhaps they write strongly accusatory letters that cannot be erased once written.

Because God is greater than the problem, we can always live with the hope of resolution. That hope will enable us to look beyond the hurt to the day when we will rejoice in a relationship restored. And that, in turn, should cause us to temper our actions and reactions. Therefore, it is always best to get the help of others who are less emotionally involved in the conflict to guide us. Because they are detached from the situation, they may be able to see things more clearly and advise us to act more wisely.

Ministering hope to people. A good summary of hope-filled ministry is found in Paul's words to the timid Timothy (1 Tim. 4:12; 2 Tim. 1:6–7): "Timothy, my son, I give you this instruction in keeping with the prophecies once made about you, so that by following them you may fight the good fight" (1 Tim. 1:18). What drives Paul here are the "prophecies once made about" Timothy—prophecies that became the basis of his hope in the possibilities of grace in Timothy's life and ministry. They gave him confidence to expect great things from Timothy.

Many people are being crushed in our competitive society as the law of the jungle (i.e., the survival of the fittest) reigns. The Christian leader looks beyond shallow estimates of what fitness is and dwells in the realm of the possibilities of grace. That fires hope about what can be achieved through people whom the world thinks are useless. We will all find scores of dejected people who have been rejected by our fast-moving, results-oriented society. God is waiting to use us to open their lives to the inexhaustible riches of God's grace.

The Irishman Adam Clarke was the great theologian of the early Methodist movement. His massive eight-volume commentary of the Bible (1810–26) remains in print to date and earned him the title "the Prince of Commentators" from Charles Spurgeon. But at school Clarke was slow to learn. One day a distinguished visitor paid a visit to the school, and the teacher singled out Clarke and said, "That is the stupidest boy in the school." But before he left the school, the visitor came to the boy and said, "Never mind, my boy, you may be a great scholar someday. Don't be discouraged but try hard, and keep on trying." William Barclay, after relating this story, asks, "Who knows?—it may well have been that word of hope which made Adam Clarke what he one day became."[19]

Itinerant ministry today. The features about itinerant ministry listed above are relevant today too. (1) Should itinerant preachers always travel in a team? This seems to be the way both Jesus and the traveling preachers of

---

19. William Barclay, *The Letters to the Corinthians*, rev. ed. *The Daily Study Bible Series* (Philadelphia: Westminster, 1975), 124.

437

Acts did it. It is certainly the ideal way to travel, as we showed in our discussion of Acts 3. We should try to always take somebody along. But today there may be situations where we cannot afford to take someone. Then we should ensure that there is a team "at home" backing us and that we have as our temporary team members the people with whom we are ministering. This can be done by staying in their homes, praying with them, spending time in fellowship with them so that they are truly one in spirit with the traveling person, and sharing personal concerns with them.

What we must strenuously avoid is the common situation where gifted people are working alone. They have a private life in their travels that others do not share. Such people can get into serious spiritual trouble. They can lose their cutting edge by not having colleagues who provoke them as iron sharpens iron (Prov. 27:17). They can succumb to the many temptations that traveling people face and begin to live in a world of defeat with no one to help them. All traveling people should seek to have team ministry in some way or other.

(2) Should we expect itinerant preachers to be both evangelists and teachers? We know that some itinerant preachers are not equally gifted in both strengthening ministry and evangelistic ministry. But usually they should be available to do at least some ministry in both areas. Usually we do a little of all types of ministries (other than those we are definitely not gifted in, e.g., public singing for a person who cannot sing in tune!), though we specialize in a few areas.

(3) We should apply the principle of having a group in our home base who sends us out, who prays for us, and to whom we are accountable. Such support and accountability is vital for effective ministry, for much strength comes from such people. They can also help us manage our finances. As the misuse of finances has caused the downfall of many a traveling preacher, it is helpful to have others to whom we are accountable keep watch over the finances pertaining to our traveling ministries.

Nurturing a team of prayer warriors at home while we travel takes commitment on our part. A heroic figure of recent missionary history, James O. Fraser, was forced, much against his wishes, to do a lot of lone pioneering work among the Lisus in the mountains of China. Yet he had a band of friends in England who were committed to pray for him. He kept them motivated by sending them regular letters with detailed descriptions of his needs, victories (which were few for a long time), and struggles. A recent biography of Fraser gives helpful hints on how to get others to pray for us.[20]

---

20. Eileen Grossman, *Mountain Rain* (Robesonia, Pa. and Sevenoaks, Kent: OMF Books, 1988).

Each of the three principles just given runs counter to the individualism that has hit our generation. Even those who travel in teams can live in their private worlds without real spiritual accountability. In Paul's team there was openness among the team members. This is why he could say to Timothy, "You, however, know all about my teaching, my way of life, my purpose, faith, patience, love, endurance, persecutions, sufferings—what kinds of things happened to me in Antioch, Iconium and Lystra, the persecutions I endured" (2 Tim. 3:10–11). Paul had opened his life to Timothy. It is strange that many Christian leaders still persist in maintaining closed private lives in spite of the scriptural models and of the many cases of fallen leaders who had no accountability. It indicates how the lifestyle of the world has overcome the scriptural lifestyle. In this area we must be clearly countercultural.

Taking on pain. When we were teenagers, we had a tract that helped us much in the path of discipleship, entitled *Others May, You Cannot*. Others might avoid the pain of subjecting themselves to circumcision, but for Timothy to succeed in ministry he had to take this on. This was the pain of identification with people. One who loves to eat meat may need to become a vegetarian if he finds that eating meat will be a stumbling block to the Buddhists he is trying to reach. Certainly one who likes hunting will have to give that up if one is to work with Buddhists (who consider killing animals a serious sin). A missionary may need to take on the tough task of learning a new language in order to identify with the people. One who is trying to reach people in the slums may need to live near the place where the people she wants to reach live. As a result she may have to endure the pain and terror of having her house broken into. In a society where people are allergic to pain, these things are difficult to endure. Most people will avoid such things, but we should voluntarily take these things on in order to bear fruit that really lasts.

Submissive visionaries. Paul was a visionary who planned ahead and developed strategies for reaching the lost and taking the gospel to the farthest corners of the world. In Romans 15:23–29 he refers to some of his visions, which included visiting Rome. But he always lived in submission to God's will. Thus, he goes on to say, "pray that I may be rescued from the unbelievers . . . so that by God's will I may come to you" (15:31–32). As we saw in our passage, he submitted his plans to God for rejection, acceptance, or modification.

How can we discover whether God is telling us not do something we have planned to do? We are told that the Spirit stopped Paul, but we are not told how he became aware of that message. There are many ways in which God can communicate his will to us on such matters. It may be through a miraculous means, like prophecy or a dream. When the community meets prayerfully to discuss a given plan or when it is being discussed at a personal level,

God may speak through the wisdom of someone there. Sometimes there is what people call "a check" in the inner spirit, when there is a sense that this may not be right. It may come through a feeling of reservation inside us about some aspect of the plan, through some obstacles that come along that are seen as signs from God to desist, or through the reservations of someone else whom we trust.

When that happens, we must go into earnest prayer and discussion over the issue, seeking clarification from God. We should be careful about pushing through projects when we have reservations about them. After all, we will be unable to give our heart and soul to such projects. It is better then to take the time to grapple with God to find out what his will is.

When we are in an attitude of earnestly looking to God for guidance, God may guide us in an unusual way, as he did with Paul through a vision. We do not know how long Paul had to wait before God came to him in this vision. But it seems to have been a considerably long time. Such times can be frustrating. But believing in the promises of God we look to him, awaiting his word with patient hope, doing all that we know we can do under the circumstances. When we sense that God has spoken, we must respond immediately, as Paul did (16:10), and launch out in faith.

When I went to the United States to study in seminary, I went with the plan of coming back to Sri Lanka to work with Youth for Christ. But in seminary, several teachers and friends advised me against such a step, saying that my giftedness seemed to be for another kind of ministry (either the pastorate or teaching). I wrote home about this, asked whomever I could for advice, and prayed much. But no sense of direction emerged for several months. Then I got a letter from the national director of our program, Sam Sherrard, in which he said that he was moving to another YFC program and asked me to take his place. I suddenly sensed that this was the leading that I had been seeking from God. I showed the letter to one of my professors, Dr. J. T. Seamands, who concurred. I went back home to the job that I have had for the past twenty-one years.

Thus, we will dream great things for God, which become the stuff out of which our visions emerge. But we will seek God's face to know his will and be always eager to submit to that will. And during the sometimes frustrating times of waiting, until we know God's will, we must do whatever we know we should do, realizing that the times of frustration we dread will one day yield a rich harvest of blessing.

Acts 16:11–40

❦

FROM TROAS WE put out to sea and sailed straight for Samothrace, and the next day on to Neapolis. [12]From there we traveled to Philippi, a Roman colony and the leading city of that district of Macedonia. And we stayed there several days.

[13]On the Sabbath we went outside the city gate to the river, where we expected to find a place of prayer. We sat down and began to speak to the women who had gathered there. [14]One of those listening was a woman named Lydia, a dealer in purple cloth from the city of Thyatira, who was a worshiper of God. The Lord opened her heart to respond to Paul's message. [15]When she and the members of her household were baptized, she invited us to her home. "If you consider me a believer in the Lord," she said, "come and stay at my house." And she persuaded us.

[16]Once when we were going to the place of prayer, we were met by a slave girl who had a spirit by which she predicted the future. She earned a great deal of money for her owners by fortune-telling. [17]This girl followed Paul and the rest of us, shouting, "These men are servants of the Most High God, who are telling you the way to be saved." [18]She kept this up for many days. Finally Paul became so troubled that he turned around and said to the spirit, "In the name of Jesus Christ I command you to come out of her!" At that moment the spirit left her.

[19]When the owners of the slave girl realized that their hope of making money was gone, they seized Paul and Silas and dragged them into the marketplace to face the authorities. [20]They brought them before the magistrates and said, "These men are Jews, and are throwing our city into an uproar [21]by advocating customs unlawful for us Romans to accept or practice."

[22]The crowd joined in the attack against Paul and Silas, and the magistrates ordered them to be stripped and beaten. [23]After they had been severely flogged, they were thrown into prison, and the jailer was commanded to guard them carefully. [24]Upon receiving such orders, he put them in the inner cell and fastened their feet in the stocks.

²⁵About midnight Paul and Silas were praying and singing hymns to God, and the other prisoners were listening to them. ²⁶Suddenly there was such a violent earthquake that the foundations of the prison were shaken. At once all the prison doors flew open, and everybody's chains came loose. ²⁷The jailer woke up, and when he saw the prison doors open, he drew his sword and was about to kill himself because he thought the prisoners had escaped. ²⁸But Paul shouted, "Don't harm yourself! We are all here!"

²⁹The jailer called for lights, rushed in and fell trembling before Paul and Silas. ³⁰He then brought them out and asked, "Sirs, what must I do to be saved?"

³¹They replied, "Believe in the Lord Jesus, and you will be saved—you and your household." ³²Then they spoke the word of the Lord to him and to all the others in his house. ³³At that hour of the night the jailer took them and washed their wounds; then immediately he and all his family were baptized. ³⁴The jailer brought them into his house and set a meal before them; he was filled with joy because he had come to believe in God—he and his whole family.

³⁵When it was daylight, the magistrates sent their officers to the jailer with the order: "Release those men." ³⁶The jailer told Paul, "The magistrates have ordered that you and Silas be released. Now you can leave. Go in peace."

³⁷But Paul said to the officers: "They beat us publicly without a trial, even though we are Roman citizens, and threw us into prison. And now do they want to get rid of us quietly? No! Let them come themselves and escort us out."

³⁸The officers reported this to the magistrates, and when they heard that Paul and Silas were Roman citizens, they were alarmed. ³⁹They came to appease them and escorted them from the prison, requesting them to leave the city. ⁴⁰After Paul and Silas came out of the prison, they went to Lydia's house, where they met with the brothers and encouraged them. Then they left.

Original Meaning

IN TROAS PAUL had received the vision to go to Macedonia. After concluding with his colleagues that God was calling them to minister there, they left immediately for that area. They sailed across the Aegean sea and disembarked at Neapolis, the port city for Philippi, where they made their first evangelistic contacts.

Lydia's Household Converted in Philippi (16:11–15)

VERSE 11 GIVES a detailed log of the journey, which "is typical of the latter part of Acts."[1] We find specific descriptions of the time taken and the places passed through; this is understandable since the author himself participated in this trip. Samothrace was a common stopover for ships "as captains preferred to anchor there rather than face the hazards of the sea at night."[2] Philippi was about ten miles inland, so they landed at Neapolis. From Neapolis Paul and company used the Egnatian Way, a famous Roman road running east-west with Neapolis as its eastern terminus. Some cobbled sections of this road are still visible.

The region of Macedonia was separate from Greece at this time; now it is mostly part of Greece, with a portion in the former Yugoslavia and Bulgaria. Two famous Macedonian kings, Philip II (356–336 B.C.) and his son Alexander (334–323 B.C.), had led a united Graeco-Macedonian empire. Macedonia became a Roman province in 146 B.C. Philippi was a Roman colony, which means its constitution was patterned after that of Rome.[3] "It was governed by two annually appointed chief magistrates (called praetors), whose police attendants were called lictors."[4] Note that Paul and Silas were brought "before the magistrates" (plural, v. 20).

On the Sabbath Paul and his friends went to the river outside the city gate, expecting to find "a place of prayer" (v. 13). Though "place of prayer" was used in those days for synagogues,[5] this must have been simply a place where people met to worship God. It was necessary to have ten men to organize a synagogue,[6] but only women were gathered here. Being by a river facilitated any ceremonial washing rituals. One of the first converts in Philippi was Lydia, a seller of purple cloth from Thyatira, a city renowned for purple dye. It belonged to the ancient kingdom of Lydia (part of Asia in the first century). This accounts for her name, which may have been a trade name—"she may have been known as the Lydian lady."[7]

---

1. Gempf, "Acts," 1090.

2. Longenecker, "Acts," 459. Longenecker cites Philo, *Natural History*, 4:23 here.

3. There has been some confusion over Luke's words, "the leading [or first; *protes*] city of that district of Macedonia," to describe Philippi. Amphipolis and Thessalonica had a more valid claim for that title politically. Bruce solves the problem by having "first" modify district rather than city (*Acts*, NICNT, 309–10). Keener thinks that Luke intended to say that Philippi was also a leading city along with Thessalonica, not the only leading city (*BBC*, 367–68). Longenecker opts for translating it as "the leading city of the district of Macedonia" and understands this expression as "an indication of Luke's pride in his city" ("Acts," 460).

4. Bruce, *Steps*, 32.

5. Boring, *Hellenistic Commentary*, 324; Ferguson, *Backgrounds*, 539.

6. Ferguson, *Backgrounds*, 546.

7. Stott, *Acts*, 263.

The interplay between the divine and human parts in evangelism is well expressed in verse 14. Paul and his companions went to the people and shared the message, but God was the ultimate evangelist: "The Lord opened her heart to respond to Paul's message." After her whole household (possibly including her employees) was baptized, she asked them to stay at her home. Verse 15b suggests that it took some persuading for Paul and company to decide to go there. This may have been because she was a woman, possibly a single woman. Were the team members reluctant to go there because it was a Gentile home? We cannot be sure, but it is unlikely that Paul would have had such hesitancy. Luke's interests in hosts is seen with the mention of hospitality in the homes of Lydia and the jailer (v. 34).

A Slave Girl Is Healed (16:16–24)

THE STORY OF the slave girl who was delivered from an evil spirit has similarities with episodes involving evil spirits in Jesus' life. The spirits seem to have had supernatural powers that enabled them to recognize the divine source of the ministries of Jesus and of Paul's team (v. 17; cf. Luke 4:34, 41; 8:28). Some suggest that the "cry could represent the little girl's confused cry of desire to know God."[8] The girl is said to have "a spirit of divination" (NRSV, NASB, etc.) or "a spirit by which she predicted the future" (NIV).[9] Today too soothsayers predict the future for gain; some are fakes while others do it through supernatural powers. This girl seems to have belonged to the latter category. Though what she proclaimed affirmed Paul's ministry, he is "troubled" by it (*diaponeomai*, v. 18, which means "to be strongly irked or provoked at something or someone";[10] cf. 4:2). Why Paul delayed responding for a few days remains a mystery. But when he did attend to it, the power of God overcame the demonic hold over the girl's life.

This miracle, which caused a significant loss of income for her owners, brought about opposition to the gospel (cf. also 19:23–28). Their official reason for opposition was that Paul and Silas were "advocating customs unlawful for us Romans to practice" (v. 21)—which the authorities had to take as a serious complaint. Clearly an attempt was made to alienate the missionaries and cause the magistrates to side with "us Romans." Little did they know that the missionaries were Romans too (v. 37).

---

8. Ed Murphy, *The Handbook for Spiritual Warfare* (Nashville: Thomas Nelson, 1992), 325. This explanation is only suggested, not dogmatically stated, by Dr. Murphy and by Knowling, "Acts," 347.

9. For a description of how what is literally "a spirit of the python" (*pneuma pythona*, v. 16), or "a pythonic spirit" (Bruce, *Acts*, NICNT), came to mean a spirit of divination, see the standard commentaries on Acts.

10. Louw and Nida, 763.

The treatment Paul and Silas received should not have been given to Roman citizens.[11] They were "dragged . . . into the marketplace to face the authorities" (v. 19), "stripped," (v. 22), "severely flogged," and "thrown into prison" (v. 23) "without a trial" (v. 37). They were sent to the maximum security "inner cell" of the prison, and their feet were fastened in the stocks (v. 24). Brian Rapske explains, "The stocks normally caused extreme discomfort as the prisoner had to sleep either in a sitting position or lying down on the floor. Changing position to avoid cramping was nearly impossible."[12] It is not surprising, then, to find them awake at midnight (v. 25). The treatment Paul and Silas received shows that they "were considered wrongdoers entirely lacking legal and social merit."[13]

A Jailer's Household Is Converted (16:25–34)

DESPITE THE HUMILIATION and pain they had experienced through being stripped, flogged, and imprisoned, Paul and Silas were "praying and singing hymns" around midnight (v. 25). "Songs in the night" of suffering have been a common response to suffering by the faithful throughout the ages. "The other prisoners were listening to them" (v. 25b), and it is interesting that they did not escape when their chains became loose after the earthquake (vv. 26–28). Gemph writes: "Paul may have taken some deliberate control over the rest of the prisoners (as he seems to have taken up the leader's role as a prisoner on board ship in ch. 27), or they may have just been too frightened to leave when he and Silas were staying."[14] The jailer's near suicide over the possibility that prisoners had escaped (v. 27) is understandable when we remember that Peter's escape from prison resulted in the execution of the guards (12:19) and that the soldiers planned to kill the prisoners after the shipwreck en route to Rome rather than letting them escape (27:42).

In an amazing turn of events the jailer rushed toward Paul and Silas, fell down trembling before them, and blurted out, "Sirs [or lords, *kyrioi*], what must I do to be saved?" (v. 30). He presumably knew that, as the girl had said, they proclaimed "the way to be saved" (v. 17). Most people ignore such messages when they first hear of them. But significant events can make them open to the message—such as a miracle, an act of kindness, or (as here) the events of the evening. He wanted to know what he had to "do" to be saved, but actually there was nothing that he needed to do, for everything had already been done for him by Christ. All he was required was to believe

---

11. Brian Rapske, *Paul in Roman Custody*, vol. 3, *BAFCS*, 123–29.
12. Ibid., 127.
13. Ibid., 127.
14. Gempf, "Acts," 1092.

(v. 31). Those who say that Paul in his letters is different from the Paul of Acts must reckon with this statement, which is in accord with his letters (and of Jesus in John's Gospel).

The first part of verse 31, "Believe in the Lord Jesus, and you will be saved," presents the condition for salvation. Later on Paul will write to the Romans, "How can they believe in the one of whom they have not heard? And how can they hear without someone preaching to them?" (Rom. 10:14). Thus, Paul follows the offer of salvation by explaining the way of salvation "to him and to all the others in his house," which Luke describes as "the word of the Lord" (Acts 16:32). This again accords with what Paul tells the Romans, "Consequently, faith comes from hearing the message, and the message is heard through the word of Christ" (Rom. 10:17).

When Paul extends the offer of salvation to the jailer's household, is he saying that his faith will convert his entire household (v. 31b)? We should infer that Paul is offering salvation to everyone in his household on the same terms as he is offering to the jailer. We should not infer that his faith will save his whole family. As both the jailer and his household listened to the word of God, we must assume that they all believed before they were baptized. This verse does tell us that "the New Testament takes the unity of the family seriously, and when salvation is offered to the head of the household, it is as a matter of course made available to the rest of the family group (including dependents and servants) as well (cf. 16:15)."[15]

As is often the case in Acts, baptism follows immediately after conversion, and here the whole household is baptized. Were infants included in this baptism? We are not told, and thus this passage cannot be used as giving conclusive evidence for infant baptism. The midnight hospitality in the jailer's home includes the compassionate washing of wounds and the serving of a meal, and it is spiced with joy over salvation (vv. 33—34).

Paul and Silas Released (16:35—40)

THE MAGISTRATES MUST have felt that the punishment meted out to Paul and Silas was sufficient, considering the trivial nature of their offense. Thus, they sent word to the jailer to release them (v. 35). Yet for the two missionaries to leave without protesting the way they were treated "could have set a dangerous precedent for the future treatment of missionaries and also could have left the Christians in Philippi exposed to arbitrary treatment from the magistrates."[16] Therefore they insisted on a public apology, which would ultimately influence the public standing of the mission and the church there.

---

15. Marshall, *Acts*, 273.
16. Ibid., 274.

Paul's claim to Roman citizenship proved to be a turning point again in Jerusalem (22:25–29).

Paul and Silas made a final visit to Lydia's home to encourage the believers before leaving.[17] According to verse 40, "they [note *third person* plural] left" Philippi. Presumably, therefore, Luke stayed on in Philippi and joined Paul again after his return visit to Philippi, at which time the first person plural reappears (20:6).

OF THE MANY conversions in Philippi Luke highlights three of people with significantly different backgrounds: a businesswoman (who may have been single), a slave girl under bondage to a spirit of divination, and a jailer in a Roman prison. This choice is in keeping with the prominent emphasis in Acts on the fact that Christ breaks barriers that separate humans and so creates a new humanity. This theme of the church as consisting of believers from diverse backgrounds has often been neglected by evangelicals despite its prominence in the Scriptures.

Principles of reaching the unreached. This passage gives us a helpful example of how to witness for Christ, especially among the unreached. This was Paul's first ministry in what we now call Europe. He started in Philippi, a key city, which accords with his pattern of going to key cities. Four principles of evangelism merit special mention.

(1) In Philippi Paul looked for what church planters sometimes refer to as a bridgehead. Shenk and Stutzman explain that "in military operations, a bridgehead is formed when troops successfully land behind enemy lines and are able to establish a small, defensible foothold which is expanded as more troops join the force. That first foothold is the bridgehead."[18] Paul's bridgehead here was the place of prayer, where people met to pray to the same God whom Paul proclaimed (v. 13). This was the case in most cities he visited: If there was a synagogue, that was where he started. In Athens he went both to the synagogue and the marketplace (17:17). As we will see, this was because the Athenians discussed philosophy in public places. Their religious and philosophical bent made it possible for Paul to go to the Gentiles right away.

(2) Note the interplay between human initiative in witnessing and divine quickening in the evangelistic process. Paul took the initiative to go to the people and began to converse with them (v. 13). Usually people do not come

---

17. Note that the first person plural ("we/us") stopped at 16:17, after which Paul and Silas took center stage.

18. Shenk and Stutzman, *Creating Communities of the Kingdom*, 58.

to us in search of Christ, so we must go to them and seek for ways to turn the conversation to the things of God. Witness calls for Spirit-led boldness. We should also, like Paul, seek to persuade the people about the truth of the gospel. But ultimately it is the Lord who opens the "heart to respond to [the] message" (v. 14). Without divine quickening human witness is ineffective. Therefore the witness always depends on the Holy Spirit to bring about conviction and a receptive heart among one's hearers.

(3) This section contains two instances of whole households coming to Christ at the same time (vv. 15, 34). This happened in Corinth too, with the "entire household" of Titius Justus (18:7). This is not, however, mass conversion, where individuals do not have a will of their own. It is the conversion of all the members of a social unit (a household). While this is not the only way people come to Christ, it is a common way in the Scriptures and in the history of the church.

(4) The final principle derives from Paul's refusal to leave the prison without an apology from the magistrates (v. 37), in order to maintain the public standing of the church and to protect it from further harassment. On the one hand, we rejoice when we are persecuted for Christ's name, and we know that persecution yields a plentiful harvest. Thus, we must never compromise our calling in order to avoid persecution. But we also know that the freedom to proclaim the gospel unhindered can be a great aid to its forward march. Thus, we must always seek to secure this freedom if we can do so without compromising our principles.

Partnership in mission through hospitality. Earlier we noted why it is helpful for traveling preachers to stay in the homes of Christians.[19] Here we will reflect on the importance hosts have as partners in the missionary enterprise. Acts often mentions the names of the hosts who opened their homes for missionaries to live in and/or to stay at for meals or meetings: Simon (9:43), Simon and Peter (10:23), Cornelius (10:48), Mary (12:12), Lydia (16:15), the Philippian jailer (16:34), Jason (17:5–7), Aquila and Priscilla (twice: 18:2–3, 26), Titius Justus (18:7), Philip (21:8), Mnason (21:16), and Publius (who was at first not a believer, 28:7). John Koenig, in his book *New Testament Hospitality*, titles his chapter on the Lukan writings, "Guests and Hosts, Together in Mission."[20] Hosts clearly played an important role in the mission of the church in Acts, and they should do so today as well.

Responding to the demonic. Paul's reaction to the utterances of the slave girl regarding his ministry (vv. 17–18) is instructive to us who live in an age when many forces are doing "good" deeds using supernatural powers. What

19. See the study on 9:31–43.
20. John Koenig, *New Testament Hospitality* (Philadelphia: Fortress, 1985), 85–123.

she said was correct and affirming of his ministry, but Paul was greatly irked by it because it came from a demonic source. James says that even demons believe "that there is one God" (James 2:19). In other words, truth can be uttered by people through demonic power. But it must not be tolerated, for it further immerses people in demonic deception and bondage. As a result, Paul cast out the evil spirit from her.

Our passage clearly proclaims Christ's power over the demonic. When Mark recorded the appointing of the twelve apostles, he gave a threefold reason for the appointments: "that they might be with him and that he might send them out to preach and to have authority to drive out demons" (Mark 3:14–15). With Paul's act of delivering the girl of the spirit of divination (v. 18) the apostles were continuing the ministry of driving out demons. This type of ministry was so effective in Ephesus that some Jewish exorcists even tried to invoke the name of Jesus in their activities (19:11–16). The calling to engage the demonic applies to us today.

Religion as business. Opposition to the gospel in Philippi (and later in Ephesus) was caused by loss of income (v. 19). Opportunity to earn money can be so important that it overrides nobler motivations for one's behavior. The employers of the girl must have known that she was in a miserable state and that what Paul had done for her was, in effect, a deliverance from bondage. But they had lost a means of income, so they opposed Paul. Yet they couched their opposition in noble terms, stating that the stability of the city was at stake because Paul and his team were "advocating customs unlawful for us Romans to accept or practice" (vv. 20–21).

Songs in the night. The emotions of Paul and Silas presumably were greatly affected by the humiliation, injustice, and pain they experienced. Later Paul presented this experience as part of his qualifications for being a servant of Christ (2 Cor. 11:23). But when they prayed and sang in the prison (v. 25), they were resorting to a time-tested method of responding to suffering. Numerous psalms have been written from out of the depths of despair (e.g., Ps. 27; 42; 43). Singing helps us focus on the glorious eternal realities that may be clouded by the gloomy temporary realities. It helps us especially because, when we cannot produce words of our own, we can use words of others. Note that the prayer of the early church following the outlawing of evangelism was also saturated with citations from the Scriptures (4:24–30).

Usually in times of distress, our minds hold on to eternal realities as articles of faith, but that does not necessarily influence our feelings. Our hearts remain engulfed by the problems. Songs help truth travel down to the heart, and the use of music, the language of the heart, helps speed that process. The objective truths we get from biblical songs challenge our subjective feelings; our theology addresses our experience. Moreover, the permanent triumphs over the temporary, and we are able to praise God from the heart (see, e.g., Ps. 73).

Joy over salvation. Luke's report of joy over salvation in the home of the jailer (v. 34) is evidence of one of the most important themes in his writings. Nearly 24 percent (79 of the 326 instances) of words for joy in the New Testament appear in Luke's Gospel (53) and Acts (24).[21] The angels heralded the coming of Christ as "good news of great joy that will be for all the people" (Luke 2:10). The sinner Zacchaeus "welcomed [Jesus] gladly" into his house (19:6), and salvation came to that home. When people find salvation, there is great rejoicing in heaven (15:7, 10). Even when believers are persecuted, they are to contemplate their heavenly reward and "rejoice ... and leap for joy" (6:23).

After Jesus' resurrection the dominant emotion of the disciples that Luke records is joy (Luke 24:41, 52–53). It is not surprising, then, that the fellowship of the first Christian community was characterized by "unaffected joy" (Acts 2:46).[22] Their joy withstood the test of persecution. After the apostles were flogged, they "left the Sanhedrin, rejoicing because they had been counted worthy of suffering disgrace for the Name" (5:41). After Paul and Barnabas had been driven out of Pisidian Antioch, "the disciples were filled with joy and with the Holy Spirit" (13:52). Just as joy characterizes our entrance into the kingdom, it characterizes our life from that point on.

APPLYING THE FOUR **principles of evangelism.** The four principles of reaching the unreached as presented above are relevant today. (1) We must always be looking for bridgeheads in order to penetrate a community with the gospel. Often the best way is to find some point of contact with someone in the community we wish to reach. Such a point of contact is usually established through a common interest. The interest may be related to a felt need that we know Christ can answer (e.g., sickness, insecurity, fear, marital problems). It can also be commonly held religious convictions, which is what Paul looked for when he made contact in a new community by attending a synagogue or a place of prayer. In Athens it was the philosophical bent of the Athenians (17:21–22). We have found that the love of sports, music, drama and adventure, and the need for extra tuition beyond what students receive in school can be effective means of making contact with unreached youth in Sri Lanka.

---

21. William G. Morrice, *Joy in the New Testament* (Exeter: Paternoster, 1984), 91.
22. Morrice's translation in *Joy in the New Testament*, 97.

(2) The interplay between human initiative and divine quickening identifies our responsibility and reminds us that God is the one who ultimately gives the results. This dual perspective helps us avoid not only being lethargic about witness but also feeling ourselves under a bondage of having to produce evangelistic results. Our call is to be faithful in going out and in using the best methods we know; God will look after the results.[23]

(3) The principle that conversion often takes place through whole groups coming to Christ needs some explanation. These have been called people movements. One of the pioneers in this method of evangelism was an American missionary to India, J. Waskom Pickett (1890–1981), who studied what he called "mass movements" in India.[24] He "pointed out that the principle of urging [individual] people to believe in Christ worked very well in the United States where Christianity was the major religion, and people could become Christians without separating from their families and friends." "The one by one method, however, did not work in India among Hindus, because if only one person became a Christian he was thrown out of his family and caste, and suffered social dislocation."[25]

Pickett's studies had a great influence on Donald McGavran, the father of the church growth movement. According to McGavran, "at least two thirds of all converts in Asia, Africa, and Oceania have come to Christian faith through people movements."[26] People movements are not instances of "group conversion." Rather, he refers to this as "multi-individual, mutually interdependent conversion."[27] Each person exercises saving faith, but this is done in consultation with and along with others in the group. In whatever culture one ministers, when working with non-Christians it is always helpful to take into account the wider contacts of the persons we reach. In our youth work, the moment we make contact with a non-Christian youth, we also make contact with his or her family. This step sometimes leads to the conversion of the family and always results in the reduction of persecution from the family if and when the youth becomes a Christian.

(4) As with Paul and Silas, we should do all we can to protect the freedom to practice and propagate Christianity wherever we are. If an unconstitutional law hinders the practice of Christianity (e.g., if Christian

---

23. For a fuller discussion on this see comments on 25:1–26:32.

24. J. Waskom Pickett, *Christian Mass Movements in India* (Nashville: Abingdon, 1933).

25. J. T. Seamands, "J. Waskom Picket, 1890–1981—Social Activist and Evangelist of the Masses," *Mission Legacies*, ed. Gerald H. Anderson, et al. (Maryknoll, N.Y.: Orbis, 1994), 352.

26. Donald A. McGavran, *Understanding Church Growth* (Grand Rapids: Eerdmans, 1970), 298.

27. Ibid., 302.

organizations and churches are required to hire practicing homosexuals onto their staff teams), they should do all they can to stop this. But while an organized "sit-in"[28] like Paul's may be acceptable, violent measures, such as those sometimes used outside abortion clinics, are never acceptable.

Sometimes because of the Christian principle of forgiveness we may refuse to prosecute those who have been unkind to us if we realize that such a course will do nothing to enhance the freedom to practice and propagate Christianity. Western powers crushed the Boxer uprising of 1900 in China, in which approximately 30,000 Chinese Christians died. The Chinese were forced by the Western powers into agreeing to pay high compensation for losses. Hudson Taylor's China Inland Mission and several other Christians refused this compensation in accordance with the spirit of Christ. Arthur Glasser reports:

> The Chinese were amazed. In Shanshi province a government proclamation was posted far and wide extolling Jesus Christ and his principles of forbearance and forgiveness.... This official endorsement served to diminish the antiforeign spirit of the people and contributed not a little to the growth of the church in China in the years that followed.[29]

Mission through hospitality today. We have already described how hospitality can aid in fulfilling the mission of the church.[30] Today, however, with people getting busier and guarding their private lives more, much of what used to be done in homes is being done in restaurants and hotels. Are our homes as significant for mission as they were in the first century? The amazing effectiveness of home cell groups as means of evangelism and nurture should elicit a resounding "Yes" to that question. So should a consideration of the hazards of a traveling ministry in today's world.[31]

The key to returning to this practice in the church is for Christians to open their hearts and homes so that others can benefit from their hospitality.[32] We described how this attitude was expressed in a church in Argentina in our discussion on 4:32–35. Members gifted their homes to the church, but the church returned it the them saying, "The Lord ... wants a house with you inside taking care of it. He wants ... everything ready for him."[33] They were to be ready to open their homes for whatever God would require.

---

28. Stott, *Acts*, 268, quoting A. N. Triton, *Whose World?* (Leicester: Inter-Varsity, 1970), 48.

29. Arthur F. Glasser, "China," *The Church in Asia*, ed. Donald E. Hoke (Chicago: Moody, 1975), 171.

30. See the discussions on 9:31–43 and 10:1–33.

31. See the discussion on 9:31–43.

32. See Karen Burton Mains, *Open Heart—Open Home* (Elgin, Ill.: David C. Cook, 1976).

33. From Juan Carlos Ortiz, *Disciple: A Handbook for New Believers* (Orlando: Creation House, 1995), 36.

A key to recovering hospitality in the church's life is to liberate it from the performance trap. When hospitality becomes a performance, it becomes a strain on the host, hinders true fellowship, and makes both the hosts and the guests feel uneasy. A week before I wrote this, I spent two days with my son in the four-roomed house of Albert Lee, the Youth for Christ director in Singapore. Because of some miscommunication, it turned out that along with four family members, there were six guests in the home at that time. Amazingly, I did not sense a strain here. That family had been liberated from the performance trap. Thus, I had the freedom to make a cup of tea whenever I wanted one (which, in true Sri Lankan fashion, was often)! I did not feel I needed to ask my hosts, for they had given me the freedom to get what I needed without feeling that they had to do that for me. A basic breakfast was at the table when we got up (which was late as a result of jet lag), and we prepared what we wanted. It was a lesson to me of a servant spirit that sought not to perform but to make us feel comfortable. Families that open their homes in this way can become key players in fulfilling the mission of the kingdom.

Opposing demonically inspired actions. Paul's attitude of opposition to demonic power that told the truth about his ministry is relevant today. We live in an age that is both pluralistic and is experiencing a rediscovery of spirituality. Pluralism causes many people to assign roughly equal status to all religious approaches; spirituality causes them to welcome different expressions of the spiritual and the supernatural. This combination has brought about a supermarket approach to religion, where people are encouraged to shop for the gods that best suit them.

Consequently, the Indian "god-man" Satya Sai Bäba, who claims to be an incarnation of the god Shiva, is gaining disciples in both the East and the West. He performs miracles, directs people away from sinful sensuality, and utters words of wisdom that help them live "better" lives. His followers say that he is the Christ who has come for this particular age. According to the pluralistic ideal we should welcome the service rendered by Sai Bäba to humanity and affirm that his way is indeed good and helpful.

But the biblical approach is different. Jesus warned that in the last days people will say, "Look, here is the Christ!" and, "Look, there he is!" But, he said, "Do not believe it" (Mark 13:21). Our Lord went on to explain, "For false Christs and false prophets will appear and perform signs and miracles to deceive the elect—if that were possible" (13:22). These powerful "god-men" who are gaining many disciples and influencing people to move in directions that seem to be good for them are false prophets. We must be alert to this and seek to rescue people from their influence, just as Paul did with the Philippian girl.

This is not popular in today's pluralistic environment, where acceptance and affirmation of other faiths is almost mandated as a part of healthy living. But it must be done because we believe that these forces, despite the temporary good they may perform, serve to further entrench people in bondage to Satan. After our Youth for Christ magazine in Sri Lanka had published an article about Sai Bäba, a top government official (who was a nominal Christian and an admirer of Sai Bäba), told me, "Isn't it better to be safe than sorry?" This is a typical pluralist attitude in such situations: "It may not be relevant to me, but it is relevant to others, and I will just leave it alone without poking my finger into it. After all, it could be genuine."[34] Paul was motivated by such a deep love for people that he could not endure the pain of seeing them under the grip of deception. He had to act, and so must we.

The demonic in Christian ministry. Except in a few pockets the ministry of exercising authority over demons was lacking in the Protestant church until the charismatic movement brought it back into focus. This may be because the Protestant church was influenced by the rationalism that characterized the modern era, unlike the Roman Catholic Church, where exorcisms have been carried out throughout the centuries. There is now a greater recognition of the demonic among people from all shades of evangelical thought.

Still today, however, there is a reluctance among many Christians to attribute problems they face to the demonic and to engage the demonic in their ministries. They point to the many abuses that have taken place through those who minister in this realm. Often demons are blamed for our sins and weaknesses so that people take no responsibility for their actions and no grappling is done with these areas. Sometimes demons are blamed for psychological and physical problems in such a way that legitimate remedies for these problems are bypassed and energies are expended trying to cast out nonexistent demons. Such abuses should cause us to be careful about attributing anything to demons without considering all the factors. It would be helpful for all ministers to read a biblically sound book on this type of ministry.[35]

When dealing with problems in our ministries, we should always ask whether there is a cause for the problem that needs to be cleared through direct action against the demonic. In doing this it would be best to act with the support of other Christians, remembering that Jesus never sent disciples for this type of ministry alone. We may also refer the case to one who is

---

34. This attitude is similar to that of Gamaliel, which (as noted in comments on 5:33–40) was not necessarily correct, though it did help the fledgling church.

35. I would recommend Mark I. Bubeck, *The Adversary: The Christian Versus Demon Activity* (Chicago: Moody, 1975); Murphy, *Handbook for Spiritual Warfare*; Timothy M. Warner, *Spiritual Warfare: Victory Over the Powers of This Dark World* (Wheaton: Crossway, 1991).

particularly gifted in this area. But we must always remember that even though we may be nervous and feel weak as we combat demonic powers, we are ministering in the name and with the authority of Jesus, who has conquered evil and the demonic. He is stronger than the forces we are combating, and his strength is available for us to use.[36]

Opposition to God's work for monetary reasons. A monk gets angry when he loses a source of regular alms as a result of the conversion of some of his donors. The leaders of a church get angry that their members are giving money to a parachurch group that is doing a good work for Christ. The leader of a parachurch group gets angry when a leader from another region but working for the same group raises funds from people in his region. These are all ways in which opposition to God's work for monetary reasons can be manifested today.

Here is an area where the principle, "It is better to be safe than sorry," may work. We are well aware of Paul's warning: "For the love of money is a root of all kinds of evil. Some people, eager for money, have wandered from the faith and pierced themselves with many griefs" (1 Tim. 6:10). Thus, we must be cautious when it comes to opposing anyone if our own financial stability is an issue. Insecurity about our such issues can cause us to act sinfully. We may choose to "play it safe" and not act when it comes to opposing someone who is threatening our stability.

Disciplining the mind in times of distress. Considering the number of Christians today who have not won the battle with bitterness over misfortunes they have faced, the prescription hinted at by Paul's praying and singing may be important to us. The failure to win this battle results in a miserable Christian life. If we are hit by a painful or humiliating blow, we can plan revenge, give in to self-pity, or immerse ourselves in an attempt to get out of the problem. While this last option may be appropriate, if we still carry an unhealed wound, we may eventually act in unchristian ways. We must discipline ourselves to let the eternal truths of God impact the situation, so that the sting of the pain is removed. With that perspective we can react positively to the crisis—and singing along with prayer helps give birth to that perspective.

Sometimes, however, we do not want the perspective of God's sovereignty to break through with the message that this problem will be turned into something good. We would rather keep our self-pity and anger and hold on to the myth that we have been permanently harmed. But if the perspective of God's sovereignty breaks through, we will be able to have the blessings mentioned in Paul's prayer in Romans 15:13: "May the God of hope fill you with all joy and peace as you trust in him, so that you may overflow

---

36. On this see Murphy, *Handbook for Spiritual Warfare*, 326.

with hope by the power of the Holy Spirit." The new perspective feeds our trust, which enables us to look at the problem through the eyes of hope. That, in turn, produces joy and peace.

Emphasizing joy. It is important to underscore the biblical emphasis on joy in today's entertainment-oriented society. Through relentless media onslaught of an unchristian understanding of pleasure, we may be tempted to think that to be fully entertained, we must indulge in something that is displeasing to God. To counteract such thinking, Christians have long been motivated to follow Christ by the so-called debtor's ethic, which says, "He did so much for us. Now the least we can do is to live in obedience to him." But when faced with the strong force of temptation, the debtor's ethic proves powerless. Sinners look at us with pity and insinuate that we do not enjoy life. At such a time our resolve to repay our debt to God can be overcome by the promise of pleasure, and we can easily yield to the temptation.

John Piper, in his book *The Purifying Power of Living by Faith in Future Grace,* challenges the idea that the Bible teaches a debtor's ethic.[37] As one who has preached this ethic, I took up the challenge, but I could find no evidence for this method of motivation in the Bible. What I did find was that when Bible writers appeal to God's goodness and sacrificial love to us, it is to show that he can be trusted to give us everything we need. As Paul said, "He who did not spare his own Son, but gave him up for us all—how will he not also, along with him, graciously give us all things?" (Rom. 8:32).[38]

One of God's greatest gifts to us is the incomparable pleasure of true joy. As David said, "You have made known to me the path of life; you will fill me with joy in your presence, with eternal pleasures at your right hand" (Ps. 16:11). What if we seek to pursue such pleasure in life? In our time of temptation to passing pleasure we can see how much more enjoyable is the incomparable pleasure that Christ gives. We will want to guard that pleasure and not let it be spoiled by lesser pleasures.

---

37. John Piper, *The Purifying Power of Living by Faith in Future Grace* (Sisters, Ore.: Multnomah, 1995), 30–49.

38. Piper regards this verse to be one of the most important verses in the Bible for Christian living (ibid., 110–18).

Acts 17:1-15

❦

WHEN THEY HAD passed through Amphipolis and Apollonia, they came to Thessalonica, where there was a Jewish synagogue. ²As his custom was, Paul went into the synagogue, and on three Sabbath days he reasoned with them from the Scriptures, ³explaining and proving that the Christ had to suffer and rise from the dead. "This Jesus I am proclaiming to you is the Christ," he said. ⁴Some of the Jews were persuaded and joined Paul and Silas, as did a large number of God-fearing Greeks and not a few prominent women.

⁵But the Jews were jealous; so they rounded up some bad characters from the marketplace, formed a mob and started a riot in the city. They rushed to Jason's house in search of Paul and Silas in order to bring them out to the crowd. ⁶But when they did not find them, they dragged Jason and some other brothers before the city officials, shouting: "These men who have caused trouble all over the world have now come here, ⁷and Jason has welcomed them into his house. They are all defying Caesar's decrees, saying that there is another king, one called Jesus." ⁸When they heard this, the crowd and the city officials were thrown into turmoil. ⁹Then they made Jason and the others post bond and let them go.

¹⁰As soon as it was night, the brothers sent Paul and Silas away to Berea. On arriving there, they went to the Jewish synagogue. ¹¹Now the Bereans were of more noble character than the Thessalonians, for they received the message with great eagerness and examined the Scriptures every day to see if what Paul said was true. ¹²Many of the Jews believed, as did also a number of prominent Greek women and many Greek men.

¹³When the Jews in Thessalonica learned that Paul was preaching the word of God at Berea, they went there too, agitating the crowds and stirring them up. ¹⁴The brothers immediately sent Paul to the coast, but Silas and Timothy stayed at Berea. ¹⁵The men who escorted Paul brought him to Athens and then left with instructions for Silas and Timothy to join him as soon as possible.

Original
Meaning

AFTER LEAVING PHILIPPI, Paul, Silas, and probably Timothy passed through Amphipolis and Apollonia, possibly spending the night in those cities. They traveled ninety to one hundred miles along the great Roman road, the Egnatian Way, until they reached Thessalonica (now called Salonika) (v. 1). In this city their next ministry began.

Ministry in Thessalonica (17:1–10a)

THESSALONICA WAS THE capital of the whole province of Macedonia and its largest and most prosperous city. "As his custom was, Paul went into the synagogue" and spoke there on three Sabbaths (v. 2). He must have stayed there much longer than three weeks, for he later writes that he worked day and night in Thessalonica so as not to burden the people there (1 Thess. 2:9; 2 Thess. 3:8), and that while in that city he also received "aid again and again when [he] was in need" from the church in Philippi (Phil. 4:16). The result of the ministry of Paul and Silas was the conversion of several Jews and God-fearers (v. 4). Paul's comment in 1 Thessalonians 1:9 indicates also that many of those converted were pagans: "You turned to God from idols to serve the living and true God." Six key words describe the evangelism of Paul and Silas in Acts 17:2–4, which will help us in constructing a biblical theology of evangelistic proclamation (see below).

Seeing that their influence over various people had diminished, the Jews were jealous (cf. 5:17), and they resorted to ignoble means to fight the missionaries. They used "some bad characters from the marketplace . . . and started a riot" (17:5a). It was not the last time that religious people used the very people they were supposed to be transforming into good people to do their dirty work. Because Paul and Silas had probably been taken to a safe place, their host Jason and some brothers were taken to the city officials (vv. 5b–6a). The title Luke uses for the city officials, *polytarches*, has "been found in inscriptions ranging from the second century B.C. through the third century A.D. and applied almost exclusively to Macedonian cities." Evidence from five inscriptions referring to Thessalonica indicate that "a body of five politarchs ruled the city during the first century A.D."[1]

Portraying the evangelists as "men who have caused trouble all over the world" (v. 6b) is severe. But it is true that turmoil often results when the gospel challenges people to change their lives, and usually such turmoil originates with those who reject this challenge. The charge against Paul and Silas was that they had defied Caesar, "saying that there is another king," Jesus.

---

1. Longenecker, "Acts," 469.

Many scholars feel that it was sensitivity to this charge that caused Paul to decrease the emphasis on the kingdom of God and the kingship of Jesus in his letters "lest Gentile imperial authorities misconstrue them to connote opposition to the empire and emperor."[2]

There had been trouble in Rome in connection with the Jews for some time. The events in Thessalonica may have occurred in the spring of A.D. 50, shortly after Claudius expelled Jews from Rome (in 49) following riots associated with Jews and Christians.[3] The authorities would not have wanted a repetition of such problems, and the Jewish opponents would have exploited that fact. Jason was released after posting bond, probably assuring the politarchs that he and the "other brothers" would not cause any more problems and would see to it that Paul and Silas left the city. This is the presumed background behind Paul's statement that he, Silas, and Timothy were torn away from the Thessalonians and that Satan stopped them from returning (1 Thess. 2:17–18).

Ministry in Berea (17:10–15)

PAUL PROCEEDED SOUTH from Thessalonica rather than following the Egnatian Way, which continued west toward Rome. His next stop is Berea (present-day Verria). Berea was not as important a city as Philippi and Thessalonica, but it was a Greek-speaking town unlike the western towns that belonged to the section known as "free Macedonia." David Gill feels that this may reflect Paul's "desire to remain within the Greek-speaking world rather than have to cope with the problems of different cultures." The three Christian communities he founded on this trip were in a position to take the gospel westward (see 1 Thess. 1:8). Gill suggests that Paul may have visited "free Macedonia" on his next trip.[4]

In keeping with their usual practice the team started off at the synagogue (v. 10) and made the pleasant discovery that "the Bereans were of more noble character than the Thessalonians" (v. 11a). Luke gives two reasons for this commendation: "They received the message with great eagerness and examined the Scriptures every day to see if what Paul said was true" (v. 11b). As we will show below, they expressed an attitude of humble receptivity that lies at the heart of faith.

Luke records that among the converts in Berea were many Jews and "also a number of prominent Greek women and many Greek men" (v. 12).

2. Ibid.
3. On the problems in Rome, see F. F. Bruce, *New Testament History* (Garden City, N.Y.: Doubleday, reprint of 1969 ed.), 295–300.
4. David W. J. Gill, "Macedonia," *BAFCS*, vol. 2, *Graeco-Roman Setting* (1994), 416.

One of the converts, Sopater, accompanied Paul on his last journey to Jerusalem. Both in Thessalonica and Berea prominent women were among those converted (vv. 4, 12). It seems that in Athens too prominent people were converted (17:34).

But Paul had to make a sudden and rushed exit from Berea as well. Jews from Thessalonica arrived and roused the crowds in Berea, just as they had done in Thessalonica. Paul was sent with a group from Berea to the coast and traveled to Athens. The first few weeks in the life of a new church are most important, and the new believers need to be provided for. Therefore Silas and Timothy stayed on in Berea with instructions to join Paul as soon as possible (vv. 14–15).[5]

Note Paul had to flee from all three Macedonian cities in which he ministered. This must have been difficult for him to take, but he left behind three stable churches.

Bridging Contexts

A BIBLICAL THEOLOGY of evangelistic proclamation. Six key words (all verbs) describe the evangelism of Paul and Silas; they are helpful in the construction of a biblical theology of evangelistic proclamation (vv. 2–4). (1) Paul "reasoned" (*dialegomai*) in the synagogues (v. 2). This Greek word occurs ten times in Acts 17–24 in reference to Paul's ministry[6] and became "a technical term for Paul's teaching in the synagogue."[7] Scholars have not reached a consensus about the meaning of this term. In two of its other three occurrences in the New Testament (Mark 9:34; Jude 9) *dialegomai* has the idea of "argue, fight with words." In Acts, however, "it approaches the meaning of give an address, preach."[8]

Many have given *dialegomai* the meaning of dialogue, but that does not seem to be the primary focus of that word. Fürst thinks that the audience was permitted to ask questions.[9] According to Marshall, in Acts "dialogue or debate arises ... as a result of the initial proclamation.... The objective is always to correct misunderstandings of the gospel."[10] David Williams suggests

---

5. Luke had earlier probably stayed on in Philippi (see our comments on 16:40).

6. See 17:2, 17; 18:4, 19; 19:8, 9; 20:7, 9; 24:12, 25.

7. D. Fürst, *NIDNTT*, 3:821.

8. Ibid.

9. Ibid.

10. I. Howard Marshall, "Inter-Faith Dialogue in the New Testament," *Evangelical Review of Theology*, 13, 3 (July 1989): 199. BAGD (185) states that this word refers to "lectures which were likely to end in disputations." G. Schrenk ("διαλέγομαι," TDNT, 2:94–95) does not leave room for that interpretation.

that "instead of straight teaching, as in the synagogues of the East, [Paul] seems to have proceeded by means of 'discussion.'" The appearance of *dialegomai* "here for the first time in Acts ... may indicate a change of style in response to a different environment."[11] A recent detailed study of Paul's preaching by D. W. Kemmler also suggests that dialogue may be included along with formal and continuous discourse.[12]

Whether or not the word *dialegomai* implies discussions, the record in verses 2−3 shows that the viewpoints of the hearers were given due weight in Paul's evangelistic preaching. Yet we should note that *dialegomai* is not used in Acts in the philosophical sense in which it is used in classical Greek. As Schrenk explains, "in the sphere of revelation there is no question of reaching an idea through dialectic."[13] God has spoken, and we are called to proclaim that message by expounding it. But in our proclamation we will face objections and questions that need to be carefully answered in order to prove (*paratithemi*, v. 3; see [3], below) the validity of the Christian scheme. Today we call this apologetics.

(2) How the reasoning that constituted apologetics was done is explained in verse 3 with two more key words: "explaining" (*dianoigo*) and "proving" (*paratithemi*). *Dianoigo* literally means to open, and the idea behind this word is well expressed in Luke 24:32: "Were not our hearts burning within us while he talked with us on the road and *opened* the Scriptures to us?" The subject expounded from the Scriptures was that "the Christ had to suffer and rise from the dead" (Acts 17:3a).

(3) Such an exposition would have encountered opposition from Jews, to whom the cross was a stumbling block (1 Cor. 1:23). Thus, to the exposition Paul added "proving" (*paratithemi*), which means he carefully answered questions posed to him, responded to their objections, and demonstrated the validity of his claims.[14]

(4) Paul "proclaimed" (*katangello*) a clear message about Jesus Christ to the Thessalonians (v. 3b). The outline of his preaching given in verse 3 resembles the summary of his gospel presented in 1 Corinthians 15:3−4. David Williams observes, "If there were any doubts earlier about the centrality of the death of Jesus in Paul's preaching ... they are dispelled."[15] As we pointed out earlier (see comments on faith in 16:31), the Paul of the letters and the Paul of Acts had the same message.

---

11. Williams, *Acts*, 294.

12. D. W. Kemmler, *Faith and Human Reason: A Study of Paul's Method of Preaching As Illustrated by 1−2 Thessalonians and Acts 17, 24* (Leiden: Brill, 1975), 35. Cited in Larkin, *Acts*, 245.

13. Schrenk, "διαλέγομαι," 2:94.

14. My discussion of these two words has been influenced by A. T. Robertson, *Word Pictures*, vol. 3, *Acts*, 267−68.

15. Williams, *Acts*, 294−95.

(5) The next two words, "persuaded" and "joined" (v. 4), describe the response to the message. The aim of apologetics is not simply discussion so that we can know what each other believes. Rather, it is to "persuade" (*peitho*). This verb is particularly relevant because Luke uses it seven times in Acts to describe Paul's evangelism.[16] In 2 Corinthians 5:11 Paul himself said, "We try to persuade men." This use of *peitho* has been defined as "to convince someone to believe something and to act on the basis of what is recommended."[17] Such confidence in our message derives from the conviction that we are bearers of the definitive revelation from God to the human race. If the Creator and Lord of the universe has given a final message to the human race and we know it, then we must do everything in our power and within our principles to bring people to appropriate that message into their lives. Evangelism, in other words, aims at a response, a response so comprehensive that it can be called a conversion.

(6) Conversion is also implied in the word translated "joined" (*proskleroo*), which appears only here in the New Testament. There is some question about its exact meaning, but whatever it is, the idea is that the new believers joined the company of the apostles.[18] Their minds had been changed and they had made a decision about the truth. They took the next step: "They attached themselves to the missionaries, casting their lot with them, come what may."[19]

The above discussion shows us that evangelism involves proclaiming the message of Christ, especially his death and resurrection. The proclamation may[20] include discussion, and it aims at persuading people so that they will be converted to Christ and incorporated into the church. This is not a comprehensive definition of evangelism, but we can say that all biblical evangelism must have these features.

Evangelism and opposition. As noted above, whenever the gospel challenges people to change their course of action, turmoil often results, instigated by those who reject this challenge (vv. 5–9, 13). Jesus predicted this in Matthew 10:34–36:

---

16. See 17:4; 18:4; 19:8, 26; 26:28; 28:23, 24; cf. 2 Cor. 5:11. It appeared six times in Acts before chapter 17, but 17:4 is the first time it appears in connection with Paul's evangelism.

17. Louw and Nida, 423.

18. In this context *proskleroo* can mean something like "'to throw in one's lot with' or 'to identify themselves with' or 'to become a part of the same group as'" (Louw and Nida, 449). Zerwick and Grosvenor, on the other hand, take it as a "theological passive" (*Analysis*, 407), that is, a passive used in order to avoid directly naming God as agent (Zerwick, *Greek*, 76). This would yield the meaning, "were allotted to Paul and Silas by God."

19. Harrison, *Acts*, 276.

20. This "may" implies that discussion is not basic but is almost always helpful.

Do not suppose that I have come to bring peace to the earth. I did not come to bring peace, but a sword. For I have come to turn

"a man against his father,
　　a daughter against her mother,
　a daughter-in-law against her mother-in-law—
　　a man's enemies will be the members of his own household."

While persecution and antagonism are inevitable, we know from Paul's actions in Acts that he did all he could to reduce opposition and to establish legal legitimacy for the Christian movement. This is why he cited his Roman citizenship when under attack (16:37; 22:25–28; 23:27), and this is the most probable reason why he appealed to Caesar later on (25:11).[21]

Paul's fleeing from all three churches in Macedonia must have been hard for him to take, and he was deeply affected by it. Shortly after these events he wrote the Thessalonians, "Brothers . . . we were torn away from you" (1 Thess. 2:17). He also told them, "We had previously suffered and been insulted in Philippi" (2:2). Bruce thinks that this is why, writing about the visit he made to Corinth a few weeks later, he said, "I came to you in weakness and fear, and with much trembling" (1 Cor 2:3).[22] Moreover, the new Christians were also persecuted. Paul was so distressed about this that he sent Timothy to encourage them (1 Thess. 3:1–6).

But the news Paul eventually received about them from Timothy was encouraging (1 Thess. 3:6–9). In fact, Paul held up the Macedonian churches as examples to other churches on how to face "severe suffering" (1:6–7) and on how to express rich generosity in the midst of trial (2 Cor. 8:1–6). The tone of his letters to the Philippians and Thessalonians suggests that these churches brought him the greatest joy.[23] Suffering experienced during evangelism may not be as big a tragedy as we think when we first experience it.

The heart of noble character. When Luke makes a complimentary statement about the character of people, we do well to examine that character trait and seek to emulate it. He explains the noble character expressed in Berea: "They received the message with great eagerness and examined the Scriptures every day to see if what Paul said was true" (v. 11b). It was the Bereans' eagerness to hear from God and respond to what they heard that made them noble. We will show below that this lies at the heart of nobility for all people, even those who have been converted.

---

21. See Bruce, *Paul*, 363–66.

22. Bruce *Steps*, 35.

23. The churches established in Macedonia still exist, almost twenty centuries after Paul's painful visits.

Social levels in Paul's churches. The mention of prominent people as converts through Paul's ministry (vv. 4, 12) raises questions about the long-held consensus that the early Christians were for the most part poor people. This view may have been influenced by the late second-century writing of Celsus,[24] who was "the first pagan author we know of who took Christianity seriously enough to write a book against it."[25] There he caricatures Christians as poor, ignorant people from the lower strata of society.[26] But a consensus seems to be emerging now that "a Pauline congregation generally reflected a fair cross-section of urban society,"[27] with prominent members of society and poorer people coming together in the same church. In fact, some of the wealthier members seem to have acted as patrons, upon whose generosity the churches depended.[28]

Wayne Meeks's influential book *The First Urban Christians* conveniently summarizes the evidence for the existence of wealthier people in the Pauline churches. But Meeks, who worked primarily with the Pauline letters, does not think that there were people from "the extreme top ... of the Greco-Roman scale" in the Pauline churches.[29] Even this is now contested by David Gill, who, after discussing the material in both Acts and the Pauline letters, concludes that "there are now good reasons to think that the Christian communities became established in part through élite families of the main urban centres in the eastern provinces."[30]

Earlier we noted that the Jerusalem church and the church in Antioch were heterogeneous churches.[31] This characteristic was carried over into the Pauline congregations.

Contemporary Significance

PROCLAMATION IN A pluralistic age. The key words for Paul's evangelistic preaching apply today. Paul expounded the death and resurrection of Christ even though it was a stumbling block to the Jews. In our eagerness to be relevant and sensitive to people's

---

24. Though Celsus' book has not survived to this day, a large portion of its contents are found in Origen's comprehensive response to it, *Against Celsus*. See H. Chadwick, *Origen: Contra Celsum* (Cambridge: Cambridge Univ. Press, 1980).

25. Wayne A. Meeks, *The First Urban Christians: The Social World of the Apostle Paul* (New Haven: Yale Univ. Press, 1983), 51.

26. This view received further impetus from the writing of Adolf Deissmann earlier in this century (see his *Paul, a Study in Social and Religious History*, trans. William E. Wilson [New York: Harper and Row, 1957]).

27. Meeks, *First Urban Christians*, 73.

28. Ibid., 77–80.

29. Ibid., 73.

30. David W. J. Gill, "Acts and the Urban Élites," *BAFCS*, vol. 2, *Graeco-Roman Setting*, 117.

31. See the discussions on 6:1–7 and 12:25–13:12.

needs, we may be tempted to ignore the cross. Since many people have lost the sense of a holy God, they may not be aware of the seriousness of sin. Thus, as we seek to present Christ as the answer to their problems, we may feel tempted to concentrate on their felt needs rather than the needs they should be addressing. A good way to solve this problem is to start by showing the relevance of the gospel to felt needs and to deal with the questions people are asking. Once we have won their attention through this "bridgehead," we can move to the questions they should be asking—how to be saved from sin in order to be right with a holy God—which Christ answered on the cross.

In other words, in the preliminary process of proclamation, healing and discussions on contemporary problems are helpful. But we must always look for a way to bring up the message of Christ and his death and resurrection. It seems to me that while the contemporary church is developing effective models to meet people's felt needs, it is not looking seriously enough for effective ways of communicating the message of the cross and empty tomb.[32]

The philosophical idea of *dialegomai* in classical Greek (reaching an idea through dialectic) represents a closer model to understanding contemporary evangelistic proclamation than the biblical idea. It fits in with the pluralistic philosophy that has swept through much of our society. Pluralists are calling for apologetics to be replaced by dialogue. But the dialogue they speak about is a meeting of minds where no one wants to cause another to change religions. Rather, each one seeks to enrich the other.[33] John Stott represents a more biblical approach:

> Although there is an important place for "dialogue" with men of other faiths ... there is also need for "encounter" with them, and even for "confrontation," in which we seek both to disclose the inadequacies and falsities of non-Christian religion and to demonstrate the adequacy and truth of, absoluteness and finality of the Lord Jesus Christ.[34]

Receiving feedback as to what our hearers are thinking through questions, observations, or objections is a necessary part of evangelism, especially when witnessing to non-Christians. It enables us to find out how they

---

32. For an attempt to do this see my *Supremacy*.

33. For example, see Wesley Ariarajah, *The Bible and People of Other Faiths* (Geneva: World Council of Churches, and Maryknoll, N.Y.: Orbis, 1985), 61–71. For a defense of the validity of apologetics within interreligious dialogue, see Paul J. Griffiths, *An Apology for Apologetics: A Study in the Logic of Interreligious Dialogue* (Maryknoll, N.Y.: Orbis, 1991).

34. John R. W. Stott, *Christian Mission in the Modern World* (Downers Grove, Ill.: Inter-Varsity, 1975), 69. For helpful discussions on dialogue see Stott, *Christian Mission*, 58–81; Glasser and McGavran, *Contemporary Theologies*, 215–19.

have understood what we have communicated. After giving an evangelistic message on John 3:16 at a Youth for Christ meeting I spoke to a Buddhist youth who had been in the audience. He told me that his religion says the same thing as I had said, whereas I thought this message showed clearly the difference between Christianity and Buddhism. He had filtered my Christian terminology through the Buddhist way of thinking in his mind and emerged with a Buddhist message from my talk!

Commitment to proclamation does not preclude listening to others. When people describe their views, we must give them full attention. Sometimes, in a witnessing situation, we may listen more than talk, for we should not rudely interrupt someone else's description of his or her views. We are servants, and it should not bother us if they dominate a conversation. Of course, love for this person will cause us to look for every opportunity to share the liberating news of Jesus. Part of our listening may involve reading what non-Christian writers have to say about their religion, rather than only reading apologetic material written by Christians (cf. comments on Paul's ministry in Athens [17:16–34]).

I want to add here that there is another type of dialogue that often takes place between Christians and those of other faiths that should not be classed under evangelism but nevertheless may be a valid activity. It is a natural expression of what Jesus meant when he said of his disciples, "My prayer is not that you take them out of the world but that you protect them from the evil one. They are not of the world, even as I am not of it. . . . As you sent me into the world, I have sent them into the world" (John 17:15–16, 18). Though we are not of the world, we do go into the world and participate in its activities. Jesus, for example, ate with tax collectors and sinners and earned the criticism: "Here is a glutton and a drunkard, a friend of tax collectors and 'sinners'" (Matt. 11:19). We meet with people who are different from us but among whom we live, and we talk and socialize with them. Among the things we talk about is religion.

As a result, we may have discussions where people of different religions participate and share each other's views. When I was in my late teens and early twenties, I did this regularly with a group of students in our neighborhood. We met in a Muslim home on Saturday nights. The majority of those who met were Muslims; there was also an atheist (a disciple of Bertrand Russell) and a somewhat nominal Christian. We discussed many things, including politics, sports, world affairs, philosophy, and religion. I always went there as a witness of Christ and often talked about my faith. I yearned for the salvation of these people, and they knew that (only the nominal Christian came to faith in Christ). Our meetings were not strictly evangelistic events, yet what I learned from them has been important in my own pilgrimage.

Evangelicals have generally shied away from this type of dialogue, especially since many of a liberal persuasion have substituted such dialogue for evangelism. But this is not evangelism at all. It is an exercise in community living and learning, just like discussions that take place on marketing, management, sports, politics, or technology. It can be conducted in a formal setting or an informal setting.[35] Of course, in our heart of hearts we long for the conversion of these people. But sometimes the rules of the discussion prevent us from using persuasion in the way that is usually practiced in evangelism. Such personal discussions can help in understanding other faiths in a much richer way than other means (e.g., reading books) provide. Such understanding will help our proclamation and can also open people to being receptive to the Christian message.[36] Let me emphasize again that this is not evangelism and thus does not really belong in a discussion of Paul's theology of proclamation in Acts. But I discuss it here because it is a key issue today that is often discussed in connection with dialogue in evangelism.

Paul not only expounded the gospel from the Scriptures, but he also practiced apologetics. Those who seek to be biblical in evangelism should become both expounders and apologists. In my early years of ministry I saw myself as a Bible expositor, and part of my expository ministry was to explain the gospel to non-Christians. But they began to present objections and ask questions I found difficult to respond to. As I kept searching for answers, I began to realize that to be an effective witness for Christ meant getting into apologetics too.

In other words, we aim to persuade people so that they will accept the truth of the gospel. It is not surprising that, like apologetics, persuasion is also frowned upon in regard to religion as an expression of intolerance and of disrespect for others. This is strange because, as Donald McGavran reminds us, persuasion is "the basis of all learning, progress and commerce."[37] For example, it lies at the heart of marketing and political campaigning. In reality, persuasion is an expression of our respect of individuals and our belief in their potential under God. If we know that someone who has the potential of receiving eternal life is holding to a false belief that is hindering that life, we will seek to persuade that person about the truth. But we will do so in a way that reflects the respect we have for the individual.

---

35. I am grateful to my colleague Ivor Poobalan for alerting me to this point. For more on this type of dialogue, see Stephen Neill, *Salvation Tomorrow* (London: Lutterworth, 1976), 22–43; E. Stanley Jones, *Christ at the Round Table* (London: Hodder and Stoughton, 1928).

36. See Stott, *Christian Mission*, 74–79. Stott cites helpful insights here from Bishop Kenneth Cragg's book *The Call of the Minaret* (London: Lutterworth, 1956).

37. In Glasser and McGavran, *Contemporary Theologies*, 231.

There are, of course, disrespectful ways of persuasion. One way is *imposition*, which John Stott describes as "the crusading attempt to coerce people by legislation to accept the Christian way."[38] Another way is *manipulation*, where factors not basic to the gospel are brought to bear on people to cause them to change their religion. Manipulation can take place through the stirring of the emotions so that people lose control of their wills. It can occur when someone offers incentives, like the promise of jobs, if one converts to a religion. Some cults manipulate people through a process of brainwashing or the force of strong personality, where they surrender their wills to the group.[39]

Peter describes the proper balance between conviction and respect in proclamation in these words: "Always be prepared to give an answer to everyone who asks you to give the reason for the hope that you have. But do this with gentleness and respect, keeping a clear conscience" (1 Peter 3:15b–16a).

Responding to opposition. When, out of sacrificial love, we share the good news with people and encounter opposition and misrepresentation, that fact can be difficult to accept. But the gospel is so radical that many will see it as a cause that is turning the world upside down (v. 6, ASV, KJV). We must never forget that. Note what Jesus said: "Remember the words I spoke to you: 'No servant is greater than his master.' If they persecuted me, they will persecute you also" (John 15:20). The history of the churches in Macedonia teaches us that suffering is the matrix out of which strong and healthy churches can emerge.

If we remember this, we will not be surprised and angry over the opposition we face. Anger over opposition is a trap that many fall into, and it results in blunting their witness and dampening their joy in the Lord. The biblical approach has been well expressed by Paul to the Thessalonians: "You became imitators of us and of the Lord; in spite of severe suffering, you welcomed the message with the joy given by the Holy Spirit" (1 Thess. 1:6). A key for facing this suffering, then, is to ensure that we have "the joy given by the Holy Spirit."

However, as we discussed in our study of Paul's ministry in Philippi, we must also be careful to ensure that we do everything in our power to show that proclaiming the gospel is within the bounds of legality, and we should do nothing to antagonize our opponents unnecessarily. This is the probable reason why Paul left Thessalonica against his wishes (1 Thess. 2:17). He would rather leave the area than antagonize his opponents further, for that would make life more difficult for the believers in Thessalonica.

---

38. John Stott, *Decisive Issues Facing Christians Today* (Old Tappan, N.J.: Revell, 1990), 46.

39. For a discussion of issues involving persuasion see my *The Christian's Attitude Toward World Religions* (Wheaton, Ill.: Tyndale, 1987), 147–59.

How to be like the Bereans today. Does Luke's attribution of nobility to the Bereans mean that they were more deserving of salvation than other people? Did they have an inherent qualification that caused them to merit salvation? That would go against the biblical teaching that no one merits salvation. On the contrary, their nobility lay in their willingness to acknowledge their need, resulting in an eagerness to hear from God and to receive what they heard. This in turn resulted in their salvation. They came down from their pedestals as people of high standing (cf. v. 12, "prominent Greek women") or as people of high Jewish heritage ("many of the Jews") and, like hungry children in need of food, they sought God's Word.

In the Bible, nobility is childlikeness—the refusal to make claims of nobility for oneself. Jesus said, "Unless you change and become like little children, you will never enter the kingdom of heaven. Therefore, whoever humbles himself like this child is the greatest in the kingdom of heaven" (Matt. 18:3–4). The character trait that Jesus recommends here is an attitude of repentance—of need, of admission that one possesses no merit. Such people are open to learn from God what he wishes to teach and receive from God what he wishes to give.

This is the heart of Christian faith: an attitude that makes people continue to go to the Scriptures in order to learn more and to grow. Just as salvation is through faith, so is growth in the Christian life. When we study the Bible, it is not some meritorious act through which we can claim to have grown spiritually. Bible study that pleases God is an expression of faith. It is an attitude that says, "I am needy. You alone can satisfy my need. You have spoken a message and it is recorded in the Bible. I will go to that book as a hungry baby seeks her mother for milk."

In 2 Timothy 3:14–17 Paul shows how the same attitude to the Word that opens the door to salvation also opens the door to Christian growth. Verse 15 connects Scripture with salvation: "and how from infancy you have known the holy Scriptures, which are able to make you wise for salvation through faith in Christ Jesus." Paul then connects Scripture with growth (vv. 14, 16–17):

> But as for you, continue in what you have learned and have become convinced of, because you know those from whom you learned it. . . .
> All Scripture is God-breathed and is useful for teaching, rebuking, correcting and training in righteousness, so that the man of God may be thoroughly equipped for every good work.

The attitude we are describing is well expressed in a memorable quote from John Wesley:

> To candid, reasonable men I am not afraid to lay open what have been the inmost thoughts of my heart. I have thought: I am a creature

of a day, passing through life as an arrow through the air. I am a spirit come from God and returning to God; just hovering over the great gulf till, a few moments hence, I am no more seen, I drop into an unchangeable eternity! I want to know one thing: the way to heaven, how to land safe on that happy shore. God himself has condescended to teach the way; for this very end he came from heaven. He hath written it down in a book. O give me that book! At any price, give me the book of God! I have it: here is knowledge enough for me. Let me be *homo unius libri* [a man of only one book]. Here then I am, far away from the busy ways of men. I sit down alone—only God is here. In his presence I open, I read his book from this end, to find the way to heaven.[40]

It is not easy today to get people to receive a message with great eagerness or to examine the Scriptures as the Bereans did (v. 11). In this postmodern world the emphasis is on personal truth that resides inside of us. Truth is viewed as subjective, and people resist the idea of objective knowledge and of eternal, unchanging truths. People are getting less and less used to studying books. Expository preachers even find it difficult to get people to become alert enough to direct their eyes to the Bibles in front of them. They prefer to look with glassy eyes at the preacher, often with their mind on something very different to what is being preached!

Thousands of aids to Bible study are in print today, which are supposed to simplify the task of studying the Scriptures. They may simplify study, but often they become a substitute to careful study of the Word. Without examining the Scriptures for answers, people read the answers that others have given to the questions they ask. Moreover, this is an age when people are so used to receiving predigested material from television that they find going to the Scriptures to do inductive study to be something strange.

There is an urgent need, then, to lead our people to discover what Oletta Wald has called *The Joy of Discovery* in Bible study.[41] And it is indeed a great joy to discover God's truth through personal study of the Word. We need a new generation of Christian leaders who will first of all set apart time to do this for themselves. They will then communicate their enthusiasm for Bible study to those they lead. They will help raise up a new crop of Berean Christians.

---

40. "Preface" to *Sermons on Several Occasions*, vol. 1 (1746), from *John Wesley*, ed. Albert C. Outler (New York: Oxford Univ. Press, 1964), 89.

41. Oletta Wald, *The Joy of Discovery* (Minneapolis: Bible Banner, 1956). This book is a helpful guide to inductive Bible study (see also Oletta Wald, *The Joy of Teaching Discovery Bible Study* [Minneapolis: Augsburg, 1976]). One of my teachers, Robert A. Traina, has written a more advanced book that describes inductive study, entitled *Methodical Bible Study* (Grand Rapids: Zondervan, 1985 [reprint]).

Heterogeneous churches. We have already discussed the significance of the heterogeneous churches found in Acts.[42] Here we will only repeat the fact that having Christians of different social and cultural backgrounds within the same local church not only accords with the biblical pattern but also demonstrates in a vivid way the power of the gospel to unite humanity. In a world that is being torn asunder by ethnic strife, this may be one of the most powerful contemporary demonstrations of the glory of the gospel we have to offer the world.

We need to be specialized in our efforts to evangelize different cultural groups, as the church growth specialists rightly advocate. But we must also do all we can to incorporate people from these groups into the wider church, both to demonstrate the power of the gospel to unite people and to mutually enrich us through the contributions they make to our understanding of the gospel.

---

42. See the discussions on 6:1–7 and 12:25–13:12.

Acts 17:16–34

HILE PAUL WAS waiting for them in Athens, he was greatly distressed to see that the city was full of idols. [17]So he reasoned in the synagogue with the Jews and the God-fearing Greeks, as well as in the market-place day by day with those who happened to be there. [18]A group of Epicurean and Stoic philosophers began to dispute with him. Some of them asked, "What is this babbler trying to say?" Others remarked, "He seems to be advocating foreign gods." They said this because Paul was preaching the good news about Jesus and the resurrection. [19]Then they took him and brought him to a meeting of the Areopagus, where they said to him, "May we know what this new teaching is that you are presenting? [20]You are bringing some strange ideas to our ears, and we want to know what they mean." [21](All the Athenians and the foreigners who lived there spent their time doing nothing but talking about and listening to the latest ideas.)

[22]Paul then stood up in the meeting of the Areopagus and said: "Men of Athens! I see that in every way you are very religious. [23]For as I walked around and looked carefully at your objects of worship, I even found an altar with this inscription: TO AN UNKNOWN GOD. Now what you worship as something unknown I am going to proclaim to you.

[24]"The God who made the world and everything in it is the Lord of heaven and earth and does not live in temples built by hands. [25]And he is not served by human hands, as if he needed anything, because he himself gives all men life and breath and everything else. [26]From one man he made every nation of men, that they should inhabit the whole earth; and he determined the times set for them and the exact places where they should live. [27]God did this so that men would seek him and perhaps reach out for him and find him, though he is not far from each one of us. [28]'For in him we live and move and have our being.' As some of your own poets have said, 'We are his offspring.'

[29]"Therefore since we are God's offspring, we should not think that the divine being is like gold or silver or stone—an image made by man's design and skill. [30]In the past God over-

looked such ignorance, but now he commands all people everywhere to repent. ³¹For he has set a day when he will judge the world with justice by the man he has appointed. He has given proof of this to all men by raising him from the dead."

³²When they heard about the resurrection of the dead, some of them sneered, but others said, "We want to hear you again on this subject." ³³At that, Paul left the Council. ³⁴A few men became followers of Paul and believed. Among them was Dionysius, a member of the Areopagus, also a woman named Damaris, and a number of others.

ATHENS (LIKE CORINTH) was in the province of Achaia¹ and is the capital of modern Greece. Today "the heart of the city is sufficiently cleared for the great monuments of its classical past to be conspicuously visible."² In Paul's day it had lost some of its grandeur, but it "remained the *symbol* of the great philosophers in popular opinion,"³ being the place where Socrates, Plato, and Aristotle had shone. Keener says, "From an aesthetic standpoint, Athens was unrivaled for its exquisite architecture and statues."⁴ On the Acropolis (the elevated part of a Greek city) is the Parthenon, the temple of Athene (the city's patron goddess), built in 447 B.C. Even today it "is one of the most visually satisfying buildings to be seen anywhere in the world."⁵

Ministry in Athens (17:16–21)

WHEN PAUL SAW these exquisite works of pagan art, he was "greatly distressed" (v. 16). As in 16:18, Luke uses a strong, though different, word (*paroxynomai*) for Paul's reaction to seeing the city so full of idols. This word has been defined as "to be provoked or upset at someone or something involving severe emotional concern."⁶

Though Paul was in a rage when he saw the idols, he acted with restraint and respect in his outward behavior among the idolaters. Thus, "he reasoned in the synagogue . . . as well as in the marketplace day by day with those who

---

1. "In 46 B.C. . . . the whole of Greece, under the name of Achaia, was transformed into a Roman province; this was divided into two provinces, Macedonia and Achaia, in 27 B.C." (J. E. Harry, "Achaia," *ISBE*, 1:30).

2. Bruce, *Steps*, 36.

3. Keener, *BBC*, 372.

4. Ibid.

5. Bruce, *Steps*, 36.

6. Louw and Nida, 763.

happened to be there" (v. 17). "Reasoned" here is *dialegomai* (cf. comments on 17:2–4), which probably involved proclamation but left room for discussion at the end. The "marketplace" he spoke at was the *agora*, the main public place in the city, adorned with public buildings and colonnades. It was the economic, political, and cultural heart of the city.[7] An ancient description of Socrates has him in the marketplace when it was most crowded, where he conversed with whomever he met.[8] When Paul evangelized this city of Socrates, he used the method of Socrates.

Paul debated with "a group of Epicurian and Stoic philosophers" (v. 18). The Epicurians were "a philosophical school that valued pleasure (the absence of pain and disturbance) and disbelieved in the gods of ancient myths."[9] "They were influential only in the educated upper classes, and their views about God were similar to deism (he was uninvolved in the universe and irrelevant)."[10] Stoicism was "the most popular form of Greek philosophy in Paul's day. Although most people were not Stoics, many Stoic ideas were widely disseminated."[11] Though they believed in a supreme God, it was in a pantheistic way. The Stoics saw the world as determined by fate and advocated that "human beings must pursue their duty, resigning themselves to live in harmony with nature and reason, however painful this might be, and develop their own self-sufficiency."[12]

From the time of Chrysostom[13] interpreters have suggested that some Athenians thought Paul was proclaiming two gods: Jesus and Anastasis (*anastasis* means "resurrection"; v. 18b). This is typical of how people with a different worldview misunderstand us as we proclaim the gospel.[14] The accusation against Paul (v. 18) reminds us of a similar charge against Socrates, which resulted in his being taken to the Areopagus and condemned to death.[15]

The Areopagus was the main administrative body and the chief court of Athens.[16] We are not sure whether Paul was taken (v. 19) into this council for a proper trial or just to the location of the hill after which the council was named.[17] These Athenians seem to have been curious philosophically (v. 21),

---

7. This description is gleaned from Bruce, *Steps*, 38, and David W. J. Gill, "Achaia," *BAFCS*, vol. 2, *Graeco-Roman Setting*, 445.

8. See Knowling, "Acts," 365.

9. Keener, *BBC*, 824.

10. Ibid., 372.

11. Ibid., 831.

12. Stott, *Acts*, 280–81.

13. John Chrysostom, "Homilies on the Acts," 233.

14. See comments on 17:1–15.

15. Conrad Gempf, "Paul at Athens," *DPL*, 52.

16. Gill, "Achaia," 447.

17. Gempf, "Athens," 52.

and thus they were willing to give the "strange ideas" of Paul an official hearing (vv. 19–20).

The Areopagus Speech and Its Results (17:22–34)

PAUL'S SPEECH BEFORE the Areopagus remains a model of sensitive but forthright confrontation of an intellectual audience with the claims of the gospel. "Very religious" in Paul's opening statement (v. 22) is a general word that can mean several things depending on the context. It could be a criticism, as is implied by the KJV translation: "Ye are too superstitious," though this is an unlikely way to start an evangelistic speech. It was probably not a compliment, for according to an ancient writer Lucian, "complimentary exordia [beginnings] to secure the goodwill of the Areopagus court were discouraged."[18] Most likely, therefore, it was a simple observation, opening the way for Paul's comment about the altar to the unknown god (v. 23a).

Ancient literature contains references to altars to unknown gods.[19] Gempf points to a writing by Diogenes Laertius that presents the practice of anonymous worship as a "safety precaution.... The thinking was that if the gods were not properly venerated they would strike the city. Hence, lest they inadvertently invoke the wrath of some god in their ignorance of him or her, the city set up these altars to unknown gods (Diogenes 1.110–113)."[20] Paul, then, is highlighting an acknowledged need of the Athenians, and he presents the God whom he proclaims as the answer to that need (v. 23b).

Paul introduces his God and offers a critique of the Athenian gods, which took the form of idolatry (vv. 24–29). His basic statement is that God is the Creator of everything in the world and that he is Lord of heaven and earth (v. 24).[21] His comments about God are calculated to not only show the futility of idolatry, but also to demonstrate that God is the supreme Lord of creation and therefore worthy of our allegiance.

Against idolatry Paul insists that God does not live in temples (v. 24) and does not need our insignificant offerings for he himself is the provider of everything (v. 25). The apostle continues by focusing both on God's sovereignty over the affairs of the human race (v. 26) and on his creation in human beings of an innate thirst to find him, an incurable religiosity (v. 27). Since God is the immanent sustainer of creation, everyone's life depends on him (v. 28).

---

18. Cited in Bruce, *Acts: Greek Text*, 380.

19. See Hemer, *Acts*, 117.

20. Gempf, "Athens," 51.

21. Note that Paul had adopted the same strategy in Lystra, where he presented God as the living God who is the Creator of everything (14:15).

All these points lead to the conclusion (note "therefore" in v. 29) that idolatry is unnecessary and give weight to Paul's call to repentance that follows (v. 30). If this God is indeed the supreme Lord of creation, the wisest thing to do is to turn to him. This turning to God is not an optional extra that merely adds a new dimension to one's life. It is a command that goes out to all people everywhere. But the wisdom of such a step becomes all the more evident when we realize that this God is someday going to judge the world (v. 31).

Along the way Paul has answered another question that would have arisen in the mind of a philosophically oriented person. If there is a God who is supreme, why does he allow people to live in such open defiance of him without punishing them? His answer has three aspects: God overlooked their ignorance in the past, but now he "commands all people everywhere to repent" (v. 30), and a judgment day is coming (v. 31a). In other words, God will not tolerate sin forever, for he is indeed just. The wicked who openly defy God may prosper for a time, but one day they will have to pay for their sin if they do not repent.

Paul has made some astounding claims—especially that the representative of this supreme God through whom he will accomplish his work is a man called Jesus. How does Paul know that these things are true? What proof does he have of these claims? Paul answers that this supreme God "has given proof of this to all men by raising [Jesus] from the dead" (v. 31b).

This basic feature of the Christian message brings the growing sense of unease within some in Paul's audience to a head, and they begin to sneer at him (v. 32). Others, however, want to hear more, and the gathering ends on that note (v. 33). Luke rounds off the story with a report about some of the results of Paul's ministry in Athens (v. 34). A member of the Areopagus, Dionysius, is among those converted, as is a woman named Damaris, who must have been converted through Paul's earlier ministry in Athens (women were traditionally not invited to meetings of the Areopagus).[22]

Paul's strategy of reasoning for the gospel with the Athenians is instructive. His message does not contain direct quotations or appeals to the Old Testament as did his talks to Jews and God-fearers. Such appeals would have meant nothing to hearers who did not accept the authority of the Scriptures. But in spite of that, the message was thoroughly scriptural. As Bruce writes, "His argument is firmly based on biblical revelation; it echoes throughout the thought, and at times the very language, of the Old Testament."[23] Interestingly, Paul quoted from writers whom the Athenians looked up to (v. 28). Of the two statements in verse 28 there is a question whether the first

---

22. Keener, BBC, 374–75.
23. Bruce, Acts, NICNT, 335.

is actually a quotation, but the second certainly is.[24] Paul would not, of course, have agreed with the philosophical system out of which the statement arose, but he did agree with this individual statement and thus used it to buttress his argument.

It is helpful to know that Paul did not create his arguments in this speech *ex nihilo.* Keener observes that "defenders of Judaism had worked for centuries to make their faith philosophically respectable, and here, as in his letters, Paul draws heavily on his Jewish predecessors' arguments."[25] As a scholar schooled in the highest educational structures that Judaism could offer, Paul had access to this Jewish wisdom of the ages. He made use of that when developing the case for Christianity to present to the pagan mind.

A FAILED MISSION?[26] There are many who consider this effort in Athens a failure and therefore an example to avoid rather than to follow. They claim that in his effort to be relevant to the philosophical Athenians, Paul compromised the gospel and did not present a clear-cut Christian message.[27] Especially missing was the cross. These scholars claim that this is why he wrote regarding his ministry in Corinth (his next stop on this journey): "I did not come with eloquence or superior wisdom. . . . For I resolved to know nothing while I was with you except Jesus Christ and him crucified" (1 Cor. 2:1–2). They also assert that the low number of converts indicates the error of Paul's strategy at Athens.

I maintain, however, that the record of Paul's ministry in Athens suggests that it was not one of compromise but of forthright confrontation with idolatry. Though the cross is missing in this summary report of his talk, the death of Christ must have been mentioned for him to mention the resurrection, and there is nothing to say that this was not clearly presented during his reasoning with the people of Athens prior to this event. It could also be that Paul was hoping to talk about the cross (which was "foolishness to Gentiles," 1 Cor. 1:23) after presenting the victory of the resurrection; but he could not get to that point because of the response of his audience.

---

24. From the fourth century B.C. writer Aratus of Soli in Cicilia (see Boring, *Hellenistic Commentary,* 328).

25. Keener, *BBC,* 373.

26. Paul's ministry in Athens is the basis for much of my book, *The Christian's Attitude Toward World Religions* (Wheaton, Ill.: Tyndale, 1987). Much of the material below is found there.

27. This is the verdict of M. Dibelius in "Paul on the Areopagus," *Studies in the Acts of the Apostles,* ed. H. Greeven (New York: Scribners, 1956), 57–63 (cited in Gempf, "Athens," 52).

Note, too, that those who work with non-Christians know that even a small number of converts from a highly intellectual audience can be considered a huge success. One of those converted was actually from the Areopagus, the cream of Athenian society. Converts from this segment of society are few and far between in the church worldwide. As Keener points out, "modern readers who judge Paul's work in Athens a failure on the basis of 1 Corinthians 2:1 have missed Luke's point entirely.... The emphasis on Acts is on his success, and the original readers of Acts could not simply turn to 1 Corinthians."[28]

In this study we will use Paul's ministry as an example of effective evangelism among people without a biblical heritage (i.e., Gentiles who were not God-fearers). Finding ways of evangelizing such people has always been important to Christians in non-Christian lands. But now it has become equally important in the so-called post-Christian West, where many people from non-Christian lands now reside and where many descendants of Christians are more pagan than Christian in their beliefs.

In Athens we find Paul ministering in three important arenas.[29] (1) He ministered in the synagogue to those with a biblical background, which is somewhat equivalent to evangelism today among Jews and, in broader applications, among Muslims and nominal Christians. (2) He ministered in the marketplace, in what we might call street evangelism. (3) He witnessed to what might be called the academy—the leaders of a highly intellectual town. We are impressed by the way Paul adapted his method and strategy to the audiences he faced.

Attitudes toward non-Christians. When Paul reacted so strongly to the idols he saw (v. 16), he was reflecting God's reaction to idolatry. In Isaiah 65:3 God describes Israel as "a people who continually provoke me to my very face, offering sacrifices in gardens and burning incense on altars of brick." When human beings made in the image of God dishonor him by doing the exact opposite to what he created them to do—trust in him—it should infuriate us, for three reasons: (1) Human beings are missing the reason for which they were created. (2) God is greatly dishonored by this blatant defiance of his will. God said, "I am the LORD; that is my name! I will not give my glory to another or my praise to idols" (Isa. 42:8). (3) The consequences of unbelief in this world and the next are terrible (see Rom. 1:18–32).

This provocation, then, comes as a result of holiness and love: holiness that responds to the unholiness of unbelief and idolatry, and love that responds to the dishonoring of God and the demeaning of humanity. Of course, we must add that we may not always react with the same emotional

---

28. Keener, *BBC*, 374.
29. See Stott, *Acts*, 281.

intensity as Paul. This passage does not insist that all react precisely as Paul did, but his reaction is instructive in pointing to the seriousness of unbelief and idolatry.

Though Paul's spirit was provoked by idols, his behavior was restrained by wisdom and respect (vv. 17–19). That too is a biblical attitude toward unbelief. True, this was not the attitude of the Old Testament prophets, but they were ministering among a people who had received a clear revelation from God. They should have known better, so they are severely rebuked. But the Gentiles to whom Paul was speaking had not been influenced by God's special revelation. They had to be presented God's message, and a display of anger would have forfeited an opportunity to win a hearing among them. Paul did ultimately call these people to repentance, but he approached the issue without thundering accusations against the people.

Into this mix of restrained provocation must come the recognition of those things that we can agree with in other religions. Paul agreed with what he could agree in those faiths and used those elements as stepping-stones to presenting the gospel. Such points of agreement can be traced back to general revelation.[30] In fact, if we are to be effective in reaching those of other faiths, we must study their religions—preferably by reading their own writers, by observing their practices, and by talking to their adherents. Here Paul quotes from a Greek writer, Aratus, and uses it as a point of contact even though he does not agree with the philosophical system Aratus advocated. We too can agree with certain elements without compromising the gospel. As Bruce points out, we "may quote appropriate words from a well-known writer or speaker without committing ourselves to their total context or background of thought."[31] And we must also remember that the arguments Paul used in his Areopagus address had been used by other Jews before him. We too can gain much from the apologetic writings of Christians who have sought to respond to other religions.

I should reemphasize, however, that while Paul may have agreed with features in other faiths, he did not agree with their overall systems. If Christianity and other religions are represented by circles, the centers of the circles are distant and the points of intersection are only on peripheral matters.

---

30. Elsewhere I have shown that this general revelation consists of "reminiscent knowledge" (which can be traced to God's original revelation to humanity), of "intuitional knowledge" (which arises from the fact that humans are made in the image of God and that vestiges of that image still remain even in fallen humanity), and of "inferential knowledge" (which is traced to the knowledge of God that is revealed in his creation). See my *Christian Attitude*, 103–13; Bruce A. Demarest, *General Revelation: Historical Views and Contemporary Issues* (Grand Rapids: Zondervan, 1982), 227–62.

31. F. F. Bruce, *First Century Faith* (Leicester: Inter-Varsity Press, 1977), 45.

For example, there is much admirable material in the ethical discipline of Buddhism with which we can agree and which we can use as stepping-stones in sharing the gospel. But we must remember that these good features can be used by Satan to keep people from the truth. By finding satisfaction in trying to earn their own salvation, Buddhists can assuage the conviction of sin and guilt and of their need for a Savior and thus resist the invitation to respond to God's gracious offer of salvation.

Contextualization. In the city of Socrates, Paul adapted to his audience both in style and content. His speech to the philosophical members of the Areopagus was, as John Wesley aptly remarked, "a divinely philosophical discourse."[32] He began by referring to a need his audience was conscious of (which necessitated setting up a temple to an unknown God). Though his substance was entirely biblical, he did not quote from the Scriptures as he did when he spoke to Jews and God-fearers. In fact, he quoted from the writings of their own philosophers (v. 28). We call such adapting *contextualization*. Paul explains how he did this in 1 Corinthians 9:19–23, where he climaxes his description with these words: "I have become all things to all men so that by all possible means I might save some." Contextualization occurs when the presentation and outworking of the gospel is done in a manner appropriate to the context in which it is found.

We are sobered by the fact that with all his contextualization Paul's message was misunderstood by some of his hearers (v. 18b). It points to the urgent need to work hard at communicating the gospel to those outside our faith. At the same time, we must also avoid the pitfall of syncretism (see below). What is most important is faithfully to proclaim the gospel. If we can find points of contact with our audience along the way, we should use them, but the gospel is always what is primary.

Acceptable aspiration or acceptable worship? When Paul said that he proclaimed what the Athenians worshiped as unknown (v. 23b), he was not saying, as some have claimed, that God accepted their worship of the anonymous god. The Indian theologian Raimundo Panikkar, in his influential book *The Unknown Christ of Hinduism,* uses this passage to explain his theory that Hindus really worship God and that Christ is at work in the Hindus even though he is not known by them.[33] But N. B. Stonehouse has pointed out that the emphasis here is on the ignorance, not on the worship.[34] At this stage of

---

32. John Wesley, *Explanatory Notes*, 464.

33. Raimundo Panikkar, *The Unknown Christ of Hinduism: Towards an Ecumenical Christophany*, rev. ed. (Maryknoll, N.Y.: Orbis, 1981), 168.

34. N. B. Stonehouse, *Paul Before the Areopagus and Other New Testament Studies* (London: Tyndale, 1957), 19.

his message, Paul was not making any value judgments. He did this subsequently with his forthright attack on idolatry (v. 29) and his comment that such "ignorance" was no longer excusable, making it necessary for "all people everywhere to repent" (v. 30). Throughout Acts the evangelists focused on felt needs and legitimate aspirations and then presented Christ as the answer to those needs.

There are other legitimate aspirations addressed in this message. Verse 27 refers to the incurable religiosity of the human being. God's actions in creation cause people to "seek him and perhaps reach out for him and find him." This must have been an important theme in Paul's evangelistic preaching for he also used it in Lystra (14:17).

Some have claimed Paul was implying that through this feeling after God that people could find him and be saved apart from the gospel. Gempf argues that this is unlikely because the verb "finding" is weakened in three ways. (1) "The first is the grammatical construction: the use of the optative mood in Greek introduces a tone of uncertainty, coupled with a phrase (*ei ara ge*) which is best translated 'if perhaps.' The finding is by no means certain." (2) "The force of the verb is weakened by being paired with the colorful verb 'groping' (*pselaphao*), a verb used in such sources as Homer's *Odyssey* (9.416) and the Greek version of Deuteronomy (28:29) to mean a 'blind feeling around.'" (3) "The verb phrase is followed by the clause 'although he is not far.' The concessive nature of this clause only makes sense if a groping is not successful."[35]

In other words, Paul is not saying here that people can find God solely by following their felt needs and aspirations. They need the gospel, which alone truly fulfills those needs and aspirations. Christians must be sensitive to people's needs and aspirations, see how Christ meets them, and use them as stepping-stones for communicating the gospel.

Establishing the fact of God. Paul's practice, followed in Lystra and Athens, of beginning his exposition of the gospel by introducing God (14:15–17; 17:24–29) must surely become standard procedure when we preach the gospel to people without a biblical worldview.[36] It is so important to establish the fact of God before we share the message of Christ. It is not an accident that the Bible and the evangelistic tract written by John to trigger belief (John 20:31) starts with a description of God as Creator of everything (Gen. 1; John 1:1–3).

Familiar evangelistic themes. The Gentile audience of Athens required evangelistic themes that were not needed when preaching to audiences of

---

35. Gempf, "Athens," 52.
36. See comments on unfolding God's plan for humanity in the study on 13:13–52.

Jews and God-fearers, such as the reality of the supremacy of God and the futility of idolatry. But in this message we find some familiar themes, which appeared in the earlier addresses and have been already discussed: the centrality of Christ (v. 31), the summons from God to repent (v. 30),[37] the value of the resurrection as an accreditation of the gospel (v. 31),[38] and the key place that judgment has in building a case for Christianity and in appealing to people to turn to God (vv. 30–31).[39] These points come at the latter part of the message. We must know where people are in their understanding of the biblical worldview. Once the foundational truths have been established, we can proceed to present the heart of the gospel, which is God's work in and through Jesus Christ.

REACHING ALL SEGMENTS **of society.** The importance of reaching all segments of society and of creative strategizing in order to do this stands out in this passage. Blessed is the nation that has people with such versatility as Paul, who could reach such a wide spectrum of people. If we do not have one person who can do as much as Paul did, we should ensure that different people are engaging all segments of society with the gospel. Just as Paul evangelized synagogue worshipers, we need people who will evangelize the Jews and Muslims as well as nominal Christians within the church.

We also need people who will hit the streets with the gospel. Stott says, "The equivalent of the *agora* will vary in different parts of the world. It may be a park, city square or street corner, a shopping mall or market place, a 'pub,' neighborhood bar, café, discothèque or student cafeteria, wherever people meet when they are at leisure."[40] And we must reach the intelligentsia. Let one of this generation's great mentors of such people, John Stott, speak again:

> There is an urgent need for more Christian thinkers who will dedicate their minds to Christ, not only as lecturers, but also as authors, journalists, dramatists and broadcasters, as television script-writers, producers and personalities, and as artists and actors who use a variety of art forms in which to communicate the gospel.[41]

Paul was undoubtedly one of the greatest intellects the church has been gifted with. He devoted his mind to the cause of the gospel—to penetrating

---

37. See discussion of 2:14–41.
38. See discussion of 2:14–41.
39. See discussion of 10:34–11:18.
40. Stott, *Acts*, 281.
41. Ibid.

the unreached with the message of Christ. This is not the only type of person God uses, but such people are needed to develop strategies to reach unreached groups of people. It is no accident that some of the best minds in the history of the Western world were released for this vital task—such as Henry Martyn, Stephen Neill, Lesslie Newbigin, and Stanley Jones.[42] Particularly lacking is the penetration of the highest (and lowest) strata of society. The church should be challenging people to engage the intellectuals of our day so that, as in the early church, there would be converts like Dionysius.

Restrained provocation today. Paul's strong reaction to idolatry found expression in the life of the great missionary to Muslims, Henry Martyn, who has been called one of the most heroic figures of nineteenth-century British history. After doing brilliant work at Cambridge University, he shunned various possibilities for advancement in life through marriage and employment in order to go as a missionary to India. When he arrived in India, his friends wanted him to stay in the city of Calcutta to minister with the Westerners, but he wanted to go where the unreached were. He wrote in his diary about this dilemma: "I almost think that to be prevented from going among the heathen as a missionary would break my heart.... I feel pressed in spirit to do something for God.... I have hitherto lived to little purpose more like a clod than a servant of God; now let me burn out for God."[43]

During this time he went to see a Hindu procession, and he describes his response to this in his diaries: "Before the stumps of images, for they were not better, some of the people prostrated themselves, striking the ground twice with their foreheads." And his response? "This excited more horror in me than I can well express.... I thought that if I had words I would preach to the multitudes all day if I lost my life for it." With such passion Martyn persevered as a missionary to the Muslims. In his lifetime he probably saw only one person openly converted through his ministry. But he translated the Bible into what was then called the Hindustani[44] language and then into the Persian language. He also left an amazing legacy through his personal diaries, which were used to motivate large numbers of people to respond to the missionary call.

Paul's and Martyn's reaction to idolatry contrasts widely with that of many Christians today. When they are confronted with the same expressions of devotion, they may admire such devotion without reflecting on the fact that it is wrong for people created in the image of God to be worshiping idols.

---

42. See discussion on 12:25–13:12.

43. Constance E. Padwick, *Henry Martyn: Confessor of the Faith* (New York: George H. Doran. n.d.), 152.

44. The modern Urdu language.

But both Paul and Martyn reasoned with the people they met. They expressed what I have called restrained provocation. They also studied these religions and were familiar with the way of life and thought of the people whom they sought to lead to Christ.

This issue of studying other religions has come into special focus in recent times. The past 150 years has seen a fresh discovery in the Western world of the cultural and religious heritage of many non-Christian cultures. As Stephen Neill puts it, "As these 'treasures of darkness' penetrated the consciousness of educated men and women, something of a gasp of astonishment arose. Surprise was followed by appreciation and even admiration."[45]

I have seen two unbiblical reactions to non-Christian religions in the West. (1) One borders on paranoia in that it sees non-Christians only as being under the grip of demonic powers, thus making social interchange impossible. Such people cannot identify with non-Christians in order to open the door for witness. When we meet non-Christians and find things that we can admire in them, we should not need to be afraid to acknowledge it. Christians in the West can actually learn from their neighbors who have come from another land. For example, they can learn many things from features of family life that have evolved in an Eastern culture, especially in view of the crisis in family life in the West.

(2) The second unbiblical attitude to these faiths is what we might call uncritical approval. I have detected an attitude among some in the West that tends to accept anything that comes from the Eastern religions while being critical of much that has to do with Christianity. Our measure of truth must always be the Scriptures. If the Bible agrees with something that another religion teaches, we do not need to be afraid about affirming it. But if Scripture disagrees, we must respectfully say so and seek to show why it is wrong, as Paul did in Athens.

But many are afraid to enter into these spheres and engage the non-Christian mind. They fear that if they affirm the good in other faiths, they will deny the supremacy of Christ. In answer, I suggest that a proper view of the glory of God's revelation, especially his revelation in Christ, will take away that fear. God's special revelation is so glorious that if we have discovered it, all other truths are but a poor shadow. These people also fear compromise. They point to many people who, after studying other faiths in recent years, have ended up as pluralists or syncretists. Syncretism takes place when, in the presentation and outworking of Christianity, elements essential to the gospel are dropped or elements incompatible with the gospel are taken on in our efforts to identify with non-Christians.

---

45. Stephen Neill, *Crises of Belief* (London: Hodder and Stoughton, 1984), 10.

If we are to maintain our fervor for biblical mission while we engage other religions in study and encounter, we should have three disciplines that we regularly practice in our lives. (1) We must live under the Scriptures. The biblical attitude to life is so different to the world's attitudes that we can easily get drawn into the world's way of thinking unless we are regularly impacted by the Scriptures. A healthy trust in the authority and sufficiency of Scripture along with comprehensive regular input from all the segments of Scripture into our lives will enable us to remain scriptural in our attitudes.

(2) We need the discipline of community. When we live under the yoke of spiritual accountability within a community, we find ourselves challenged by others if we try something new. While such challenges may be difficult to endure, it is healthy for our spiritual stability. Our friends can confront us if we veer away from the path of biblical Christianity.

(3) We must live under the discipline of witness. There are few things that energize the soul and enable us to maintain our passion for the gospel as much as an evangelistic lifestyle. When we get close to people, see their lives, and yearn for their salvation, we realize afresh how vital the gospel is for their salvation and we experience afresh the power of energizing for witness by the Spirit (1:8). Such cutting-edge living is an effective safeguard against compromise.[46]

The challenge of contextualization.[47] Churches seeking to be faithful to Christ's call to go to the unreached must take the challenge of contextualization seriously. When we made a conscious decision in our ministry to focus on non-Christian youth rather than only on nominal Christians, we found ourselves ill-equipped for the task. Thus, we began to study the Buddhist, Hindu, and Muslim cultures. We realized that though youth could be effectively reached through drama and music, our styles of drama and music were different from theirs. We therefore sent our staff to learn these art forms from non-Christians. We began to write our own music and stage plays. We stopped using the games we played, which the non-Christians did not enjoy, and learned new games that they enjoyed. We went to political meetings, especially when good orators were speaking, in order to learn their art of oratory. We were uncomfortable with some of these things. During the early years we would have liked to do ministry differently. But gradually our ministry was transformed into one that began to reach large numbers of non-Christians for Christ. We have had to keep changing our methods because the youth culture has kept changing.

Each context into which Christians are called differs. It may be the Greek culture of Athens or the Afro-American culture of New York or the Sinhala

---

46. On this, see my *Christian Attitude*, 91−102.

47. For more on contextualization see the discussions of 6:8−7:53 and 19:8−41.

Buddhist culture of rural Sri Lanka. Each culture has unique challenges that call for a creative departure from the comfort zones of the Christian witness. All this calls for a passion for God and for people, which will give us the courage to try new things and to pay the price of doing so. That passion comes when we draw near to the heart of our missionary God, and it is maintained through a close personal tie with God and his Word. If we remain near to God's Word, we know that our contextualization will not degenerate into syncretism.

Emphasizing felt needs and aspirations. I have already shown how important it is for evangelists to focus on felt needs and aspirations and to show that Christ answers those needs.[48] Once we have won the attention of people and their interest in following Christ by showing how Christ meets these needs, we can proceed to other burning issues that they may not consciously acknowledge as needs, such as the need for forgiveness and acceptance by a holy God.

Let us examine some of the felt needs that we may encounter today. For several years it has been acknowledged that in the so-called Third World countries fear is an important felt need in the lives of most people—fear of demons, of sickness and death, of the future, of the "evil eye" of jealous people, of reprisals by gods who have been neglected or rejected, and of powerful people in society. But recently fear has become a dominant emotion in the affluent West too; fear of the unknown (esp. the future) is leading many people to turn to astrology or to go to witches and mediums for advice. More recently there is the rampant fear because of insecurity in the workplace. These fears provide us with an opportunity to present God as sovereign over history and more powerful than all the forces of this world.

The growing interest in spirituality in the West (cf. esp. New Age spirituality and the charismatic movement) is an indication that people have realized that mere technology is not enough. This is an expression of the incurable religiousness of the human being (cf. v. 27). The quest for a meaningful spiritual experience is a key aspect of the shift from modernism (with its ultra-rationalism) to postmodernism (with its rejection of rationalism). Unfortunately many see the church as a child of modernism and infer that it will not meet this need. But we know that the legitimate aspiration for authentic spiritual existence can be fulfilled only in Christ, who came that we might have life to the full (John 10:10). Included in this full life is the fulfillment of all legitimate human aspiration. In other words, we must rediscover biblical spirituality, which alone fulfills the human thirst for the divine.

Christ fulfills the acknowledged human need for meaning in life, for living a righteous life, for having a clear conscience, and for victory over weak-

---

48. See the studies on 2:14—41 and 16:11—40.

ness and illness. He meets the need for peace, joy, and love. The church must face the challenge to love people enough to observe them carefully so that we may know what their felt needs and aspirations are. Once we know them, we must seek to make the connection between what they are looking for and what Christ can and will give them. We must point out that without Christ they are missing the purpose of life; the resulting unfulfillment can be satisfied only by Christ.

God's of this age or God of the ages?[49] It is vital to lay the foundation of who God is early in our gospel presentation to those who do not have a biblical worldview. How can people realize the need for a Savior from sin unless they realize the seriousness of sin and its consequences? And how can they realize the seriousness of sin unless they know about the holy God against whom our sin is committed? How can they appreciate what Christ did for them unless they understand God's horror over sin and the price he paid to redeem us? Why should they go through the hassle of changing religions unless they realize that to turn to God is to turn to the supreme Creator and Lord of the universe?

If this is who God is, then the wisest thing his creatures can do is to align themselves with the Lord God. Threats of reprisals from false gods and from family and friends keep people from accepting the gospel. This deterrent to commitment will lose its power if people realize that displeasing the sovereign Creator and Lord of the universe is far more serious than displeasing mere creatures. So Paul's wisdom in presenting God as the Creator and Lord of all is evident.

As we take the gospel out today, we will encounter a wide variety of erroneous understandings of God. Secular humanists think that the idea of God is a crutch, perhaps needed by weak people, but not by self-made people like themselves. Atheists and scientific materialists claim that science has proved that there is no God and that the existence of the world can be accounted for without bringing God into the equation. Many Buddhists think of the gods as inferior to the Buddha, perhaps needed to perform small favors but certainly not worthy of the position of Lord of their lives. Animists and polytheists see several gods responsible for different aspects of life, who can be appeased by following magic-like formulas. Many Buddhists and Hindus, and even some Roman Catholics, have given God-like status to images of their gods or to holy men. Muslims see God as so transcendent and distant from humanity that we can only be slaves, depending on his mercy, not children basking in his love. Pantheistic Hindus and New Age adherents see God as being in everything, including oneself.

---

49. This is the title of a book by Carl F. H. Henry (Nashville: Broadman & Holman, 1994).

Even those in contact with the church may not fully apprehend the gospel because of a false idea of God. The children of tyrannical or unfaithful fathers may recoil from the idea of the fatherhood of God and be repelled by our presentation of God. A person attracted to Christianity through a felt need that God satisfied through prayer may relate to God as one relates to a doctor. They will go to him with their needs but not think of yielding to his lordship over their lives. The person introduced to the love of God without an understanding of his holiness may take sin lightly and be unafraid to keep on sinning and going back to God to receive forgiveness.

The above list of misconceptions about God shows us again that we have much homework to do to ensure that in sharing the gospel we build our message on the right foundation. The seriousness of our evangelistic task and the need to dedicate ourselves to it with all our energies and creative powers are themes seen throughout the book of Acts. Paul's ministry in Athens is particularly vivid in presenting us with these challenges.

Acts 18:1-22

⚜

AFTER THIS, PAUL left Athens and went to Corinth. ²There he met a Jew named Aquila, a native of Pontus, who had recently come from Italy with his wife Priscilla, because Claudius had ordered all the Jews to leave Rome. Paul went to see them, ³and because he was a tent-maker as they were, he stayed and worked with them. ⁴Every Sabbath he reasoned in the synagogue, trying to persuade Jews and Greeks.

⁵When Silas and Timothy came from Macedonia, Paul devoted himself exclusively to preaching, testifying to the Jews that Jesus was the Christ. ⁶But when the Jews opposed Paul and became abusive, he shook out his clothes in protest and said to them, "Your blood be on your own heads! I am clear of my responsibility. From now on I will go to the Gentiles."

⁷Then Paul left the synagogue and went next door to the house of Titius Justus, a worshiper of God. ⁸Crispus, the synagogue ruler, and his entire household believed in the Lord; and many of the Corinthians who heard him believed and were baptized.

⁹One night the Lord spoke to Paul in a vision: "Do not be afraid; keep on speaking, do not be silent. ¹⁰For I am with you, and no one is going to attack and harm you, because I have many people in this city." ¹¹So Paul stayed for a year and a half, teaching them the word of God.

¹²While Gallio was proconsul of Achaia, the Jews made a united attack on Paul and brought him into court. ¹³"This man," they charged, "is persuading the people to worship God in ways contrary to the law."

¹⁴Just as Paul was about to speak, Gallio said to the Jews, "If you Jews were making a complaint about some misdemeanor or serious crime, it would be reasonable for me to listen to you. ¹⁵But since it involves questions about words and names and your own law—settle the matter yourselves. I will not be a judge of such things." ¹⁶So he had them ejected from the court. ¹⁷Then they all turned on Sosthenes the synagogue ruler and beat him in front of the court. But Gallio showed no concern whatever.

¹⁸Paul stayed on in Corinth for some time. Then he left the brothers and sailed for Syria, accompanied by Priscilla and Aquila. Before he sailed, he had his hair cut off at Cenchrea because of a vow he had taken. ¹⁹They arrived at Ephesus, where Paul left Priscilla and Aquila. He himself went into the synagogue and reasoned with the Jews. ²⁰When they asked him to spend more time with them, he declined. ²¹But as he left, he promised, "I will come back if it is God's will." Then he set sail from Ephesus. ²²When he landed at Caesarea, he went up and greeted the church and then went down to Antioch.

AFTER PAUL LEFT Athens, he went further south to Corinth, the capital of Achaia and the third largest city in the Roman empire in the first century A.D., next only to Rome and Alexandria. It is said to have had a population of about 200,000, at least twenty times that of Athens. Because modern Corinth is three miles away from ancient Corinth, the latter has been accessible to archaeological exploration.

Paul in Corinth (18:1)

CORINTH WAS SITUATED on the Isthmus of Corinth, the narrow neck of land that joins central Greece to the Peloponnese, the peninsula that forms the southern part of mainland Greece. It had two harbors, one on the east of the isthmus and the other on the west, and it had a three-and-one-half-mile long railroad of wooden logs over which ships were dragged from one harbor to the other. The main north-south land routes also converged here. Thus, Corinth became a prosperous city, having the feel of an economic "boom town." It was the center for the worship of Aphrodite, the Greek goddess of love, and had a temple with a thousand sacred prostitutes. From the fifth century B.C. on, the verb "to corinthianize" meant to be sexually immoral.[1]

Paul reports that he came to Corinth "in weakness and fear, and with much trembling" (1 Cor. 2:3). This is understandable considering the pain he had endured in his last few stops. Despite the divine call to Macedonia, he had been driven out of all three Macedonian cities in which he ministered. From Athens he "was dismissed with polite contempt rather than being violently driven out."[2] He was worried about the situation in Thessalonica and

---

1. The above description of Corinth has been gleaned from Bruce, *Steps*, 41–42; Longenecker, "Acts," 480; S. J. Hafemann, "Letters to the Corinthians," *DPL*, 172–73.
2. Longenecker, "Acts," 479.

eagerly awaited the arrival of Silas and Timothy from there (1 Thess. 2:17–3:5). Paul may not have anticipated encountering much receptivity to his message in Corinth because of its prosperity and reputation for immorality. But he stayed here for over a year and a half and saw the founding of "a large and gifted, if volatile, church." Bruce writes, "It is plain from his two letters to the Corinthians that the church which he planted there caused him many a headache; it was turbulent and unruly, but it was undoubtedly alive, and remains so to this day."[3]

Evangelizing Corinth (18:2–11)

IN CORINTH PAUL, without his companions Silas and Timothy, was blessed with the acquaintance of Aquila and Priscilla, who had recently been expelled from Rome along with other Jews (v. 2).[4] We cannot be sure whether this husband and wife were already Christians, though most scholars have assumed they were, especially since Paul went to live with them. Like Paul, they were "tentmakers," and they soon became business partners.

What exactly is meant by the term *tentmaker* is disputed. Tents in those days were either made of leather or of *cilicium*, a cloth of woven goat's hair named after Paul's native province Cilicia.[5] Paul worked on tents during the week (v. 3), probably doing some personal witnessing along the way, and had a more public ministry in the synagogue every Sabbath (v. 4). This ministry is described in familiar words: "reasoned" (*dialegomai*) and "trying to persuade" (*peitho*).[6] In every new city Paul visited, he looked for a bridgehead from which he could launch his ministry.[7] Here it was his trade and his contacts in the synagogue.

While Paul was doing this work, his colleagues Silas and Timothy arrived from Macedonia with great news of how the church there was thriving under persecution (v. 5a; 1 Thess. 3:6–10). They probably brought gifts from Macedonia for support of his work (2 Cor. 11:8–9; Phil. 4:15–16), and as a result he was able to devote "himself exclusively to preaching" (v. 5b). While this probably means that he gave up his tentmaking to go into full-time evangelism, the word translated "devoted" (*synecho*)[8] can also be translated "began to be engrossed,"[9] which may suggest that the arrival of his colleagues with

---

3. Bruce, *Steps*, 44.

4. On this expulsion see comments on 17:1–10.

5. See Polhill, *Acts*, 383.

6. See comments on 17:2–4.

7. See the discussion of 16:11–40

8. This word is translated "constrains" or "compels" in 2 Cor. 5:14: "For Christ's love compels us."

9. See the discussion in Zerwick and Grosvenor, *Analysis*, 412.

such good news acted as a shot in the arm to Paul and thus propelled him into more intense ministry. Robertson translates this word with the next phrase in the Greek (*to logo:* "in reference to the word") as "was constrained by the word" and adds the comment: 'The coming of Silas with gifts from Macedonia . . . set Paul free from tent-making for a while so that he began to devote himself . . . with fresh concentration to preaching."[10]

Paul's proclamation is described as "testifying to the Jews that Jesus was the Christ" (v. 5c). The word translated "testifying" (*diamartyromai*) appears fifteen times in the New Testament (nine in Acts); it is usually translated "warn" or "testify" and has been defined as "to make a serious declaration on the basis of presumed personal knowledge."[11] It reminds us that while evangelism is a joyous privilege, it is also an awesome responsibility. Verse 6 further illustrates a sense of the seriousness of the message as it describes Paul's response when the Jews became abusive (*blasphemeo*): "He shook out his clothes in protest" of their blasphemous attitude and as an expression of his exemption from further responsibility for them.[12] He then explicitly stated this exemption with the familiar words: "Your blood be on your own heads! I am clear of my responsibility," and announced his intention to concentrate on the Gentiles.

Leaving the synagogue, Paul went to the home of Titius Justus, which became the center of the young church in Corinth (v. 7) and was probably where its first house church met.[13] Romans 16:23 refers to Gaius, who provided hospitality for the whole church in Corinth, but Gaius may be another name of Titius.[14] If Gaius provided hospitality to the whole church, he must have had a big house, which meant he was wealthy. The Corinthian letters indicate that the church in Corinth had a few wealthy "urban élites,"[15] but that the majority of the members were "at the lower end of the socioeconomic ladder."[16] Recently there has been much discussion on the social composition of the Corinthian church.[17] It seems that the few wealthy members of the congregation exercised "an influence all out of proportion to their numbers."[18]

---

10. Robertson, *Word Pictures: Acts*, 296.

11. Louw and Nida, 413.

12. Longenecker, "Acts," 483.

13. On house churches, see discussion of 2:42—47.

14. Leon Morris, *The Epistle to the Romans* (Grand Rapids: Eerdmans, 1988), 544.

15. David W. J. Gill, "Acts and the Urban Élites," *BAFCS*, vol. 2, *Graeco-Roman Setting* (1994), 109—13.

16. Gordon Fee, *The First Epistle to the Corinthians*, NICNT (1987), 4.

17. Wayne A. Meeks, *The First Urban Christians: The Social World of the Apostle Paul* (New Haven: Yale Univ. Press, 1983).

18. Craig Blomberg, *1 Corinthians*, NIVAC (Grand Rapids: Zondervan, 1994), 20. Blomberg explains that these richer members may have acted as "patrons," who considered

In addition to the open door provided by Titius, the conversion of "Crispus, the synagogue ruler" (v. 8), must have done much to encourage Paul in his disappointment over his rejection by his kinsmen, the Jews. We note here again that we have an instance of a whole household coming to Christ.[19] But the biggest encouragement came from a vision Paul had in which the Lord promised to protect him and told him that he had "many people [*laos*] in this city" (vv. 9−10). The use of *laos* for the prospective Corinthian believers is the usual designation for Israel as the people of God. This shows that now the people of God "embraces all believers without distinction, Gentiles as well as Jews."[20] As a result of these encouraging signs, Paul stayed in Corinth "for a year and a half, teaching them the word of God" (v. 11).

Gallio's Crucial Verdict (18:12−17)

LUKE DOES NOT describe Paul's relatively long ministry in Corinth in much detail. His emphasis is on the response to Christianity of the proconsul Gallio, who was a well-known figure in the Roman empire. His proconsulship of Achaia is attested in an inscription found in Delphi dated around A.D. 52 and in the writings of his famous brother, the Stoic philosopher Seneca.[21] His positive response toward Christianity was a key building block in the church's case for a positive legal standing in the Roman empire.

The Jews brought Paul to Gallio, charging him with "persuading the people to worship God in ways contrary to the law" (v. 13). The reason behind making this charge was to show that Christianity was not truly Jewish and therefore could not be included with Judaism or claim protection under Roman law. Gallio did not even give time for Paul to speak. Rather, he said that what Paul was doing was not a crime for him to judge; it was instead a matter of Jewish law, and he was not going to tackle issues pertaining to their theology (vv. 14−15). The ejection of the Jews from the court (v. 16) resulted in the ruler of the synagogue being beaten by the people (not Christians, we hope!). Unfortunately, Gallio did not interfere to stop the beating (v. 17).

Itinerating En Route to Antioch (18:18−22)

THANKS TO GALLIO'S favorable ruling, Paul was able to stay on in Corinth after he had been brought to trial. But after some time he set off for Antioch, taking Aquila and Priscilla with him (vv. 18−19a). Paul went into the synagogue

---

the poorer members as their "clients," thus perpetuating the class structure that was prevalent in Corinth.

19. See the discussion on 16:11−40.

20. Bruce, *Acts*, NICNT, 349. On this see Gooding, *True to the Faith*, 316−21.

21. Hemer, *Acts*, 168−69.

in Ephesus, reasoned with the Jews (v. 19b), and won an invitation to spend more time with them. He declined it with the promise that he would return if it was God's will (vv. 20–21). It is interesting that earlier too he had "been kept by the Holy Spirit from preaching the word in the province of Asia" (16:6). Now for a second time he seemed to discern that the time was not ripe for a full-blown ministry in Ephesus.

Paul left Aquila and Priscilla behind in Ephesus and set off for Caesarea, where he "greeted the church and then went down to Antioch" (v. 22). One would not go "down" to an inland city from a coastal city. This has led scholars to assume that the church he greeted was the church in Jerusalem, from which we could then speak of Paul traveling "down" to Antioch.[22] This ended Paul's second missionary journey.

Luke adds a note about Paul's having his hair cut in connection with a vow he had taken before leaving Cenchrea, the eastern port of Corinth (v. 18). Hair was cut (usually shaven) after completion of a vow. It would probably be taken to Jerusalem and offered to God. Many have felt that Paul took this vow when he was in a discouraged state at the start of his ministry in Corinth, or perhaps in connection with the vision he received with the promise of God's blessing. If so, cutting his hair was an act of thanksgiving for protection while in Corinth.[23]

EVANGELISM IN PROFLIGATE **places**. It is significant that the church in the notoriously profligate city of Corinth was founded by Paul, whom we know as being forthright in his call for moral purity among Christians and strict about dealing with immorality in the church. He was obviously uneasy when he went to Corinth for more reasons than one (1 Cor. 2:3). But he persevered in ministry and was responsible for founding a church that still exists almost twenty centuries later. While Christians may be reluctant to work in such places, those living there also need the Savior and are not beyond redemption.

Of course the Corinthian church was a scandal-ridden church. Just as Isaiah had said that while living among a people of unclean lips, his lips too had become unclean (Isa. 6:5), the church in Corinth was not immune to influence by the sins of the culture around it. Some will succumb to temptations that come from the environment around them. But such an environ-

---

22. See Bruce, *Acts*, NICNT, 357. Bruce directs us to 11:27, which says that a group of prophets "came down" to Antioch from Jerusalem.

23. On Paul's vow see the comments in Longenecker, "Acts," 488.

ment did not cause Paul to give up on this church. He wrote urgent letters to it, two of which made their way into the Bible, presenting remedies for their maladies. We too are challenged to have a burden for the evangelization of the Corinths of today.

Tentmaking. Paul sometimes did manual labor as a tentmaker in order to meet his needs (v. 3), and the term *tentmaking* is much in vogue today. Christians who work at a paid job with the hope that it will open doors for Christian ministry are called tentmakers. From Paul's words regarding this activity we see that he did this for two reasons: out of necessity and out of a desire to maintain his credibility as a servant of Christ.[24]

This does not mean that it is unscriptural for so-called "full-time" Christian workers to be paid for their services. Paul argues that the church should pay its workers adequately (1 Cor. 9:1–12a). "But," he says, "we did not use this right. On the contrary, we put up with anything rather than hinder the gospel of Christ" (9:12b). Thus, while we must not relegate paid workers to a lower status because they are paid for their services,[25] we must remember that there is a great tradition in the Bible of people, such as Nehemiah and Daniel, who while doing other jobs, fulfilled great tasks usually associated with paid workers.

Evangelism as a serious responsibility. This passage clearly illustrates the seriousness of one's personal responsibility to evangelism. Our look at the word translated "testify" (*diamartyromai*; v. 5) pointed to the personal responsibility of those who have found the truth to testify to it. This serious responsibility is illustrated in the Old Testament story of the four lepers outside the starving city of Samaria. They discovered that not only had the besieging army left, but they had also left behind food and treasures. After a hearty meal and a plundering session they realized that their wonderful discovery also brought with it a great responsibility. So they said, "We're not doing right. This is a day of good news and we are keeping it to ourselves. If we wait until daylight, punishment will overtake us. Let's go at once and report this to the royal palace" (2 Kings 7:9).

This idea appears again in Ezekiel 3:18–19, which presents the prophet as God's watchman who must warn the wicked of their sin and of impending judgment:

> When I say to a wicked man, "You will surely die," and you do not warn
> him or speak out to dissuade him from his evil ways in order to save

---

24. See also 20:34; 1 Cor. 4:12; 9:3–18; 1 Thess. 2:9; 2 Thess. 3:8; cf. 2 Cor. 11:7.

25. This is hardly a problem in today's church. Even volunteers are sometimes paid for their services, and the concept of making great personal sacrifices for the sake of the gospel, though part of the basic biblical lifestyle, is becoming less and less popular.

his life, that wicked man will die for his sin, and I will hold you accountable for his blood. But if you do warn the wicked man and he does not turn from his wickedness or from his evil ways, he will die for his sin; but you will have saved yourself.

While we are responsible to share the message faithfully, we are not responsible for the response of our audience. In fact, if we face continued refusal to consider the claims we present, we may come to the stage where we can wash our hands of the responsibility and move to a more receptive group of people (cf. v. 6).

God's encouragement. Paul arrived in Corinth as a discouraged man. The reaction of the Jews to his message did not help improve this situation (cf. v. 6). But in this passage we have four clear instances of God's encouragement, which did much to enable him to persevere with his ministry there for eighteen months. (1) Paul established a friendship with fellow tentmakers Aquila and Priscilla, who became his partners in ministry (vv. 2–3). Few things encourage a lonely traveler as much as welcoming him or her into a loving Christian family. (2) As the synagogue doors were closing to Paul, God opened the door of the home next door (v. 7). (3) Although by and large the Jews rejected the gospel, the synagogue ruler, Crispus, and his entire family were converted (v. 8). (4) The greatest of encouragement was the Lord's vision to Paul (vv. 9–10). We have already seen how God reassures his troubled servants at crucial times (4:31).[26] Here we see this comfort from the Lord with even greater clarity. Such comfort is an almost essential ingredient for persevering ministry in a fallen world.

Are vows for us? Many readers may be surprised to find Paul performing vows (v. 18), which they see as alien to the spirit of Christianity. The New Testament, outside Acts, says little about vows except to warn about their misuse (Matt. 5:34–37). But we have two instances in Acts in which Paul made vows, which may suggest that they deserve a second look. This is especially so because they were an integral part of biblical religion in the Old Testament. Paul, being a Jew, continued to practice this discipline, which, though not mandatory, was regarded as helpful for one's spiritual health.

Vows have always been important within Roman Catholicism, but the Reformers reacted to them "on the grounds that, amongst other things, they implied a form of righteousness by works, [and] imposed human obligations that were not demanded by Christ."[27] R. J. Song has shown that John Calvin, however,

---

26. See the discussion on 4:23–31.
27. R. J. Song, "Promises," *NDCEPT*, 695.

regarded them as a valuable tool for personal spiritual discipline and laid down rules for their use.... Handled discerningly and with imagination, vows could be a God-given resource to strengthen resolve and enable one to rise above immediate circumstances, and to restore continuity to our lives fractured by the pressures of a disorienting world.[28]

We should take a second look at this practice as a source of spiritual help.

EVANGELIZING THE CORINTHS of today. As we think of the challenge of evangelizing the Corinths of today, we might be compelled to conclude that the whole world has become a Corinth. The rampant disregard for moral standards is no longer confined to a few cities. It is brought right into homes through television. The church is inevitably affected by it. Just as some Corinthian Christians succumbed to the temptations surrounding them, contemporary Christians also give in to the loose moral lifestyles portrayed in the media. Sadly, it seems that far too many have been doing this, so much so that in certain Western countries the percentage of Christians involved in extramarital sexual activity is not different from the percentage in the rest of society.[29] Even Christian ministers and evangelists succumb to immorality. There is equal cause for concern in the Third World church.

What is equally as bad, churches seem reluctant to be forthright in condemning these sins. Some leaders think that they have no right to pry into the personal lives of other people, so they ignore what they hear about their members. Perhaps with the marketing orientation that has hit ecclesiastical thinking (large congregations being seen as a sign of success), preachers are afraid to condemn sin because they might lose some of their people to the church "down the road."

This is all contrary to Paul's attitude. He urged the church in Corinth to take urgent action against such sins in the church. "And you are proud! Shouldn't you rather have been filled with grief and have put out of your fellowship the man who did this?... God will judge those outside. 'Expel the wicked man from among you.'" (1 Cor. 5:2, 13). The fact that the Corinthians

---

28. Ibid., citing John Calvin, *Institutes of the Christian Religion*, 4.12.

29. Statistical evidence for this is given in Gene Edward Veith Jr., *Postmodern Times: A Christian Guide to Contemporary Thought and Culture* (Wheaton: Crossway, 1994), 17–18. As an occasional visitor to the West, I must say that I am amazed at the risks some Christians take in their relationships with those of the opposite sex. They seem to be quite oblivious to the warnings in the Bible about caution in this area.

lived in an immoral culture did not cause Paul to lower his moral standards. God calls us to go out into this immoral world as witnesses not only to his love but also to his holiness. The church must show the world that one can be morally pure and that this is the best, the happiest, way to live.

Today's tentmakers. There has been a surge of interest in tentmaking ministry over the past two decades.[30] Situations today may require tentmakers for the same two reasons that Paul had: economic necessity and credibility. In certain situations, where there is no trust yet concerning the Christian workers, it may be best for them not to take support from the people to whom they minister (cf. 1 Cor. 9). Sometimes a work cannot afford to support a worker. This is true of churches in poorer areas and in predominantly non-Christian cultures.

Sometimes a church may have some workers who are full-time and others who are tentmakers. I know of vibrant churches in Sri Lanka and the United States where the senior pastors do so-called "secular" jobs while some paid full-time workers are also on the staff. Tentmakers bring great enrichment to a ministerial team in that they have much more intimate contact with the world, which can enhance the team's relevance and impact on the culture. Ruth Siemens writes, "The secular job is not an inconvenience, but the God-given context in which tentmakers live out the gospel in a winsome, wholesome, non-judgmental way, demonstrating personal integrity, doing quality work and developing caring relationships."[31]

It is on the mission field that tentmaking is becoming most valuable. In fact Ruth Siemens feels that the international job market, a key feature in today's business world, "is an argument for tentmaking because it does not exist by accident, but by God's design." She describes it as God's "'repopulation program,' transferring millions of hard-to-reach people into freer countries (Turks to Germany, Algerians to France, Kurds to Austria, etc.), and opening doors for Christians in hard-to-enter countries—so that many can hear the gospel!"[32] Here are some of the examples she gives:

A tentmaker couple translated the New Testament for five million Muslims while he did university teaching and she tutored English! A science teacher evangelized his students in rural Kenya, and preached

---

30. See Don Hamilton, *Tentmakers Speak* (Glendale: Regal, 1987); Ruth Siemens, "Tentmakers Needed for World Evangelization," *Perspectives on the World Christian Movement: A Reader,* eds. Ralph D. Winter and Steven C. Hawthorne, rev. ed. (Pasadena: William Carey Library, 1992), D–246–54; J. Christy Wilson Jr., *Today's Tentmakers* (Wheaton, Ill.: Tyndale, 1979); Tetsunao Yamamori, *God's New Envoys* (Portland: Multnomah, 1987).

31. Siemens, "Tentmakers," D–247.

32. Ibid., D–249.

every third Sunday in the local church. A symphony violinist in Singapore had Bible studies with fellow musicians. A faculty person and an engineer set up a Christian bookstore in the Arab Gulf region.[33]

I know of Christians who sometime take jobs in difficult and unreached areas of their own country, such as the inner city or a remote village, so that they can witness in those places. Thus, when challenging Christians to missions, which we should all be doing, we can also place before them the possibility of going as tentmakers to needy places.

Implications of "evangelism as responsibility" thinking. With almost embarrassing repetitiveness this commentary has been highlighting the priority of evangelism in a church's agenda.[34] The focus in this study of the Corinthian ministry is on the personal responsibility of Christians to testify to God's truth. With today's aversion to guilt (possibly because our generation does not know the freedom of forgiveness), many are reluctant to push this aspect of personal responsibility in the church. We speak of how we should witness and the joy of doing it. But sometimes the anticipation of joy in witness is overcome by fear of rejection and failure or by spiritual lethargy, so that we do not fulfill our calling to witness for Christ. At such times a sense of responsibility can be a great help. We may not feel like doing it, but we know we should be doing it, and so we do it. And after doing it we are usually glad, for we have become channels through which the Spirit's love flows.

Yet we are sobered by the knowledge that, just as the master evangelist Paul experienced rejection, so will we. Our own people may reject the message. We may have to give them stern words of warning, as Paul did with the Jews. We may even move away from them because of their contempt for the truth. But, like Paul, we will not lose our yearning for them. We will mourn their rejection of the gospel (Rom. 9:1–3) and pray for their salvation (10:1). And may Paul's stern rebuke to the hardhearted Jews never be used as an excuse for anti-Semitism!

We must be careful about making absolute principles out of Paul's action of moving away from ministering to the Jews in Corinth (v. 6). Some people have a worldview so different to ours that it may take a long time for them to understand the gospel or be receptive to it. God may be calling us to dedicate an entire career in ministry to serve among a resistant people and not see any visible fruit. Our calling may be to prepare unproductive ground for a harvest that comes after we die. But this passage does give us freedom to ask whether groups we are seeking to reach for Christ have hardened their

33. Ibid., D–247.
34. See the section on "importance of evangelism" in the index at the back.

hearts so much through their blasphemous attitude that we are released from our responsibility to them, so that we can concentrate on others.

Winter sunshine. In an earlier study we noted how God's specific acts of encouragement can give us a strong sense of his presence and assist us to persevere in our calling.[35] Here we will look at the great blessing that flows from God's specific intervention on our behalf. All of life is tinged with pain and frustration. That is an inevitable result of the curse that accompanied the Fall (Rom. 8:20). So the familiar song—"Oh what a beautiful morning! O what a beautiful day! I've got a beautiful feeling, Everything's going my way!"—is almost never true. Yet we have a capacity for pleasure and enjoyment that cannot be denied. Can we be happy if life is tinged with frustration and if the possibility of pain always looms above us?

A peasant living in the woods composed a brilliant piece of music called "Winter Sunshine." In this piece, "against a subdued and even somber background, there stood out melodious patches of remarkable beauty and infectious gaiety." When asked about the inspiration behind this piece, he replied that he "had always held that the happiest man on the face of the earth is the man who can make most of the sunshine that breaks up and brightens the winter."[36] For a Christian the bursts of sunshine that God gives us in the midst of our deepest crises are evidences that he is with us, that he will see us through. Such truths provide a sudden release from the grip of gloom, and we are liberated to give ourselves to unfettered celebration. Only the grasp of the eternal God can help us to be truly happy in the midst of trouble. And if we can have happiness in the winter, we are truly happy people.

Evangelicals and vows. Most Protestants today have little place for vows. Why? (1) We have seen vows used in an unbiblical way by both Christians and non-Christians. People have used vows in a somewhat magical way: "We will do this so that we can get that." The vow does not affect daily life or enhance commitment; rather, it is a means of getting what we want. A Christian use of vows in a given situation should be different. Rather than being an act of bargaining with God, it is a means of affirming that we do not trust in ourselves but in him alone. Viewed in this way, vows will help us focus on God. We should always welcome that, given our tendency to focus on the things of the world rather than on God.

(2) We have neglected the symbolic in our understanding of Christianity, in part because we have spiritualized the Old Testament ritual. Now that the real thing has come in Christ, we feel these shadows are unnecessary. This is, to a great extent, true. Only people who do not experience the real thing—

---

35. See comments on 4:23–31.
36. F. W. Boreham, *The Last Milestone* (London: Epworth, 1961), 36.

a heart-to-heart relationship with God—need symbols. But we know that even in this era of the new covenant with its intimate tie with God through the Spirit, we are at times prone to forget certain spiritual truths as we get engrossed in the affairs of life.

This is one reason why we still need the Lord's Day—to remind us that every day belongs to the Lord. We still need the Lord's Supper to remind us of the significance of what Christ did for us. In a similar way, we may still find vows helpful to bring to special focus spiritual realities that we are prone to forget. If the climax of Paul's vow focused on thanksgiving, then it touches on an area that we are often weak in. We pray earnestly for something, but neglect to thank God after he answers the prayer. Bringing in a structure like a vow can help us avoid this serious oversight. We will do well, then, to incorporate into our spiritual walk certain special spiritual exercises like vows to help us put first things first in life.

Acts 18:23–19:7

A FTER SPENDING SOME time in Antioch, Paul set out from there and traveled from place to place throughout the region of Galatia and Phrygia, strengthening all the disciples.

24Meanwhile a Jew named Apollos, a native of Alexandria, came to Ephesus. He was a learned man, with a thorough knowledge of the Scriptures. 25He had been instructed in the way of the Lord, and he spoke with great fervor and taught about Jesus accurately, though he knew only the baptism of John. 26He began to speak boldly in the synagogue. When Priscilla and Aquila heard him, they invited him to their home and explained to him the way of God more adequately.

27When Apollos wanted to go to Achaia, the brothers encouraged him and wrote to the disciples there to welcome him. On arriving, he was a great help to those who by grace had believed. 28For he vigorously refuted the Jews in public debate, proving from the Scriptures that Jesus was the Christ.

19:1While Apollos was at Corinth, Paul took the road through the interior and arrived at Ephesus. There he found some disciples 2and asked them, "Did you receive the Holy Spirit when you believed?"

They answered, "No, we have not even heard that there is a Holy Spirit."

3So Paul asked, "Then what baptism did you receive?"

"John's baptism," they replied.

4Paul said, "John's baptism was a baptism of repentance. He told the people to believe in the one coming after him, that is, in Jesus." 5On hearing this, they were baptized into the name of the Lord Jesus. 6When Paul placed his hands on them, the Holy Spirit came on them, and they spoke in tongues and prophesied. 7There were about twelve men in all.

LUKE NOW RECORDS the start of another missionary journey for Paul, as he sets out from Antioch for a third time. Most of what happens in these verses occurs in Ephesus, the most prominent city in the Roman province of Asia and the city where Aquila and Priscilla stayed after they and Paul left Corinth (18:19).

Paul's Third Journey Begins (18:23)

PAUL'S THIRD MISSIONARY journey began from Antioch with visits to Galatia and Phrygia, regions that he had previously evangelized. Galatia had been evangelized during Paul's first journey. Phrygia is mentioned two other times in Acts: There were people from Phrygia in Jerusalem on the day of Pentecost (2:10), and Paul traveled through that region during his time of uncertainty before he received his Macedonian call (16:6). In these two regions Paul "traveled from place to place . . . strengthening all the disciples." He had done this type of strengthening ministry before (14:21–22; 15:41; cf. 9:32).

The Completion of Apollos (18:24–28)

THOUGH PERGAMUM WAS the capital of Asia, Ephesus (in modern Turkey) was the real seat of provincial administration. Being on the western shore of Asia Minor, it connected the Greco-Roman world with Asia Minor. In the first century it was a predominantly Greek city. It had a seaport on the mouth of the Caystar River, but it was subject to constant silting, which required dredging. Once the city diminished in importance, this dredging was not done; as a result, the site of Ephesus is now seven miles inland. The ancient harbor is now a marshy waste, though it can still be discerned in photographs.[1] Ephesus was at the end of the Arcadian Way—a magnificent paved road that is still visible—which led from the center of town to the harbor. Because it does not have any modern settlements, it is, in Bruce's words, "an archaeologist's paradise."[2]

Ephesus was the center of the worship of the Greek goddess Artemis (Roman Diana), the multibreasted goddess of fertility. It boasted a magnificent temple to Artemis, which was considered one of the seven wonders of the ancient world. In Paul's time the city had lost some of its importance as a political and commercial center and was turning more to the temple to support its economy.[3] In Christian tradition the city is associated more with John than with Paul. The second-century church father Irenaeus wrote that John went there after his exile on the Isle of Patmos and lived there to be an old man.[4]

A learned Old Testament scholar, Apollos, receives an important place in this narrative because he played a significant role in the growth of the early church. Luke thus interrupts his description of Paul's journey to insert a section on the "completion" of Apollos's understanding of the gospel. This provides the only Christian contact we have in the New Testament with the

---

1. See the photograph in Bruce, *Steps*, 45 (which is also the cover photo).
2. Ibid., 46.
3. Longenecker, "Acts," 493.
4. Irenaeus, *Against Heresies*, 3.3.4, in *The Ante-Nicene Fathers*, ed. Alexander Roberts and James Donaldson (Grand Rapids: Eerdmans, 1996 reprint), 416.

Egyptian city of Alexandria (18:24),[5] which became the intellectual center of Christianity and produced some of the greatest scholars of early Christianity (notably Clement and Origen). It had a large Jewish population, which included (until about A.D. 50) the famous philosopher Philo.[6] Apollos's eloquence was surely a foretaste of things to come from that city. "He appears to have been an itinerant Jew of a type not uncommon in the first Christian century—a commercial traveler who engaged in religious teaching as well as in trade."[7]

We are not told from where Apollos first heard about Jesus. The Western Text's addition to verse 25 says that he had been instructed "in his own country," implying that Christianity had reached Alexandria by about A.D. 50.[8] It may be that disciples of John who accepted Christ as the Messiah had gone there and taught him, for we are told that "he knew only the baptism of John" (v. 25). But we cannot say for sure where he had been deficient in his teaching.

Apollos's effectiveness as a preacher is put down to three factors. (1) "He was a learned man with a thorough knowledge of the Scriptures" (18:24b), having been well "instructed in the way of the Lord" (18:25a). (2) "He spoke with great fervor" (18:25b). (3) He "taught about Jesus accurately" (18:25c). He not only had a good knowledge of the Word, but he also knew how to communicate it accurately—that is, he had developed skills in Bible teaching. And when he taught, he did so with enthusiasm and fervency.

Into this situation Priscilla and Aquila entered (18:26). Luke has changed the order of their names from his first mention of them (18:2), giving the wife's name first (see also 18:18–19).[9] On two occasions when Paul sends greetings to this couple, he mentions Priscilla first (Rom. 16:3; 2 Tim. 4:19), while Aquila is mentioned first when they send greetings through Paul (1 Cor. 16:19). On that occasion "it is quite credible that Priscilla insisted that her husband's name be put first."[10] Priscilla may have been the more prominent of the two.

We are not told whether Apollos lodged in Priscilla and Aquila's home, but this act of inviting Apollos into their home is typical of the open home attitude that this couple had. Though Apollos "was a learned man, with a thorough knowledge of the Scriptures" (18:24b), he was willing to learn

---

5. The city is mentioned in 6:9; 27:6; 28:11, but not in connection with Christians being there.

6. The Septuagint (LXX) had been translated there around the third century B.C.

7. Bruce, Circle, 52.

8. Metzger, Textual, 466.

9. In his letters, Paul uses the more formal name Prisca (though the NIV renders it as Priscilla).

10. Bruce, Circle, 45.

from his hosts when they took him home to "complete his education." We will see that this is a characteristic of a true student of God's Word.

We are not told whether Apollos was rebaptized, as were the Ephesian disciples whom Paul brought to a more complete knowledge of the truth (19:5). Apollos was probably a true believer in Christ with a deficient knowledge. Though there is much dispute about the status of the twelve Ephesian disciples, they had probably made less progress on the way to salvation. The believers in Ephesus sent off Apollos to Achaia with a letter of commendation. The sending of such letters was a common practice in those days (see Rom. 16:1–2).[11]

Luke focuses on Apollos's ministry of apologetics among the unbelieving Jews (18:27–28). This has caused some to suggest that Apollos wrote the letter to the Hebrews; the Pauline elements in this letter are traced to the influence of Priscilla and Aquila and to the believers in Corinth. It seems apparent that the more wealthy and sophisticated members of the church were so impressed by Apollos's eloquence that they clung to him and depreciated the ministry of Paul, who spoke in such a way that the simplest people could understand (1 Cor. 1:12; 4:6). We cannot blame Apollos for this, however. This type of unhealthy comparison still happens among those who do not understand the biblical pattern of a variety of gifts within the body of Christ.

The Completion of Twelve Ephesians (19:1–7)

PAUL HAD WANTED to come to Ephesus for major ministry for quite some time, but he had to wait for God's time (16:6; 18:21), which had now come. It was an important place because from here he could reach the entire province of Asia (19:10). He took the most direct "interior" route from Phrygia-Galatia over mountainous terrain rather than the more customary route closer to the coast (19:1). This enabled him to visit Lystra, Iconium, and Pisidian Antioch. There were believers in Ephesus when he arrived (18:27). They had probably become Christians during Paul's earlier short ministry here, through Priscilla and Aquila, or through someone else (cf. 2:9).

Paul also found some people who are called "disciples" but who were seriously deficient in their beliefs, even though they are said to have "believed" (19:1–2). The debate will continue as to whether or not they were true believers.[12] What is significant is that Paul specifically asked them whether they received the Holy Spirit when they believed (19:2). This suggests that people can really know when they receive the Holy Spirit. The response of these disciples was that they had not even heard that there was a Holy Spirit. Stott is

---

11. Gempf, "Acts," 1096.

12. On the affirmative, see Arrington, Acts, 191; Stronstad, Charismatic Theology of St. Luke, 68–69. On the negative, see Longenecker, "Acts," 493; Stott, Acts, 304.

probably correct that they would have known about the Holy Spirit through the Old Testament and John's prophecy, but that they did not know that John's prophecy had been fulfilled. "They were ignorant of Pentecost."[13] Bruce translates their answer, "We never even heard that the Holy Spirit is available."[14]

The problem was that they had only received John's baptism (19:3). Unlike Apollos, they had not progressed much beyond John's teaching. Hence they needed to be told about believing in Jesus, which led to baptism in his name (19:4—5). This suggests that they were not true believers until then. How then could Luke call them "disciples" (v. 1), and how could Paul refer to them as having "believed" (v. 2)? Longenecker says, "Luke's practice is to portray the spiritual condition of his characters by their actions without always evaluating it." Note how Luke

> speaks of Simon of Samaria as having "believed" (cf. 8:13), of the Judaizers as "believers" (cf. 15:5), of the seven sons of Sceva as exorcising demons "in the name of Jesus," and of Sceva their father as "a Jewish chief priest" (cf. 19:13—14).... Here it seems, both from their own statements and from how Paul deals with them, that we should consider these men as sectarians with no real commitment to Jesus at all.[15]

Verses 5—6 suggest that it was after they were baptized that "Paul placed his hands on them," resulting in the Spirit's coming on them accompanied by tongues and prophecy.

KEYS TO AN effective Bible teaching ministry. Apollos's ministry reveals three features that characterize an effective Bible teaching ministry: a knowledge of the Word, skill in method, and fervency of spirit (18:24—25). Apollos acquired his basic knowledge of the Word through the instruction he received. But he himself must have diligently given himself to study the Word. The skills of accurate interpretation of the story of Jesus would have come again through instruction by the church and through his applying himself carefully to improve this skill.

But what of fervency? Is this a personality trait that only some have, which enables them to be good preachers? One's personality may be an asset to preaching, but it is not what lies at the heart of fervency. Fervency comes from a confidence in the truth and power of what we proclaim. This, of course,

---

13. Stott, *Acts*, 304.
14. Bruce, *Acts*, NICNT, 362.
15. Longenecker, "Acts," 493.

is ignited by the Holy Spirit. Such confidence is necessary on our part, and it comes through lingering with the Word in trustful meditation, study, and obedience.

Paul cited this as an attitude required of all Christians when he said, "Never be lacking in zeal, but keep your spiritual fervor, serving the Lord" (Rom. 12:11). The same words used there for "spiritual fervor" are used in Acts 18:25 of Apollos. Such people exhibit the fervency of knowledge on fire. They become like Jeremiah, to whom God said, "I will make my words in your mouth a fire" (Jer. 5:14).[16] In other words, time spent in God's Word and confidence in the message give the knowledge, skills, and fervency needed to make a good Bible teacher.

How Bible scholars learn new truths. The learned and eloquent Apollos, who already had "a thorough knowledge of the Scriptures," had still more to learn. Several factors helped facilitate this learning. (1) The graciousness of Aquila and Priscilla was an important element. When they saw a deficiency in his teaching, they did not publicly point it out. Rather, they took him aside privately and invited him into their home (18:26). In the warmth of that accepting environment they taught him what was lacking in his theology.

(2) Apollos's teachable attitude must surely have helped. The truth of God is so vast that we will never plumb its depths or scale its heights. Thus, until the day we die we can be learning. Usually the more we know, the more we recognize that we have so much more to learn. At the heart of a biblical attitude to the Word is a childlike eagerness to be fed. Peter urged, "Like newborn babies, crave pure spiritual milk, so that by it you may grow up in your salvation, now that you have tasted that the Lord is good" (1 Peter 2:2–3). This applies to both new and mature Christians. We are all disciples of Christ, which means we are all learners. The graciousness of the helper and the teachableness of the helpee give an environment conducive to great scholars taking the role of helpee and learning new truths.

Opening our homes to help others in need. The New Testament gives three instances of Priscilla and Aquila's opening their home for service to God: They kept the apostle Paul in their home in Corinth (18:3), they hosted a house church in Rome (Rom. 16:3–5), and they brought Apollos to their home in Ephesus to complete his education (Acts 18:26). This latter is an important type of hospitality—bringing people to our homes to help them in a time of special need. We do not know whether Apollos lodged at this home, but we know that his theological deficiencies were dealt with in the

---

16. This statement inspired the title for Donald G. Miller's book on preaching, *Fire in Thy Mouth* (Nashville: Abingdon, 1954). Cited in Donald E. Demaray, *Preacher Aflame* (Grand Rapids: Baker, 1972), 16.

warmth of a home. We too can use our homes to help people in need. This provides the fourth type of hospitality presented in Acts.[17]

Interpreting the Ephesian Pentecost. What can we make of the Ephesian Pentecost (19:6)? It seems clear that the special experience of the Holy Spirit came to these former disciples of John.[18] The experience of the Spirit was a clearly distinguishable experience, not something that was accepted by faith without being felt. Through that experience they felt the fullness of the Spirit. This agrees with our conclusion presented earlier that baptism with the Holy Spirit implies a fullness, a subjective experience of the Spirit.[19]

But whether the baptism with the Spirit and the subjective experience of him implied in that baptism always take place at the same time or at different times is uncertain. What we insist on is that the Spirit must be experienced. Those who say that the baptism with the Spirit takes place at initiation, that it is only an objective initiation, and that it is not necessarily a subjective experience of the Spirit are missing the point behind the descriptions of the baptism with the Spirit in the Bible. We showed earlier[20] that the baptism implies a fullness and that those who are not experiencing this are having a subbiblical experience.

What should we make of tongues and prophecy? They are certainly the normal signs of the coming of the Spirit in the instances described in Acts. As such we can expect them to be common phenomena today. But to insist on them as normative and essential is going beyond what Scripture permits us to say. What is important is that we have what the baptism implies: an immediacy and fullness of the Spirit, which gives power to witness and live the Christian life. This has been neglected by many evangelicals, and we are thankful for groups like the Wesleyan holiness and the charismatic movements, which have recently helped refocus attention on this.

BIBLE TEACHING: A **lost art?** There have been mixed reports about the status of Bible teaching in the church today. Some feel it is a lost art, whereas others, especially in Britain, feel that a recovery of it within the church may have recently begun. With the reduction of the habit of reading, contemporary Christians have reduced the aver-

---

17. The other three types are evangelistic (2:42–47; 10:1–33), hosting traveling preachers (9:43; 16:15), and hosting informal fellowship and house churches (2:42–47).

18. Some say much later, while others say almost immediately after being baptized (with the laying on of hands).

19. See discussion on 1:1–8.

20. Ibid.

age time spent with the Word. This is true of preachers too. The thousands of study aids prepared to "take the sweat out of Bible study" may have done just that: taken away the thrill that comes from grappling with Scripture. Today's activist generation finds it difficult to set apart quiet time simply to sit and study the Scriptures. We have developed a laziness about reading and inductive study.

The result is that much of so-called biblical preaching is not very biblical and gives evidence of shoddy Bible study. I am convinced that one of the reasons why Bible exposition has gone out of fashion today is that preachers are not willing to devote the time necessary to study in order to teach the Bible effectively. When we spend time in the Word with a heart open to hearing from God, it will begin to glow because it "is living and active. Sharper than any double-edged sword . . ." (Heb. 4:12). The result will be fervency.

In his classic book *Power in Preaching*, British Methodist preacher W. E. Sangster gives seven basics of good preaching. One of them is fervor or passion, and he entitles his chapter on it, "Glow Over it." He writes, "The glow must be the outward radiance of some burning light within."[21] This characteristic is not limited to those whom we may describe as vibrant personalities. Sangster says, "At the point when one man declaims and gesticulates and uses the whole range of his voice (naturally and convincingly), another stands motionless, his voice almost a quiet monotone but a white heat burning at the heart of all he says."[22] As an example of this second type of intensity, he describes one of the last public speeches of British Archbishop William Temple (1881–1944), given at the Westminster Central Hall of which Sangster was minister. "Standing quite still, without a gesture and without a note, he unwound the sinuous argument which burned from time to time with a terrible intensity."

As Stephen Neill has pointed out, there is "one notable characteristic to be found in all the greatest teachers," whether from the East or from the West, and that is what he calls "intense seriousness."[23] There was a time when people were attracted to the gospel through the passion of the preacher. Benjamin Franklin said he often went to hear George Whitefield preach because there, before his eyes, he could watch a man burn.[24]

Sangster also reports on the description that a powerful Afro-American preacher gave on how he prepared his messages, which may give us a key to how our preaching can have fervency. He said that he "read himself full,"

---

21. W. E. Sangster, *Power in Preaching* (Grand Rapids: Baker, 1958 [repr. 1976]), 87.
22. Ibid., 89.
23. Stephen Neill, *The Supremacy of Jesus* (London: Hodder and Stoughton, 1984), 55.
24. Cited in Demaray, *Preacher Aflame*, 14.

"thought himself clear," and "prayed himself hot."[25] Study, reflection, and prayer are three keys to fervency, to having knowledge on fire.

Today, unfortunately, passion is being replaced by entertainment as a means of attracting people. Since we do not have the skills and discipline to develop informed, wise, and relevant preaching that can be passionately presented because it is true, we resort to a skill that is common in today's world: the ability to entertain. Sometimes that medium becomes so important that the message ends up taking a back seat. We fill our pews with people who come to church for the entertainment but who are unable to overcome the powerful temptations they face, for their worldview has not been shaped by the Word. The seriousness of Christianity has not been communicated to them through passionate preaching; they do not see it as a matter of life and death. The challenge in this media-oriented age is to package the truth with such quality and intensity that people will want to come and be fed, even if they are not entertained.

Creating an environment conducive to leaders learning. Unlike what happened with Priscilla, Aquila, and Apollos, we have encountered situations of potential learning today that have gone sour. Often this is because the teachers have not been wise in the way they confronted a leader whose knowledge was defective. Unfortunately, some people are so uncomfortable with personal encounter that they prefer to resort to public denouncing or to writing letters or, worse still, writing articles, rather than talking privately with the person concerned. The result is much hurt and usually little teaching that gets through.

Yet leaders will not learn unless they are teachable. The teachable attitude we described above should be true of anyone who truly understands the nature of Scripture. On the one hand, its vastness makes us realize that our knowledge will always be limited. On the other hand, its glory makes us eager to learn whatever new thing we can. These two factors combine with the attitude of childlike faith, which is basic to the Christian life, and prepare us for a lifetime of learning. The teacher-learner distinction subsides as a result of the eagerness to learn more of God's truth. The teacher enters into every teaching situation humbled by the realization that God's truth is so vast that there is more to learn and that some of this learning may come from unexpected sources, such as students or simple, unlearned Christians.

Applications of the open-home principle. Just as Priscilla and Aquila opened their home to help Apollos in his time of need, so we too can open our homes to people in need. The following texts imply that this is a basic aspect of Christian discipleship.

---

25. Sangster, *Power in Preaching*, 90.

- "Share with God's people who are in need. Practice hospitality" (Rom. 12:13).
- "Is not this the kind of fasting I have chosen? . . . Is it not to share your food with the hungry and to provide the poor wanderer with shelter—when you see the naked, to clothe him, and not to turn away from your own flesh and blood?" (Isa. 58:6–7).
- "For I was hungry and you gave me something to eat, I was thirsty and you gave me something to drink, I was a stranger and you invited me in, I needed clothes and you clothed me, I was sick and you looked after me" (Matt. 25:35–36).
- "God sets the lonely in families . . ." (Ps. 68:6).[26]

Let us apply this principle of opening our homes in order to meet needs. Christian homes can be places where unwanted or abused people are welcomed and even kept for a considerable length of time. A great opportunity of welcoming aliens today is having foreign students over at our homes for a weekend or at least for a meal. I remember with great gratitude the refreshment this brought to me when I was a student in the United States. It is sobering that most foreign students in America never enter an American home before they leave for their home countries.[27]

In our church in Sri Lanka we try to ensure that single people who live alone are taken to the home of another member when they get sick. Just the day before I wrote this, we had a mother and her two children stay in our home for a night because her husband was seeking to harm her physically. Christian workers who work under difficult circumstances have told me of the refreshment they have received through Christians who opened their homes to them for a few days of "rest and recuperation." How about those who come to a big city for medical treatment? Should they check into a hotel? Wouldn't a loving Christian home help in creating an atmosphere more conducive to healing? Those under special mental turmoil especially benefit from such hospitality. George O'Carroll says, "We've found that the vast majority of people do not need a professional psychiatrist. They need, first of all, someone to listen to them, someone to love them, and something to feel a part of, a family in particular. This is usually ninety percent of the problem."[28]

---

26. These references are gleaned from David and Ruth Rupprecht, *Radical Hospitality* (Phillipsburg, N.J.: Presbyterian and Reformed, 1983).

27. Groups like International Students Incorporated and InterVarsity Christian Fellowship are trying to change this statistic and are performing a great service on university campuses.

28. Quoted in Rupprecht, *Radical Hospitality*, 11.

Acts 19:8–41

❦

PAUL ENTERED THE synagogue and spoke boldly there for three months, arguing persuasively about the kingdom of God. ⁹But some of them became obstinate; they refused to believe and publicly maligned the Way. So Paul left them. He took the disciples with him and had discussions daily in the lecture hall of Tyrannus. ¹⁰This went on for two years, so that all the Jews and Greeks who lived in the province of Asia heard the word of the Lord.

¹¹God did extraordinary miracles through Paul, ¹²so that even handkerchiefs and aprons that had touched him were taken to the sick, and their illnesses were cured and the evil spirits left them.

¹³Some Jews who went around driving out evil spirits tried to invoke the name of the Lord Jesus over those who were demon-possessed. They would say, "In the name of Jesus, whom Paul preaches, I command you to come out." ¹⁴Seven sons of Sceva, a Jewish chief priest, were doing this. ¹⁵One day the evil spirit answered them, "Jesus I know, and I know about Paul, but who are you?" ¹⁶Then the man who had the evil spirit jumped on them and overpowered them all. He gave them such a beating that they ran out of the house naked and bleeding.

¹⁷When this became known to the Jews and Greeks living in Ephesus, they were all seized with fear, and the name of the Lord Jesus was held in high honor. ¹⁸Many of those who believed now came and openly confessed their evil deeds. ¹⁹A number who had practiced sorcery brought their scrolls together and burned them publicly. When they calculated the value of the scrolls, the total came to fifty thousand drachmas. ²⁰In this way the word of the Lord spread widely and grew in power.

²¹After all this had happened, Paul decided to go to Jerusalem, passing through Macedonia and Achaia. "After I have been there," he said, "I must visit Rome also." ²²He sent two of his helpers, Timothy and Erastus, to Macedonia, while he stayed in the province of Asia a little longer.

²³About that time there arose a great disturbance about the Way. ²⁴A silversmith named Demetrius, who made silver shrines of Artemis, brought in no little business for the crafts-

men. ²⁵He called them together, along with the workmen in related trades, and said: "Men, you know we receive a good income from this business. ²⁶And you see and hear how this fellow Paul has convinced and led astray large numbers of people here in Ephesus and in practically the whole province of Asia. He says that man-made gods are no gods at all. ²⁷There is danger not only that our trade will lose its good name, but also that the temple of the great goddess Artemis will be discredited, and the goddess herself, who is worshiped throughout the province of Asia and the world, will be robbed of her divine majesty."

²⁸When they heard this, they were furious and began shouting: "Great is Artemis of the Ephesians!" ²⁹Soon the whole city was in an uproar. The people seized Gaius and Aristarchus, Paul's traveling companions from Macedonia, and rushed as one man into the theater. ³⁰Paul wanted to appear before the crowd, but the disciples would not let him. ³¹Even some of the officials of the province, friends of Paul, sent him a message begging him not to venture into the theater.

³²The assembly was in confusion: Some were shouting one thing, some another. Most of the people did not even know why they were there. ³³The Jews pushed Alexander to the front, and some of the crowd shouted instructions to him. He motioned for silence in order to make a defense before the people. ³⁴But when they realized he was a Jew, they all shouted in unison for about two hours: "Great is Artemis of the Ephesians!"

³⁵The city clerk quieted the crowd and said: "Men of Ephesus, doesn't all the world know that the city of Ephesus is the guardian of the temple of the great Artemis and of her image, which fell from heaven? ³⁶Therefore, since these facts are undeniable, you ought to be quiet and not do anything rash. ³⁷You have brought these men here, though they have neither robbed temples nor blasphemed our goddess. ³⁸If, then, Demetrius and his fellow craftsmen have a grievance against anybody, the courts are open and there are proconsuls. They can press charges. ³⁹If there is anything further you want to bring up, it must be settled in a legal assembly. ⁴⁰As it is, we are in danger of being charged with rioting because of today's events. In that case we would not be able to account for this commotion, since there is no reason for it." ⁴¹After he had said this, he dismissed the assembly.

ACTS 19 DESCRIBES Paul's ministry in Ephesus in some detail, though there is no sampling of the message he preached there. Luke has already given us ample records of Paul's messages to both Jewish (13:16–41, in Antioch of Pisidia) and Gentile (14:15–17; 17:22–31, in Lystra and Athens) audiences outside Palestine.

The Evangelization of Asia (19:8–10)

AS IN OTHER cities, Paul uses the synagogue as his bridgehead for evangelism. Ephesus was somewhat different from other cities he went to, for a few believers and "semi-believers" were already there. He established contact with them and even ministered to them at the start of his stay (19:1–7). Yet Paul was not content with a smattering of believers in Ephesus. He wanted everyone to hear the gospel, and in his remarkable stay of at least twenty-seven months, he succeeded in bringing the gospel to the entire population of the province of Asia (v. 10).

Luke uses some familiar words to describe Paul's evangelism. In the synagogue he "spoke boldly" (v. 8; Gk. *parresiazomai,* which appears six times in Acts, each time to describe the ministry of Paul).[1] In general, this word describes his ministry among Jews.[2] Preaching the gospel to Jews who were so close to and yet so far from the gospel required much boldness because of their animosity to it. Paul's boldness is also expressed in his "arguing persuasively" (*dialegomai* and *peitho*) about the kingdom of God.[3]

Though the message of the kingdom of God does not appear as much in Acts as in the Gospels, it is mentioned seven times in Acts—to describe the preaching of Jesus (1:3), of Philip (8:12), and of Paul (14:22; 19:8; 20:25; 28:23, 31). Peter also echoed this message in his Pentecost speech, though he did not use the expression "kingdom of God." The sequence we have seen elsewhere is repeated here in Acts 19, for the Jews rejected the gospel (v. 9b). But here there was a slight difference in that Paul spoke at the synagogue for as long as three months, and only "some" (not most) of the Jews "became obstinate."

Paul then moved to "the lecture hall of Tyrannus" and held "discussions [*dialegomai* again] daily" (v. 9b). Tyrannus was either the lecturer who taught there or the owner of the hall, who rented it out to Paul. According to the Western Text, Paul had the use of the hall from 11 A.M. to 4 P.M. Bruce writes,

---

1. See 9:27, 28; 13:46; 14:3; 18:26; cf. 26:26.
2. The only possible exception is 14:3, though we take King Agrippa (26:26) to be a Jew.
3. See the discussion on 17:1–15 for comments on these two words.

"Whatever the textual basis of this reading may be, it probably represents what actually happened."[4] During those hours public activity came to a standstill in cities in this region and people took an afternoon nap. Paul's hearers must have been motivated to come for discussions at this time. The apostle himself probably gave mornings and evenings to tentmaking (see 20:34) and came to the lecture hall to teach the people in the intervening time.

The result of this two-year stint (v. 10) was that "all the Jews and Greeks who lived in the province of Asia heard the word of the Lord" (v. 10b). This was in part achieved through people who came to the big city of Ephesus from other places in the province, heard the gospel, and took it back to their hometowns. It also took place through colleagues of Paul, who brought the gospel to the other towns in Asia. Epaphras, for example, took the gospel to Colosse, Laodicea, and Hierapolis and founded the churches there (cf. Col. 1:7–8; 2:1; 4:12–13). Presumably the seven churches of Asia addressed in Revelation 2–3 were founded at this time.

After several divinely ordained delays, therefore, the mission to Asia Minor finally took off. Christianity persisted in this province for centuries after the Turkish conquest of the region. It "disappeared only with the wholesale exchange of Greek and Turkish populations which followed the Graeco-Turkish war of 1923."[5]

Extraordinary Miracles (19:11–22)

AFTER LUKE'S SUMMARY of the ministry in Ephesus, he records a few incidents or pictures that help us understand the unique experiences Paul had there. Verses 11–12 summarize the apostle's ministry in the miraculous. As discussed in other sections, the apologist who marshaled arguments for the gospel was also the healer.[6] The expression "extraordinary miracles" indicates that something unusual happened in Ephesus.

Some background information on Ephesus will help us understand Paul's ministry. This city had a reputation as a center for the learning and practice of magical arts. "Its reputation in this respect is indicated by the fact that the phrase 'Ephesian writings' (*Ephesia grammata*) was commonly used in antiquity for documents containing spells and formulae."[7] In other words, in addition to Paul's evangelistic ministry (vv. 8–10), he also had a ministry that can be classed as a "power encounter," where Christ's power over the forces that bound the people was clearly demonstrated. Clinton Arnold, in his

---

4. Bruce, *Acts,* NICNT, 366.
5. Bruce, *Steps,* 50.
6. See comments on 3:1–26.
7. Bruce, *Paul,* 291.

study *Ephesians, Power and Magic,* points out the significance of the fact that Paul's most complete study of spiritual powers and of the battle Christians face against them comes in his letter to Ephesus.[8]

Many of the actions that took place in Ephesus are related to this need to demonstrate the power of God over these forces. Bruce suggests that the "handkerchiefs and aprons that had touched him [and] were taken to the sick" (v. 12) may have been "those which Paul used in his tentmaking or leather-working—the sweat rags for tying round his head and aprons for tying round his waist."[9] We cannot be sure whether Paul deliberately adopted this strategy or whether, as with the healing that took place through a woman's touching the edge of Christ's cloak (Luke 8:44), others took these objects representing Paul to the sick.

In a culture where people were steeped in the use of such items, it is understandable that they would use them in connection with healing in the name of Jesus. Luke, however, is eager to stress that God was the one who "did extraordinary miracles through Paul," not Paul himself or the aprons. As a result, the people's "illnesses were cured and the evil spirits left them" (v. 12). It is not surprising that the casting out of demons, which is more prominent in the Gospels than in Acts, gains prominence in a place under the grip of occult practices.

The next picture Luke gives us is of "seven sons of Sceva, a Jewish chief priest" (v. 14). They were among the "Jews who went around driving out evil spirits [and who] tried to invoke the name of the Lord Jesus over those who were demon-possessed" (v. 13). According to Bruce, "among practitioners of magic in ancient times Jews enjoyed high respect, for they were believed to have exceptionally effective spells at their command." He writes that "the fact that the name of God was not pronounced by vulgar lips was generally known among pagans, and misrepresented by them according to regular magical principles." By contrast, "the Jewish high priest was the one man who was authorized to pronounce the otherwise ineffable name.... Such a person would therefore enjoy prestige among magicians." Bruce thinks, therefore, that "Jewish chief priest" may have been a self-designation, taken on by Sceva.[10]

The evil spirit in the person being exorcised by the sons of Sceva attacked these exorcists, leaving them naked and bleeding (v. 16). As Ed Murphy points out, this was a case of evil spirits battling each other—that is, the

---

8. Clinton E. Arnold, *Ephesians, Power and Magic* (Cambridge: Cambridge Univ. Press, 1989), 39. Cited in Ed Murphy, *The Handbook for Spiritual Warfare* (Nashville: Thomas Nelson, 1992), 345.

9. Bruce, *Acts,* NICNT, 367.

10. Ibid., 368.

evil spirit in the possessed person battled the demonized exorcists.[11] How can we harmonize this fact with Christ's statement that Satan will not be divided against Satan? Demons can expel and attack other demons to enhance the control of demons over people. Such demon-to-demon attacks only increase Satan's hold over people.

Luke goes on to paint the picture of a people seized with fear and holding the name of Jesus in high honor (v. 17). This came as a direct result of the demonstration of God's power and, as we will see, was an important aspect of effective evangelism among those under the grip of occult power. Related to this was the open confession of evil deeds, culminating in a grand scroll-burning session (vv. 18–19). "Openly confessed" (v. 18) probably refers to these people's revealing the content of their spells. "According to magical theory, the potency of a spell is bound up with its secrecy; if it be divulged, it becomes ineffective. So these converted magicians renounced their imagined power by rendering their spells inoperative."[12]

The scrolls burned were valued at fifty thousand drachmas, which was equivalent to about fifty thousand days' wages of an average worker—a great value. The scrolls burned must have been documents containing spells and formulae for which Ephesus was famous. "Magical papyri were rolled up in small cylinders or lockets used as amulets around the neck."[13]

Luke's customary summary statement about the growth of the church had a significant emphasis for a place like Ephesus: "In this way the word of the Lord spread widely and grew in power" (v. 20). The word was, as always, primary. But the mention of growth in power is relevant among a people living under bondage to demonic powers.

Verses 21–22 summarize Paul's plans for moving on from Ephesus. The apostle made his plans for leaving with joy, seeing that a strong church had been established there. He wanted to go to Jerusalem and from there to Rome. But he decided first to go to Macedonia and Achaia and complete the work on the contribution to the church in Jerusalem. His plan was to bring the gift there personally (see Rom. 15:25–28; 1 Cor. 16:1–11; 2 Cor. 8–9). He sent two helpers ahead of him to Macedonia and planned to join them shortly (v. 22).

The Riot Subdued (19:23–41)

LUKE HAS ONE more picture to give us from Paul's lengthy ministry in Ephesus. He seems to have omitted the battle with what Paul calls "wild beasts" (1 Cor. 15:32) as well as the hardships that caused him to despair "even of

---

11. Murphy, *Handbook for Spiritual Warfare*, 349.

12. Bruce, *Acts*, NICNT, 369.

13. Keener, *BBC*, 379.

life" (2 Cor. 1:8–10). Many scholars think Paul may have been imprisoned in Ephesus for a period of time.[14] But the riot—especially its conclusion in the acquittal of the Christians—fits in with a theme that Luke considered important: opposition to the gospel (here cited as "great disturbance about the Way," v. 23). Luke consistently stresses the real reasons behind such opposition, especially because opposition was usually for reasons other than the content of the gospel.

Here in Ephesus (as elsewhere, see 5:17; 13:45; 17:5) the root of the opposition was jealousy. As in Philippi (16:19), it had primarily an economic reason, though it was couched in religious and patriotic terms when presented in public. The temple of Artemis was a key to the economic stability of Ephesus, for foreigners traveled there to worship and deposited money in the temple. This had become more significant in the time of Paul since the city was beginning to lose its significance as a center for international trade.

Demetrius must have been the president of the guild of silversmiths. In those days "members of the same trade united to form professional guilds, or *collegia*, which set standards for their own trade and united to defend their economic interests."[15] The silversmiths made "silver shrines of Artemis" (v. 24), that is, "miniature silver niches, containing an image of the goddess, which her votaries [devotees] bought to dedicate in the temple."[16] Archaeologists have found "silver reproductions of her image and terra-cotta [clay] models of her temple."[17] In his speech to his colleagues, Demetrius is frank about the way Paul's preaching had hit them economically (vv. 24–26). But it would hit the honor of the goddess (v. 27). That was the line they would take in their public agitation (v. 28).

The silversmiths succeeded in getting the whole city into an uproar and seized two of Paul's colleagues (v. 29). The apostle wanted very much to take the place of his colleagues, but the wisdom of the believers and Paul's influential friends prevailed, and he remained in hiding (vv. 30–31). The word translated "officials of the province" is *Asiarchai* (Asiarchs). While there is some uncertainty about the exact duties of these high government officials, their presence in Ephesus during the first four centuries has been clearly attested. Strabo, writing only one generation before the date of this story, refers to the Asiarchs of Tralles as a group.[18] In other words, Paul had wealthy and powerful friends at Ephesus.

---

14. C. E. Arnold, "Ephesus," *DPL*, 252.

15. Keener, *BBC*, 380.

16. Bruce, *Acts*, NICNT, 374.

17. Bruce, *Steps*, 49.

18. A. N. Sherwin-White, *Roman Society and Roman Law in the New Testament* (Grand Rapids: Baker, 1973, repr. 1963 ed.), 90 (he cites Strabo, *Geography*, 14.1.42).

Luke's terminology and description of the proceedings has remarkable parallels with the evidence that is emerging about the social structure of Asia, especially of Ephesus, in the mid-first century.[19] The people gathered in the great theater of Ephesus, where meetings of the assembly were held (vv. 30–31). This was an unofficial or informal assembly, which Luke calls the *ekklesia* (vv. 32, 41) and distinguishes from "legal assembly" (*te ennomo ekklesia*), which had its regular official meetings (see v. 39). The Jews seem to have become nervous about trouble coming to them, so they wanted to distance themselves from Paul by thrusting a certain Alexander to the forefront. But he had no chance to speak for a mob mentality has taken over. The result is a two-hour-long shouting session (vv. 33–34).

At this stage the city clerk[20] took over (v. 35). He appealed to the heritage of the city, which believed that the many-breasted image of the goddess Artemis had fallen down from heaven (v. 35) and was thus of divine workmanship. His point was that the security of having such facts should cause them not to panic and do something rash (v. 36). Besides, there were legal ways to handle such issues: "The courts are open and there are proconsuls"[21] (v. 38). This statement "reflects the Roman practice in Asia of holding courts under the proconsul in nine or more principal cities which served as district capitals."[22]

The concerns of the clerk about a bad report going to the Romans have been reflected by another writer, Dio of Prusa, who wrote about fifty years later.[23] City assemblies were on their way out at that time, because Rome wanted to eliminate these democratic elements. According to Sherwin-White, "this was the last age of civic autonomy in the ancient world." By the late second and early third centuries "civic politics in the old pattern of the city-state, with its assemblies and councils," had come to an end.[24] The clerk must have been fearing these trends when he cautioned his people about the Roman reaction to this commotion (v. 40).

Luke saw this event as another victory for the cause of the gospel. In his estimation, the existing legal system, if properly administered, could be relied upon to give the Christians a fair trial (cf. also the decision of the proconsul Gallio in Corinth in 18:12–17; see comments).

---

19. This is carefully documented in A. N. Sherwin-White's *Roman Society and Roman Law* (ibid., 83–92). See also Hemer, *Acts*, 120–24.

20. "There is fairly copious evidence about [the office of city clerk] at Ephesus and other cities of Asia minor" (Sherwin-White, *Roman Society*, 86).

21. Differing explanations have been given for the appearance of the plural "proconsuls" here. See Hemer, *Acts*, 123; Bruce, *Acts*, NICNT, 379.

22. Hemer, *Acts*, 123.

23. See Sherwin-White *Roman Society and Roman Law*, 84.

24. Ibid.

WORKING WITH PEOPLE **influenced by magic and the occult.** This passage gives us helpful keys to working with people who have been influenced by the occult and by other forms of satanic magic. Like the other descriptions of evangelistic ministry in Acts, this one offers a good example of effective contextualization. Some aspects of evangelism, such as the basic content of the gospel, are necessary in every place where it occurs. Thus, when Luke describes the growth of the church, while he includes a note about growth in power (which was relevant to Ephesus), his primary focus is on how "the word of the Lord spread" (v. 20).

Each culture, however, has certain features that particularly keep people away from God, that hold them in bondage, or that make them receptive to the gospel. A contextualized ministry will deal effectively with these features. Peter in Jerusalem and Paul in Antioch of Pisidia focused on the Jewish hope for a Messiah and how Christ fulfills that. In Athens Paul attacked the intellectual base for idolatry. In Ephesus Paul's ministry addressed the bondage to magic of the people living there. It is therefore helpful to see the incidents at Ephesus as examples of power encounter with the demonic.

There has been much discussion on this topic in recent times, and the term *power encounter* is often used in a broad sense to include everything that we usually associate with spiritual warfare. I have found it more helpful to follow Ed Murphy in restricting the use of this expression to crisis points in the ongoing spiritual warfare, where issues are brought to a head and the battle for allegiance takes a decisive turn.[25] This is the type of thing that happened in Ephesus, with people not only forsaking their magical practices, but also "openly confess[ing] their evil deeds" (v. 18) and burning the scrolls through which they practiced magic (v. 19). It also occurred between two demonic forces: those possessing an individual who needed to be exorcised and those performing the exorcisms (the seven sons of Sceva). The latter were comprehensively defeated in that encounter (vv. 14–16).

Does the use of "handkerchiefs and aprons" in Ephesus (v. 12) give us the freedom to use such methods today? We should be careful about banning such things outright, as some do. But we should also note that we are not sure whether this method was actively advocated by Paul. At the same time, in a culture influenced heavily by magic (where the symbolic is important), God used symbols to reveal himself to the people. Could the use of these methods be an example of God's accommodating himself to human frailty rather than a pattern for all to follow? Conrad Gempf thinks so: "The incarnation

---

25. Murphy, *Handbook for Spiritual Warfare*, 341–43.

has always been about God limiting himself in dramatic, nearly absurd, ways in order to communicate to a fallen and absurd people."[26] If this is the case, we can glean the principle that, in the process of contextualization, we may need to accommodate ourselves to people's frailty so long as it does not contradict biblical principles.

Luke's description of fear being among the people as a result of the demonstration of power suggests that fear played an important role in bringing people to God in Ephesus (vv. 17–18). We have already looked at the place fear (resulting from the demonstration of God's miraculous power) has in the gospel program.[27] Here the focus is on fear in a background heavily influenced by the occult. Even today people go to magical or occult sources for guidance and help primarily because of fear of the unknown. They are held in the grip of satanic influence by fear, for they are afraid of displeasing these forces. That God is greater than these forces can be an important means to helping them shift their allegiance to God. As Jesus said, "Do not be afraid of those who kill the body but cannot kill the soul. Rather, be afraid of the One who can destroy both soul and body in hell" (Matt. 10:28). Many reject the gospel because they fear to displease gods and other powers. Actually, they should be accepting the gospel out of fear of displeasing the supreme God. While this is not the heart of the gospel, it is an important element.

What do we make of the burning of the scrolls (v. 19)? This incident has been used throughout the centuries as a basis for burning books and destroying idols. Does it give us a precedent? The practice of burning books to repudiate their contents was common in Paul's day.[28] But this was more than that; it was also a case of destroying spells deemed to have magical power. A key to understanding what happened in Ephesus is remembering that people under bondage to occult forces needed to be delivered from their hold on them. This was a situation of power encounter; the same applies to people under the grip of the occult today.

The law as protector. Though the legal system was not influenced by Christianity in the first century, Luke shows that several times it protected Christians from unfair treatment. Shortly after this Paul wrote to the Christians in Rome about the positive contribution made by the state:

> For rulers hold no terror for those who do right, but for those who do wrong. Do you want to be free from fear of the one in authority? Then do what is right and he will commend you. For he is God's

---

26. Gempf, "Acts," 1096.
27. See discussion on 4:36–5:11.
28. Keener, *BBC,* 379.

servant to do you good. . . . Therefore, it is necessary to submit to the authorities, not only because of possible punishment but also because of conscience. (Rom. 13:3–5)[29]

In Ephesus the fact that Paul was friendly with the Asiarchs (v. 31) may have helped him to get a fair trial. Luke's emphasis of the place of the state and its response to Christianity shows us that we too should think of how the church relates to the state.

THE PLACE OF truth in contextualized ministry. We hear many voices today downplaying the value of truth-centered evangelism. Such people, including many who class themselves as evangelicals, claim we live in an age when people no longer think in categories that value truth. In its place, they advocate a needs-based evangelism, which shows Jesus as the answer to felt needs. Sensitivity to needs was certainly a key to Paul's evangelistic strategy (cf. Paul's ministry in Ephesus and elsewhere). But basic to his gospel presentation was the primacy of its truth. This will always be so, for Christianity is a religion that claims to have God's complete revelation to humanity. Those who downplay the truthfulness and content of the gospel have sadly betrayed its heart and have given in to syncretism.[30]

Ministering in occult-related situations. Millions of people both in the East and the West have been influenced by the occult world. Fear of evil spirits and of the unknown was the dominant emotion in Ephesus, as it is throughout the world today. The presence of an astrology page in many newspapers and magazines gives evidence of that. Moreover, many visit mediums, astrologers, and the like for guidance. Therefore the presentation of God as the all-powerful Supreme Being, higher than all the other forces that people are going to, is relevant.

The use of symbols, as we saw in use of handkerchiefs and aprons in Ephesus, may also have new significance in today's world. Evangelicals have generally attributed a negative value to religious symbols. That probably springs from a history of opposition to what happened in Roman Catholic and

---

29. On the question of our attitude to the state, see John Stott, *The Cross of Christ* (Leicester: Inter-Varsity Press, 1986), 298–309.

30. One of the most eloquent spokespersons for the primacy of truth in recent times has been a man who has had ample experience in ministering to human need in India and Britain, Bishop Lesslie Newbigin. See his books *The Gospel in a Pluralist Society* (Grand Rapids: Eerdmans and Geneva: WCC Publications, 1989); *Truth to Tell: The Gospel as Public Truth* (Grand Rapids: Eerdmans and Geneva: WCC Publications, 1991); *Proper Confidence: Faith, Doubt and Certainty in Christian Discipleship* (Grand Rapids: Eerdmans, 1995).

Orthodox churches, where symbols were often viewed as mediating salvation and became substitutes to faith. In the Bible, however, God gave a high place to symbols as means through which his message could be burned into the minds of people. We must, of course, be careful about focusing so much on the symbols that we miss the emphasis that God is the one who does the healing (cf. v. 11). That is, the symbols must not achieve a magical status. But today too we may use symbols to help people realize the victory that Christ has won for them over the forces of darkness.

Baptism by immersion may be a significant symbol to communicate God's cleansing to a person who had repented from a life of great immorality. Physical objects pointing to a spiritual truth that can get easily obliterated may be used with caution in our ministries. I often have key verses, which I need to sustain me through a crisis, pasted on the wall of my room. People wear their wedding ring when they travel, and one among many reasons for this is to ward off the temptation to get too close to someone other than one's spouse. Churches give the right hand of fellowship to new members to express their welcome to the family (Gal. 2:9). Leaders lay hands on and pray for people in special need.[31] James recommends anointing the sick with oil when they are prayed over (James 5:14). These are all symbols to remind us of a deeper truth that can be forgotten or to proclaim a truth that people need to know.

It is also important that, just as there was open confession and the burning of paraphernalia related to the practice of magic, there should be an open repudiation of all occult connections by the converted person. This is because once we give Satan a foothold, he can continue to have an insidious hold on our lives. His influences must be decisively repudiated. Because occult paraphernalia were sources of security for an individual, these may not be as easy to renounce as it seems. A friend of mine in the university who accepted Christ soon realized that he had to throw away a charm that he had bought from a Buddhist monk for his protection. It had cost a lot of money and had at one time been a source of security. But when he decided that it had to be disposed of, he did not sell the charm or return it to the monk. Instead, he threw it into a field in a decisively symbolic act of repudiation.

The above discussion also suggests that what happened in Ephesus does not give us the license to ask all people publicly to burn religious books and break idols.[32] In Ephesus the magicians did this of their own accord. Even though Paul held "that man-made gods are no gods at all" (v. 26), he did not

---

31. See Acts 6:6; 8:17; 9:12; 13:3; 19:6; 28:8.

32. Note that the public destruction of idols in the Old Testament was with a people who had clearly been given God's Word about the evils of idolatry.

require their destruction, or if he did, it was only with those who had accepted Christ. I have heard of Christians who have gone to non-Christian homes and, even before these people accepted Christ, asked them to destroy idols in their homes. The result has been severe unrest in the community and unnecessary animosity towards Christianity.

Paul's strategy was to argue against idolatry so that people, realizing the futility of idols, would put them away themselves. If they were going to accept Christ, they had to reject idols and cease to depend on any other non-Christian religious practice. I usually do this with Buddhists and Hindus before they pray a prayer of commitment to Christ. I do not lead them into the step of commitment unless they are willing to forsake all other gods. This sometimes elicits opposition.

With people who have dabbled in the occult, there must always be some dramatic form of cleansing from the past. The burning of photographs of satanic groups, the destruction of charms, prayers for God's cleansing of homes where occult practices have taken place, prayers for deliverance from all remaining vestiges of occult power for people who have backgrounds of occult involvement—these will all be necessary when ministering with today's occult-ridden people. Recently I was asked to come and pray at a home that had some occult paraphernalia, into which a Christian friend of mine had just moved. We had a service where we asked for God's protection upon the house and those who lived in it; then a colleague and I took the paraphernalia away with us and threw it into a garbage dump.

A sequence similar to what happened in Ephesus took place recently in Resistencia, Argentina, where over a three-year period the evangelical community grew about 500 percent. They had a series of evangelistic rallies at the end of these three years. And as part of these meetings a book-burning ceremony was held every evening. The leader, Ed Silvoso, explains what happened.

> A 100-gallon drum was set up to the left of the platform to dispose of satanic paraphernalia. As people came forward, they dumped all kinds of occult-related items into it. Before praying for the people, gasoline was poured on the contents of the drum, a match was struck and every evil thing inside went up in flames.[33]

While the burning was taking place, some people experienced spontaneous deliverances. Christians in the West who think that this does not apply to them may be surprised to find out how many of those whom they are working with have a background in occult-related practices.

---

33. Ed Silvoso, *That None Should Perish* (Ventura, Calif.: Regal, 1994), 50. Cited in Wagner, *Blazing the Way*, 170.

Acting wisely in connection with the state. The reaction of the state to Christianity was an important issue to Luke. We too should regard this with utmost seriousness. But how does this flesh itself out in daily life? Many of us know of situations where people make use of a special connection they have to influence unfairly the process of justice. Surely Luke is not advocating this. Rather, he seems to be implying that there are non-Christian judges who are reasonable and who abide by the law. In times of difficulty we can appeal to such for protection under the law. Such protection may be necessary for Christian activity to go on. Christians have done this throughout history to good effect. With certain repressive states, of course, such attempts may end in disaster. But that does not exempt Christians living in those states from thinking how best they can relate to the law of their land.

In recent years as opposition to evangelism has mounted in Sri Lanka, we have been grateful for a constitution that ensures the people's right to practice and propagate the religion of their choice. In times of crisis we have appealed to that. The fact that some Christians know influential people in the government has also helped in enabling us to get the protection that is rightfully ours. But there are rumblings afoot now to change this constitution, which will result in the curtailment of freedom of religious practice and propagation. Some Christian leaders are therefore trying to prevent such changes, using every opportunity they have to influence our leaders. Some are writing articles and publishing them in secular forums, just as the early apologists did in defense of the Christian practice of evangelism. Some are meeting their friends in the government to lobby support for the cause. Some are alerting the world Christian community in the hope that others will speak up on behalf of Christians in Sri Lanka.

A few years ago the president of a Muslim country ordered the banning of a new Bible just a few days before its release. The protests and pleas of the Christians in that country were of no avail. This president visited the West around this time. On this trip a U.S. Senator told him that he was the first president in the history of the world to ban a Bible. The Pope also talked to him about this ban. As a result, he removed the ban as soon as he returned home!

Should we, then, go after friendships with influential people? Should we give time and energy to "hobnob with the big wigs"? This depends on one's personal call. The influential people in a society also need Christ, and we should attempt to make friends with them so that we can witness to them. We must assume that Paul presented the gospel to the Asiarchs, just as he did to everyone he met. Some may be called to move in those circles in order to influence them to give the work of the gospel the protection it requires. Such should be supported by the Christian group that they are accountable to. This group can help them avoid breaking Christian principles as they move around with those who live on this high social plane.[34]

Like Joseph, Nehemiah, Esther, and Mordecai, we should use any esteem we have won with national leaders to represent the cause of God's kingdom and to highlight the need for the protection of his people. While the church in Acts was possibly too young to produce politicians, the biblical attitude to society has a place for devout Christians to enter into the sphere of national life so as to influence it through kingdom principles.

---

34. On this, see my book *Spiritual Living in a Secular World* (Grand Rapids: Zondervan, 1993), 46—56.

Acts 20:1–38

WHEN THE UPROAR had ended, Paul sent for the disciples and, after encouraging them, said good-by and set out for Macedonia. ²He traveled through that area, speaking many words of encouragement to the people, and finally arrived in Greece, ³where he stayed three months. Because the Jews made a plot against him just as he was about to sail for Syria, he decided to go back through Macedonia. ⁴He was accompanied by Sopater son of Pyrrhus from Berea, Aristarchus and Secundus from Thessalonica, Gaius from Derbe, Timothy also, and Tychicus and Trophimus from the province of Asia. ⁵These men went on ahead and waited for us at Troas. ⁶But we sailed from Philippi after the Feast of Unleavened Bread, and five days later joined the others at Troas, where we stayed seven days.

⁷On the first day of the week we came together to break bread. Paul spoke to the people and, because he intended to leave the next day, kept on talking until midnight. ⁸There were many lamps in the upstairs room where we were meeting. ⁹Seated in a window was a young man named Eutychus, who was sinking into a deep sleep as Paul talked on and on. When he was sound asleep, he fell to the ground from the third story and was picked up dead. ¹⁰Paul went down, threw himself on the young man and put his arms around him. "Don't be alarmed," he said. "He's alive!" ¹¹Then he went upstairs again and broke bread and ate. After talking until daylight, he left. ¹²The people took the young man home alive and were greatly comforted.

¹³We went on ahead to the ship and sailed for Assos, where we were going to take Paul aboard. He had made this arrangement because he was going there on foot. ¹⁴When he met us at Assos, we took him aboard and went on to Mitylene. ¹⁵The next day we set sail from there and arrived off Kios. The day after that we crossed over to Samos, and on the following day arrived at Miletus. ¹⁶Paul had decided to sail past Ephesus to avoid spending time in the province of Asia, for he was in a hurry to reach Jerusalem, if possible, by the day of Pentecost.

¹⁷From Miletus, Paul sent to Ephesus for the elders of the church. ¹⁸When they arrived, he said to them: "You know how

I lived the whole time I was with you, from the first day I came into the province of Asia. ¹⁹I served the Lord with great humility and with tears, although I was severely tested by the plots of the Jews. ²⁰You know that I have not hesitated to preach anything that would be helpful to you but have taught you publicly and from house to house. ²¹I have declared to both Jews and Greeks that they must turn to God in repentance and have faith in our Lord Jesus.

²²"And now, compelled by the Spirit, I am going to Jerusalem, not knowing what will happen to me there. ²³I only know that in every city the Holy Spirit warns me that prison and hardships are facing me. ²⁴However, I consider my life worth nothing to me, if only I may finish the race and complete the task the Lord Jesus has given me—the task of testifying to the gospel of God's grace.

²⁵"Now I know that none of you among whom I have gone about preaching the kingdom will ever see me again. ²⁶Therefore, I declare to you today that I am innocent of the blood of all men. ²⁷For I have not hesitated to proclaim to you the whole will of God. ²⁸Keep watch over yourselves and all the flock of which the Holy Spirit has made you overseers. Be shepherds of the church of God, which he bought with his own blood. ²⁹I know that after I leave, savage wolves will come in among you and will not spare the flock. ³⁰Even from your own number men will arise and distort the truth in order to draw away disciples after them. ³¹So be on your guard! Remember that for three years I never stopped warning each of you night and day with tears.

³²"Now I commit you to God and to the word of his grace, which can build you up and give you an inheritance among all those who are sanctified. ³³I have not coveted anyone's silver or gold or clothing. ³⁴You yourselves know that these hands of mine have supplied my own needs and the needs of my companions. ³⁵In everything I did, I showed you that by this kind of hard work we must help the weak, remembering the words the Lord Jesus himself said: 'It is more blessed to give than to receive.'"

³⁶When he had said this, he knelt down with all of them and prayed. ³⁷They all wept as they embraced him and kissed him. ³⁸What grieved them most was his statement that they would never see his face again. Then they accompanied him to the ship.

CHAPTER 20 DESCRIBES Paul's ministry of encouraging the churches, most of which he had helped start. It goes through this fairly extended ministry rather quickly and then gives a sampling of one of the messages he gave on this journey. We can fill in some details from what Paul wrote in 2 Corinthians and Romans, composed during this time.

Encouraging the Churches in Macedonia and Greece (20:1–6)

AFTER ENCOURAGING THE Ephesians Paul leaves for Macedonia (v. 1). He travels through the area speaking many words of encouragement; eventually he reaches Greece (v. 2). Luke strangely omits the fact that from Ephesus Paul first went to Troas and restlessly waited for Titus to come with news of the situation in Corinth. Because the latter did not arrive there, Paul "had no peace of mind"; as a result, he went to Macedonia, where he received good news of the situation in Corinth (2 Cor. 2:12–14; 7:6–7).[1]

Encouragement is a key theme of this chapter. The verb *parakaleo* ("to encourage") appears three times (vv. 1, 2, 12), and verses 18–35 give a sample of the content of the encouragement Paul gave. The wording of verse 2 suggests that he spent a substantial time in Macedonia, unlike his first visit where he had to leave three Macedonian cities in a hurry. Some scholars suggest that he stayed one to two years in this area. During this time he wrote 2 Corinthians. He may have done some pioneer evangelism—for example, in Illyricum (which occupies the lands of the former Yugoslavia), the province northwest of Macedonia (see Rom. 15:18–19).[2] By now Paul had established churches in a good portion of the Greek world. His next plan was to reach the Latin world, possibly using Rome as his base of operations.

Paul may have wanted to go to Jerusalem in time for the Passover. He was about to sail from Corinth on a ship bound for Syria, which possibly carried Jewish pilgrims on their way to Jerusalem for this feast. But he found out about a plot against him, possibly by some of the people traveling on this ship (v. 3). As a result, he decided to take the long route on foot through Macedonia, traveling north instead of east. He spent Passover in Philippi (v. 6), a city that had had such a small Jewish population that it did not even have a

---

1. Though Titus is mentioned thirteen times in Paul's letters, including a letter addressed to him, he does not appear in Acts. Presumably there is a reason for this omission, but no one seems to be sure what it is.

2. Wagner, *Blazing the Way*, 187. Romans was written during Paul's three-month stay in Greece (actually Corinth), where he went after leaving Macedonia (v. 2).

---

synagogue. According to his revised plan, he hoped to be in Jerusalem in time for the next feast, Pentecost (v. 16).

An important task during these days was to raise a substantial gift for the poor in the church in Jerusalem. There is only one allusion to this collection in Acts (24:17), but it was a topic Paul often brought up in his letters (Rom. 15:25–32; 1 Cor. 16:1–4; 2 Cor. 8–9). Just as prominent representatives of the Diaspora Jewish communities took their annual temple tax to Jerusalem,[3] Paul was planning to take this contribution of the churches as a tangible expression of the solidarity of the Gentile Christians with the church from which the gospel first radiated. The long list of traveling companions mentioned in verse 4 probably represented the churches that had made contributions. Almost all of Paul's Gentile churches are mentioned. Corinth is not mentioned, but that may be either because Paul represented Corinth or because of strained relations between him and the Corinthian church.[4] Philippi is also not mentioned, but Luke, who has now joined the group, probably represents Philippi. The "we" section that came to a stop after the first visit to Philippi (16:16) starts again here (v. 6).

A Midnight Miracle in Troas (20:7–12)

FROM PHILIPPI PAUL and Luke sailed to Troas (v. 6), where there is a church that had probably not been started by Paul. There the Christians meet "on the first day of the week . . . to break bread" (v. 7). Here is the first clear reference in Scripture to the believers meeting for worship on the first day of the week.[5] We are not sure whether Sunday worship had already become a regular practice in the church or whether this meeting's being on a Sunday was coincidental. By the time the Didache was written (late first or early second century) Sunday worship seems to have become commonplace.[6] As friends often did in those days when they met after a long absence, they talked into the night (v. 7b).[7] Luke may be referring here to conversation rather than a long sermon, for he uses the word *dialegomai* in verse 7.[8]

---

3. Keener, *BBC*, 382.

4. Longenecker mentions these two options ("Acts," 506).

5. See also John 20:19, 26; 1 Cor. 16:2. The Jewish way of reckoning days had a day starting at sunset, whereas the Roman system had the day beginning at midnight. Thus, this meeting may have begun on Saturday night (if the Jewish system was used) or on Sunday afternoon (if the Roman system was used).

6. "On the Lord's own day gather together and break bread and give thanks, having first confessed your sins, so that your sacrifice may be pure" (Didache 14:1, in *Apostolic Fathers*, 267).

7. Keener, *BBC*, 383.

8. Bruce, *Acts: Greek Text*, 425. The word appears in v. 9 also.

Luke adds an observation about "many lamps in the upstairs room" (v. 8), possibly to clear his hero Paul of responsibility for Eutychus's falling asleep.[9] Bruce explains what seems to have happened: "The hot, oily atmosphere caused by the crowd and the torches made it difficult for a youth who may have put in a hard day's work to keep awake, despite the priceless opportunity of learning truth from apostolic lips."[10] Doctor Luke must have been satisfied that Eutychus was indeed dead, unlike in Lystra, where Paul's opponents thought he was dead but were mistaken (14:19). Paul's comment, "Don't be alarmed, he's alive!" (v. 10b), refers to the young man's state after he was healed. This is the last of eight occurrences of raising the dead in the Bible.

This occurrence has similarities with the two resurrections performed through Elijah and Elisha (1 Kings 17:17–24; 2 Kings 4:32–37).[11] "Paul . . . threw himself on the young man and put his arms around him" (v. 10a). The embrace was an extension of the more common practice of laying hands on a person during the act of healing. J. A. Alexander is probably right that "it was intended to connect a miraculous effect with the person by whom it was caused or brought about."[12] Note how "Jesus realized that power had gone out from him" when the woman with an issue of blood was healed (Mark 5:30), suggesting a close connection between the healing and the medium through whom the miracle was performed. After breaking bread, Paul talked until daylight and left (v. 11), with the Christians greatly encouraged (*parakaleo* again).

Traveling on to Miletus (20:13–16)

PAUL'S COMPANIONS TOOK a ship bound for Assos, but Paul left a little later and journeyed on foot (v. 13b). Was this so that he could avoid choppy weather? Did he want to stay a little longer to ensure that young Eutychus was well? Or did he just want to be alone? Or did he keep changing his plans because he was carrying a lot of money for the Christians in Jerusalem and did not want others (apart from his close colleagues) to know where he would be at a particular time? Whatever the reason, the twenty-mile walk alone would have done him a lot of good. From Assos Paul headed for Miletus by ship (vv. 14–15). These two ports were on the western coast of the mainland of Asia Minor. Between them were the island ports of Mitylene, Kios, and Samos. Paul avoided going to Ephesus (v. 16) possibly to save time since he was subject to the schedule of the ship or possibly because it would have been dangerous for him to go there.

---

9. Longenecker, "Acts," 509.
10. Bruce, *Acts: Greek Text*, 426.
11. The other five are in Luke 7:11–16; 8:49–56; 24:6; John 11:43–44; Acts 9:36–42.
12. Alexander, *Acts*, 232.

Encouraging the Ephesian Elders (20:17–38)

THOUGH PAUL AVOIDED Ephesus, he sent for the elders of that church to come to Miletus (about thirty miles by land), possibly while the ship was loading and unloading its cargo. His talk to this group follows the form of farewell speeches familiar at that time.[13] The language of this speech is more like Paul's than Luke's. Keener observes that "because presumably Luke had little access to Paul's letters (they were not collected from various churches until long after Paul's death), he must have learned Paul's style from direct contact with him."[14]

This is the only record we have of a speech that Paul gave to believers, and its contents are remarkably similar to his letters (also addressed to believers). This is a strong point against those who allege that Acts cannot be historically reliable because of alleged differences between the Paul of Acts and of the letters. The Pastoral Letters were written to elders, and they have a remarkable number of points in common with this speech.[15]

Paul's talk has three main themes. (1) He defends his behavior, presenting it as an example to Ephesian elders (vv. 18–27, 33–35). (2) He presents a charge along with a warning (vv. 28–30). (3) Finally, he commits them to God (v. 32).

Paul's example (20:18–27). The first and most prominent theme of the speech is Paul's example—an element typical of farewell addresses. He says he was an example in four things. (1) *He identified with the people,* living among them (v. 18), serving God with humility and tears (v. 19), and going from house to house (v. 20). This enabled him to know what they needed to hear, so that he

---

13. "The farewell discourse is a genre present throughout Scripture (Gen. 47:29–49:33; Deut. 31:14–33:29; Josh. 23:1–24:30; 1 Sam. 12:1–25; 2 Kings 2:1–14; Matt. 28:18–20; John 13–17; 2 Tim.; 2 Peter....). The departing leader's life is reviewed as an example for imitation and an apologetic for his conduct. There are warnings concerning future dangers to the faith, exhortations to faithfulness and God's benediction in an affectionate, sorrowful, prayerful farewell" (Larkin, *Acts,* 292–93).

14. Keener, *BBC,* 383.

15. Both have autobiographical sections (vv. 18–27, 33–35; 1 Tim. 1:12–16; 2 Tim. 2:8–10; 4:6–18) and both emphasize the importance of example (Acts 20:18–27, 31, 33–35; 1 Tim. 4:12; Titus 2:7), of finishing the race (Acts 20:24; 2 Tim. 4:7), of hard work (Acts 20:18–21, 35; 2 Tim. 2:6), of suffering (Acts 20:22–25; 2 Tim. 1:8, 12; 2:3, 9–10; 4:6), of impending trouble (Acts 20:22–25; 2 Tim. 4:6–7), of communicating a body of truth carefully (Acts 20:20, 26–27, 32; 1 Tim. 6:20; 2 Tim. 2:2, 15), of false teachers coming from within the church (Acts 20:29–31; 2 Tim. 4:3–4), of being on guard against certain people (Acts 20:30–31; 2 Tim 4:14–15), of the importance of leaders looking after their own lives (Acts 20:26; 1 Tim. 4:7, 15–16; 2 Tim. 2), of tears of concern (Acts 20:19, 31; 2 Tim. 1:4), of the primacy of the ministry of the Word (Acts 20:20, 26–27, 32; 1 Tim. 4:13–14; 2 Tim. 4:2), of the ability of the Word to help keep people in the faith (Acts 20:32; 2 Tim. 3:16–17), etc.

was able to preach everything that was helpful to them (v. 20a). He obviously had what might be called an openhearted approach to ministry. This is why he could spend a whole night chatting with the believers in Troas (vv. 9–10), and this is why he shed so many tears among the Ephesians (vv. 19, 31).

(2) *Paul was a teacher.* He taught the Ephesians everything that was helpful to them, and did so publicly and from house to house (v. 20). His teaching was relevant to their needs.

(3) *Paul was a witness to the gospel* (v. 21). Paul uses the word *diamartyromai*, translated "declared" here (cf. comments on 18:5). This word conveys the idea that evangelism is a serious responsibility as it calls people to repentance and faith. Later Paul says that the preaching was comprehensive in that he did not hesitate "to proclaim to [them] the whole will of God" (v. 27). Because of that he was able to declare that he was innocent of their blood (v. 26). Verses 21, 26–27 remind us of the call to be a watchman, with a responsibility to warn people adequately as described in Ezekiel 3:16–21; 33:1–9.

(4) Paul's commitment to evangelism is closely tied in with the fourth area where he was an example: *Paul suffered because of obedience.* In verses 22–23 he attributes two actions to the Holy Spirit: a compulsion that is now driving him to Jerusalem and a regular warning (*diamartyromai*) that he will suffer if he goes to Jerusalem. Verse 24 explains how these two seemingly contradictory messages can be reconciled: the goal of life is not to preserve our lives but to be faithful to our calling to testify to the gospel. If such faithfulness involves suffering and imprisonment, then such experiences will be taken on willingly.

After presenting what the Holy Spirit has communicated to him, Paul presents a personal conviction that he will not see them again (v. 25). That, in turn, prompts his declaration that he is "innocent of the blood of all men" because he has warned them of God's truth (vv. 26–27).

A charge and a warning (20:28–31). Paul is aware of the danger of things going wrong in Ephesus. He therefore both charges them and sternly warns them. The charge consists of three points. (1) Most important, the elders must keep watch over themselves (v. 28).

(2) They must watch over the flock as overseers (v. 28). The word translated "overseer" (*episkopos*) has often been rendered "bishop." As elsewhere in Scripture it is a synonym for "elder" (see v. 17). Whereas "elder" focuses on the maturity of the individual, "overseer" focuses on the function, which is to take care of the people. In this verse (and in Heb. 13:17) this task takes the form of keeping watch over them. Believers are to be especially on guard for "savage wolves," who will come even from within the church and distort the truth (vv. 29–30). When Paul was there he had warned people about this danger day and night with tears (v. 31).

(3) The elders must shepherd the flock (see also 1 Peter 5:2–3), which is so valuable that it was bought by Christ's own blood. Shepherding involves "tending, caring for, feeding, protecting, and leading."[16] The reference to Christ's act of purchasing the church with his own blood reminds us that just as the good shepherd gave his life for the sheep (cf. John 10:11), we too must give our lives for the sheep.

Committing the people to God and his word (20:32). Paul finally commits the elders "to God and to the word of his grace." The message they received will enable them to stay close to God. Today we have this message in the Scriptures. Though Paul may not have intended both Old and New Testament here, we can legitimately extend it to the entire Bible, for unlike the time of the first apostles, when their message carried final authority, today we have the Word of God in which that message is contained.

Paul's example (again) (20:33–35). Paul concludes his speech by once more presenting the challenge of his own life as an example for the elders to follow. When he was with them, he showed sincere commitment. He did not covet what others had (v. 33). Rather, he worked hard with his own hands to provide for the needs of the team (v. 34), and in the process he demonstrated one of the Christian aims for earning money: helping those who are in need (see also Eph. 4:28). There is a ring of credibility to his appeals for money for the poor because he himself led the way by being generous in his own giving.

The farewell (20:36–38). The grief expressed at Paul's departure gives us an indication of how much he was loved. He had paid the price of opening his life to these people. They, in turn, reciprocated by opening their lives to him. They now accompany him to the ship, and he proceeds on his journey to Jerusalem—just like his Master, who also "resolutely set out for Jerusalem" (Luke 9:51), knowing that death awaited him there.

Bridging Contexts

WE SEE TWO significant themes that seem repeated in this section:[17] the complex situations involving Paul and the Jews, and his encouraging the churches.

Paul and the Jewish reaction. Though it is perhaps a secondary theme to this passage, the issue of Paul and the Jewish reaction to the gospel is an

---

16. Daniel L. Akin, "Overseer," *EDBT*, 586.

17. I originally planned to do two separate studies on this chapter. But I found that these two themes were equally found in both sections. As a result, I was forced to opt for one long study on the whole chapter.

important part of the tension that Luke is building up as he moves toward the close of his book. Twice Luke records plots against him (vv. 3, 19), and the plots in Asia were described as severe tests to Paul (v. 19). He describes his impending visit to Jerusalem as promising hardship to him (vv. 22–24). Paul specifically mentions his faithfulness in proclaiming the message to the Jews (v. 21). We are also told about Paul in relation to the Jewish festivals (vv. 6, 16). We know that this trip will result in his arrest, and that a patriotic act of Paul will be interpreted as having defiled the temple.

The Jews reacted to Paul's message in the same way as they reacted to Jesus' message (see Luke 4:16–31). In his Gospel Luke built up the tension relating to the significant final trip that Jesus made to Jerusalem. This begins as early as 9:51: "As the time approached for him to be taken up to heaven, Jesus resolutely set out for Jerusalem." Immediately after that he said that "the people [of Samaria] did not welcome him, because he was heading for Jerusalem" (9:53). A little later Luke mentioned that "Jesus went through the towns and villages, teaching as he made his way to Jerusalem" (13:22). Jesus himself said in connection with his journey that "surely no prophet can die outside Jerusalem!" (13:33). This prompted the lament: "O Jerusalem, Jerusalem, you who kill the prophets and stone those sent to you, how often I have longed to gather your children together" (13:34).

Later Luke again reported that Jesus was on his way to Jerusalem (Luke 17:11), and Jesus added that he would die and be raised up (18:31–33). As he neared Jerusalem the people thought that the kingdom of God was going to appear at once (19:11), prompting a parable. This buildup came to climax with the events of Palm Sunday, when Jesus entered Jerusalem triumphantly, but the leaders rejected the people's welcoming cries. Jesus wept over Jerusalem and predicted its destruction. Then he cleared the temple of the money changers and continued to teach, while the leaders looked for a way to kill him (ch. 19). A comment by the disciples about the grandeur of the temple prompted him to give a discourse about the coming events, particularly Jerusalem's doom (ch. 21). The next climax, of course, was the death of Jesus.

With what drama and pathos Luke has recorded how God's people rejected the Son of God! Luke records a similar drama and pathos in his second volume in his report on the journey of one of the great sons of the Israelites to Jerusalem. As with Jesus there are ominous signs of trouble, but Paul persists with the same assurance of impending crisis and the same resoluteness that Jesus had (Acts 20:22–25). Rejection by his own people was not easy for Paul to take. In fact he "was severely tested by the plots of the Jews" (v. 19). It was during this period of his life that he wrote the letter to the Romans, with his sublime theological reflection on the Jewish rejection of the gospel. This theological discourse begins with an expression of his deep sorrow over this rejection (Rom. 9:1–4a).

> I speak the truth in Christ—I am not lying, my conscience confirms it in the Holy Spirit—I have great sorrow and unceasing anguish in my heart. For I could wish that I myself were cursed and cut off from Christ for the sake of my brothers, those of my own race, the people of Israel.

What principles can we derive from this for us today? (1) It describes for us the mysterious phenomenon of Jewish rejection of the gospel. Like Paul we too should say, "My heart's desire and prayer to God for the Israelites is that they may be saved" (Rom. 10:1). We too should, like Paul, yearn for the salvation of the Jews and support Jewish evangelism.[18]

(2) I believe, however, that this biblical phenomenon of God's representatives being rejected by their own people has a wider application. It speaks a word of comfort and challenge to all those who in obedience to God are living as pilgrims, are paying the price of obedience, and are rejected by those who should know better. Jesus "came to that which was his own, but his own did not receive him" (John 1:11). We should not expect anything different for ourselves. Jesus said, "'No servant is greater than his master.' If they persecuted me, they will persecute you also." But Jesus said immediately thereafter: "If they obeyed my teaching, they will obey yours also" (John 15:20). Along with disappointments will be a few successes that make the price paid worthwhile.

More on Luke's theology of suffering. Paul's approach to his impending suffering adds a new dimension to Luke's theology of suffering, an important theme of Acts. Paul received a dual message from the Spirit: He must go to Jerusalem, and if he goes there he will suffer. Of course, as Calvin reminds us, he did "not rashly rush into the midst of dangers."[19] Thus, he took the longer route to Jerusalem, arriving there later than originally planned (v. 3). But if obedience was at stake, he willingly suffered. This was not suffering just for the sake of suffering; rather, it came out of a deep ambition that drove Paul—the ambition to finish the race and complete the task God gave him (v. 24). That ambition overcame the legitimate, though secondary, task of protecting his life. This approach to life is consistent with what Paul wrote in his letters. The instinct to self-preservation and personal advancement was always subsumed by his ambition to see God's kingdom grow through his obedience.

---

18. The issue of evangelizing Jews will be discussed in more detail in our study of 28:16–31.

19. Calvin, *Acts 14–28*, 168.

Paul's primary issue was the fulfilling of his mission. Second Corinthians 4 is a key passage here. In verse 7 he presents his glorious mission: "But we have this treasure in jars of clay to show that this all-surpassing power is from God and not from us." This body—this person—of ours, which people give so much time and energy trying to nurture and beautify, is just a jar of clay when considered from the perspective of eternal realities. Only in connection with those realities does life find its worth. Thus Paul writes in verses 8–12 that he was willing to be subjected to pain and hardship if it helped further this cause that gave him significance:

> We are hard pressed on every side, but not crushed; perplexed, but not in despair; persecuted, but not abandoned; struck down, but not destroyed. We always carry around in our body the death of Jesus, so that the life of Jesus may also be revealed in our body. For we who are alive are always being given over to death for Jesus' sake, so that his life may be revealed in our mortal body. So then, death is at work in us, but life is at work in you.

This perspective convinces Paul that he is not really at a loss through his sacrifices: "Therefore we do not lose heart. Though outwardly we are wasting away, yet inwardly we are being renewed day by day. For our light and momentary troubles are achieving for us an eternal glory that far outweighs them all" (2 Cor. 4:16–17). In a similar vein, in 1 Corinthians 9, after listing the many sacrifices he made on behalf of the gospel, Paul exclaims, "What then is my reward? Just this: that in preaching the gospel I may offer it free of charge, and so not make use of my rights in preaching it.... I do all this for the sake of the gospel, that I may share in its blessings" (vv. 18, 23). In other words, Acts 20 and Paul's letters tell us that the cause of the gospel is so great that any price is worth paying in order to advance it (v. 24).

It is important to note that in Acts 20 Paul presents his willingness to suffer for the gospel as part of his attempt to encourage the Ephesian elders to be faithful to their task. This is a common theme with Paul. He often appeals to his own sufferings when he wants to influence his readers about something important (see 1 and 2 Corinthians; Gal. 6:17; Eph. 4:1). Note also what Hebrews says: After writing how Jesus, "for the joy set before him endured the cross, scorning its shame, and sat down at the right hand of the throne of God," the author goes on: "Consider him who endured such opposition from sinful men, *so that you will not grow weary and lose heart*" (Heb. 12:2–3, italics added). Leaders who suffer encourage others to take on suffering themselves.

Related to this is the point hinted at in Acts 20:28, that leaders are shepherds who die for their flock. Since this thought rarely comes to our minds when we think of leadership, we need to expand it from Scripture. Jesus is our model, so that what he did for us, we do for others (cf. John 13:14). As the Father sent him into the world, we are sent into the world (20:21)— which means that as he laid down his life for us, we must be willing to lay down our lives for our friends (15:12–13). The good shepherd is so committed to the sheep that he dies for them (10:11–15). Paul specifically asks us to follow the example of Jesus, who "though he was rich, yet for your sakes he became poor, so that you through his poverty might become rich" (2 Cor. 8:9).

Paul's life fully exemplified this principle. He informs us how he took on the death of Christ in his body for the sake of the church (2 Cor. 4:10–11): "So then, death is at work in us, but life is at work in you. . . . All this is for your benefit, so that the grace that is reaching more and more people may cause thanksgiving to overflow to the glory of God" (4:12, 15; see Col. 1:24– 25). Therefore, a leader's calling is to shepherd the flock by being willing to die for it.

In summary, then, this passage teaches us three things about suffering. (1) Christians take on suffering that they can easily avoid because of their commitment to the glorious gospel of Christ, a cause that makes such suffering worthwhile. (2) People will be motivated to suffer for the gospel when they see their leaders suffer for it. (3) Leaders not only suffer for the gospel, they suffer for those whom they lead.

The itinerant ministry of encouragement. Encouragement is the major theme of this chapter. This is why Paul visits each city, and encouragement is indicated by the threefold repetition of the word *parakaleo*. Paul's speech (vv. 18–35) gives a sampling of the content of his "many words of encouragement" (v. 2). Note that the evangelistic preacher is an encourager here. In the Bible evangelism and encouragement are often done by the same person—a healthy combination for anyone doing evangelism. There is no place in the Bible for a specialist evangelist who concentrates solely on his public ministry, leaving personal ministry to others.

Like God, Paul encouraged the people through three means. (1) God encourages us through his presence, expressed in the incarnation of Christ and through the indwelling Holy Spirit. Similarly Christian leaders encourage other Christians through their being with people and identifying with them. (2) Just as God encourages us through his Word, human encouragers do it through expounding the Word in teaching. (3) As God encourages us through his actions on our behalf, we encourage others through deeds of kindness. Let us look at these three means of encouragement in more detail.

(1) Paul encouraged people through his *presence.* The arrival of the key leader of the Gentile mission in a city must have been an event of great

encouragement to the believers there, especially since the visit was made primarily to encourage them. Paul's presence was not the detached presence of a specialist who does his public ministry and then retreats to his private world. He really became one with the people, identifying with their hurts and aspirations. The speech to the Ephesians shows that Paul's presence was manifested in costly identification with the people (vv. 18–20, 31, 35). Perhaps the best example of identification through presence is the way he chatted through the night with the people (vv. 7, 9, 11); this is something friends do. Paul's method of encouragement also included getting alongside people in their homes (v. 20).

When Paul got alongside people, they were able to observe him. He says to them here: "You know how I lived the whole time I was with you" (v. 18). He later told Timothy, "You, however, know all about my teaching, my way of life, my purpose, faith, patience, love, endurance, persecutions, sufferings—what kinds of things happened to me in Antioch, Iconium and Lystra, the persecutions I endured" (2 Tim. 3:10–11). Timothy knew Paul through and through because his life was like an open book. Therefore, he could send Timothy out on a mission as his representative and claim, "He will remind you of my way of life in Christ Jesus, which agrees with what I teach everywhere in every church" (1 Cor. 4:17).

In this process of identification and open friendship close ties developed, which made Paul vulnerable to being hurt. And he was hurt, for three times in this passage we find references to tears or weeping (vv. 19, 31, 37). But that is the cost of openhearted identification.

(2) Paul encouraged people through his *words*. He "traveled through that area, speaking many words of encouragement to the people" (v. 2). Verses 7 and 9 report the marathon talking session in Troas. Verses 18–35 give a sample of his message of encouragement. Teaching the Word, of course, is vital in encouragement. Thus, while Paul's first visits to most of the places mentioned in our passage were for evangelism, the second visits were primarily for teaching. Barnabas and Saul, who were outstanding evangelists, taught for a whole year in Antioch (11:26). Earlier we noted that in the evangelism in Acts, the evangelists preached and taught the gospel and also demonstrated it through their actions, especially through miracles.[20] Now we see that this is the same for nurture. Just as conversion takes place through faith, growth in grace also takes place through faith. The faith awakened through the evangelist by word and deed is nurtured through the encourager by word and deed. In the Bible the evangelist and the encourager are often the same person (cf. 20:20–21).

---

20. See the discussion on 3:1–25; 19:8–41.

The above evidence should make us cautious about driving a wedge between evangelism and nurture, between preaching and teaching. While we are grateful for people like C. H. Dodd, who highlighted the importance of the *kerygma* (the proclaimed gospel) in distinction to the *didache* (the teaching), we must not draw too much of the distinction between the two.

Paul's identification with the people undoubtedly helped make his teaching concrete. He knew the Word and the people to whom he spoke, so that he was able to teach relevantly to their situation. If we live close to people, our teaching becomes relevant to them. Note too Paul's final comment to these people before leaving them: He commits them "to God *and to the word of his grace*" (v. 32, italics added). God's work of keeping his children safe is done primarily through the truth of the gospel, which is now contained in the written Word, the Bible. This passage, then, challenges us to teach the Word relevantly to our people for that will help them remain close to God.

(3) Paul encouraged people through his *actions*. The great encouragement of the people in verse 12 is directly connected with the raising up of Eutychus. Paul's house-to-house visits (v. 20) can be regarded as acts of kindness, as is whatever was involved in his "[serving] the Lord with great humility and with tears" (v. 19). He also worked hard with his hands and showed them that "by this kind of hard work we must help the weak" (v. 35). These are all actions that helped encourage these Christians.

Priorities for leaders. Paul's solemn parting charge to the elders (vv. 28–31) gives three significant priorities for leaders. (1) They must keep watch over themselves (v. 28a). We are reminded of Paul's charge to Timothy: "Watch your life and doctrine closely. Persevere in them, because if you do, you will save both yourself and your hearers" (1 Tim. 4:16). The biggest battle the Christian leader has is to ensure that his or her life is in order. We are reminded of the comment by Robert Murray McCheyne, "My people's greatest need is my personal holiness." Paul's charge to Timothy to "persevere in them" reminds us that some who start well do not end well because they have not kept watch over themselves.

(2) Leaders must be overseers of the flock (v. 28a). One way to do that is to be alert to false teaching (vv. 29–30), just as Paul was (v. 31). Christianity is a religion of revelation from a God, whose thoughts are higher than ours (Isa. 55:8–9). It is therefore easy for human wisdom to supplant or radically reinterpret God's Word because it seems so unreasonable to those whose minds are not in tune with him. This danger will be with us always, and we must continue to warn people about the danger of aberrations of the truth entering the church.

(3) They must shepherd the flock (v. 28b) (this element is discussed above in the context of Luke's theology of suffering).

REJECTION BY OUR own. We noted that just as Jesus and Paul were rejected by their own, we too may face rejection from our own people. The day before I wrote this I was at the police station, try-ing to secure the release of my assistant, who is like a son to me. He is from the other major race in our country. Some from his race are trying to divide our land through civil war. He was arrested and had the humiliation of stay-ing twelve hours in a smelly, crowded, warm, and humid cell. He felt rejected by the nation he loves, having been arrested under suspicion of belonging to a group whose activities he himself detests.

A highly qualified professional rejects many lucrative offers of jobs in order to work for the state for a much lower salary but where she can per-form a great service to the most needy people in the land. Rather than being appreciated and praised for the sacrifices she makes, she encounters jealousy and a mass of red tape that takes away much pleasantness from her job.

There are many people like this today. Some work in banking projects that help the poor build houses. Some teach in inner-city schools, where they are considered a nuisance by parents, students, and colleagues who have little ambitions for the students. Some work with AIDS patients, who in their bit-terness reject the love caregivers try to bestow. Some have parents who are angry about the sacrifices their children have made for the sake of the kingdom.

As both Jesus and Paul found rejection emotionally difficult to take, we too will find this hard on our emotions. That is inevitable, for we have a special love for these people and rejection by them is tough to take. Jesus wept over Jerusalem. Paul had great sorrow and unceasing anguish in his heart over the Jews. We too should not be surprised if we struggle with bit-terness over rejection by our own. But we must fight such feelings and remain obedient to God's call. We must keep yearning for these people until the day we die, remembering that we are pilgrims who may see the fruit of our labors only in heaven.

Bringing back the theology of suffering to the church. It is well known that church leaders today find it difficult to motivate others to suffer for the cause of Christ. In fact, they often find it difficult to motivate Christians even to take on inconvenience for the sake of Christ. The three principles about suffering gleaned from this passage can help us here. (1) Realizing the greatness of the cause of Christ should fire us with an ambition to take on suffering as a natural response (v. 24). Have we presented the glory of this cause in our proclamation? Or has our proclamation been so this-worldly, so related to our little human desires, that people have lost sight of the glory of the gospel cause? In focusing so much on felt needs, have we neglected the grand theme of the kingdom of God, which is a cause worth dying for? This passage challenges us to rethink our proclamation so that our people will be fired up by the greatness of the cause of Christ. Then they too can say with Paul, "When I preach the gospel, I cannot boast, for I am compelled to preach. Woe to me if I do not preach the gospel!" (1 Cor. 9:16).

How important it is to recover this biblical sense of the glory of suffering for a great cause. Perhaps because people have become obsessed with lesser causes today, those who suffer for the gospel are viewed as failures and are pitied in the church rather than admired. Fatigue, unpopularity, inconvenience, or loss of prestige on earth, taken on because of obedience, are regarded as signs of weakness and folly rather than strength and wisdom. This is particularly a problem in richer countries, where economic and technological advancement have made it possible for people to have many conveniences. Convenience itself has become a major goal in life. Even Christians today avoid inconvenience for the gospel and resent it when they are inconvenienced.

This pattern has posed a major problem to churches in poorer countries. They send some of their most capable people to richer countries for education, and these people return expecting convenience. They have become soft and do not want to suffer; when they do, they resent it. Not only do they end up having ineffective ministries, they also drag the church down to their low level of commitment. We should work hard at trying to restore a sense of the glory of suffering in the church.

(2) Leaders can motivate others to suffer for the gospel by themselves being examples of suffering. It is no secret that commitment breeds commitment. When a leader is willing to die for a cause, those who follow are also fired by enthusiasm. A leader's willingness to die impresses others of the urgency of the task they are involved in, thrills them with its significance, and motivates them to commitment. Our Youth for Christ ministry in Sri Lanka works primarily through volunteers. One of the things we have found is that if the leader works hard at personal cost to himself or herself, that leader usually can recruit and keep committed volunteers. If the leader does not work hard, volunteers often get demotivated and are unwilling to pay a price.

(3) To this discussion we must add the third priority of leadership gleaned from verse 28: Leaders are good shepherds who die for their sheep. Not only do we die for the cause, we also die for the people we lead. This principle is often violated by Christian leaders today. A gifted pastor leaves a struggling church that needs him badly when he receives an invitation to go to a vibrant church that pays a much higher salary. A professor leaves the struggling seminary of her small denomination that is desperately short of teachers, to go to a famous school that offers her a bigger salary for teach-

ing less hours, along with a generous package that gives time for writing. A Sunday school teacher rejects the request of a distraught student to go home with him to help resolve a crisis with his parents because it is after 11:00 P.M. These people are not willing to die for their flock. Such lack of commitment begets a selfish Christianity.

One of the keys to solving the commitment crisis in the church is for a few people to be willing to die for their flock. When a leader is willing to die for those whom he or she leads, they in turn become willing to die for the movement or church they are part of. We need to raise up a generation of radical Christians willing to pay the necessary price for us to shake this world with the revolutionary message of Christ. Most leaders are not willing to die for others because no one has been willing to die for them. They have not had a model to follow. But we do have the model of Jesus and Paul. If we start using that model, we may breed a new generation of leaders who will die for others and help multiply generations of committed Christians.

Evangelists who encourage. The combination of evangelist and encourager is an important one for the health of the church. The Bible has no place for specialist evangelists who do nothing but preach publicly. Unfortunately, with specialization growing in today's church, this is becoming more common. We have evangelists who do little more than speak at public meetings. The rest of the time they spend in their hotels, often leaving a meeting before the audience is dismissed so as not to be disturbed by the people. True, we must ensure that those in public ministry not be overtaxed, resulting in physical and emotional exhaustion. But we must also guard against the other extreme—having them do so little personal work that they lose touch with the people. This will ultimately render their message ineffective.

Jesus, Peter, and Paul are the most prominent evangelists in the New Testament. The portrait presented of them is of people who excelled in personal ministry. This has been my experience with some of the famous evangelists of today. Though the Christian world knows people like Billy Graham, John Stott, and Leighton Ford through their public ministry, many of us Christian workers know them more through their encouraging words and letters to us.

My first experience of speaking at an international conference was at the Amsterdam '83 conference for itinerant evangelists. I was thirty-four years old and felt inadequate to address 4,000 evangelists. I spoke on the call for senior evangelists to disciple younger evangelists. One of my points was that evangelists should take younger people with them when they travel and so have a "traveling Bible school," as Paul did. Billy Graham was not on the platform when I spoke. But at the end of the meeting he came to the platform, thanked me for my message, and told me that he would like to travel with me some day to learn how to minister in Asia. I was stunned! His word of encouragement filled me with joy and multiplied my resolve to encourage younger Christian workers.

Openhearted identification. We must not forget that at the heart of Paul's ministry of encouragement was his identification with people. Today identification has become a science that is studied in technical ways by anthropologists, sociologists, and missiologists. I do not want to downplay the importance of such studies. They give people an appreciation of cultures that will help people avoid mistakes that some missionaries have made in the past. But far more important is being with the people—being friends with them and chatting with them. Often we have such busy schedules that we find this inconvenient. Consequently, we substitute it with our studies, which can be done under conditions we can control. But this way it is difficult to get to the heart of where a people are..Much of their heart-cry comes out through friendship, and friendship is forged through lingering, as Paul did all night in Troas. This was not an isolated exception, for Jesus did the same thing with two of John's disciples who became his disciples after a long chatting session (John 1:38–42).

Paul's ability to linger with those whom he nurtured was the key to his ability to make friends. Bruce, in a book about the friends of Paul, says, "Paul attracted friends around him as a magnet attracts iron filings. His genius for friendship has been spoken of so often that it has become proverbial—almost cliché."[21] The main reason why Paul was able to make such close friends was that he opened his life to them.[22] Unfortunately this openhearted approach to ministry is getting less and less popular today. We value our privacy so much that we prefer to keep our private lives and our ministerial lives separate. Even the so-called accountability groups of many Christians are not with colleagues in their ministry (who can observe them best and so help them most) but with people they don't work closely with. We are not used to bearing the pain of being close to people. Our generation is so committed to feeling good that it fears the experience of such pain. The result is a shallow ministry.

A key to openhearted ministry is lingering in conversation, as Paul did in Troas. Lingering creates an atmosphere for openness. Things come up that would not have come up in a more formal meeting. Such elements are usually the keys to a person's heart.[23] Again, there is a trend against this type of relationship in ministry. I have heard people say that leaders should not get too close to those they lead for they will not be able to lead them properly

---

21. Bruce, *Circle*, 8–9.

22. On this see my book *Leadership Lifestyle: A Study of 1 Timothy* (Wheaton, Ill.: Tyndale, 1985), 15–25.

23. On lingering and this type of friendship in general, see my *Friendship*, esp. 28–35.

because of their friendship. That may be the way secular organizations work, but it is alien to a Christian understanding of leadership. Jesus himself told his disciples: "I no longer call you servants, because a servant does not know his master's business. Instead, I have called you friends, for everything that I learned from my Father I have made known to you" (John 15:15). That is the openhearted ministry we are talking about. Such ministry has great rewards. Few earthly pleasures can match the joy of true Christian friendship.

People are often afraid of this openhearted approach to ministry because of a fear of burnout, which has reached epidemic proportions in helping professions today. This can happen, of course, and we must be careful to avoid it.[24] Three things implied about Paul's ministry here helped him avoid burnout. (1) His approach left room for relaxed lingering with friends, which is a great antidote to burnout. Driven people are most prone to burnout, and many are so busy with their "mission" that they have no time or inclination to nurture deep friendships.

(2) Paul knew how to be alone, especially with God; this is an even greater antidote to burnout. His huge prayer list (which emerges from the letters) must have taken a long time to cover. Few things refresh us more than being in God's presence interceding for people. Paul's twenty-mile walk from Troas to Assos (v. 13) may have been just for the purpose of being alone. Having a day off (a day of Sabbath rest) is important for Christian workers, especially in today's rushed society.[25] We know that when Jesus tried to take time off from the crowds, it was difficult. He said to his disciples, "Come with me by yourselves to a quiet place and get some rest. So they went away by themselves in a boat to a solitary place" (Mark 6:31-32). But the people caught up with them (v. 33; see also 7:24). Yet he persevered, trying hard to find time to be alone, and finally he succeeded (6:46; see 1:35).

The importance of these two points of enrichment through friends and through aloneness with God is well expressed by the fourth-century bishop of Milan, Ambrose, who writes in his work *Duties of the Clergy*, "Am I to suppose that he is fit to give me advice who never takes it for himself, or am I to believe that he has time to give me when he has none for himself? . . . How can a person have time for giving counsel when one has none for quiet?"[26]

---

24. On burnout see, Donald E. Demaray, *Watch Out for Burnout: A Look at Signs, Prevention and Cure* (Grand Rapids: Baker, 1983); D. G. Kehl, "Burnout: The Risk of Reaching too High," *Christianity Today* (Nov. 20, 1981); Archibald Hart, "Recovery From Stress and Burnout," *Pastors at Risk*, H. B. London Jr. and Neil B. Wiseman, ed. (Wheaton: Victor, 1993), 157–72; John A. Sanford, *Ministry Burnout* (New York: Paulist, 1982).

25. See Hart's comments in "Recovery From Stress and Burnout," 59–60, 68–69.

26. *A Select Library of the Nicene and Post-Nicene Fathers of the Christian Church*, 2d series, ed. H. Wace and P. Schaff (New York: Christian), 10:53; cited in Thomas C. Oden, *Classical Pastoral Care*, vol. 1, *Becoming a Minister* (Grand Rapids: Baker, 1994), 13.

(3) Working in a team was important to Paul. In team ministry leaders will not do everything that needs to be done and run themselves into the ground. They depend a lot on others. Thus, a good leader must give high priority to equipping others to do the work. Paul, of course, was a master at this. This is why he called only the leaders of Ephesus to come to Miletus. Though he had a general concern for the entire church at Ephesus, he took on the special responsibility of equipping leaders. When he started churches, he soon appointed leaders (14:23). He gave special instruction to these leaders, as we see here and in the Pastoral Letters. He sent them as his representatives on missionary assignments. He could trust people like Timothy and Titus because he had opened himself to them and taught them comprehensively (1 Cor. 4:17).

Paul's openhearted approach to ministry is well expressed in a statement he made to the Corinthians, who had closed their hearts to him. Without reciprocating their closure, Paul responded by persisting in his openness since that was the best way to win them back: "We have spoken freely to you, Corinthians, and opened wide our hearts to you. We are not withholding our affection from you, but you are withholding yours from us. As a fair exchange . . . open wide your hearts also" (2 Cor. 6:11–13).

The teaching ministry. On several occasions we have discussed the challenge of teaching in today's world.[27] Two unique points about teaching are mentioned in our passage. (1) As a result of Paul's identification with the people, his teaching was relevant to their needs. We must know the Scriptures and know our people. The best way to know the people is to get close to them. (2) Paul believed in the keeping power of the Word, which caused him to commit them "to God and to the word of his grace" (v. 32). I am reminded of what Susanna Wesley told her son John: "This book will keep you from sin or sin will keep you from this book."

Watching over ourselves. Given the fact that appearance and success are so important in our pragmatic society, Paul's charge to keep watch over ourselves (v. 28) is significant. We have become used to measuring success by indicators that can be maintained without a holy life—such as the technical quality of our programs, their popularity, and the ability to balance our budgets. We have also become increasingly privatized so that the private life of many leaders remains known only to members of their families, who generally do not publicize the faults of other family members. Sometimes even they are in the dark about what is happening inside a leader. Thus it is possible to go on ministering and appearing successful while our personal lives are in shambles. But in God's sight we will be disqualified. Therefore Paul said, "I beat my body and make it my slave so that after I have preached to others,

---

27. See the studies on 1:1–8; 2:42–27; 6:1–7; 17:1–15.

I myself will not be disqualified for the prize" (1 Cor. 9:27). A. W. Tozer once wrote, "Do you know who gives me the most trouble? Do you know who I pray for the most in my pastoral work? Just myself."[28]

Combating false teaching. Seeing that one of the priorities of an overseer is to be alert to the possibility of false teaching affecting the church (vv. 28–31), we should discuss this in light of the theological battles of this century. In the late nineteenth and early twentieth century our spiritual ancestors, especially in North America, had to battle for the truth of the gospel against skepticism regarding the supernatural and the trustworthiness of Scripture and an unbiblical optimism about human nature, which opened the door to a lot of other unbiblical doctrines. These teachings came to be known as liberalism.[29] The battles were bruising, with extreme reactions on both sides. Evangelicals—or fundamentalists, as they were called then—reacted against many excesses by discarding some truths that had been an important part of the evangelical tradition, such as social concern[30] and intellectual engagement with the culture.[31]

Around the middle of the twentieth century a fresh brand of evangelicalism arose, which had warmer ties with Christians of other perspectives and was more committed to social concern[32] and intellectual engagement.[33] It was led by scholars like Carl F. H. Henry and Edward John Carnell and churchmen like Harold John Ockenga. Fuller Theological Seminary was its most prominent intellectual center[34] and *Christianity Today* its most prominent periodical. The

---

28. A. W. Tozer, *Whatever Happened to Worship?* comp. and ed. Gerald B. Smith (Camp Hill, Pa.: Christian Publications, 1985), 78.

29. See George M. Marsden, *Fundamentalism and the American Culture: The Shaping of Twentieth-Century Evangelicalism: 1870–1925* (Oxford and New York: Oxford Univ. Press, 1980).

30. See Donald W. Dayton, *Discovering an Evangelical Heritage* (New York: Harper and Row, 1976).

31. Some great evangelical scholars did emerge at this time, however, like B. B. Warfield and J. Gresham Machen. See Machen, *The Origin of Paul's Religion* (New York: Macmillan, 1921; repr. Grand Rapids: Eerdmans, 1973); idem, *Christianity and Liberalism* (New York: Macmillan, 1923; repr. Grand Rapids: Eerdmans); idem, *The Virgin Birth of Christ* (New York: Harper and Row, 1930; repr. Grand Rapids: Baker, 1974); Warfield, *Works of Benjamin Warfield*, 10 vols. (New York: Oxford Univ. Press, 1927–1932). See the reprint, Warfield, *The Inspiration and Authority of the Bible*, ed. Samuel G. Craig (Philadelphia: Presbyterian and Reformed, 1948).

32. See Carl F. H. Henry, *The Uneasy Conscience of Modern Fundamentalism* (Grand Rapids: Eerdmans, 1948).

33. See Edward John Carnell, *An Introduction to Christian Apologetics: A Philosophic Defense of the Trinitarian-Theistic Faith* (Grand Rapids: Eerdmans, 1948); idem, *A Philosophy of the Christian Religion* (Grand Rapids: Eerdmans, 1952; repr. Grand Rapids: Baker, 1980).

34. See George M. Marsden, *Reforming Fundamentalism: Fuller Seminary and the New Evangelicalism* (Grand Rapids: Eerdmans, 1987).

National Association of Evangelicals was a rallying point and Billy Graham its most prominent preacher. Though British evangelicalism did not have such a serious battle, it produced scholars like F. F. Bruce and churchmen like John R. W. Stott, who advocated a similar brand of evangelicalism.

Many reacted negatively to these changes, which they saw as compromise. Under people like Carl McIntire, they formed rival structures that kept the fundamentalist cause alive. The second half of the century too has seen some bruising battles among evangelicals on such issues as engagement in politics, the charismatic movement,[35] and the inerrancy of Scripture.[36]

With such a background of battling, some of which went to extremes and became unnecessarily acrimonious, many within the evangelical movement have lost interest in theological battles and focused on the experiential aspects of religion. This seems to be fairly representative of mainstream evangelicalism. Many scholars have expressed alarm over this trend[37] while others, like Roger Nicole, point to the growth of evangelical scholarship, especially the many evangelical systematic theologies published recently, as evidence of health within evangelicalism.[38] However, contemporary surveys reveal an appalling lack of biblical literacy among lay Christians today. Consequently, this situation calls for a serious response.

Whatever our history, we must look to the Scriptures for guidance about our agenda. The Bible gives ample evidence that combating false teaching is an important part of the agenda of the church and of the ministry of Christian leaders.[39] History teaches us to be careful when making unguarded accusations against others without fully understanding what they are saying. It should make us cautious about going to extremes and rejecting certain truths that false teachers have carried to an extreme (such as social concern, which became the social gospel). But history also shows us that just as wrong teaching caused havoc in the church throughout the past twenty centuries, it can happen today too. We must therefore be constantly alert to aberrations from the truth. We should also teach our people the truth so that they themselves will be able to discern error when confronted by it.

---

35. For the anticharismatic view see John F. MacArthur Jr., *Charismatic Chaos* (Grand Rapids: Zondervan, 1992). For a response and defense of the charismatic position see Gary S. Greig and Kevin N. Springer, *The Kingdom and the Power* (Ventura, Calif.: Regal, 1993); Jack Deere, *Surprised by the Power of the Spirit* (Grand Rapids: Zondervan, 1993).

36. See Harold Lindsell, *The Battle for the Bible* (Grand Rapids: Zondervan, 1976).

37. See from different perspectives, David F. Wells, *No Place for Truth: Or Whatever Happened to Evangelical Theology* (Grand Rapids: Eerdmans, 1993); Mark A. Noll, *The Scandal of the Evangelical Mind* (Grand Rapids: Eerdmans, 1994).

38. Roger Nicole, "What Evangelicalism Has Accomplished," *Christianity Today* (Sept. 16, 1996), 31–34.

39. See, for example, Gal. 1:6–9; 1 Tim. 1:3–10, 18–20; 4:1–16; 2 Tim. 1:12–14; 4:3–5, 14–15; 2 Peter 3:16–18.

Acts 21:1-36

A FTER WE HAD torn ourselves away from them, we put
out to sea and sailed straight to Cos. The next day we
went to Rhodes and from there to Patara. ²We found a
ship crossing over to Phoenicia, went on board and set sail.
³After sighting Cyprus and passing to the south of it, we sailed
on to Syria. We landed at Tyre, where our ship was to unload
its cargo. ⁴Finding the disciples there, we stayed with them
seven days. Through the Spirit they urged Paul not to go on
to Jerusalem. ⁵But when our time was up, we left and continued on our way. All the disciples and their wives and children
accompanied us out of the city, and there on the beach we
knelt to pray. ⁶After saying good-by to each other, we went
aboard the ship, and they returned home.

⁷We continued our voyage from Tyre and landed at Ptolemais, where we greeted the brothers and stayed with them for
a day. ⁸Leaving the next day, we reached Caesarea and stayed
at the house of Philip the evangelist, one of the Seven. ⁹He
had four unmarried daughters who prophesied.

¹⁰After we had been there a number of days, a prophet
named Agabus came down from Judea. ¹¹Coming over to us,
he took Paul's belt, tied his own hands and feet with it and
said, "The Holy Spirit says, 'In this way the Jews of Jerusalem
will bind the owner of this belt and will hand him over to the
Gentiles.'"

¹²When we heard this, we and the people there pleaded
with Paul not to go up to Jerusalem. ¹³Then Paul answered,
"Why are you weeping and breaking my heart? I am ready not
only to be bound, but also to die in Jerusalem for the name of
the Lord Jesus." ¹⁴When he would not be dissuaded, we gave
up and said, "The Lord's will be done."

¹⁵After this, we got ready and went up to Jerusalem.
¹⁶Some of the disciples from Caesarea accompanied us and
brought us to the home of Mnason, where we were to stay.
He was a man from Cyprus and one of the early disciples.

¹⁷When we arrived at Jerusalem, the brothers received us
warmly. ¹⁸The next day Paul and the rest of us went to see
James, and all the elders were present. ¹⁹Paul greeted them

and reported in detail what God had done among the Gentiles through his ministry.

²⁰When they heard this, they praised God. Then they said to Paul: "You see, brother, how many thousands of Jews have believed, and all of them are zealous for the law. ²¹They have been informed that you teach all the Jews who live among the Gentiles to turn away from Moses, telling them not to circumcise their children or live according to our customs. ²²What shall we do? They will certainly hear that you have come, ²³so do what we tell you. There are four men with us who have made a vow. ²⁴Take these men, join in their purification rites and pay their expenses, so that they can have their heads shaved. Then everybody will know there is no truth in these reports about you, but that you yourself are living in obedience to the law. ²⁵As for the Gentile believers, we have written to them our decision that they should abstain from food sacrificed to idols, from blood, from the meat of strangled animals and from sexual immorality."

²⁶The next day Paul took the men and purified himself along with them. Then he went to the temple to give notice of the date when the days of purification would end and the offering would be made for each of them.

²⁷When the seven days were nearly over, some Jews from the province of Asia saw Paul at the temple. They stirred up the whole crowd and seized him, ²⁸shouting, "Men of Israel, help us! This is the man who teaches all men everywhere against our people and our law and this place. And besides, he has brought Greeks into the temple area and defiled this holy place." ²⁹(They had previously seen Trophimus the Ephesian in the city with Paul and assumed that Paul had brought him into the temple area.) ³⁰The whole city was aroused, and the people came running from all directions. Seizing Paul, they dragged him from the temple, and immediately the gates were shut. ³¹While they were trying to kill him, news reached the commander of the Roman troops that the whole city of Jerusalem was in an uproar. ³²He at once took some officers and soldiers and ran down to the crowd. When the rioters saw the commander and his soldiers, they stopped beating Paul.

³³The commander came up and arrested him and ordered him to be bound with two chains. Then he asked who he was and what he had done. ³⁴Some in the crowd shouted one thing

and some another, and since the commander could not get at the truth because of the uproar, he ordered that Paul be taken into the barracks. ³⁵When Paul reached the steps, the violence of the mob was so great he had to be carried by the soldiers. ³⁶The crowd that followed kept shouting, "Away with him!"

THE SORROW OF the Ephesian elders at their parting from Paul and his company (20:37–38) was such that they had to tear themselves away from them (21:1). The travelers then get back on board the ship and set sail with the ultimate goal of reaching Jerusalem by Pentecost.

In Tyre and Caesarea (21:1–16)

AS PAUL AND his friends sail eastward, they stop first at the main port on the island of Rhodes and then at Patara on the mainland (v. 2). There they board a larger ship that travels on the high seas. After sighting Cyprus along the way, they arrive in Tyre, a city in Phoenicia (v. 3). The unloading and loading process takes a week, but they have made good time. Thus Paul's plans to get to Jerusalem before Pentecost (20:16) remain intact. The traveling group makes contact with the church in Tyre (v. 4)—a church probably founded by Christians who "had been scattered by the persecution in connection with Stephen [some of whom] traveled as far as Phoenicia" (11:19). Paul is not acquainted with this church, for the word translated "finding" (*aneurisko*, v. 4) means "to learn the location of something by intentional searching."[1]

"Through the Spirit" (i.e., probably through the operation of a prophetic gift) the Christians in Tyre "urged Paul not to go on to Jerusalem" (v. 4b). How do we reconcile this with Paul's statement that his trip to Jerusalem was "compelled by the Spirit" (20:22)? The Spirit could not possibly have given two contradictory messages in such quick succession. Perhaps the solution lies in the fact that Paul himself placed the Spirit's prediction about impending persecution alongside the compulsion of the Spirit to go to Jerusalem. What the Christians in Tyre received from the Spirit was a prophecy that Paul would have trouble in Jerusalem. Out of that they may have inferred that the Spirit was prompting Paul not to go to Jerusalem. This explains why "through the Spirit they urged Paul not to go on to Jerusalem."

In the short time of one week a warm tie of love in Christ developed between Paul's team and the Christians in Tyre, so that they come with their

---

1. Louw and Nida, 331.

families to see them off. J. G. S. S. Thomson observes, "Since it was customary to stand when praying (Mark 11:25; Luke 18:11–13) the kneeling posture in public here reveals the intensity, solemnity and sincerity of the prayer for Paul's protection and their perseverance."[2]

In Ptolemais, a few miles south of Tyre, Paul and his company stay only one day but again they greet believers there (v. 7). Next they come to Caesarea, where they stay in the house of Philip—one of the Seven (6:5), who is called "the evangelist" here (21:8). We saw his giftedness as both a public evangelist through his ministry in Samaria and a personal evangelist with the Ethiopian (ch. 8). Luke notes that Philip had "four unmarried daughters who prophesied" (v. 9). Keener thinks that the word Luke uses here for Philip's daughters (parthenoi; lit., virgins) probably indicates that they "are young, under the age of sixteen."[3]

In the early church prophesy was one of the most cherished gifts (1 Cor. 14:5, 39), but in that culture unmarried women normally did not have high standing. This may be Luke's way of pointing out that low-status people were included in positions of prominence in the church.[4] Eusebius refers to these daughters twice,[5] mentioning that they lived and were buried in Hierapolis, which is in Phrygia in Asia Minor. Papias, bishop of Hierapolis, said that these daughters were sources of valuable information of what happened in the early years of Christianity. Philip and his daughters may have been one of Luke's information sources.

In Caesarea the prophet Agabus, who had predicted the famine in Judea that prompted a collection from the church in Antioch (11:28–30), predicts that Paul will be bound and handed over to the Jews (vv. 10–11). He uses the form of an acted prophecy—a familiar method used by Old Testament prophets.[6] The people plead with Paul not to go to Jerusalem, though Agabus apparently does not do this (v. 12). For the first time, it seems, Paul's traveling companions (cf. Luke's "we") also join in the plea. The people weep as they try to persuade Paul (v. 13a; see 20:37). Paul's answer that they are breaking his heart shows how hard all this is on him (v. 13a). But he explains his stand: He is not only willing to be bound but also to die for the cause (v. 13b). Finally the people give up, resigning themselves to "the Lord's will" (v. 14).

The journey from Caesarea to Jerusalem was sixty-four miles, so the company stops over somewhere along the way—we are not sure where—at the

---

2. Thomson, "Studies in the Acts of the Apostles—22," n.d., 88.

3. Craig S. Keener, BBC, 385.

4. See Gempf, "Acts," 1099.

5. Eusebius, The History of the Church from Christ to Constantine, 3:31, 39, trans. G. A. Williamson, rev. and ed. Andrew Louth (London: Penguin, 1989), 94 and 103.

6. See Isa. 20:2; Jer. 13:4–11; 19:1–15; Ezek. 4–5.

home of Mnason (v. 16). Like Barnabas, he is from Cyprus and one of the early disciples. He too may have provided Luke with valuable information about the early days of the church.

Paul Meets the Jerusalem Christians (21:17–26)

PAUL IS WARMLY received by the believers on his arrival in Jerusalem (v. 17). The next day he and his company meet James and the elders (v. 18). His report of what God has done elicits praise to God, though there is no mention of the gift Paul brought (vv. 19–20a; but cf. 24:17). The "we" sections stop here and start again only with the journey to Rome (27:1), at which point Luke again shares common experiences with Paul. In the intervening events Luke is probably a bystander.

The sensitive nature of what the believers tell Paul is evidenced by the tone in which they introduce their point (vv. 20b, 22b). For the sake of the many Christians who are zealous for the Jewish law, they think it a good idea for him to dispel misrepresentations about his stand on the law by showing a willingness to submit to the law publicly. He can do this by paying for the expenses of four fellow Christians who have taken a vow. In order to do this he must purify himself along with these people (v. 24, 26). Lest Paul misunderstand their position, they affirm that they are in agreement with the position of the Jerusalem Council regarding requirements of Gentile Christians (v. 25).

Longenecker explains the procedure that Paul subjects himself to:

> Coming from abroad, Paul would have had to regain ceremonial purity by a seven day ritual of purification before he could be present at the absolution ceremony of the four Jewish Christians in the Jerusalem temple. This ritual included reporting to one of the priests and being sprinkled with water of atonement on the third and seventh days.

This is not the same as taking upon himself a Nazirite vow. Rather, Paul must "report to the priest at the start of the seven days of purification, inform him that he was providing the funds for the offerings of the four ... men ... and return to the temple at regular intervals during the week for the appropriate rites."[7]

Is Paul being inconsistent here? We must remember that Paul himself took a vow a few years before (18:18), so we know that he was convinced about the value of vows for Christians. But what about his opposition to works of the law in the letters? This was opposition to the belief that such works were necessary for salvation. He himself was not opposed to the law per se. We must not forget what Paul wrote in 1 Corinthians 9:20: "To the

---

7. Longenecker, "Acts," 520.

Jews I became like a Jew, to win the Jews. To those under the law I became like one under the law (though I myself am not under the law), so as to win those under the law." His actions in Jerusalem are consistent with the approach expressed in this verse.

Paul Is Arrested (21:27–36)

AS PAUL WAS coming to the end of his responsibilities regarding the vows, some Jews from Asia saw him in the temple. They had earlier seen Paul in the city with Trophimus (20:4), a Gentile companion from Asia, and they assumed that he was also in the temple. Had this been true, it would have desecrated the temple, for Gentiles could go only up to the outer court of the temple ("the Court of the Gentiles"). They incited the Jewish people to attack Paul (vv. 27–29).

Bruce explains the seriousness of their charge: "The Roman authorities were so conciliatory of Jewish religious scruples in this regard that they authorized the death sentence for this trespass even when the offenders were Roman citizens." Citing evidence from Josephus and Philo, Bruce says that notices in Latin and Greek were fixed to the barrier between the inner and outer courts, warning Gentiles that death was the penalty for going any further.[8] "The whole city was aroused" (v. 30a), and the people dragged Paul out of the temple. The gates of the temple were shut (v. 30b), possibly to avoid defiling the temple from the chaos.

The rioters began beating Paul to death. The timely intervention of the Roman commander and some of his soldiers prevented this from happening (vv. 31–32). Paul was arrested so that he could be given a proper trial (v. 33), but because of the turmoil of the crowd he had to be carried by the soldiers (v. 35). The crowd kept shouting, "Away with him" (v. 36). Luke must surely have felt the significance of the fact that some twenty-seven years earlier, another crowd had shouted, "Away with this man!" at a spot nearby (Luke 23:18).

PHILIP'S DAUGHTERS. LUKE'S mention of Philip's daughters (v. 9) highlights the fact that people not regarded as being of high status did have positions of prominence in the church. The breaking of human barriers in Christ is one of the main subthemes of Acts.[9] Luke has given prominence to women in different ways. They were with the disciples during the pre-Pentecostal prayer meetings of the church (1:14). Because the

8. Bruce, *Acts*, NICNT, 409.
9. For an analysis of this, see the discussions on 6:1–7; 10:1–33; 12:25–13:12.

Grecian widows were neglected, the apostles made a major administrative advance in the church (6:1–7). Dorcas was an exemplary woman of good deeds (9:36–42). The Gentile Lydia, probably single, hosted the apostolic team in Philippi (16:15), and Priscilla was the more prominent of an exemplary husband-wife team (18:18–19). The present passage records single women exercising what the New Testament regards as a key gift for the church.[10]

The New Testament letters affirm that women and men are equals in God's kingdom (see Gal. 3:28; 1 Peter 3:7) and give guidelines about the different roles each has in the church[11] and home.[12] These passages have been the subject of much controversy and debate, a discussion of which is beyond the scope of this commentary. Acts teaches us that women, especially women marginalized by society, have a prominent role in fulfilling the agenda of the kingdom.

Warm, open community life. In this chapter Luke gives us an unadorned description of Christian community at work, seen especially in his repetition of the response of believers to Paul. He records warm affection with weeping, embracing, and kissing (20:37), which made it difficult for Paul to leave the Ephesian elders, so much so that they had to tear themselves away (v. 1). Even the newfound friends in Tyre expressed warm affection as they came with their families to send off Paul and his team and pray on their knees on the beach. In a similar vein Paul's team had a warm reception in Jerusalem (v. 17), along with praise to God over the reports of his ministry (v. 20a).

Prophetic insight resulted in warnings to Paul about impending persecution in Jerusalem (vv. 4, 10–12). Believers can warn others of danger through the miraculous gifts of prophecy or insight. The community's love, however, took a different turn when believers tried to persuade Paul against going to Jerusalem (vv. 4, 12). This proved to be hard for him, for they began to weep as they pleaded with him, breaking his heart in the process (v. 13). Even his close colleagues were swayed and joined in the chorus of dissent over his plans (v. 12). This reminds us that people who love us may try to shield us from the cross. We take community life seriously, but at times our own people will take stands that must be rejected.

Paul's response to the misplaced concern of his friends is instructive. He expressed his frustration and pain over their approach (v. 13a). The openness that walking in the light requires in order to maintain fellowship (1 John

---

10. In Luke's Gospel we see a similarly prominent place given to women; see Luke 1:7, 25, 27; 4:38–39; 7:11–17, 36–50; 8:1–3, 40–56; 10:38–42; 13:10–17; 18:1–8; 21:1–4; 23:55–56; 24:1–11 (cf. Robert H. Stein, *Luke*, NAC 24 [Nashville: Broadman/Holman, 1992], 50).

11. See 1 Cor. 11:12–16; 14:34–36; 1 Tim. 2:8–15.

12. See 1 Cor. 7; Eph. 5:21–33; Col. 3:18–19; Titus 2:1–6; 1 Peter 3:1–7.

1:7) necessitates such open expressions of pain. But Paul also explained what lay behind his decision to go ahead with his journey to Jerusalem: He was ready not only to be bound but also to die for the cause (v. 13b).

All of us, if we are obedient to Christ, will face death of some sort, for the cross is a nonnegotiable prerequisite of discipleship. Our Christian loved ones may not understand or appreciate the path we are taking. If they oppose us, it is not because they reject God's ways but because in their misplaced love they want to help us avoid pain. We must explain what lies behind our decisions and help them understand and accept the way we have chosen. Those who respect the will of God will relent from their opposition since they fear opposing God. This is what happened in Caesarea when believers said, "The Lord's will be done."

As another aspect of our community commitments, we may sometimes agree to do things we feel are unnecessary for us personally but help maintain unity. Paul did this in his involvement with the four men who took a vow. He bent over backwards and submitted to the will of the body, in keeping with what he taught in Ephesians 5:21: "Submit to one another out of reverence for Christ." But was this a mistake? Some have thought so. We would do well, of course, to heed the warning "to guard against seeing Acts 21:17–26 as too positive a model inasmuch as the whole plot backfires (vv. 27–36)."[13] While it does not present a model as such, I believe it shows us how seriously Paul viewed the unity of the church and how he was willing to do everything possible to please those who were different in perspective from himself.

The plot did indeed backfire, but the Jerusalem Christians were surely grateful for the price Paul was willing to pay to express his solidarity with them. I sometimes wonder whether the ease with which commentators dub this action of Paul as a mistake indicates how far the church has strayed from viewing suffering owing to commitments as an essential ingredient of Christian community.

Moreover, Paul's participation in the vows of the four men is consistent with his teaching in his letters. As he wrote in 1 Corinthians 9, for evangelistic purposes he was willing to change his behavior according to his audience. He advocated the same flexibility in order to preserve the unity of the body, especially because some actions that certain Christians thought were legitimate could be a stumbling block to weaker Christians (Rom. 14; 1 Cor. 8). One who has died to self has a love that "does not insist on its own way" (1 Cor. 13:5, NRSV). To Paul the unity of the church was so important that a

---

13. William W. Klein, Craig L. Blomberg, and Robert L. Hubbard Jr., *Introduction to Biblical Interpretation* (Dallas: Word, 1993), 349.

big price was well worth paying in order to preserve it. We ought to recover this perspective in today's church.

More on Paul and the Jews. Luke must surely have considered the interplay between Paul and the Jewish people as important, for he writes about it so many times in Acts. In this section, even though Paul was primarily called to evangelize the Gentiles, he never gave up trying to minister to Jews and to build bridges between Judaism and Christianity. The attempt here ended in disaster, but he kept trying to win them over. In fact, the last chapter of Acts gives considerable space to describing Paul's efforts at evangelizing the Jews in Rome. There too he had the same response, with the majority of the Jews rejecting what he said so that he turned to concentrate on the Gentiles (28:28). But he never gave up trying to win the Jews.

This pattern ought to inspire us to persevere with what may be called "the establishment" and not give up on it. Perhaps we cannot derive a binding principle here. But this section helps us appreciate the efforts of those who try to bring renewal to old structures that seem confined to traditional ways of doing things and closed to considering change.

 THE PROMINENT ROLE of women in God's agenda. How can we apply the principle evident in Luke's writings that women and other people marginalized in society have a prominent place in God's kingdom? We ought to follow Luke in demonstrating to such people that they are truly important to God and to the church. Our application of Scripture should be relevant to all segments of God's people. We must show how biblical principles apply to men and women, to the rich and the poor, and to adults, youth, and children. In our illustrations, we should be representative in our use of examples.[14] For us in poorer nations, where much of our literature comes from the richer nations, we should look diligently for examples from our part of the world. In multiethnic societies, we should look for examples from the different ethnic groups.

We should also avoid examples that entrench people in their prejudices. Things have become a bit sensitive recently because of an overemphasis on political correctness, and inclusive language has been used even for God. While we deplore such excesses, that should not prevent us from using language that does not eliminate one group of people (e.g., women). What was legitimate a generation ago may mean something different today, as meanings attributed to words change over time.

---

14. See Ruth A. Tucker, *The Christian Speaker's Treasury: A Sourcebook of Anecdotes and Quotes* (San Francisco: Harper & Row, 1989), which has many good items relevant to women.

Having said this, we must also remember that the New Testament letters say some things about the roles of men and women that grate against the way many people are thinking today. We should be careful about radically reinterpreting these passages to mean something Paul did not mean. Insofar as our cultural backgrounds can cause us to be blind to certain facets of scriptural truth, we should always be willing to submit traditional interpretations to fresh study. But we have no mandate to reject a passage or to reinterpret it so that it ends up saying something clearly not intended by the author. This is a difficult issue, as the plethora of books with conflicting conclusions from authors, all of whom are firmly committed to the authority of Scripture, shows. But whatever our views, there should be no doubt in the minds of all biblical Christians about the equality, importance, and significance of those whom society considers unequal, unimportant, or insignificant.

Fallible Christians expressing community love. In our discussion of Acts 20 we looked at the happiness that comes from warm ties of love and commitment. These warm ties are illustrated in the present passage. But committed relationships can also bring much pain and inconvenience— experiences that may cause Christians to shun such relationships in preference for a life that guards their privacy. Yet one of the many blessings of committed relationships is the joy of being loved by fellow Christians. This joy Paul had, and it would have more than compensated for the pain that came with such commitments. In a world filled with lonely people, such love and commitment are so important.

At the same time, we also noted that even Paul's close friends did not understand the path he was taking. Heroes are usually admired only from a distance. When they are actually doing the work that ultimately leads to their becoming heroes, it seems so costly, strange, and foolish. Their loved ones see the cross of suffering and want to spare them the pain. For example, many missionaries go out to the field against the wishes of their parents. When they find the going tough, they write home, and the parents get upset at their children or accuse the sending agency of causing them harm.

Because our rewards are in heaven, we usually do not have much to show by way of earthly success. Paul himself appeared to be such a failure that at the end of his life everyone had deserted him (2 Tim. 4:16). All this is hard on the emotions of God's servants. They know there was an element of risk in what they were doing, and they cannot help but question if they have been mistaken after all. But a compulsion of the Spirit is what helps them to go on (cf. 20:22).

Yet when no one understands us, we should not reject everyone and go it alone. Rather, we should try to change people's minds. And many do change their minds, as we see with Paul's trip to Jerusalem. Luke himself eventually changed his mind. He joined in the pleas to Paul not to go to

Jerusalem (v. 12). But he stuck with Paul not only in Jerusalem but throughout his imprisonments. At least seven years later, Paul wrote to Timothy from prison in Rome, "Only Luke is with me" (2 Tim. 4:11).

We cannot avoid the sad fact that some Christians will not understand the path we are taking. Some parents will remain opposed to the decision their children have taken to follow Christ along a difficult path. Some of those who oppose us are good, godly people. As I mentioned earlier, the great evangelical social reformer, the Earl of Shaftesbury, known as "the poor man's Earl," once announced that after much study he was convinced that the Salvation Army was clearly the Antichrist![15] But passion for obedience to Christ helps us to go on with our vision.

The request of the Jerusalem Christians for Paul to be involved in the funding of the vows of four brothers is another good example of fallible Christians trying to express Christian love. We cannot be certain whether this act was a mistake. But it shows us how serious Paul was about preserving unity in the body of Christ. He was willing to do everything possible to please Christians who were different from him. This perspective needs emphasis in an age where individualism has hit the church so hard that church splits are even being viewed as a desirable means of church growth! This surely is an expression of worldliness in this age where the supposed quest for self-fulfillment has devalued the importance of lasting commitments[16] and where, because of the pragmatic attitude, growth at the cost of another is regarded as acceptable.

The idea of the survival of the fittest at the cost of the weak may be the law of the jungle and of the marketplace, but it is not the law of the kingdom. In a study on cooperating in world evangelism, John Stott comments, "An empirical fact is not necessarily a biblical truth.... We must not assume that the world is necessarily to be a model for the church."[17] Paul reacted with horror over divisions in the body of Christ. With biting irony he asked, "Is Christ divided?" (1 Cor. 1:13). The damage this does to Christian witness is immense.

Just two days before I wrote this, our daily newspaper carried a letter to the editor, presumably from a Buddhist, where the writer sarcastically expressed his feelings about divisions among the Protestants as opposed to

---

15. Bramwell Booth, *Echoes and Memories* (New York: George H. Doran, 1925), 27. Cited in Warren W. Wiersbe and Lloyd M. Perry, *The Wycliffe Handbook of Preaching and Preachers* (Chicago: Moody, 1984), 185.

16. See Daniel Yankelovich, *New Rules: Searching for Self-fulfillment in a World Turned Upside Down* (New York: Random House, 1981).

17. John R. W. Stott, "Theological Preamble," *Co-operating in World Evangelization,* ed. Keith A. Price (Wheaton and London: Lausanne Committee for World Evangelization, 1983), 10.

the unity of the Roman Catholics. He ended the letter with the words, "The structure of the Christian church seems so confusing at times!"[18] Paul's willingness to submit himself to the request of the Jerusalem leaders challenges us to greater sensitivity about Christians who are different and to greater efforts at cooperation with them.

On one of Paul's earlier visits to Jerusalem, the leaders of the church agreed that while Peter would specialize in Jewish evangelism, Paul would specialize in Gentile evangelism (Gal. 2:7–8). But that did not prevent Paul from being sensitive to the sensibilities of Jewish Christians. This is what we call the kingdom perspective. Within the one kingdom of God we may have different roles, but we work for the same King; therefore, we will help each other at personal cost to ourselves and never do things that will hurt the other. That is, the Baptist Church should not do anything to hurt the Assembly of God church down the road, and an Inter-Varsity chapter should not attempt to grow at the expense of a Navigators chapter on the same campus. Recognizing our different roles and submitting to scriptural teaching about the body of Christ, we should try to help each other whenever possible and modify our plans if we find they are hurting another Christian group.

Persevering with the establishment. Paul's perseverance with the Jewish "establishment" should encourage us to persevere with what we today see as the establishment. As noted above, this may not be a binding principle that applies to everyone; it may have to do with each one's individual calling. Some devout Christians, for example, leave older denominations out of a sense of outrage over the way they have compromised biblical Christianity. But other equally devout people stay on in these denominations, seeking to be agents of renewal. They will face frustration and even persecution, but that is to be expected in this fallen world (cf. Rom. 8:20). They may groan, looking forward to their ultimate redemption, which will come only in the new heaven and the new earth (8:23). Many give up because they feel it is a waste of time. But Paul was willing to "waste" his time with resistant Jews in every town he went to before going to the more receptive Gentiles and God-fearers. In most of these towns some Jews were converted.

God may be calling some Christians to attempt to facilitate a renewal of biblical Christianity within older churches that others are prone to dismiss as unredeemable. God does not call all Christians to do this. But Paul's example of persevering with the Jews should make us reluctant to criticize those who are trying to bring renewal in older churches. In fact, even those who are not called to this work ought to pray for and encourage their brothers and sisters who have stayed.

---

18. *The Island* (March 22, 1997), 9.

Acts 21:37–23:11

A
S THE SOLDIERS were about to take Paul into the barracks, he asked the commander, "May I say something to you?"

"Do you speak Greek?" he replied. 38"Aren't you the Egyptian who started a revolt and led four thousand terrorists out into the desert some time ago?"

39Paul answered, "I am a Jew, from Tarsus in Cilicia, a citizen of no ordinary city. Please let me speak to the people."

40Having received the commander's permission, Paul stood on the steps and motioned to the crowd. When they were all silent, he said to them in Aramaic: 22:1"Brothers and fathers, listen now to my defense."

2When they heard him speak to them in Aramaic, they became very quiet.

Then Paul said: 3"I am a Jew, born in Tarsus of Cilicia, but brought up in this city. Under Gamaliel I was thoroughly trained in the law of our fathers and was just as zealous for God as any of you are today. 4I persecuted the followers of this Way to their death, arresting both men and women and throwing them into prison, 5as also the high priest and all the Council can testify. I even obtained letters from them to their brothers in Damascus, and went there to bring these people as prisoners to Jerusalem to be punished.

6"About noon as I came near Damascus, suddenly a bright light from heaven flashed around me. 7I fell to the ground and heard a voice say to me, 'Saul! Saul! Why do you persecute me?'

8"'Who are you, Lord?' I asked.

"'I am Jesus of Nazareth, whom you are persecuting,' he replied. 9My companions saw the light, but they did not understand the voice of him who was speaking to me.

10"'What shall I do, Lord?' I asked.

"'Get up,' the Lord said, 'and go into Damascus. There you will be told all that you have been assigned to do.' 11My companions led me by the hand into Damascus, because the brilliance of the light had blinded me.

12"A man named Ananias came to see me. He was a devout observer of the law and highly respected by all the Jews living there. ¹³He stood beside me and said, 'Brother Saul, receive your sight!' And at that very moment I was able to see him.

¹⁴"Then he said: 'The God of our fathers has chosen you to know his will and to see the Righteous One and to hear words from his mouth. ¹⁵You will be his witness to all men of what you have seen and heard. ¹⁶And now what are you waiting for? Get up, be baptized and wash your sins away, calling on his name.'

¹⁷"When I returned to Jerusalem and was praying at the temple, I fell into a trance ¹⁸and saw the Lord speaking. 'Quick!' he said to me. 'Leave Jerusalem immediately, because they will not accept your testimony about me.'

¹⁹"'Lord,' I replied, 'these men know that I went from one synagogue to another to imprison and beat those who believe in you. ²⁰And when the blood of your martyr Stephen was shed, I stood there giving my approval and guarding the clothes of those who were killing him.'

²¹"Then the Lord said to me, 'Go; I will send you far away to the Gentiles.'"

²²The crowd listened to Paul until he said this. Then they raised their voices and shouted, "Rid the earth of him! He's not fit to live!"

²³As they were shouting and throwing off their cloaks and flinging dust into the air, ²⁴the commander ordered Paul to be taken into the barracks. He directed that he be flogged and questioned in order to find out why the people were shouting at him like this. ²⁵As they stretched him out to flog him, Paul said to the centurion standing there, "Is it legal for you to flog a Roman citizen who hasn't even been found guilty?"

²⁶When the centurion heard this, he went to the commander and reported it. "What are you going to do?" he asked. "This man is a Roman citizen."

²⁷The commander went to Paul and asked, "Tell me, are you a Roman citizen?"

"Yes, I am," he answered.

²⁸Then the commander said, "I had to pay a big price for my citizenship."

"But I was born a citizen," Paul replied.

²⁹Those who were about to question him withdrew immediately. The commander himself was alarmed when he realized that he had put Paul, a Roman citizen, in chains.

³⁰The next day, since the commander wanted to find out exactly why Paul was being accused by the Jews, he released him and ordered the chief priests and all the Sanhedrin to assemble. Then he brought Paul and had him stand before them.

²³:¹Paul looked straight at the Sanhedrin and said, "My brothers, I have fulfilled my duty to God in all good conscience to this day." ²At this the high priest Ananias ordered those standing near Paul to strike him on the mouth. ³Then Paul said to him, "God will strike you, you whitewashed wall! You sit there to judge me according to the law, yet you yourself violate the law by commanding that I be struck!"

⁴Those who were standing near Paul said, "You dare to insult God's high priest?"

⁵Paul replied, "Brothers, I did not realize that he was the high priest; for it is written: 'Do not speak evil about the ruler of your people.'"

⁶Then Paul, knowing that some of them were Sadducees and the others Pharisees, called out in the Sanhedrin, "My brothers, I am a Pharisee, the son of a Pharisee. I stand on trial because of my hope in the resurrection of the dead." ⁷When he said this, a dispute broke out between the Pharisees and the Sadducees, and the assembly was divided. ⁸(The Sadducees say that there is no resurrection, and that there are neither angels nor spirits, but the Pharisees acknowledge them all.)

⁹There was a great uproar, and some of the teachers of the law who were Pharisees stood up and argued vigorously. "We find nothing wrong with this man," they said. "What if a spirit or an angel has spoken to him?" ¹⁰The dispute became so violent that the commander was afraid Paul would be torn to pieces by them. He ordered the troops to go down and take him away from them by force and bring him into the barracks.

¹¹The following night the Lord stood near Paul and said, "Take courage! As you have testified about me in Jerusalem, so you must also testify in Rome."

Original Meaning

THE PREVIOUS STUDY ended with Paul narrowly escaping being beaten to death. He must have been badly bruised and shaken, but soon he recovers his composure sufficiently to ask permission to speak to the crowd, and he gives his audience an eloquent defense of himself.

Paul Speaks to the Mob (21:37–22:21)

THE COMMANDER ORIGINALLY thought that Paul was an Egyptian who had tried to lead some people in revolt against Rome (21:37–38). This Egyptian took a large number of people to the Mount of Olives, promising them God's intervention, but the revolt was aborted by Governor Felix with the loss of much life but the escape of the Egyptian.[1] The commander expressed surprise at Paul's ability to speak Greek, but the response he received to his query about Paul's citizenship in Tarsus (21:39) did not impress the commander as much as the fact he found out later—that Paul was a Roman citizen (22:26–29).

Luke's mention of the language Paul used to speak to the Jewish crowd (*Hebraidi dialekto*) is probably a loose expression for Aramaic (21:40). This was "the vernacular of much of rural Syria-Palestine and all lands to the east."[2] The fact that Paul spoke fluent Aramaic caused the people to become "very quiet" (22:2). Any who may have thought he was a Diaspora collaborator with the Gentiles would probably have realized that they were wrong.[3]

Paul began his address respectfully, calling his audience "brothers and fathers," just as Stephen had addressed a similar audience (7:2). Paul's first point demonstrated his excellent Jewish credentials (22:3): "educated at the feet of Gamaliel according to the strictness of the ancestral law" (lit. trans.); that is, he had a thorough training as a Pharisee under the most revered teacher of the era. The description of his activity as a persecutor of Christians (22:4–5) opened the way for him to describe his conversion.

Paul's report of his conversion here is similar to that in chapter 9, but there are some interesting points that complement the earlier account. The present one focuses on his call rather than his conversion. He defends his work with the Gentiles and shows that he is still a good Jew. This account has a greater emphasis on light than Acts 9: Paul specifies that it was around noon when he saw the light, which would make it a very strong light indeed (22:6). The first account reports that the men with Paul heard the sound but did not see anyone (9:7). Here Paul says that his companions saw the light but did not understand the voice speaking to him (22:9).

Paul does not mention Ananias's dialogue with the Lord, where he was commanded to go to Paul (9:10–16), but he adds a new point, important to his audience, about Ananias's being "a devout observer of the law and highly respected by all the Jews living" in Damascus (22:12). Also new is the word from God communicated by Ananias that Paul was to be a "witness to all men"

---

1. See Josephus, *Antiquities of the Jews*, 20.7.6; *Wars of the Jews*, 2.13.5; in Josephus, *Complete Works*, 422, 483 resp.
2. Keener, *BBC*, 389.
3. Ibid.

and that he must be baptized (22:14–16). Ananias's phrases are typically Jewish (e.g., "the God of our fathers,"[4] "the Righteous One"[5]). We know from Paul's talk with Herod Agrippa that God also gave this commission directly to Paul (26:17). But here it was important for Paul to tell his audience that a respected Jew had shared the vision of his future ministry with him. In keeping with the emphasis on light and the response to it, Ananias said that Paul was chosen "to know [God's] will and to see the Righteous One and to hear words from his mouth" (22:14). He was to witness of what he has "seen and heard" (22:15).[6]

Another new point in this account is Paul's description of a vision he had while praying in the temple some later time, where God told him to leave Jerusalem (22:17–21). Paul had expressed to God his personal desire to stay in Jerusalem and witness to the Jews, considering his unique background. There is probably a hint that the Jews listening to Paul now should have accepted the validity of his message but would not because of the stubbornness of their hearts.

Luke's earlier description of the circumstances surrounding Paul's departure from Jerusalem is from a different perspective. The brothers heard about a plot against Paul and escorted him to Caesarea, from where he was sent off to Tarsus (9:29–30). Bruce comments that "this is not the only place in our narrative where divine direction and human action coincide."[7]

Paul Uses His Roman Citizenship (22:22–29)

PAUL'S STATEMENT IN 22:21 that the Lord had decided to send him to the Gentiles served as a trigger for another outburst from the Jewish crowd. They shouted for his death, threw off their cloaks, and flung dust into the air (22:22–23). The latter two actions expressed both their frustration and their horror at blasphemy, possibly through their connecting the word "Gentiles" with Paul's alleged desecration of the temple. The crowd was too unruly for anything constructive to take place, so the commander had him taken into the barracks in order to give him third-degree treatment—questioning through torture with hope of getting at the bottom of the wrong that Paul had committed about which the Jews were so angry (22:24).

The planned flogging was probably the Roman brutal scourging with a whip that had thongs weighted with rough pieces of bone or metal. It could

---

4. See Gen. 43:23; Ex. 3:13, 15, 16; 4:5; Deut. 1:11, 21; 4:1; 6:3; 12:1; etc.

5. See for the idea 2 Sam. 23:3; Isa. 32:1; 53:11; Zech. 9:9.

6. The possible inference that verse 16 teaches baptismal regeneration is contradicted in our discussion of a similar statement in 2:38.

7. Bruce, *Acts*, NICNT, 419.

cause great harm and even leave people crippled for life. As Paul was about to be flogged, he told the centurion that he was a Roman citizen. Though Roman citizens who had been convicted of some crime could have scourging decreed as a punishment, they were exempt from it as a method of inquiry before trial.[8] The commander was therefore saved from breaking the law any further, for he was wrong to even order the flogging. Thus, his alarm (22:29) was understandable. He talked of the bribe that he had had to pay to acquire Roman citizenship (22:28),[9] while Paul said he had inherited his citizenship through birth.

Paul Before the Sanhedrin (22:30–23:11)

THE COMMANDER STILL had to get to the bottom of the case. As it obviously concerned a religious issue, he decided to order the Sanhedrin to look into the matter (22:30). Longenecker explains that "as a Roman military commander, he had no right to participate in the Sanhedrin's deliberations. But as the Roman official charged with keeping peace with Jerusalem, he could order the Sanhedrin to meet to determine the cause of the riot."[10] When Luke says that Paul was "released" (22:30), he probably meant that he was released from confinement to appear before the Sanhedrin.[11]

Paul's first statement to the Sanhedrin proclaimed that he had fulfilled his "duty to God in all good conscience" (23:1). This is consistent with what he said elsewhere (24:16; Phil. 3:6). He was not talking about fulfilling requirements for salvation through a life of obedience. He clearly argued that no one can do that (Rom. 2–3). Rather, by Jewish standards of measuring faithfulness relative to conscience, he had lived a blameless and exemplary life.[12]

The high priest Ananias orders that Paul be struck on the mouth for this statement (23:2). Paul responds with a typically human reaction to this slap. He calls the high priest a hypocrite and says that God will strike him too, for he had violated the law in commanding this (23:3). It was a miscarriage of justice to strike a person before being convicted, and in this case he had

---

8. The information on scourging is from ibid., 420–21.

9. Bruce cites evidence for the fact that "this form of bribery reached scandalous proportions under Claudius" (Acts, NICNT, 421).

10. Longenecker, "Acts," 530. This would answer Haenchen (Acts, 640), who discounts the historicity of this passage on the grounds that it was "naive" to think that the commander would take Paul to the council.

11. This is an ambiguous statement. Luke "could refer either to his having his chains removed, or to his being released from confinement in order appear before the Sanhedrin. The latter seems more likely, since the removal of his chains is implied in 23:29" (Polhill, Acts, 467 n.61).

12. The significance of this claim will be discussed in the next study.

not even been properly charged. Paul's comment about Ananias proves to be prophetic, for within ten years the high priest had to flee to Herod's palace, his house was burned, and he was eventually killed.[13] He was known as a greedy, corrupt, and violent man.[14]

When Paul was told that he had spoken these strong words to the high priest, he made a godly retraction of his typically human reaction (23:5). Why did he not recognize the high priest? Sir William Ramsay's suggestion that this was because the meeting was run like a Roman assembly, presided over by the commander, is now generally rejected.[15] The explanation I heard in my youth was that Paul suffered from poor eyesight, perhaps because of the blinding that took place on the road to Damascus (as evidence, Gal. 4:13—15 is often cited, where Paul said that the Galatians would have given their eyes to him). Longenecker is probably nearer the truth: Since this was not a regular meeting of the Sanhedrin, the high priest was likely not in his usual seat or wearing his robes of office. Also, because Paul had visited Jerusalem only sporadically during the previous twenty years and Ananias had become high priest in A.D. 48, about ten years before these incidents, Paul would not have recognized him.[16]

As Paul's first line of reasoning was not going to work, he adopted a new line. The issue at stake here was the resurrection of the dead, which the Pharisees accepted but the Sadducees rejected. Was this simply a crafty ploy used by Paul to divide the group? Certainly there is wisdom, possibly even shrewdness, here. But he was also using a strategy that pointed to the heart of the Christian gospel, which was indeed a fulfillment of Pharisaism, so much so that a real Pharisee should actually become a Christian. He even calls himself a Pharisee here (23:6).

Bruce's paraphrase of verse 6b helps us understand his point: "The charge on which I am now being examined concerns the national hope, which depends for its fulfillment on the resurrection of the dead."[17] Paul agreed with the Pharisees that the Jews' national hope depended on a future resurrection. Here he is saying that the first stage of this resurrection has been fulfilled with the resurrection of Jesus. Paul clearly presented the connection between the resurrection of Christ and the hope of the Jews in his speech to Agrippa (26:8, 23)[18] and in 1 Corinthians 15:16—28.

---

13. See Josephus, *Wars of the Jews*, 2.17.6, 9 (in Josephus, *Complete Works*, 491, 492 resp.).

14. On Ananias's character and acts, see Josephus, *Antiquities of the Jews*, 20.9.2, 4 (in Josephus, *Complete Works*, 424).

15. Ramsay, *BRD*, 90—95.

16. Longenecker, "Acts," 531.

17. Bruce, *Acts*, NICNT, 427.

18. See our discussion of that passage.

Paul's statement results in total confusion in the Sanhedrin, some siding with Paul and others against him. Some even consider the possibility that an angel or a spirit revealed Paul's message to him (23:9). The commander has to intervene and take Paul away from the scene. The next night the Lord stands near Paul and encourages him by telling him that he is going to testify in Rome (23:11). Amidst all of the confusion of these days, the apostle receives assurance that God is working out his purposes, and that one of Paul's great dreams is going to be fulfilled—he will go to Rome.

THE REACTION OF **Paul and of the Jews to God's revelation.** On the Damascus road, Paul was blinded by a bright light (22:11). But he responded to that light, and not only was his blindness taken away (v. 13), he was also transformed by the revelation (v. 14). He was now to witness of what he had seen and heard (v. 15). Jewish tradition valued the light of God and viewed Israel as its guardians and agents, who were to give it to the Gentiles (Isa. 42:6; 49:6). This tradition Paul shared with his Jewish audience (Acts 22:3).

Yet as John later explains, "The light shines in the darkness, but the darkness has not understood it" (John 1:5). In other words, Jesus "came to that which was his own, but his own did not receive him. Yet to all who received him, to those who believed in his name, he gave the right to become children of God" (1:11–12). The Jewish mob belonged to the majority of God's people who were rejecting the light; Paul belonged to the minority who received him and carried on the tradition of bearing the light. But when he as God's servant told them about God's command to take the light to the Gentiles, as promised in the Scriptures,[19] they cried, "Rid the earth of him! He's not fit to live!" (Acts 22:22).

Paul also shared a common commitment to the biblical tradition with the Pharisees in the Sanhedrin. This tradition, however, had now become traditionalism.[20] When they were now confronted with a necessary implication of their tradition—the resurrection of Jesus as the forerunner of the resurrection for which they hoped—they rejected it and persecuted any who accepted it. Too much of their comfortable traditionalism had to be given up if they were to accept the truth that their tradition implied. This incident shows how a theologically orthodox people can become so comfortable in their orthodoxy that they become hardened to change. The conservatism

---

19. See Gen. 12:3; 1 Kings 8:41–43; Isa. 2:2–4; 11:9–10; 42:1–7; 66:18–20; Dan. 7:14; Joel 2:28; Zech. 2:11; 8:20–23; 14:16–17.
20. Willimon, *Acts,* 169.

of the Jews had become a dead traditionalism, which persecuted the agents of change whom God sent their way.

Paul's three visions. This passage gives us three visions of Paul. (1) He saw the risen Lord, which resulted in his conversion and which he considered as a resurrection appearance (22:6–10).[21] On the place of visions in the conversion process, we can say that a vision is one of many ways that God can use to confront people. It has happened enough times in the Bible and in history (see 10:1–33) to be listed as one of the ways God reveals himself to people.

(2) Three years after his conversion (cf. Gal. 1:18), God warned Paul of the dangers of staying in Jerusalem and told him to leave (22:18). In this vision God gave Paul direction for his life. This vision has similarities with the one Peter received (10:9–16). In both the subject was in prayer when God spoke in a vision.[22] Prayer attunes us to God and makes us receptive to his voice. While Paul was in this attitude of prayer, God warned him about the dangers of something he was eager to do. His "heart's desire and prayer to God for the Israelites [was] that they may be saved" (Rom. 10:1). Paul felt positive that he would be the one to fulfill this ambition, that because of his background he was eminently qualified for the job (22:19–20). But God did not see it in that way. Paul was mistaken, for what he thought might give him openings for the gospel would not do so. This vision shows us that we must be open to God and place our ambitions before him so that he may direct us in the way that is best for us.

(3) The third vision encouraged Paul (23:11)—a feature that occurs several times in Acts. At times of special need, God appears to his servants in some supernatural way and gives them a glimpse of himself that encourages them to persevere in the task they have been given (4:31; 18:9–10; 27:23). We can call this the comfort of the God of all comfort (cf. 2 Cor. 1:3–4). God knows when we need special help to overcome discouragement and to persevere in a difficult call. And at just the right time he sends us that comfort. The comfort Paul received was in the form of an affirmation of the sovereignty of God. This time of uncertainty eventually resulted in Paul's fulfilling one of his greatest ambitions: to preach the gospel in Rome.[23]

Paul's use of his Roman citizenship. We have reflected much on the call to suffer in this commentary because it is such an important theme in Acts. The apostles, including Paul, were happy to suffer for the sake of Christ (5:41; 21:13). Before Paul arrived in Jerusalem, he was given ample warning

---

21. This was discussed at length in our comments on 9:1–31.

22. See the discussion of Peter's vision for the place prayer has in opening us to God's direction.

23. For more on God's comfort through visions, see the study on 18:1–22.

from God that he would be persecuted, and he came prepared to suffer (20:23–24; 21:4, 10–13). But he was not a masochist who took on suffering unnecessarily. He indicated he was willing to die in Jerusalem (21:13), but when the Romans tried to give him a scourging to get him to talk, he appealed to his citizenship to stop the process (22:25).[24]

To Paul, a ruler "is God's servant to do you good" (Rom. 13:4). If a ruler does not do that, then we can urge him to do so. Besides as representatives of a just God, we as believers are committed to combating injustice on earth. Sometimes we may even need to fight injustice against ourselves. The Bible does give us guidelines here. For example, Paul says it is better to be wronged or cheated than to go to secular courts against another believer (1 Cor. 6:6–7). But as a general rule, we can appeal to the law for our protection if we are attacked or persecuted in a way that clearly violates the law of the land.

TRADITION, TRADITIONALISM, AND **the light.** The traditionalism of the Jews resulted in their rejecting the great truth that their tradition implied. Though some Pharisees (15:5) and "a large number of priests" (6:7) did accept the message of Jesus' resurrection, many refused to do so, and they even persecuted those who did. In the same way, throughout the history of the church, traditionalists have persecuted those from within their tradition who have launched out into a new direction that was permitted and indeed implied by their tradition.

When Martin Luther, for example, began to proclaim what the Bible clearly taught, he was branded a heretic by the very church that in theory accepted the Bible as one of its two main sources of authority (the other being tradition). At the Diet of Worms (1521), the Catholic scholar Johann Eck asked Luther whether he wished to retract what he had taught. Luther's famous reply was as follows:

> Since your serene majesty and your lordships seek a simple answer, I will give it in this manner, neither horned nor toothed: unless I am convinced by the testimony of the Scriptures or by clear reason . . . I am bound by the Scriptures I have quoted, and my conscience is captive to the Word of God. I cannot and will not retract anything, since it is neither safe nor right to go against conscience.[25]

---

24. Cf. also 16:37: When he was unjustly beaten and imprisoned in Philippi, he protested the action without meekly leaving after his (and Silas's) release.

25. From A. Skevington Wood, *Captive to the Word. Martin Luther: Doctor of Sacred Scripture* (Grand Rapids: Eerdmans, 1969), 72.

As a result, Luther was excommunicated. For his safety his friend, the elector of Saxony, Frederick the Wise, staged a kidnapping and hid him in a castle in Wartburg.

Similarly, when some younger scholars of the fundamentalist movement began to open themselves to certain truths and academic disciplines compatible with the fundamentals of the faith, they were brutally attacked by traditionalists within the fundamentalist camp. Some of them (e.g., E. J. Carnell) were deeply hurt and permanently bruised by these attacks.[26] When a South African friend of mine with an effective evangelistic ministry included some of the political implications of the gospel in his preaching in the 1980s, other evangelicals branded him as having abandoned the gospel. In other words, those who respond in obedience to the light may find that others who consider themselves as guardians of the light oppose them.

Personal ambition and God's warning. On several occasions God had to curb Paul's personal ambitions with his guidance. When he wanted to go to Asia, his efforts were thwarted until it was God's time (16:6–10; 19:1). Acts 22:17–21 reflects God's curbing of Paul's ambition to be the witness par excellence to the Jews. The apostle honestly thought that his background would give him such credibility that he would be a powerful witness to his people. But this was not going to be so, and God knew it. Thus, God directed him to leave Jerusalem.

This does not mean that ambition is wrong. Paul also had a great ambition to go to Rome (Rom. 1:10–15; 15:22–32), and the Lord fed that ambition in a vision by telling him, "Take courage! As you have testified about me in Jerusalem, so you must also testify in Rome" (23:11). It is good to dream great dreams, but we must place all these dreams at the altar of God and bow to his sovereignty, believing that he knows what is best for us. And we should also be conscious of the fact that when it comes to our ambitions, it is easy for fleshly desire to cloud godly ambition. Since it is difficult for us to distinguish between these two, we must look to God to send obstacles along the way that alert us to dangers.

We should note too that the other Christians in Jerusalem had a part to play in Paul's leaving Jerusalem (see 9:29–30). In other words, the Christian community can be agents of God's warning regarding our ambitions. We usually resent these blocks that come our way and seemingly hinder us from achieving our goals. But we need to discipline ourselves to accept the perspectives of other believers as gifts sent by God, who in his sovereignty knows what is best.

---

26. See Gordon R. Lewis's analysis of the "traumatic effects" of these attacks on Edward John Carnell in *Handbook of Evangelical Theologians*, ed. Walter A. Elwell (Grand Rapids: Baker, 1993), 332.

Recently we have heard many sad stories of capable Christian leaders whose uncontrolled ambitions led them to break Christian principles and to end up with shameful failure. Many such people have testified later that their ambition led to their downfall and that they did not have frank advisors who could have helped them avoid the pitfalls.[27] This is why the Bible advises us to seek advice regarding our plans (Prov. 11:14; 15:22; 20:18).

This does not mean that we should give up our visions whenever hindrances develop. Paul's plans to go to Asia Minor and Rome were often hindered, but he finally got to both places. Believers also tried to stop Paul from going to Jerusalem at this time, but he strongly felt the Spirit was directing him to go. A key ingredient of faithfulness is a willingness to persevere amidst discouragements. Most, if not all, people who have achieved great things for God have done so by persevering through circumstances that would have caused others to give up.

Often our visions are fulfilled by others, and our role may be to motivate them. We can then back this work with our prayers, rejoice when we see it happening, and help wherever we can. Long after Paul's vision of the Lord in the temple, for example, he agreed that Peter had the call to go to the Jews while his own call was to go to the Gentiles (Gal. 2:7–8). Yet Paul never lost his burden for the Jews (Rom. 9:1–4), and he kept praying for their conversion (10:1). Wherever he went he started by witnessing to them. Although God took him away from ministry in Jerusalem, when he heard about a need there, he took immediate steps to do something about it. This was what had brought him to Jerusalem on this visit—to bring gifts from the Gentile churches for the Jewish Christians. We conclude this discussion with the wise words of Proverbs 16:9: "In his heart a man plans his course, but the LORD determines his steps."

No unnecessary suffering. Even though Paul was willing to suffer death for Christ's sake, he did not take on unnecessary suffering (21:13). Some second-century Christians are said to have gloried in suffering so much that they desired it in unhealthy ways.[28] New Testament Christians did not give in to such excessive morbidity. Today too we can challenge people through the law to ensure our own rights and protection as long as we do not dishonor God. Especially when Christians are being illegally ill-treated because of their principles, it may be good for them (and for society in general) if they protest the way they are being treated.

I do not think God intends a battered wife to bear her pain silently when she is being physically abused and treated as a subhuman by her husband. A

---

27. See Jim Bakker, *I Was Wrong* (Nashville: Thomas Nelson, 1996).

28. See Philip Schaff, *History of the Christian Church*, vol. 2, *Ante-Nicene Christianity* (Grand Rapids: Eerdmans, 1952, repr. 1910 ed.), 48.

child must be encouraged to protest sexual abuse that he or she may be facing. Workers who are underpaid should appeal to their employers to be fair. Furthermore, if the Bible leaves room for us to speak up on behalf of ourselves for our protection, how much more important it is for us to speak up for others who are being dehumanized or treated unjustly.

Because of the sinfulness of the human race, in spite of all the advances in labor rights in the world, there are still situations where laborers are badly exploited. Christians ought to speak up on their behalf and try to secure their legitimate rights. These are results of Christians getting close to people. They see needs and realize that as Christians they can and must do something. The early Methodist movement rightly got involved in encouraging the labor movement. Christian laborers began to talk in their small groups about their troubles, and their fellow Christians realized they had to do something to alleviate those sufferings.[29]

---

29. This point was made in a lecture on John Wesley's method of pastoral care by Dr. Allan Coppedge at the Ministers' Conference at Asbury Theological Seminary in February 1989.

Acts 23:12–24:27

THE NEXT MORNING the Jews formed a conspiracy and bound themselves with an oath not to eat or drink until they had killed Paul. ¹³More than forty men were involved in this plot. ¹⁴They went to the chief priests and elders and said, "We have taken a solemn oath not to eat anything until we have killed Paul. ¹⁵Now then, you and the Sanhedrin petition the commander to bring him before you on the pretext of wanting more accurate information about his case. We are ready to kill him before he gets here."

¹⁶But when the son of Paul's sister heard of this plot, he went into the barracks and told Paul.

¹⁷Then Paul called one of the centurions and said, "Take this young man to the commander; he has something to tell him." ¹⁸So he took him to the commander.

The centurion said, "Paul, the prisoner, sent for me and asked me to bring this young man to you because he has something to tell you."

¹⁹The commander took the young man by the hand, drew him aside and asked, "What is it you want to tell me?"

²⁰He said: "The Jews have agreed to ask you to bring Paul before the Sanhedrin tomorrow on the pretext of wanting more accurate information about him. ²¹Don't give in to them, because more than forty of them are waiting in ambush for him. They have taken an oath not to eat or drink until they have killed him. They are ready now, waiting for your consent to their request."

²²The commander dismissed the young man and cautioned him, "Don't tell anyone that you have reported this to me."

²³Then he called two of his centurions and ordered them, "Get ready a detachment of two hundred soldiers, seventy horsemen and two hundred spearmen to go to Caesarea at nine tonight. ²⁴Provide mounts for Paul so that he may be taken safely to Governor Felix."

²⁵He wrote a letter as follows:

²⁶Claudius Lysias,

To His Excellency, Governor Felix:

Greetings.

²⁷This man was seized by the Jews and they were about
to kill him, but I came with my troops and rescued him, for
I had learned that he is a Roman citizen. ²⁸I wanted to
know why they were accusing him, so I brought him to
their Sanhedrin. ²⁹I found that the accusation had to do
with questions about their law, but there was no charge
against him that deserved death or imprisonment. ³⁰When I
was informed of a plot to be carried out against the man, I
sent him to you at once. I also ordered his accusers to present to you their case against him.

³¹So the soldiers, carrying out their orders, took Paul with
them during the night and brought him as far as Antipatris.
³²The next day they let the cavalry go on with him, while
they returned to the barracks. ³³When the cavalry arrived in
Caesarea, they delivered the letter to the governor and
handed Paul over to him. ³⁴The governor read the letter and
asked what province he was from. Learning that he was from
Cilicia, ³⁵he said, "I will hear your case when your accusers
get here." Then he ordered that Paul be kept under guard in
Herod's palace.

²⁴:¹Five days later the high priest Ananias went down to
Caesarea with some of the elders and a lawyer named Tertullus, and they brought their charges against Paul before the
governor. ²When Paul was called in, Tertullus presented his
case before Felix: "We have enjoyed a long period of peace
under you, and your foresight has brought about reforms in
this nation. ³Everywhere and in every way, most excellent
Felix, we acknowledge this with profound gratitude. ⁴But in
order not to weary you further, I would request that you be
kind enough to hear us briefly.

⁵"We have found this man to be a troublemaker, stirring
up riots among the Jews all over the world. He is a ringleader
of the Nazarene sect ⁶and even tried to desecrate the temple;
so we seized him. ⁸By examining him yourself you will be able
to learn the truth about all these charges we are bringing
against him."

⁹The Jews joined in the accusation, asserting that these things were true.

¹⁰When the governor motioned for him to speak, Paul replied: "I know that for a number of years you have been a judge over this nation; so I gladly make my defense. ¹¹You can easily verify that no more than twelve days ago I went up to Jerusalem to worship. ¹²My accusers did not find me arguing with anyone at the temple, or stirring up a crowd in the synagogues or anywhere else in the city. ¹³And they cannot prove to you the charges they are now making against me. ¹⁴However, I admit that I worship the God of our fathers as a follower of the Way, which they call a sect. I believe everything that agrees with the Law and that is written in the Prophets, ¹⁵and I have the same hope in God as these men, that there will be a resurrection of both the righteous and the wicked. ¹⁶So I strive always to keep my conscience clear before God and man.

¹⁷"After an absence of several years, I came to Jerusalem to bring my people gifts for the poor and to present offerings. ¹⁸I was ceremonially clean when they found me in the temple courts doing this. There was no crowd with me, nor was I involved in any disturbance. ¹⁹But there are some Jews from the province of Asia, who ought to be here before you and bring charges if they have anything against me. ²⁰Or these who are here should state what crime they found in me when I stood before the Sanhedrin—²¹unless it was this one thing I shouted as I stood in their presence: 'It is concerning the resurrection of the dead that I am on trial before you today.'"

²²Then Felix, who was well acquainted with the Way, adjourned the proceedings. "When Lysias the commander comes," he said, "I will decide your case." ²³He ordered the centurion to keep Paul under guard but to give him some freedom and permit his friends to take care of his needs.

²⁴Several days later Felix came with his wife Drusilla, who was a Jewess. He sent for Paul and listened to him as he spoke about faith in Christ Jesus. ²⁵As Paul discoursed on righteousness, self-control and the judgment to come, Felix was afraid and said, "That's enough for now! You may leave. When I find it convenient, I will send for you." ²⁶At the same time he was hoping that Paul would offer him a bribe, so he sent for him frequently and talked with him.

²⁷When two years had passed, Felix was succeeded by Porcius Festus, but because Felix wanted to grant a favor to the Jews, he left Paul in prison.

THE APOSTLE PAUL has now been placed in prison, partly for his own protection. He obviously does not know at this time that he will be in prison for the next four years. During these long years he must have taken comfort from the fact that the Lord had promised him that eventually he would get to Rome and witness to Jesus in the capital city of the empire (23:11).

Paul Moved to Caesarea (23:12–35)

AS PAUL SAT in prison, some Jews devised a plot that began the long process that would send him from Palestine to Rome (23:12). The intensity of the resolve of these men is evidenced by their decision to have a total fast until they have killed Paul.

At this stage Paul's nephew enters the story with his tip-off to Paul (23:16). He was able to get in touch with Paul and even with the centurion because Paul was an unconvicted Roman citizen and had to be treated with due respect. When Paul said that he lost all the things that he could claim from a human standpoint because of the gospel (Phil. 3:4–8), this must have included his family. His father, probably a wealthy person, likely disowned him. But something of family affection must have remained for his sister's son to take the risk of spilling out the plot of this murderous group.

The centurion took immediate action on hearing about the plot and made arrangements to transfer Paul to Caesarea, where the governor of Judea usually resided (he went to Jerusalem only at important times, such as during festivals). An unusually large military contingent accompanied Paul, possibly because of the threat of a revolt in Jerusalem and also because of the group that was waiting to kill Paul (23:23–24). Once they were a safe distance from Jerusalem in Antipatris (about thirty-five miles away) and the danger to Paul's life was diminished, a portion of the group returned to Jerusalem (23:32).

The centurion sent a letter along to the governor, describing the circumstances of Paul's arrest and trial in Jerusalem. The account embellished the story about Paul with an untruth about the commander's rescuing him upon discovering he was a Roman citizen (23:27). The commander specifically mentions that "there was no charge against him that deserved death or imprisonment" (23:29); rather, Paul was being sent to Caesarea for protection (23:30). Luke's stress on Paul's blamelessness before the Roman law is a major theme of this entire passage.

Felix had became procurator of Judea in A.D. 52, which means that he had been governor for about five years when Paul was brought to him. Felix came from a somewhat lowly background but rose to a high position because of his brother Pallas, who was for a number of years the head of the imperial civil service. The governor successively married three women of royal birth. His current wife was his third, Drusilla, the daughter of Herod Agrippa I.

There were many insurgent uprisings during Felix's term of office, which he ruthlessly put down. The Roman historian Tacitus said that Felix "exercised the power of a king with the mind of a slave."[1] After reading the letter Felix ascertained that Paul was from Cilicia and decided to hear his case (23:34–35). Had he been from a neighboring area, Felix could have sent him to that governor, just as Pilate sent Jesus to Herod when he found that he was from Galilee. Paul was kept under guard in the palace that Herod the Great built for himself, which was now the governor's headquarters.[2]

The Trial Before Felix (24:1–23)

THE SERIOUSNESS WITH which the Jewish leaders took this case is apparent in that the high priest himself made the sixty-five-mile journey to Caesarea along with the elders and the lawyer Tertullus (24:1). The speeches of Tertullus and Paul (as well as Paul's speech before Agrippa in ch. 26) follow the form of forensic speeches of the time.[3]

Tertullus begins with a typical exordium (introduction), "acknowledging the judge's authority on the matter phrased to win favor and goodwill."[4] He expresses the gratitude of the Jews for the peace that they have enjoyed under him. This was not really true, for there had been many insurrections that had been brutally stamped out by Felix. Gempf suggests that, rather than being nonsense (as some have alleged), this could be "Tertullus' attempt to remind Felix that the stability had been purchased through severe action against troublemakers, of which, he goes on to argue, Paul was one causing 'riots all over the world'"[5] (24:5a).

---

1. Tacitus, *History*, 5.9. This quotation and the other information on Felix is from Bruce, *Acts*, NICNT, 436–37.

2. Luke calls it "Herod's praetorium" (*praitorion* being a technical term for the commander-in-chief's headquarters; see Bruce, *Steps*, 54).

3. Bruce W. Winter, "Official Proceedings and the Forensic Speeches in Acts 24–26," *BAFCS*, vol. 1, *Ancient Literary Setting*, 305–36.

4. Gempf, "Acts," 1102.

5. Ibid.

Tertullus then brings several charges against Paul. His causing riots may refer to the trouble he supposedly caused in Asia. Paul is also charged with being a ringleader of the Nazarene sect, and he tried to desecrate the temple (24:5b–6).[6] The term *Nazarene* probably derives from the fact that Jesus grew up in Nazareth (Matt. 2:23) and was used of Jesus in the Gospels (Matt. 2:23; Mark 14:67; 16:6). This is the only time it is used of the church. Tertullus asserts that an examination of Paul will show that the charges they bring are true (24:8).

Paul's exordium also points to the competence of Felix to judge the case, but he is less lavish than Tertullus with his compliments (24:10). His speech is, in Bruce Winter's words, "a well ordered defense. . . . Paul conducted his defense in an able manner against a professional forensic orator."[7] Each statement recorded by Luke in this summary makes a telling point that convinces Felix of Paul's innocence (cf. 24:22–27). Felix can verify when Paul arrived in Jerusalem (v. 11). His accusers did not find him doing anything anywhere in Jerusalem that might suggest he was causing trouble (v. 12); they have no proof of any of their charges (v. 13). Paul does admit that he is a member of the Way, but he goes on to show that this sect has similar beliefs to the Jews (vv. 14–15); this is a sect just like the Pharisees and Sadducees.[8] Next Paul asserts his blamelessness (v. 16). No one can point a finger at him regarding his personal life—a powerful state indeed for an ambassador of Christ to be in. The word translated "strive" in verse 16 (*askeo*) was originally used for athletic strife. It means "to engage in some activity, with both continuity and effort."[9]

Paul then gets specific about his visit to Jerusalem, giving the clearest reference in Acts to the gifts for the poor he brought with him (v. 17). He also mentions bringing "offerings," a statement that has been variously interpreted. This may be referring to the gifts for the poor, to offerings he presented at the temple possibly in connection with a vow, or to what he did in the temple in connection with the Nazirites, who had taken a vow. Kistemaker may be correct in saying that "since Luke often compresses material, the term 'offering' is a shortened form meant to bring to mind the episode in the temple (21:26–27)."[10]

---

6. The Western Text includes a statement of complaint against the commander in Jerusalem, which is included as a footnote in the NIV (v. 7): "[We] . . . wanted to judge him according to our law. But the commander, Lysias, came and with the use of much force snatched him from our hands and ordered his accusers to come before you." The standard Greek New Testament does not include the text (see Metzger, *Textual*, 490). Bruce thinks that, considering its tone, it may be a genuine statement (*Acts*, NICNT, 441).

7. Winter, "Forensic Speeches," 327.

8. Gempf, "Acts," 1103.

9. Louw and Nida, 663.

10. Kistemaker, *Acts*, 846.

Then Paul denies the specific charges against him. He was ceremonially clean when he was found in the temple, there was no crowd with him, and he was not involved in any disturbance (v. 18). If the charge about his causing trouble all over the world (24:5) refers to the trouble in Ephesus, then the people from Asia should be there to press charges (v. 19). One by one he has refuted all the charges against him.

But Paul has one more point to make: He was tried by the Sanhedrin, but they also found no suitable charge to bring against him (v. 20). In his full talk the apostle may have mentioned the confusion in the Sanhedrin during his trial. He certainly implies that when he says that he had to shout a statement about the resurrection (v. 21), which divided the Sanhedrin. He admits to one possible point against him—a doctrinal issue that really was not within Felix's jurisdiction.

Felix should have released Paul, but he was reluctant to displease the Jews (see 24:27). So he delayed making a decision until the commander came (v. 22). But he gave Paul relative freedom (v. 23). Felix's delaying tactics went on for two whole years, at which time he was removed from his job (v. 27). Luke leaves us with no doubt that this Roman governor thought Paul was innocent of any crime against the state.

Felix and the Gospel (24:24–27)

THE CONVERSATIONS PAUL had with Felix and his wife give us a good description of how many top officials respond to the gospel (see discussion below). Included in Paul's discussions about the gospel (v. 24) was discourse about "righteousness, self-control and the judgment" (v. 25a). These discussions made Felix afraid, which expressed itself in a couldn't-care-less attitude ("When I find it convenient, I will send for you"—v. 25b). We also see how mixed his motives were, for he was looking for a bribe (v. 26) and did not want to displease the Jews even if that meant being unjust to Paul (v. 27). He probably thought that one who was a Roman citizen and who had just brought a substantial gift for the poor must have had access to substantial wealth. Josephus tells us that Felix would have been severely punished after he was removed from office if not for the influence of his brother, Pallas.[11]

DEFENDING CHRISTIANITY BEFORE the state. We have frequently noted one of Luke's aims in Acts of demonstrating that Christianity was not a dangerous religious group, especially that there was no truth to the charge of subversion against Rome. The record of Paul's trials

---

11. Josephus, *Antiquities of the Jews*, 20.8.9 (*Complete Works*, 422–23).

before Jewish and Roman crowds, councils, and tribunals (chs. 21−26) clearly shows this. In this section this theme appears in several ways. Luke gives the impression that the key Roman authority Felix, who concluded that Paul was innocent and kept him in custody only to please the Jews, knew the facts about what happened in Palestine. Both Tertullus and Paul refer to Felix's long service in Judea (24:2, 10). Luke says that he was well acquainted with Christianity (v. 22) and that his wife was a Jewess (v. 24).

Another key factor in demonstrating the legitimacy of Christianity is the high quality and persuasiveness of Paul's defense. He exposed many holes in the arguments of his opponents, giving at least six telling points that would stand up in the court.

- No one could not prove the charges against him (24:13).
- The Jews from Asia should have been there to substantiate some of the accusations (24:19).
- The Sanhedrin was unable to come up with clear charges (24:20).
- As far as Rome was concerned, Christianity is a sect within Judaism, just like the Sadducean and Pharisaic sects (24:14−15).
- As for Paul's personal life, he could honestly say he was blameless before God and humankind (24:16).
- Paul's belief about the resurrection might indeed be an issue (24:21), but that was a theological matter and did not really concern the Roman state.

Clearly Paul outwitted Tertullus and rendered void all his arguments. We remember a comment made about Stephen that his opponents "could not stand up against his wisdom or the Spirit by whom he spoke" (6:10). All this points to our call to be competent in our defense of Christianity against the attacks that come to it from the world.

One of the points given above merits special mention because it is found in all three of the formal speeches of Paul that appear in this last division of Acts. This is Paul's statement that he was blameless before God and the world (23:1; 24:16; 25:8). The blamelessness of Christians was an important part of the case for Christianity in New Testament times. The early Christians not only outthought their opponents, they also outlived them.

Felix and the gospel. Luke gives us some details of Felix's response not only to the legal case against Paul but also to the gospel that Paul taught. This in turn gives us some insights on how people in positions of power and authority often respond to the truth of the gospel. (Luke does the same with Agrippa later, 26:25−29.) The Bible is concerned with the conversion of all people, including the rich and powerful. Thus when Luke included these sections, he must have intended to teach something about the reactions of high officials to the gospel. We will list Felix's reactions as we examine each one in the "Contemporary Significance" section.

ELOQUENT SPOKESPERSONS. LIKE Paul, we should be competent in our defense of Christianity from the world's attacks. This requires that we know the world and understand its criticisms against Christianity. Then we should formulate answers to those criticisms that are credible and convincing.

Paul presented a speech that fitted in with the best forms of rhetoric required for a legal defense. In the following centuries the church produced great apologists, such as Justin Martyr, who attempted to create sympathy and understanding for Christianity among pagan emperors and intellectuals.[12] Many great thinkers of the church today write only to defend the truth against attacks from within the church. Each generation ought to develop thinkers who will engage the prominent non-Christian minds of the day. Though we must all do this to some small extent, the church must nurture those who are particularly gifted in this work. We should encourage these people, give them sufficient time to devote themselves to needed study and writing, see how we ourselves can complement their ministry, and back it with their prayers.

A good example of how the church backed one who engaged the political leaders of his day on behalf of God's truth comes from the political career of William Wilberforce, who, after a long battle, had slavery abolished in the British empire. He was supported by a group of like-minded Christians who lived near Clapham, England, thus becoming known as "the Clapham Sect." They spent three hours daily in prayer as a group. During Wilberforce's later years, Zachary Macaulay, one of the members, provided him with the facts and figures he needed for his debates. When there were critical debates in parliament, Christians all over England united in prayer.[13]

Ours is an age when the world is influencing the church in such subtle ways that we do not even realize that it is happening. Postmodernism has been presenting a new approach to truth. Christian stands on issues like homosexual practice, abortion on demand, euthanasia, and labor rights are being attacked as bigotry and/or folly. Christians in some countries are facing

---

12. See Robert M. Grant, *Greek Apologists of the Second Century* (Philadelphia: Westminster, 1988).

13. The facts on Wilberforce come from Richard Lovelace, *Dynamics of Spiritual Life* (Downers Grove, Ill.: InterVarsity, 1979), 370; John Pollock, *Wilberforce* (Herts and Belleville, Mich.: Lion, 1986 repr.), 177.

persecution because of their stands. Modern society strongly objects to the Christian insistence on the need for conversion; in some nations conversion is illegal. Many countries are enacting laws that restrict evangelistic activity. In some places minorities are treated as second-class citizens. All such situations call for an eloquent Christian response. The church must get ready for such challenges by encouraging capable people to argue for the Christian viewpoint.

Blameless spokespersons. As noted above, the early Christians not only outthought their opponents, they also outlived them. Paul said of himself, "I strive always to keep my conscience clear before God and man" (24:16). In the writings of the early Christian apologists, the behavior of the Christians was a key aspect used in defense of Christianity.[14] The force of blameless lives has been powerful in defending Christianity against attacks from outside in every age.

The challenge to the church today to be blameless before the world has become acute, considering the great moral crisis facing the world today. In the West, there has been a general rejection of the Christian worldview that formed its moral basis for centuries. Many of its structures were based on moral absolutes. For example, much of American society operates on the principle of trust. With the current rejection of moral absolutes in postmodern Western society, one wonders how it can survive without deteriorating into serious confusion.

Theologians like Carl Henry and scholars like Allan Bloom have been charting this trend.[15] One can imagine that sooner or later many millions of Westerners are going to look for an alternative to this confusion. When they realize the ravages of sexual indiscipline and seek a purer sexual morality, will they see Christians as people who not only remain pure but have a wholesome enjoyment that is much more refreshing than the extreme asceticism that many opt for? When they realize the ravages of living without integrity, will they see Christians as people who live with a clear conscience before God and humankind?

Although many Westerners, tired of the materialism and moral indiscipline of Western society, are turning to Eastern spirituality for answers, they will soon realize that this resource is equally bankrupt. There is no ethical system within Hinduism that enables people to live holy lives. While Buddhism has a strong ethical system to strive for, Buddhists are finding that they do

---

14. See the writings of Justin, Tertullian, Ignatius, and in 1 Clement (see Grant, *Greek Apologists*, 66–67).

15. Carl F. H. Henry, *Twilight of a Great Civilization* (Westchester: Crossway, 1988); Allan Bloom, *The Closing of the American Mind* (New York: Simon and Schuster, 1987).

not have the spiritual resources to overcome the onslaught of modern immorality to which they are being exposed in the media. Most countries in the so-called Third World are unable to make progress because of rampant corruption. There is a growing disenchantment with existing structures since people have not been able to shake off the corruption destroying the fabric of many nations.

I spoke about this recently with theologian Bruce Nicholls, a New Zealander who has been a missionary for forty years in India. He observed that the recent growth of fundamentalist movements among Hindus, Muslims, and Buddhists is an attempt to stem this tide of moral degradation sweeping Asian nations. He felt that this is a time of unprecedented opportunity for the church to demonstrate the power of the gospel.

We do have a dynamic from the Creator of human nature that alone can satisfy this homesickness for morality in the human soul. But how have we fared? The church seems to have become a reflection of the maladies of society rather than a witness to these maladies. We have been so enslaved by pragmatism that morality has been subsumed in our quest for results. Elsewhere in this book we have spoken of the valuable place that signs and wonders have as means of attracting people to Christ. But it is easy to be so enamored by such display of power that we neglect the priority of holiness over power.

Many churches that emphasize the miraculous today are weak in their teaching and reflections on Christian morality. As a result, people who are testifying to miraculous answers to prayer are underpaying their workers, are guilty of racial prejudice, or lie to make a sale. Evangelists who minister in the miraculous can get so enamored by their power that they give little attention to pursuing holiness. They find refuge in their ministries and thus ignore the voice of conscience that tells them that all is not well in their lives.

This neglect of moral instruction is seen in other branches of the evangelical movement too. Some churches are afraid to confront members who are living privately in sin. In keeping with the thinking of society around us, they do not want to pry into the private lives of others. Preachers are afraid to speak forthrightly against sins condemned in Scripture, fearing that they will be branded as bigoted and will lose members as a result.

I am thankful that prayer has seen a resurgence in many evangelical churches. There is much talk about the place of prayer and fasting in mission. Warfare prayer for breaking down strongholds and the place of prayer in evangelism are receiving fresh emphasis today. But there is little emphasis on praying for personal holiness, on fasting and praying for the revival of holy living in the church. If we examine the New Testament letters that teach about living the Christian life, we will find much more teaching on holy living than on warfare. While we do not discount the value of instruction on warfare and rejoice over its return to the life of the church, we must keep a scriptural balance.

We may be neglecting one of the most urgent warfares that has to be waged for the Christian worldview and ethic. This is an intellectual and moral warfare that influences the spiritual lives of us all. Carl Henry describes it well:

> A half-generation ago the pagans were still largely threatening at the gates of Western culture; now the barbarians are plunging into the oriental and occidental mainstream. As they seek to reverse the inherited intellectual and moral heritage of the Bible, the Christian world-life view and the secular world-life view engage as never before in rival conflict for the mind, the conscience, the will, the spirit, the very selfhood of contemporary man.[16]

Paul spoke of striving (*askeo*) to keep his "conscience clear before God and man" (24:16). The pursuit of holiness is an exercise that must be carried out with utmost diligence. If we exaggerate in the pulpit, we must correct it in the pulpit, even though it may be humiliating. If we fail at home in front of our children, we must apologize in their presence. We must strongly refuse any temptation to pay a bribe or tell a lie to get something done. We must follow the laws of the land even if they may seem silly. We must do our work conscientiously in our offices even if no one else is doing so and it may be embarrassing for us to be the only ones. Though all the churches nearby underpay their custodians, we must refuse to do so even if we are financially less stable. We must openly admit personal weaknesses to our Christian colleagues and spouses and have them check on us so that they may "spur [us] on toward love and good deeds" (Heb. 10:24).

The church, then, must rediscover the priority of holiness and look for the ways prescribed in the Scriptures to release the dynamic of the Holy Spirit, who enables Christians to live holy lives. This is why Christianity is so unique. Other religions also teach us to be good, but Christianity gives us the power to become good. Note Paul's words: "May God himself, the God of peace, sanctify you through and through" (1 Thess. 5:23).

Why the rich and powerful find it hard to enter the kingdom. We now examine the principles from Luke's portrayal of the interaction between Felix and Paul, which shows us features typical of the response of rich and powerful people to the gospel.

(1) Felix showed an interest in the gospel by sending for Paul and listening "to him as he spoke about faith in Christ Jesus" (24:24). Top officials and

---

16. Henry, *Twilight of a Great Civilization,* 27.

powerful people commonly show a cordial interest in what religious leaders say. We can use this as a stepping-stone to sharing the gospel with them, as Paul did with Felix and Agrippa. But we must remember that, though many such people will be interested in the gospel and testify to being blessed by it, they may not be willing to repent of their sin and turn to God alone for salvation. Nebuchadnezzar saw God's hand acting powerfully on two occasions and even praised God and made pronouncements about him (Dan. 2–3). But he was not converted until he was brought to the end of himself and was forced to affirm that the Most High God reigns (Dan. 4).

We should therefore be careful about proclaiming that a famous person has been converted until there is evidence of conversion. Too often we assume that because a famous person did something (e.g., ask a preacher to come and see him or testify to an answer to prayer), that means that the individual has become a Christian. In reality, some professions of religious commitment made by famous people are nothing more than public relations gimmicks.

(2) Paul brought up the topics of "righteousness, self-control and the judgment to come" with Felix so that he even became afraid (24:25). The Bible offers ample evidence that one of the ways to present the gospel to powerful people is to confront them with the reality of judgment. God did this with Nebuchadnezzar (Dan. 4); John the Baptist did this with the Pharisees and Sadducees (Matt. 3:7); Peter did this with Cornelius (10:42) and Paul with the Athenians (17:31). But we tend to neglect this today. Leaders often call for Christians and ask them to pray for them. We must respond positively to such requests and pray for the person. Participating in prayer can open powerful people to the gospel. But we must not forget to confront them with the challenge of a holy God, who calls them to leave their sin behind in order to follow him. The role of the Holy Spirit is to "convict the world of guilt in regard to sin and righteousness and judgment" (John 16:8). As his agents, we can become the medium through which he performs that role.[17]

These topics are relevant to powerful people, for they respect power. Many of them look at Christians as weak people who need the crutch of a merciful God to enable them to face up to the strains of life. They regard themselves as "self-made persons," who do not need that crutch. They must be confronted with the holiness and sovereignty of God, to be told that "it is a dreadful thing to fall into the hands of the living God" (Heb. 10:31), who is "a consuming fire" (12:29). In their careers they have learned to respect and negotiate wisely with powerful forces and people. They must be made to realize that they also need to come to grips with the power of Almighty God if they want assurance of a secure future.

---

17. On proclaiming judgment see my *Crucial Questions About Hell* (Wheaton: Crossway, 1994), 125–80.

The failure to bring up the important topics of righteousness, self-control, and judgment can result in powerful people professing commitments to Christ but without a change in lifestyle. When the idea of being born again had become almost a fad in North America in the 1970s, the publisher of a famous pornographic magazine made much news by professing a born-again experience. Unfortunately he did not think it was necessary for him to stop publishing pornography. During this same era a powerful aide to President Richard Nixon, Charles Colson, professed conversion and with that confessed to an obstruction of justice charge in connection with the Watergate affair. As a result, he was imprisoned for seven months.[18] It is no accident that Colson is one of our generation's greatest spokespersons for the holiness of God. Throughout history other wealthy and powerful people, when confronted with the holiness of God and their own sin, have responded with repentance and restitution and thus brought honor to God (e.g., the king of Nineveh [Jonah 3] and Zacchaeus [Luke 19:8–10]).

(3) Felix's behavior gives us at least three reasons why it is so hard for the rich and powerful to enter the kingdom of God (cf. Luke 18:24–25). (a) They are able to camouflage their insecurity by pretending to be in control of their lives. Verse 25a says that Felix was afraid after Paul had talked to him about righteousness, self-control, and judgment. But he was able to brush off his unease through his power to control his schedule. "That's enough for now!" he said, "You may leave. When I find it convenient, I will send for you" (24:25b). We must be aware of such bluffs and, if possible, keep exposing the powerful to the primacy of their relationship with God. We must tell them, "You may be sure that your sin will find you out" (Num. 32:23).

(b) The rich and powerful are often controlled by an insatiable greed, and they usually find convenient ways to express this. Felix was so blinded by greed that he even hoped for a bribe from the one who had talked to him about righteousness, self-control, and judgment (24:26)! Paul gave a severe warning about this when he wrote, "People who want to get rich fall into temptation and a trap and into many foolish and harmful desires that plunge men into ruin and destruction. For the love of money is a root of all kinds of evil. Some people, eager for money, have wandered from the faith and pierced themselves with many griefs" (1 Tim. 6:9–10). The power of these traps are often so strong that people come to their senses only after they have fallen into a deep pit of failure. The evangelist's role is to keep challenging people with the truth of God's Word so that people may come to their senses and be delivered from any enslavement.

(c) Those who are at the top feel that they have to please many people if they want to stay in their position and thrive in society. This may hinder

---

18. See Charles Colson, *Born Again* (Old Tappan, N.J.: Chosen, 1976).

them from doing what they know to be right. Ultimately, Paul was denied justice "because Felix wanted to grant a favor to the Jews" (24:27). Ironically, Felix could not stay on like this, for he was finally dismissed from his job, and a deputation of Jews went to Rome to accuse him of wrongdoing. He avoided punishment for his failures in Judea only because of his influential brother, Pallas. But in the present passage we see how difficult it was for him to do justice by Paul.

The three factors that make it difficult for the rich to come into the kingdom are true of all people, but they particularly come into focus with the rich since they have greater opportunities to give in to their evil desires. Christian communicators must warn the rich about the deceit of wealth. As Paul says, we must "command those who are rich in this present world not to be arrogant nor to put their hope in wealth, which is so uncertain, but to put their hope in God, who richly provides us with everything for our enjoyment" (1 Tim. 6:17). One good way to avoid this trap is to become lavish in generosity: "Command them to do good, to be rich in good deeds, and to be generous and willing to share" (6:18). Generosity is not only an antidote to the maladies associated with wealth, it is also a wise investment: "In this way they will lay up treasure for themselves as a firm foundation for the coming age, so that they may take hold of the life that is truly life" (6:19).

How true it is! The reality of judgment colors our attitudes to wealth. Wealth is fleeting in comparison to eternity, and the wise person prepares for eternity.

Acts 25:1–26:32

THREE DAYS AFTER arriving in the province, Festus went up from Caesarea to Jerusalem, ²where the chief priests and Jewish leaders appeared before him and presented the charges against Paul. ³They urgently requested Festus, as a favor to them, to have Paul transferred to Jerusalem, for they were preparing an ambush to kill him along the way. ⁴Festus answered, "Paul is being held at Caesarea, and I myself am going there soon. ⁵Let some of your leaders come with me and press charges against the man there, if he has done anything wrong."

⁶After spending eight or ten days with them, he went down to Caesarea, and the next day he convened the court and ordered that Paul be brought before him. ⁷When Paul appeared, the Jews who had come down from Jerusalem stood around him, bringing many serious charges against him, which they could not prove.

⁸Then Paul made his defense: "I have done nothing wrong against the law of the Jews or against the temple or against Caesar."

⁹Festus, wishing to do the Jews a favor, said to Paul, "Are you willing to go up to Jerusalem and stand trial before me there on these charges?"

¹⁰Paul answered: "I am now standing before Caesar's court, where I ought to be tried. I have not done any wrong to the Jews, as you yourself know very well. ¹¹If, however, I am guilty of doing anything deserving death, I do not refuse to die. But if the charges brought against me by these Jews are not true, no one has the right to hand me over to them. I appeal to Caesar!"

¹²After Festus had conferred with his council, he declared: "You have appealed to Caesar. To Caesar you will go!"

¹³A few days later King Agrippa and Bernice arrived at Caesarea to pay their respects to Festus. ¹⁴Since they were spending many days there, Festus discussed Paul's case with the king. He said: "There is a man here whom Felix left as a prisoner. ¹⁵When I went to Jerusalem, the chief priests and elders of the Jews brought charges against him and asked that he be condemned.

¹⁶"I told them that it is not the Roman custom to hand over any man before he has faced his accusers and has had an opportunity to defend himself against their charges. ¹⁷When they came here with me, I did not delay the case, but convened the court the next day and ordered the man to be brought in. ¹⁸When his accusers got up to speak, they did not charge him with any of the crimes I had expected. ¹⁹Instead, they had some points of dispute with him about their own religion and about a dead man named Jesus who Paul claimed was alive. ²⁰I was at a loss how to investigate such matters; so I asked if he would be willing to go to Jerusalem and stand trial there on these charges. ²¹When Paul made his appeal to be held over for the Emperor's decision, I ordered him held until I could send him to Caesar."

²²Then Agrippa said to Festus, "I would like to hear this man myself."

He replied, "Tomorrow you will hear him."

²³The next day Agrippa and Bernice came with great pomp and entered the audience room with the high ranking officers and the leading men of the city. At the command of Festus, Paul was brought in. ²⁴Festus said: "King Agrippa, and all who are present with us, you see this man! The whole Jewish community has petitioned me about him in Jerusalem and here in Caesarea, shouting that he ought not to live any longer. ²⁵I found he had done nothing deserving of death, but because he made his appeal to the Emperor I decided to send him to Rome. ²⁶But I have nothing definite to write to His Majesty about him. Therefore I have brought him before all of you, and especially before you, King Agrippa, so that as a result of this investigation I may have something to write. ²⁷For I think it is unreasonable to send on a prisoner without specifying the charges against him."

²⁶:¹Then Agrippa said to Paul, "You have permission to speak for yourself."

So Paul motioned with his hand and began his defense: ²"King Agrippa, I consider myself fortunate to stand before you today as I make my defense against all the accusations of the Jews, ³and especially so because you are well acquainted with all the Jewish customs and controversies. Therefore, I beg you to listen to me patiently.

⁴"The Jews all know the way I have lived ever since I was a child, from the beginning of my life in my own country, and

also in Jerusalem. ⁵They have known me for a long time and can testify, if they are willing, that according to the strictest sect of our religion, I lived as a Pharisee. ⁶And now it is because of my hope in what God has promised our fathers that I am on trial today. ⁷This is the promise our twelve tribes are hoping to see fulfilled as they earnestly serve God day and night. O king, it is because of this hope that the Jews are accusing me. ⁸Why should any of you consider it incredible that God raises the dead?

⁹"I too was convinced that I ought to do all that was possible to oppose the name of Jesus of Nazareth. ¹⁰And that is just what I did in Jerusalem. On the authority of the chief priests I put many of the saints in prison, and when they were put to death, I cast my vote against them. ¹¹Many a time I went from one synagogue to another to have them punished, and I tried to force them to blaspheme. In my obsession against them, I even went to foreign cities to persecute them.

¹²"On one of these journeys I was going to Damascus with the authority and commission of the chief priests. ¹³About noon, O king, as I was on the road, I saw a light from heaven, brighter than the sun, blazing around me and my companions. ¹⁴We all fell to the ground, and I heard a voice saying to me in Aramaic, 'Saul, Saul, why do you persecute me? It is hard for you to kick against the goads.'

¹⁵"Then I asked, 'Who are you, Lord?'

"'I am Jesus, whom you are persecuting,' the Lord replied. ¹⁶'Now get up and stand on your feet. I have appeared to you to appoint you as a servant and as a witness of what you have seen of me and what I will show you. ¹⁷I will rescue you from your own people and from the Gentiles. I am sending you to them ¹⁸to open their eyes and turn them from darkness to light, and from the power of Satan to God, so that they may receive forgiveness of sins and a place among those who are sanctified by faith in me.'

¹⁹"So then, King Agrippa, I was not disobedient to the vision from heaven. ²⁰First to those in Damascus, then to those in Jerusalem and in all Judea, and to the Gentiles also, I preached that they should repent and turn to God and prove their repentance by their deeds. ²¹That is why the Jews seized me in the temple courts and tried to kill me. ²²But I have had God's help to this very day, and so I stand here and testify to

small and great alike. I am saying nothing beyond what the prophets and Moses said would happen—²³that the Christ would suffer and, as the first to rise from the dead, would proclaim light to his own people and to the Gentiles."

²⁴At this point Festus interrupted Paul's defense. "You are out of your mind, Paul!" he shouted. "Your great learning is driving you insane."

²⁵"I am not insane, most excellent Festus," Paul replied. "What I am saying is true and reasonable. ²⁶The king is familiar with these things, and I can speak freely to him. I am convinced that none of this has escaped his notice, because it was not done in a corner. ²⁷King Agrippa, do you believe the prophets? I know you do."

²⁸Then Agrippa said to Paul, "Do you think that in such a short time you can persuade me to be a Christian?"

²⁹Paul replied, "Short time or long—I pray God that not only you but all who are listening to me today may become what I am, except for these chains."

³⁰The king rose, and with him the governor and Bernice and those sitting with them. ³¹They left the room, and while talking with one another, they said, "This man is not doing anything that deserves death or imprisonment."

³²Agrippa said to Festus, "This man could have been set free if he had not appealed to Caesar."

Original Meaning

AS REPORTED IN the last section, Paul was incarcerated in Caesarea during the final two years of Felix's governorship over Palestine. After he was removed from office and replaced by Festus, the Jews made another attempt to move Paul's case forward. Indirectly, the apostle must also have been happy to see a break in the status quo.

Paul Appeals to Caesar (25:1–12)

GOVERNOR FESTUS MADE his first visit to Jerusalem three days after arriving in the province. He met with the Jewish leaders, who were quick to bring up the issue of Paul (25:1–2). Even two years after Paul's arrest their urgency over this case and their plans to kill him had not diminished. The first favor they requested of Festus was to have Paul brought to Jerusalem, with the intent that they might kill him on the way (25:3). Festus apparently preferred to conduct most of his business from Caesarea, particularly in cases that could be drawn out. So he asked the Jews to come to Caesarea with him and promised to take up the case on his return (25:4–6).

As in the trial before Felix, the Jews made serious charges against Paul, which they could not prove (25:7). Again Paul proclaimed his blamelessness before the Jewish law, the temple, and Caesar (25:8; see 23:1; 24:16). He should have been released at this stage. But Festus bowed to Jewish pressure and, wishing to grant them a favor, asked Paul whether he would be willing to go to Jerusalem for trial. Luke uses the word "favor" three times in the space of ten verses (24:27; 25:3, 9), showing that the chances of a fair trial for Paul were bleak.

Since the process of justice had been stalled for two years, Paul now realized that there was no hope of his getting a fair trial in Judea. Instead, his life was in great danger. The famous Roman justice system that had served him well under Gallio (18:17) could not operate for his good here because of the influence of powerful locals. Paul must have felt that this problem would not be as serious in Rome. Besides, the Lord had told him that he would testify in Rome (23:11). Thus, he decided to appeal to Caesar (25:11)—a privilege granted to Roman citizens.[1] Felix must have been relieved by Paul's appeal to Caesar, for he could now wash his hands of the case. It was clearly beyond his abilities to judge, considering his unfamiliarity with Jewish customs and beliefs. He conferred with his council and declared the appeal valid (25:12).

Festus Consults King Agrippa (25:13–22)

FESTUS WAS HAPPY to use a visit from Herod Agrippa II and his sister Bernice to consult on the puzzling case of Paul (25:13–14). Agrippa II was the son of Agrippa I (the grandson of Herod the Great and the "King Herod" mentioned in Acts 12). He was in his early thirties. Rumors were rife about an incestuous relationship between Agrippa and Bernice,[2] both of whom did not live exemplary private lives. Agrippa held the vestments of the Jewish high priest and had the right to appoint him.[3] Paul acknowledged that Agrippa was "acquainted with all the Jewish customs and controversies" (26:3). Thus, "the Romans would consult him on religious matters."[4]

Festus explained the events up to that point (25:14–21). It was a straightforward explanation, and it is interesting to note that he saw the resurrection of Jesus as a pivotal point in this case (25:19–20). When Agrippa expressed

---

1. See Bruce, *Acts*, NICNT, 453, for the background of this privilege.
2. Josephus, *Antiquities*, 20.7.3 (*Complete Works*, 420–21).
3. Ibid., 15.9.4 (*Complete Works*, 335).
4. H. W. Hoehner, "Herod," ISBER, 2, 697.

a desire to hear Paul, arrangements were made for a meeting to be held the next day (25:22).

Paul's Speech Before Agrippa (25:23–26:23)

THE APPEARANCE OF Agrippa and Bernice with great pomp to hear Paul speak at a gathering that included "high ranking officers and the leading men of the city" (25:23) reminds us of the prediction God made to Ananias that Paul would appear before the kings of the Gentiles (9:15). Though Agrippa cannot himself be called a Gentile, the territory he ruled included many Gentiles. Luke's expression "with great pomp" may suggest the transitory character and vanity of all the outward show.[5] Kistemaker remarks, "The contrast between the dazzling garb of the high and mighty and the humble clothes of the chained prisoner suddenly becomes meaningless, for Paul displays the quiet dignity of a man with a message."[6]

Festus's recounting of the events surrounding Paul shows that he was not impressed by the mob approach of the Jews ("shouting that he ought not to live any longer" [25:24]) and expresses his conviction that Paul was innocent (25:25). His immediate dilemma was that he did not have any specific charges against Paul to present to Caesar when he sent him to Rome (25:25–26).

Paul's speech once again follows the standard pattern of defense speeches of the first century. It starts with the *exordium* (introductory address to the king [26:2–3]), proceeds to the *narratio* (the narration of events [26:4–18]), and ends with the *argumentio* (the proof of his case [26:19–23]).[7] Paul acknowledges the acquaintance of the young king with "Jewish customs and controversies," thus implying his suitability to hear his "defense" (26:2–3). Technically this was not a legal defense, but the word is used in a general sense here.

The *narratio* gives Paul's testimony. This is his fullest testimony in Acts because it discusses his pre-Christian activity, his conversion, and his calling, which drives his mission. Nothing is said about the role played by the devout Jew Ananias, who had an important role in the testimony given before the Jerusalem crowd (cf. 22:12–16). After saying that the Jews know his past well, Paul affirms his strict background as a Pharisee (26:4–5). Then he says that it is because of the hope of the Jewish people that he is on trial (26:6–7) and immediately affirms that his audience should not consider it incredible that God raises the dead (26:8). The hope of Israel and the resurrection of Christ are intimately bound together, as we will see later.

---

5. Harrison, *Acts*, 397.

6. Kistemaker, *Acts*, 884.

7. Keener, *BBC*, 398.

Paul insists that he once had the same attitude toward Christianity as his opponents now do (26:9–11). He vividly describes the vehemence with which he opposed the gospel and persecuted Christians; he was an official representative of the chief priests and their main prosecutor (26:10a). His statement that he cast his vote against those who were put to death (26:10b) has led some to conclude that he was a member of the Sanhedrin, where such a vote may have been taken. But he was too young to be a member of the Sanhedrin at that time (see 7:58). Rather, it signifies that Paul was one of the major leaders in the campaign against Christianity and that he was actively involved in prosecuting Christians. He "went from one synagogue to another" (26:11), by which Paul shows to Agrippa that at that time the believers were still participating in the life of the Jewish synagogues.

Verses 12–18 give the third account in Acts of Paul's conversion and divine call. Here he recounts that Jesus spoke to him in Aramaic, suggesting that this was Christ's first language. Also to his words are added the comment, "It is hard for you to kick against the goads" (26:14). This proverb has been used to buttress the idea that Paul was a troubled person, fighting his conscience prior to his conversion. In our study of chapter 9, we discounted this view on the grounds that the autobiographical statements of Paul leave no room for such psychological unrest in the apostle. This proverb appears often in classical writings.[8] Daniel Fuller explains that it was "often used by the Greeks to express the futility of striving against fate or against the gods, and its meaning to Paul on the Damascus road was that it was now futile for him to try any longer to work against Christ as it would be for an ox to kick against the plowman's goad."[9]

Also unique to this narrative of Paul's conversion was his commissioning by Jesus himself (26:16–18). The account in Acts 22 mentioned two commissionings—one by Ananias (22:14–16) and a later one by Jesus (22:21). Here Paul mentions a direct commissioning from Jesus right on the Damascus road, where he was appointed as a servant and a witness of Christ and of what he would show him (26:16). Like the other apostles, then, Paul was to be a witness to the resurrection. Based on this commissioning Paul claimed apostleship.

Two factors qualified a person to be an apostle in the early church with the uniqueness that the twelve apostles had: seeing the risen Lord (1 Cor. 9:1; 15:8; see Acts 1:22) and being personally commissioned by him (cf. Rom. 1:1; 1 Cor. 1:1; Gal. 1:1; 2:7). Both these things happened to Paul during his Damascus road experience.[10] Paul cites one more feature as qualifying him

---

8. See Bruce, *Acts: Greek Text*, 501, for a list of occurrences.

9. Daniel P. Fuller, *Hermeneutics* (Pasadena: Fuller Theological Seminary, 1974), VIII.9.

10. See further the discussion of 9:1–31; Seyoon Kim, *The Origin of Paul's Gospel* (Grand Rapids: Eerdmans, 1982).

for apostleship: his effectiveness in ministry (1 Cor. 9:2; 2 Cor. 12:12; Gal. 2:8–9). This feature is also presented in the speech to Agrippa (26:19–23). A key to understanding his ministry is that he was obedient to a vision from heaven (26:19). Through a study of Paul's description of his commissioning and his ministry here, we discover a comprehensive view of the evangelistic process (see discussion below).

Festus and Agrippa Respond to Paul's Speech (26:24–32)

PAUL'S SPEECH IS too much for the practical Roman official, Festus, who knows little about the intricacies of Jewish theology. He recognizes that Paul is a learned man, but he cries out that his learning has driven him insane (26:24). Paul responds by affirming that what he is saying is both true and reasonable (26:25). Had Paul been addressing Festus primarily, he would have presumably presented his words in a way that Festus would have understood. But here he is speaking to Agrippa, and Paul knows that the king understands what he is talking about (26:26a). He is positive that Agrippa already knows many of the facts about Christianity because these things were "not done in a corner" (26:26b).

Paul zeros in at this stage with a direct challenge to Agrippa: "King Agrippa, do you believe the prophets? I know you do" (26:27). This challenge is for Agrippa to compare what the prophets foretold with what happened in Christ. The king is in a dilemma. As an expert on the Jewish Scriptures, he knows what Paul is speaking about. But he cannot afford to make connections between what he knows and what Paul is saying because then he will have to make a decision about Christianity. He therefore brushes off the challenge with an evasive comment that means something like, "In short you are trying to persuade me to act the Christian" (26:28).[11] Agrippa has not come to this gathering with a view to making such a serious commitment. He simply wants to help Festus out by giving him advice about this case. He may also have looked forward to meeting one of the top leaders of this growing sect. Paul's response shows that he desires all to come to Christ—including rulers (26:29). Later he tells Timothy to pray for kings for God "wants all men to be saved and to come to a knowledge of the truth" (1 Tim. 2:1–4).

As the gathering is adjourned, the general sense of everyone there is that Paul has done nothing to deserve punishment (26:31–32). Agrippa specifically states, "This man could have been set free if he had not appealed to Caesar." It was easy for the consultant Agrippa to say this after Paul made his appeal. Before that, for two whole years, Paul was kept in prison because the leaders did not have the moral courage to release him even though they knew he was innocent.

---

11. Bruce, *Acts*, NICNT, 470, n. 44.

Bridging Contexts

THE LIMITS OF **the law in practice.** Earlier in Acts Luke presented the Roman justice system in a positive light. There were fair officials, and in Corinth, Ephesus, and Jerusalem they had even protected Paul from harm (chs. 18; 19; 21). Some key Romans were converted in Caesarea and Philippi, and in Philippi the officials recanted the harm done to Paul unjustly (chs. 10; 16).

But now we see Roman procedures in a different light. There is almost an element of absurdity here. Serious charges have been made against Paul (25:7, 24), and Festus is at a loss, not knowing what to do (25:20, 26–27). Yet many times the Roman officials express their belief that Paul is innocent (25:7, 18–19, 20, 25–26; 26:31). This culminates with Agrippa's statement, "This man could have been set free if he had not appealed to Caesar" (26:32). This was easy for Agrippa to say since he had no responsibility for the case. But those who did have responsibility (Felix and Festus) were afraid to take a stand that would antagonize the majority.

In other words, though Roman law was a noble system that Christians used for their protection, its implementers were sometimes reluctant to antagonize the majority. This is why Luke uses the word "favor" three times (24:27; 25:3, 9). On one occasion the Jewish leaders asked for this favor, and the other two times the Roman officials acted in order to grant the Jews a favor. After the process of justice had been stalled for two years, Festus tried to escape from the responsibility by having Paul transferred to Jerusalem. Thus, Paul was forced to look for a more favorable climate for a fair trial and appealed to Rome. While we should use the law to look after us, we should not naively think that resorting to the law will automatically provide justice.

The centrality of the resurrection to the Christian message. In our study of the Pentecost message we saw how important the resurrection is to the Christian message; it was God's accreditation of Jesus as the Messiah.[12] In Paul's speech to Agrippa we see another reason why the resurrection is so central. As the first to rise from the dead (26:23), Christ fulfilled the hope of Israel (26:6–8). That is, he started the process of the regeneration of Israel and actually of the new Israel, which consists of all the redeemed—Gentiles and Jews. With the resurrection of Christ, "eternal life ... appeared in the midst of mortality"[13] and will be consummated at the end of time. G. E. Ladd puts this succinctly in the language of biblical theology:

> The resurrection of Jesus is an eschatological event that occurred in history and gave rise to the Christian church. It sounds a note that provides

---

12. See the study on 2:14–41.
13. Ladd, *Theology*, 363.

the clue for understanding the character and message of the primitive church. The church was brought into being by an eschatological event; it is itself an eschatological community with an eschatological message. In some real sense, the events that belong to the end of the age and the eschatological consummation have invaded history.[14]

Paul's explanation of evangelism. Paul's speech before Agrippa provides the most comprehensive defense of his evangelistic ministry in Acts. The fact that people were being converted to Christianity had caused much anger among the Jews. Paul explains to this "Jewish" king how and why this takes place. Undoubtedly Luke records this speech in some detail so that his readers will understand what happens in the evangelistic process.

(1) *God calls and enables* people to be witnesses for him. He appoints us as servants and witnesses to what we have experienced of Jesus (26:16). He commissions us to go to the people (26:17), protects us from our opponents (26:17), and helps us throughout our ministry (26:22a). Christ himself, the first to rise from the dead, proclaims light to Jews and to Gentiles (26:23).

(2) In *our role as witnesses for Christ,* we must respond obediently to God's call (26:19). We must testify to both small and great (26:22b), and in so doing we open their eyes to the truth of God. To achieve this end we must say things that are true and reasonable (26:25) so that people will be persuaded about the gospel (26:28–29). Behind all of this is our hope and prayer that all the people we encounter will experience salvation (26:29).

(3) Paul also makes several points about *the evangelistic message.* We preach that people should repent and turn to God and prove their repentance by their deeds (26:20). We say nothing beyond what the prophets and Moses said would happen (26:22c). We testify that the Messiah had to suffer and that, as the first to rise from the dead, he proclaims light to the people (26:23).

(4) The result of this ministry is that *people are saved.* Their eyes are opened; they turn from darkness to light and from the power of Satan to God (26:18a). On their part they must have faith in Jesus (26:18b), repent of their sins, turn to God, and prove their repentance by their deeds (26:20). On God's part, he forgives their sins and gives them a place among those who are sanctified (26:18b).

The divine and human sides of evangelism. This list of the elements of the evangelistic process shows us that effective Christian mission includes both divine and human activity. The initiator of everything is God. He calls, commissions, equips, and protects the evangelists (26:16, 17, 22). But we have a responsibility to obey the heavenly vision (26:19), testifying to both small and great (26:22b). When we proclaim the gospel, God is actually

---

14. Ibid.

speaking through us and makes our words become fruitful, and Jesus is the one proclaiming light to the people (26:23).

Agrippa uses the word *peitho* ("to persuade") to describe what he sees Paul trying to do to him. This word is used seven times in Acts to describe Paul's evangelism[15] and means to work with persons until their minds are changed and they accept the message proclaimed.[16] From the content of Paul's speech here, it is clear that he worked hard to convince others about what he believed. He tells Festus that what he says is true and reasonable (26:25). Thus, in all his proclamation Paul used reason (cf. 17:1–15). While it is true that we proclaim a divine wisdom that is higher than human wisdom, we do so reasonably.[17]

This interplay between the divine and human sides is also seen in the response of the individual. On the one hand, Paul "preached that [people] should repent and turn to God and prove their repentance by their deeds" (26:20). This suggests that conversion is something we do (cf. also 17:30). Paul's letters also speak of our obligation to obey the gospel (2 Thess. 1:8; cf. 1 Peter 4:17). On the other hand, Jesus told Paul that people "receive forgiveness of sins and a place among those who are sanctified by faith in me" (26:18b). That is, forgiveness and a place among the sanctified are gifts given by God (though the word "faith" suggests also that a person is not a passive recipient of this gift).

In Paul's prayer for the conversion of the lost (26:29) we see his combining of the divine and the human sides of evangelism most clearly. We pray to God, and what happens on earth is his answer to our prayers.

RECKONING WISELY WITH the law. We said that while we should try to use the law on our behalf, we should not naively think that by resorting to the law we will automatically get justice. Even the best legal system is administered by fallen individuals, who may choose expediency over what is right. This calls for wisdom on the part of the Christian, so that we take a course of action that will best serve the cause of Christ. In this case, Paul appealed to Caesar, thinking that this would be the best way to get justice and avoid assassination by the Jews. We too should weigh the options wisely when appealing to the law. We should also seek advice from

---

15. See 17:4; 18:4; 19:8, 26; 26:28; 28:23, 24; cf. 2 Cor. 5:11.

16. See comments on this word in the study of 17:1–15.

17. There has been some disagreement within the church on this issue, which will be discussed below.

fellow Christians and from those who are more conversant with the law than ourselves. This buttresses the view presented in the last study that some of the best minds in the church should give themselves to the task of dealing with the knotty issues involving church and state.

This challenge of wisdom in relation to the state is going to become more and more significant as both religious fundamentalism and pluralism continue to grow. These two diverse approaches to truth oppose Christian evangelism because they are incompatible with the view that, since Christ is absolute truth, we must urge all to convert to him. The fundamentalists say, "Don't touch our people"; the pluralists say, "Don't say yours is the only way." In the coming years we can anticipate a growing opposition to biblical Christianity. We must let some of our best minds—our Pauls—tackle this great challenge.

Proclaiming the message of the resurrection. While the resurrection is the cornerstone of Christianity (both proof of the message of Jesus and the onset of Israel's eschatological blessings), many within the church do not know how to proclaim that message. The victory of the resurrection is one that must be emphasized because, in our pragmatic world, we find it difficult to visualize how an event like this can affect our daily lives.

Through the stress given to the cross in evangelical preaching in this century, we have come to understand at least some of the deep meaning of the cross. But we may not have come to a corresponding understanding of the resurrection and its significance. Yet this is a key message for today's church because, with all our pragmatism and focus on how to live the Christian life, Christians seem to lack the theological and spiritual muscle needed to overcome the onslaught of the world upon the church. The answer to the moral and ethical poverty of today's church is not only more instruction to weak people on how to live. It is a good dose of theological truth that will enable them to understand the meaning of Christ's victory won through his work. Believers will then realize that in Christ they have the spiritual and theological power to withstand the onslaughts that come from the world, the flesh, and the devil.

Early in my ministry, my colleagues asked me to give a series of four messages on the resurrection at an evangelistic youth camp. I thought that would be easy, considering that I had come to agree with my teacher George Ladd's affirmation that "the cornerstone of the entire New Testament is the resurrection."[18] But as I looked for material to go into this series, I struggled, partly because I had not heard much evangelistic preaching on the resurrection. I realized a great need for Christians to rediscover the meaning of the resur-

---

18. George Eldon Ladd, *I Believe in the Resurrection of Jesus* (Grand Rapids: Eerdmans, 1975), 43.

rection and to learn how best to communicate it to both Christians and non-Christians. In my book *The Supremacy of Christ* I have shown how the resurrection provides proof about the person of Christ, about his plan of salvation, about his Lordship over all, about the wonderful new life he opens up for us, and about his and our victory over death.[19]

The debate over divine and human activity in evangelism. The issue of the divine and human sides in Christian activity has caused much controversy in the church throughout history.[20] This is understandable, considering the paradox of human and divine involvement as presented in our passage. It is easy to get carried away with one aspect of this paradox and exclude the other. Given the difficulty of fallen human beings to achieve perfect balance, I suppose this conflict of emphases is something we will continue to face within the church.

Some Christians object to praying for the conversion of the lost, saying that human prayers cannot influence God here, for he has sovereignly decreed who are elected to salvation and who are not. They may pray that they will be good witnesses, but they do not think it biblical to pray for the conversion of the lost. Yet Paul clearly prays for the salvation of those whom he encounters (26:29; see Rom. 10:1; 1 Tim. 2:1–4). Those from the Reformed tradition who seek to come to grips with the biblical insistence on the important place that human instruments play in the evangelistic process should see that God uses means, such as prayers and persuasion, to bring in the elect.[21]

The issue of using means to receive what God has decreed came to a head over the so-called "new measures" advocated by the evangelist and scholar Charles G. Finney (1792–1875). Jonathan Edwards and other preachers of the Great Awakening in the eighteenth century had seen revivals as "surprising works of God"—that is, inexplicable outpourings of God's Spirit. Finney, on the other hand, claimed that revival is a "result of the right use of constituted means" (the new measures).[22]

Each of these streams of the church had latched onto a scriptural truth, which they emphasized to such an extent that they virtually eliminated the other side of the coin. Earlier in this commentary we said that when William

---

19. See my *Supremacy*, 225–42.

20. For an attempt to explain these two sides in evangelism, see J. I. Packer, *Evangelism and the Sovereignty of God* (Downers Grove, Ill.: InterVarsity, 1961).

21. See, for example, C. Samuel Storms, "Prayer and Evangelism Under God's Sovereignty," *The Grace of God and the Bondage of the Will*, vol. 1, *Biblical and Practical Perspectives on Calvinism*, ed. Thomas R. Schreiner and Bruce A. Ware (Grand Rapids: Baker, 1995), 215–31.

22. This description is from Earle E. Cairns, *An Endless Line of Splendor: Revivals and Their Leaders From the Great Awakening to the Present* (Wheaton, Ill.: Tyndale, 1986), 130.

Carey advocated foreign missions by talking about the means through which the nations were going to hear the gospel, he was discouraged by a high Calvinism that produced the famous statement, "Sit down young man! When God chooses to convert the heathen he will do it without your aid or mine!"[23] The idea was that if we start talking about human means to achieving the mission of the church, we undermine God's sovereignty.

This is particularly true of persuasion techniques as means of evangelism. Some feel that since God sovereignly effects the regeneration of the elect, seeking to persuade people denies his role in the salvation process. They object to public invitations, especially those that plead with people to "come forward." In this view, those who have been regenerated by God do not need such persuasion. Instead, at an evangelistic meeting, preachers should ask those who sense that they have been found by God to quietly meet the pastor or someone else to indicate this.

On the other extreme, some preachers place far too much emphasis on the human element in evangelism. Evangelists can exert undue pressure when inviting people to respond to the gospel, almost with the notion that the success of the evangelistic event depends on their ability to urge people to come forward. They can be seen as manipulating the audience. The invitation does not seem to be given in confidence and thus lacks the authority of a herald of Christ.

I personally suffered from a nervousness in this regard in my early years in evangelism and was greatly helped by the wise counsel of the Presbyterian evangelist Leighton Ford. He reminded me that the sovereign God was the one doing the inviting and drawing of people to himself. I had to rest in the confidence that he would draw people to himself through my words. This was not an excuse for reducing my preparation; rather, I continued to work hard at preparing my message, including the invitation. But this was a liberating truth that took away the crippling fear that sometimes gripped me as I invited people to turn to Christ.

The use of reason in evangelism. Another aspect of the divine and human in evangelism is the use of reason in proclamation. In 26:25 Paul says, "What I am saying is true and reasonable." Some, however, appeal to the fact that God's wisdom and thoughts are higher than ours (Isa. 55:8–9) to back their belief that we should not use reason to try to win people to Christ. These people refer to Paul's discounting of human wisdom in evangelism in 1 Corinthians 1:17–25 to show how useless it is to appeal to people's intellect in

---

23. Kellsye M. Finnie, *William Carey: By Trade a Cobbler* (Eastbourne: Kingsway Publications, 1986), 32. Finnie says that we do not know for certain whether such a statement was really made.

evangelism. Instead, they say, our work is to simply preach Christ crucified and leave it to God to open the eyes of people. But this approach contradicts the method used by Paul (cf. the discussions on Acts 17).

One of the keys in this issue is to understand the nature of fallen humanity. As a result of the Fall human reason has been warped; we think in ways that are foolish (e.g., believing that sin satisfies and that we can save ourselves). Naturally, then, God's thoughts and ways are higher than ours. But sin has not obliterated human reason. In proclamation we may appeal to the remnants of reason within the human mind. Like God, we may appeal to sinful people with these words, "Come now, let us reason together" (Isa. 1:18). Our fallen nature may revolt against such reasoning, for we do not want to turn from our sin and self-sufficiency. But when God opens people's minds, they will follow our reasoning, and to them it will be good news. The Calvinist may say that those whom God enlightens cannot resist his grace, whereas the Arminian may say that God's enlightenment can be resisted by a rebellious heart. But in practice that should not cause a difference in our methodology. We do not know who the elect are. Insofar as God can use our reason to bring people in, our job is to reason with them.

To understand Paul's rejection of human wisdom in 1 Corinthians 1 we must note the context of that passage. He is referring there to disunity in the church. People had latched onto those they considered to be their leaders (e.g., Paul, Cephas, and Apollos); division had resulted in the church. Bruce Winter explains that in that culture the pupils of secular teachers had to give exclusive loyalty to their masters and thus there was often rivalry among different teachers. This is what was happening in the Corinthian church.

Moreover, in the first century, rhetoric was so important that the careful crafting of a speech was even more important than its content. Orators "spoke to gain the adulation of their audiences."[24] Paul, on the other hand, says that he was sent "to preach the gospel—not with words of human wisdom [lit., not by means of the wisdom of rhetoric], lest the cross of Christ be emptied of its power" (1 Cor. 1:17). Had Paul focused on rhetoric, he would have promoted himself and diverted attention away from the cross to himself. But "Christ sent him to preach the gospel and not to secure a personal following."[25] Thus, the wisdom he was against was a focus on rhetoric that directed attention away from the cross to the speaker.

Paul went on to say that the preaching of the cross was folly to the Gentiles (1 Cor. 1:23). He rejected the wisdom of such worldlings who scoffed at the idea of the cross. That is, he rejected any presentation of the gospel that

---

24. Bruce Winter, "1 Corinthians," *NBCTCE*, 1164.
25. Ibid.

downplayed the cross so as to appeal to the intelligentsia. Communicating the message of the cross was far more important than winning the audience. Instead of using a human wisdom that rejected the cross, he proclaimed the wisdom of God, that is, Christ (1 Cor. 1:24). But since God created reason, the wisdom of God is not unreasonable. Therefore we may reason with people and show them both the folly of all ways that reject God's wisdom and the reasonableness and truthfulness of the gospel. We can leave it to God to enlighten their eyes so that they may accept and act upon what we share.

Evangelism as obedience to a vision. Paul's statement about not being "disobedient to the vision from heaven" (26:19) presents a key to the effectiveness of a servant of God. Shenk and Stutzman have a helpful discussion on this. They point out that "vision has become a catchword in today's language."[26] A leader must have a clear picture of what is desirable and must be able to articulate that vision so that others also can grasp it. "The word vision shows what is ahead and uncharted. It is in the future tense." They agree that visionary leadership is a key to motivating others to give themselves to a task or movement.

But Shenk and Stutzman make an important distinction between the above model of vision and the biblical model. After referring to the visions of Paul on the Damascus road, Peter on the rooftop, and John on the island of Patmos, they acknowledge that in the Bible "vision had vital implications for the future. But the vision was not a humanly constructed picture of what was to come. The vision came from God as an instruction for action." This is something that we too easily overlook as we speak on vision today.

When we plan for the future, draw up our goals, and develop a vision statement, we often use methods of research that the business world gives us. These can indeed help in developing a vision. But much more important is waiting to hear from God. Peter and John were seeking God's face when they received their respective visions (Acts 10:9; Rev. 1:10). The church of Antioch was "worshiping the Lord and fasting" (Acts 13:2) when God gave them the vision that gave birth to the first formal foreign missionary movement in the church. Leaders must earnestly ask God, both privately and in community, for a vision of what he wants done through them.

Once God's vision has been discovered, leaders must express it to their people enthusiastically so that they too will catch the vision. It should be communicated practically so that others will realize that this is something that can be done and that they can have a part in achieving it. We have shown

---

26. See Shenk and Stutzman, *Creating Communities of the Kingdom,* 64–65; they refer to a book by Warren Bennis and Burt Nanus, *Leaders: The Strategies for Taking Charge* (New York: Harper and Row, 1985), which argues that to be successful in business, vision is essential.

how Jesus did this with the Great Commission.[27] When people are excited with the vision, they will pay the price to see it fulfilled.

Leaders must also order their lives in order to give priority to the vision.[28] There are so many "urgent" demands on our lives that it is easy to neglect the "important" (to use a distinction popularized by Charles Hummel in his influential booklet, *The Tyranny of the Urgent*[29]). Leaders must constantly divest themselves of weights that, though they are good in themselves, keep them from doing the truly important things in life. Often our devotional life and personal ministry are the first things affected by being overcommitted. But dropping these will hinder us from fulfilling our visions. Without a healthy devotional life we will become spiritually dry and will not have the spiritual resources to motivate people to receive their fullest potential under God. Without personal work we will soon find that we are left with no people to motivate. It is personal ministry that breeds committed workers in a ministry.

We must always stretch ourselves because Christian leadership is never easy or convenient. We may need to take on the cross of tiredness and strain. But let that strain come from fulfilling the vision God gave us, not from doing things that we should have avoided.

---

27. See the discussion on 1:1–8.
28. See Shenk and Stutzman, *Creating Communities*, 65.
29. Charles Hummel, *The Tyranny of the Urgent* (Downer's Grove, Ill.: InterVarsity, 1967).

Acts 27:1–28:15

𝖜

W HEN IT WAS decided that we would sail for Italy,
Paul and some other prisoners were handed over
to a centurion named Julius, who belonged to the
Imperial Regiment. ²We boarded a ship from Adramyttium
about to sail for ports along the coast of the province of Asia,
and we put out to sea. Aristarchus, a Macedonian from Thessalonica, was with us.

³The next day we landed at Sidon; and Julius, in kindness
to Paul, allowed him to go to his friends so they might provide for his needs. ⁴From there we put out to sea again and
passed to the lee of Cyprus because the winds were against
us. ⁵When we had sailed across the open sea off the coast of
Cilicia and Pamphylia, we landed at Myra in Lycia. ⁶There the
centurion found an Alexandrian ship sailing for Italy and put
us on board. ⁷We made slow headway for many days and had
difficulty arriving off Cnidus. When the wind did not allow us
to hold our course, we sailed to the lee of Crete, opposite
Salmone. ⁸We moved along the coast with difficulty and came
to a place called Fair Havens, near the town of Lasea.

⁹Much time had been lost, and sailing had already become
dangerous because by now it was after the Fast. So Paul
warned them, ¹⁰"Men, I can see that our voyage is going to be
disastrous and bring great loss to ship and cargo, and to our
own lives also." ¹¹But the centurion, instead of listening to
what Paul said, followed the advice of the pilot and of the
owner of the ship. ¹²Since the harbor was unsuitable to winter
in, the majority decided that we should sail on, hoping to
reach Phoenix and winter there. This was a harbor in Crete,
facing both southwest and northwest.

¹³When a gentle south wind began to blow, they thought
they had obtained what they wanted; so they weighed anchor
and sailed along the shore of Crete. ¹⁴Before very long, a wind
of hurricane force, called the "northeaster," swept down from
the island. ¹⁵The ship was caught by the storm and could not
head into the wind; so we gave way to it and were driven
along. ¹⁶As we passed to the lee of a small island called
Cauda, we were hardly able to make the lifeboat secure.

¹⁷When the men had hoisted it aboard, they passed ropes under the ship itself to hold it together. Fearing that they would run aground on the sandbars of Syrtis, they lowered the sea anchor and let the ship be driven along. ¹⁸We took such a violent battering from the storm that the next day they began to throw the cargo overboard. ¹⁹On the third day, they threw the ship's tackle overboard with their own hands. ²⁰When neither sun nor stars appeared for many days and the storm continued raging, we finally gave up all hope of being saved.

²¹After the men had gone a long time without food, Paul stood up before them and said: "Men, you should have taken my advice not to sail from Crete; then you would have spared yourselves this damage and loss. ²²But now I urge you to keep up your courage, because not one of you will be lost; only the ship will be destroyed. ²³Last night an angel of the God whose I am and whom I serve stood beside me ²⁴and said, 'Do not be afraid, Paul. You must stand trial before Caesar; and God has graciously given you the lives of all who sail with you.' ²⁵So keep up your courage, men, for I have faith in God that it will happen just as he told me. ²⁶Nevertheless, we must run aground on some island."

²⁷On the fourteenth night we were still being driven across the Adriatic Sea, when about midnight the sailors sensed they were approaching land. ²⁸They took soundings and found that the water was a hundred and twenty feet deep. A short time later they took soundings again and found it was ninety feet deep. ²⁹Fearing that we would be dashed against the rocks, they dropped four anchors from the stern and prayed for daylight. ³⁰In an attempt to escape from the ship, the sailors let the lifeboat down into the sea, pretending they were going to lower some anchors from the bow. ³¹Then Paul said to the centurion and the soldiers, "Unless these men stay with the ship, you cannot be saved." ³²So the soldiers cut the ropes that held the lifeboat and let it fall away.

³³Just before dawn Paul urged them all to eat. "For the last fourteen days," he said, "you have been in constant suspense and have gone without food—you haven't eaten anything. ³⁴Now I urge you to take some food. You need it to survive. Not one of you will lose a single hair from his head." ³⁵After he said this, he took some bread and gave thanks to God in

front of them all. Then he broke it and began to eat. ³⁶They were all encouraged and ate some food themselves. ³⁷Altogether there were 276 of us on board. ³⁸When they had eaten as much as they wanted, they lightened the ship by throwing the grain into the sea.

³⁹When daylight came, they did not recognize the land, but they saw a bay with a sandy beach, where they decided to run the ship aground if they could. ⁴⁰Cutting loose the anchors, they left them in the sea and at the same time untied the ropes that held the rudders. Then they hoisted the foresail to the wind and made for the beach. ⁴¹But the ship struck a sandbar and ran aground. The bow stuck fast and would not move, and the stern was broken to pieces by the pounding of the surf.

⁴²The soldiers planned to kill the prisoners to prevent any of them from swimming away and escaping. ⁴³But the centurion wanted to spare Paul's life and kept them from carrying out their plan. He ordered those who could swim to jump overboard first and get to land. ⁴⁴The rest were to get there on planks or on pieces of the ship. In this way everyone reached land in safety.

²⁸:¹Once safely on shore, we found out that the island was called Malta. ²The islanders showed us unusual kindness. They built a fire and welcomed us all because it was raining and cold. ³Paul gathered a pile of brushwood and, as he put it on the fire, a viper, driven out by the heat, fastened itself on his hand. ⁴When the islanders saw the snake hanging from his hand, they said to each other, "This man must be a murderer; for though he escaped from the sea, Justice has not allowed him to live." ⁵But Paul shook the snake off into the fire and suffered no ill effects. ⁶The people expected him to swell up or suddenly fall dead, but after waiting a long time and seeing nothing unusual happen to him, they changed their minds and said he was a god.

⁷There was an estate nearby that belonged to Publius, the chief official of the island. He welcomed us to his home and for three days entertained us hospitably. ⁸His father was sick in bed, suffering from fever and dysentery. Paul went in to see him and, after prayer, placed his hands on him and healed him. ⁹When this had happened, the rest of the sick on the island came and were cured. ¹⁰They honored us in many ways and

when we were ready to sail, they furnished us with the supplies we needed.

¹¹After three months we put out to sea in a ship that had
wintered in the island. It was an Alexandrian ship with the figurehead of the twin gods Castor and Pollux. ¹²We put in at
Syracuse and stayed there three days. ¹³From there we set sail
and arrived at Rhegium. The next day the south wind came
up, and on the following day we reached Puteoli. ¹⁴There we
found some brothers who invited us to spend a week with
them. And so we came to Rome. ¹⁵The brothers there had
heard that we were coming, and they traveled as far as the
Forum of Appius and the Three Taverns to meet us. At the
sight of these men Paul thanked God and was encouraged.

THE LAST TWO chapters of Acts record the fulfillment of Paul's great ambition to go to Rome
(cf. Rom. 1:10–13; 15:22–32). Luke records the
event with the crisp, "And so we came to Rome"
(Acts 28:14). This was politically the most powerful city of the time and
Paul had been a citizen of it from birth. He had planned to go there several
times but had been prevented from doing so (Rom. 1:13). He had spent the
twenty-seven years or so after his conversion in the eastern parts of the
empire (15:19–20) and had dreams of taking the gospel westward as far as
Spain, hopefully using Rome as a base for this stage of his career (15:22–29).

About three years before, Paul had written to the Roman church his testament of faith, the letter to the Romans, in preparation for his visit. In a time
of crisis, the Lord had buttressed this dream through a vision in which he was
told that he "must also testify in Rome" (Acts 23:11). But he probably never
imagined that he would reach Rome as a prisoner. The description of the way
he got there reads like an excerpt from an exciting novel. We can feel the
drama and excitement of the events through Luke's vivid description. These
two chapters also contain details typical of the record of one who was part
of the travel group (this is a "we" section).

One of the most helpful resources for the study of this passage is a book
written more than a century ago by James Smith, *The Voyage and Shipwreck of
St. Paul.* As an experienced yachtsman and classical scholar, Smith "made a
careful study of Luke's narrative in relation to the route which it maps out—
a part of the Mediterranean with which he himself was acquainted—and
formed the most favorable estimate of the accuracy of Luke's account of each

stage of the voyage."[1] Smith says about Luke's style and content, "No sailor would have written in a style so little like that of a sailor; no man not a sailor could have written a narrative of a sea voyage so consistent in all its parts, unless from actual observation."[2]

Fortunately for us, Colin J. Hemer has made available many of the findings of Smith and of others in arguing his case for the historical accuracy of the book of Acts.[3]

The Journey Begins (27:1–12)

LUKE RETURNS TO the first person plural ("we/us") (27:1) after leaving off with his arrival in Jerusalem (21:18). He may have been in Caesarea during the two intervening years and collected valuable information for his two-volume work (see Luke 1:3).[4] Others in the traveling party included the centurion, Julius, his soldiers, other prisoners, and "Aristarchus, a Macedonian from Thessalonica" (27:2). The latter had been traveling with Paul for some time (19:21; 20:4); he is described as Paul's "fellow prisoner" in Colossians 4:10 and "fellow worker" in Philemon 24. These two letters were probably written from Rome in the early sixties.

In tracing this journey it is helpful to have a map open. In the Phoenician city of Sidon (about sixty-nine miles north of Caesarea), the centurion, in the first of his many acts of kindness to Paul, permitted him to visit "his friends"—probably members of the Christian community there (27:3; see 11:19). Interestingly, this was a privilege also given to Ignatius, bishop of Antioch, when he made his journey to martyrdom in Rome.[5] The western winds that blow during the summer months caused the ship to go east and north of Cyprus (traveling off the coast of Cilicia and Pamphylia). Luke must have made note of this fact since this was opposite to the route they used when coming to Tyre two years earlier (21:3).

The ship arrived in Myra in Lycia and the passengers boarded an Alexandrian ship there (27:6)—probably one of the large Alexandrian grain ships that headed west from there.[6] A strong northwest wind probably caused them to make "slow headway" (27:7) and even to travel southwest, along the southern coast of Crete, rather than due west (27:8).

---

1. Bruce, *Acts*, NICNT, 475–76.

2. J. Smith, *The Voyage and Shipwreck of St. Paul* (London: Longmans Green, 1848, 4th. ed. 1880); cited in E. F. Harrison, *Acts*, 412.

3. Hemer, *Acts*, 132–58.

4. Bruce, *Acts*, NICNT, 476.

5. Eusebius, *The History of the Church from Christ to Constantine*, 3.36, trans. G. A. Williamson, rev. and ed. Andrew Louth (London: Penguin, 1989), 98.

6. Hemer, *Acts*, 134.

With difficulty the ship arrived in Fair Havens, which, despite its name, was not a suitable place to face the rigors of winter. The group had already been delayed, for it was "after the Fast" (i.e., the Day of Atonement or Yom Kippur, 27:9), which fell around October 5 that year.[7] Paul felt it was not safe to venture out to find a better place for the winter (27:10). This advice may have been given informally at a consultation with the owner/master of the ship, its pilot, and the centurion, to which Paul was included "as a man of standing and experience who had won Julius' respect."[8] We do not know whether this advice was given through direct divine guidance or through Paul's human wisdom. We know that on one point he was not accurate, for he predicted the loss of life if they ventured out, and that did not happen.

Paul was a seasoned traveler, who had already been shipwrecked three times and had spent a night and a day in the open sea (2 Cor. 11:25). But he was overruled by the majority, who decide to go a short distance further west to the better harbor at Phoenix (27:12). They needed to travel four miles west and about thirty-four miles west-northwest across a bay.[9]

The Storm (27:13–26)

"A GENTLE SOUTH wind" seemed to be ideal for the journey to Phoenix, so the crew weighed anchor (27:13). But "there was a noted tendency of a south wind in these climes to back suddenly to a violent north-easter, the well known *gregale*."[10] Unfortunately Paul's ship had to confront a northeaster with all its force. They eventually decided that they could not fight it, so they gave in and let it carry them along in the opposite direction, away from the island (27:14–15). The little island of Cauda gave them a temporary reprieve from the gale (27:16), and they were able to take some emergency measures necessary under these conditions. The lifeboat that may have been towed behind the ship was hauled in (27:17a), and the crew passed ropes under the ship "to hold together and reinforce the hull against the battering of the waves."[11]

As they were being driven along, a new fear confronted them—the dreaded shallows and quicksands off the shore of Cyrene in North Africa called "Syrtis" (27:17b), which "inspired an obsessional fear constantly mentioned in first-century literature."[12] The crew "lowered the equipment or instrument" (lit.), an action that has been given numerous explanations as

7. Ibid., 137.
8. Ibid., 138.
9. Ibid., 141.
10. Ibid.
11. Ibid., 143.
12. Ibid., 144. Hemer has a long list of references from first-century literature.

Luke is not specific about this instrument. This may be because Luke did not know what the instrument was or had forgotten its technical name.[13] It was probably a floating anchor that "was dragged astern at the end of a rope of suitable length so as to offer maximum resistance every time the ship plunged down from the crest of the wave."[14]

As with the storm in the story of Jonah (Jonah 1:5), the next step the sailors took was to throw their cargo overboard (27:18) and then the ships tackle or the spare gear (27:19). By doing this they hoped to decrease the danger of the ship if it offered too much resistance to the storm. The sun or stars did not appear "for many days" (27:20a), which meant that they could not now determine which direction they should go. They finally came to the stage of giving up hope of being saved (27:20b).

As a result of this storm, most of the people on board would have become seasick and not have eaten for several days. In this hopeless situation Paul came with a word of encouragement, having himself been encouraged by God (2 Cor. 1:3–4) through a vision. When he said that they should have taken his advice (27:21), he was not making an "I told you so" statement but trying to win their attention. Twice he asked them to keep up their courage (27:22, 25), basing that appeal on his vision. God had a job for him in Rome, and because of that everyone would be saved (27:24). After expressing his faith in God, he predicted the ship would run aground on an island (27:25–26). From this point on, Paul seems to have assumed a leadership role in the ship.

The Shipwreck (27:27–44)

LUKE MENTIONS "STILL being driven along the Adriatic sea" (27:27), that is, the central Mediterranean. James Smith made careful inquiries from experienced Mediterranean navigators and calculated the time it would take for a ship drifting and trying to avoid the Syrtis to do the trip that Paul's ship made. He came up with thirteen days, plus one hour and twenty-one minutes, thus giving credence to Luke's mention of the fourteenth night when the sailors sensed they were approaching land (27:27).[15] They wisely decided to drop anchor and wait until it was day so that the ship would not dash onto rocks of these unknown seas (27:29).

Paul asserted his leadership again when the sailors tried to escape from the ship and ensured that they would stay on for the crucial time when the people had to go to shore (27:30–32). His leadership is again seen when he urged the people to eat (27:33–34). They needed energy for the final chal-

---

13. Bruce, *Acts*, NICNT, 486.
14. Ibid.
15. Smith, *Voyage*, 126–28; cited in Bruce, *Acts*, NICNT, 489.

lenge and would not be strong on empty stomachs. They found courage to eat when they saw Paul eating after giving thanks to God (27:35–36).

Some have been skeptical about Luke's report that there were 276 people on board (27:37), but Hemer lists ample evidence from the literature of the time of ships plying this route carrying larger numbers of people.[16] The crew saw a bay, which was probably what is now known as St. Paul's Bay in Malta, but they did not recognize the land. They decided to sail toward land and run the ship aground near the shore, but it struck a sandbar further out and became stuck (27:39–41a). The waves were too strong for the battered ship and it broke to pieces (27:41b). The soldiers would have faced severe punishment if the prisoners escaped,[17] so they planned to kill them; but they were saved because the centurion wanted to save Paul's life (27:42–43a). Again, therefore, people's lives were saved because of Paul's presence on the ship. As Paul had predicted, "everyone reached land in safety" (27:44).

Ministering in Malta (28:1–10)

THE PROPOSED FORTY-MILE trip from Fair Havens to Phoenix ended two weeks later on the island of Malta, which was scarcely a day's voyage from the great port of Syracuse in Sicily. But the people had to wait three months in Malta because it was winter. The word "islanders" (28:2) is *barbaroi* (lit., "barbarians"), which was how those who did not speak Greek were referred to in those days.[18] The islanders showed the shipwrecked travelers "unusual kindness." And Paul, despite his exhaustion from the preceding events, joined in setting up a fire, which was probably needed because of the cool autumn temperature (28:2–3).

The viper that stuck to Paul has caused problems to scholars. While present-day Malta has vipers that stick onto their victims, they are not poisonous. This may be the species referred to here. But if so, the islanders would not have expected Paul to swell up or fall down dead (28:6). Perhaps there was a species of poisonous viper in first-century Malta, which has since been exterminated by the islanders.[19] The reaction that Paul was probably a murderer (28:4) is typical of superstitious people who see others going through misfortune—they assume that they are paying for their wrong deeds. When nothing happened to Paul, their superstition led them to change their verdict, saying that he was a god (28:6).

---

16. Hemer, *Acts,* 149.

17. Ibid., 152.

18. The Maltese spoke a Phoenician dialect. It seems that the word *barbaros* came out of the fact that the speech of foreigners sounded like "bar-bar" to the Greeks. The word need not carry a pejorative meaning. See the article by F. D. Gealy in *IDB,* 1:354.

19. This would be possible in a small but densely populated island like Malta (see Hemer, *Acts,* 153).

As was typical, Paul had a healing ministry in the town following the healing of the chief official's father (28:8–9). The prayer and the placing of hands on him is similar to other healing miracles. The hospitality of the people was truly generous, for they even supplied the travelers' needs when they left three months later (28:10).

Rome at Last (28:11–15)

THE SHIP THAT took Paul and company to Italy was also an Alexandrian ship, with a figurehead of the "Heavenly Twins," Castor and Pollux. These were "patrons of navigation and favorite objects of sailors' devotion. Their constellation, Gemini, was considered a sign of good fortune in a storm."[20] If they left three months after the shipwreck, that would have been around February 8, rather early in the shipping season.[21] They first stopped at Syracuse in Sicily and then at Rhegium at the toe of the Italian mainland. They finally reached Puteoli, the port of Neapolis (modern Naples), where they disembarked (28:12–13). It is interesting that Paul was allowed to accept the invitation to spend a week with the Christians in Puteoli. Longenecker is probably right in suggesting that Julius likely had to stay for some time in Puteoli.[22]

During this week news of Paul's arrival in Italy reached the church in Rome, presumably through someone who went to Rome from Puteoli. Some believers decided to meet Paul on the way (28:15). Paul traversed "the oldest, straightest and most perfectly made of all Roman roads,"[23] the Appian Way (*Via Appia*), which connected Neapolis and Rome. Some Christians met him at the famous Forum (or market) of Appia, forty-three miles from Rome, others at the Three Taverns (a settlement that had grown around an isolated inn by that name[24]), thirty-three miles from Rome. "At the sight of these men Paul thanked God and was encouraged" (v. 15).

It was almost two and a half difficult years after the divine assurance given to Paul in Jerusalem that he would go to Rome. He finally met Christians in Rome, people whom he had longed with much eagerness to see. Luke's mention of arrival in Rome in verse 14 rather than in verse 16 has been variously explained. Longenecker is probably right in suggesting "that it reflects Luke's eagerness to get to the climax of his story and that this eagerness led him to anticipate their arrival in Rome."[25]

---

20. Bruce, *Acts*, NICNT, 501.
21. See Hemer, *Acts*, 154, for an attempt to explain this.
22. Longenecker, "Acts," 566.
23. Ibid., 568.
24. Keener, *BBC*, 405.
25. Longenecker, "Acts," 567.

Bridging Contexts

IT IS SURPRISING to find fifty-nine verses devoted to a journey in a history book with a strong theological orientation. As we seek to apply this passage the most important questions to ask are, "Why did Luke devote so much space to this journey?" and "What does he want to achieve from this passage?"

Luke was there. The narrative is so vivid that we can almost feel what was happening. In light of this I suppose we can understand the conclusion of R. I. Prevo that Acts should be classified along with popular novels and historical romances.[26] Hopefully the discussion above and what has been said in other studies about the historicity of Acts has shown that this passage, like the rest of the book, is historically reliable. When we reckon with the fact that Luke was there and that his emotions must have been severely affected by such a tumultuous journey, we can understand the reason for the vividness of his description.

A little over a year prior to writing these words, traveling from a YFC center that was not accessible by road because of the war in our country, I made a seven-hour journey on a ship that must have been about the size of Paul's ship. We ran into bad weather, and that experience of battling relatively less severe winds is etched vividly in my mind. How much more would a two-week ordeal be etched in Luke's mind! This gives us the first reason for the great length of this record of Paul's journey to Rome: Luke was there.

God's sovereignty is at work. A second reason is that here we see vividly illustrated the mysterious providence of God as he works out his purposes amidst the apparent misfortunes encountered while living in this fallen world. This is a major subtheme of Acts.[27] Our passage shows how again God worked good out of a difficult situation. Earlier we saw God work out his purposes despite human sinfulness. Here he works despite the unpredictability of nature and despite human errors in judgment (i.e., the decision to spend the winter in Phoenix [27:12]). God spoke to Paul at a crucial time so that he could maintain his courage and trust in God's sovereignty; buoyed by that belief, Paul acted with calm at a time when others were panicking.

Paul, the leader. Luke also wanted to present his hero Paul as an example of leadership in the midst of difficult circumstances. This situation is what we might call a "secular situation," where the others do not have even

---

26. R. I. Prevo, *Profit With Delight: The Literary Genre of the Acts of the Apostles* (Philadelphia: Fortress, 1987).

27. See the discussions of 4:23–31; 7:54–8:4; 28:16–31.

a nominal allegiance to Christian principles.[28] Because of Paul's strength of character he rose to the occasion and gradually became more and more influential as a leader, even though he was still a prisoner.

Ernst Haenchen is not impressed by all of this. He discounts the historicity of this passage, claiming that the events reported simply could not have happened.[29] He thinks that the author of Acts, using "a constructive imagination," adds to his source "edifying supplements which extol Paul." The source was "a journal of reminiscences which could not report anything special about Paul."[30] In response to Haenchen, E. F. Harrison maintains that "this prominence [given to Paul] would indeed stand out like a sore thumb if the apostle had not displayed extraordinary qualities elsewhere." He continues:

> But his personal magnetism and sterling character, his outstanding leadership, and his Spirit-filled life, affecting enemies and friends alike, are so clearly etched on the history as a whole that there is no good reason for distrusting this portion of the narrative. He was no less dynamic as a prisoner than as a free man; and for this information we are not dependent simply on Luke, for after reaching Rome Paul made a profound impression both on the praetorian guard and on others in the imperial service (Phil. 1:13).[31]

We will look at this passage, then, to find significant things about leadership in what we might call "secular" situations, which are the situations in which Christians find themselves most often. Paul was an agent of hope, a wise person, one who had an attitude of servanthood, and one whose testimony was clear and appropriate. Paul also found encouragement from fellow Christians amidst the strain of the challenges facing him.

THE SOVEREIGNTY OF God over circumstances. We noted that this passage is unique to the exposition of God's sovereignty amidst hardship in Acts because here the hardship comes not from the sinfulness of people but from the forces of nature and the folly of humans. Paul and his team would have avoided the storm if the ship's officers had heeded his words of wisdom. This passage provides a needed check to prevent overapplication of the story of Christ's stilling the storm (see Luke 8:22–

---

28. See the "Contemporary Significance" section for various leadership features Paul demonstrated here.

29. See Haenchen's comments in *Acts*, 708–11.

30. Ibid., 709.

31. Harrison, *Acts*, 422.

25). Indeed, Christ can still every storm, but he does not immunize Christians from problems that others in the world also face. Sometimes he miraculously delivers Christians from such situations, while at other times he gives Christians courage to endure natural and other disasters.[32] We thank him for performing miracles but also for his sufficient grace that provides endurance in the midst of storms (2 Cor. 12:7–10).

Some Christians will testify how God has saved them from investing in a venture that went bankrupt while others ponder the mysterious providence that permitted them to invest in the same venture after making all the necessary inquiries about it and praying about the decision to invest. One Christian will testify how a traffic jam caused him to miss an ill-fated flight, while the godly mother of three little children will face an uncertain future because her husband died on that flight. We should never say that the one who was saved was any more godly than the one who was not. In fact, the one who suffered perhaps had a stronger faith, so that God felt that he or she was able to go through this circumstance. We must never glibly pronounce that a calamity faced by a Christian is a judgment from God. This may be so, but most often it is not, and by making such a pronouncement we may unnecessarily intensify the suffering of the righteous (cf. what Job's friends did to him).

What use is it to refer to God's sovereignty in view of the Christian who was not spared the experience of disaster? Though Christ can still the storm, we can have the courage to face it when he does not, for we know that through the crisis God's sovereignty will work out something good (Rom. 8:28). We live under God's promises, and these promises brace us to face the challenge. The American poet John Greenleaf Whittier (1907–92) meditated on the mysterious providence of God in a beloved hymn:

> Here in the maddening maze of things,
> When tossed by storm and flood,
> To one fixed ground my spirit clings;
> I know that God is good!

But what if the trial is too heavy for us? Whittier anticipates this situation:

> And if my heart and flesh are weak
> To bear an untried pain,
> The bruiséd reed he will not break,
> But strengthen and sustain.

---

32. See the discussion on 12:1–24, where I noted how in the terrible riots that engulfed our land in 1983, some Christians testified to miraculous deliverances that glorified God and others faced arson, looting, and death.

Paul experienced such strengthening from God when an angel brought him a reassuring message, reminding him about the Lord's promise (27:23–24).

Leadership in "secular" situations. That Paul should take a leadership role in this situation while being a prisoner is so amazing that Haenchen thinks it never happened.[33] But this is typical of the way Paul acted elsewhere in this book. It is important for Christian witness and for the general welfare of people for Christians to be actively involved in the affairs of society. If they are gifted in leadership, they can take a lead and have a wide influence for good. But even those not called to be leaders can learn from Paul's actions here.

Being agents of hope. Since Paul believed so strongly in the sovereignty of God, he could look beyond the bleak situation and anticipate good to come out. A vision of sovereignty may not come to us at once because our natural tendency may be to panic in a difficult situation. If so, we must grapple with God until we come out of that situation and are able to go to the people with a word from God rather than with a public display of anxiety.

The psalmist in Psalm 73, for example, pondered the mysterious providence of God that can permit the wicked to prosper while the righteous suffer. After a sustained reflection on his doubts, he said, "If I had said, 'I will speak thus,' I would have betrayed your children" (Ps. 73:15). As a result, without publicly proclaiming his doubts, he went to the sanctuary to battle it out with the Lord (73:17). There he received a vision of God's sovereignty, and in the rest of the psalm he praised God. We too must grapple until we see things the way God sees them. This will give us the confidence to be agents of hope in this hopeless world.

Twice in this passage Paul asked the people to take courage (27:22, 25). He then buttressed these words by eating. Thereupon, "they were all encouraged and ate some food" (27:36). Our words and actions can cause us to be agents of hope in a world that often seems hopeless. One of the most powerful messages we can give to the world is that God is sovereign and that there is therefore hope amidst the gloom that may temporarily engulf us.

Both words and actions can communicate this hope. Jeremiah's purchase of a plot of land in Anathoth at a time when he himself was prophesying the defeat and exile of his people was a symbolic act of hope (Jer. 32:6–16). God asked him to do so because after seventy years of exile, he promised that the Jews would return to their land. When people lose hope, it shows in their meaningless actions, which make situations even worse. Christians, by their constructive and meaningful actions, can bring hope to others and thus help transform society.

---

33. Haenchen, *Acts*, 709–10.

At a time when the war was raging in the north of Sri Lanka, the people there had fallen into a state of hopelessness and despondency. Roads were littered with filth and the yards of homes were unkempt. The YFC leader for northern Sri Lanka at that time, Suri Williams, decided to keep a happy and beautiful home in spite of all the terror and confusion around him. He and his family carefully tended their flower plants even though bombs were destroying many yards and many others had given up on their yards. One day they decided that not only would they keep their yard clean, they would also clean up the road outside their home. An Indian army officer[34] from a camp nearby saw this being done and challenged his soldiers to start a clean-up campaign of the roads near their camp. Neighbors were also encouraged to improve the areas surrounding their houses. Keeping a tidy home in a time of war became a symbolic act of hope.

The unspoken witness to the gospel through such acts of hope is immense and will result in people who observe others seeking out Christ. When John Wesley was on his voyage to North America as a missionary from England, his ship encountered a terrible storm, so bad that they feared for their lives. The English immigrants on the ship were shrieking with fear. Wesley examined himself, as he usually did in all circumstances, "and found to his horror that he was afraid, mortally afraid of dying." But a group of Moravian Christians from Germany were singing hymns amidst the storm. After the storm had subsided, Wesley went to one of them and asked, "Were you not afraid?" The man replied, "I thank God, no!" Wesley persisted, "But were not your women and children afraid?" "No," came the reply, "our women and children are not afraid to die."[35] This experience had a profound influence on Wesley, and these and other Moravians had a big part to play in his subsequent experience of evangelical conversion that sparked off the eighteenth-century revival in England.

Human wisdom. Several times Paul acted with a wisdom that came out of a knowledge of life in the world. For example, his warning about the danger of leaving Fair Havens for Phoenix (27:10) probably came out of his experience of sea travel. Later, Paul sensed that the sailors were trying to abandon the ship, and his advice enabled the officials to keep them on board so that their expertise would be available when it is most needed (27:30–31). Paul's wisdom is also seen in his advice to those on board to take some food (27:34). Barclay aptly observes, "He knew that hungry men are not efficient men."[36]

---

34. There was an Indian peace-keeping force in northern Sri Lanka at the time.

35. The sections within quotes are from Ingvar Haddal, *John Wesley: A Biography* (Nashville: Abingdon, 1961), 50–51.

36. Barclay, *Acts*, 186.

The media often portrays religious people as nice people who, however, do not know much about what is happening in the world. They are of little use in emergencies, for they lack the wisdom needed. Paul did not fit into this stereotype, nor did Joseph, Moses, Joshua, David, Solomon, Daniel, Mordecai, Nehemiah, or a host of others known for both their wisdom and their godliness. We are challenged to be alert to what is happening in the world and to seek wisdom on the best ways to live and work in this world. While some may be gifted with more wisdom than others, this is essentially something we acquire through alert observation, through conversations with people active in fields different from ours, through reading periodicals and books, through viewing programs that give us information about the world around us, and through involvement in the affairs of the societies and nations in which we live.

Clear and appropriate testimony. Luke does not cite any aggressive evangelism during this journey, though Paul must have been involved in personal verbal witness on the trip. Yet Luke does mention that when Paul can say a word for God, he does so. For example, he gave reassuring words to the people on board the ship, explaining that the one who spoke to him was "an angel of the God whose I am and whom I serve" (27:23)—a most appropriate way to introduce God to a non-Christian. When he partook of the food, he "gave thanks to God in front of them all" (27:35). At a time of seeming hopelessness these words of thanks must have provided a strong contrast to the mood of the rest.

Such quiet and appropriate acts of affirming our faith play a role in orienting people positively toward God. I have heard tennis player Michael Chang, ranked third in the world at the time of my writing, winsomely mention God when answering a question on television: "I am hoping to win, if it is God's will." On another occasion I heard television commentators discuss why he takes longer than other players to sign his autograph. Chang not only signs his name, he also writes, "God bless you." On that occasion a commentator remarked, "What a good model he is for the younger generation!" Years ago in the West it was common to mention God in a conversation or a public statement. But with mounting hostility to the Christian idea of God even in Western society, statements about God now have to be slipped in at appropriate times, but they can do their part in adding to the total witness of the church in a given society.

A servant's lifestyle. Wherever we are (in church, at home, or in society) and whatever our role may be (leader, follower, Christian minister, worker in a secular job, etc.), our attitude should always be that of a servant (Phil. 2:5–8). In our study of Paul's address to the Ephesian elders (20:17–35), we saw that he adopted a servant lifestyle in his ministry. Now we see him adopting a similar lifestyle in his activity in society. Though he must have been exhausted from the strenuous trip and though the Maltese people were doing their best to help the people from the ship, Paul was busy gathering wood for the fire that the Maltese people were building (28:2–3). Commenting on this Barclay says, "It is only the little man who refuses the little task."[37]

Paul was, of course, following the example set by Jesus, who washed the feet of his disciples—a servant's task that none of the disciples seemed willing to do (John 13:4–9). I have in my dossier of photographs from my travels a photo of an Australian Anglican bishop, Reg Piper, kneeling on the floor beside my bed making it up. He was my roommate at a conference, and coming from a warm climate where blankets were unnecessary, I was at a loss to know how to make up my bed, so he took the job over. I rushed to my camera and snapped the scene, as I felt that a remembrance of this Christlike act needed to be preserved.

Another servant-like act of Paul in this passage is his going to see the sick father of Publius (28:8). In religions like Buddhism and Hinduism one has to pay to receive the services of religious workers, and devotees have to either go to them or provide transport for them to come and perform their service (at a funeral, wedding, almsgiving, etc.). In Christianity the religious worker is a servant, so he does his work without demanding any privileges except that of serving the people. This is a powerful testimony for Christ.

An article by an anti-Christian journalist in an Indian newspaper on the conversion of large numbers of tribal people in India to Christianity attributed the success of Christianity with these people to three reasons. (1) Christian workers went to places where no one else would go. Even government census workers did not bother to go to remote tribal villages in the mountains (they simply wrote down estimates). But Christian evangelists not only went to these places, they even lived among these people. (2) Christian evangelists handed over leadership of the churches to locals very soon and thus empowered the people. (3) Christianity is a "cheap" religion. By that the author meant that it did not cost the people a lot in order to get the services of a Christian minister.[38] These three points of attraction of Christianity have to do with the servant lifestyle of the Christian. How powerful might the testimony be of a legislator, a government official, a bus driver, or a school teacher if he or she went into his or her work with a desire to be a servant!

Encouragement from fellow Christians. The task of being a Christian witness in a secular society is a difficult one. It is emotionally draining and often

---

37. Ibid., 188.

38. The report on this article was related to me by Indian Christian leader, Dr. Samuel T. Kamaleson.

discouraging. Paul must have been drained as he was coming to the end of his trip. Luke points out that when Paul saw the Romans who had come to meet him on the way, "[he] thanked God and was encouraged" (28:15). They had walked at least thirty-three miles from Rome to meet him—a sacrificial expression of kindness and of warmth. Though they could have welcomed him when he arrived in Rome, they made the considerably long walk to meet him on the way. That kind gesture lifted his spirits.

Christians who have boldly stood for Christ and his principles in public testify how acts of affirmation by fellow Christians do much to encourage them along the way. Let us take time to do this to people who live under pressure. A short letter of appreciation of services rendered may be just what a person involved in a lonely battle for God needs to spur him or her on at a time of discouragement.

Acts 28:16–31

❦

WHEN WE GOT to Rome, Paul was allowed to live by himself, with a soldier to guard him. ¹⁷Three days later he called together the leaders of the Jews. When they had assembled, Paul said to them: "My brothers, although I have done nothing against our people or against the customs of our ancestors, I was arrested in Jerusalem and handed over to the Romans. ¹⁸They examined me and wanted to release me, because I was not guilty of any crime deserving death. ¹⁹But when the Jews objected, I was compelled to appeal to Caesar—not that I had any charge to bring against my own people. ²⁰For this reason I have asked to see you and talk with you. It is because of the hope of Israel that I am bound with this chain."

²¹They replied, "We have not received any letters from Judea concerning you, and none of the brothers who have come from there has reported or said anything bad about you. ²²But we want to hear what your views are, for we know that people everywhere are talking against this sect."

²³They arranged to meet Paul on a certain day, and came in even larger numbers to the place where he was staying. From morning till evening he explained and declared to them the kingdom of God and tried to convince them about Jesus from the Law of Moses and from the Prophets. ²⁴Some were convinced by what he said, but others would not believe. ²⁵They disagreed among themselves and began to leave after Paul had made this final statement: "The Holy Spirit spoke the truth to your forefathers when he said through Isaiah the prophet:

²⁶"'Go to this people and say,
    "You will be ever hearing but never understanding;
        you will be ever seeing but never perceiving."
²⁷For this people's heart has become calloused;
        they hardly hear with their ears,
        and they have closed their eyes.
    Otherwise they might see with their eyes,
        hear with their ears,
        understand with their hearts
    and turn, and I would heal them.'

²⁸"Therefore I want you to know that God's salvation has been sent to the Gentiles, and they will listen!"

³⁰For two whole years Paul stayed there in his own rented house and welcomed all who came to see him. ³¹Boldly and without hindrance he preached the kingdom of God and taught about the Lord Jesus Christ.

THE WAY LUKE ends Acts is abrupt, but an examination of these last verses suggests that he is giving a summary of what happened all through the section of Acts that focused on the evangelism of the Gentiles (11:19–28:31). Paul went first to the Jews, but most of them rejected the message. So he went to the Gentiles, and we close the book with him chained to a soldier while the gospel was unchained as he shared it with the many who came to him.

A Rented Home in Rome (28:16)

ONCE PAUL ARRIVED in Rome he was "allowed to live by himself," which means he must have rented a house (see v. 30). He had a soldier to guard him, and Paul was probably chained to him by the wrist. This soldier would be relieved every four hours or so. As a result, Paul and the gospel became a talking point among the members of the palace guard (Phil. 1:13). The environment was not ideal, but it was adequate for Paul to have a bold and unhindered witness in Rome for two years (Acts 28:30–31).

Paul and the Jews in Rome (28:17–28)

LUKE DOES NOT refer anymore to Paul's relations with the Roman Christians. Instead, he concludes his book by describing Paul's attempts at witnessing to the Jewish community and by giving a summary of his other evangelistic activity. These have been key themes in Acts. Paul first called the Jewish leaders to meet him (v. 17), which was the correct protocol in communities that had a strong sense of solidarity. He explained to them the circumstances of his coming to Rome, climaxing with the statement, "It is because of the hope of Israel that I am bound with this chain" (v. 20b).

The leaders replied that they had not received any letters from Judea concerning Paul (v. 21). This is surprising, considering the urgency with which the Judean leaders hounded Paul while he was there. Also surprising is the fact that the Jewish leaders said that they did not know much about Christianity in spite of a Christian community in Rome (v. 22). Haenchen uses these two facts and the fact that Luke does not talk much of the Christian church in Rome to discount the historicity of this passage.[1]

The first point can be explained in two different ways. Perhaps a letter or representative had been sent but was delayed because of the complexities of winter travel.[2] Equally plausible is that the leaders in Judea did not think that they had much of a chance of success in Rome after failing in Judea, where the Roman leaders were eager to do them favors (24:27; 25:3, 9). They may have preferred to let the case go by default, especially since Roman law was severe on unsuccessful prosecutors.[3] Gempf explains the relative ignorance of the Jews about Christianity on the grounds that the Jews had been expelled for a time in A.D. 49 (Paul arrived in Rome in 60). "In the interim, the church would have become predominantly gentile in make-up, and the recently returned Jewish community may have had no contact with them in this big city."[4]

We see a familiar sequence in verses 23–28. The Jews showed an interest in Christianity and a meeting was arranged (v. 23a). Paul tried "to convince them about Jesus from the Law of Moses and from the Prophets" (v. 23b). The familiar word *peitho* ("persuade, convince") appears twice in these verses (vv. 23–24). Some are convinced, "but others would not believe" (v. 24). Those who rejected the message had stubborn hearts that did not want to believe. The result of that meeting was unpleasant for Paul (v. 25). There isn't much new here. Luke underscores the tragedy of Jewish rejection of the gospel. What is new is Paul's use of a familiar text (Isa. 6:9–10) about hardened hearts to explain Jewish resistance to the gospel (vv. 26–27).

Bold Preaching and Teaching (28:30–31)

ACTS DOES NOT conclude on the note of Jewish rejection of the gospel. Rather, Luke's conclusion presents a more glorious reality: The Gentiles hear the gospel, and Paul has two years of bold witness about "the kingdom of God and . . . the Lord Jesus Christ" (v. 31). At the start of Acts Luke gave his key verse (1:8), which predicted that through the Holy Spirit the gospel would be proclaimed "to the ends of the earth." The book ends with that prediction being fulfilled.

Paul had more freedom than a typical prisoner because he was able to live in his own rented house and welcome all who came to see him (v. 30). Bruce, Marshall, and others think that the Greek here is better translated "at his

---

1. Haenchen, *Acts*, 726–32.
2. Bruce, *Acts*, NICNT, 506.
3. Hemer, *Acts*, 157; Williams, *Acts*, 452.
4. Gemph, "Acts," 1107.

own expense" (see NRSV, REB), that is, "on his own earnings" rather than "in his own rented house" (NIV; cf. NASB).[5] Marshall points out that "prisoners could in certain circumstances carry on their own trades." Perhaps Paul was able to carry on his "tentmaking" although this would have been awkward if he was continually chained by the wrist to a soldier.[6] Paul probably wrote his Prison Letters—Philippians, Ephesians, Colossians, and Philemon—at this time, though scholars are not unanimous about this.

Why does the book of Acts end so abruptly? Is it because Acts was written shortly after the two years mentioned in this conclusion? There is a strong case for this, and many scholars date the book of Acts in the early to mid-sixties.[7] We cannot be sure of what Paul did after the events described in Acts. Tradition affirms that he was released from this imprisonment, had more evangelistic campaigns, and probably visited friends in Macedonia and Asia. Did he go to Spain during this time, as he had wished to (Rom. 15:24, 28)? We cannot be sure.

Paul was probably arrested again and wrote the Pastoral Letters during his second imprisonment in Rome. The last of these, 2 Timothy, speaks of his impending death. He was martyred some time between A.D. 64 and 67.[8]

THOUGH ACTS COMES to an abrupt end, Luke's conclusion is a summary of the whole book, with the gospel being taken to both Jew and Gentile. Does the Holy Spirit want to communicate to us through this conclusion something about what we should be doing with the gospel? Lloyd Ogilvie thinks so: "The abrupt ending leaves us with the challenge and opportunity to allow the Spirit to write the next chapter in the Book of Acts today in and through us!"[9]

The tragedy of Jewish unbelief. Of the different things Paul did after arriving in Rome, the one thing that Luke focused on most was his witness to the Jews (28:16—29). Luke does not mention the witness to the palace guard as a result of Paul's imprisonment and the encouragement that the brothers received as a result (see Phil. 1:12—14). The Gentile Luke seems to have chosen at the close of this book to report on Jewish evangelization

---

5. Bruce, *Acts,* NICNT, 509; Marshall, *Acts,* 425.

6. Bruce, *Acts,* NICNT, 509—10.

7. E.g., E. M. Blaiklok, J. Munck, F. V. Filson, D. Guthrie, A. J. Mattill, B. Reike, E. F. Harrison, J. A. T. Robinson, R. E. Longenecker, C. Gempf. See the full list in Hemer, *Acts,* 367—70.

8. For a discussion on the last days of Paul, see Bruce, *Paul,* 441—55.

9. Ogilvie, *Acts,* 357.

because that was an important theme to him. While Paul gave up on specific Jews in his ministry when they became obstinate, he never gave up on the race as such.[10] He lived with a constant ache in his heart over their unbelief (Rom. 9:1–3) and kept trying to do what he could to bring them to Christ.

Paul used a familiar text (Isa. 6:9–10) to explain Jewish resistance to the gospel (Acts 28:26–27; cf. Mark 4:12 for the reaction of some to Jesus' teaching through parables). In his exposition on Jewish unbelief in Romans, Paul used two Old Testament texts (Deut. 29:4; Isa. 29:10) to convey a similar idea (Rom. 11:8). That verse implies that God gave a spirit of stupor, which caused the Jews to resist the gospel. In keeping with a general principle elaborated in Romans 1:18–32, the hardness of the heart of the Jews is God's punishment for their rebellion against him. Paul confirms the direction of their decision to oppose God by hardening their hearts so that they could not see and understand the light of the gospel. Yet in Romans Paul also says that when the Jews see the blessings of God coming to the Gentiles, they will be provoked to jealousy and turn to God (Rom. 11:11–16). In other words, Gentile Christians have a vital part in the process leading to the conversion of Jewish people.

To Luke, then, Jewish evangelism was an important theme. While he wants us to understand the phenomenon of their rejection of the gospel, he does not want us to give up evangelizing them. He closes Acts by presenting this challenge. In the light of that, we should have sorrow over the Jewish rejection of the gospel (Rom. 9:1–3), and every Christian should desire to see Jews accept Christ. We too should be saying with Paul, "Brothers, my heart's desire and prayer to God for the Israelites is that they may be saved" (Rom. 10:1).

Evangelism basics. After a somewhat detailed description of Paul's attempts at building bridges with and evangelizing the Jewish community in Rome, Luke closes his two-volume work with two short verses that give us a picture of how evangelism happens (vv. 30–31). This is an appropriate way for Luke to end his book, for, as we said above, this was the great activity that formed its agenda, beginning with the Great Commission (1:8). The gospel was taken to Jerusalem, to Judea, to Samaria, and then to the ends of the earth. Now it has come to the most politically powerful city in the world. There too evangelism takes place.

It is helpful for us as well to close this commentary by gleaning from these two verses what it means to evangelize. They tell us some things about the type of person who is effective in evangelism and about the message and the methods used. Pervading this whole passage is the theme of the priority of evangelism for the Christian.

---

10. Gempf, "Acts," 1107.

JEWISH EVANGELISM TODAY. We must never forget Paul's affirmation of his passion for mission: Salvation was "first for the Jew, then for the Gentile" (Rom. 1:16). However, as the founder of Jews for Jesus, Moishe Rosen, said at the Lausanne II Congress in Manila in 1989, the Jewish people are among the most gospel-resistant people in the world. The report of that congress gives reasons for this: "Folk memories of the horrors of the Middle Ages die hard: to many Jewish people, the name of Christ invokes only the remembrance of state persecution; the cross only the image of the sword, and the very word *mission*, only the experience of coercive proselytization."[11] Unlike in Paul's day, the Christian evangelist should go to the Jews with an attitude of repentance for what Christians have done to them in the past.[12]

Not everyone in the church agrees on the need for Jewish evangelism. Some oppose it, saying that since we have so many things in common with the Jews, we should be cooperating with them in common causes and dialoguing with them rather that seeking to convert them to Christ.[13] Missiologist Gerald Anderson writes: "It is ironic that whereas the first major controversy in the primitive church was whether anyone *other than* Jews should be discipled, today the controversy is just the opposite—whether Jews themselves should be discipled."[14]

Even some who hold a high view of Scripture waver on this issue on the grounds that God has two separate covenants, one for the Jews and one for Christians. While we affirm that the Bible speaks of a special place given to the nation of Israel, we also affirm with Anderson that "God's covenant with Israel was fulfilled by Jesus, who proclaimed, 'I have come not to destroy but to fulfill' (Matt. 5:17, anticipated in Jer. 31:31−33)."[15]

In the book of Acts one of the burning issues was whether Gentiles needed to become Jews when they became Christians. I think today one of the important points that needs stressing is that Jews do not have to become

---

11. J. D. Douglas ed., *Proclaim Christ Until He Comes: Calling the Whole Church to Take the Whole Gospel to the Whole World* (Minneapolis: World Wide Publications, 1990), 445.

12. This, of course, does not mean that Christians should be blind to the legitimate aspirations of the Palestinian people, a good many of whom are Christian.

13. See Allan R. Brockway, "Learning Christology Through Dialogue With Jews," *Journal of Ecumenical Studies* 25 (1989): 351.

14. Gerald H. Anderson, "Theology of Religions and Missiology: A Time of Testing," *The Good News of the Kingdom,* ed. Charles Van Engen, Dean S. Gilliland, and Paul Pierson (Maryknoll, N.Y.: Orbis, 1993), 206 (italics his).

15. Ibid., 207.

Gentiles when they become Christians.[16] Much progress has been made on this in recent years with the emergence of the phenomenon of messianic or fulfilled Jews and of messianic synagogues. The church should always be reflecting on how best to fulfill the task of Jewish evangelism.[17]

Conclusion: evangelism basics. The description of Paul's evangelism in verses 30−31 shows us various factors that go to make an effective evangelistic process and that are as relevant today as they were in the first century.

People under God's sovereignty have confidence to evangelize. Acts affirms the sovereignty of God in the various situations Christians faced: in the first persecution of believers, which resulted in a prayer that reflected on sovereignty (4:24−30); in the scattering of believers that became the scattering of the seed of the gospel as refugees were transformed into missionaries (8:1, 4); in the mysterious way in which Paul was brought to Rome (chs. 27−28). Evangelism thrives under the shadow of sovereignty. We know that God is marching on with his agenda, even through what humans consider tragedies, and we may join in the stream of God's sovereignty by being active in his agenda. To one who lives under sovereignty, success is obedience to God. That is, even though Paul was bound to a chain in Rome, he was a success.

With his confidence in God's sovereignty, Paul carried on with his ministry as if nothing had happened! In Rome he probably continued his tentmaking, wrote his four great Prison Letters (including Ephesians, "the Quintessence of Paulinism"[18]), and carried on his openhearted ministry as he welcomed all who came to him (v. 30). The palace guards ended up talking about Christ, and the other Christians were "encouraged to speak the word of God more courageously and fearlessly" (Phil. 1:13−14). Thus Paul affirmed: "What has happened to me has really served to advance the gospel" (1:12).

The depth and effectiveness of Paul's ministry was greatly enhanced by this mingling of deprivation, sovereignty, and obedience. This has been so throughout the history of the church. It is well-known that suffering is often the context out of which great creativity emerges.[19] When you add to that the operation of the sovereign God, who can turn tragedies into triumphs, you realize that deprivation is not something to fear but an occasion for God to express his glory.

---

16. On this see David H. Stern, *Restoring the Jewishness of the Gospel* (Jerusalem: Jewish New Testament Publications, 1988). Stern is himself a messianic Jew.

17. See *Christian Witness to the Jewish People*, Lausanne Occasional Papers. No. 7 (Wheaton, Ill.: Lausanne Committee for World Evangelization, 1980); David F. Wells, *Turning to God: Biblical Conversion in the Modern World* (Grand Rapids: Baker; and Exeter: Paternoster, 1989), 97−109; Moishe and Ceil Rosen, *Witnessing to Jews: Practical Ways to Relate the Love of Jesus* (San Francisco: Jews for Jesus, 1998).

18. Bruce, *Paul*, 424.

19. See Paul Tournier, *Creative Suffering* (London: SCM, 1982).

Next to the Bible probably the best-selling Christian book in history has been John Bunyan's *Pilgrim's Progress.* Bunyan (1628–88) spent a total of twelve years in prison. He was arrested a year after his second marriage. When he went to prison, he left his young wife to look after the four children from his first marriage. In prison he went through downcast times, but he did not give up on life. In order to support his wife and children he made and sold hundreds of long-tagged thread laces for riding boots and other footwear. In the first six years of his imprisonment he wrote nine books. During his second imprisonment of six years he published only two books, possibly because he was working on his greatest work, *Pilgrim's Progress.*

He wrote to people outside who sought his counsel after reading his books. He conducted worship services for others in the prison (and sometimes was given leave from the prison to secretly conduct services outside too!). He shaped the rail of his prison stool into a flute, carefully hollowing the wood and using his candle flame to burn the small holes in the barrel. He would play the flute when the jailer was not around and would hurriedly put it back when he came to find out what the strange noise was![20] Buoyed by the vision of God's sovereignty, Bunyan made the best of his situation in prison.

Though we belong to the triumphant kingdom of the Lord of the universe, we may sometimes feel as if we are living under circumstances of defeat. The witness of Acts should encourage us to see obedience to God as the ultimate success and triumph in life. Some churches in the West that were once powerful in national life are gradually losing their power and political clout. I see Christians bemoaning this fact and responding sometimes aggressively against this loss of earthly power. Perhaps they should not be worried, for great spiritual power is often unleashed from environments of great deprivation. Paul's (and Bunyan's) imprisonment shows us that the greatest activities of life can be successfully carried out in such situations.

The message is about the kingdom of God and Jesus Christ. Luke summarizes the message preached as being about "the kingdom of God and ... the Lord Jesus Christ" (v. 31). This too has much to tell us today. The kingdom of God has been a neglected topic among evangelicals in this century. But mission theologian Arthur Glasser, after tracing various emphases that characterized evangelical mission theology in the postwar era, states that the reaffirming of the kingdom of God was the most significant trend.[21] Preach-

---

20. These facts come from Ernest W. Bacon, *Pilgrim and Dreamer, John Bunyan: His Life and Work* (Exeter: Paternoster, 1983), 111–18.

21. Starting with affirming the Great Commission and follow-up in the 1940s Glasser traced successively the following emphases: church growth and anthropology, the struggle for a holistic gospel, and the charismatic movement and the Holy Spirit ("The Evolution of Evangelical Mission Theology Since World War II," *International Bulletin of Missionary*

ing about the kingdom of God presents the greater purpose of God rather than just what God can do to an individual. It affirms that God is working out his purposes through the vicissitudes of history and that his plan will finally be accomplished, with his kingdom ruling the world. We ask people to join in this great march forward with the Lord of the universe. In this world, where people are wracked by the fear of demons, enemies, economic reversals, and failure, this is liberating news.

If the truth of the kingdom were added to our evangelistic preaching, our evangelism would yield much stronger Christians. In today's evangelism we tend to focus on how Jesus meets our personal needs. This topic is, of course, appropriate. But sooner or later Christians are going to find that God does not meet some needs they consider to be urgent. At such times they may be are tempted to stray from Christ and seek help elsewhere. But if the grand picture of the kingdom is firmly rooted in their minds, they will never forsake the Lord of the universe for a smaller, less powerful deity or force.

Also necessary to evangelistic preaching is a focus on Jesus. Again we do not only tell what he can do for us in connection with our present needs. We also describe who he is and what he has done and is doing in the world. We must emphasize the Jesus as preached in Acts. Such a portrayal of Christ will leave us feeling secure, confident, and complete.

The method is to be open to people and to preach and to teach. We noted how Paul opened his home and welcomed all who came to him (v. 30; cf. 20:20, 31). Elsewhere we called this the openhearted approach to ministry.[22] If we are to truly identify with those whom we are trying to reach, we must open our lives to them as Paul did.

In such situations, Paul preached and taught (v. 31). Preaching (*kerysso*) refers to a proclamation of the message that appeals primarily to the will of the individual. In teaching (*didasko*) the emphasis is more on challenging the mind. Often in Acts evangelism is described as teaching (5:21, 25, 28). Especially when evangelizing people who do not have a Christian worldview, teaching is important in order for them to understand what Christians are saying and thus make an intelligent decision. However impressed they may be by our oratory in preaching, they will interpret our message by sending its words through the grid of their own worldview. They may make a decision in response to our invitation, but they have not understood the gospel.

Research 9 [January 1985]: 9–13). See also Paul G. Hiebert, "Evangelism, Church and Kingdom," and J. Robertson McQuilkin, "An Evangelical Assessment of Mission Theology of the Kingdom of God," in *The Good News of the Kingdom*, 153–61 and 172–78 respectively.

22. See comments on 20:1–38.

The evangelistic discussions that Paul had with his audiences[23] undoubtedly helped the truth of the gospel sink into their minds. Two days before writing this I spoke at a YFC evangelistic camp. About 70 percent of the youth in the audience were Buddhist, Hindu, or Muslim. I spoke on who Jesus is, explaining things that the Gospels said about him. The speakers before me had spoken on creation, the Fall, and the affects of sin on personal life and relationships. After my talk we had a seventy-five-minute discussion about what Christians believe. Much of what happened up to that time had been teaching truths about Christianity through talks and discussions. When an evangelist spoke the night after I had spoken, many people were ready to commit their lives to Christ. Though this was an evangelistic camp, the teaching was as critical as the preaching.

Since a majority of the people in the West today have rejected Christianity, their worldview too is not Christian. Therefore witnesses in the post-Christian West face the same challenge that we in so-called non-Christian countries do. A key to effective evangelism in both these environments is teaching people what Christians believe and being sensitive to their reactions. Teaching does not have to be boring! I have heard people say of some Christian communicators that they are teachers, not preachers. But what they really meant was that they were boring speakers. Teachers must use a wide variety of means to attract and keep the attention of the audience.

The priority of evangelism. Luke's decision to close his book with a report of ongoing evangelism reminds us that evangelism is the passion that ignites our activity. God has acted decisively in Christ to save the human race. Herein lies the ultimate answer to the problems of the human race. If we love this world as God does, we will want to tell it of this liberating good news. This business will consume our passion to the day we die.

---

23. See discussion on 17:1–15.

Scripture Index

Scripture Index

Subject Index

This index lists the topics discussed. Some of these topics arise not from what Acts teaches but from implications of or questions that arise from what Acts teaches. However, we can glean from this index many of the basic teachings of this book. On a few occasions, where a given topic appears in Acts but is not commented on, the page number given in this index is the page where the Scripture text is printed.

Subject Index